COMPLETE
ATLAS
OF THE WORLD

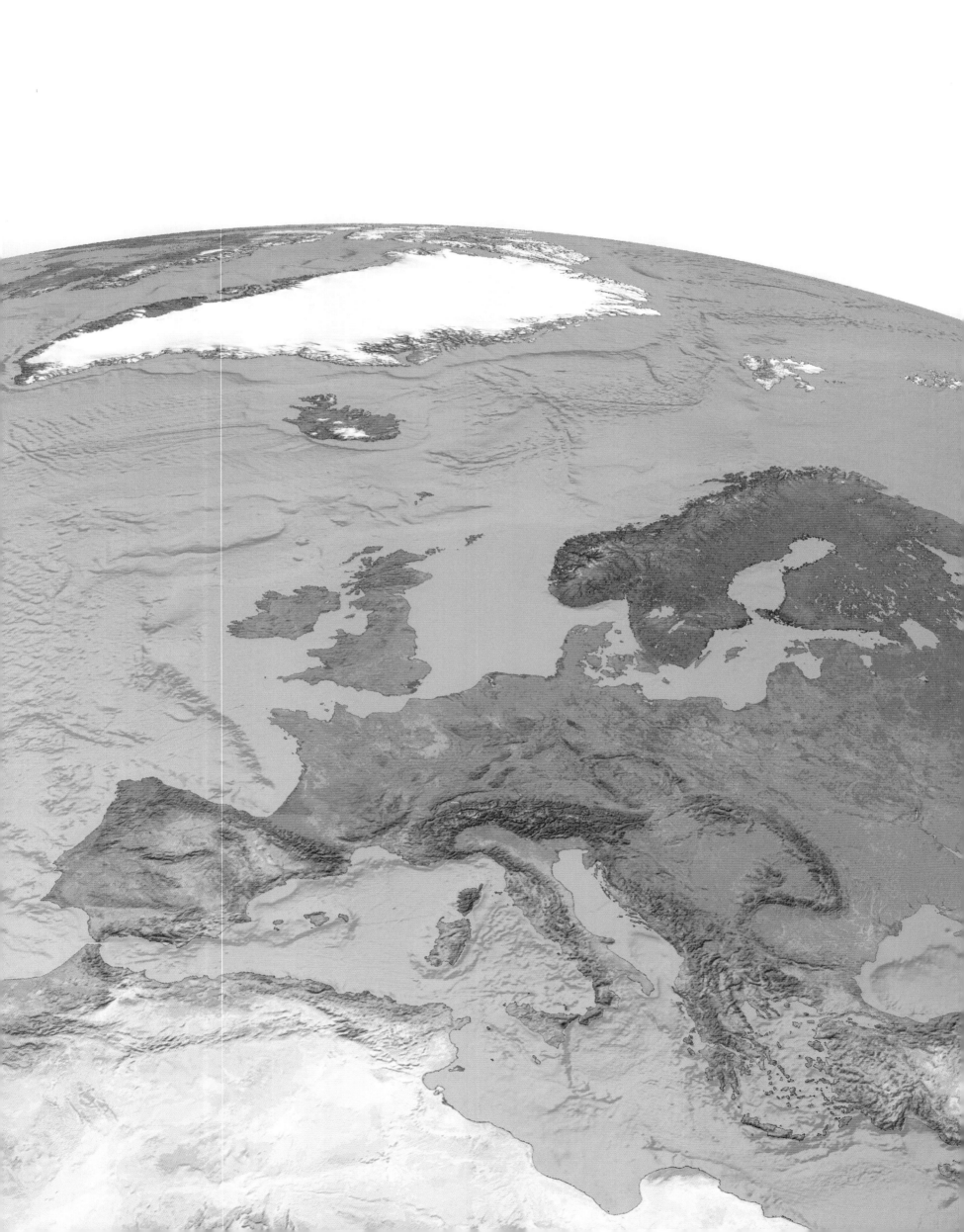

COMPLETE
ATLAS
OF THE WORLD

LONDON, NEW YORK, MELBOURNE, MUNICH AND DELHI

Publishing Director
Jonathan Metcalf

Art Director
Bryn Walls

Managing Editor
David Roberts

Senior Cartographic Editor
Simon Mumford

Digital Map Suppliers
Advanced Illustration, Congleton, UK • Cosmographics, Watford, UK
Encompass Graphics, Brighton, UK • Lovell Johns Ltd., Long Hanborough, UK
Netmaps, Barcelona, Spain

Digital Terrain Data
Digital terrain data and continental panoramic images created by Planetary Visions Ltd, Farnham, UK

Cartographers
Paul Eames, Edward Merritt, John Plumer, Rob Stokes, Iorwerth Watkins

Cartographic Editors
Tony Chambers, John Dear, Ruth Hall, Andrew Johnson, Belinda Kane, Lynn Neal, Ann Stephenson

Indexing and Database
T-Kartor, Sweden
Francesca Albini, Eleanor Arkwright, Renata Dyntarova, Edward Heelas, Britta Hansesgaard

Editor
Robert Dinwiddie

Designers
Nicola Liddiard, Yak El-Droubie

Picture Research
Louise Thomas, Jenny Baskaya

Jacket Desginers
Lee Ellwood, Duncan Turner

Systems Coordinator
Philip Rowles

Production Controllers
Linda Dare, Melanie Dowland

Flags courtesy of The Flag Institue, Cheshire, UK

First American Edition, 2007

Published in the United States by DK Publishing, 375 Hudson Street, New York, New York 10014

07 08 09 10 11 10 9 8 7 6 5 4 3 2 1

Published in Great Britain by Dorling Kindersley Limited.

A catalog record for this book is available from the Library of Congress.

ISBN: 978-0-7566-2859-8

DK books are available at special discounts when purchased in bulk for sales promotions, premiums, fund-raising, or educational use.
For details, contact: DK Publishing Special Markets, 375 Hudson Street, New York, New York 10014 or SpecialSales@dk.com

Color reproduction by MDP Ltd, Wiltshire, UK
Printed and bound by Tien Wah Press, Singapore

Discover more at www.dk.com

Introduction

The World at the beginning of the 21st Century would be a place of unimaginable change to our forefathers. Since 1900 the human population has undergone a fourfold growth coupled with an unparalleled development in the technology at our disposal. The last vestiges of the unknown World are gone, and previously hostile realms claimed for habitation. The advent of aviation technology and the growth of mass tourism have allowed people to travel further and more frequently than ever before

Allied to this, the rapid growth of global communication systems mean that World events have become more accessible than ever before and their knock on effects quickly ripple across the whole planet. News broadcasts bring the far-flung corners of the world into everyone's lives, and with it, a view of the people and places that make up that region. The mysteries of the World that once fueled global exploration and the quest to discover the unknown are behind us; we inhabit a world of mass transportation, a world where even the most extreme regions have been mapped, a world with multi faceted view points on every event, a World of communication overload.

However, does this help us make sense of the World? It is increasingly important for us to have a clear vision of the World in which we live and such a deluge of information can leave us struggling to find some context and meaning. It has never been more important to own an atlas; the *DK Complete Atlas of the World* has been conceived to meet this need. At its core, like all atlases, it seeks to define where places are, to describe their main characteristics, and to locate them in relation to other places. By gathering a spectacular collection of satellite imagery and draping it with carefully selected and up-to-date geographic information this atlas filters the World's data into clear, meaningful and user-friendly maps.

The World works on different levels and so does the *DK Complete Atlas of the World*. Readers can learn about global issues of many kinds or they can probe in a little further for the continental context. Delving even further they can explore at regional, national or even sub-national level. The very best available satellite data has been used to create topography and bathymetry that reveal the breathtaking texture of landscapes and sea-floors. These bring out the context of the places and features selected to appear on top of them. The full-spread map areas purposefully overlap to emphasis the connectivity and interdependence of our World.

The *DK Complete Atlas of the World* not only allows you to travel around our planet without leaving your seat but perhaps more importantly, helps you to understand the World around you.

David Roberts
Managing Editor

Contents

The atlas is organized by continent, moving eastwards from the International Date Line. The opening section describes the world's structure, systems and its main features. The Atlas of the World which follows, is a continent-by-continent guide to today's world, starting with a comprehensive insight into the physical, political and economic structure of each continent, followed by detailed maps of carefully selected geopolitical regions.

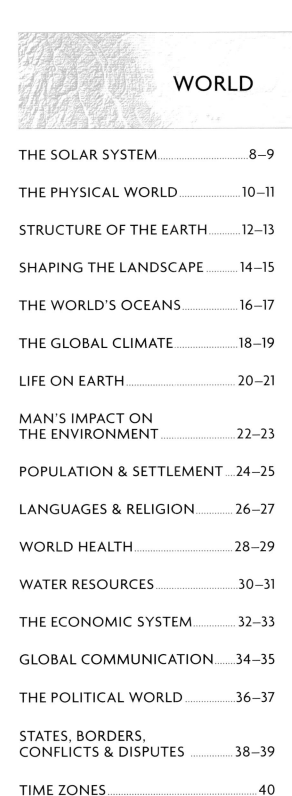

WORLD

NORTH AMERICA

SOUTH AMERICA

AFRICA

EUROPE

ASIA

AUSTRALASIA & OCEANIA

INDEX & GAZETTEER

Key to regional maps

Physical features

elevation

6000m / 19,686ft
4000m / 13,124ft
3000m / 9843ft
2000m / 6562ft
1000m / 3281ft
500m / 1640ft
250m / 820ft
100m / 328ft
sea level
below sea level

▲ elevation above sea level (mountain height)
▲ volcano
✕ pass
▼ elevation below sea level (depression depth)

sand desert
lava flow
coastline
reef
atoll

sea depth

sea level
-250m / -820ft
-500m / -1640ft
-1000m / -3281ft
-2000m / -6562ft
-3000m / -9843ft

▲ seamount / guyot symbol
▼ undersea spot depth

Drainage features

main river
secondary river
tertiary river
minor river
main seasonal river
secondary seasonal river
canal
waterfall
rapids
dam
perennial lake
seasonal lake
perennial salt lake
seasonal salt lake
reservoir
salt flat / salt pan
marsh / salt marsh
mangrove
wadi
○ spring / well / waterhole / oasis

Ice features

ice cap / sheet
ice shelf
glacier / snowfield
· · · · summer pack ice limit
winter pack ice limit

Graticule features

lines of latitude and longitude / Equator
Tropics / Polar circles
45° degrees of longitude / latitude

Communications

motorway / highway
motorway / highway (under construction)
major road
minor road
⊢····⊣ tunnel (road)
main line
minor line
⊢···⊢ tunnel (rail)
✈ international airport

Borders

full international border
undefined international border
disputed de facto border
disputed territorial claim border
indication of country extent (Pacific only)
indication of dependent territory extent (Pacific only)
demarcation/ cease fire line
autonomous / federal region border
2nd order internal administrative border
3rd order internal administrative border

Miscellaneous features

═══════ ancient wall
◇ site of interest
⊙ scientific station

Settlements

built up area

settlement population symbols

■ more than 5 million
◉ 1 million to 5 million
◉ 500,000 to 1 million
◎ 100,000 to 500,000
⊕ 50,000 to 100,000
○ 10,000 to 50,000
○ fewer than 10,000

■● ● country/dependent territory capital city
■● ● autonomous / federal region / 2nd order internal administrative center
■● ⊕ 3rd order internal administrative center

Typographic key

Physical features

landscape features ... *Namib Desert*
Massif Central
ANDES

headland .... *Nordkapp*

elevation / volcano / pass .... Mount Meru 4556 m

drainage features .... *Lake Geneva*

rivers / canals
spring / well /
waterhole / oasis /
waterfall /
rapids / dam .... *Mekong*

ice features .... *Vatnajökull*

Physical features (continued)

sea features .... *Golfe de Lion*
Andaman Sea
INDIAN OCEAN

undersea features ... *Barracuda Fracture Zone*

Regions

country .... ARMENIA

dependent territory with parent state ..... NIUE (to NZ)

autonomous / federal region .... MINAS GERAIS

2nd order internal administrative region .... MINSKAYA VOBLASTS'

3rd order internal administrative region .... Vaucluse

cultural region .... New England

Settlements

capital city .... BEIJING

dependent territory capital city .... FORT-DE-FRANCE

other settlements ... Chicago
Adana
Tizi Ozou
Yonezawa
Farnham

Miscellaneous

sites of interest / miscellaneous .... Valley of the Kings

Tropics / Polar circles .... *Antarctic Circle*

The Solar System

The Solar System consists of our local star, the Sun, and numerous objects that orbit the Sun – eight planets, three recognized dwarf planets, over 165 moons orbiting these planets and dwarf planets, and countless smaller bodies such as comets and asteroids. Including a vast outer region that is populated only by comets, the Solar System is about 9,300 billion miles (15,000 billion km) across. The much smaller region containing just the Sun and planets is about 7.5 billion miles (12 billion km) across. The Sun, which contributes over 99 percent of the mass of the entire Solar System, creates energy from nuclear reactions deep within its interior, providing the heat and light that make life on Earth possible.

THE MOON'S PHASES

As the Moon orbits Earth, the relative positions of Moon, Sun and Earth continuously change. Thus, the angle at which the Moon's sunlit face is seen by an observer on Earth varies in a cyclical fashion, producing the Moon's phases, as shown at right. Each cycle takes 29.5 days.

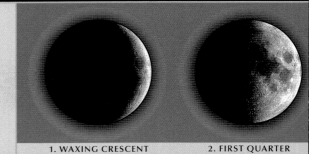

1. WAXING CRESCENT   2. FIRST QUARTER

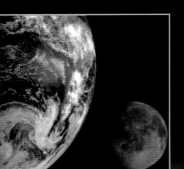

The Earth and Moon's relative sizes are clear in this long-range image from space.

The Moon

Earth's only satellite, the Moon, is thought to have formed 4.5 billion years ago from a cloud of debris produced when a large asteroid hit the young Earth. The Moon is too small to have retained an atmosphere, and is therefore a lifeless, dusty and dead world. However, although the Moon has only about 1 percent of the mass of the Earth, its gravity exerts an important influence on Earth's oceans, manifest in the ebb and flow of the tides.

What is a Planet?

The International Astronomical Union defines a Solar System planet as a near-spherical object that orbits the Sun (and no other body) and has cleared the neighborhood around its orbit of other bodies. A dwarf planet is a planet that is not big enough to have cleared its orbital neighborhood. Extra-solar planets are objects orbiting stars other than the Sun.

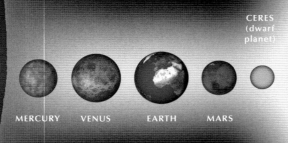

MERCURY   VENUS   EARTH   MARS

CERES (dwarf planet)

The Sun

The Sun is a huge sphere of exceedingly hot plasma (ionized gas), consisting mainly of the elements hydrogen and helium. It formed about 4.6 billion years ago, when a swirling cloud of gas and dust began to contract under the influence of gravity. When the center of this cloud reached a critically high temperature, hydrogen nuclei started combining to form helium nuclei – a process called nuclear fusion – with the release of massive amounts of energy. This process continues to this day.

JUPITER

SOLAR ECLIPSE

A solar eclipse occurs when the Moon passes between Earth and the Sun, casting its shadow on Earth's surface. During a total eclipse (below), viewers along a strip of Earth's surface, called the area of totality, see the Sun totally blotted out for a short time, as the umbra (Moon's full shadow) sweeps over them. Outside this area is a larger one, where the Sun appears only partly obscured, as the penumbra (partial shadow) passes over.

INSIDE THE SUN

The Sun has three internal layers. At its center is the core, where temperatures reach 27 million°F (15 million°C) and nuclear fusion occurs. The radiative zone is a slightly cooler region through which energy radiates away from the core. Further out, in the convective zone, plumes of hot plasma carry the energy towards the Sun's visible surface layer, called the photosphere. Once there, the energy escapes as light, heat and other forms of radiation.

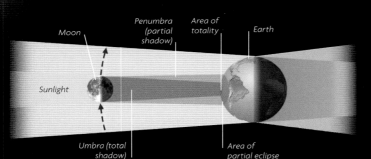

Moon
Penumbra (partial shadow)
Area of totality
Earth
Sunlight
Umbra (total shadow)
Area of partial eclipse

Photosphere

Core

Radiative zone

Convective zone

Sunspots mark cooler areas of surface

Prominences are loops of gas arching above the photosphere

| 3. WAXING GIBBOUS | 4. FULL MOON | 5. WANING GIBBOUS | 6. LAST QUARTER | 7. WANING CRESCENT | 8. NEW MOON |

PLANETS									DWARF PLANETS		
	MERCURY	VENUS	EARTH	MARS	JUPITER	SATURN	URANUS	NEPTUNE	CERES	PLUTO	ERIS
DIAMETER	4875 km (3029 miles)	12,104 km (7521 miles)	12,756 km (7928 miles)	6780 km (4213 miles)	142,984 km (88,846 miles)	120,536 km (74,898 miles)	51,118 km (31,763 miles)	49,528 km (30,775 miles)	950 km (590 miles)	2304 km (1432 miles)	2300-2500 km (1429-1553 miles)
AVERAGE DISTANCE FROM THE SUN	57.9 mill. km (36 mill. miles)	108.2 mill. km (67.2 mill. miles)	149.6 mill. km (93 mill. miles)	227.9 mill. km (141.6 mill. miles)	778.3 mill. km (483.6 mill. miles)	1431 mill. km (889.8 mill. miles)	2877 mill. km (1788 mill. miles)	4498 mill. km (2795 mill. miles)	414 mill. km (257 mill. miles)	5,915 mill. km (3675 mill. miles)	10,210 mill. km (6344 mill. miles)
ROTATION PERIOD	58.6 days	243 days	23.93 hours	24.62 hours	9.93 hours	10.65 hours	17.24 hours	16.11 hours	9.1 hours	6.38 days	not known
ORBITAL PERIOD	88 days	224.7 days	365.26 days	687 days	11.86 years	29.37 years	84.1 years	164.9 years	4.6 years	248.6 years	557 years
SURFACE TEMPERATURE	-180°C to 430°C (-292°F to 806°F)	480°C (896°F)	-70°C to 55°C (-94°F to 131°F)	-120°C to 25°C (-184°F to 77 °F)	-110°C (-160°F)	-140°C (-220°F)	-200°C (-320°F)	-200°C (-320°F)	-107°C (-161°F)	-230°C (-380°F)	-243°C (-405°F)

ERIS (dwarf planet)

PLUTO (dwarf planet)

NEPTUNE

URANUS

THE OUTER PLANETS

SATURN

Orbits

All the Solar System's planets and dwarf planets orbit the Sun in the same direction and (apart from Pluto) roughly in the same plane. All the orbits have the shapes of ellipses (stretched circles). However in most cases, these ellipses are close to being circular: only Pluto and Eris have very elliptical orbits. Orbital period (the time it takes an object to orbit the Sun) increases with distance from the Sun. The more remote objects not only have further to travel with each orbit, they also move more slowly.

THE OUTER PLANETS

The four gigantic outer planets – Jupiter, Saturn, Uranus and Neptune – consist mainly of gas, liquid and ice. All have rings and many moons. The dwarf planet Pluto is made of rock and ice.

THE INNER PLANETS

The four planets closest to the Sun – Mercury, Venus, Earth and Mars – are composed mainly of rock and metal. They are much smaller than the outer planets, have few or no moons, and no rings.

THE INNER PLANETS

AVERAGE DISTANCE FROM THE SUN

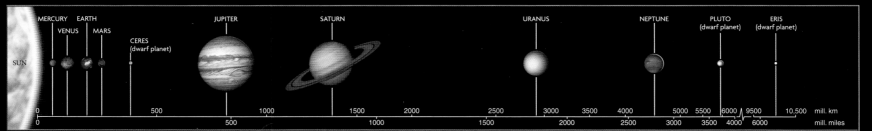

The Physical World

Earth's surface is constantly being transformed. Movements of the rigid tectonic plates that make up this surface are continuously, if slowly, shifting its landmasses around, while the land itself is constantly weathered and eroded by wind, water, and ice. Sometimes change is dramatic, the spectacular results of earthquakes or floods. More often it is a slow process lasting for millions of years. A physical map of the world represents a snapshot of Earth's ever-evolving architecture. The terrain maps below and at right show the planet's whole surface, including variations in ocean depth as well as the mountain-rippled texture of Earth's continents.

THE WORLD'S OCEANS

Earth's surface is dominated by water. The hemisphere shown here, centered around the southwest Pacific, is nearly all ocean, with the waters interrupted only by Antarctica, a part of South America, Australia, and the numerous islands of Australasia & Oceania, and southeast Asia.

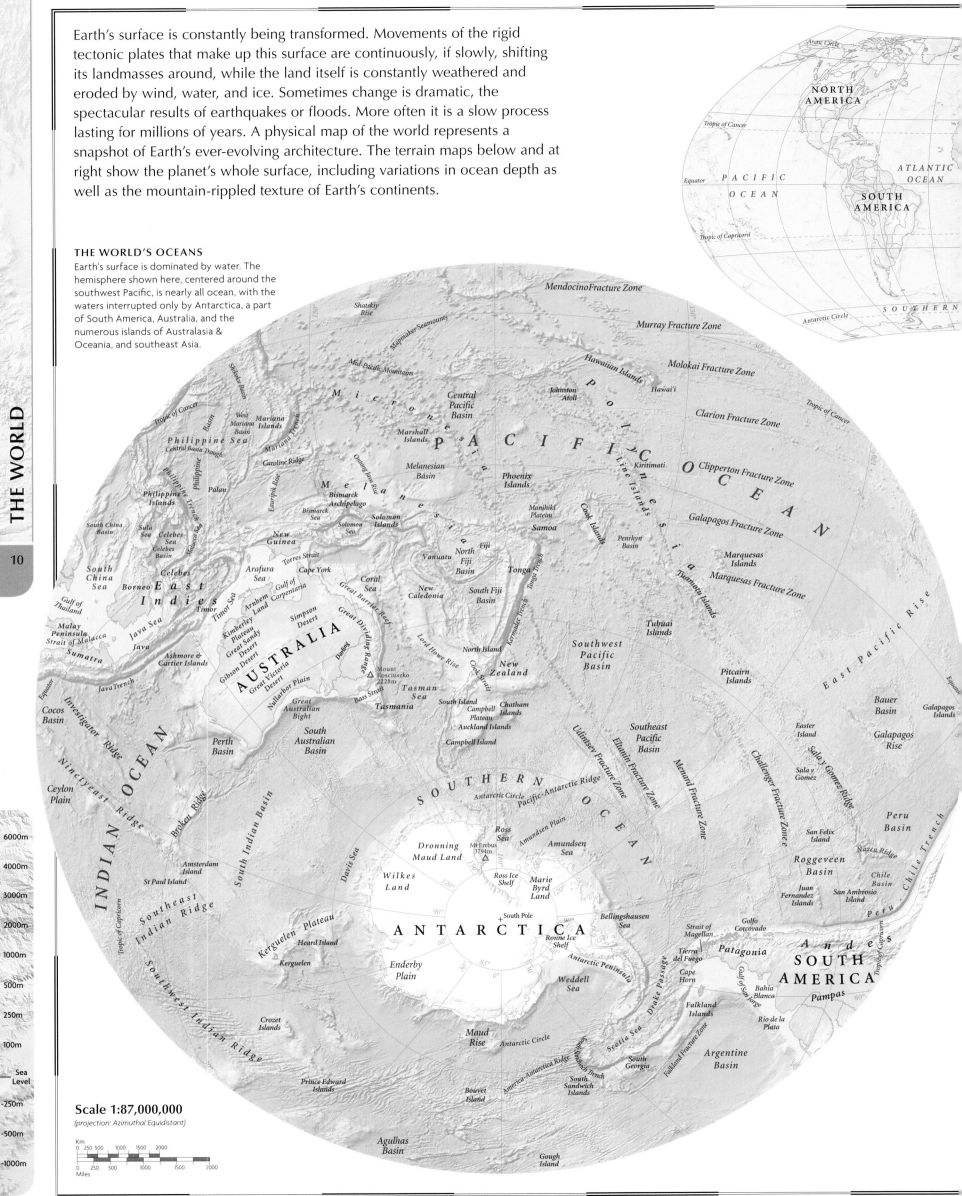

Scale 1:87,000,000
(projection: Azimuthal Equidistant)

6000m
4000m
3000m
2000m
1000m
500m
250m
100m
Sea Level
-250m
-500m
-1000m

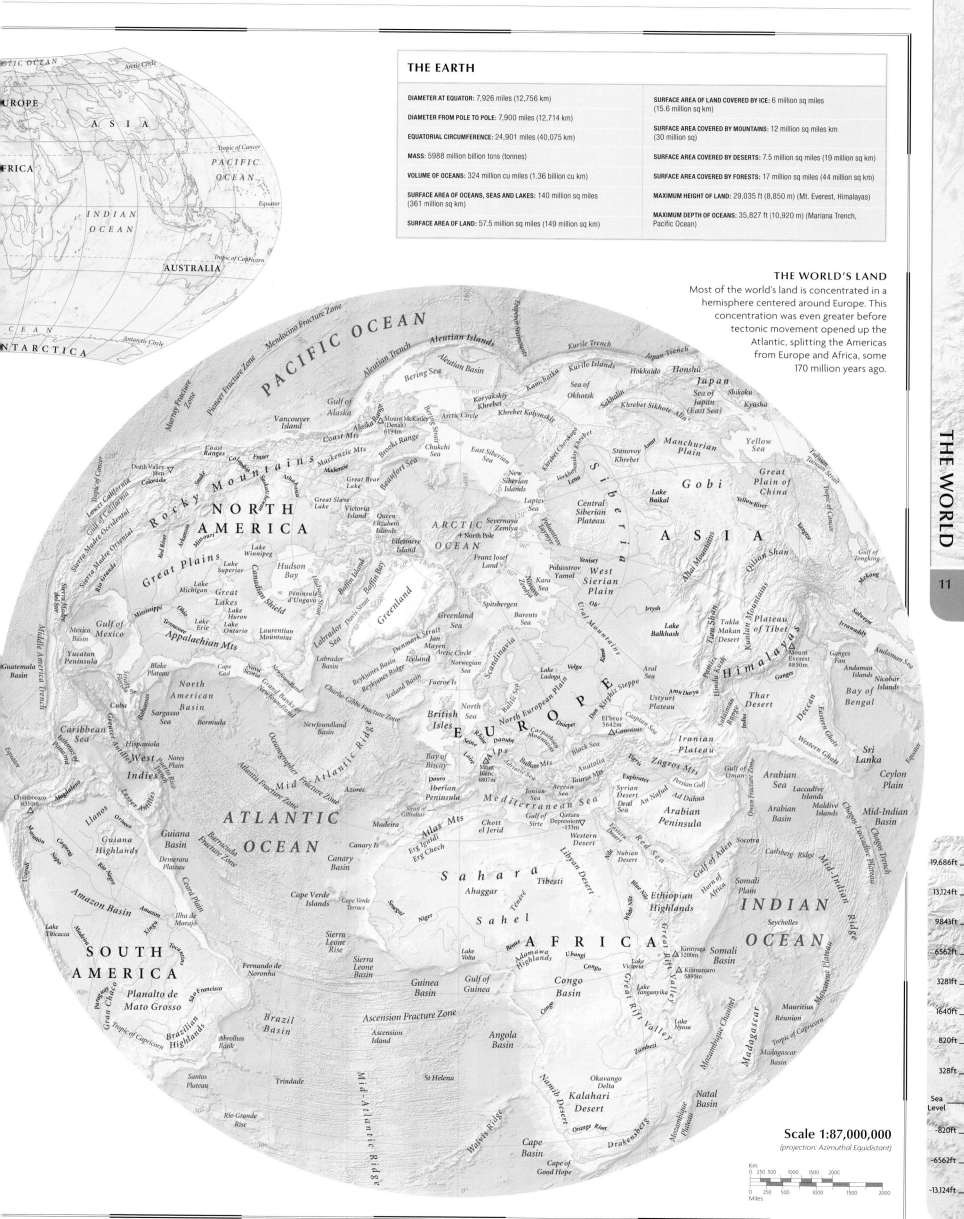

THE EARTH

DIAMETER AT EQUATOR: 7,926 miles (12,756 km)

DIAMETER FROM POLE TO POLE: 7,900 miles (12,714 km)

EQUATORIAL CIRCUMFERENCE: 24,901 miles (40,075 km)

MASS: 5988 million billion tons (tonnes)

VOLUME OF OCEANS: 324 million cu miles (1.36 billion cu km)

SURFACE AREA OF OCEANS, SEAS AND LAKES: 140 million sq miles (361 million sq km)

SURFACE AREA OF LAND: 57.5 million sq miles (149 million sq km)

SURFACE AREA OF LAND COVERED BY ICE: 6 million sq miles (15.6 million sq km)

SURFACE AREA COVERED BY MOUNTAINS: 12 million sq miles km (30 million sq)

SURFACE AREA COVERED BY DESERTS: 7.5 million sq miles (19 million sq km)

SURFACE AREA COVERED BY FORESTS: 17 million sq miles (44 million sq km)

MAXIMUM HEIGHT OF LAND: 29,035 ft (8,850 m) (Mt. Everest, Himalayas)

MAXIMUM DEPTH OF OCEANS: 35,827 ft (10,920 m) (Mariana Trench, Pacific Ocean)

THE WORLD'S LAND

Most of the world's land is concentrated in a hemisphere centered around Europe. This concentration was even greater before tectonic movement opened up the Atlantic, splitting the Americas from Europe and Africa, some 170 million years ago.

Scale 1:87,000,000

(projection: Azimuthal Equidistant)

The Structure of the Earth

Earth is an almost perfect sphere consisting of a partly liquid core overlain by a deep, semisolid layer, called the mantle, and two types of surface crust, known as continental and oceanic crust. Our planet has constantly evolved since it formed some 4.5 billion years ago. Its continents are neither fixed nor stable. Over the course of history, gradual movements of rocky material within Earth's mantle, resulting from massive internal flows of heat, have caused the great slabs of material that make up the planet's surface, known as tectonic plates, to shift around. The plates have moved, collided, joined together, and sometimes split apart. These processes continue to mold Earth's surface, causing earthquakes and volcanic eruptions, and creating oceans, mountain ranges, rift valleys, deep ocean trenches, and island chains.

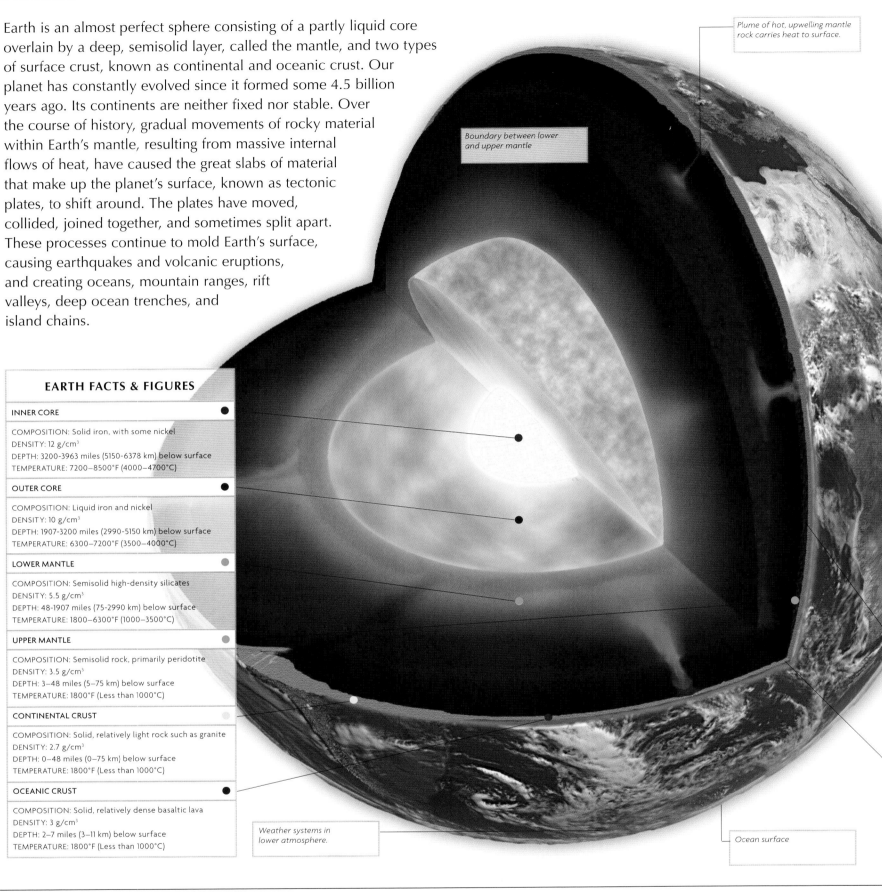

Plume of hot, upwelling mantle rock carries heat to surface.

Boundary between lower and upper mantle

Weather systems in lower atmosphere.

Ocean surface

EARTH FACTS & FIGURES

INNER CORE

COMPOSITION: Solid iron, with some nickel
DENSITY: 12 g/cm³
DEPTH: 3200-3963 miles (5150-6378 km) below surface
TEMPERATURE: 7200–8500°F (4000–4700°C)

OUTER CORE

COMPOSITION: Liquid iron and nickel
DENSITY: 10 g/cm³
DEPTH: 1907-3200 miles (2990-5150 km) below surface
TEMPERATURE: 6300–7200°F (3500–4000°C)

LOWER MANTLE

COMPOSITION: Semisolid high-density silicates
DENSITY: 5.5 g/cm³
DEPTH: 48-1907 miles (75-2990 km) below surface
TEMPERATURE: 1800–6300°F (1000–3500°C)

UPPER MANTLE

COMPOSITION: Semisolid rock, primarily peridotite
DENSITY: 3.5 g/cm³
DEPTH: 3—48 miles (5–75 km) below surface
TEMPERATURE: 1800°F (Less than 1000°C)

CONTINENTAL CRUST

COMPOSITION: Solid, relatively light rock such as granite
DENSITY: 2.7 g/cm³
DEPTH: 0—48 miles (0—75 km) below surface
TEMPERATURE: 1800°F (Less than 1000°C)

OCEANIC CRUST

COMPOSITION: Solid, relatively dense basaltic lava
DENSITY: 3 g/cm³
DEPTH: 2—7 miles (3–11 km) below surface
TEMPERATURE: 1800°F (Less than 1000°C)

FROM THE BIG BANG TO THE PRESENT DAY

The Big Bang

first galaxies form

Milky Way galaxy forms

13,700 million years ago (mya)

12,000 mya

11,000 mya

10,000 m

1000 mya

2000 mya
first multi-celled organisms

3000 mya
first landmasses

Phanerozoic Eon

543 mya

present day

Phanerozoic Eon (right) has been enlarged to show geological eras, periods and epochs

ERA	Paleozoic - age of ancient life						
PERIOD	Cambrian	Ordovician	Silurian	Devonian	Carboniferous		Permian
EPOCH					Mississippian	Pennsylvanian	

543   490   443   418   354   323   290

Continental drift

Although Earth's tectonic plates move only a few inches (centimeters) each year, over hundreds of millions of years, its landmasses have moved many thousands of miles (kilometers), to create new continents, oceans, and mountain chains.

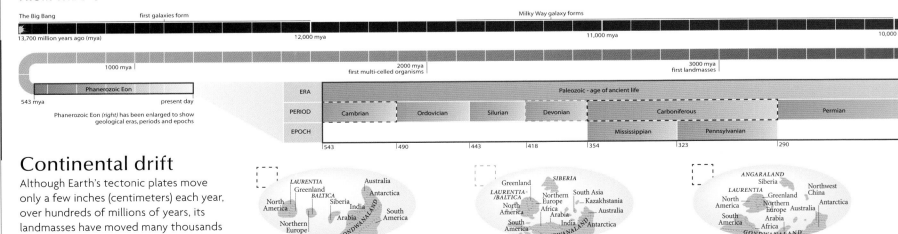

Cambrian 543–490 million years ago

Devonian 418–354 million years ago

Carboniferous 354–290 million years ago

Dynamic Earth

Earth's surface is split up into several rigid, closely-fitting sections, called tectonic plates. Each of the plates contains some oceanic crust, and most also contain some continental crust. The plates constantly move relative to one another. Movements at different types of plate boundary produce various types of geological structure and activity.

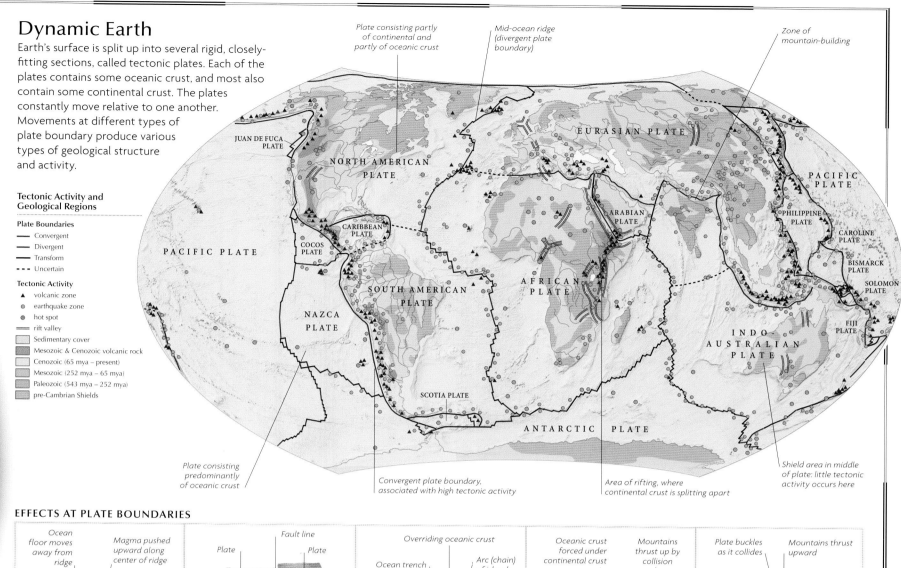

Plate consisting partly of continental and partly of oceanic crust

Mid-ocean ridge (divergent plate boundary)

Zone of mountain-building

JUAN DE FUCA PLATE

NORTH AMERICAN PLATE

EURASIAN PLATE

PACIFIC PLATE

PHILIPPINE PLATE

ARABIAN PLATE

CAROLINE PLATE

CARIBBEAN PLATE

BISMARCK PLATE

SOLOMON PLATE

COCOS PLATE

PACIFIC PLATE

SOUTH AMERICAN PLATE

AFRICAN PLATE

FIJI PLATE

NAZCA PLATE

INDO-AUSTRALIAN PLATE

SCOTIA PLATE

ANTARCTIC PLATE

Plate consisting predominantly of oceanic crust

Convergent plate boundary, associated with high tectonic activity

Area of rifting, where continental crust is splitting apart

Shield area in middle of plate: little tectonic activity occurs here

Tectonic Activity and Geological Regions

Plate Boundaries
— Convergent
— Divergent
— Transform
--- Uncertain

Tectonic Activity
▲ volcanic zone
● earthquake zone
● hot spot
~ rift valley
Sedimentary cover
Mesozoic & Cenozoic volcanic rock
Cenozoic (65 mya – present)
Mesozoic (252 mya – 65 mya)
Paleozoic (543 mya – 252 mya)
pre-Cambrian Shields

EFFECTS AT PLATE BOUNDARIES

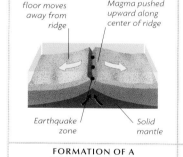

Ocean floor moves away from ridge

Magma pushed upward along center of ridge

Earthquake zone

Solid mantle

FORMATION OF A MID-OCEAN RIDGE

Plate

Fault line

Plate

Earthquake zone

SLIDING PLATES (TRANSFORM BOUNDARY)

Overriding oceanic crust

Ocean trench

Arc (chain) of islands

Oceanic crust pushed down

Volcanic activity

FORMATION OF ISLAND ARC AND OCEAN TRENCH

Oceanic crust forced under continental crust

Mountains thrust up by collision

Earthquake zone

Continental crust

SUBDUCTION OF OCEANIC CRUST UNDER CONTINENTAL CRUST

Plate buckles as it collides

Mountains thrust upward

Crust thickens in response to the impact

Earthquake zone

BLOCKS OF CONTINENTAL CRUST COLLIDE TO FORM MOUNTAINS

Boundary between upper mantle and crust

Sea floor made of oceanic crust

CONVECTION CURRENTS

Deep within Earth's core, temperatures may exceed 8100°F (4500°C). The heat from the core warms rocks in the mantle, which become semimolten and rise upward, displacing cooler rock below the solid oceanic and continental crust. This rock sinks and is warmed again by heat given off from the core. The process continues in a cyclical fashion, producing convection currents below the crust. These currents lead, in turn, to gradual movements of the tectonic plates over the planet's surface.

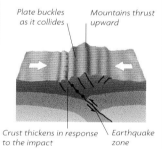

Subduction zone

Movement of plate

Mid-ocean ridge

Convection current

Continental crust

Inner core

Outer core

Oceanic crust

Mantle

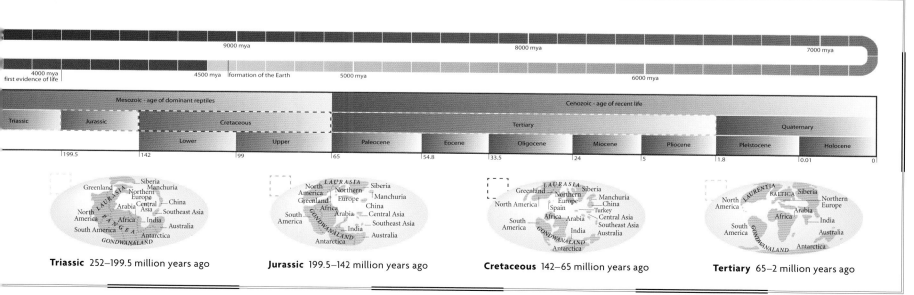

9000 mya

8000 mya

7000 mya

4000 mya
first evidence of life

4500 mya formation of the Earth

5000 mya

6000 mya

Mesozoic - age of dominant reptiles

Cenozoic - age of recent life

Triassic | Jurassic | Cretaceous | Tertiary | Quaternary

Lower | Upper | Paleocene | Eocene | Oligocene | Miocene | Pliocene | Pleistocene | Holocene

199.5 | 142 | 99 | 65 | 54.8 | 33.5 | 24 | 5 | 1.8 | 0.01 | 0

Greenland | Siberia | Manchuria | China | Southeast Asia | Australia | India | Antarctica
LAURASIA
North America | Northern Europe | Central Asia | Arabia | Africa | South America
PANGAEA
GONDWANALAND

Triassic 252–199.5 million years ago

North America | Greenland | LAURASIA | Siberia | Manchuria | China | Central Asia | Southeast Asia | Australia | India | Antarctica
Northern Europe | Africa | Arabia
South America
GONDWANALAND

Jurassic 199.5–142 million years ago

Greenland | LAURASIA | Siberia | Manchuria | China | Turkey | Central Asia | Southeast Asia | Australia | India | Antarctica
North America | Northern Europe | Spain | Arabia | Africa
South America
GONDWANALAND

Cretaceous 142–65 million years ago

North America | LAURENTIA | BALTICA | Siberia | Northern Europe | Arabia | India | Australia | Antarctica
Africa
South America
GONDWANALAND

Tertiary 65–2 million years ago

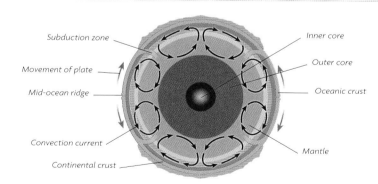

Shaping the Landscape

The basic material of Earth's surface is solid rock: valleys, deserts, soil, and sand are all evidence of the powerful agents of weathering, erosion and deposition that constantly transform Earth's landscapes. Water, whether flowing in rivers or grinding the ground in the form of glaciers, has the most clearly visible impact on Earth's surface. Also, wind can transport fragments of rock over huge distances and strip away protective layers of vegetation, exposing rock surfaces to the impact of extreme heat and cold. Many of the land-shaping effects of ice and water can be seen in northern regions such as Alaska *(below)*, while the effects of heat and wind are clearly visible in the Sahara *(far right)*.

FJORD
A valley carved by an ancient glacier and later flooded by the sea is called a fiord.

Ice and water

Some of the most obvious and striking features of Earth's surface are large flows and bodies of liquid water, such as rivers, lakes, and seas. In addition to these are landforms caused by the erosional or depositional power of flowing water, which include gullies, river valleys, and coastal features such as headlands and deltas. Ice also has had a major impact on Earth's appearance. Glaciers—rivers of ice formed by the compaction of snow—pick up and carry huge amounts of rocks and boulders as they pass over the landscape, eroding it as they do so. Glacially-sculpted landforms range from mountain *cirques* and U-shaped valleys to fiords and glacial lakes.

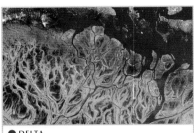

DELTA
A delta, such as that of the Yukon River (above), is a roughly triangular or fan-shaped area of sediment deposited by a river at its mouth.

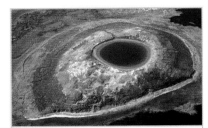

PINGO
These blister-like mounds, seen in regions of Arctic tundra, are formed by the upward expansion of water as it freezes in the soil.

TIDEWATER GLACIER
Glaciers of this type flow to the sea, where they calve (disgorge) icebergs. Like all glaciers, they erode huge amounts of rock from the landscape.

LANDSLIDE
The freezing and later thawing of water, which occurs in a continuous cycle, can shatter and crumble rocks, eventually causing landslides.

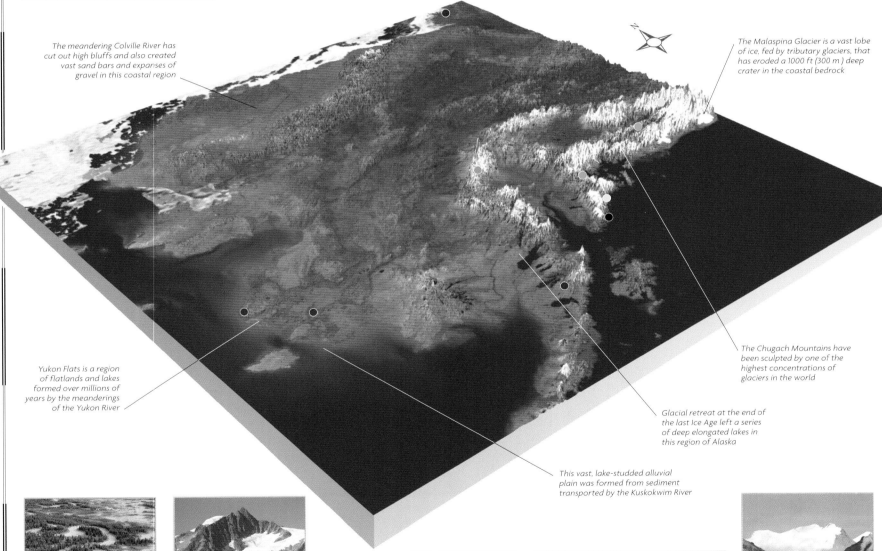

The meandering Colville River has cut out high bluffs and also created vast sand bars and expanses of gravel in this coastal region

The Malaspina Glacier is a vast lobe of ice, fed by tributary glaciers, that has eroded a 1000 ft (300 m) deep crater in the coastal bedrock

Yukon Flats is a region of flatlands and lakes formed over millions of years by the meanderings of the Yukon River

The Chugach Mountains have been sculpted by one of the highest concentrations of glaciers in the world

Glacial retreat at the end of the last Ice Age left a series of deep elongated lakes in this region of Alaska

This vast, lake-studded alluvial plain was formed from sediment transported by the Kuskokwim River

MEANDERING RIVER
In their lower courses, some rivers carve out a series of looping bends called meanders.

CIRQUE
A cirque is a hollow formed high on a mountain by glacial action. It may be ice-filled.

POSTGLACIAL FEATURES
Glacially-polished cliffs like these are a tell-tale sign of ancient glacial action. Other signs include various forms of sculpted ridge and hummock.

RIVER VALLEY
Over thousands of years, rivers erode uplands to form characteristic V-shaped valleys, with flat narrow floors and steeply-rising sides.

GULLIES
Gullies are deep channels cut by rapidly flowing water, as here below Alaska's Mount Denali.

Heat and wind

Marked changes in temperature—rapid heating caused by fierce solar radiation during the day, followed by a sharp drop in temperature at night—cause rocks at the surface of hot deserts to continually expand and contract. This can eventually result in cracking and fissuring of the rocks, creating thermally-fractured desert landscapes. The world's deserts are also swept and scoured by strong winds. The finer particles of sand are shaped into surface ripples, dunes, or sand mountains, which can rise to a height of 650 ft (200 m). In other areas, the winds sweep away all the sand, leaving flat, gravelly areas called desert pavements.

DESERT LANDSCAPES

In desert areas, wind picks up loose sand and blasts it at the surface, creating a range of sculpted landforms from faceted rocks to large-scale features such as *yardangs*. Individually sculpted-rocks are called ventifacts. Where the sand abrasion is concentrated near the ground, it can turn these rocks into eccentrically-shaped "stone mushrooms." Other desert features are produced by thermal cracking and by winds continually redistributing the vast sand deposits.

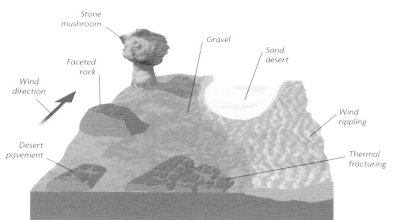

FEATURES OF A DESERT SURFACE

● **DUST STORM**
A common phenomenon in some deserts, dust storms result from intense heating of the ground creating strong convection currents.

● **LOESS DEPOSIT**
A deposit of silt that has been transported over long distances by wind, then compacted. Loess is found in a few marginal areas of the Sahara.

● **YARDANG**
A yardang is a ridge of rock produced by wind erosion, usually in a desert. Large yardangs can be many miles long.

● **DESERT PAVEMENT**
Dark, gravelly surfaces like this result from wind removing all the sand from an area of desert.

Part of the Grand Erg Oriental, this region is a vast wind-sculpted sea of sand, much affected by sand storms

This area of complex dune morphology has resulted from two different types of dunes overlapping and coalescing

Wind erosion of the sandstone rocks in this area (the Tassili n'Ajjer) has created nearly 300 natural rock arches

The Tefedest is an impressive, sun-baked, wind-eroded, granite massif located in southern Algeria

This highland region, called the Ahaggar Mountains, has largely been blasted free of sand and is heavily eroded throughout

● **TRANSVERSE DUNES**
This series of parallel sand ridges lies at right angles to the prevailing wind direction.

● **VENTIFACT**
A ventifact is a rock that has been heavily sculpted and abraded by wind-driven sand.

● **CRACKED DESERT**
Intensely heated and dried-out desert areas often developed geometrically-patterned surface cracking.

● **WADI**
Wadis are dried out stream beds, found in some desert regions, that carry water only during occasional periods of heavy rain.

● **BARCHAN DUNE**
This arc-shaped type of dune migrates across the desert surface, blown by the wind.

The World's Oceans

Two-thirds of Earth's surface is covered by the five oceans: the Pacific, Atlantic, Indian, Southern (or Antarctic), and Arctic. The basins that form these oceans, and the ocean floor landscape, have formed over the past 200 million years through volcanic activity and gradual movements of the Earth's crust. Surrounding the continents are shallow flat regions called continental shelves. These shelves extend to the continental slope, which drops steeply to the ocean floor. There, vast submarine plateaus, known as abyssal plains, are interrupted by massive ridges, chains of seamounts, and deep ocean trenches.

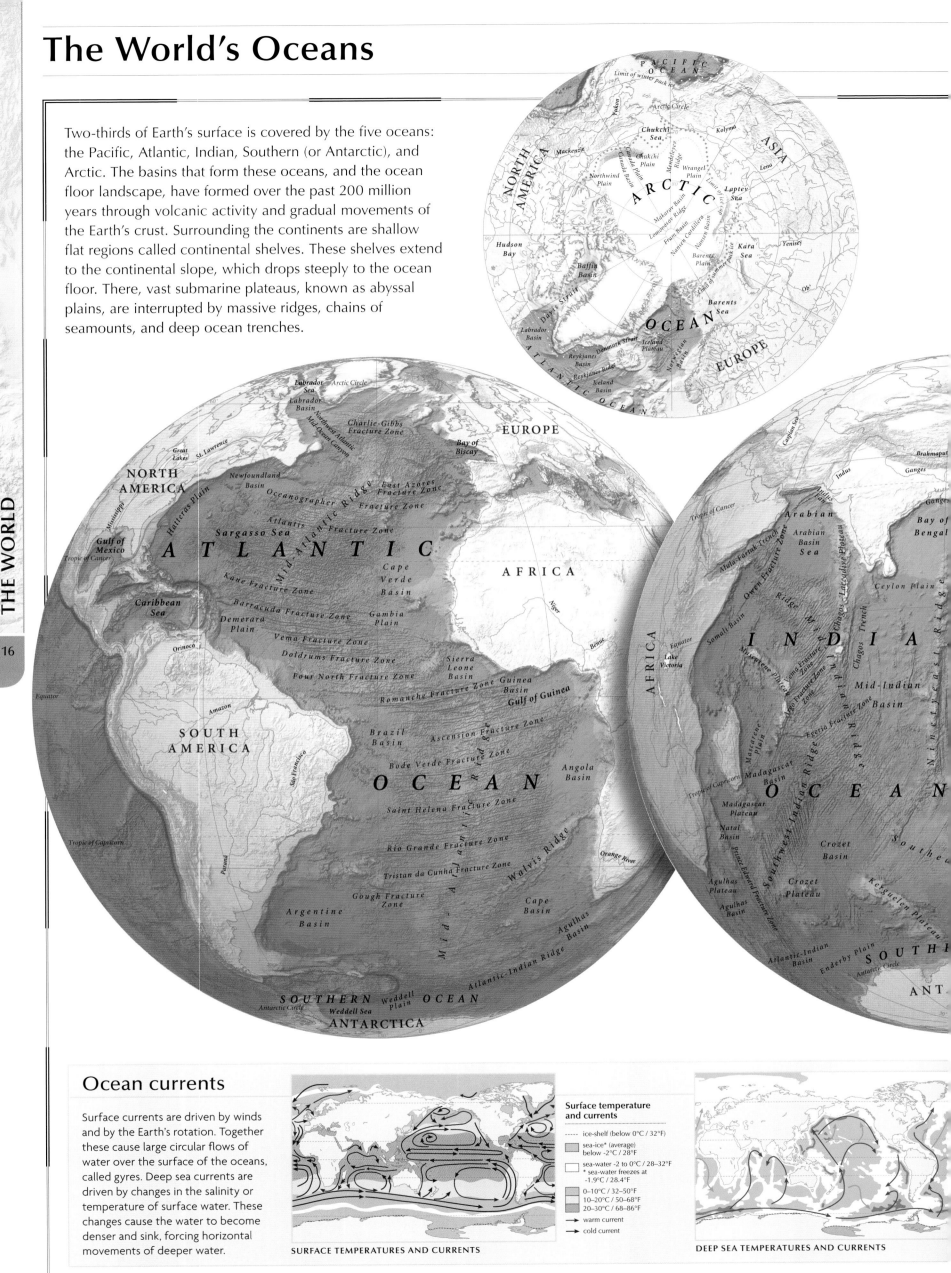

Ocean currents

Surface currents are driven by winds and by the Earth's rotation. Together these cause large circular flows of water over the surface of the oceans, called gyres. Deep sea currents are driven by changes in the salinity or temperature of surface water. These changes cause the water to become denser and sink, forcing horizontal movements of deeper water.

Surface temperature and currents

- - - - - ice-shelf (below 0°C / 32°F)
- sea-ice* (average) below -2°C / 28°F
- sea-water -2 to 0°C / 28–32°F
  * sea-water freezes at -1.9°C / 28.4°F
- 0–10°C / 32–50°F
- 10–20°C / 50–68°F
- 20–30°C / 68–86°F
- → warm current
- → cold current

SURFACE TEMPERATURES AND CURRENTS

DEEP SEA TEMPERATURES AND CURRENTS

The ocean floor

The ages of seafloor rocks increase in parallel bands outward from central ocean ridges. At these ridges, new oceanic crust is continuously created from lava that erupts from below the seafloor and then cools to form solid rock. As this new crust forms, it gradually pushes older crust away from the ridge.

Ages of the ocean crust

- 0–5 million years
- 5–21 million years
- 21–38 million years
- 38–65 million years
- 65–140 million years
- 140–190 million years
- continental shelf
- no data

Tides

Tides are caused by gravitational interactions between the Earth, Moon, and Sun. The strongest tides occur when the three bodies are aligned and the weakest when the Sun and Moon align at right angles.

Strongest tides

Weakest tides

Gravitational pull from the Sun

Tidal bulges created by gravitational interactions

Earth

Moon

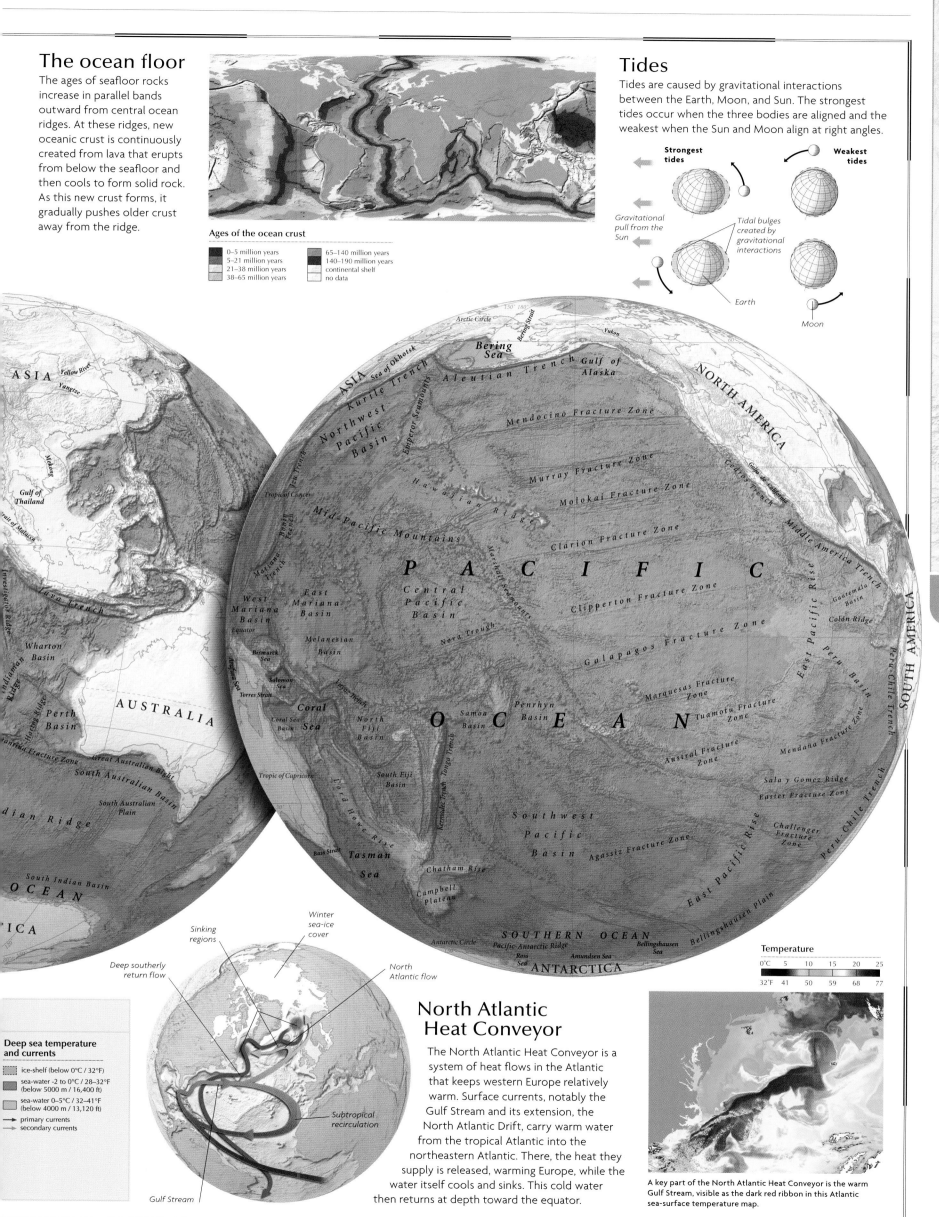

Deep sea temperature and currents

- ice-shelf (below 0°C / 32°F)
- sea-water -2 to 0°C / 28–32°F (below 5000 m / 16,400 ft)
- sea-water 0–5°C / 32–41°F (below 4000 m / 13,120 ft)
- → primary currents
- → secondary currents

Sinking regions

Deep southerly return flow

Winter sea-ice cover

North Atlantic flow

Subtropical recirculation

Gulf Stream

North Atlantic Heat Conveyor

The North Atlantic Heat Conveyor is a system of heat flows in the Atlantic that keeps western Europe relatively warm. Surface currents, notably the Gulf Stream and its extension, the North Atlantic Drift, carry warm water from the tropical Atlantic into the northeastern Atlantic. There, the heat they supply is released, warming Europe, while the water itself cools and sinks. This cold water then returns at depth toward the equator.

Temperature

0°C 5 10 15 20 25
32°F 41 50 59 68 77

A key part of the North Atlantic Heat Conveyor is the warm Gulf Stream, visible as the dark red ribbon in this Atlantic sea-surface temperature map.

Global Climate

The climates of different regions on Earth are the typical long-term patterns of temperature and humidity in those regions. By contrast, weather consists of short-term variations in factors such as wind, rainfall, and sunshine. Climates are determined primarily by the Sun's variable heating of different parts of Earth's atmosphere and oceans, and by Earth's rotation. These factors drive the ocean currents and prevailing winds, which in turn redistribute heat energy and moisture between the equator and poles, and between sea and land. Most scientists think that major changes are currently occurring in global climate due to the effects of rising carbon dioxide levels in the atmosphere.

The atmosphere

Earth's atmosphere is a giant ocean of air that surrounds the planet. It extends to a height of about 625 miles (1000 km) but has no distinct upper boundary. The Sun's rays pass through the atmosphere and warm Earth's surface, causing the air to move and water to evaporate from the oceans.

Global air circulation

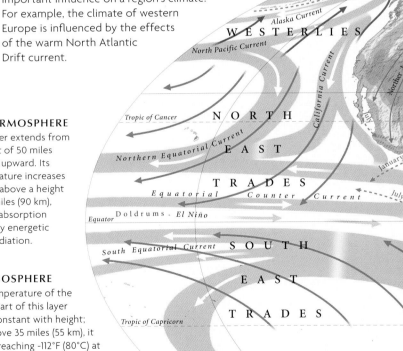

Polar cell
Cool air subsides at North Pole
Polar easterly blowing away from high pressure over North Pole
Air rises in subpolar region
Ferrell cell
Hadley cell
Air descends in subtropics
Air rises near equator
Southwesterly caused by Coriolis deflection of surface air flow in Ferrell cell
Subtropical jet stream
Northeasterly trade wind, caused by Coriolis deflection of surface air flow in Hadley cell
Polar-front jet stream
Roaring Forties
Southeasterly trade wind

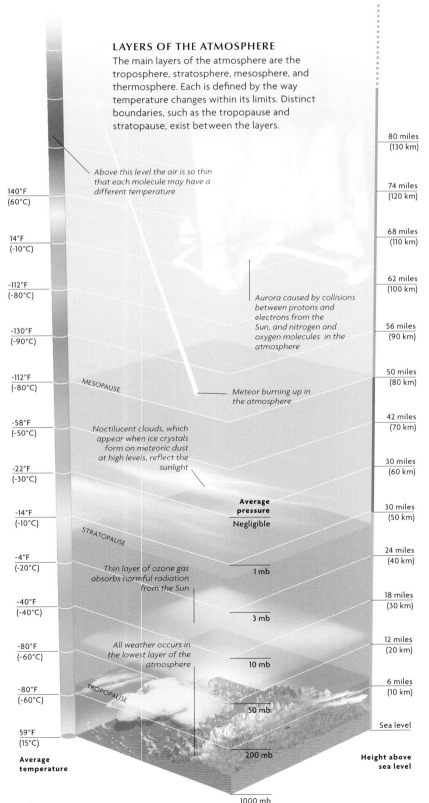

LAYERS OF THE ATMOSPHERE
The main layers of the atmosphere are the troposphere, stratosphere, mesosphere, and thermosphere. Each is defined by the way temperature changes within its limits. Distinct boundaries, such as the tropopause and stratopause, exist between the layers.

Above this level the air is so thin that each molecule may have a different temperature

Aurora caused by collisions between protons and electrons from the Sun, and nitrogen and oxygen molecules in the atmosphere

MESOPAUSE

Meteor burning up in the atmosphere

Noctilucent clouds, which appear when ice crystals form on meteoric dust at high levels, reflect the sunlight

STRATOPAUSE

Thin layer of ozone gas absorbs harmful radiation from the Sun

All weather occurs in the lowest layer of the atmosphere

TROPOPAUSE

Average temperature		Height above sea level
	80 miles (130 km)	
140°F (60°C)	74 miles (120 km)	
14°F (-10°C)	68 miles (110 km)	
-112°F (-80°C)	62 miles (100 km)	
-130°F (-90°C)	56 miles (90 km)	
-112°F (-80°C)	50 miles (80 km)	
-58°F (-50°C)	42 miles (70 km)	
-22°F (-30°C)	30 miles (60 km)	
-14°F (-10°C)	Average pressure Negligible	30 miles (50 km)
-4°F (-20°C)	1 mb	24 miles (40 km)
-40°F (-40°C)	3 mb	18 miles (30 km)
-80°F (-60°C)	10 mb	12 miles (20 km)
-80°F (-60°C)	50 mb	6 miles (10 km)
		Sea level
59°F (15°C)	200 mb	
	1000 mb	

Winds, currents, and climate

Earth has 12 climatic zones, ranging from ice-cap and tundra to temperate, arid (desert), and tropical zones. Each of these zones features a particular combination of temperature and humidity. The effects of prevailing winds, ocean currents of both the warm and cold variety, as well as latitude and altitude, all have an important influence on a region's climate. For example, the climate of western Europe is influenced by the effects of the warm North Atlantic Drift current.

● **THERMOSPHERE**
This layer extends from a height of 50 miles (80 km) upward. Its temperature increases rapidly above a height of 60 miles (90 km), due to absorption of highly energetic solar radiation.

● **MESOSPHERE**
The temperature of the lower part of this layer stays constant with height; but above 35 miles (55 km), it drops, reaching -112°F (80°C) at the mesopause.

● **STRATOSPHERE**
The temperature of the stratosphere is a fairly constant -76° F (-60°C) up to an altitude of about 12 miles (20 km), then increases, due to absorption of ultraviolet radiation.

● **TROPOSPHERE**
This layer extends from Earth's surface to a height of about 10 miles (16 km) at the equator and 5 miles (8 km) at the poles. Air temperature in this layer decreases with height.

Arctic Circle
WESTERLIES
Alaska Current
North Pacific Current
California Current
Tropic of Cancer
NORTH
EAST
Northern Equatorial Current
TRADES
Equatorial Counter Current
Doldrums El Niño
Equator
South Equatorial Current
SOUTH
EAST
TRADES
Tropic of Capricorn
WESTERLIES
West Wind D
Antarctic Circ

Air moves within giant atmospheric cells called Hadley, Ferrell, and polar cells. These cells are caused by air being warmed and rising in some latitudes, such as near the equator, and sinking in other latitudes. This north-south circulation combined with the Coriolis effect *(below)* produces the prevailing surface winds.

THE CORIOLIS EFFECT

Air moving over Earth's surface is deflected in a clockwise direction in the northern hemisphere and counterclockwise in the south. Known as the Coriolis effect, and caused by Earth's spin, these deflections to the air movements produce winds such as the trade winds and westerlies.

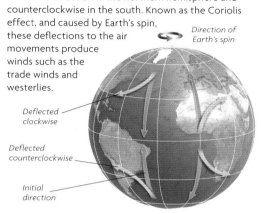

Direction of Earth's spin

Deflected clockwise

Deflected counterclockwise

Initial direction

Temperature and precipitation

The world divides by latitude into three major temperature zones: the warm tropics, the cold polar regions; and an intermediate temperate zone. In addition, temperature is strongly influenced by height above sea level. Precipitation patterns are related to factors such as solar heating, atmospheric pressure, winds, and topography. Most equatorial areas have high rainfall, caused by moist air being warmed and rising, then cooling to form rain clouds. In areas of the subtropics and near the poles, sinking air causes high pressure and low precipitation. In temperate regions rainfall is quite variable.

AVERAGE JANUARY TEMPERATURE

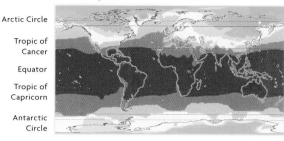

Arctic Circle
Tropic of Cancer
Equator
Tropic of Capricorn
Antarctic Circle

AVERAGE JANUARY RAINFALL

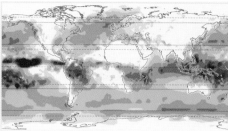

AVERAGE JULY TEMPERATURE

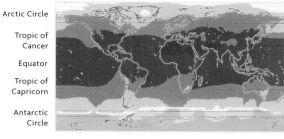

Arctic Circle
Tropic of Cancer
Equator
Tropic of Capricorn
Antarctic Circle

AVERAGE JULY RAINFALL

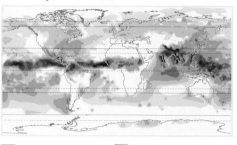

- below - 30°C (-22°F)
- -30 to - 20°C (-22 to -4°F)
- -20 to - 10°C (-4 to 14°F)
- -10 to 0°C (14 to 32°F)
- 0 to 10°C (32 to 50°F)
- 10 to 20°C (50 to 68°F)
- 20 to 30°C (68 to 86°F)
- above 30°C (86°F)

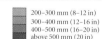

- 0–25 mm (0–1 in)
- 25–50 mm (1–2 in)
- 50–100 mm (2–4 in)
- 100–200 mm (4–8 in)
- 200–300 mm (8–12 in)
- 300–400 mm (12–16 in)
- 400–500 mm (16–20 in)
- above 500 mm (20 in)

Ocean currents, winds and climatic regions

Climate zones

- ice-cap
- subarctic
- tundra
- continental
- temperate
- warm temperate
- mediterranean
- semi-arid
- arid
- hot humid
- humid-equatorial
- tropical

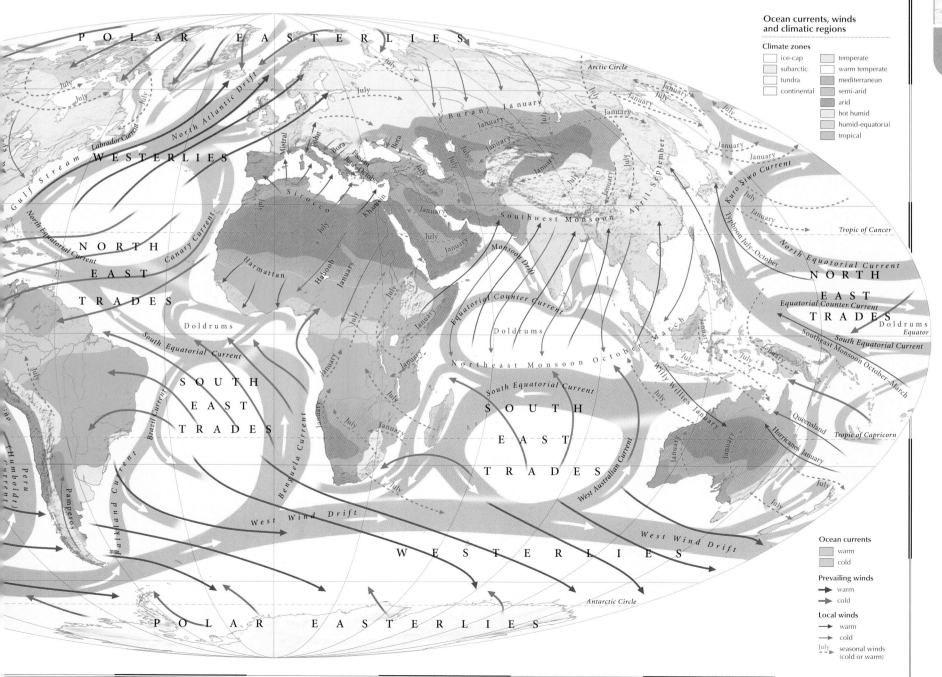

P O L A R   E A S T E R L I E S

W E S T E R L I E S

N O R T H   E A S T   T R A D E S

S O U T H   E A S T   T R A D E S

Doldrums

S O U T H   E A S T   T R A D E S

W E S T E R L I E S

P O L A R   E A S T E R L I E S

N O R T H   E A S T   T R A D E S

Doldrums

Equator

Arctic Circle

Tropic of Cancer

Tropic of Capricorn

Antarctic Circle

Gulf Stream
North Atlantic Drift
Labrador Current
North Equatorial Current
Canary Current
South Equatorial Current
Brazil Current
Falkland Current
Peru (Humboldt) Current
Benguela Current
West Wind Drift
North Equatorial Current
Equatorial Counter Current
South Equatorial Current
Northeast Monsoon October–March
Southwest Monsoon April–September
Monsoon Drift
Kuro Siwo Current
Typhoon July–October
West Australian Current
Queensland Current
Hurricanes January
Southeast Monsoon October–March
Willy Willies January
Pampero
Pamperos
West Wind Drift

Buran January
Bora
Föhn June–October
Mistral
Sirocco
Khamsin
Harmattan
Hajoob

Ocean currents
- warm
- cold

Prevailing winds
- warm
- cold

Local winds
- warm
- cold
- July seasonal winds (cold or warm)

Life on Earth

A unique combination of an oxygen-rich atmosphere and plentiful surface water is the key to life on Earth, where few areas have not been colonized by animals, plants, or smaller life-forms. An important determinant of the quantity of life in a region is its level of primary production—the amount of energy-rich substances made by organisms living there, mainly through the process of photosynthesis. On land, plants are the main organisms responsible for primary production; in water, algae fulfil this role. These primary producers supply food for animals. Primary production is affected by climatic, seasonal, and other local factors. On land, cold and aridity restrict the quantity of life in a region, whereas warmth and regular rainfall allow a greater diversity of species. In the oceans, production is mainly affected by sunlight levels, which reduce rapidly with depth, and by nutrient availability.

POLAR REGIONS
Ice restricts life in these regions to just a few species, such as polar bears in the Arctic.

Biogeographical regions

Earth's biogeographical regions, or biomes, are communities where certain species of plants and animals coexist within the constraints of particular climatic conditions. They range from tundra to various types of grassland, forest, desert, and marine biomes such as coral reefs. Factors like soil richness, altitude and human activities such as deforestation can affect the local distribution of living species in each biome.

TEMPERATE GRASSLAND
Also known as steppe or prairie, grassland of this type occurs mainly in the northern hemisphere and in South America (the Pampas).

NEEDLELEAF FOREST
These vast forests of coniferous trees cover huge areas of Canada, Siberia, and Scandinavia.

TROPICAL GRASSLAND
This type of grassland is widespread in Africa and South America, supporting large numbers of grazing animals and their predators.

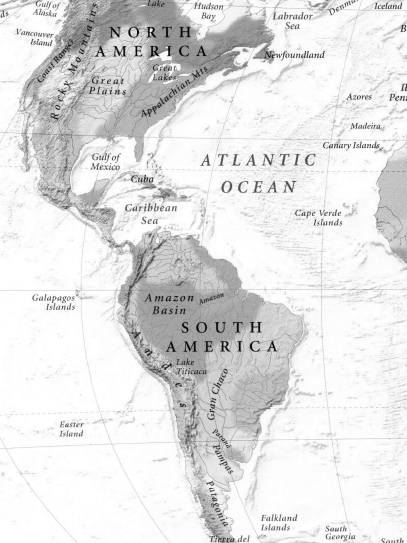

World biomes
- polar
- tundra
- needleleaf forest
- broadleaf forest
- temperate rainforest
- temperate grassland
- cold desert

Animal diversity

The number of animal species, and the range of genetic diversity within the populations of those species, determines the level of animal diversity within each country or other region of the world. The animals that are endemic to a region—that is, those found nowhere else on the planet—are also important in determining its level of animal diversity.

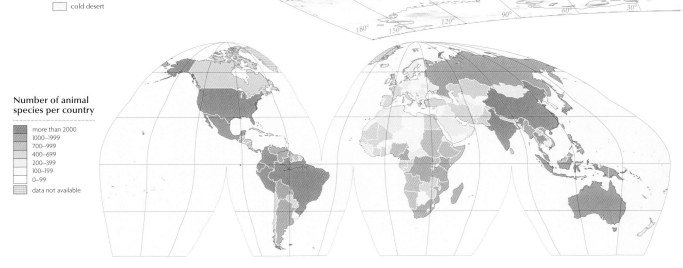

Number of animal species per country
- more than 2000
- 1000–1999
- 700–999
- 400–699
- 200–399
- 100–199
- 0–99
- data not available

TUNDRA
With little soil and large areas of frozen ground, the tundra is largely treeless, though briefly clothed by small flowering plants in summer.

TEMPERATE RAIN FOREST
Occurring in mid-latitudes in areas of high rainfall, these forests may be predominantly coniferous or mixed with deciduous species.

CORAL REEFS
Occurring in clear tropical waters, coral reefs support an extraordinary diversity of species, especially fish and many types of invertebrate.

MOUNTAINS
In high mountain areas only a few hardy species of plant will grow above the tree-line.

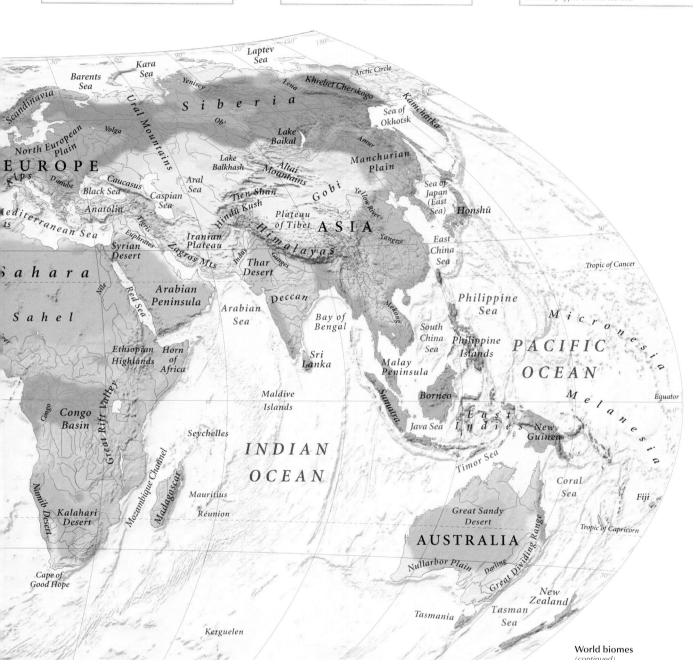

TROPICAL RAINFOREST
Characterized by year-round warmth and high rainfall, tropical rainforests contain the highest diversity of plant and animal species on Earth.

HOT DESERT
Only a few highly adapted species can survive in hot deserts, which occur mainly in the tropics.

World biomes
(continued)

- mediterranean
- hot desert
- tropical grassland
- dry woodland
- tropical rainforest
- mountain
- wetland

OPEN OCEAN
Earth's largest biome, the oceans are home to a vast diversity of fish, mammals, invertebrates, and algae.

Number of plant species per country

- more than 50,000
- 7000–49,999
- 3000–6999
- 2000–2999
- 1000–1999
- 600–999
- 0–599
- data not available

Plant diversity

Environmental conditions, particularly climate, soil type, and the extent of competition with other living organisms, influence the development of plants into distinctive forms and thus also the extent of plant diversity. Human settlement and intervention has considerably reduced the diversity of plant species in many areas.

Man and the Environment

The impact of human activity on the environment has widened from being a matter of local concern (typically over the build-up of urban waste, industrial pollution, and smog) to affect whole ecosystems and, in recent decades, the global climate. Problems crossing national boundaries first became a major issue over acid rain, toxic waste dumping at sea, and chemical spillages polluting major rivers. Current concerns center on loss of biodiversity and vital habitat including wetlands and coral reefs, the felling and clearance of great tropical and temperate forests, overexploitation of scarce resources, the uncontrolled growth of cities and, above all, climate change.

OZONE HOLE
Man-made chlorofluorocarbons (CFCs), used in refrigeration and aerosols, damaged the ozone layer in the stratosphere which helps filter out the sun's harmful ultraviolet rays. When a seasonal ozone hole first appeared in 1985 over Antarctica, a shocked world agreed to phase out CFC use.

1980   1985

CO₂ emissions in 2003
(million tonnes)

- over 4000
- 1000–4000
- 500–1000
- 100–500
- 50–100
- 10–50
- 2–10
- 0–2
- no data

Kyoto Protocol
- △ countries that have reached targets
- ▽ countries that have not reached targets
- ● industrialised countries that have not ratified

Climate change

Global warming is happening much faster than Earth's normal long-term cycles of climate change. The consequences include unpredictable extreme weather and potential disruption of ocean currents. Melting ice-caps and glaciers, and warmer oceans, will raise average sea levels and threaten coastlines and cities. Food crops like wheat are highly vulnerable to changes in temperature and rainfall. Such changes can also have a dramatic affect on wildlife habitats.

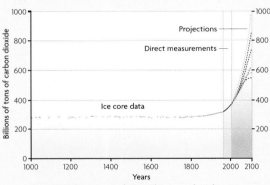

Since 1800 the amount of CO₂ in the atmosphere has risen sharply. Urgent worldwide action to control emissions is vital to stabilize the level by the mid 21st century.

THE GREENHOUSE EFFECT
Some solar energy, reflected from the Earth's surface as infra red radiation, is reflected back as heat by "greenhouse gases" (mainly carbon dioxide and methane) in the atmosphere. Nearly all scientists now agree that an upsurge in emissions caused by humans burning fossil fuel has contributed to making the resultant warming effect a major problem.

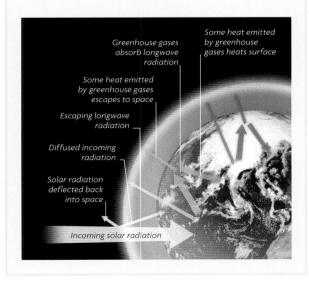

FOOD AND LAND USE
The world has about five billion hectares of agriculturally useful land, well under one hectare per person. The majority of this is pasture for grazing. Crops are grown on about 30 percent (and nearly a fifth of cropland is artificially irrigated). Mechanized farming encouraged vast single crop "monocultures," dependent on fertilizers and pesticides. North America's endless prairies of wheat and corn, huge soybean plantations, and southern cotton fields are mirrored in Ukraine (wheat), Brazil and Argentina (soya) and Uzbekistan (cotton). Elsewhere, scarce farmland can be squeezed by the housing needs of growing urban populations. Current interest in crop-derived "biofuels" means further pressure to grow food more productively on less land.

Intensive farming. Satellite photography picks up the greenhouses that now cover almost all the land in this Spanish coastal area southwest of Almeria.

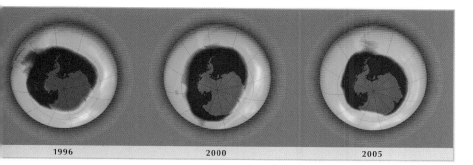

1996   2000   2005

DEFORESTATION

At current rates of destruction, all tropical forests, and most old-growth temperate forest, will be gone by 2090. The Amazon rain forest is a valuable genetic resource, containing innumerable unique plants and animals, as well as acting as a crucial natural "sink" for absorbing climate-damaging carbon dioxide. Stemming the loss of these precious assets to logging and farming is one of the major environmental challenges of modern times.

Over 25,000 sq miles (60,000 sq km) of virgin rain forest are cleared annually by logging and agricultural activities, destroying an irreplaceable natural resource.

Deforestation

- frontier forest
- degraded forest
- frontier forest 8000 years ago

GLACIATION

The world's glaciers and ice sheets have been in retreat for decades, forming less new ice at high altitudes than they lose by melting lower down. The loss of ice from Greenland doubled between 1996 and 2005, with alarming implications for rising sea levels. Other dramatic evidence of global warming includes the rapid thinning of ice in the Himalayas, and the highly symbolic loss of the snowcap on Africa's Mount Kilimanjaro.

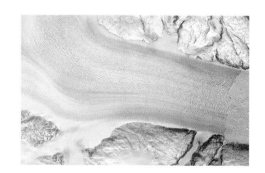

Helheim Glacier 2001
The Helheim glacier *(above)* almost completely fills this image, with the leading edge visible on the righthand side, and was in a relatively stable condition.

Helheim Glacier 2005
By 2005 *(right)* it had retreated by 2.5 miles (4 km).

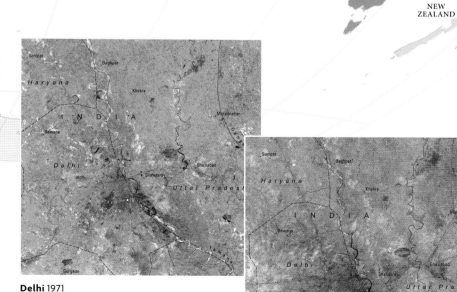

Delhi 1971
In 1971 Delhi *(above)* occupied an area of about 190 sq miles (500 sq km).

Delhi 1999
By 1999 *(right)* it had sprawled to cover 500 sq miles (1300 sq km). It vies with Mumbai in the southwest to be the sub-continent's most populous city, fast approaching 20 million people.

CITY GROWTH

The world in 2006 had five cities with populations over 20 million—Tokyo, Mexico City, Seoul, New York City, and São Paulo. The number of cities with populations between 10 and 20 million has reached 20 and continues to rise. The search for work, and the hope of escape from rural poverty, drives migration from rural to urban areas across the developing world. Urban dwellers now amount to more than half the world's population, and consume more resources than their rural counterparts.

Population and Settlement

Earth's human population is projected to rise from its current level of 6.5 billion to between 7.6 and 11 billion by the year 2050. The distribution of this population is very uneven and is dictated by climate, terrain, and by natural and economic resources. Most people live in coastal zones and along the valleys of great rivers such as the Ganges, Indus, Nile, and Yangtze. Deserts cover over 20 percent of Earth's surface but support less than 5 percent of its human population. Over half the world's population live in cities—most of them in Asia, Europe, and North America—as a result of mass migrations that have occurred from rural areas as people search for jobs. Many of these people live in so-called "megacities"—sprawling urban areas that have populations higher than 10 million.

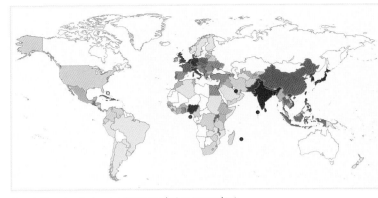

Population density by country (population per sq km)

over 1000	100–149	25–49
300–999	75–99	10–24
150–299	50–74	0–9

Population density

A few regions, including Europe, India, and much of eastern Asia, have extremely high population densities. Within these areas, a few spots, such as Monaco and Hong Kong, have densities of over 12,900 per sq mile (5000 people per sq km). Other regions (mostly desert, mountain, ice cap, tundra, or thickly forested areas) have densities close to zero –examples include large areas of Australia, western China, Siberia, North Africa, Canada, Greenland, and much of the Amazon rain forest region.

NORTH AMERICA

World population 9% **World land area** 17.0%

EUROPE

World population 14% **World land area** 7.1%

SOUTH AMERICA

World population 5.5% **World land area** 11.8%

ANTARCTICA

World population 0.0% **World land area** 8.9%

Population density
(persons per sq km)

200–1000
100–200
50–100
20–50
10–20
5–10
1–55
0–1

Million-person cities

In the year 1900 there were fewer than 20 cities in the world with a population that exceeded one million. By 1950 there were 75 such cities, and by the year 2000 there were more than 300 such cities, 40 of them in China alone, with another 30 in India, 14 in Brazil, and 10 in Japan.

Million-cities in 1900

• Cities over 1 million in population

Million-cities in 1950

Million-cities in 2006

Tokyo urban sprawl

—— City boundary, 1860 ⋯⋯ City boundary, 1964

GREATER TOKYO

The Greater Tokyo Area is the most populous urban area in the world, with an estimated head count in 2006 of 35.5 million. It includes Tokyo City, which has a population of about 12 million, and adjoining cities such as Yokohama. This satellite photograph shows the Greater Tokyo Area today, and also the boundaries of Tokyo City in 1860 (red) and 1964 (yellow).

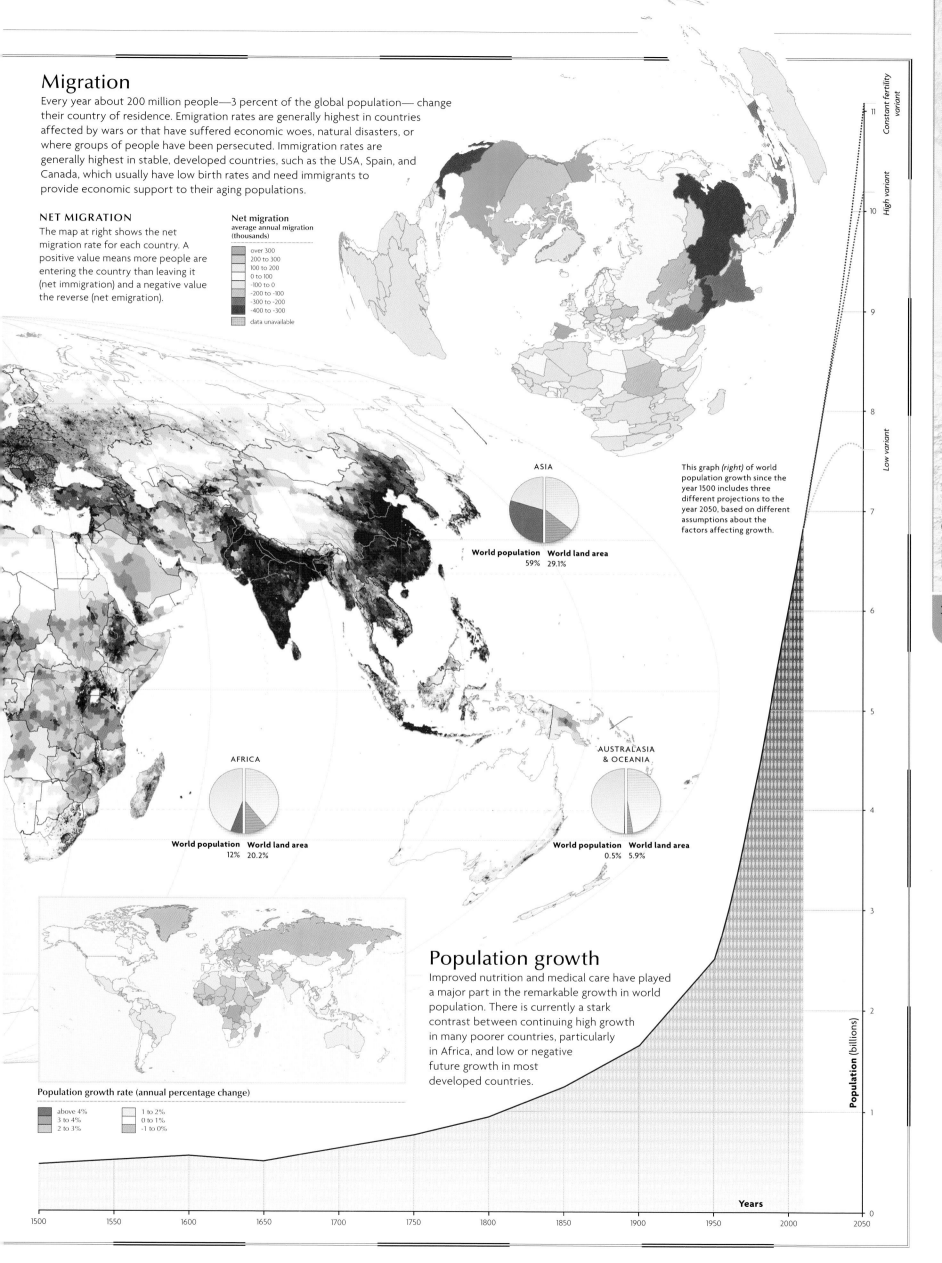

Migration

Every year about 200 million people—3 percent of the global population— change their country of residence. Emigration rates are generally highest in countries affected by wars or that have suffered economic woes, natural disasters, or where groups of people have been persecuted. Immigration rates are generally highest in stable, developed countries, such as the USA, Spain, and Canada, which usually have low birth rates and need immigrants to provide economic support to their aging populations.

NET MIGRATION

The map at right shows the net migration rate for each country. A positive value means more people are entering the country than leaving it (net immigration) and a negative value the reverse (net emigration).

Net migration
average annual migration (thousands)

- over 300
- 200 to 300
- 100 to 200
- 0 to 100
- -100 to 0
- -200 to -100
- -300 to -200
- -400 to -300
- data unavailable

ASIA

World population 59% World land area 29.1%

AFRICA

World population 12% World land area 20.2%

AUSTRALASIA & OCEANIA

World population 0.5% World land area 5.9%

This graph *(right)* of world population growth since the year 1500 includes three different projections to the year 2050, based on different assumptions about the factors affecting growth.

Population growth

Improved nutrition and medical care have played a major part in the remarkable growth in world population. There is currently a stark contrast between continuing high growth in many poorer countries, particularly in Africa, and low or negative future growth in most developed countries.

Population growth rate (annual percentage change)

- above 4%
- 3 to 4%
- 2 to 3%
- 1 to 2%
- 0 to 1%
- -1 to 0%

Constant fertility variant

High variant

Low variant

Population (billions)

11
10
9
8
7
6
5
4
3
2
1
0

Years

1500 1550 1600 1650 1700 1750 1800 1850 1900 1950 2000 2050

Language

Over 6800 different languages exist throughout the world, each one with its own unique evolutionary history and cultural connotations. Most of these languages are spoken only by small groups of people in remote regions. Sadly these minority tongues are dying out—it is estimated that about a third will have disappeared by the year 2100. The relatively small number of widely-spoken languages have gained their current predominance and pattern of distribution through a variety of historical factors. Among these have been the economic, military, or technological success of certain peoples and cultures, differing population growth rates, and the effects of migrations and colonization.

The European Union (EU) embraces the diversity of its 27 countries and 23 official languages by providing a translation and interpretation service for the majority of its meetings and documentation. This costs around US$ 650 million per year, which equates to 1 percent of the EU budget.

Main international languages

- Chinese
- Spanish
- Arabic
- Hindi
- English
- French
- Russian
- Portuguese
- English/Spanish
- Spanish/other
- Arabic/French
- French/other
- English/other
- Arabic/other
- Hindi/English/other
- Chinese/other
- Russian/other
- English/French
- Portuguese/other
- other language

Bantu language group
Mari other language

uninhabited land

The colonial powers

Colonialism between the 15th and 20th centuries had a major influence in establishing the world prevalence of various, mainly European, languages. Britain, for example, was the colonial power in Canada, the USA (until 1776), the Indian subcontinent, Australia, and parts of Africa and the Caribbean. Hence, English is still the main (or a major) language in these areas. The same applies to France and the French language in parts of Africa and southeast Asia, and to Spain and the Spanish language in much of Latin America. For similar reasons, Portuguese is the main language in Brazil and parts of Africa, and there are many Dutch speakers in Indonesia.

This dual language sign, written in both in Hindi and English, stands outside Shimla railway station in northern India. The sign reflects India's past—the British used Shimla as their summer capital during the colonial period.

TOP TEN LANGUAGES

About 45 percent of people speak one of just ten languages as their native tongue. Mandarin Chinese is spoken by far the largest number—a situation likely to persist, as minority language speakers in China are encouraged to switch to Mandarin. English usage is also increasing, as it is the most favored language on the internet and in business circles. Wherever English is not the mother tongue, it is often the second language.

THE TEN MOST SPOKEN LANGUAGES
(number of native speakers)

- Mandarin Chinese (1.1 billion)
- English (330 million)
- Spanish (300 million)
- Hindi/Urdu (250 million)
- Arabic (200 million)
- Bengali (185 million)
- Portuguese (160 million)
- Russian (160 million)
- Japanese (125 million)
- German (100 million)

Colonial Empires in 1914

- Austro-Hungarian
- Belgian
- British
- Chinese
- Danish
- Dutch
- French
- German
- Italian
- Japanese
- Ottoman
- Portuguese
- Russian
- Spanish
- United States
- Independent
- Disputed

Religion

The spread of religion

By their nature, religions usually start off in small geographical areas and then spread. For Christianity and Islam, this spread was rapid and extensive. Buddhism diffused more slowly from around 500 BCE into a large part of Asia. The oldest religion, Hinduism, has always been concentrated in the Indian subcontinent, although its adherents in other parts of the world now number millions following migrations from India.

1ST–7TH CENTURY

During this period, Christianity spread from its origins in the eastern Mediterranean, while Hinduism and forms of Buddhism spread in Asia. Islam became established in Arabia.

Rise and spread of the classical religions to 650 CE

- Buddhist heartland
- Chinese Confucianism/ Daoism and indigenous primal traditions
- Converted to Christianity by 600 CE
- Hinduism
- Islam under Muhammad
- Mahayana Buddhism
- Shintoism
- Zoroastrianism
- → spread of Buddhism
- → spread of Christianity
- → spread of Hinduism
- → dispersion of Jews, to 500 CE

7TH–16TH CENTURY

Islam later spread further through Asia and into parts of Africa and Europe. Christianity diffused through Europe and was then carried to many other parts of the world by colonialists and missionaries. Buddhism spread further in Asia.

World religions c.1500 CE

- Catholic Christianity
- area converted to Catholic Christianity
- Hinduism
- Islam
- Mahayana Buddhism and Confucianism, Daoism and Shinto
- Mahayana Buddhism and Confucianism, Daoism
- Russian Orthodoxy
- Theravada Buddhism
- Tibetan Buddhism
- Aztec Empire
- Inca Empire
- → spread of Catholicism
- → spread of Islam
- → spread of Protestantism
- → spread of Russian Orthodoxy

About 83 percent of the world's population adheres to a religion. The remainder adopt irreligious stances such as atheism. In terms of broad similarities of belief, there are about 20 different religions in the world with more than 1 million adherents. However, the larger of these are split into several denominations, which differ in their exact beliefs and practices. Christianity, for example, includes three major groupings that have historically been in conflict—Roman Catholicism, Protestantism, and Orthodox Christianity—as well as hundreds of separate smaller groups. Many of the world's other main religious, such as Islam and Buddhism, are also subdivided.

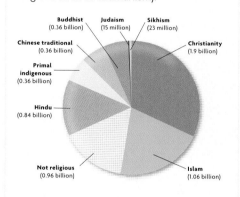

Each year millions of Muslims visit Mecca during the the Islamic pilgrimage known as the *Hajj*

RELIGION AROUND THE WORLD

About 72 percent of humanity adheres to one of five religions: Christianity, Islam, Hinduism, Buddhism, and Chinese traditional religion (which includes Daoism and Confucianism). Of the remainder, many are adherents of primal indigenous religions (a wide range of tribal or folk religions such as shamanism).

Pie chart:
- Buddhist (0.36 billion)
- Judaism (15 million)
- Sikhism (23 million)
- Christianity (1.9 billion)
- Chinese traditional (0.36 billion)
- Primal indigenous (0.36 billion)
- Hindu (0.84 billion)
- Not religious (0.96 billion)
- Islam (1.06 billion)

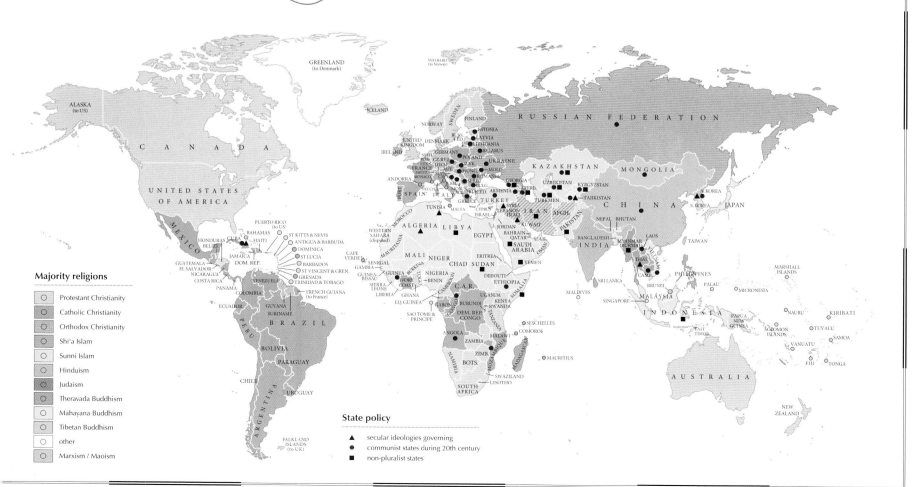

Majority religions

- Protestant Christianity
- Catholic Christianity
- Orthodox Christianity
- Shi'a Islam
- Sunni Islam
- Hinduism
- Judaism
- Theravada Buddhism
- Mahayana Buddhism
- Tibetan Buddhism
- other
- Marxism / Maoism

State policy

- ▲ secular ideologies governing
- ● communist states during 20th century
- ● non-pluralist states

Health

On most health parameters, the countries of the world split into two distinct groups. The first of these encompass the richer, developed, countries, where medical care is good to excellent, infant mortality and the incidence of deadly infectious diseases is low, and life expectancy is high and rising. Some of the biggest health problems in these countries arise from overeating, while the two main causes of death are heart disease and cancer. The second region consists of the poorer developing countries, where medical care is much less adequate, infant mortality is high, many people are undernourished, and infectious diseases such as malaria are major killers. Life expectancy in these countries is much lower and in some cases is falling.

Life expectancy

Life expectancy has risen remarkably in developed countries over the past 50 years and has now topped 80 years in many of them. In contrast, life expectancy in many of the countries of sub-Saharan Africa has fallen well below 50, in large part due to the high prevalence of HIV/AIDS.

Many people in developed countries are now living for 15–20 years after retirement, putting greater pressure on welfare and health services.

Infant deaths and births

Infant mortality is still high in many developing nations, especially some African countries, due in part to stretched medical services. As well as lower infant mortality, the world's developed countries have much lower birth rates—greater female emancipation and easier access to contraceptives are two causative factors.

World infant mortality rates (deaths per 1000 live births)

■ above 125	■ 75–124	■ 35–74	□ 15–34	□ below 15

Number of births (per 1000 people)

■ above 40	■ 30–39	■ 20–29	□ below 20

Nutrition

Two-thirds of the world's food is consumed in developed nations, many of which have a daily calorific intake far higher than is needed by their populations. By contrast, about 800 million people in the developing world do not have enough food to meet basic nutritional needs.

Daily calorie intake per capita

■ above 3000	■ 2500–2999	■ 2000–2499	□ below 2000

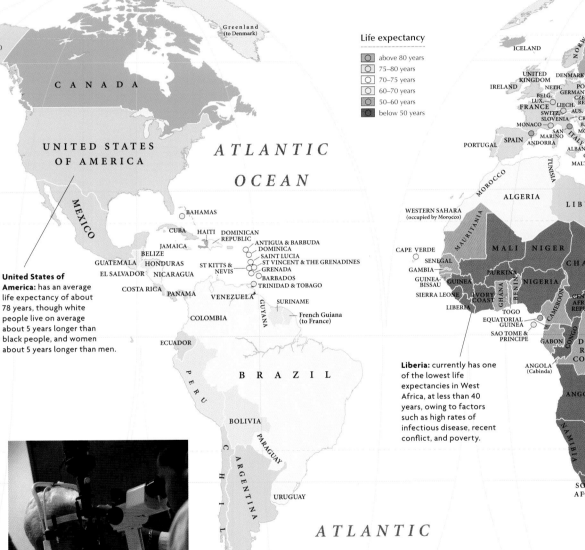

Life expectancy

◯	above 80 years
◯	75–80 years
◯	70–75 years
◯	60–70 years
◯	50–60 years
●	below 50 years

United States of America: has an average life expectancy of about 78 years, though white people live on average about 5 years longer than black people, and women about 5 years longer than men.

Liberia: currently has one of the lowest life expectancies in West Africa, at less than 40 years, owing to factors such as high rates of infectious disease, recent conflict, and poverty.

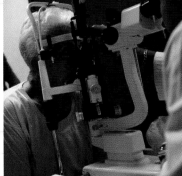

The extensive public healthcare system in Cuba provides for around 6 doctors per 1000 people, one of the highest ratios in the world.

Healthcare

An indicator of the strength of healthcare provision in a country is the number of doctors per 1000 population. Some communist and former communist countries such as Cuba and Russia score well in this regard. In general, healthcare provision is good or adequate in most of the world's richer countries but scanty throughout much of Africa and in parts of Asia and Latin America.

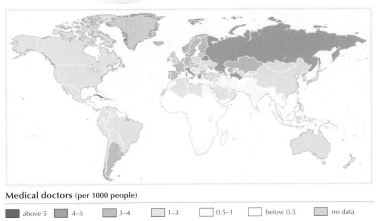

Medical doctors (per 1000 people)

■ above 5	■ 4–5	■ 3–4	□ 1–3	□ 0.5–1	□ below 0.5	■ no data

Smoking

Cigarette smoking—one of the most harmful activities to health—is common throughout much of the world. Smoking prevalence is generally highest in the richer, developed countries. However, awareness of the health risks has seen cigarette consumption in most of these countries stabilize or begin to fall. By contrast, more and more people, especially males, are taking up the habit in poorer developing countries.

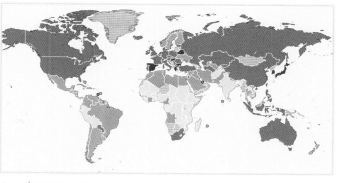

Annual cigarette consumption (per person)

- above 2500
- 1500–2499
- 500–1499
- 1–499
- no data

RUSSIAN FEDERATION

KAZAKHSTAN · MONGOLIA · NORTH KOREA · SOUTH KOREA · JAPAN · CHINA · UZBEKISTAN · KYRG. · TURKMEN. · TAJ. · AFGHANISTAN · NEPAL · BHUTAN · PAKISTAN · INDIA · BANGLADESH · MYANMAR (BURMA) · LAOS · THAILAND · VIETNAM · CAMBODIA · PHILIPPINES · TAIWAN · SRI LANKA · MALDIVES · MALAYSIA · SINGAPORE · BRUNEI · INDONESIA · PAPUA NEW GUINEA · EAST TIMOR

TURKEY · GEORGIA · ARMENIA · AZERB. · SYRIA · LEBANON · IRAQ · IRAN · WEST BANK · JORDAN · KUWAIT · BAHRAIN · QATAR · UAE · OMAN · SAUDI ARABIA · YEMEN · ERITREA · DJIBOUTI · ETHIOPIA · SOMALIA · KENYA · RWANDA · BURUNDI · TANZANIA · SEYCHELLES · COMOROS · MOZAMBIQUE · MADAGASCAR · MAURITIUS · ZIMBABWE · SWAZILAND · LESOTHO

PACIFIC OCEAN · INDIAN OCEAN

MICRONESIA · MARSHALL ISLANDS · PALAU · NAURU · SOLOMON ISLANDS · VANUATU · AUSTRALIA · NEW ZEALAND

Japan: has one of the world's highest life expectancies, at over 81 years—a fact commonly put down to the typical Japanese low-fat diet of rice, fish, and soy products.

Swaziland: currently has the lowest life expectancy in the world, at less than 33 years, due to widespread HIV/AIDS.

Communicable diseases

Despite advances in their treatment and prevention, infectious diseases remain a huge problem, especially in developing countries. Three of the most common and deadly are tuberculosis (TB), HIV/AIDS, and malaria. Of these, active TB affects about 15 million people (often as a complication of AIDS), with a particularly high prevalence in parts of Africa. HIV/AIDS has spread since 1981 to become a global pandemic. Malaria affects about 400 million people every year.

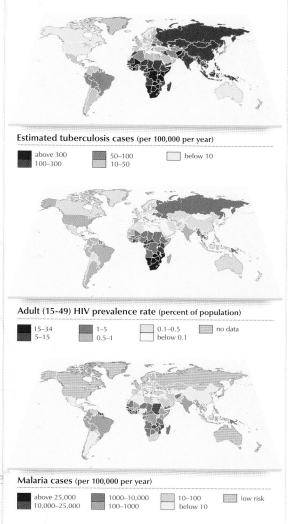

Estimated tuberculosis cases (per 100,000 per year)

- above 300
- 100–300
- 50–100
- 10–50
- below 10

Adult (15-49) HIV prevalence rate (percent of population)

- 15–34
- 5–15
- 1–5
- 0.5–1
- 0.1–0.5
- below 0.1
- no data

Malaria cases (per 100,000 per year)

- above 25,000
- 10,000–25,000
- 1000–10,000
- 100–1000
- 10–100
- below 10
- low risk

Preventive medicine

Throughout the world, doctors recognize that the prevention of disease and disease transmission is just as important as the treatment of illness. Preventive medicine has many aspects and includes advice about diet and nutrition; education about the avoidance of health-threatening behaviors such as smoking, excess alcohol consumption, and unprotected sex; and the use of vaccines against diseases such as typhoid, polio and cholera. In developing countries, some of the main priorities in preventive medicine are the provision of pure water supplies and proper sanitation, as well as measures against malaria, including the use of antimalarial drugs and mosquito nets.

The use of mosquito nets greatly reduces the transmission of malaria and the risk of infection.

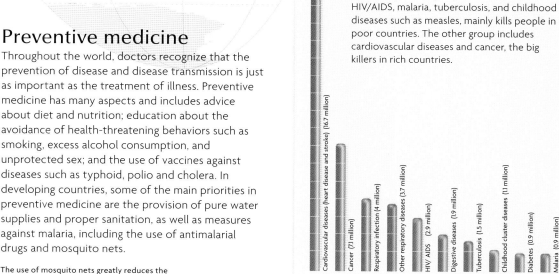

TOP TEN KILLER DISEASES, 2004

The world's biggest killer diseases fall into two main groups. One group, which includes HIV/AIDS, malaria, tuberculosis, and childhood diseases such as measles, mainly kills people in poor countries. The other group includes cardiovascular diseases and cancer, the big killers in rich countries.

- Cardiovascular diseases (heart disease and stroke) (16.7 million)
- Cancer (7.1 million)
- Respiratory infection (4 million)
- Other respiratory diseases (3.7 million)
- HIV/AIDS (2.9 million)
- Digestive diseases (1.9 million)
- Tuberculosis (1.5 million)
- Childhood cluster diseases (1.1 million)
- Diabetes (0.9 million)
- Malaria (0.9 million)

Water Resources

Water covers 71 percent of Earth's surface, but only 2.5 percent of this is fresh water, and two thirds of that is locked up in glaciers and polar ice sheets. Patterns of human settlement have developed around fresh water availability, but increasing numbers of people are now vulnerable to chronic shortage or interruptions in supply. Worldwide, fresh water consumption multiplied more than sixfold during the 20th century as populations increased and agriculture became more dependent on irrigation, much of it hugely wasteful because of evaporation and run-off. Industrial water demand also rose, as did use in the home, for washing, flushing, cooking, and gardening.

Amid the desert of Wadi Rum, Jordan, crops grow on circular patches of land irrigated with water from an underground aquifer.

Water withdrawal

Agriculture accounts for 70 percent of water consumption worldwide. Industry and domestic use each account for 15 percent. Excessive withdrawal of water affects the health of rivers and the needs of people. China's Yellow River now fails to reach the sea for most of the year.

Percentage of freshwater withdrawal by agriculture

79–100	66–79	47–66	31–47	16–31	0–16

Percentage of freshwater withdrawal by industry

79–100	66–79	47–66	31–47	16–31	0–16

Percentage of freshwater withdrawal by domestic use

60–81	45–60	30–45	15–30	0–15	no data

Availability of fresh water
total renewable
(cubic metres/capita/per year)

- less than 1000 (water scarcity)
- 1000–1699 (water stress)
- 1700–2999 (insufficient water)
- 3000–9999 (relatively sufficient)
- 10,000 or more (plentiful supplies)
- major drainage basin
- over 50% of water resource originating from outside country

Drought

The disruption of normal rainfall patterns can cause drought problems even in temperate zones, with consequences ranging from domestic water usage restrictions to low crop yields to forest fires. In regions of the developing world where monsoon rains fail, or water is perennially scarce, drought is a life or death issue. Parts of central and east Africa, for instance, have suffered severe and recurring droughts in recent decades, with disastrous results including destruction of livestock, desertification, famine, and mass migration.

In a severe drought, river beds may dry up (above left), leaving stranded fish to die, as here in Florida.

A Chinese farmer waters dry fields (above) in China's southern province of Guangdong. This picture was taken in May 2002, but the image is timeless; it could be August 2006 in Sichuan province, to the northwest of here—or almost any year in water-stressed northern China.

Water stress

A region is under "water stress" when the rate of water withdrawal from its rivers and aquifers exceeds their natural replenishment, so that people living there are subject to frequent shortages. Currently 1.7 billion people live in "highly stressed" river basins worldwide. This is a major potential cause of conflict, particularly when several countries share one river; the Euphrates, running through Turkey, Syria, and Iraq, or the rivers of southern China running south into Korea, are just two examples.

Freshwater stress in 1995 Water withdrawal (% of total available)

■ above 40	■ 20–40	■ 10–20	■ below 10

Freshwater stress in 2025 Water withdrawal (% of total available)

■ above 40	■ 20–40	■ 10–20	■ below 10

WATER AVAILABILITY

(by percentage of world's population)

relative sufficiency

- Plentiful 16.3%
- Water scarcity 8%
- Water stress 24.5%
- Relatively sufficient 24.5%
- Insufficient 16.7%

insufficiency

Clean drinking water

Sub-Saharan Africa is among the most deprived regions for lack of access to safe drinking water. Worldwide, this terrible health hazard affects over a billion people—at least 15 percent of the population. One of the agreed United Nations "millennium goals" for international development is to halve this proportion by 2015, by tackling chemical pollution from agriculture and industry, and by introducing essential purification facilities and local supply systems. In the industrialized world, people have come to expect clean drinking water on tap, even if they face rising prices for its treatment and supply.

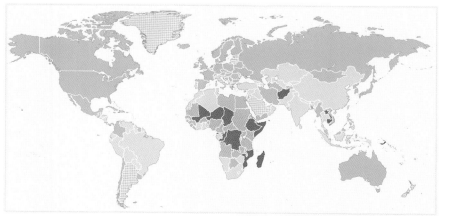

Mozambican children *(above)* fetch precious water in metal pans.

Gujarati villagers gather to draw water from a huge well *(above left)* in Natwarghad, western India. Many wells and village ponds ran dry in the severe drought of 2003, leaving local people to wait for irregular supplies brought in by state-run tankers.

Access to safe drinking water source
(percentage of population)

■ 91%–100%	■ below 50%
■ 76%–90%	□ no data
■ 50%–75%	

Economic Systems

The world economy is now effectively a single global system based on "free market" capitalist principles. Few countries still cling, like North Korea, to the "command economy" formula developed in the former communist bloc, where centralized state plans set targets for investment and production. In the West, state ownership of companies has greatly diminished thanks to the wave of privatization in the last 25 years. Major companies move capital and raw materials around the globe to take advantage of different labor costs and skills. The World Trade Organization (WTO) promotes free trade, but many countries still use subsidies, and protect their markets with import tariffs or quotas, to favor their own producers.

Balance of trade

Few countries earn from their exports exactly as much as they spend on imports. If the imbalance is persistently negative, it creates a potentially serious problem of indebtedness. The European Union's (EU) external trade is broadly in balance, but the US balance of trade has been in deficit since the 1970s, partly because it imports so many consumer goods. This deficit has recently spiralled to over US$ 800 billion a year.

Enormous volumes of trade pass through the world's stock markets making them key indicators of the strength of the global economy.

Balance of trade
(million US$)

over 30,000	
10,000–29,000	
1000–9999	Surplus
0–999	
0–999	
1000–9999	
10,000–29,999	Deficit
over 30,000	
data unavailable	

TOP TEN GLOBAL COMPANIES

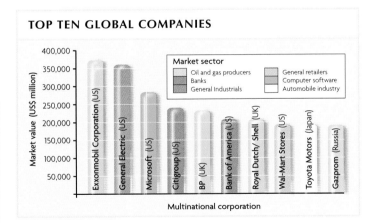

Market value (US$ million) vs Multinational corporation

Market sector:
- Oil and gas producers
- Banks
- General Industrials
- General retailers
- Computer software
- Automobile industry

Companies: Exxonmobil Corporation (US), General Electric (US), Microsoft (US), Citigroup (US), BP (UK), Bank of America (US), Royal Dutch/ Shell (UK), Wal-Mart Stores (US), Toyota Motors (Japan), Gazprom (Russia)

Energy

Countries with oil and gas to sell (notably in the Middle East and Russia) can charge high prices; trade in fuel was worth US$ 1.4 trillion in 2005. The US and others are turning back to nuclear power (despite safety fears) for generating electricity. China relies heavily on (polluting) coal. Renewable technologies promise much, but so far make relatively minor contributions.

World Energy consumption (quadrillion British thermal units)

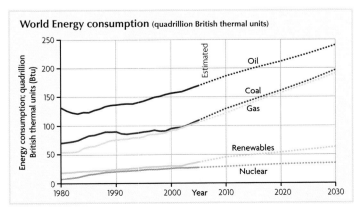

Energy consumption; quadrillion British thermal units (Btu) — Oil, Coal, Gas, Renewables, Nuclear — Estimated — Year 1980–2030

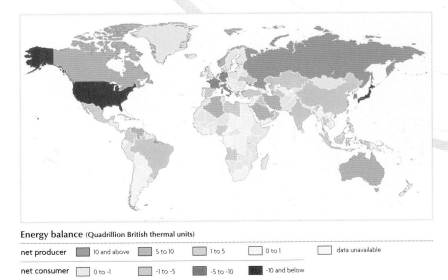

Energy balance (Quadrillion British thermal units)

net producer	10 and above	5 to 10	1 to 5	0 to 1	data unavailable
net consumer	0 to -1	-1 to -5	-5 to -10	-10 and below	

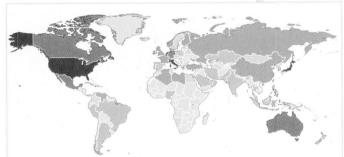

SOUTH AMERICA

New York

London

EUROPE

AFRICA

International debt
(as percentage of GDP)

- above 100%
- 70–99%
- 50–69%
- 30–49%
- 10–29%
- below 10%

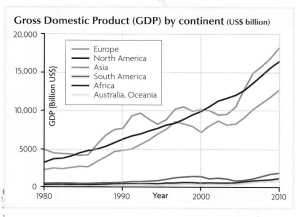

International debt

Saddled with crippling debts from past borrowing, the world's poorest countries are still paying off US $100 million a day. This is despite recent successful campaigns to get some of their debts cancelled to allow them to use their limited resources for development. Most international debt, however, is owed by developed countries to one another. The US owes literally trillions of dollars, nearly a third of it's total debt, to Japan.

Gross Domestic Product (GDP) by continent (US$ billion)

- Europe
- North America
- Asia
- South America
- Africa
- Australia, Oceania

GDP (Billion US$) vs. Year (1980–2010), scale 0–20,000

Trade sector

World trade in merchandise tops US$ 10 trillion a year. The global pattern is uneven. Latin America, Africa, the Middle East, and Russia principally export "primary" goods (agricultural produce, mining and fuel). The "secondary" manufacturing sector includes iron and steel, machine tools, chemicals, clothing and textiles, cars and other consumer goods. The West still dominates the "tertiary" or non-merchandise sector, worth US$ 2.4 trillion, in services such as insurance and banking.

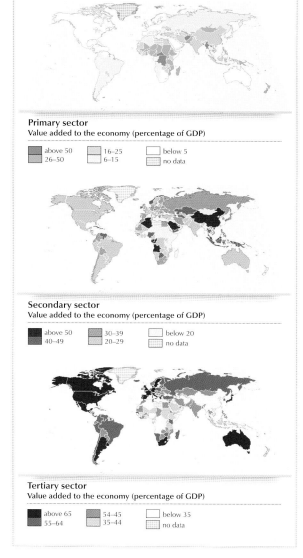

Primary sector
Value added to the economy (percentage of GDP)

- above 50
- 26–50
- 16–25
- 6–15
- below 5
- no data

Secondary sector
Value added to the economy (percentage of GDP)

- above 50
- 40–49
- 30–39
- 20–29
- below 20
- no data

Tertiary sector
Value added to the economy (percentage of GDP)

- above 65
- 55–64
- 54–45
- 35–44
- below 35
- no data

NORTH AMERICA

ASIA

Tokyo

AUSTRALIA

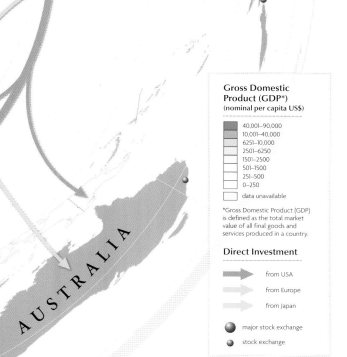

Gross Domestic Product (GDP*)
(nominal per capita US$)

- 40,001–90,000
- 10,001–40,000
- 6251–10,000
- 2501–6250
- 1501–2500
- 501–1500
- 251–500
- 0–250
- data unavailable

*Gross Domestic Product (GDP) is defined as the total market value of all final goods and services produced in a country.

Direct Investment

- from USA
- from Europe
- from Japan
- major stock exchange
- stock exchange

Average monthly salary
(US$)

- above 3000
- 2000–3000
- 1000–2000
- 500–1000
- 250–500
- below 250
- no data

Labor

China's huge low-cost labor force promotes its conquest of world markets for manufactured goods. India's educated workforce attracts call centers and other service sector jobs, while the more economically developed countries's (MEDC) caring professions, and low-wage agriculture, draw in immigrant labor.

Travel

Mass travel is now a ubiquitous feature of all developed countries, and the provision of transport and tourism facilities one of the world's biggest industries, employing well over 100 million people. The travel explosion has come about, first, through major improvements in transportation technology; and second, as a result of increasing amounts of disposable income and leisure time in the world's wealthier countries. The main reasons for travel today include leisure pursuits and tourism (accounting for well over half of the total financial outlay), work and business, pilgrimage, migration, and visits to family and friends.

There are currently around 4.2 billion air travelers a year passing through over 1600 international and domestic airports. This figure is forecast to grow by 4 percent each year, leading to increased pressure on air traffic control and ground handling systems that, in many areas, are already close to maximum capacity.

Major modes of transportation

The major transport modes for people in the 21st century are road, rail, and air travel. The most popular air routes are highly concentrated within and between the USA, western Europe, and Asia. Major roads and railroads are more evenly spread, following the general distribution of the world's population.

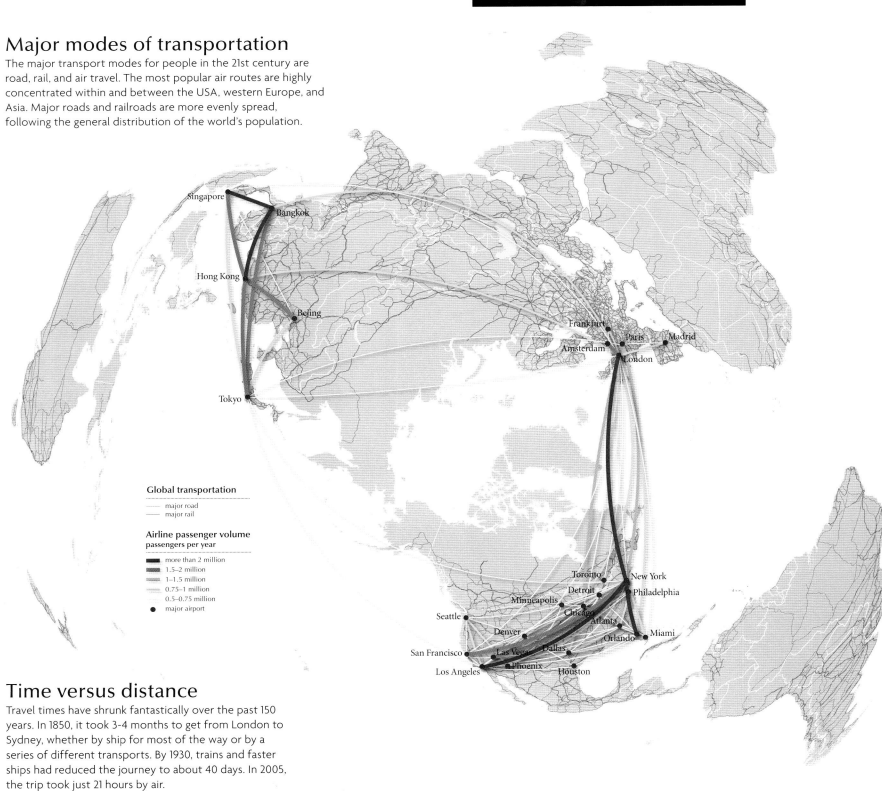

Global transportation

— major road
— major rail

Airline passenger volume
passengers per year

- more than 2 million
- 1.5–2 million
- 1–1.5 million
- 0.75–1 million
- 0.5–0.75 million
- ● major airport

Time versus distance

Travel times have shrunk fantastically over the past 150 years. In 1850, it took 3-4 months to get from London to Sydney, whether by ship for most of the way or by a series of different transports. By 1930, trains and faster ships had reduced the journey to about 40 days. In 2005, the trip took just 21 hours by air.

London

1850 — *by coach to Portsmouth and thence ship around the Cape of Good Hope*

1850 — **Istanbul** — *coach . ferry . coach . horseback* — *horseback . river boat* — **Basra** — *river b*

1930 — **Istanbul** **Basra** **Bombay** **Calcutta** **Singapore** **Sydney**
train . ferry . train | *train . river boat* | *river boat . steamship* | *train* | *steamship* | *steamship*

2005 ● ▮ ● *London–Sydney by air including one refueling stop*

DAYS | 1 | 2 | 3 | 4 | 5 | 6 | 7 | 8 | 9 | 10 | 11 | 12 | 13 | 14 | 15 | 16 | 17 | 18 | 19 | 20 | 21 | 22 | 23 | 24 | 25 | 26 | 27 | 28 | 29 | 30 | 31 | 32 | 33 | 34 | 35 | 36 | 37 | 38 | 39 | 40 | 41 | 42 | 43 | 44 | 45 | 46 | 47 | 48 | 49 | 50 | 51 | 52 | 53 | 54 | 5

Media and Communications

Over the past 50 years, the term "media" has come to denote various means of communicating information between people at a distance. These include mass media—methods such as newspapers, radio, and television that can be used to rapidly disseminate information to large numbers of people—and two-way systems, such as telephones and e-mail. Currently, the communication systems undergoing the most rapid growth worldwide include mobile telephony and various Internet-based applications, such as web sites, blogs, and podcasting, which can be considered forms of mass media.

Internet usage

Internet usage has grown extremely rapidly since the early 1990s, largely as a result of the invention of the World Wide Web. Usage rates are highest in the USA (where about 80 percent of people were using the Internet in 2006), Australia, Japan, South Korea, and Finland. They are lowest in Africa, where on average less than 5 percent of the population were Internet users in 2006.

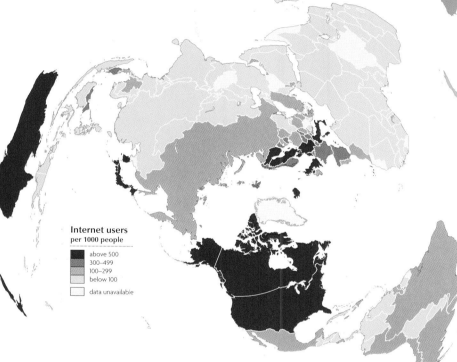

Internet users
per 1000 people

- above 500
- 300–499
- 100–299
- below 100
- data unavailable

The internet emerged in the early 1990s as a computer-based global communication system. Since then massive growth has seen user numbers increase to around 1.1 billion people, or roughly 17 percent of the world's population.

Mobile phone usage

By 2006, there were more than 2.5 billion mobile phone users worldwide. In some parts of Europe, such as Italy, almost everyone owns and uses a mobile—many possess more than one phone. In contrast, throughout much of Southern Asia and Africa, less than 10 percent of the population are users. As well as utilizing them as telephones, most users now employ the devices for the additional functions they offer, such as text messaging and e-mail.

Mobile phone users
per 1000 people

- above 900
- 700–899
- 500–699
- 300–499
- 100–299
- below 100
- data unavailable

Satellite Communications

Modern communications satellites are used extensively for international telephony, for television and radio broadcasting, and to some extent for transmitting Internet data. Many of these satellites are deployed in clusters or arrays, often in geostationary orbits—that is, in positions that appear fixed to Earth-based observers.

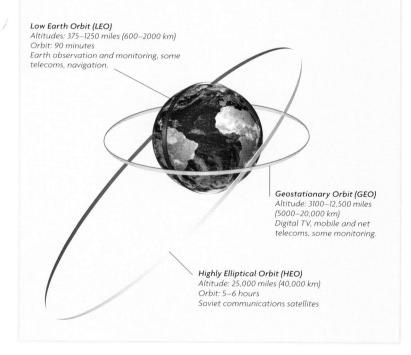

Low Earth Orbit (LEO)
Altitudes: 375–1250 miles (600–2000 km)
Orbit: 90 minutes
Earth observation and monitoring, some telecoms, navigation.

Geostationary Orbit (GEO)
Altitude: 3100–12,500 miles (5000–20,000 km)
Digital TV, mobile and net telecoms, some monitoring.

Highly Elliptical Orbit (HEO)
Altitude: 25,000 miles (40,000 km)
Orbit: 5–6 hours
Soviet communications satellites

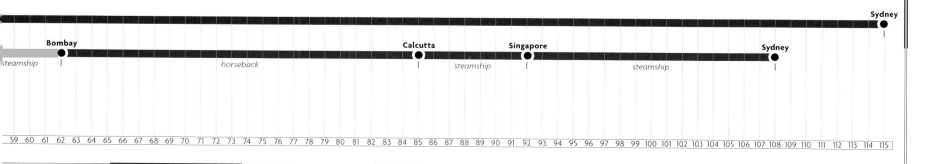

Sydney

Bombay

Calcutta

Singapore

Sydney

Sydney

steamship   horseback   steamship   steamship

59 60 61 62 63 64 65 66 67 68 69 70 71 72 73 74 75 76 77 78 79 80 81 82 83 84 85 86 87 88 89 90 91 92 93 94 95 96 97 98 99 100 101 102 103 104 105 106 107 108 109 110 111 112 113 114 115

The Political World

Today's world map shows nearly 200 independent states, compared with about 80 after World War II. The transformation is mainly due to the withdrawal of European powers from huge colonial empires; their remaining overseas dependencies are tiny by comparison. The late 20th century also saw the collapse of communism, realignment in Europe, and fragmentation in former Yugoslavia. Globally, the Soviet Union's demise left the USA as the sole superpower, though with fast-growing China and India emerging as economic giants of the future. US security preoccupations switched to combating terrorism, while looming oil and other resource shortages, and environmental constraints, underlined the need for more effective international cooperation.

CONTINENTAL FACTFILE

	Total area: sq miles	Total area: sq km	Total population
North & Central America	8,621,846	22,327,375	516.8 million
South America	6,839,892	17,715,315	380.2 million
Africa	11,617,219	30,088,602	924.6 million
Europe	3,596,737	9,341,459	711.5 million
Asia	17,469,967	45,246,231	3978.2 million
Australia & Oceania	3,275,288	8,483,003	32.7 million

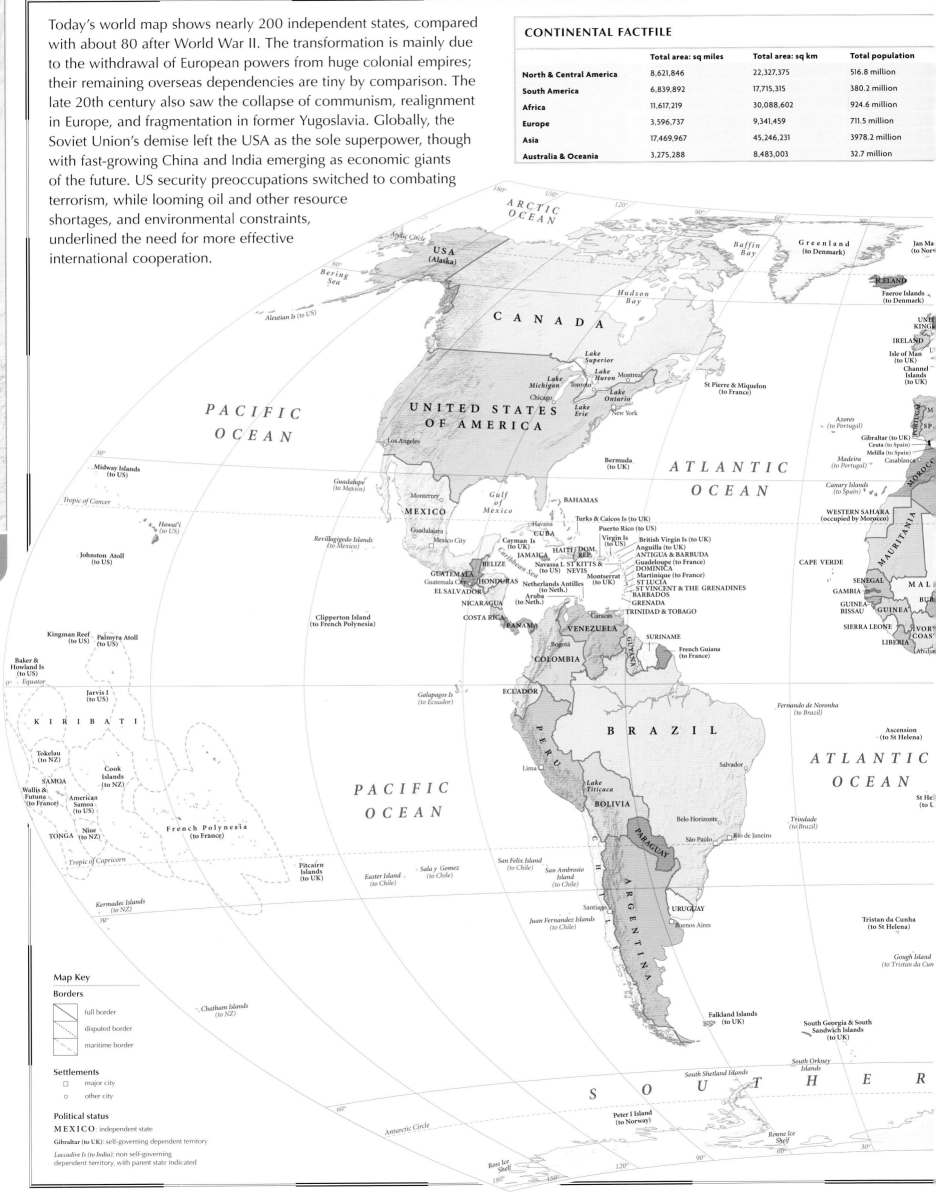

Map Key

Borders

full border

disputed border

maritime border

Settlements

□ major city

○ other city

Political status

MEXICO: independent state

Gibraltar (to UK): self-governing dependent territory

Laccadive Is (to India): non self-governing dependent territory, with parent state indicated

Countries	Largest country	Country with largest population
23	Canada 3,855,171 sq miles (9,984,670 sq km)	United States 301 million
12	Brazil 3,286,470 sq miles (8,511,965 sq km)	Brazil 188.9 million
53	Sudan 967,493 sq miles (2,505,810 sq km)	Nigeria 134.4 million
46	European Russia 1,527,341 sq miles (3,955,818 sq km)	European Russia 114 million
48	Asiatic Russia 5,065,394 sq miles (13,119,382 sq km)	China 1323.6 million
14	Australia 2,967,893 sq miles (7,686,850 sq km)	Australia 20.4 million

International borders

The world political map of today displays a complex pattern of boundaries that has evolved through history, and is still constantly changing as new countries emerge and disputes and territorial claims are slowly resolved. The map shows two main types of border. Full borders represent internationally agreed and recognized territorial boundaries. A disputed border is indicated where a *de facto* territorial boundary exists, which is not agreed or is still subject to arbitration.

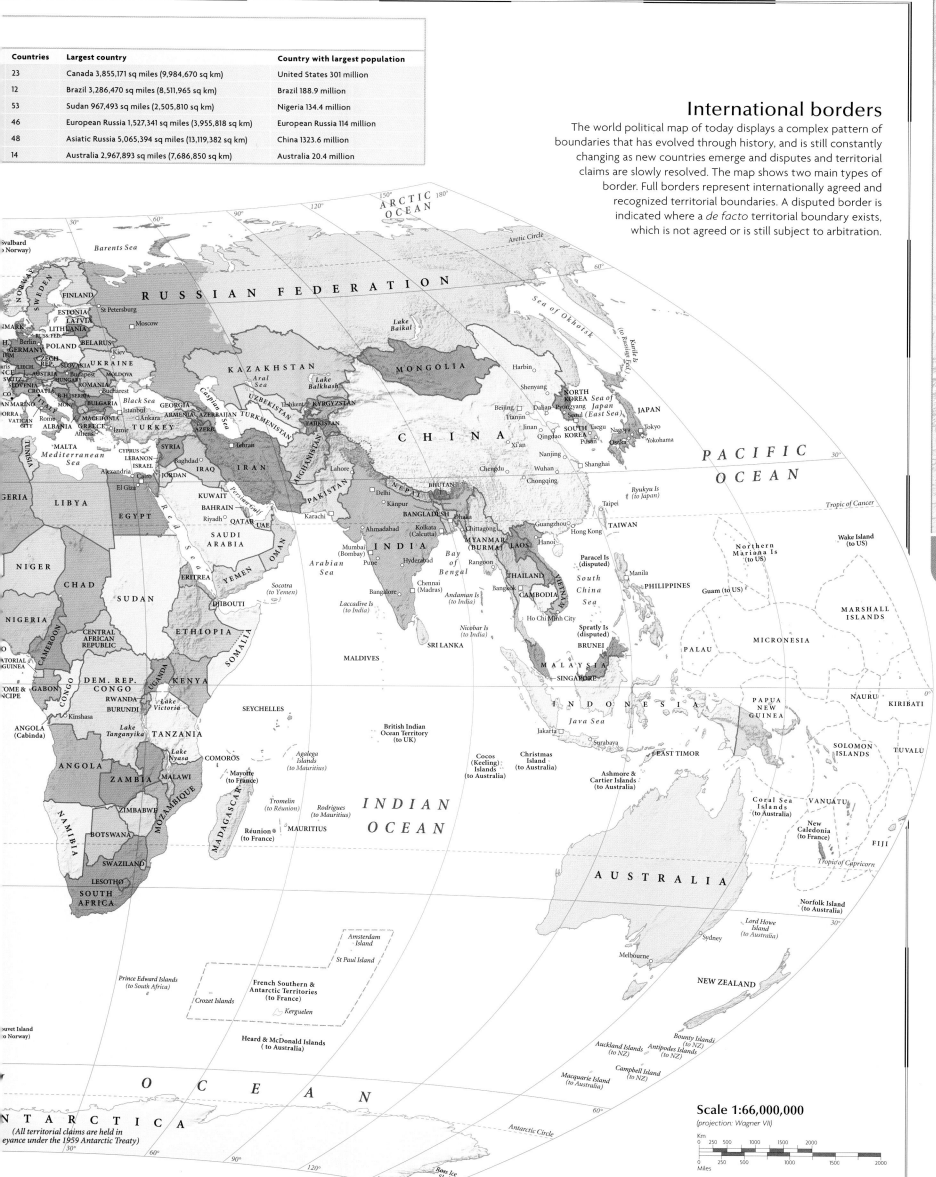

Scale 1:66,000,000

(projection: Wagner VII)

Borders, conflicts, and disputes

Conflict evolved in the 20th century from conventional land- or sea-based warfare to increasingly long-range airborne attacks. Nuclear arms from 1945 took this to the intercontinental scale. The Cold War presented a new type of conflict, underlined by the race for weapons capabilities between the US and the Soviet Union. In Korea, Vietnam, the Middle East and elsewhere, soldiers and civilians were exposed to deadly chemicals. International treaties aimed to prevent the spread of nuclear, biological and chemical "weapons of mass destruction"— especially to "pariah states" like Libya and Iran. Intercommunal conflict and "ethnic cleansing" reminded the world that horror needed no sophisticated weaponry. After 9/11, the US-led "war on terror" perceived conflict in a new light, where international terrorism knew no borders.

THE PEACEKEEPERS

Over 130 countries have contributed around a million troops to UN missions to monitor peace processes and help implement peace accords since 1948. Regional alliances such as NATO and the African Union (AU) are increasingly deploying their own multinational forces in trouble-spots, while Australia has intervened in a similar manner in nearby Pacific island states. Peacekeepers oversaw East Timor's elections in 2001 and subsequent celebration of independence (above). The US position as sole global superpower enables it to define many of its activities as peacekeeping, despite the confrontational nature of its interventions.

DARFUR

African ethnic minorities in Darfur in western Sudan have suffered appalling violence since 2003 at the hands of genocidal Arab Janjaweed militias, for which the government in Khartoum denies responsibility. Displaced in their hundreds of thousands, refugees receive inadequate protection and aid from an international community unwilling to commit to full-scale intervention.

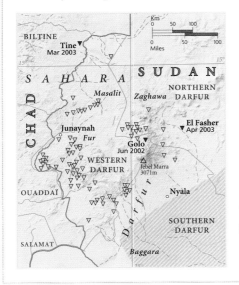

Darfur conflict

Fur ethnic group
- ▨ arabic speaking area
- ▽ villages destroyed by Janjaweed
- ▼ towns that have been attacked by rebels opposing the Sudanese government

ISRAEL

Since its creation in 1948, Israel has been at war with its Arab neighbors. The Palestinians are fighting for a separate, viable state, comprising of at least East Jerusalem, and the West Bank and Gaza Strip, territories occupied by Israel in 1967. Their struggle *(intifada)* has attracted international support, but has been met by a hard-line response from Israel, which is backed by the US.

Arab-Israeli Wars 1947-2006

MAIN MAP: Arab-Israeli Wars
- ▨ Israel in 1949
- ▨ occupied by Israel after 1967 war
- ▨ occupied by Israel after 1973 war
- ▨ occupied by Israel after 1967 war reoccupied by Egypt after 1973 war
- ▭ demilitarized zone held by UN after Israel-Syria agreement, 1974, and 2nd Sinai agreement, 1975
- ▽ Hezbollah rocket attacks 2006
- ▼ Israeli rocket attacks 2006
- —·— disputed border

INSET MAP 1: UN Partition plan in 1947
- — border of British mandate 1923
- ▨ proposed Arab State
- ▨ proposed Jewish State
- ▨ proposed international zone

INSET MAP 2: West Bank security
- ▨ Palestinian responsibility for civil affairs and internal security
- ▨ Palestinian responsibility for civil affairs; Israel responsible for security
- — Security Wall (existing and planned)

Types of government

- Multiparty democracy for more than 10 yrs
- Multiparty/transitional democracy within last 10 yrs
- Single-party government
- Military regime
- Theocracy
- Absolute monarchy

Conflicts and international disputes

- Major active territorial or border disputes
- Countries involved in internal conflict
- Active territorial or border disputes and internal conflict

Lines on the map

The determination of international boundaries can use a variety of criteria. Many borders between older states follow physical boundaries, often utilizing natural defensive features. Others have been determined by international agreement or arbitration, or simply ended up where the opposing forces stood at the end of a conflict.

WORLD BOUNDARIES

Dates from which current boundaries have existed

1990–present	1946–1965	1850–1914
1966–1989	1915–1945	1800–1849	Pre-1800

POST-COLONIAL BORDERS

Independent African countries have largely inherited the earlier carve up of the continent by European colonial powers. These often arbitrarily divided or grouped differing ethnic and religious groups which has, in turn, contributed to the tensions that underlie the many civil conflicts that have plagued post-colonial Africa.

ENCLAVES

Changes to international boundaries occasionally create pockets of land cut off from the main territory of the country they belong to. In Europe, Kaliningrad has been separated from the rest of the Russian

Federation since the independence of the Baltic States. Likewise, when Morocco was granted independence, Spain retained the coastal enclaves of Ceuta and Melilla.

GEOMETRIC BORDERS

Straight lines and lines of longitude and latitude have occasionally been used to determine international boundaries: the 49th Parallel forms a large section of the Canada–US border, while the 38th Parallel divides the Korean Peninsula. Internal administrative divisions within Canada, the US, and Australia also use geometric boundaries.

PHYSICAL BORDERS

Rivers account for one-sixth of the world's borders: the Danube forms part of the boundaries for nine European nations. Changes in a river's course or disruption of its flow can lead to territorial disputes. Lakes and mountains also form natural borders.

Lake border *(right)*
Mountain border *(below left)*
River border *(below right)*

THE GULF WAR

Although the West armed Saddam Hussein in the brutal 1980s Iran-Iraq War, his unprovoked invasion of Kuwait in 1990 was decried the world over. A US-led coalition, including Arab states, repelled his troops but left him in power. A decade of sanctions followed until, in 2003, Saddam was finally toppled by US-led forces. Following elections in 2005, Iraq has struggled to contain a violent insurgency.

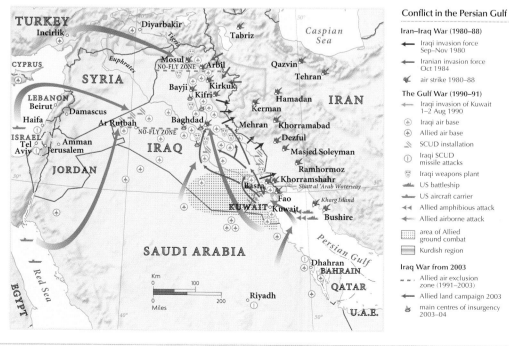

Conflict in the Persian Gulf

Iran–Iraq War (1980–88)
- Iraqi invasion force Sep–Nov 1980
- Iranian invasion force Oct 1984
- air strike 1980–88

The Gulf War (1990–91)
- Iraqi invasion of Kuwait 1–2 Aug 1990
- Iraqi air base
- Allied air base
- SCUD installation
- Iraqi SCUD missile attacks
- Iraqi weapons plant
- US battleship
- US aircraft carrier
- Allied amphibious attack
- Allied airborne attack
- area of Allied ground combat
- Kurdish region

Iraq War from 2003
- Allied air exclusion zone (1991–2003)
- Allied land campaign 2003
- main centres of insurgency 2003–04

The World's Time Zones

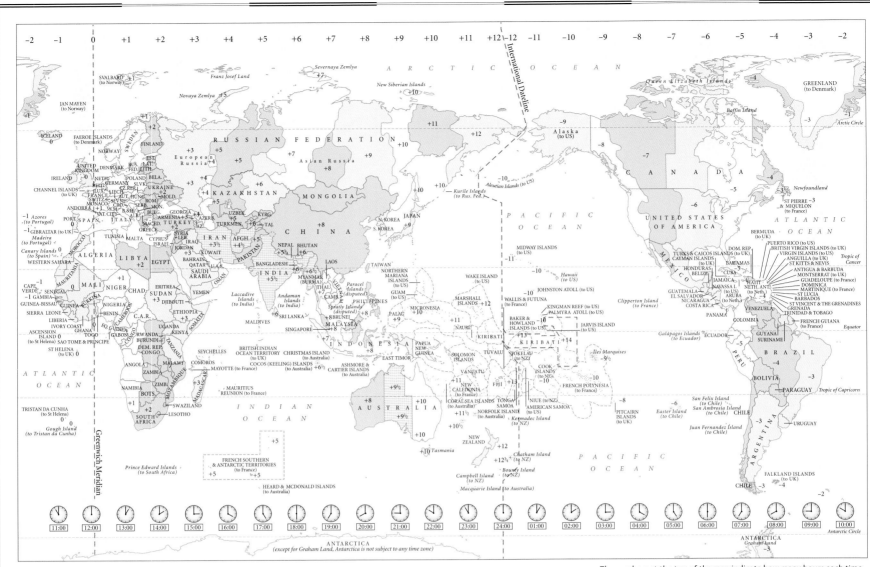

The numbers at the top of the map indicate how many hours each time zone is ahead or behind Coordinated Universal Time (UTC). The row of clocks indicate the time in each zone when it is 12:00 noon UTC.

TIME ZONES

Because Earth is a rotating sphere, the Sun shines on only half of its surface at any one time. Thus, it is simultaneously morning, evening and night time in different parts of the world (see diagram below). Because of these disparities, each country or part of a country adheres to a local time. A region of Earth's surface within which a single local time is used is called a time zone. There are 24 one hour time zones around the world, arranged roughly in longitudinal bands.

STANDARD TIME

Standard time is the official local time in a particular country or part of a country. It is defined by the time zone or zones associated with that country or region. Although time zones are arranged roughly in longitudinal bands, in many places the borders of a zone do not fall exactly on longitudinal meridians, as can be seen on the map (above),

but are determined by geographical factors or by borders between countries or parts of countries. Most countries have just one time zone and one standard time, but some large countries (such as the USA, Canada and Russia) are split between several time zones, so standard time varies across those countries. For example, the coterminous United States straddles four time zones and so has four standard times, called the Eastern, Central, Mountain and Pacific standard times. China is unusual in that just one standard time is used for the whole country, even though it extends across 60° of longitude from west to east.

COORDINATED UNIVERSAL TIME (UTC)

Coordinated Universal Time (UTC) is a reference by which the local time in each time zone is set. For example, Australian Western Standard Time (the local time in Western Australia) is set 8 hours ahead of UTC (it is UTC+8) whereas Eastern Standard Time in the United States is set 5

hours behind UTC (it is UTC-5). UTC is a successor to, and closely approximates, Greenwich Mean Time (GMT). However, UTC is based on an atomic clock, whereas GMT is determined by the Sun's position in the sky relative to the 0° longitudinal meridian, which runs through Greenwich, UK.

In 1884 the Prime Meridian (0° longitude) was defined by the position of the cross-hairs in the eyepiece of the "Transit Circle" telescope in the Meridian Building at the Royal Observatory, Greenwich, UK.

DAY AND NIGHT AROUND THE WORLD

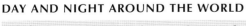

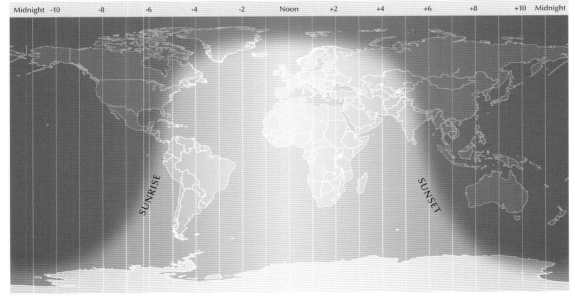

THE INTERNATIONAL DATELINE

The International Dateline is an imaginary line from pole to pole that roughly corresponds to the 180° longitudinal meridian. It is an arbitrary marker between calendar days. The dateline is needed because of the use of local times around the world rather than a single universal time. When moving from west to east across the dateline, travelers have to set their watches back one day. Those traveling in the opposite direction, from east to west, must add a day.

DAYLIGHT SAVING TIME

Daylight saving is a summertime adjustment to the local time in a country or region, designed to cause a higher proportion of its citizens' waking hours to pass during daylight. To follow the system, timepieces are advanced by an hour on a pre-decided date in spring and reverted back in the fall. About half of the world's nations use daylight saving.

ATLAS
OF THE WORLD

THE MAPS IN THIS ATLAS ARE ARRANGED CONTINENT BY CONTINENT, STARTING FROM THE INTERNATIONAL DATE LINE, AND MOVING EASTWARDS. THE MAPS PROVIDE A UNIQUE VIEW OF TODAY'S WORLD, COMBINING TRADITIONAL CARTOGRAPHIC TECHNIQUES WITH THE LATEST REMOTE-SENSED AND DIGITAL TECHNOLOGY.

North America is the world's third largest continent with
a total area of 9,358,340 sq miles (24,238,000 sq km)
including Greenland and the Caribbean islands.
It lies wholly within the Northern Hemisphere.

FACTFILE

N **Most Northerly Point:** Kap Morris Jesup, Greenland 83° 38′ N
S **Most Southerly Point:** Peninsula de Azuero, Panama 7° 15′ N
E **Most Easterly Point:** Nordøstrundingen, Greenland 12° 08′ W
W **Most Westerly Point:** Attu, Aleutian Islands, USA 172° 30′ E

Largest Lakes:
1 Lake Superior, Canada/USA 31,151 sq miles (83,270 sq km)
2 Lake Huron, Canada/USA 23,436 sq miles (60,700 sq km)
3 Lake Michigan, USA 22,402 sq miles (58,020 sq km)
4 Great Bear Lake, Canada 12,274 sq miles (31,790 sq km)
5 Great Slave Lake, Canada 10,981 sq miles (28,440 sq km)

Longest Rivers:
1 Mississippi-Missouri, USA 3710 miles (5969 km)
2 Mackenzie, Canada 2640 miles (4250 km)
3 Yukon, Canada/USA 1978 miles (3184 km)
4 St. Lawrence/Great Lakes, Canada/USA 1900 miles (3058 km)
5 Rio Grande, Mexico/USA 1900 miles (3057 km)

Largest Islands:
1 Greenland 849,400 sq miles (2,200,000 sq km)
2 Baffin Island, Canada 183,800 sq miles (476,000 sq km)
3 Victoria Island, Canada 81,900 sq miles (212,000 sq km)
4 Ellesmere Island, Canada 75,700 sq miles (196,000 sq km)
5 Newfoundland, Canada 42,031 sq miles (108,860 sq km)

Highest Points:
1 Mount McKinley (Denali), USA 20,332 ft (6194 m)
2 Mount Logan, Canada 19,550 ft (5959 m)
3 Volcán Pico de Orizaba, Mexico 18,700 ft (5700 m)
4 Mount St. Elias, USA 18,008 ft (5489 m)
5 Popocatépetl, Mexico 17,887 ft (5452 m)

Lowest Point:
▼ Death Valley, USA -282 ft (-86 m) below sea level

Highest recorded temperature:
● Death Valley, USA 135°F (57°C)

Lowest recorded temperature:
— Northice, Greenland -87°F (-66°C)

Wettest Place:
≋ Vancouver, Canada 183 in (4645 mm)

Driest Place:
— Death Valley, USA 2 in (50 mm)

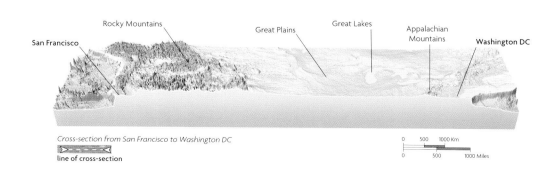

Cross-section from San Francisco to Washington DC

line of cross-section

San Francisco — Rocky Mountains — Great Plains — Great Lakes — Appalachian Mountains — Washington DC

0 500 1000 Km
0 500 1000 Miles

Political

Democracy is well established in some parts of the continent but is a recent phenomenon in others. The economically dominant nations of Canada and the USA have a long democratic tradition but elsewhere, notably in the countries of Central America, political turmoil has been more common. In Nicaragua and Haiti, harsh dictatorships have only recently been superseded by democratically-elected governments. North America's largest countries—Canada, Mexico, and the USA—have federal state systems, sharing political power between national and state or provincial governments. The USA has intervened militarily on several occasions in Central America and the Caribbean to protect its strategic interests.

Transportation

In the 19th century, railroads were used to open up the North American continent. Air transport is now more common for long distance passenger travel, although railroads are still extensively used for bulk freight transport. Waterways, like the Mississippi River, are important for the transport of bulk materials, and the Panama Canal is a vital link between the Pacific Ocean and the Caribbean. In the 20th century, road transportation increased massively in North America, with the introduction of cheap, mass-produced cars and extensive highway construction.

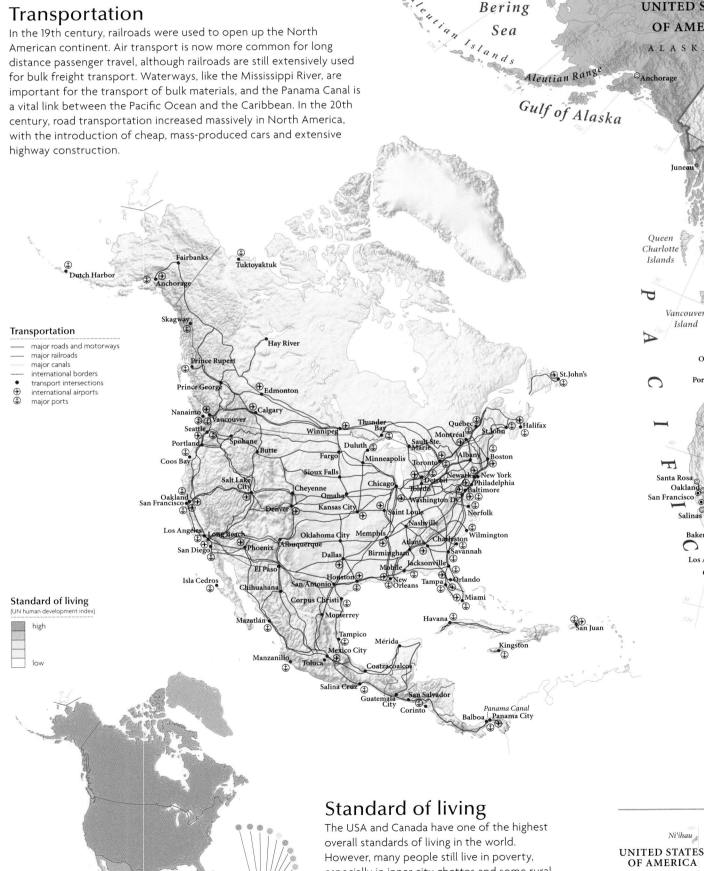

Transportation
- major roads and motorways
- major railroads
- major canals
- international borders
- • transport intersections
- ⊕ international airports
- ⊕ major ports

Standard of living
(UN human development index)

high

low

Standard of living

The USA and Canada have one of the highest overall standards of living in the world. However, many people still live in poverty, especially in inner city ghettos and some rural areas. Central America and the Caribbean are markedly poorer than their wealthier northern neighbors Haiti is the poorest country in the western hemisphere.

UNITED STATES OF AMERICA

HAWAI'I

SCALE 1:13,000,000

Km
0 50 100 150 200

0   50   100   150   200
Miles

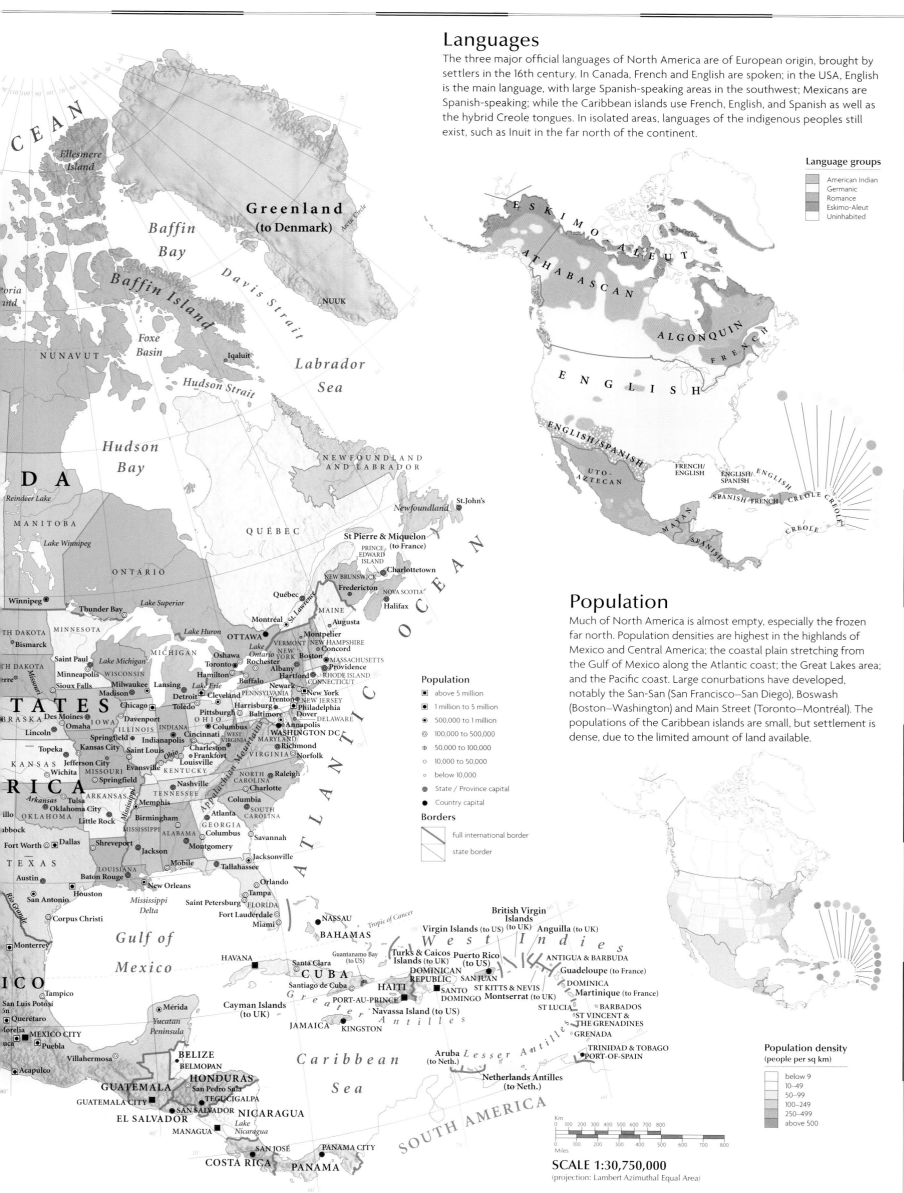

Languages

The three major official languages of North America are of European origin, brought by settlers in the 16th century. In Canada, French and English are spoken; in the USA, English is the main language, with large Spanish-speaking areas in the southwest; Mexicans are Spanish-speaking; while the Caribbean islands use French, English, and Spanish as well as the hybrid Creole tongues. In isolated areas, languages of the indigenous peoples still exist, such as Inuit in the far north of the continent.

Language groups

- American Indian
- Germanic
- Romance
- Eskimo-Aleut
- Uninhabited

Population

Much of North America is almost empty, especially the frozen far north. Population densities are highest in the highlands of Mexico and Central America; the coastal plain stretching from the Gulf of Mexico along the Atlantic coast; the Great Lakes area; and the Pacific coast. Large conurbations have developed, notably the San-San (San Francisco–San Diego), Boswash (Boston–Washington) and Main Street (Toronto–Montréal). The populations of the Caribbean islands are small, but settlement is dense, due to the limited amount of land available.

Population

- ▣ above 5 million
- ▣ 1 million to 5 million
- ◉ 500,000 to 1 million
- ◎ 100,000 to 500,000
- ⊕ 50,000 to 100,000
- ○ 10,000 to 50,000
- ◦ below 10,000
- ● State / Province capital
- ● Country capital

Borders

- full international border
- state border

Population density
(people per sq km)

- below 9
- 10–49
- 50–99
- 100–249
- 250–499
- above 500

Km
0 100 200 300 400 500 600 700 800

Miles
0 100 200 300 400 500 600 700 800

SCALE 1:30,750,000
(projection: Lambert Azimuthal Equal Area)

NORTH AMERICA – **Physical**

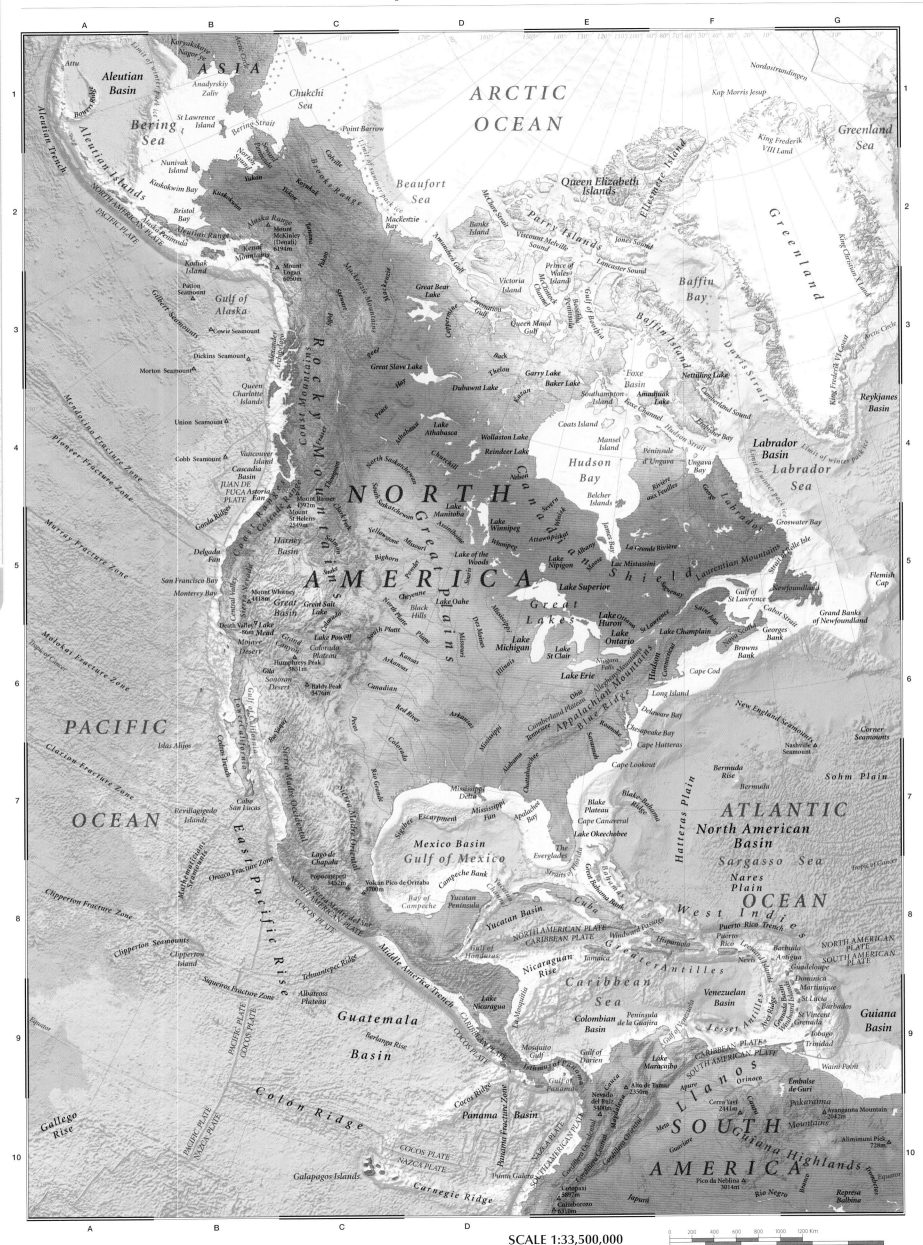

SCALE 1:33,500,000
(projection: Lambert Conformal Conic)

| 0 | 200 | 400 | 600 | 800 | 1000 | 1200 Km |
| 0 | 200 | 400 | 600 | 800 | 1000 | 1200 Miles |

Environmental Issues

Many fragile environments are under threat throughout the region. In Haiti, all the primary rain forest has been destroyed, while air pollution from factories and cars in Mexico City is among the worst in the world. Elsewhere, industry and mining pose threats, particularly in the delicate arctic environment of Alaska where oil spills have polluted coastlines and decimated fish stocks.

Environmental issues

- national parks
- acid rain
- tropical forest
- forest destroyed
- desert
- desertification
- polluted rivers
- radioactive contamination
- marine pollution
- heavy marine pollution
- poor urban air quality

Climate

North America's climate includes extremes ranging from freezing Arctic conditions in Alaska and Greenland, to desert in the southwest, and tropical conditions in southeastern Florida, the Caribbean, and Central America. Central and southern regions are prone to severe storms including tornadoes and hurricanes.

Average Rainfall

January rainfall *July rainfall*

Rainfall

- 0–25 mm (0–1 in)
- 25–50 mm (1–2 in)
- 50–100 mm (2–4 in)
- 100–200 mm (4–8 in)
- 200–300 mm (8–12 in)
- 300–400 mm (12–16 in)
- 400–500 mm (16–20 in)
- more than 500 mm (20 in)

Average Temperature

January temperature *July temperature*

Temperature

- below -30°C (-22°F)
- -30 to -20°C (-22 to -4°F)
- -20 to -10°C (-4 to 14°F)
- -10 to 0°C (14 to 32°F)
- 0 to 10°C (32 to 50°F)
- 10 to 20°C (50 to 68°F)
- 20 to 30°C (68 to 86°F)
- above 30°C (86°F)

Climate

- ice cap
- tundra
- subarctic
- cool continental
- warm humid
- semi-arid
- arid
- humid equatorial
- tropical
- daily hours of sunshine, January
- daily hours of sunshine, July
- direction of hurricanes
- tornado zones

Landuse

Abundant land and fertile soils stretch from the Canadian prairies to Texas creating North America's agricultural heartland. Cereals and cattle ranching form the basis of the farming economy, with corn and soybeans also important. Fruit and vegetables are grown in California using irrigation, while Florida is a leading producer of citrus fruits. Caribbean and Central American countries depend on cash crops such as bananas, coffee, and sugar cane, often grown on large plantations. This reliance on a single crop can leave these countries vulnerable to fluctuating world crop prices.

Using the land and sea

- cropland
- forest
- ice cap
- mountain region
- pasture
- tundra
- wetland
- desert
- major conurbations
- cattle
- goats
- pigs
- poultry
- reindeer
- sheep
- bananas
- citrus fruits
- coffee
- corn (maize)
- cotton
- fishing
- fruit
- maple syrup
- peanuts
- rice
- shellfish
- soya beans
- sugar cane
- timber
- tobacco
- vineyards
- wheat

1 VANCOUVER, BRITISH COLUMBIA, CANADA
Canada's premier west coast city occupies the delta of the Fraser river, formed among the Coast Mountains.

2 MOUNT SAINT HELENS, WASHINGTON, USA
In 1980, this volcano's catastrophic eruption devastated 270 sq miles (700 sq km) of forest almost instantly.

3 GREAT SALT LAKE, UTAH, USA
A causeway carries a railroad, blocking circulation between the northern and southern parts, the water reddened by bacteria in the more saline north.

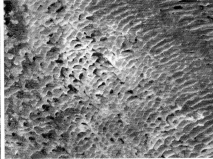

4 SAND HILLS, NEBRASKA, USA
Forming the largest sand sea in the Western Hemisphere, these hills are not classified as desert because today's relatively wet climate has allowed grasses to take hold.

9 LOS ANGELES AND LONG BEACH, CALIFORNIA, USA
Taken together, these west coast cities constitute the busiest seaport in the United States.

10 ISLA GUADALUPE, MEXICO
The volcanic island, 186 miles (300 km) off the west coast of Mexico, is a protected wildlife reserve.

11 GRAND CANYON, ARIZONA, USA
The 5250 ft (1600 m) deep canyon cuts through the Kaibab Plateau in this southwest-looking view.

12 DENVER, COLORADO, USA
Colorado's state capital nestles under the Rocky Mountains with the South Platte River running through its center.

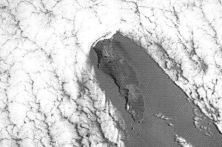

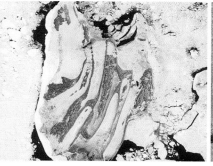

BELCHER ISLANDS, NUNAVUT, CANADA 5
These low-lying, treeless, and sparsely-
populated islands lie icebound in Hudson Bay
for much of the year.

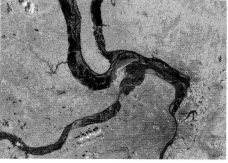

MISSISSIPPI, MISSOURI, AND ILLINOIS RIVERS, USA 6
This infrared image shows how these rivers burst their
banks in many places after heavy rains in the summer
of 1993, leading to the area's worst floods on record.

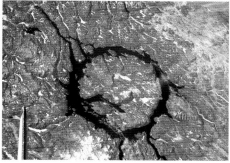

RÉSERVOIR MANICOUAGAN, QUÉBEC, CANADA 7
This unusual 62-mile (100-km) diameter annular
lake occupies the low ground between the rim
and central uplift of an ancient meteorite crater.

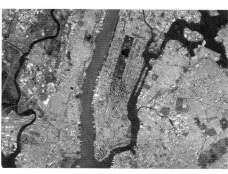

NEW YORK CITY, USA 8
The largest city in the United States, with
a population of over 8 million, it is also the
country's main financial center.

MISSISSIPPI RIVER DELTA, LOUISIANA, USA 13
This delta has developed a "bird's foot" shape
due to the shifting course of the river over
the last 6000 years.

FLORIDA, USA 14
This low-lying, subtropical peninsula is home to
thousands of lakes that have formed among its
limestone "karst" topography.

HAVANA, CUBA 15
Cuba's capital city is home to 2 million
people and was founded by the Spanish in
1519 around a natural harbor.

BARRIER REEF, BELIZE 16
The world's second-longest barrier reef lies
about 12 miles (20 km) off the coast of Belize.

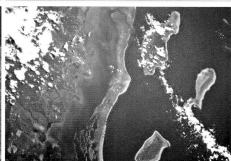

Canada

A B C D E F G

1 2 3 4 5 6 7 8 9 10

193

286

60

RUSSIAN FEDERATION

UNITED STATES OF AMERICA

ALASKA

Brooks Range

Alaska Range

Aleutian Range

Kuskokwim Mountains

Alaska Peninsula

Mount McKinley (Denali)
Mount Logan 5959m

Bering Sea
Bering Strait
Chukchi Sea
Beaufort Sea
ARCTIC OCEAN
Gulf of Alaska
PACIFIC OCEAN

Pribilof Islands

Saint Lawrence Island
Nunivak Island
Saint Matthew Island

Norton Sound
Yukon River
Kuskokwim River

Bristol Bay
Kodiak Island
Trinity Islands
Chirikof Island

Cook Inlet
Kenai Peninsula

Anchorage
Fairbanks
Juneau

North Magnetic Pole (2005)

Axel Heiberg Island
Ellef Ringnes Island
Prince Patrick Island
Mackenzie King Island
Melville Island
Banks Island
Victoria Island
Parry Islands
Bathurst Island
Queen Elizabeth Islands

Prince of Wales Island
Prince Albert Peninsula
Wollaston Peninsula

Amundsen Gulf
Coronation Gulf
Queen Maud Gulf
Viscount Melville Sound
Prince of Wales Strait
M'Clintock Channel

YUKON TERRITORY
Whitehorse
Dawson
Mayo

NORTHWEST TERRITORIES
Yellowknife
Great Bear Lake
Great Slave Lake
Lake Athabasca
Mackenzie Mountains
Mackenzie River

Inuvik
Tuktoyaktuk
Fort Good Hope
Fort McPherson
Hay River
Fort Smith
Fort Providence

BRITISH COLUMBIA
Prince George
Prince Rupert
Kamloops
Kelowna
Vancouver
Victoria
Terrace
Kitimat
Smithers

Queen Charlotte Islands
Graham Island
Moresby Island
Vancouver Island
Hecate Strait
Queen Charlotte Sound

ALBERTA
Edmonton
Calgary
Red Deer
Lethbridge
Medicine Hat
Fort McMurray
Grande Prairie
Peace River

SASKATCHEWAN
Saskatoon
Regina
Prince Albert
North Battleford
Moose Jaw
Swift Current

MANITOBA
Winnipeg
The Pas

Lake Athabasca
Reindeer Lake
Wollaston Lake
Cree Lake
Churchill Lake

WASHINGTON
Seattle
Tacoma
Everett
Spokane
Olympia

OREGON
Portland
Salem
Eugene

IDAHO
Boise

MONTANA
Helena
Missoula
Great Falls
Billings

NORTH DAKOTA
Bismarck

SOUTH DAKOTA
Rapid City

NEVADA
CALIFORNIA
Redding

WYOMING
NEBRASKA

UNITED STATES

Vancouver

Anvil Island
Gambier Island
Bowen Island
Horseshoe Bay
Cypress Provincial Park
Mount Seymour Provincial Park
North Vancouver
Vancouver
Burnaby
Coquitlam
Port Moody
Pitt Lake
Coquitlam Lake
Maple Ridge
New Westminster
Richmond
Sea Island
Vancouver Intl. Airport
Steveston
Surrey
Port Kells
Langley
White Rock
CANADA
USA
Blaine
Point Roberts
Birch Bay
Lynden
Boundary Bay
Tsawwassen
Westham Island
Ferndale
Marietta
Bellingham
Strait of Georgia
Gulf Islands
Galiano Island
Mayne Island
Pender Islands
Salt Spring Island
Saturna Island
Waldron Island
Orcas Island
Lummi Island
Burrard Inlet
Fraser River
Indian Arm

0 10 Km
0 10 Miles

Elevation scale:
6000m
4000m
3000m
2000m
1000m
500m
250m
100m
Sea Level
-250m
-500m
-1000m

ARCTIC

OCEAN

Limit of permanent ice cap

Limit of summer pack ice

Beaufort Sea

North Magnetic Pole
(2005)

Bad Weather Cape
Meighen
Island

Sverdru

Limit of permanent ice cap

Borden Island
Brock Island
Cape
Leopold McClintock
Satellite Bay
Wilkins Strait
Ballantyne Strait
Mackenzie
King
Island
Prince
Gustaf
Adolf Sea

Ellef
Ringnes
Island

Queen

Lands End
Prince
Patrick
Island
Mould
Bay
Hazen Strait
Lougheed
Island
King Christian
Island

Is

Dyer Bay
Crozier Channel
Kellet Strait
Emerald
Isle
Sabine
Peninsula
Cameron
Island
Seymour
Island

Eglinton Island
Cape Russell
Sherard
Bay
Austin Strait

Cape Prince Alfred
Cape
Wrottesley
McClure Strait
Melville Island
Parry
Bathurst
Island

Bernard Island
Liddon Gulf
Dundas
Peninsula
Hearne Point
Byam Martin
Island
Byam Channel
Lowi
Isl

Meek Point
Parry Channel
Russell
Island

Banks
Island
Passage
Point
Viscount Melville Sound
Cape John Dyer

Cape Kellett
Big
Peel
Point
Prince of Wales Strait
Richard Collinson Inlet
Stefansson
Island
Minto
Head

Sachs Harbour
Prince Albert
Peninsula
Hadley Bay
Prince of Wa
Island

Cape Dalhousie
Cape Lambton

Tuktoyaktuk
Peninsula
Cape Bathurst
Liverpool
Bay
Minto Inlet
Nunook
Cape
Richard
Collinson

Tuktoyaktuk
Franklin
Bay
Cape Parry
Cape Wollaston
Holman
Tahiryuak
Lake
Zeta
Lake
N

Eskimo Lakes
Parry
Peninsula
Darnley
Bay
Cape
Lyon
Prince Albert Sound
Norway
Bay
U

Aklavik
Siidei
Lake
Amundsen
Gulf
Cape Baring
Victoria
Island

Inuvik
Paulatuk
Wollaston
Peninsula
Quunmguq Lake
Gateshead
Island
Pelly Point

Arctic
Red River
Fort
McPherson
Dolphin and Union Strait
Washburn
Lake
Collinson
Peninsula
Cape Felix

Travaillant
Lake
Carnwath
Horton
Croker
Cape
Swinburne
Larsen Sound

Onoratue
Anderson
Aubry
Lake
Lac
Maunoir
Bluenose Lake
Rae
Kughuktuk
Dease Strait
Cambridge Bay
Victoria
Ki
Will
Isla

Mackenzie
Hare Indian
Lac Belot
Colville
Lake
Haldane
Bebensee
Lake Dismal
Lakes
Cape
Krusenstern
Byron
Bay
Kent
Peninsula
Jenny Lind
Island
Royal
Geographical Society
Islands

Fort
Good Hope
Lac des
bois
Kilekale
Lake
Coronation Gulf
Melbourne
Island
Queen Maud Gulf
Adel
Penin

Mahony
Lake
Smith Arm
Dease Arm
C
Coppermine
Inulik Lake
Melville Sound
Whitebear
Point
Bowes
Point

Norman
Wells
Whitefish River
Franklin
Fort
Deline
Point Leith
Sawmill
Bay
Echo Bay
A

Keele
Great bear
Keith
Arm
McVicar Arm
James
Hood
Banks
Peninsula
N

Tulita
Great Bear
Lake
Takijuq Lake
Burnside
MacAlpine
Lake

Hottah
Lake
Redrock Lake
Contwoyto
Lake

NORTHWEST
TERRITORIES
Point Lake
Garry Lake

Keller
Lake
Rebecca
Lake
Snare
Lakes
Little
Marten
Lake
Lac de
Gras

Lac Taché
Ray Lakes
Faber Lake
Back

Lac Grandin
Hebo
Snare
Aberdeen
Lake
Schultz Lake

Lac la Martre
Clive Lake
MacKay
Lake
Aylmer
Lake
Clinton-Colden
Lake
Hanbury

Wha Ti
Yellowknife
Lockhart
Lake
Gordon
Lake
Fletcher
Lake
Walmsley Lake
Tebesjuak
Lake

Rae
Edzo
Great
Slave Lake
McLeod Bay
Reliance
Artillery
Lake
Dubawnt
Lake

Cape
Halkett
Harrison
Bay
Prudhoe Bay
Deadhorse
Kaktovik
Martin
Point
Herschel
Island
Demarcation
Point
Shingle
Point
Mackenzie
Bay
Warren
Point

Kuparuk River
Canning River
Shublik
Mountains
Romanzof
Mountains
Konganik River

USA
ALASKA
British
Mountains
Old
Crow
Flats
Tuktoyaktuk

Franklin
Mountains
Davidson Mountains
East Fork Chandalar
River

Porcupine
Old Crow
Arctic
Red River
Peel

Arctic Circle
Eagle Plain
Porcupine
Richardson Mountains

Ogilvie
Blackstone
Snake
Rampats
Franklin

YUKON
TERRITORY
Wind
Bonnet Plume
Mackenzie Mountains

Ogilvie
Mayo
Ross River
Hess
Mountain
Carcajou
Norman
Wells

Elsa
Keno
Hill
Beaver
Macmillan
Selwyn Mountains
Backbone
Range
Redstone

Faro
Ross
Keele
Franklin
Mountains

Ross River
Mount
Hunt
Tungsten
Redstone
Root
Wrigley

Pelly
Mountains
Mount
Marsh
Nahanni
Butte
North Nahanni
Horn Plateau
Willow Lake
Birch
Lake

Wolf Lake
Upper
Liard
Watson Lake
South Nahanni
Jean Marie River
Mills Lake
Hay

Cassiar Mountains
Lower Post
Coal River
Fort Simpson

Dease Lake
Good Hope
Beaver

6000m
4000m
3000m
2000m
1000m
500m
250m
100m
Sea
Level
-250m
-500m
-1000m

Scale 1:7,500,000
(projection: Lambert Conformal Conic)

0 25 50 75 100 125 150 175 200 Km
0 25 50 75 100 125 150 175 200 Miles

Population
■ above 5 million
▣ 1 million to 5 million
◉ 500,000 to 1 million
◎ 100,000 to 500,000
⊕ 50,000 to 100,000
○ 10,000 to 50,000
∘ below 10,000

19,686ft
13,124ft
9843ft
6562ft
3281ft
1640ft
820ft
328ft
Sea Level
-820ft
-6562ft
-13,124ft

AVANNAARSUA

GREENLAND
(to Denmark)

TUNU

KITAA

Baffin Bay

Davis Strait

Limit of summer pack ice

Limit of winter pack ice

Arctic Circle

Baffin Island

NUNAVUT

Barnes Ice Cap

Cumberland Peninsula

Cumberland Sound

Foxe Basin

Foxe Channel

Hudson Strait

Ungava Bay

QUÉBEC

Péninsule d'Ungava

Southampton Island

CANADA

Scale 1:7,500,000
(projection: Lambert Conformal Conic)

0 25 50 75 100 125 150 175 200 Km
0 25 50 75 100 125 150 175 200 Miles

Population
- ■ above 5 million
- ▪ 1 million to 5 million
- ◉ 500,000 to 1 million
- ◎ 100,000 to 500,000
- ⊕ 50,000 to 100,000
- ⊙ 10,000 to 50,000
- ○ below 10,000

53

72

58

19,686ft
13,124ft
9843ft
6562ft
3281ft
1640ft
820ft
328ft
Sea Level
-820ft
-6562ft
-13,124ft

Map labels

NUNAVUT

Albert Edward Bay
King William Island
Matty Island
Lady Melville Lake
Simpson Peninsula
Pelly Bay
Committee Bay
Wales Island
Lefroy Bay
Melville Peninsula
Parry Bay
Prince Charles Island
Cape Dominion
Amadjuak Lake
Hall Peninsula
Arctic Circle

Cambridge Bay
Jenny Lind Island
Melbourne Island
Royal Geographical Society Islands
Gjoa Haven
Rasmussen Basin
Murchison
Repulse Bay
Winter Island
Foxe Basin
Bowman Bay
Aukpa
Mingo Lake
Sylvia Grinnell Lake
Iqaluit
Frobisher Bay

White Bear Point
Bowes Point
Adelaide Peninsula
Churry Inlet
Rae Isthmus
Frozen Strait
Cape Dorchester
Finnie Bay
Foxe Peninsula
Cape Dorset
Shukhuk Bay
Markham Bay
Fair Ness
Big Island
Meta Incognita Peninsula
Ice Harbour

Queen Maud Gulf
Franklin Lake
Back
Hayes
Hansine Lake
White Island
Cape Bylot
Cape Comfort
Vansittart Island
Foxe Channel
Salisbury Island
Charles Island
Kangiqsujuaq

MacAlpine Lake
Brown Lake
Wager Bay
Roes Welcome Sound
Southampton Island
Coral Harbour
Seahorse Point
Nottingham Island
Nuvuk Islands
Digges Islands
Ivujivik
Salluit
Déception
Whitley Bay
Hudson Strait

Garry Lake
Bullen
Gartu
Repulse Bay
Native Bay
Evans Strait
Cape Pembroke
Kovic Bay
Rivière de Povungnituk
Lac Klotz
Lac Payne

Aberdeen Lake
Schultz Lake
Tehek Lake
Baker Lake
Armit Lake
Landbard
Daly Bay
Cape Kendall
Bay of Gods Mercy
Cape Low
Coats Island
Mansel Island
Cape Acadia
Smith Island
Puvirnituq
Péninsule d'Ungava
Kogaluk
Lac Tassialouc
Aernuk

Mosquito Lake
Sid Lake
Kamilukuak Lake
Nowleye Lake
Angikuni Lake
North Henik Lake
South Henik Lake
Maguse Lake
Eskimo Point
Arviat
Whale Cove
Bibbyt Island
Cape Southampton
Cape Smith
Ottawa Islands
Gilmour Island
QUÉBEC
Lac Minto
Inukjuak
Cape Dufferin

Firedrake Lake
Dubawnt Lake
Tulemalu Lake
Tebesjuak Lake
Kazan
Baker Lake
Peter Lake
Meliadine Lake
Rankin Inlet
Chesterfield Inlet

Snowbird Lake
Ennadai Lake
Kaminuriak Lake
Yathkyed Lake
Kaminak Lake
Tha-anne
Thlewiaza

Anownethad Lake
Nueltin Lake
Edehon Lake
Nejanilini Lake
Caribou

Point of the Woods
Cape Churchill
Hudson Bay
Sleeper Islands
Nastapoka Islands
King George Islands
North Belcher Islands
Bakers Dozen Islands
Sanikiluaq
Lac Guillaume-Delisle
Petite Rivière de la Baleine

Shethanei Lake
Seal
Churchill
Lamprey
South Knife
North Knife
Belcher Islands
Grande Rivière de la Baleine

Tadoule Lake
Big Sand Lake
Northern Indian Lake
Owl
Herchmer
Cape Tatnam
Poste-de-la-Baleine
Kuujjuarapik
Burton Lake

Wollaston Lake
Brochet
Southern Indian Lake
Nelson
York Factory
Niskibi
Fort Severn
Cape Lookout
Cape Henrietta Maria
Long Island
Réservoir la Grande Deux Radisson
James Bay
La Grande Rivière

Reindeer Lake
Kinoosao
Lynn Lake
Waskaiowaka Lake
South Indian Lake
Weir River
Limestone
Gillam
Hayes
Gods
Shamattawa
Winisk
Shagamu
Peawanuk
Sutton Ridges
Kimasao
Chisasibi
North Twin Island
South Twin Island
Wemindji

Macoun Lake
Foster Lakes
Southend
Fox Mine
Leaf Rapids
Baldock Lake
Split Lake
Kelsey
Ilford
Shamattawa
Winisk
Sutton
Ekwan Point
Akimiski Island
Nomansland Point
Trodely Island
Eastmain

Missinipe
Churchill
Sandy Bay
Sisipuk Lake
Pukatawagan
Nelson House
Thompson
Sipiwesk
Oxford House
Stull Lake
Ekwan
Attawapiskat
Charlton Island
Rupert Bay
Hannah Bay

Lac La Ronge
Pelikan Narrows
Charles
Kississing Lake
Setting Lake
Snow Lake
Wabowden
Sipiwesk Lake
Gods Lake
Beaverhill Lake
Sachigo
Big Trout Lake
Shibogama Lake
Winisk Lake
Missa Lake
Moosonee
Moose Factory

Deschambault Lake
Amisk Lake
Creighton
Flin Flon
Cranberry Portage
Ponton
Cross Lake
Oxford Lake
Gods Lake
Sachigo Lake
Big Trout Lake
Makoop Lake
Wunnummin Lake

MANITOBA
Namew Lake
Cumberland House
The Pas
Moose Lake
Cedar Lake
Grand Rapids
Molson Lake
Island Lake
Red Sucker Lake
Sandy Lake
Wapiskew
North Caribou Lake
Attawapiskat Lake
Kesagami Lake

HEWAN
Candle Lake
Choiceland
Nipawin
Tobin Lake
Carrot River
Easterville
Westray
Barrows
Long Lake
Norway House
ONTARIO
Sandy Lake
Pipestone
Otoskwin
Lansdowne
Albany
Fort Albany
Missinaibi

Meath Park
Prince Albert
Melfort
Tisdale
Saskatchewan River
Hudson Bay
Lake Winnipegosis
Poplar
Berens River
Cat Lake
Pickle Lake
Slate Falls
Ogoki
Ogoki Lake
Little Current
Kapuskasing
Smooth Rock Falls

Black Hills
Louis
Naicam
Watson
Kelvington
Cowan
Duck Bay
Dauphin River
Gypsumville
Fisher River
Manigotagan
Red Lake
Ear Falls
Savant Lake
Armstrong
Lake Nipigon
Geraldton
Longlac
Hornepayne
Fraserdale
Abitibi
Cochrane
Iroquois Falls
Timmins

Middle Lake
Aberdeen
Lanigan
Watrous
Quill Lakes
Wynyard
Foam Lake
Wadena
Canora
Preeceville
Duck Mountain
Dauphin
Ethelbert
Riverton
Victoria Beach
Pine Falls
Sioux Lookout
Dryden
Sturgeon Lake
Nipigon
Manitouwadge
Marathon
Terrace Bay
Chapleau
Gogama

Last Mountain Lake
Strasbourg
Southey
Raymore
Jasmin
Yorkton
Grandview
Roblin
Russell
Riding Mountain
Ste-Rose du Lac
McCreary
Gladstone
MacGregor
Carberry
Arborg
Eriksdale
Winnipeg Beach
Gimli
Lac du Bonnet
Pinawa
Keewatin
Kenora
Lake of the Woods
Ignace
Eagle River
Lac Seul
Lac des Mille Lacs
St.Ignace Island
Tip Top Mountain 701m

Regina
Grenfell
Whitewood
Balcarres
Langenburg
Esterhazy
Foxwarren
Minnedosa
Neepawa
Portage la Prairie
Oak Point
St.Laurent
Warren
Selkirk
Beausejour
Rennie
Sioux Narrows
Rainy Lake
Atikokan
Namakan Lake
Kakabeka Falls
Saganaga Lake
Isle Royale
Michipicoten Island
Sault Ste Marie

Balgonie
Sedley
Kipling
Langbank
Carlyle
Hamiota
Brandon
Rivers
Souris
Holland
Carman
Morris
Winkler
Ste.Anne
St.Malo
Rainy River
Fort Frances
Au Sable Point
Keweenaw Peninsula
Keweenaw Bay
Houghton
North Channel
Gore Bay

Wives Lake
Pangman
Weyburn
Kisbey
Radville
Stoughton
Reston
Melita
Boissevain
Manitou
Pembina
Winnipeg
Emerson
Rainy River
Virginia
Thunder Bay
Lake Superior
MICHIGAN
Grand Marais
Marquette

Willow Bunch
Coronach
Minton
Tribune
Estevan
Oxbow
Carnduff
Deloraine
Killarney
Crystal
Morden
North Dakota
Grand Forks
Mud Lake
Red Lake River
Upper Red Lake
Lower Red Lake
Kabetogama
Basswood Lake
Vermilion
Chisholm
Saint Joseph's Island

OF AMERICA
NORTH DAKOTA
Minot
Devils Lake
MINNESOTA

CANADA Shield

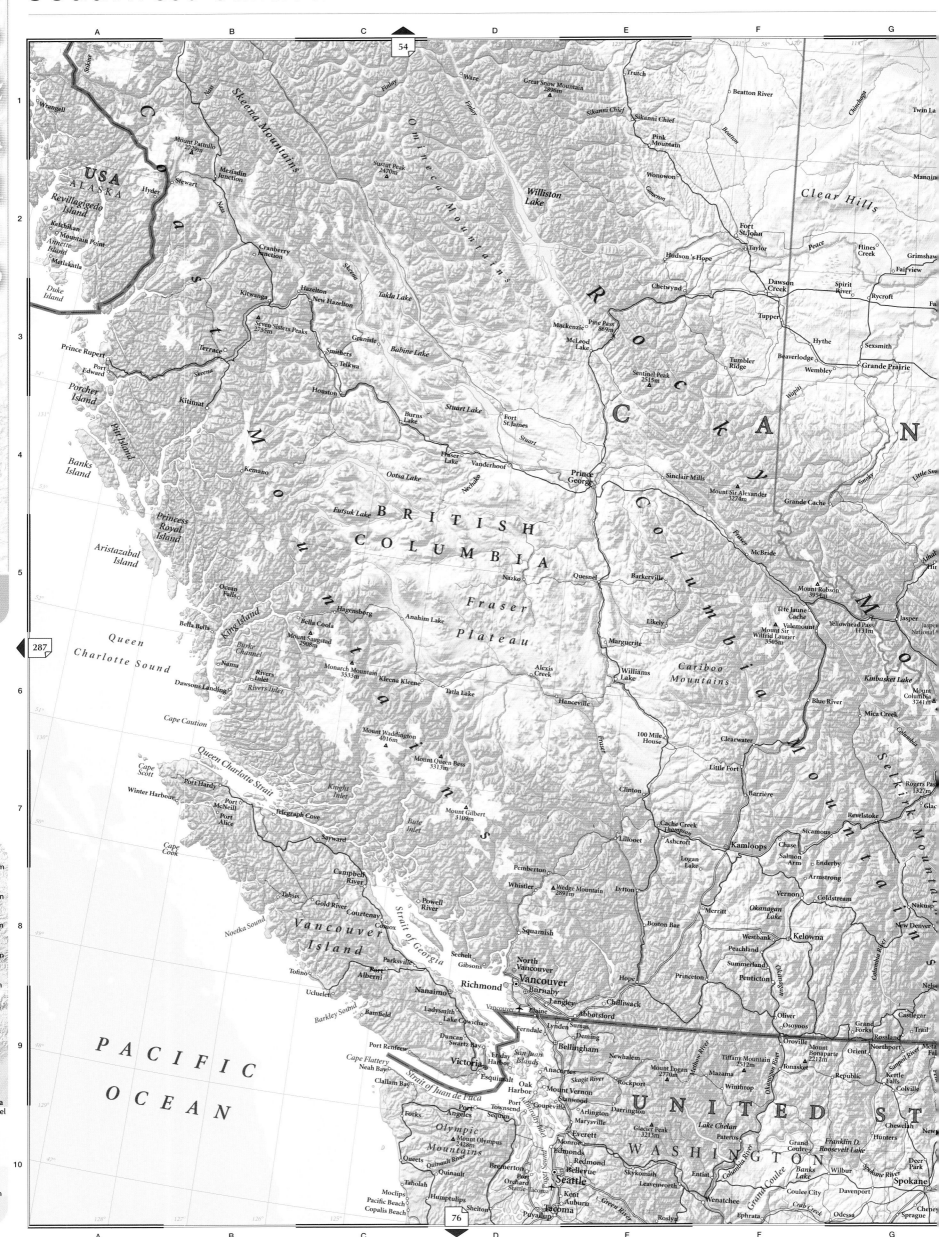

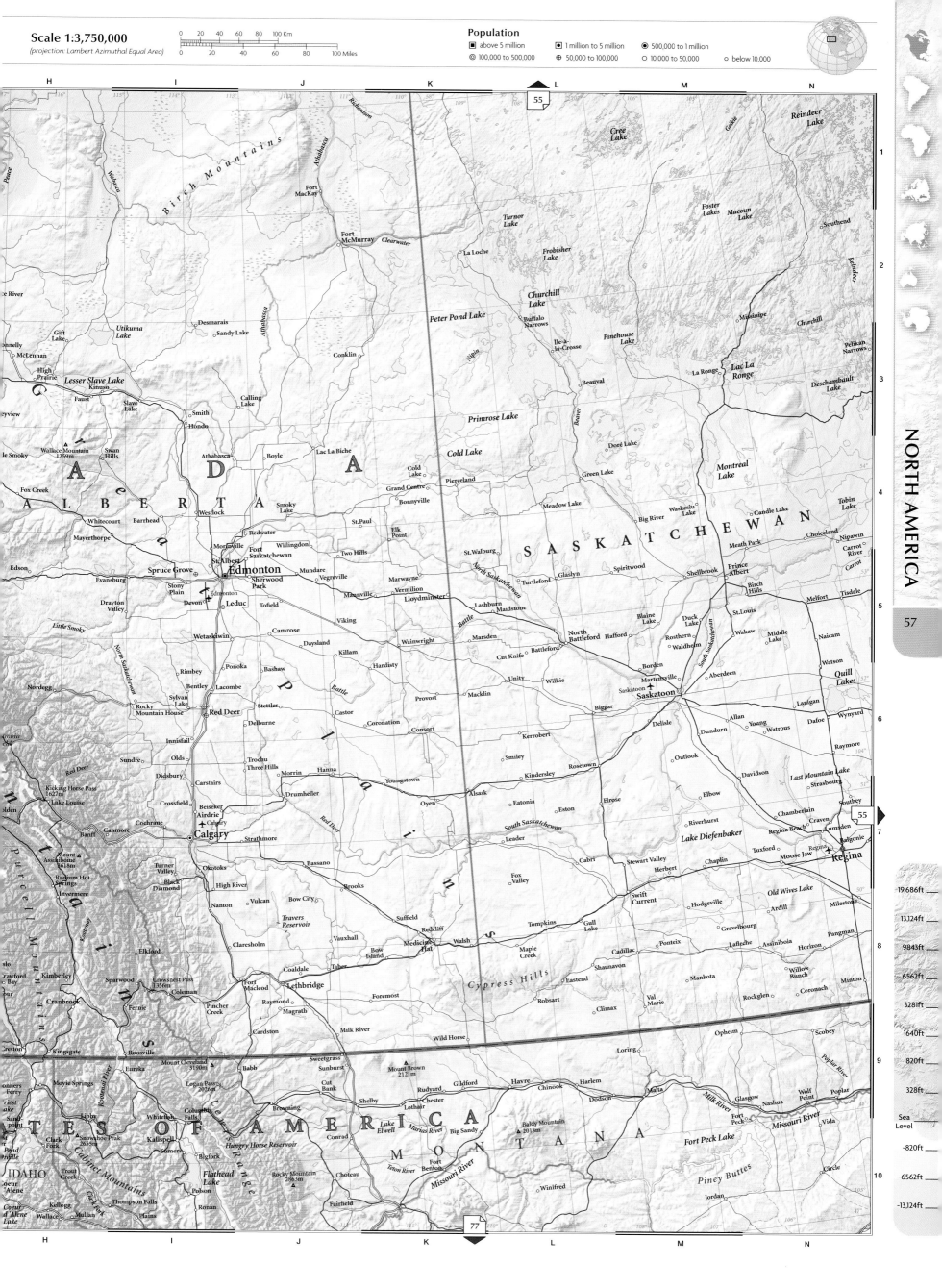

The United States of America

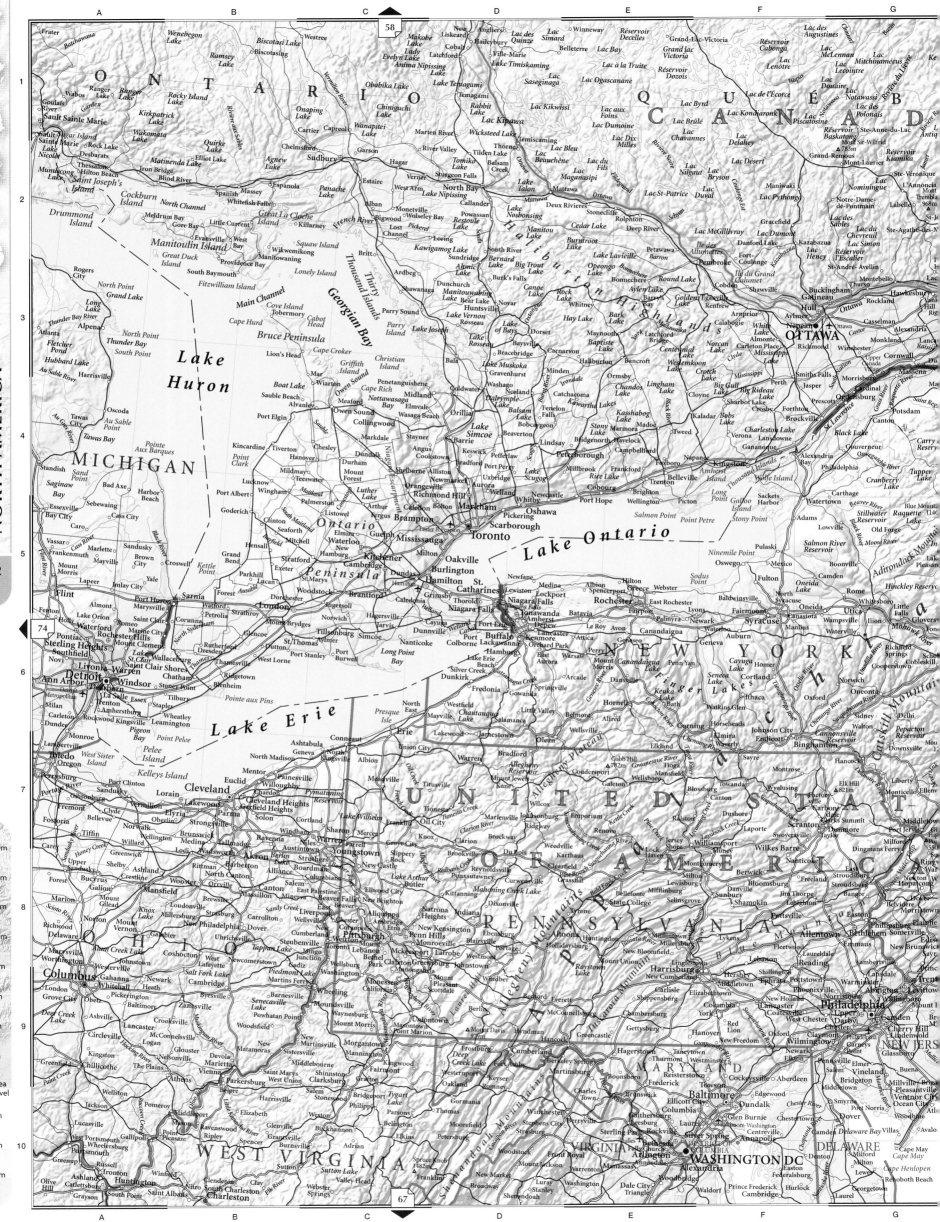

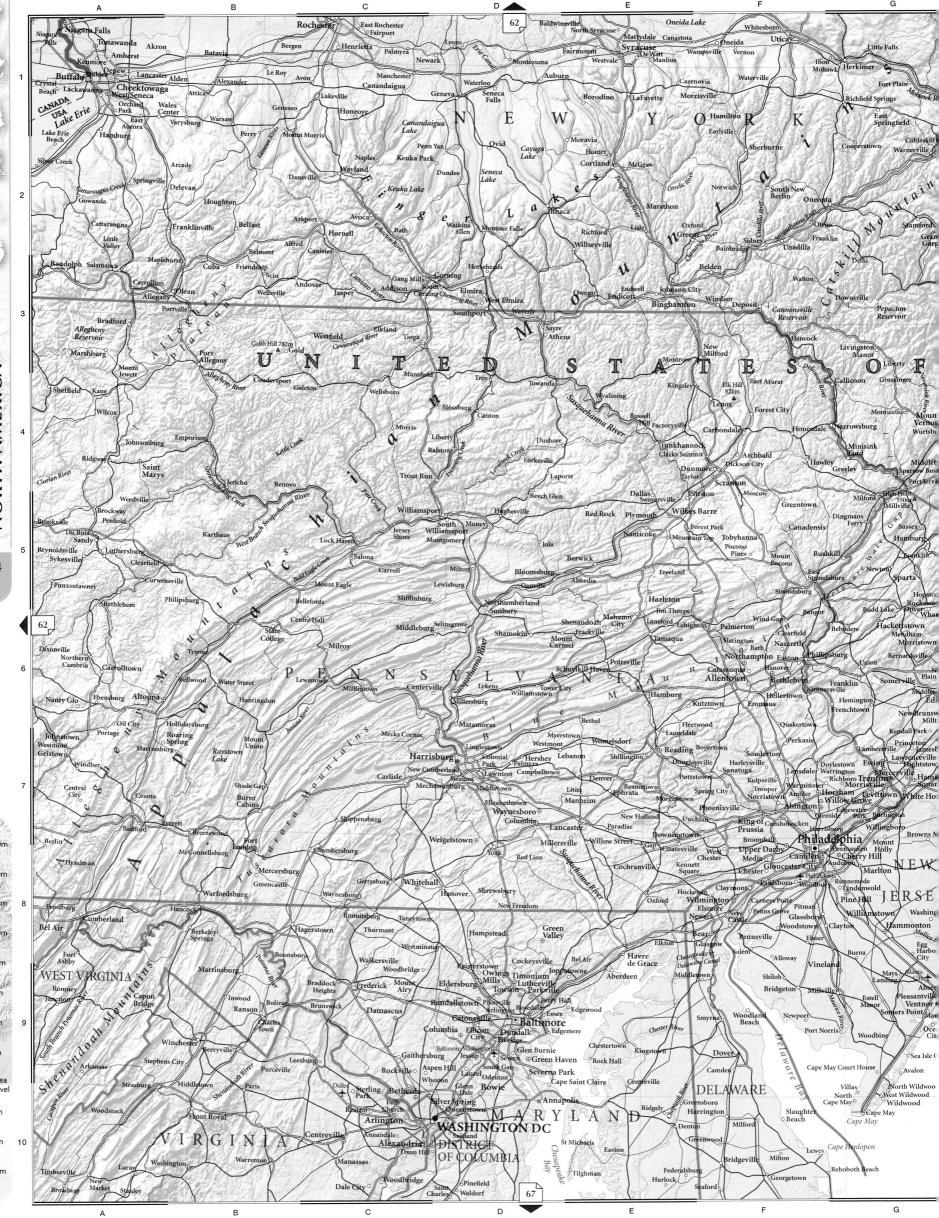

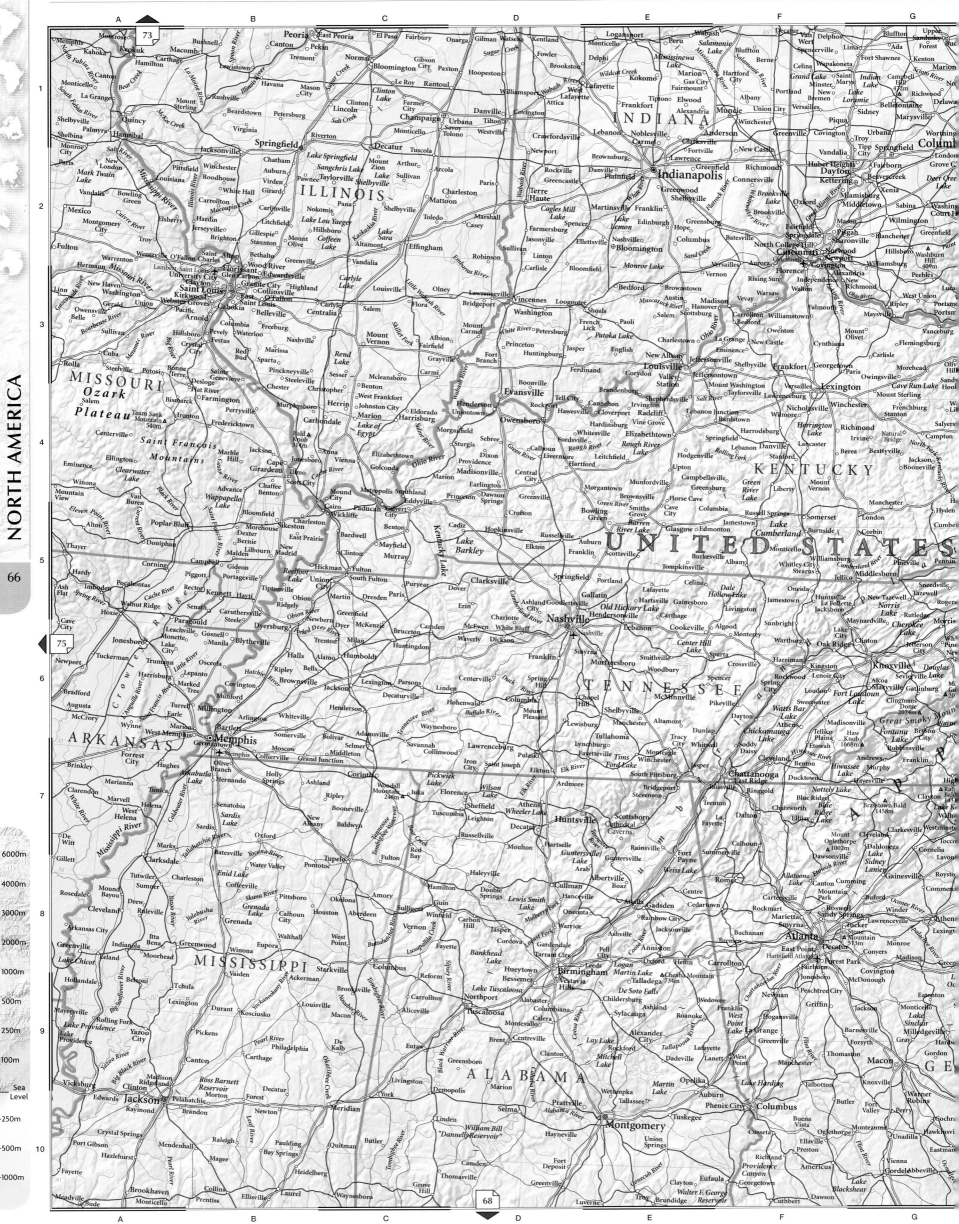

Scale 1:3,000,000
(projection: Lambert Conformal Conic)

0 20 40 60 80 100 Km
0 20 40 60 80 100 Miles

Population
- ■ above 5 million
- ◉ 100,000 to 500,000
- ▣ 1 million to 5 million
- ⊕ 50,000 to 100,000
- ◎ 500,000 to 1 million
- ○ 10,000 to 50,000
- ○ below 10,000

States and Regions

PENNSYLVANIA

NEW JERSEY

WEST VIRGINIA

VIRGINIA

MARYLAND

DELAWARE

DISTRICT OF COLUMBIA

NORTH CAROLINA

SOUTH CAROLINA

UNITED STATES OF AMERICA

ATLANTIC OCEAN

Major Cities

Pittsburgh

Philadelphia

Baltimore

WASHINGTON DC

Richmond

Charlotte

Raleigh

Columbia

Norfolk

Virginia Beach

Newport News

Charleston

Greensboro

Winston Salem

Durham

Roanoke

Huntington

Water Features

Chesapeake Bay

Delaware Bay

Albemarle Sound

Pamlico Sound

Long Bay

Onslow Bay

Raleigh Bay

Lake Gaston

John H. Kerr Reservoir

Cape Hatteras

Cape Lookout

Cape Fear

Cape Henry

Cape Charles

Hatteras Island

Ocracoke Island

Roanoke Island

Smith Mountain Lake

Bermuda Inset

BERMUDA (to UK)

HAMILTON

St George's Island
St Catherine Point
St George
St David's Island
Ireland Island North
Ireland Island South
Somerset Island
Commissioner's Point
Kindley Field
Castle Harbour
Harrington Sound
Tucker's Town
Flatts Village
Spanish Point
Great Sound
Little Sound
Gibbs Hill 73m

Scale 1:500,000
0 2.5 5 Km
0 2.5 5 Miles

ATLANTIC OCEAN

Elevation Scale

19,686ft
13,124ft
9843ft
6562ft
3281ft
1640ft
820ft
328ft
Sea Level
-820ft
-6562ft
-13,124ft

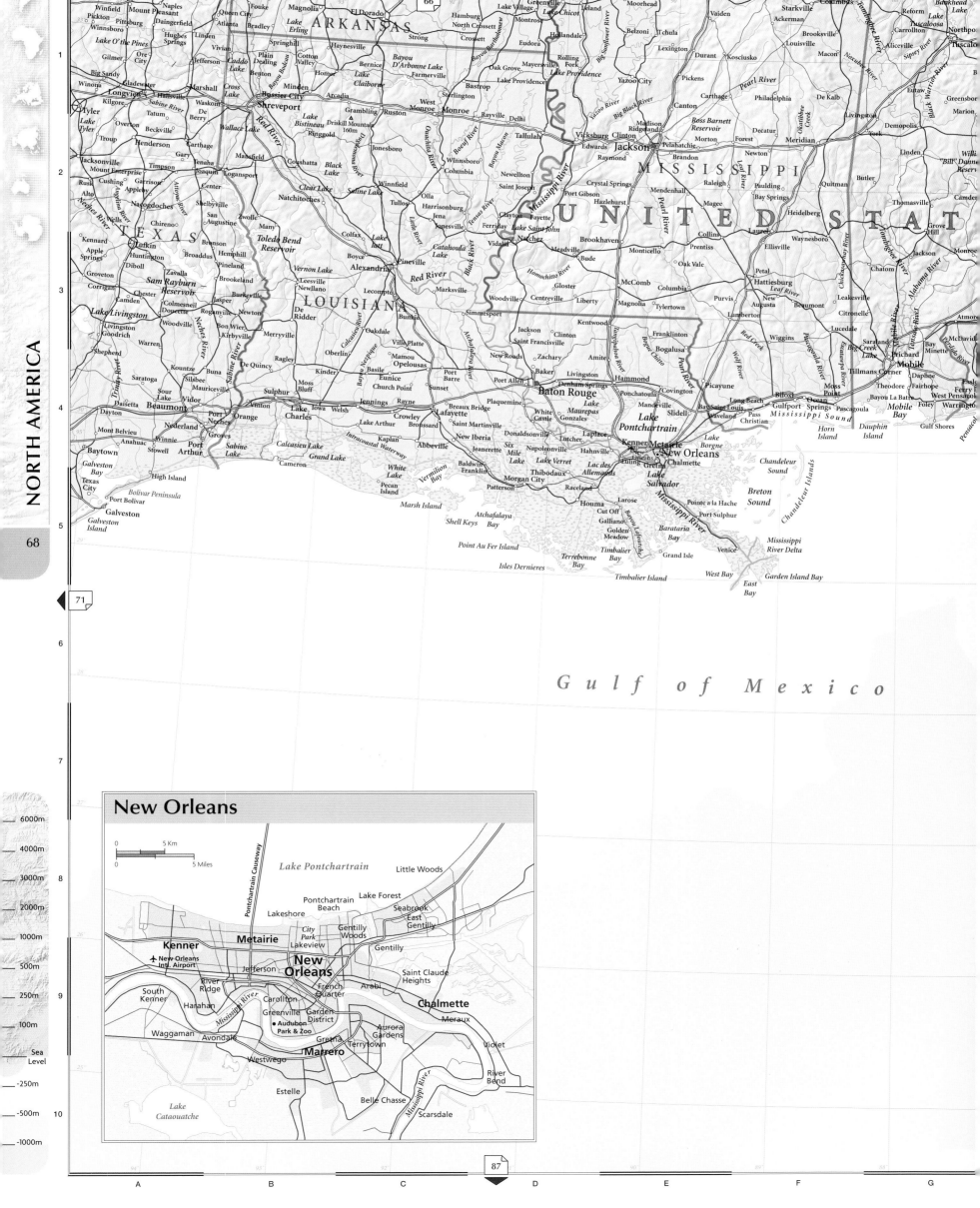

Gulf of Mexico

New Orleans

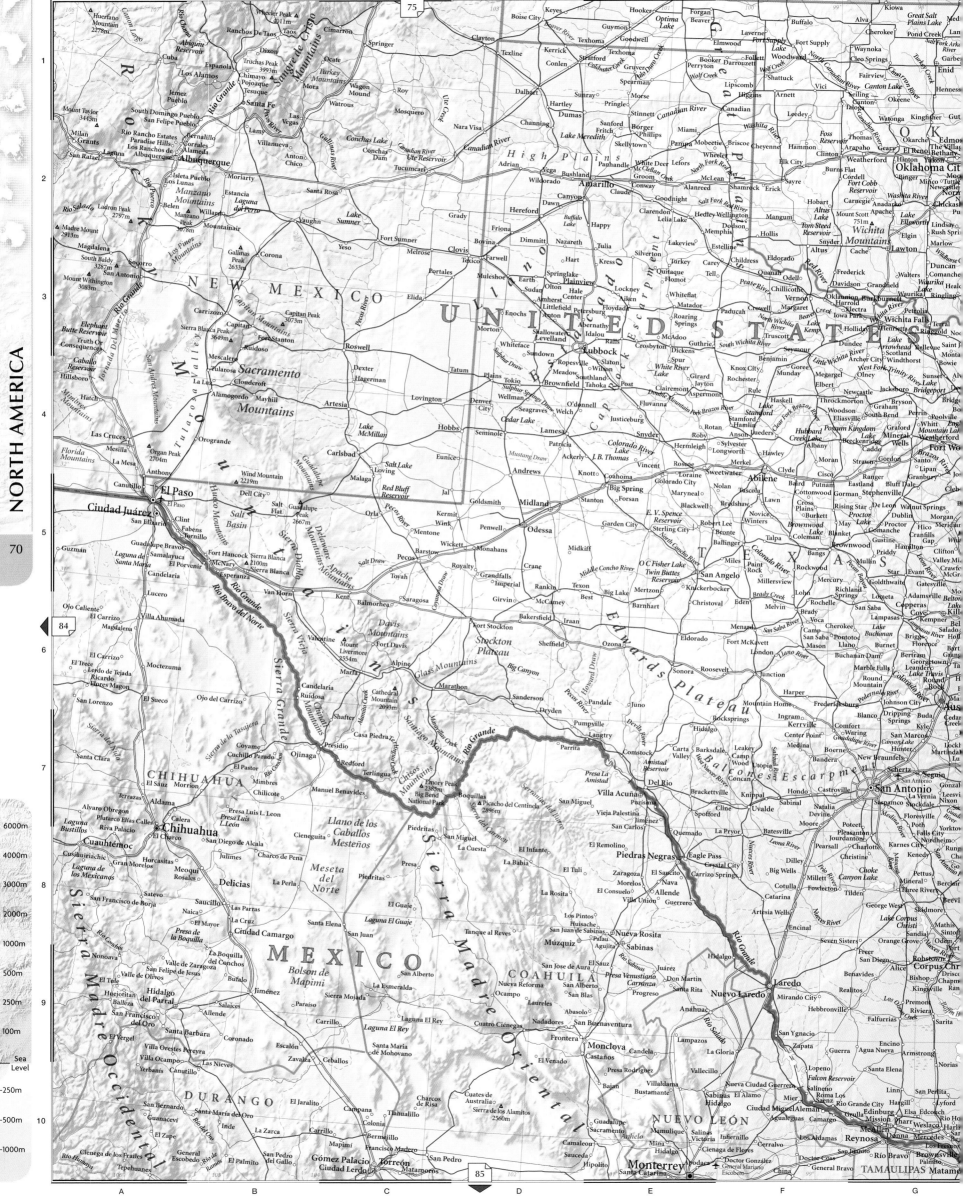

Scale 1:3,750,000
(projection: Lambert Conformal Conic)

0 20 40 60 80 100 Km
0 20 40 60 80 100 Miles

Population
■ above 5 million
■ 1 million to 5 million
◉ 500,000 to 1 million
◎ 100,000 to 500,000
⊕ 50,000 to 100,000
○ 10,000 to 50,000
∘ below 10,000

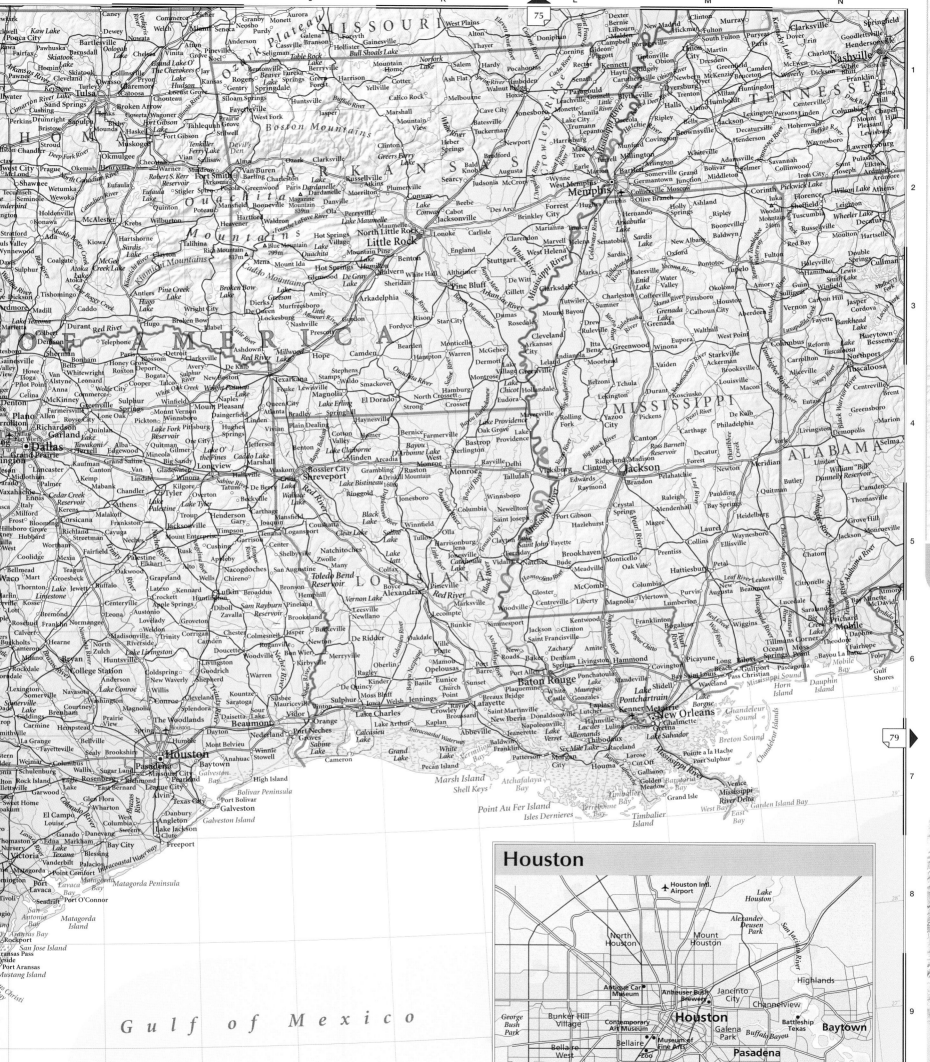

Houston

19,686ft
13,124ft
9843ft
6562ft
3281ft
1640ft
820ft
328ft
Sea Level
-820ft
-6562ft
-13,124ft

USA – Great Lake States

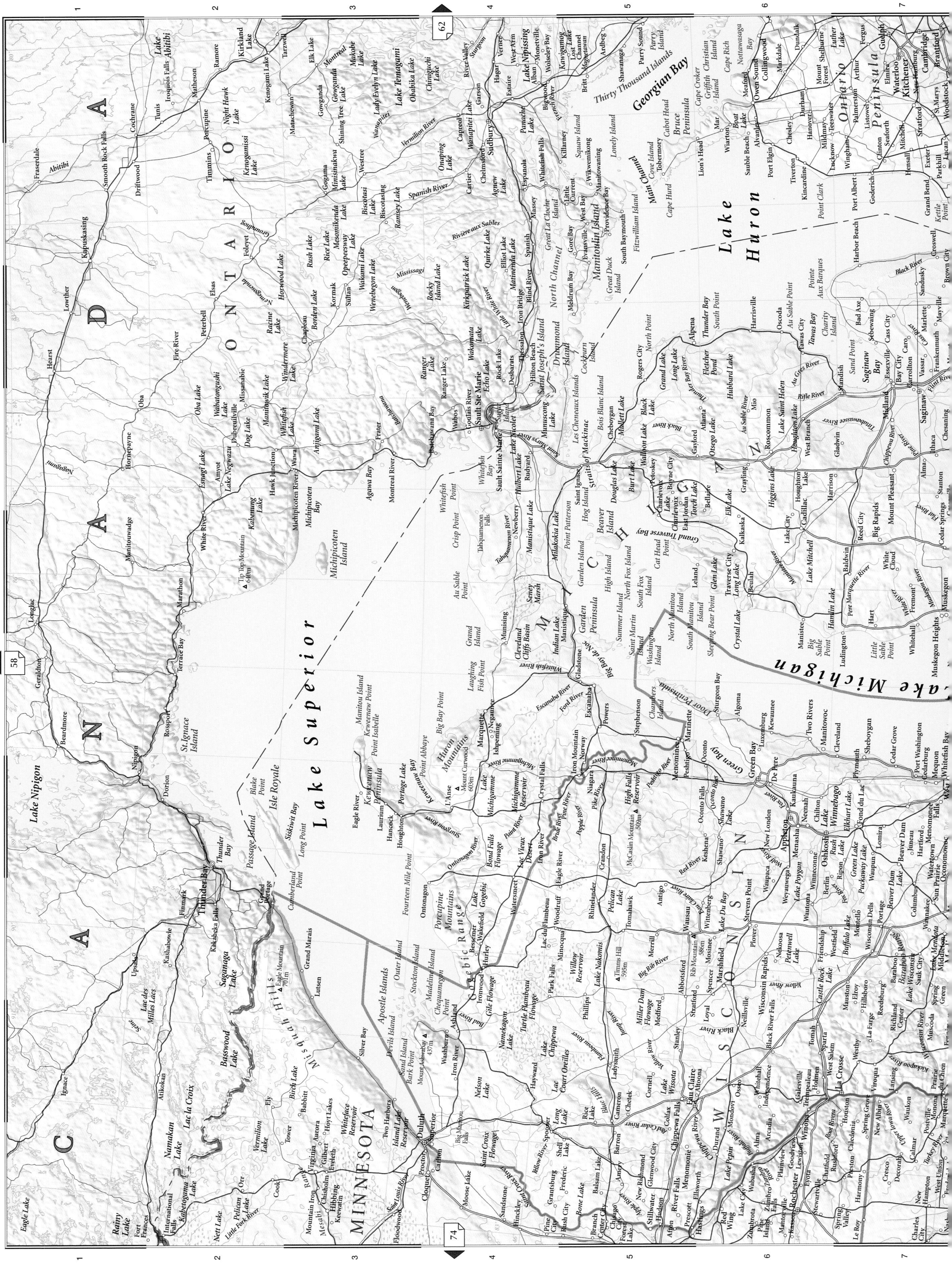

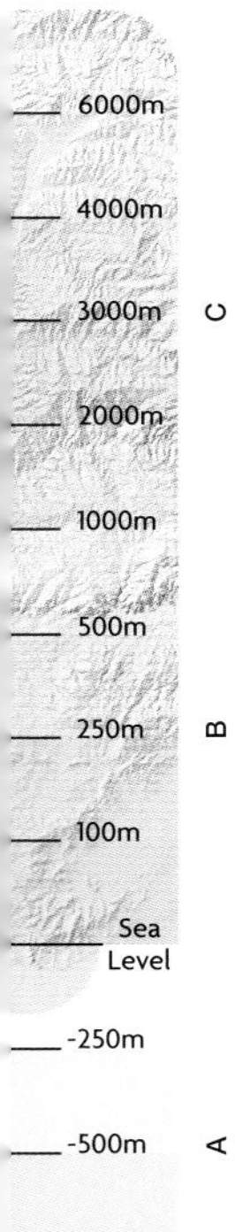

Elevation scale (m):

- 6000m
- 4000m
- 3000m
- 2000m
- 1000m
- 500m
- 250m
- 100m
- Sea Level
- -250m
- -500m
- -1000m

Major features

Lake Superior

Lake Huron

Lake Michigan

Georgian Bay

Thirty Thousand Islands

Lake Nipigon

Green Bay

Isle Royale

Michipicoten Island

Manitoulin Island

North Channel

Apostle Islands

Bruce Peninsula

Door Peninsula

Keweenaw Peninsula

Saginaw Bay

States / Provinces

CANADA

ONTARIO

MINNESOTA

WISCONSIN

MICHIGAN

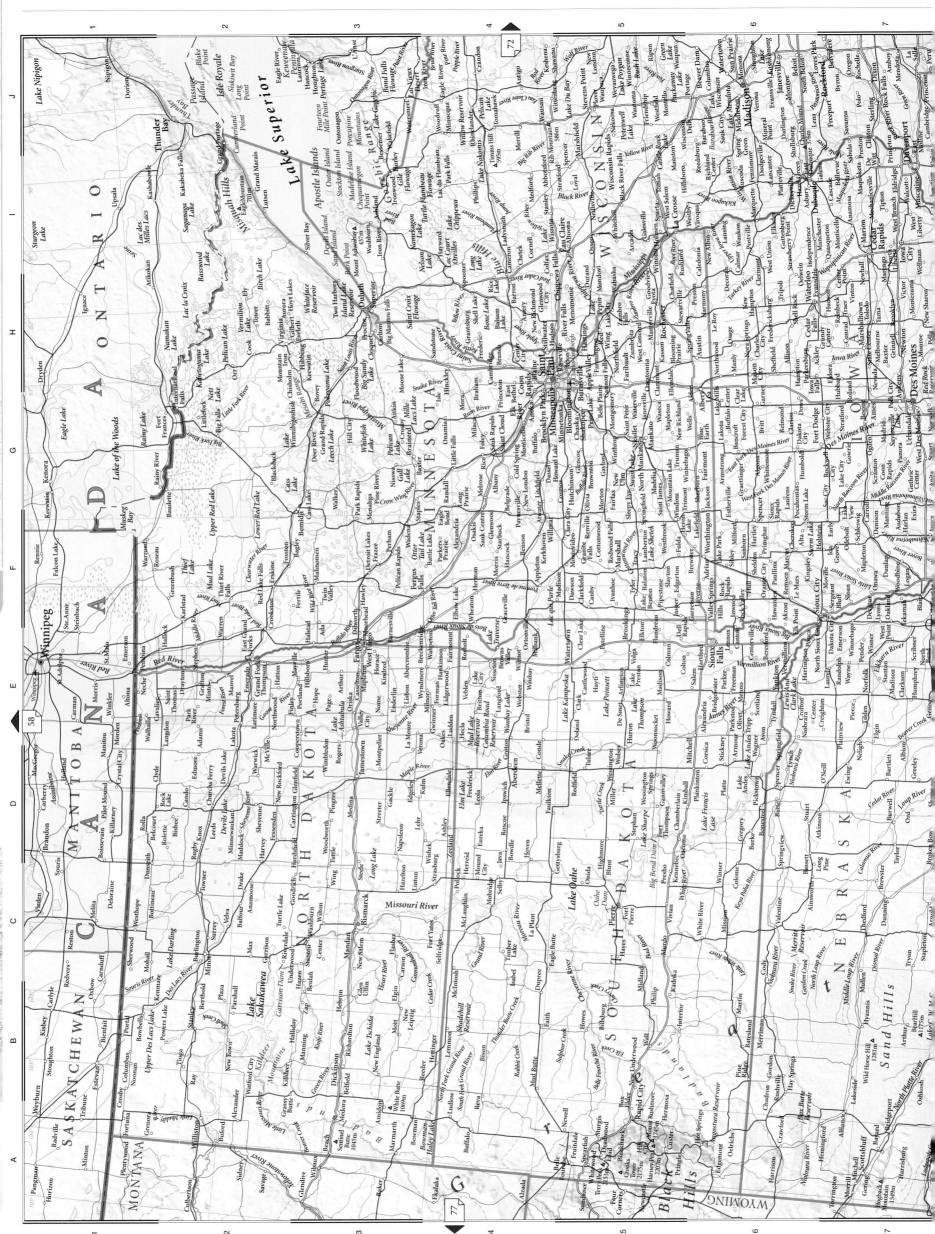

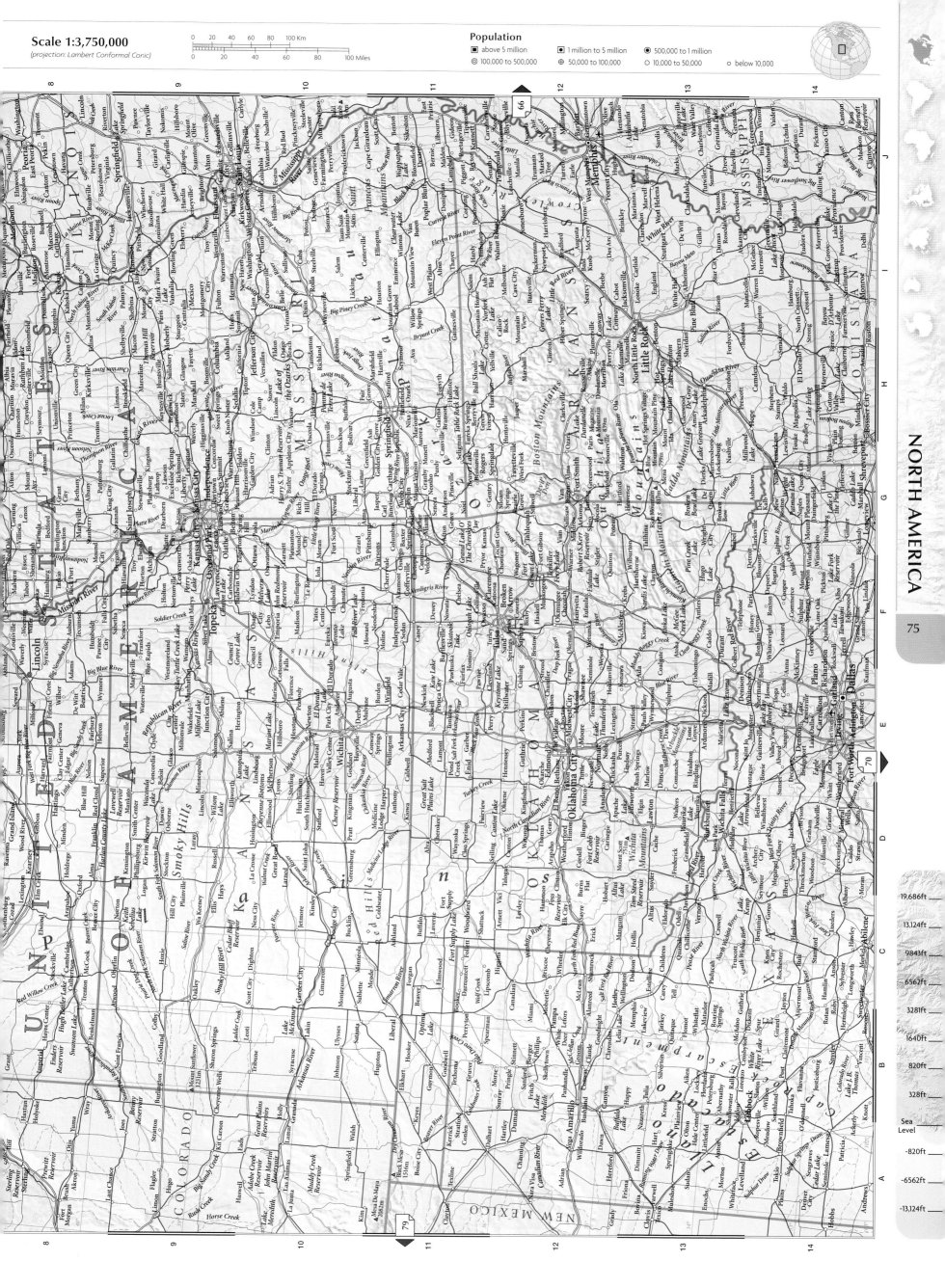

Scale 1:3,750,000
(projection: Lambert Conformal Conic)

0 20 40 60 80 100 Km
0 20 40 60 80 100 Miles

Population
- ■ above 5 million
- ◉ 100,000 to 500,000
- ▣ 1 million to 5 million
- ⊕ 50,000 to 100,000
- ◉ 500,000 to 1 million
- ○ 10,000 to 50,000
- ○ below 10,000

57

79

74

ALBERTA

SASKATCHEWAN

MANITOBA

MONTANA

NORTH DAKOTA

SOUTH DAKOTA

WYOMING

NEBRASKA

UTAH

COLORADO

Great Plains

Badlands

Cypress Hills

U N I T E D   S T A T E S   O F   A M E R I C A

C A N A D A

Regina

Great Falls

Helena

Billings

Salt Lake City

Cheyenne

Denver

Bighorn Basin

Great Divide Basin

Yellowstone National Park

Bighorn Mountains

Laramie Mountains

Uinta Mountains

Roan Plateau

Great Salt Lake

Fort Peck Lake

Lake Sakakawea

Missouri River

Yellowstone River

Snake River

Green River

North Platte River

Milk River

Elevation scale:
- 19,686ft
- 13,124ft
- 9843ft
- 6562ft
- 3281ft
- 1640ft
- 820ft
- 328ft
- Sea Level
- -820ft
- -6562ft
- -13,124ft

Scale 1:3,750,000
(projection: Lambert Conformal Conic)

0 20 40 60 80 100 Km
0 20 40 60 80 100 Miles

Population

■ above 5 million	▣ 1 million to 5 million	◉ 500,000 to 1 million
◎ 100,000 to 500,000	⊕ 50,000 to 100,000	○ 10,000 to 50,000	∘ below 10,000

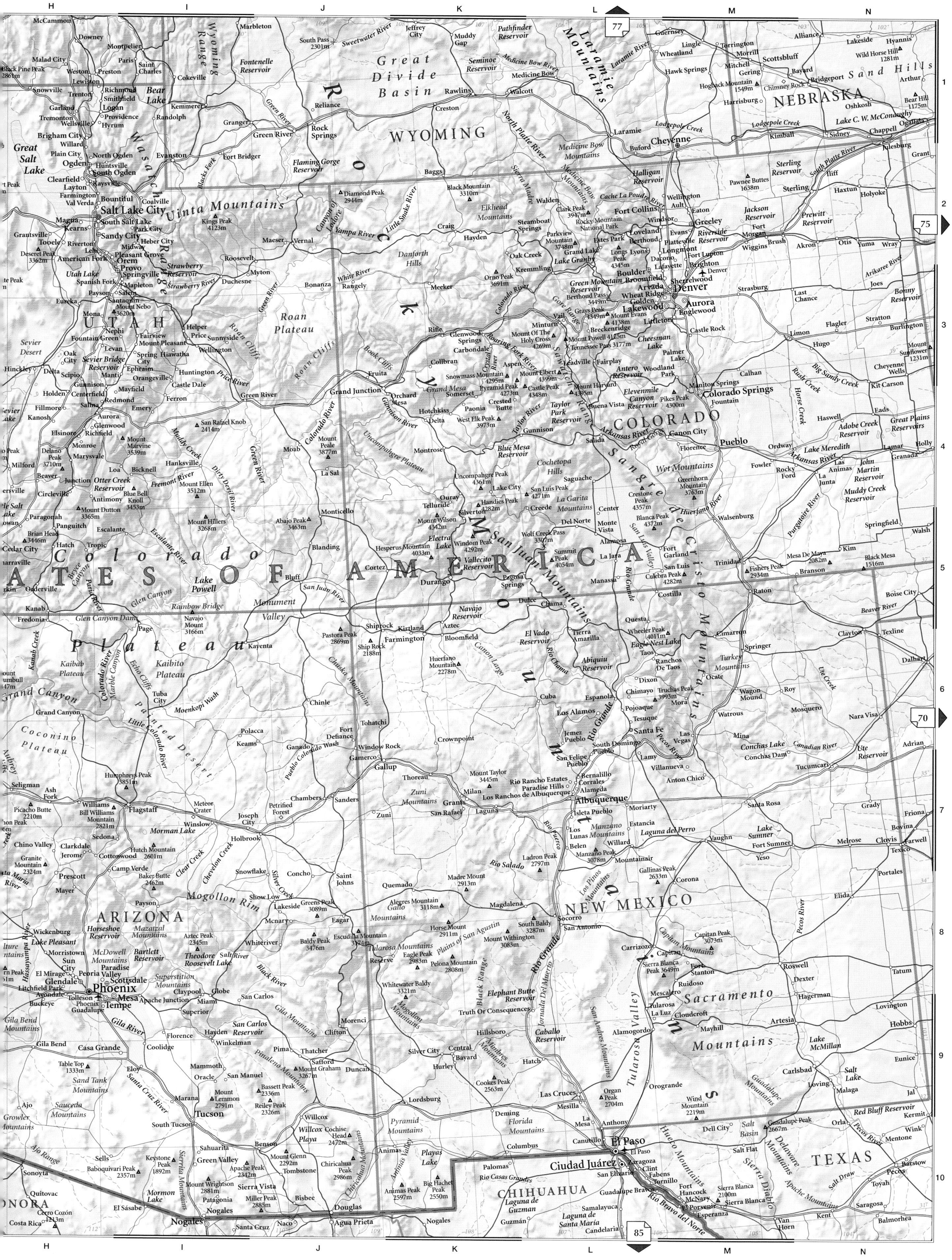

19,686ft
13,124ft
9843ft
6562ft
3281ft
1640ft
820ft
328ft
Sea Level
-820ft
-6562ft
-13,124ft

NEVADA

UNITED STATES OF AMERICA

Sierra Nevada

San Joaquin Valley

Sacramento Valley

Coast Range

Diable Range

Santa Lucia Range

Central Valley

Lake Tahoe

Reno

Sacramento

San Francisco

San Jose

Oakland

Berkeley

Fresno

Stockton

Modesto

Monterey Bay

6000m
4000m
3000m
2000m
1000m
500m
250m
100m
Sea Level
-250m
-500m
-1000m

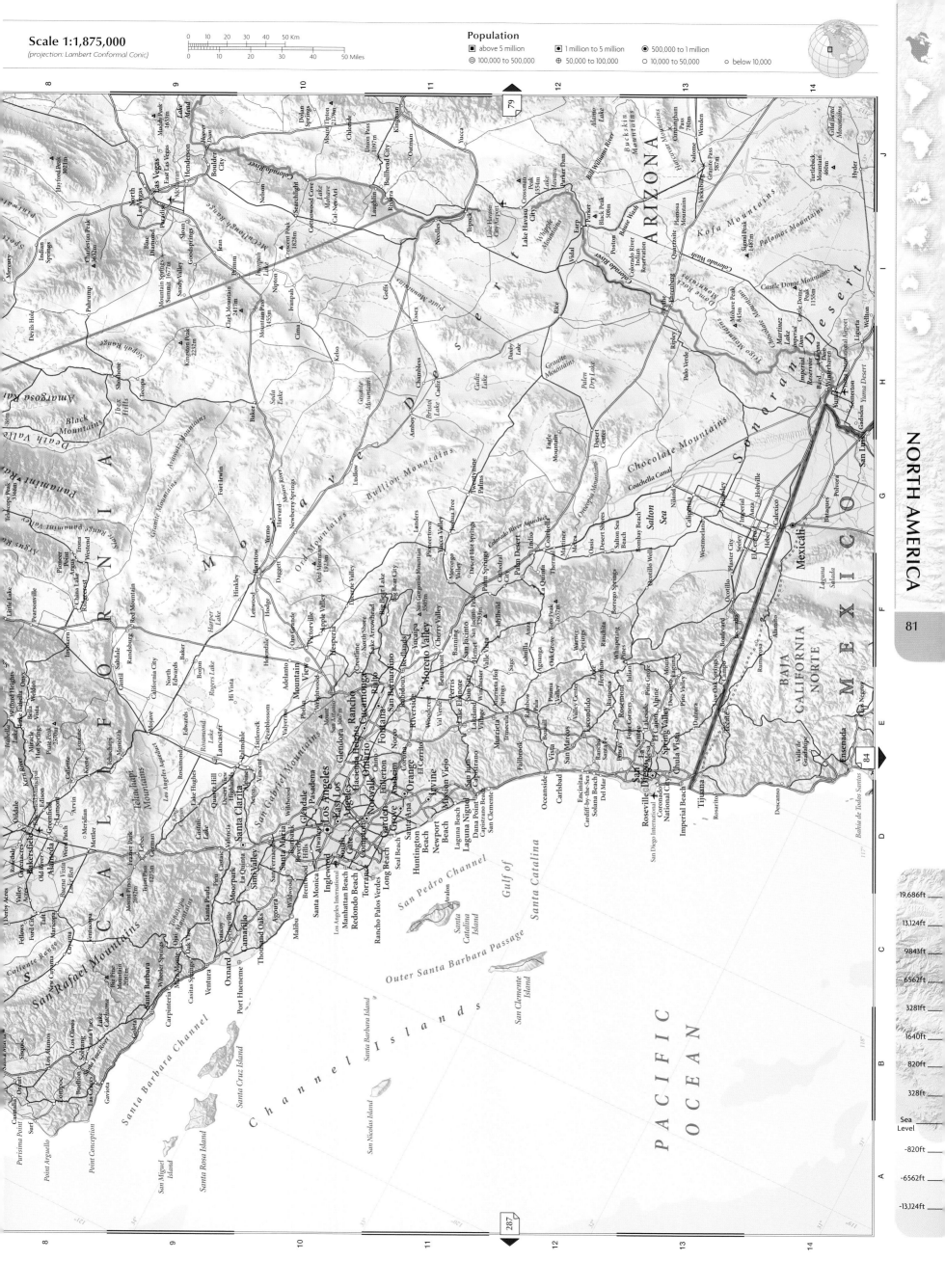

294
193
286

ARCTIC

Chukchi

Sea

UNITED STATES OF AMERICA
HAWAI'I

PACIFIC OCEAN

Hawaiian Islands

Kaua'i
Lehua Island
Pu'uwai
Ni'ihau
Kawaihoa Point
Kaulakahi Channel
Hanalei
Kekaha
'Ele'ele
Kōloa
Kilauea
Kahala Point
Kapa'a
Lihu'e

O'ahu
Kaua'i Channel
Ka'ena Point
Kahuku Point
Kahuku
Hau'ula
Waialua
Wai'anae
Makakilo City
'Ewa Beach
Pearl City
Honolulu
Diamond Head
Pearl Harbor
Ka'iwi Channel

Moloka'i
Kaunakakai
Kalaupapa
Kalohi Channel
Kalaupapa
Pailolo Channel
Nākālele Point
Lāna'i City
Lāna'i
Lahaina
Pā'ia
Kīhei
'Au'au Channel
Maui
Kailua
Haleakalā
Hāna
Pu'u 'Ula'ula (Red Hill) 3055m
'Alalākeiki Channel
Kaho'olawe
'Alenuihāhā Channel
'Upolu Point
Hāwī
Honoka'a
Laupāhoehoe
Wailea
Waimea
Keāhole Point
Mauna Kea 4205m
Pāpa'ikou
Hilo
Kalaoa
Honokōhau
Kealakekua
Kahaluu
Captain Cook
Hawai'i
Mauna Loa 4169m
Kea'au
Mountain View
Cape Kumukahi
Kīlauea Caldera
Pāhoa
Pāhala
Āpua Point
Nā'ālehu
Kaunā Point
Ka Lae (South Point)

Scale 1:5,000,000
0 20 40 60 80 100 120 Km
0 20 40 60 80 100 120 Miles

Wainwr
Icy Cape
Point Lay
Cape Lisburne
Point Hope
Point Hope
Lisburne
Ledak River
De Lo
Mishguk Mountain 1350m
Kivalina
Noatak
Tututalak Mount 1364m
Bai

Kotzebue Sound
Kotzebue
Noorvik
Cape Espenberg
Goodhope Bay
Deering
Candle
Kiwalik
Buckla
Selav
Selaw
Lak

Seward Peninsula
Enurmino
Shishmaref
Little Diomede Island
Wales
Cape Prince of Wales
Brevig Mission
Port Clarence
Teller
Kougarok Mountain 875m
Brooks Mountain 883m
Kuzitrin River
Koyuk River
Hay

Poluostrov Chukotskiy
Arctic Circle
Uelen
Lavrentiya
Bering Strait
Cape Rodney
Council
Solomon
Golovin
Elim
Koyuk
Nome
Cape Nome
Norton Bay
Shaktoolik

Norton Sound
Providèniya
Northwest Cape
Gambell
Savoonga
Saint Lawrence Island
Northeast Cape
Camp Kulowiye
Southeast Cape
Southwest Cape

Stuart Island
Stebbins
Saint Michael
Pastol Bay
Unalakleet
Hamilton
Kotlik
Emmonak
Alakanuk
Sheldons Point
Graylir
Shag
Anvik
Paradis
Bonasila Dome 551m

CHUKOTSKIY AVTONOMNYY OKRUG
Velikaya
Kamenskoye
Gora Ledyanaya 2562m

KORYAKSKOYE Nagor'ye
KORYAKSKIY AVTONOMNYY OKRUG
Korf
Tilichiki
Pakhachi
Meynypil'gyno
Khatyrka

RUSSIAN FEDERATION
Olyutorskiy Zaliv
Mys Olyutorskiy
Beringovskiy
Mys Navarin

Anadyrskiy Zaliv

Mountain Village
Scammon Bay
Pitkas Point
Pilot Station
Saint Marys
Russian Mission
Marshall
Kals
Lower Kalskag
Hooper Bay
Chevak
Hazen Bay
Aropuk Lake
Newtok
Kasigluk
Akiachak
Bethel
Napakiak
Kwethlu
Akiak
Napaskiak
Kuskokwi
Rui
Mekoryuk
Tanunak
Toksook Bay
Tuntutuliak
Nightmute
Dall Lake
Nunivak Island
Cape Mohican
Roberts Mountain 510m
Kipnuk
Quinhagak
Chefornak
Eek
Eek River
Kwigillingok

Cape Mendenhall
Kuskokwim Bay
Goodnews
Twin
Platinum
Togiak

Bering Sea

Limit of winter pack ice
Hall Island
Saint Matthew Island
Pinnacle Island
Glory of Russia Cape
Upright Cape

Cape Newenham
Hagemeister Island

Bristol Ba

Saint Paul Island
Saint Paul
Pribilof Islands
Saint George Island
Saint George

Port Moller
Iyane
Alask
Amak Island
Cold Bay
Korovin Island
Sand Point
Squaw
King Cove
Belkofski
Deer
Nagai
False Pass
Shum
Unimak Island
Shishaldin Volcano 2857m
Pogromni Volcano 2002m
Unimak Pass
Akun Island
Makushin Volcano 2036m
Akutan
Tigalda Island
Pauloff Harbor
Avatanak Island
Sanak Islands
Aleutian Islands

Cape Wrangell
Near Islands
Attu Island
Attu
Shemya Island
Agattu Strait
Krugloi Point
Agattu Island
Cape Sabak
Buldir Island
Kiska Island
Vega Point
Segula Island
Little Sitkin Island
Rat Islands
Rat Island
Amchitka Island
Amchitka Pass
Semisopochnoi Island
Anvil Peak 1221m
Garetoi Island
Tanaga Volcano
Tanaga Island
Kanaga Volcano 1307m
Kanaga Island
Cape Kanaga
Sasmik Island
Delarof Islands
Adak Island
Kagalaska Island
Andreanof Islands
Great Sitkin Island
Atka Island
Atka
Fenimore Pass
Amlia Island
Seguam Island
Seguam Pass
Amukta Island
Amukta Pass
Yunaska Island
Islands of Four Mountains
Herbert Island
Chagulak Island
Carlisle Island
Umnak Island
Nikolski
Unalaska Island
Dutch Harbor
Fox Islands
Krenitzen Islands

Elevation scale
6000m
4000m
3000m
2000m
1000m
500m
250m
100m
Sea Level
-250m
-500m
-1000m

Scale 1:8,000,000
(projection: Lambert Conformal Conic)

0 25 50 75 100 125 150 175 200 Km
0 25 50 75 100 125 150 175 200 Miles

Population
- ■ above 5 million
- ⊡ 1 million to 5 million
- ◎ 500,000 to 1 million
- ◉ 100,000 to 500,000
- ⊕ 50,000 to 100,000
- ○ 10,000 to 50,000
- ∘ below 10,000

19,686ft
13,124ft
9843ft
6562ft
3281ft
1640ft
820ft
328ft
Sea Level
-820ft
-6562ft
-13,124ft

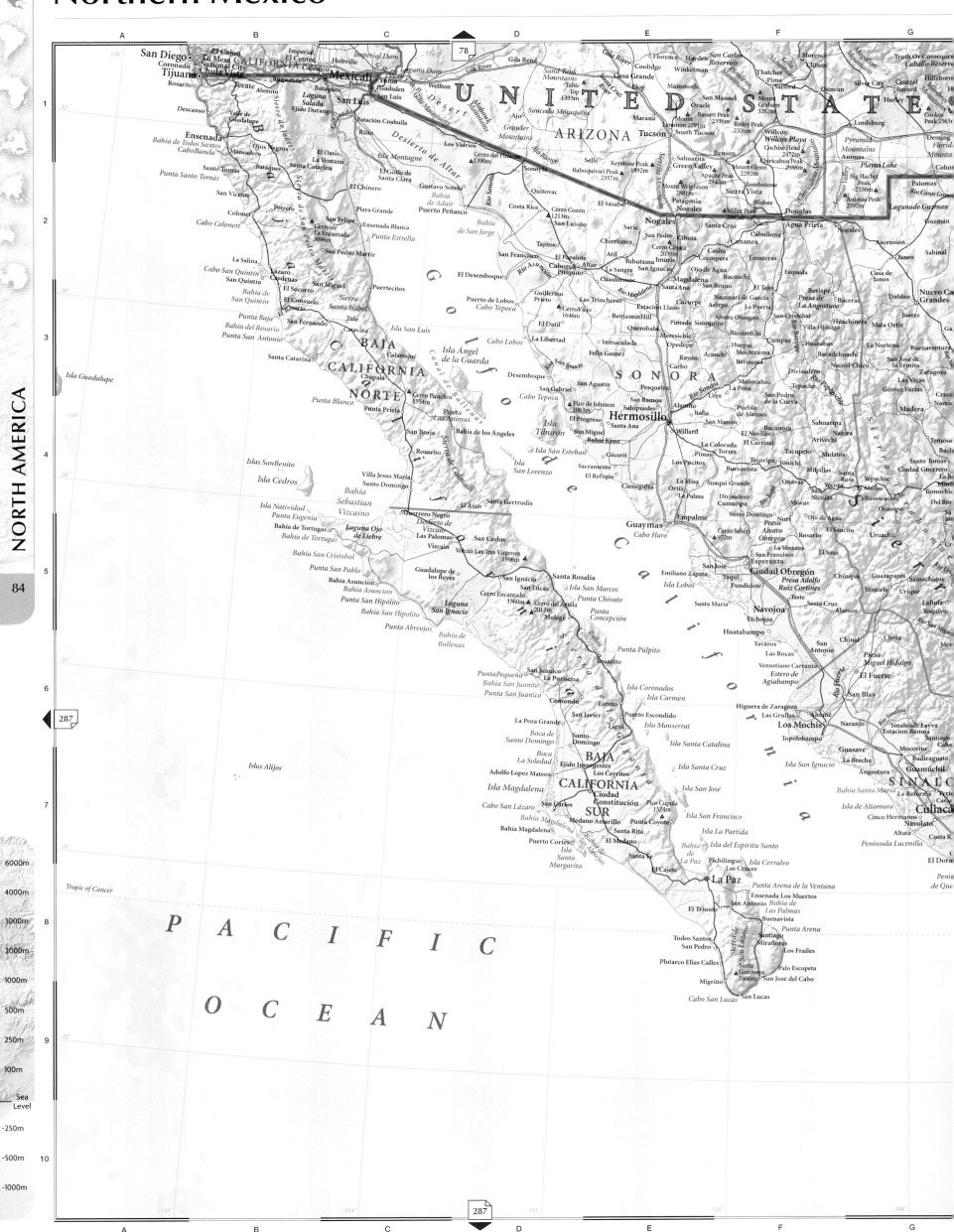

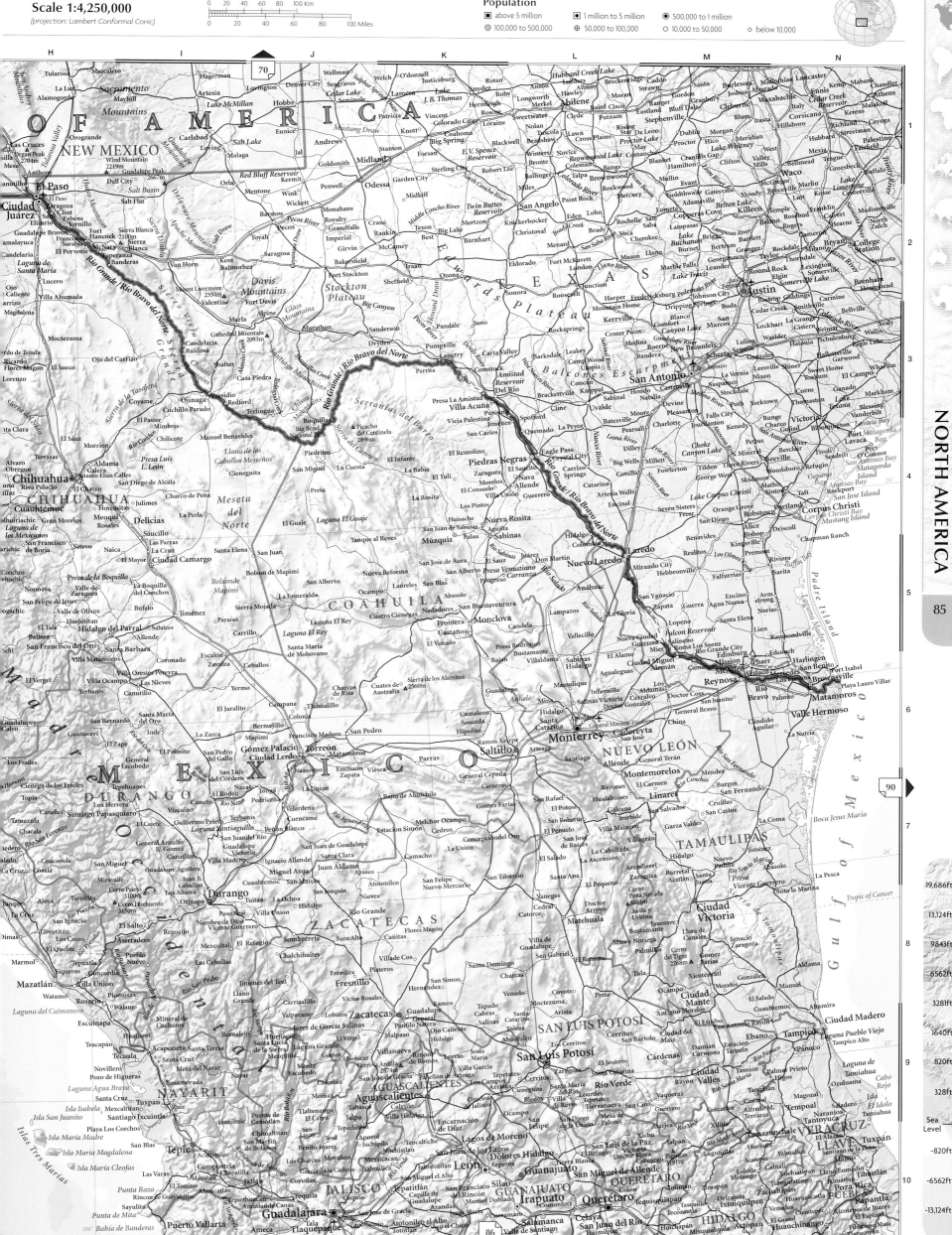

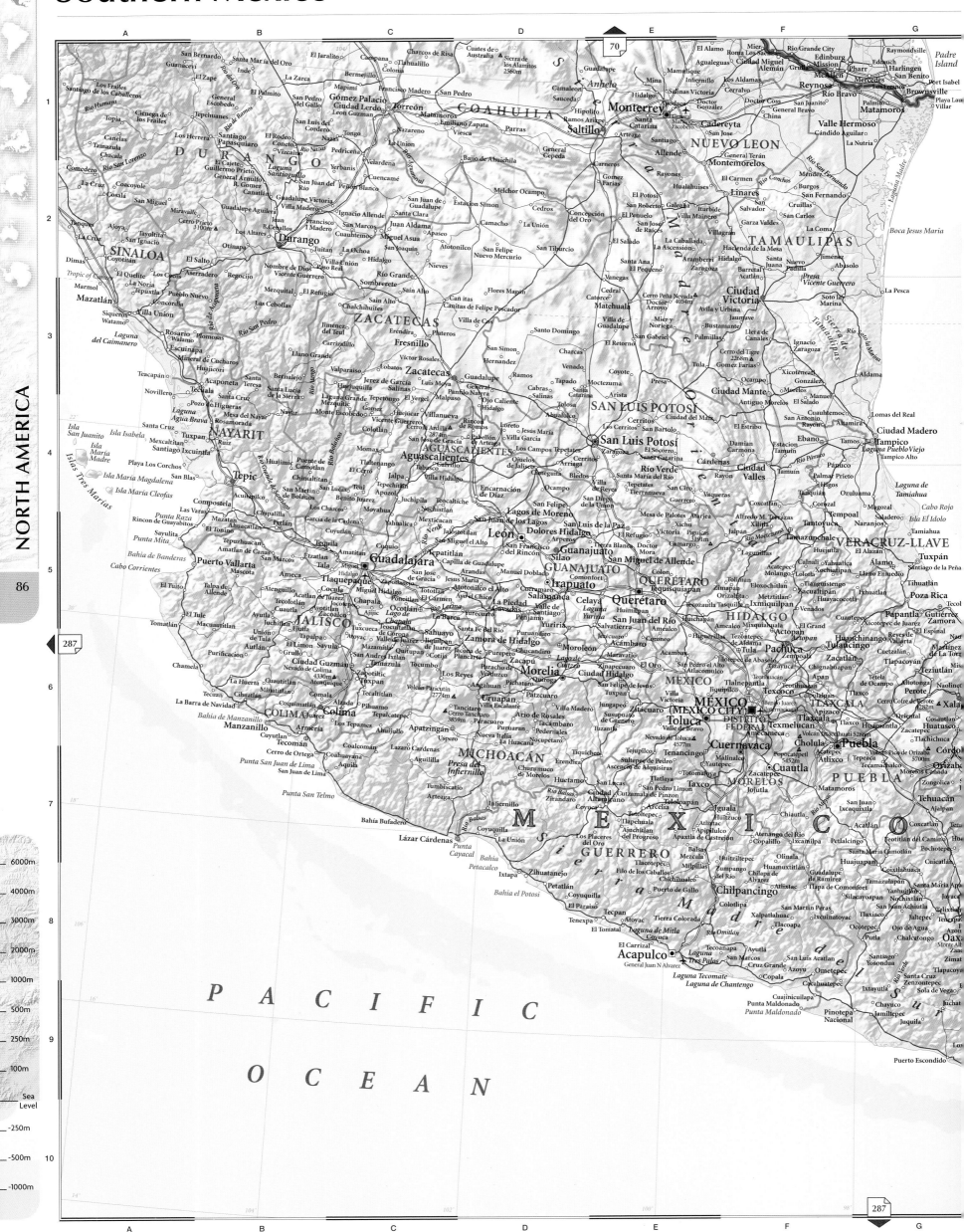

NORTH AMERICA

90

UNITED STATES OF AMERICA

Saint Petersburg
Bradenton
Sarasota
Venice
Port Charlotte
Punta Gorda
Fort Myers
Cape Coral
Bonita Springs
Naples
Lake Wales
Wauchula
Arcadia
La Belle
Immokalee
Big Cypress Swamp
The Everglades
Everglades City
Cape Romano
Cape Sable
Avon Park
Okeechobee
Lake Okeechobee
Belle Glade
Lake Worth
Boynton Beach
Pompano Beach
Fort Lauderdale
Hollywood
North Miami
Miami Beach
Miami
Hialeah
Kendall
Homestead
Florida Bay
Marathon
Dry Tortugas
Key West
Marquesas Keys
Florida Keys
Key Largo
Islamorada
Sebastian
Vero Beach
Fort Pierce
Jensen Beach
Stuart
Hobe Sound
Indiantown
West Palm Beach
West Palm Beach

FLORIDA

Gulf of Mexico

Straits of Florida

Tropic of Cancer

MEXICO
Isla Mujeres
Puerto Juárez
Cancún
Leona Vicario
Puerto Morelos
Punta Molas del Norte
Playa del Carmen
Cozumel
Isla Cozumel

Cabo Catoche

Yucatan Channel

Archipiélago de los Colorados
Minas de Matahambre
Pinar del Río
Sierra de los Órganos
Los Palacios
Consolación del Sur
Viñales
Golfo de Guanahacabibes
Cabo de San Antonio
Cabo Corrientes
Cayos de San Felipe
Nueva Gerona
Santa Fé
Isla de la Juventud
Cayo Largo
Archipiélago de los Canarreos

LA HABANA (HAVANA)
Mariel
Artemisa
Guanajay
Guanabacoa
San Cristóbal
Güira de Melena
Güines
Colón
Matanzas
Cárdenas
Jovellanos
Jagüey Grande
Santo Domingo
Cruces
Cienfuegos
Trinidad
Pico San Juan 1150m
Jatibonico
Morón
Sancti Spíritus
Ciego de Ávila
Florida
Esmeralda
Cayo Guajaba
Nuevitas

CUBA

Sagua la Grande
Caibarién
Placetas
Santa Clara
Cabaiguán
Cayo Fragoso
Isla de Buena Vista
Cayo Coco
Cayo Romano
Camagüey
Vertientes
Las Tunas
Puerto Padre
Gibara
Banes
Holguín
Cueto
Mayarí
Moa
Baracoa
Bayamo
Manzanillo
Campechuela
Jiguaní
Palma Soriano
Pilón
Santiago de Cuba
Guantánamo
Bahía de Guantánamo (to US)
Maisí
Punta de Quemado

Santa Cruz del Sur
Golfo de Ana María
Archipiélago de los Jardines de la Reina
Golfo de Guacanayabo
Sierra Maestra
Pico Turquino 1944m
Cabo Cruz

G r e a t e r

BAHAMAS

Grand Bahama Island
Great Sale Cay
Little Abaco
Coopers Town
Pelican Point
West End
Freeport
Eight Mile Rock
Marsh Harbour
Great Abaco
Cherokee Sound
Moores Island
Northwest Providence Channel
Berry Islands
Bimini Islands
Nicholls Town
Current
Eleuthera Island
Governor's Harbour
Northeast Providence Channel
Nassau
NASSAU
New Providence
Adelaide
Behring Point
Andros Town
Andros Island
Rock Sound
Bannerman Town
Arthur's Town
Cat Island
Cockburn Town
San Salvador
Columbus Point
Conception Island
Santa María
George Town
Long Island
Rum Cay
Great Exuma Island
Little Exuma
Deadman's Cay
Clarence Town
Cape Verde
Colonel Hill
Crooked Island
Samana Cay
Northeast Point
Plana Cays
Long Cay
Snug Corner
Acklins Island
Salina Point
Ragged Island Range
Kemp's Bay
Great Guana Cay
Tongue of the Ocean
Exuma Sound
Exuma Cays
Santaren Channel
Old Bahama Channel
Nicholas Channel
Cay Sal
Anguilla Cays
Archipiélago de Sabana
Archipiélago de Camagüey
Matthew Town
Great Inagua
Lake Rosa
Little Inagua
Northeast Point
West C
Caicos Pas
Mayaguana Passage
Crooked Island Passage

CAYMAN ISLANDS (to UK)
Little Cayman
Cayman Brac
Owen Roberts
Bodden Town
GEORGE TOWN
Grand Cayman

JAMAICA
Montego Bay
Sangster
South Negril Point
Savanna-La-Mar
Christiana
Mandeville
Black River
May Pen
Spanish Town
KINGSTON
Port Maria
Port Antonio
Blue Mountain Peak 2256m
Royal Norman Manley
Morant Bay
Portland Point

HAITI
Port-de-Paix
Môle St-Nicolas
Gros-Mor
Gonaïve
Golfe de la Gonâve
St-Ma
Île de la Gonâve
Jérémie
Cap Dame Marie
Dame-Marie
Corail
Miragoâ
Chardonnières
Les Cayes
Pointe à Gravois
Île à Vache
Aquin
Jac
NAVASSA ISLAND (to US)
Jamaica Channel
Windward Passage

A n

ISLAS DE LA BAHÍA
Roatán
Isla de Roatán
Isla de Guanaja
Punta Caxinas
Trujillo
Balfate
Limón
Iriona
Brus Laguna
Río Aguán
COLÓN
Sava
Río Sico Tinto
San Esteban
Gualaco
HONDURAS
Juticalpa
Catacamas
Dulce Nombre de Culmí
GRACIAS A DIOS
Puerto Lempira
Cabo de Gracias a Dios
SIERRA DE AGALTA
OLANCHO
Río Coco
Waspam
Boom
Bocay
Ulmukhuás
Río Wana
Bonanza
Siuna
Yablis
Dákura
Tuapi
Puerto Cabezas
La Rosita
San Luis
Jalapa
Jinotega
Cerro Saslaya 1590m
REGIÓN AUTÓNOMA ATLÁNTICO NORTE
Río Prinzapolka
Wounta
Prinzapolka
Prinzapolka
Matagalpa
Río Tuma
La Sirena
Barra de Río Grande
Kara
MATAGALPA
BOACO
Boaco
Río Grande de Matagalpa
Cayos Guerrero
Arrecifes de la Media Luna
Arrecife Edinburgh
Cayo Muerto
Cayos Miskitos
Cayos Londres
Cayos King
NICARAGUA
CHONTALES
Juigalpa
Santo Tomás
Muelle de los Bueyes
El Rama
Bluefields
Río Escondido
Cayos de Perlas
Islas del Maíz
Lago de Nicaragua
Volcán Concepción 1610m
Morrito
REGIÓN AUTÓNOMA ATLÁNTICA SUR
Río Punta Gorda
Monkey Point
Rivas
Isla de Ometepe
San Miguelito
San Carlos
Punta Gorda
San Juan del Sur
La Cruz
Upala
El Castillo de la Concepción
San Juan del Norte
Barra del Colorado
Liberia
Cañas
Volcán Miravalles 2028m
Volcán Arenal 1616m
Quesada
Puerto Viejo
Río San Juan
GUANACASTE
Santa Cruz
PUNTARENAS
Abangares
Puntarenas
COSTA RICA
ALAJUELA
HEREDIA
Volcán Barva 2906m
San Isidro
Guápiles
Siquirres
LIMÓN
Limón
SAN JOSÉ

C a r i b b e a n

S e a

COLOMBIA
Ríohach
Santa Marta
Dibulla
Barranquilla
Ciénaga
MAGDALENA
Pico Cristóbal 5775m
Puerto Colombia
Soledad
ATLÁNTICO
Sitionuevo
Santa Catalina
Sabanalarga
Pivija
Cartagena
Turbaco
Campo de la Cruz
Valledupar

Scale 1:2,500,000
0 5 10   20 Km
0 5 10   20 Miles

JAMAICA *(inset)*
Montego Bay
Sangster
Falmouth
Discovery Bay
St Ann's Bay
Port Maria
Lucea
Clark's Town
Browns Town
Ocho Rios
Don Christophers Point
Negril
Dolphin Head 545m
Birchs Hill 551m
The Cockpit Country
Grange Hill
Cambridge
Alexandria
Claremont
Highgate
Buff Bay
North East Point
Little London
Savanna-La-Mar
Maggotty
Mount Denham 986m
Frankfield
Linstead
Ewarton
Port Antonio
Crab Pond Point
Christiana
Mandeville
Chapelton
Bog Walk
Blue Mountain Peak 2256m
Golden Grove
Black River
Malvern 725m
Santa Cruz
Spanish Town
May Pen
Portmore
Port Royal
KINGSTON
Norman Manley
Bath
Port Morant
Morant Bay
Alligator Pond
Old Harbour
Yallahs Hill 730m
Great Pedro Bluff
Lionel Town
Long Bay
Portland Bight
Wreck Point
Portland Point
Caribbean Sea
Jamaica Channel

Caribbean Sea

Sea Level
6000m
4000m
3000m
2000m
1000m
500m
250m
100m
Sea Level
-250m
-500m
-1000m

Scale 1:6,250,000
(projection: Lambert Conformal Conic)

0 25 50 75 100 125 150 175 200 Km
0 25 50 75 100 125 150 175 200 Miles

Population
- ■ above 5 million
- ■ 1 million to 5 million
- ◉ 500,000 to 1 million
- ◎ 100,000 to 500,000
- ⊕ 50,000 to 100,000
- ○ 10,000 to 50,000
- ∘ below 10,000

GUADELOUPE (to France)

Guadeloupe Passage
Pointe de la Grande Vigie
Anse-Bertrand
Port-Louis
Grand Cul-de-Sac Marin
Morne-à-l'Eau
le Moule
Ste-Rose
Baie-Mahault
Lamentin
Pointe-à-Pitre
les Abymes
Ste-Anne
St-François
Pointe Noire
Basse Terre
Petit-Bourg
Petit Cul-de-Sac Marin
Pointe des Colibris
Vieux-Habitants
Soufrière 1467m
Canal de Marie-Galante
St-Claude
BASSE-TERRE
Capesterre-Belle-Eau
Canal des Saintes
Caribbean Sea
ATLANTIC OCEAN

Scale 1:2,500,000
0 5 10 20 Km
0 5 10 20 Miles

DOMINICA

Dominica Passage
Pointe Jaco
Vieille Case
Portsmouth
Melville Hall
Marigot
Morne Diablotins 1447m
Castle Bruce
Salisbury
St. Joseph
Canefield
Rosalie
La Plaine
ROSEAU
Berekua
Scotts Head Village
Caribbean Sea
ATLANTIC OCEAN
Martinique Passage

Scale 1:2,000,000
0 5 10 Km
0 5 10 Miles

MARTINIQUE (to France)

Martinique Passage
Grand' Rivière
Basse-Pointe
le Prêcheur
Montagne Pelée 1397m
Ste-Marie
St-Pierre
la Trinité
Schœlcher
le Lamentin
le Robert
FORT-DE-FRANCE
le François
Baie de Fort-de-France
le Diamant
les Anses-d'Arlets
Rivière-Pilote
Ste-Anne
Caribbean Sea
ATLANTIC OCEAN
Saint Lucia Channel

Scale 1:2,500,000
0 5 10 20 Km
0 5 10 20 Miles

ST LUCIA

Pointe Du Cap
Gros Islet
George F.L. Charles
CASTRIES
Anse La Raye
Dennery
Soufrière
Petit Piton 743m
Micoud
Gros Piton 798m
Laborie
Hewanorra
Vieux Fort
Ministre Point
Caribbean Sea
ATLANTIC OCEAN
Saint Vincent Passage

Scale 1:2,000,000
0 5 10 Km
0 5 10 Miles

BARBADOS

North Point
Crab Hill
ATLANTIC OCEAN
Speightstown
Bathsheba
Mount Hillaby 340m
Welchman Hall
Holetown
BRIDGETOWN
The Crane
Oistins
Grantley Adams

Scale 1:2,000,000
0 5 10 Km
0 5 10 Miles

ST VINCENT & THE GRENADINES

Saint Vincent Passage
Porter Point
Fancy
La Soufrière 1234m
Chateaubelair
Georgetown
St Vincent
Layou
Barrouallie
North Union
KINGSTOWN
Stubbs
Arnos Vale
Caribbean Sea
ATLANTIC OCEAN

Scale 1:2,000,000
0 5 10 Km
0 5 10 Miles

GRENADA

Caribbean Sea
Sauteurs
Victoria
Mount St. Catherine 840m
Gouyave
Grenville
ST.GEORGE'S
St. David's
Grand Anse
Point Salines
ATLANTIC OCEAN

Scale 1:2,000,000
0 5 10 Km
0 5 10 Miles

ATLANTIC OCEAN

Tropic of Cancer

TURKS & CAICOS ISLANDS (to UK)
North Caicos Islands
Caicos Islands
Providenciales
East Caicos
Cockburn Harbour
Grand Turk Island
COCKBURN TOWN
Turks Islands

Mouchoir Passage

Hispaniola
DOMINICAN REPUBLIC
Monte Cristi
Cabo Isabela
Cap-Haïtien
Puerto Plata
Cabo Francés Viejo
Saint-Louis-du-Nord
Dajabón
Moca
Cabrera
Santiago
Nagua
La Vega
Bahía Escocesa
San Francisco de Macorís
Río Yuna
Bahía de Samaná
Cordillera Central
Monte Plata
Hato Mayor
Bonao
Villa Altagracia
El Seibo
Higüey
Cabo Engaño
San Juan
Las Américas
San Pedro de Macorís
PORT-AU-PRINCE
Pico Duarte 3175m
SANTO DOMINGO
La Romana
Lago Enriquillo
Barahona
Punta Palenque
Isla Saona
Oviedo
Enriquillo
Isla Beata
Cabo Beata

PUERTO RICO (to US)
Aguadilla
Arecibo
SAN JUAN
Carolina
Fajardo
Mayagüez
Utuado
Bayamón
Caguas
Vieques
Isla de Vieques
Yauco
Cordillera Central
Ponce
Guayama
Isla Mona
Cabo Rojo
Mona Passage

BRITISH VIRGIN ISLANDS (to UK)
Anegada
Virgin Passage
St Thomas
ROAD TOWN
Beef Island
Tortola
CHARLOTTE AMALIE
VIRGIN ISLANDS (to US)
Frederiksted
St Croix
Christiansted

Sombrero (to Anguilla)
Anguilla Passage
ANGUILLA
THE VALLEY
Wall Blake
Anguilla
Marigot
St-Martin (to France)
Philipsburg
Sint-Maarten (to Netherlands)
St-Barthélémy (to France)
Saba
St Eustatius
NETHERLANDS ANTILLES (to Netherlands)
Golden Rock
Codrington
Barbuda
BASSETERRE
St Kitts
Newcastle
V.C.Bird
ANTIGUA & BARBUDA
Nevis
Charlestown
Redonda
ST JOHN'S
Antigua
ST KITTS & NEVIS
Falmouth
PLYMOUTH
Blackburne
MONTSERRAT (to UK)
Guadeloupe Passage
le Raizet
Port-Louis
BASSE-TERRE
Ste-Rose
Pointe-de-Pitre
la Désirade
GUADELOUPE (to France)
Basse Terre
Soufrière 1467m
Marie-Galante
les Saintes
Grand-Bourg
Dominica Passage
Portsmouth
Melville Hall
Marigot
Canefield
La Plaine
ROSEAU
DOMINICA
Montagne Pelée 1397m
Ste-Marie
St-Pierre
MARTINIQUE (to France)
FORT-DE-FRANCE
le Lamentin
Rivière-Pilote
St Lucia Channel
Vigie
Castries
ST LUCIA
Soufrière
Mount Gimie 950m
Hewanorra
Vieux Fort
St Vincent Passage
St Vincent
La Soufrière 1234m
Chateaubelair
Arnos Vale
KINGSTOWN
ST VINCENT & THE GRENADINES
Port Elizabeth
Bequia
Mustique
BARBADOS
Speightstown
BRIDGETOWN
Grantley Adams
Canouan
The Grenadines
Union Island
Hillsborough
Carriacou
Victoria
GRENADA
ST GEORGE'S
Grenville
Point Salines
Tobago
Charlotteville
Scarborough
TRINIDAD & TOBAGO
PORT-OF-SPAIN
Arima
Sangre Grande
Trinidad
Galera Point

Lesser Antilles
Leeward Islands
Windward Islands

PUERTO RICO (to US)

ATLANTIC OCEAN
Isabela
Laguna Tortuguero
Arecibo
Vega Baja
SAN JUAN
Aguadilla
San Sebastián
Manati
Río Grande
Cabezas de San Juan
Punta Higüero
Lago Dos Bocas
Bayamón
Cataño
Carolina
Fajardo
Sonda de Vieques
Culebra
Bahía de Mayagüez
Grande de Añasco
Utuado
Orocovis
Humacao
Isla de Culebra
Punta Puerca
Mayagüez
Adjuntas
Sierra de Cayey
Yabucoa
Isla de Vieques
San Germán
Cerro de Punta 1338m
Juana Díaz
Toa Vaca
Monte Pirata 301m
Cabo Rojo
Yauco
Ponce
Guayama
Guayanés
Punta Brea
Salinas
Punta Petrona
Caribbean Sea

Scale 1:2,500,000
0 5 10 20 Km
0 5 10 20 Miles

TRINIDAD & TOBAGO

Caribbean Sea
Galera Point
The Dragon's Mouth
Blanchisseuse
Matelot
Redhead
Tunapuna
PORT-OF-SPAIN
Arima
Sangre Grande
Chaguanas
Couva
Caroni River
Caroni Arena Dam
Gulf of Paria
Trinidad
Guatuaro Point
San Fernando
Rio Claro
La Brea
Princes Town
Killdeer Point
Rushville
Point Fortin
Siparia
Galeota Point
Bonasse
Moruga
The Serpent's Mouth
VENEZUELA
ATLANTIC OCEAN

Scale 1:2,500,000
0 5 10 20 Km
0 5 10 20 Miles

Lesser Antilles
ARUBA (to Netherlands)
ORANJESTAD
Reina Beatrix
Aruba
Sint Nicholaas
NETHERLANDS ANTILLES (to Netherlands)
Noordpunt
Hato Airport
Malmok
Santa Catherina
Bonaire
Curaçao
WILLEMSTAD
Kralendijk
Isla Blanquilla
Charlotteville
Scarborough

Peninsula de la Guajira
Cabo San Román
Isla La Orchila
Islas Los Testigos
Tobago
Galera Point
TRINIDAD & TOBAGO
PORT-OF-SPAIN
Puerto López
Punto Fijo
Los Taques
Puerto Nuevo
Islas Las Aves
Islas Los Roques
Arima
Sangre Grande
Trinidad
Golfo de Venezuela
Puerto Cumarebo
San Juan de los Cayos
NUEVA ESPARTA
Isla La Tortuga
Río Caribe
Puerto de Hierro
Gulf of Paria
Coro
San Luis
Mirimire
Tucacas
Juangriego
La Asunción
Cumaná
Carúpano
Irapa
Point Fortin
San Fernando
Galeota Point
LA GUAJIRA
Punta Gallinas
Uribia
Dabajuro
FALCÓN
Tocuyo de la Costa
Porlamar
Isla de Margarita
Punta de Piedras
El Pilar
Güiria
Bonasse
Siparia
Rio Claro
Maracaibo
Capatárida
La Cruz de Taratara
Boca de Pozo
Carúpano
Cariaco
Cumanacoa
San Antonio
Caripito
Pedernales
Caño Macareo
Punta Baja
ZULIA
Sinamaica
Pedregal
Morón
Puerto Cabello
La Vela de Coro
VENEZUELA
Cariaco
SUCRE
Caripe
MONAGAS
The Serpent's Mouth
San Rafael
Altagracia
Mene de Mauroa
Siquisique
VARGAS
La Guaira
Río Chico
Barcelona
Cumaná
Maturín
DELTA AMACURO
Concepción
Cabimas
Santa Rita
Ciudad Ojeda
Aguada Grande
Churuguara
Simón Bolívar
CARACAS
Petare
Puerto La Cruz
Guanta
Cerro 2438m
ANZOÁTEGUI
Cantaura
San Francisco de Yare
Los Teques
LARA
Rio Tocuyo
Yumare
Puaca
YARACUY
San Felipe
Maracay
Turmero
Cua
Valle de Guanape
Valle de la Pascua
MIRANDA
Sabaneta
Tía Juana
Quíbor
Guanare
Aroa
Valencia
Chivacoa
Villa de Cura del Tuy
Valle de Guanape
Caicara
Punta de Mata
Maracaibo

19,686ft
13,124ft
9843ft
6562ft
3281ft
1640ft
820ft
328ft
Sea Level
-820ft
-6562ft
-13,124ft

Atlanta

Bolton
Hills Park
Brookwood
Lavista
Morningside
Druid Hills
Piedmont Park
Woodruff Arts Center
Callanwolde Fine Arts Center
Rockdale
Carey Park
Center Hill
Grove Park
Margaret Mitchell House
Decatur
Atlanta Civic Center
Oakhurst
Atlanta
Inman Park
Kirkwood
East Lake
World of Coca-Cola
Martin Luther King Jr N.H.S.
West End
Hammonds House Galleries
Grant Park
Gresham Park
East Atlanta
Casacade Heights
Oakland City
Ormewood
Eastland Heights
Brookwood
Sylvan Hills
Lakewood Park
Lakewood Heights
Thomasville
East Point
South Bend Park
South River
Cornell
Constitution

2 Km
2 Miles

Chicago

Chicago O'Hare Intl. Airport
Harwood Heights
Uptown
Lake Michigan
Addison
Elmwood Park
Lincoln Park
Lincoln Park Zoo
Elmhurst
Melrose Park
Avondale
Chicago River
Sears Tower
Maywood
Oak Park
Bucktown
Lombard
Westchester
Berwyn
Chicago
Oak Brook
Cicero
Chinatown
Pilsen
Bronzeville
Bridgeport
Downers Grove
La Grange
Kenwood
Summit
Elsdon
Darien
Chicago Midway Airport
Englewood
Bedford Park
Forest Hill
Burbank
Ashburn
Waterfall Glen Forest Preserve
Des Plaines
Hickory Hills
Oak Lawn
Evergreen Park
Chicago State University

5 Km
5 Miles

Dallas

L.B. Houston Park
Meaders
Biblical Arts Center
Richardson
White Rock
Garland
Oldham
Fair Oaks Park
Town East Mall
Dallas Love Field
University Park
White Rock Lake
Uniersity of Dallas
Highland Park
Dallas Theater Center
Irving
Big Town Mall
Trinity River Greenbelt Park
Eagle Ford
Dallas
Cotton Bowl
Rochester Park
Grand Prairie
Oak Cliff
Dallas Zoo
Rochester Park
Balch Springs
Cockrell Hill
Mountain Creek Lake
Fruitdale
Trinity
Mountain Creek Lake Park
Paul Quinn Collection
Lancaster

4 Km
4 Miles

Denver

Westminster
Northglenn
Standley Lake
Federal Heights
Rocky Mountain Arsenal National Wildlife Refuge
Arvada
Welby
Commerce City
Wheat Ridge
Mile-High Stadium
Denver
Museum of Natural History
Applewood
Edgewater
Glendale
Four Mile Historic Park
Lakewood
University of Denver
Aurora
Bear Creek Lake Park
Englewood
Cherry Creek State Park
Marston Lake
Littleton Historical Museum
Cherry Hills Village
Littleton
Greenwood Village

6 Km
6 Miles

Detroit

Sterling Heights
Mount Clemens
N
Lake Saint Clair
Troy
Roseville
St. Clair Shores
Pontiac
Palmer Park
Warren
Madison Heights
Harper Woods
Birmingham
Detroit City Airport
Chandler Park
Royal Oak
Hamtramck
Grosse Pointe
Southfield
Chrysler Center
Belle Isle Park
Detroit
Redford
Joe Louis Sport Arena
Windsor
University of Windsor
USA CANADA
Livonia
Dearborn
Henry Ford Museum & Greenfield Village
Patton Park
Westland
Dearborn Heights
Lincoln Park
Canton
Taylor
Southgate
Detroit River
CANADA USA
Detroit Metro Wayne County Airport

10 Km
10 Miles

Las Vegas

Nellis Air Force Base
North Las Vegas Airport
Vegas Heights
North Las Vegas
Eastland Heights
Las Vegas Natural History Museum
Sunrise Manor
Fountain Park
Nevada State Museum and Historic Society
Freedom Park
Meadows Mall
Las Vegas
Nature Park
Las Vegas Art Museum
University
The Strip
Clark
The Strip
Las Vegas Country Club
Winchester
Spring Valley
Liberace Museum
McCarran Intl. Airport
Paradise

4 Km
4 Miles

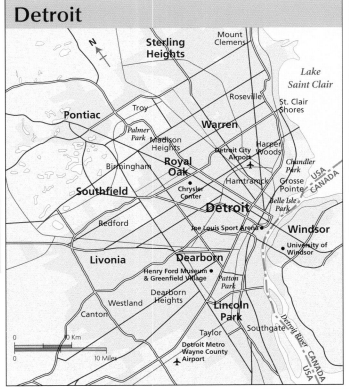
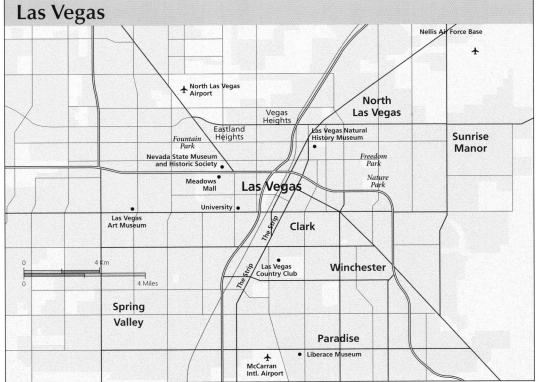
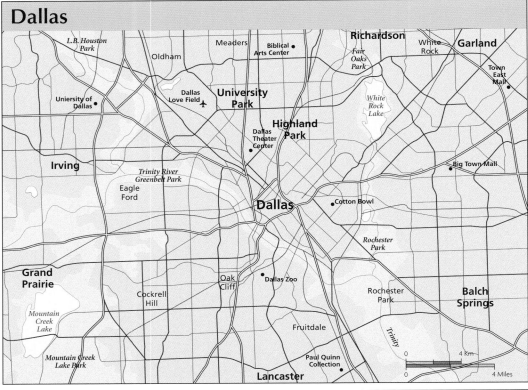
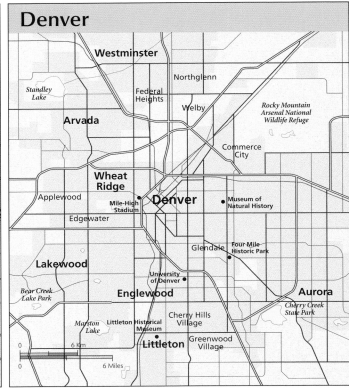

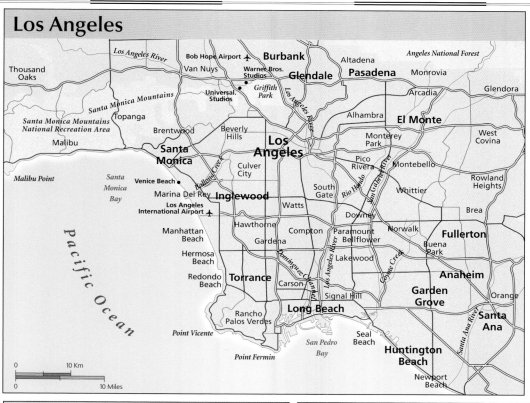

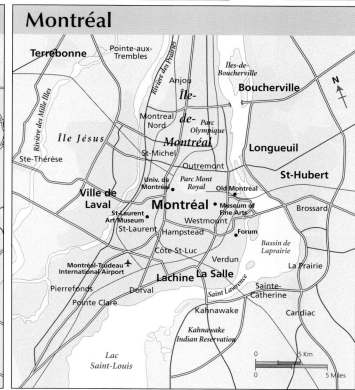

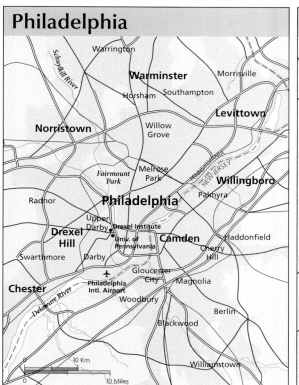

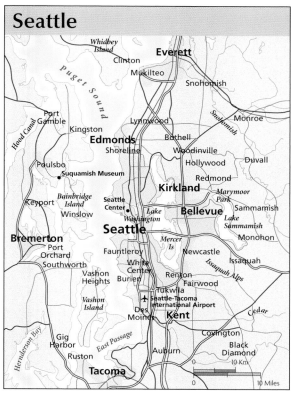

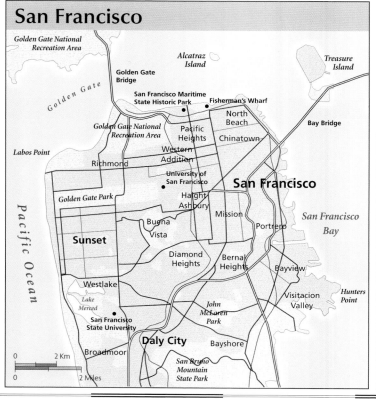

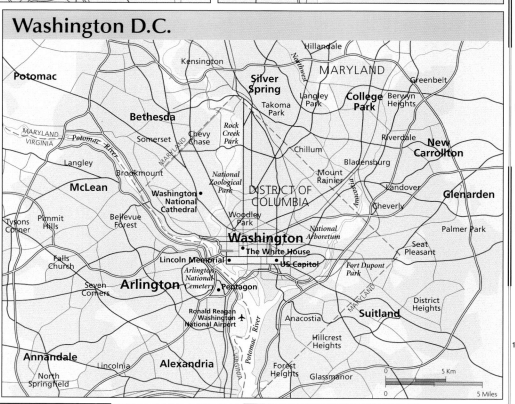

South America reaches from the humid tropics down into the cold South Atlantic, with a total area of 6,886,000 sq miles (17,835,000 sq km). It comprises 12 separate countries, with the largest, Brazil, covering almost half the continent.

FACTFILE

N **Most Northerly Point:** Punta Gallinas, Colombia 12° 28′ N
S **Most Southerly Point:** Cape Horn, Chile 55° 59′ S
E **Most Easterly Point:** Ilhas Martin Vaz, Brazil 28° 51′ W
W **Most Westerly Point:** Galapagos Islands, Ecuador 92° 00′ W

Largest Lakes:
1. Lake Titicaca, Bolivia/Peru 3141 sq miles (8135 sq km)
2. Mirim Lagoon, Brazil/Uruguay 1158 sq miles (3000 sq km)
3. Lago Poopó, Bolivia 976 sq miles (2530 sq km)
4. Lago Buenos Aires, Argentina/Chile 864 sq miles (2240 sq km)
5. Laguna Mar Chiquita, Argentina 695 sq miles (1800 sq km)

Longest Rivers:
1. Amazon, Brazil/Colombia/Peru 4049 miles (6516 km)
2. Paraná, Argentina/Brazil/Paraguay 2920 miles (4700 km)
3. Madeira, Bolivia/Brazil 2100 miles (3379 km)
4. Purus, Brazil/Peru 2013 miles (3239 km)
5. São Francisco, Brazil 1802 miles (2900 km)

Largest Islands:
1. Tierra del Fuego, Argentina/Chile 18,302 sq miles (47,401 sq km)
2. Ilha de Marajo, Brazil 15,483 sq miles (40,100 sq km)
3. Isla de Chiloé, Chile 3241 sq miles (8394 sq km)
4. East Falkland, Falkland Islands 2550 sq miles (6605 sq km)
5. Isla Wellington, Chile 2145 sq miles (5556 sq km)

Highest Points:
1. Cerro Aconcagua, Argentina 22,831 ft (6959 m)
2. Cerro Ojos del Salado, Argentina/Chile 22,572 ft (6880 m)
3. Cerro Bonete, Argentina 22,546 ft (6872 m)
4. Monte Pissis, Argentina 22,224 ft (6774 m)
5. Cerro Mercedario, Argentina 22,211 ft (6768 m)

Lowest Point:
▼ Península Valdés -131 ft (-40 m) below sea level

Highest recorded temperature:
⊕ Rivadavia, Argentina 120°F (49°C)

Lowest recorded temperature:
− Sarmiento, Argentina -27°F (-33°C)

Wettest Place:
≋ Quibdó, Colombia 354 in (8990 mm)

Driest Place:
⊖ Arica, Chile 0.03 in (0.8 mm)

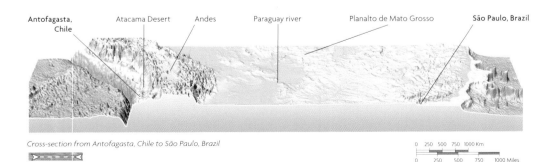

Antofagasta, Chile — Atacama Desert — Andes — Paraguay river — Planalto de Mato Grosso — São Paulo, Brazil

Cross-section from Antofagasta, Chile to São Paulo, Brazil

line of cross-section

0 250 500 750 1000 Km
0 250 500 750 1000 Miles

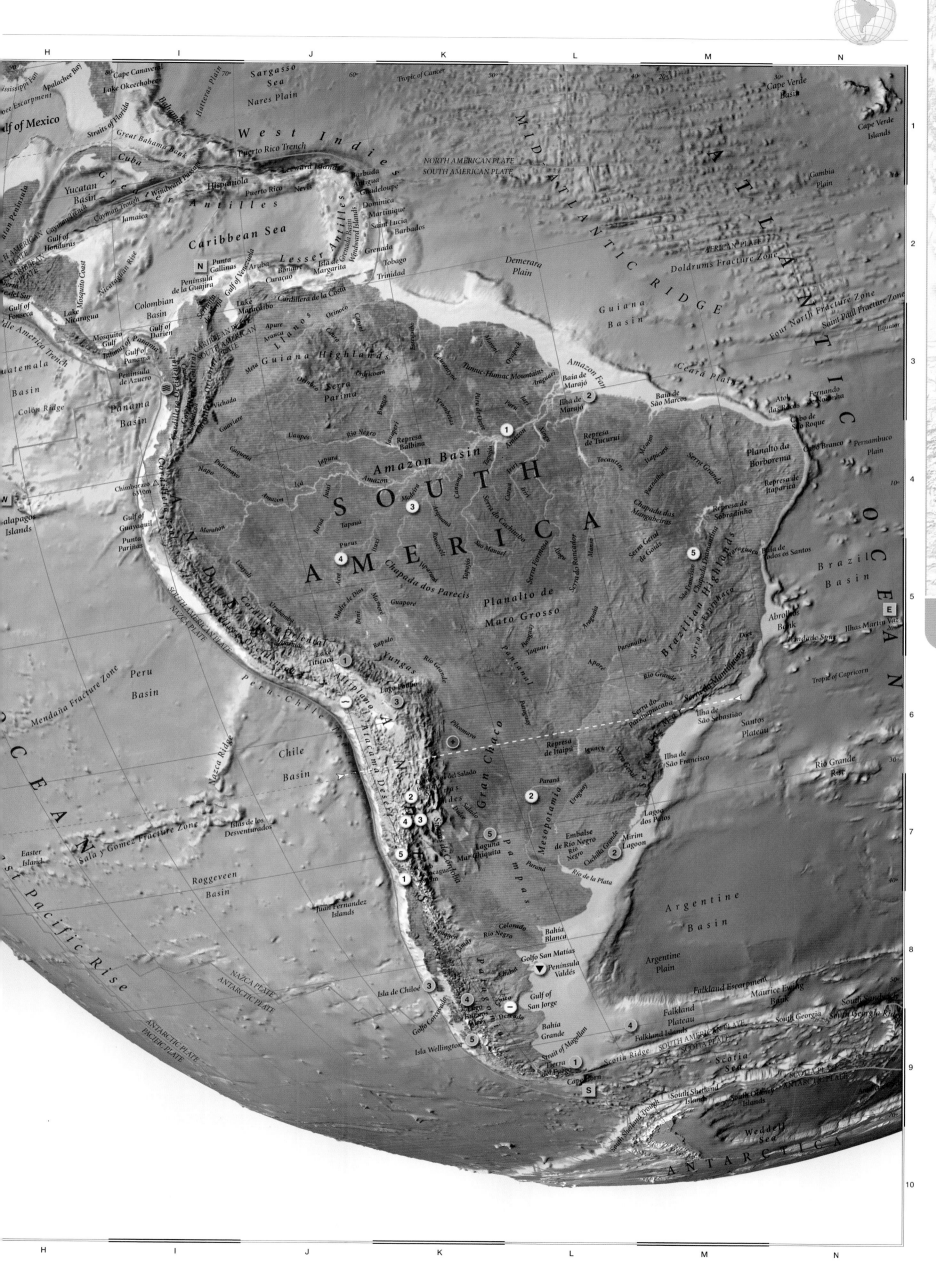

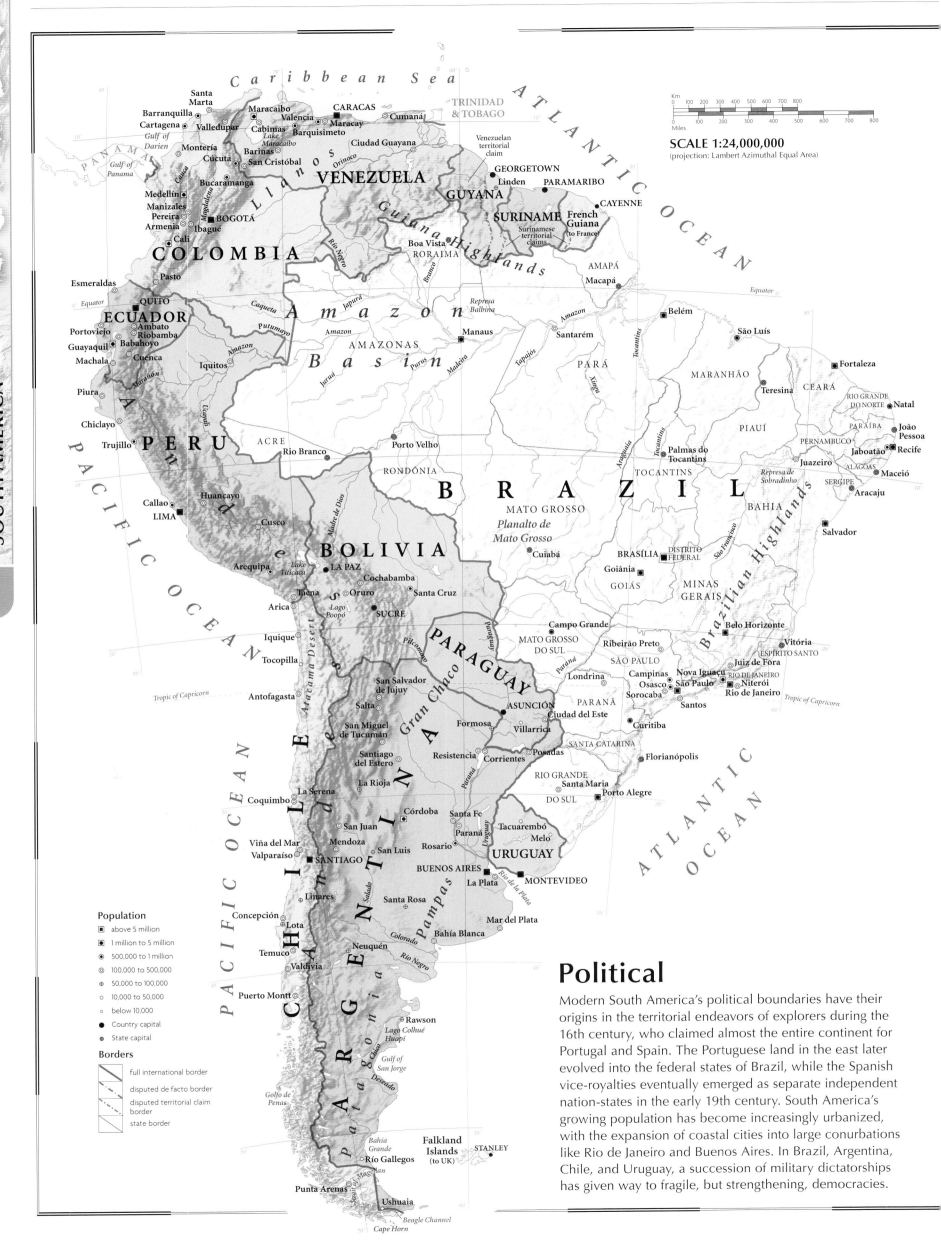

SCALE 1:24,000,000
(projection: Lambert Azimuthal Equal Area)

Km
0   100 200 300 400 500 600 700 800
Miles
0   100 200 300 400 500 600 700 800

Population
- ■ above 5 million
- ◉ 1 million to 5 million
- ◎ 500,000 to 1 million
- ◎ 100,000 to 500,000
- ⊕ 50,000 to 100,000
- ⊙ 10,000 to 50,000
- ○ below 10,000
- ● Country capital
- ◦ State capital

Borders
- full international border
- disputed de facto border
- disputed territorial claim border
- state border

Political

Modern South America's political boundaries have their origins in the territorial endeavors of explorers during the 16th century, who claimed almost the entire continent for Portugal and Spain. The Portuguese land in the east later evolved into the federal states of Brazil, while the Spanish vice-royalties eventually emerged as separate independent nation-states in the early 19th century. South America's growing population has become increasingly urbanized, with the expansion of coastal cities into large conurbations like Rio de Janeiro and Buenos Aires. In Brazil, Argentina, Chile, and Uruguay, a succession of military dictatorships has given way to fragile, but strengthening, democracies.

Languages

Prior to European exploration in the 16th century, a diverse range of indigenous languages were spoken across the continent. With the arrival of Iberian settlers, Spanish became the dominant language, with Portuguese spoken in Brazil, and Native American languages, such as Quechua and Guaraní, becoming concentrated in the continental interior. Today this pattern persists, although successive European colonization has led to Dutch being spoken in Suriname, English in Guyana, and French in French Guiana, while in large urban areas, Japanese and Chinese are increasingly common.

Language groups

- American Indian
- Germanic
- Romance

Standard of living

Wealth disparities throughout the continent create a wide gulf between affluent landowners and those afflicted by chronic poverty in inner-city slums. The illicit production of cocaine, and the hugely influential drug barons who control its distribution, contribute to the violent disorder and corruption which affect northwestern South America, destabilizing local governments and economies.

Standard of living
(UN human development index)

- low
- high

Population

Almost half of South America's population lives in Brazil but, due to the large uninhabited expanses of the Amazon Basin, its overall population density is much lower than in other countries. During the 20th century the most important population trend was the movement from rural to urban areas, giving rise to great population concentrations in cities like São Paulo, Rio de Janeiro, Caracas, Lima, Bogotá, and Buenos Aires.

Population density
(people per sq km)

- 0–4
- 5–9
- 10–14
- 15–19
- 20–29
- 30 +

Transportation

Most major road and rail routes are confined to the coastal regions by the forbidding natural barriers of the Andes mountains and the Amazon Basin. Few major cross-continental routes exist, although Buenos Aires serves as a transport center for the main rail links to La Paz and Valparaíso, while the construction of the Trans-Amazon and Pan-American Highways have made direct road travel possible from Recife to Lima and from Puerto Montt up the coast into central America. A new waterway project is proposed to transform the Paraguay river into a major shipping route, although it involves considerable wetland destruction.

Transportation

- major roads and motorways
- major railroads
- international borders
- transport intersections
- international airports
- major ports

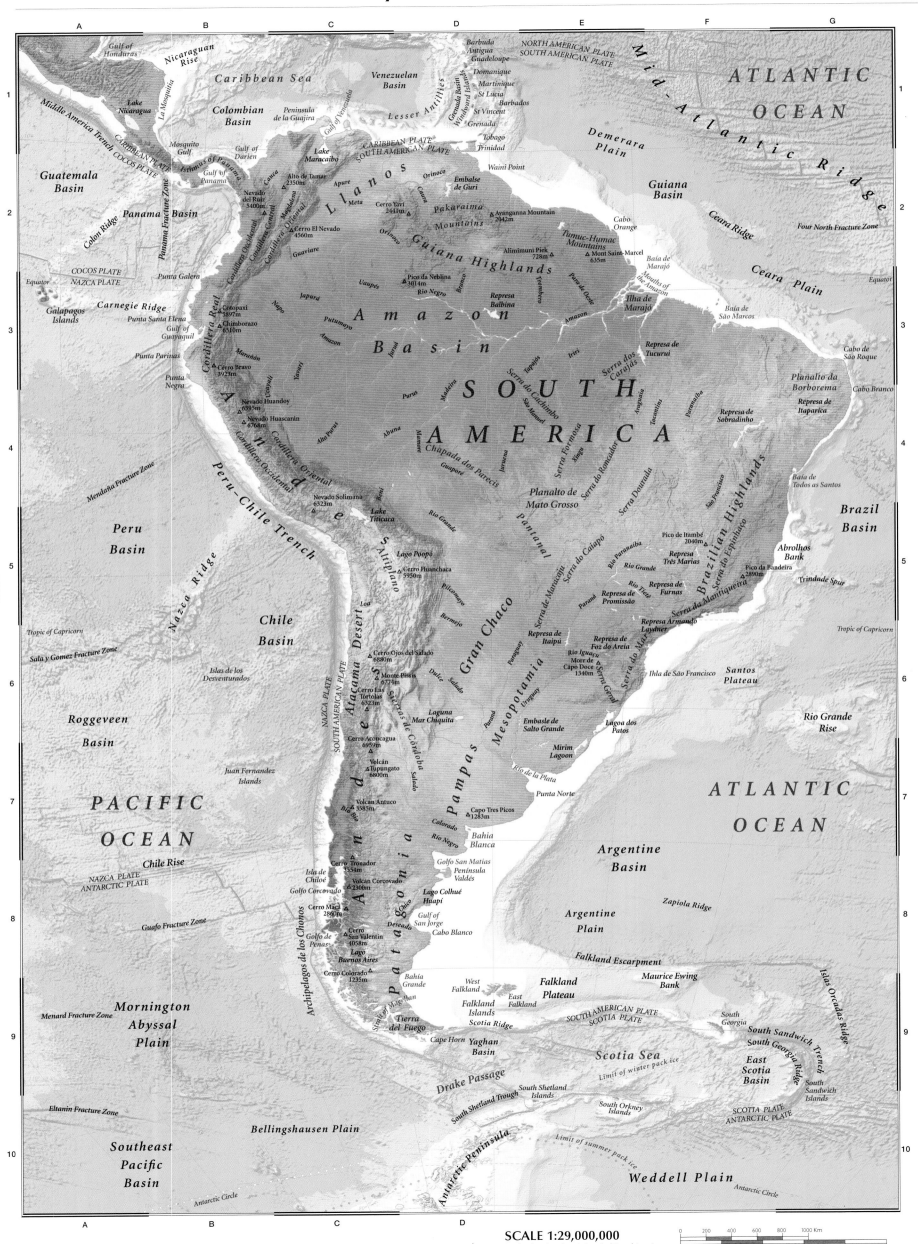

SCALE 1:29,000,000
(projection: Lambert Azimuthal Equal Area)

0   200   400   600   800   1000 Km
0   200   400   600   800   1000 Miles

Climate

The climate of South America is influenced by three principal factors:
the seasonal shift of high pressure air masses over the tropics, cold ocean currents
along the western coast, affecting temperature and precipitation, and the mountain
barrier produced by by the Andes, which creates a rain shadow over much of the south.

Average Rainfall

January rainfall

July rainfall

Rainfall
- 0–25 mm (0–1 in)
- 25–50 mm (1–2 in)
- 50–100 mm (2–4 in)
- 100–200 mm (4–8 in)
- 200–300 mm (8–12 in)
- 300–400 mm (12–16 in)
- 400–500 mm (16–20 in)
- more than 500 mm (20 in)

Average Temperature

January temperature

July temperature

Temperature
- below -30°C (-22°F)
- -30 to -20°C (-22 to -4°F)
- -20 to -10°C (-4 to 14°F)
- -10 to 0°C (14 to 32°F)
- 0 to 10°C (32 to 50°F)
- 10 to 20°C (50 to 68°F)
- 20 to 30°C (68 to 86°F)
- above 30°C (86°F)

Climate
- tundra
- cool continental
- warm humid
- semi-arid
- arid
- humid equatorial
- tropical

☼ daily hours of sunshine, January

☼ daily hours of sunshine, July

→ cold wind

Landuse

Many foods now common worldwide originated in South America.
These include the potato, tomato, squash, and cassava. Today, large
herds of beef cattle roam the temperate grasslands of the Pampas,
supporting an extensive meat-packing trade in Argentina, Uruguay and
Paraguay. Corn is grown as a staple crop across the continent and
coffee is grown as a cash crop in Brazil and
Colombia. Coca plants grown in Bolivia, Peru and
Colombia provide most of the western world's
cocaine. Fish and shellfish are caught off
the western coast, especially
anchovies off Peru, shrimps
off Ecuador, and sardines
off Chile.

Environmental Issues

The Amazon Basin is one of the last great wilderness areas
left on Earth. The tropical rain forests which grow there are a
valuable genetic resource, containing innumerable unique
plants and animals. The forests are increasingly threatened by
new and expanding settlements and "slash and burn" farming
techniques, which clear land for the raising of cattle, causing
land degradation and soil erosion.

Environmental Issues
- national parks
- tropical forest
- forest destroyed
- desert
- desertification
- polluted rivers
- marine pollution
- heavy marine pollution
- • poor urban air quality

Using the Land and Sea
- barren land
- cropland
- desert
- forest
- mountain region
- • major conurbations
- 🐄 cattle
- 🐖 pigs
- 🐑 sheep
- 🍌 bananas
- 🌽 corn (maize)
- 🍊 citrus fruits
- 🍫 cocoa
- 🌱 cotton
- ☕ coffee
- 🐟 fishing
- 🌴 oil palms
- 🥜 peanuts
- ∞ rubber
- 🦐 shellfish
- 🌿 soya beans
- sugar cane
- 🍇 vineyards
- 🌾 wheat

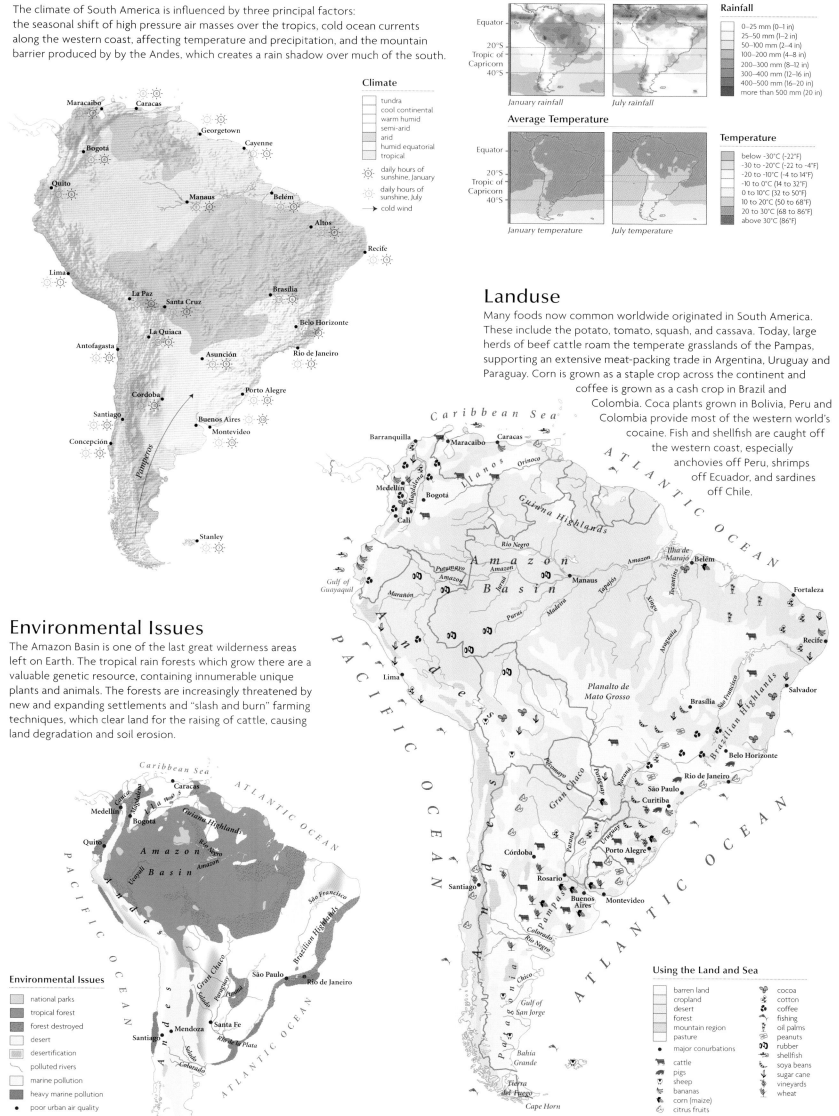

1   SANTIAGO, CHILE
Chile's capital city was founded in 1541 by Pedro de Valdivia who chose the location because it had a Mediterranean climate and was easy to defend.

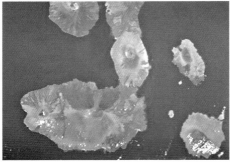

2   GALAPAGOS ISLANDS, ECUADOR
These islands are a collection of volcanoes rising from the ocean floor 621 miles (1000 km) west of the South American mainland.

3   SALAR DE UYUNI, BOLIVIA
Occupying a depression high up on the Altiplano between the volcanoes of the western Andes and the fold belts of the eastern Andes, this is the world's largest salt flat.

4   MACHU PICCHU, PERU
Perched precariously above the Urubamba valley, the lost Inca retreat was rediscovered in 1911 by Hiram Bingham, an American archaeologist.

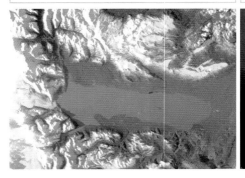

9   LAGO VIEDMA, ARGENTINA
Lago Viedma enjoys a milky-blue appearance due to the glacial sediment suspended in its waters.

10   LOS LAGOS, CHILE
A region of many lakes at the foothills of the Andes in south-central Chile, this area is an attraction for many tourists.

11   ROSARIO, ARGENTINA
Located on the west bank of the Paraná river, Rosario lies at that heart of Argentina's industrial corridor, centered on the river.

12   RIVER PLATE, ARGENTINA/URUGUAY
Fed by the Paraná and Uruguay rivers, this Atlantic Ocean inlet separates Argentina and Uruguay.

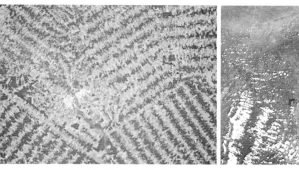

RONDÔNIA, BRAZIL 5
Pale strips of forest clearance can be seen along perpendicular tracks in this region of the Amazon Basin.

MARACAIBO, VENEZUELA 6
Maracaibo is the center of Venezuela's oil industry and its second largest city with a population of 1.6 million.

AMAZON RIVER/RIO NEGRO, BRAZIL 7
The dark, plant debris-stained waters of the Rio Negro join the beige Amazon near the city of Manaus.

EMBALSE DE GURI, VENEZUELA 8
This enormous reservoir, on the Caroni river, was completed in 1986 and its hydroelectric plant was the first to produce more than 10 gigawatts of electricity.

FOREST CLEARANCE IN SANTA CRUZ STATE, BOLIVIA 13
This infrared image shows the distinctive radial clearance patterns of original tropical dry forest with a small settlement at each center.

LAGOA DOS PATOS AND MIRIM LAGOON, BRAZIL/URUGUAY 14
These two lagoons are separated from the Atlantic Ocean by 248 miles (400 km) of sandbar.

ITAIPU DAM, BRAZIL/PARAGUAY 15
With an installed capacity of 14 gigawatts this is the world's largest hydroelectric power scheme, delivering 95% of Paraguay's energy needs and 24% of Brazil's.

POINT BALEIA, BRAZIL 16
This headland has built up through steady accumulation of silt and sediment, shaped by tides and ocean currents.

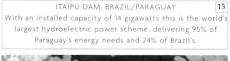

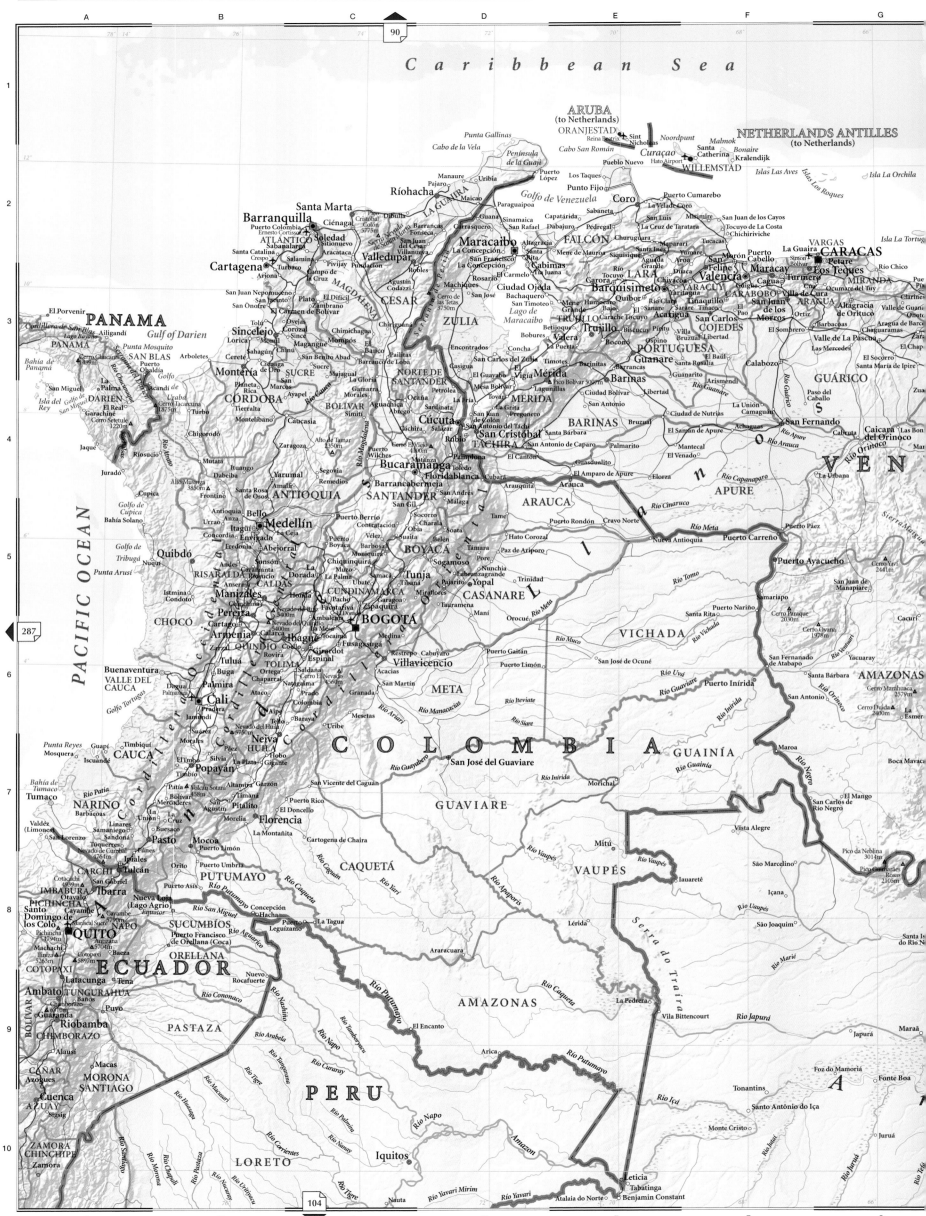

90

287

104

Caribbean Sea

ARUBA
(to Netherlands)
ORANJESTAD

NETHERLANDS ANTILLES
(to Netherlands)

Curaçao

WILLEMSTAD

Punta Gallinas
Cabo de la Vela
Península
de la Guaji

Ríohacha

Santa Marta

Barranquilla

Cartagena

PANAMA

Gulf of Darien

PANAMA

SAN BLAS

DARIEN

Golfo de
Panamá

PACIFIC OCEAN

Golfo de
Cupica

Quibdó

CHOCÓ

Buenaventura

VALLE DEL
CAUCA

CAUCA

Tumaco

NARIÑO

PUTUMAYO

ECUADOR

QUITO

PICHINCHA

COTOPAXI

CHIMBORAZO

PASTAZA

MORONA
SANTIAGO

CUENCA

AZUAY

ZAMORA
CHINCHIPE
Zamora

Iquitos

LORETO

PERU

Maracaibo

Lago de
Maracaibo

ZULIA

CESAR

Valledupar

Sincelejo

Montería

CÓRDOBA

SUCRE

BOLÍVAR

NORTE DE
SANTANDER

Cúcuta

San Cristóbal

TÁCHIRA

Bucaramanga

SANTANDER

Barrancabermeja

ANTIOQUIA

Medellín

CALDAS

RISARALDA

Manizales

Pereira

QUINDÍO

Armenia

Ibagué

TOLIMA

Cali

Palmira

Neiva

HUILA

Popayán

Pasto

CAUCA

CAQUETÁ

Florencia

PUTUMAYO

Mocoa

COLOMBIA

BOYACÁ

Tunja

CUNDINAMARCA

BOGOTÁ

Girardot

Villavicencio

META

GUAVIARE

San José del Guaviare

VAUPÉS

Mitú

AMAZONAS

Leticia

FALCÓN

Coro

CARACAS

Los Teques

Valencia

Maracay

ARAGUA

CARABOBO

YARACUY

Barquisimeto

LARA

TRUJILLO

Valera

MÉRIDA

Mérida

Barinas

BARINAS

TRUJILLO

PORTUGUESA

Guanare

COJEDES

San Carlos

San Fernando

APURE

Arauca

ARAUCA

CASANARE

Yopal

VICHADA

Puerto Carreño

GUAINÍA

GUÁRICO

Calabozo

Puerto Ayacucho

AMAZONAS

VEN

Scale 1:6,500,000
(projection: Lambert Azimuthal Equal Area)

0 25 50 75 100 125 150 175 200 Km
0 25 50 75 100 125 150 175 200 Miles

Population
- ■ above 5 million
- ■ 1 million to 5 million
- ◉ 500,000 to 1 million
- ◉ 100,000 to 500,000
- ⊕ 50,000 to 100,000
- ⊙ 10,000 to 50,000
- ○ below 10,000

Bogotá

Usaquén
Canal de Guaymaral
Molinos
Río Juan Amarillo
Monumento Lara Bonita
Aeropuerto Internacional El Dorado
Barrios Unidos
Chapinero
Engativá
Teusaquillo
Fontibón
Bogotá
Museo Nacional de Colombia
Puente Aranda
Kennedy
Río Fucha
Los Mártires
Catedral La Candelaria
Santa Fe
Antonio Nariño
San Cristóbal
Tunjuelito
Rafael Uribe

0 1 Km
0 1 Miles

ATLANTIC OCEAN

CASTRIES
George F L Charles
Mount Gimie 950m
ST LUCIA
Hewanorra
Vieux Fort
Saint Vincent Passage
St Vincent
KINGSTOWN
Arnos Vale
BRIDGETOWN
BARBADOS
Grantley Adams
ST VINCENT & THE GRENADINES
Bequia
Mustique
Canouan
Union Island
Carriacou
ST. GEORGE'S
Point Salines
GRENADA

Isla Blanquilla
Islas los Testigos
Tobago
Scarborough
Charlotteville
Isla de Margarita
Galera Point
NUEVA ESPARTA
Juangriego
La Asunción
Pampatar
Porlamar
Punta de Piedras
Carúpano
Río Caribe
PORT-OF-SPAIN
Arima
Puerto de Hierro
Piarco
Sangre Grande
Cumaná
Casanay
El Pilar
Irapa
Güiria
Río Claro
Trinidad
TRINIDAD & TOBAGO
SUCRE
San Antonio
San Fernando
Rushville
Araya
Cumanacoa
Caripe
Point Fortin
Siparia
Galeota Point
Barcelona
Catipito
Quiriquire
Bonasse
Aragua de Maturín
Punta de Mata
Pedernales
Punta Baja
Maturín
Santa Rosa
MONAGAS
Anaco
Aguasay
La Horqueta
Tucupita
Tembladar
San Tomé
San José de Guanipa
Barrancas
DELTA AMACURO
Cantaura
Guayabones
Curiapo
Waini Point
ANZOÁTEGUI
Ciudad Guayana
Río Orinoco
Waini
Soledad
El Río
El Palmar
Curupa
Port Kaituma
Ciudad Bolívar
Opata
Arakaka
Matthews Ridge
Banana River
Charity
Borbón
Embalse de Guri
Guasipati
El Manteco
Spring Garden
Essequibo Islands
Ciudad Piar
Kuracki
Cuyuni River
Parika
GEORGETOWN
VENEZUELA
Cerro Turagua 1838m
La Paragua
El Callao
Aurora
Georgetown
Trincheras
Tumeremo
New Amsterdam
El Dorado
Cuyuni River
Bartica
Rose Hall
La Casabe
Caño Negro
Canaima
Enachu Landing
Peters Mine
Corriverton
BOLÍVAR
Salto Ángel
Cerro Vernan 1563m
Kamarang
Mazaruni River
Rockstone
Linden
Nieuw Nickerie
NICKERIE
Cerro Guaiquinima 2100m
Auyan Tepuy 2950m
Uroyén
Imbaimadai
Issano
Wageningen
Friendship
Totness
Groningen
Paramaribo
Nieuw Amsterdam
WANICA
COMMEWIJNE
Santa María del Erebato
Ayanganna Mountains 2042m
GUYANA
Ituni
Mahdia
Orealla
CORONIE
SARA-MACCA
Totoso
PARAMARIBO
MAROWIJNE
Mana
Caruana de Montana
Mount Roraima 2810m
Patuni
River
Wineperu
Apoera
Wasibo
Coronie
PARA
Onverwacht
Albina
St-Laurent-du-Maroni
Iracoubo
Iles du Salut
Ile du Diable
Santa Elena de Uairén
Kaieteur Falls
Donderkamp
Kwakoegron
Bergen Dal
Citron
Sinnamary
Apatou
Centre Spatial Guyanais
Uonán
Glendor Mountainsa
Kurupukari
Coppename River
Browaswey
Brokopondo
Pokigron
St-Élie
Kourou
Tonate
CAYENNE
Pakaraima Mountains
Kaalcher River
Hendrik Top 957m
BROKOPONDO
Grand-Santi
Apatou Herminadorp
Cayenne
Rémire Matoury
G
u
i
a
n
a
Glendor
Mahu
Berbice River
Boti-Pasi
Djoemoe
W.J. van Blommesteinmeer
Cacao
Roura
Normandia
Tafelberg 1026m
FRENCH GUIANA
Pointe Béhague
Conceição do Maú
Rupununi River
SURINAME
Wilhelmina Gebergte
Poeketi
(to France)
Régina
Cabo Orange
Uraricoera
Lethem
Juliana Top 1230m
Baie de l'Oyapok
Boa Vista
Kanuku Mountains
Apetina
Tupanahony River
Maripasoula
Pédima
Camopi
Rio Oiapoque
BOLÍVAR
Saúl
l'Oyapock River
Santa Rosa
Sauriwauñawa
SIPALIWINI
Montagnes Bellevue de l'Inini
Rio Catrimani
Lucie Rivier
Counantyne River
Ouanary
Uaicás
(Venezuela claims all of Guyana west of the Essequibo river)
Kuyuwini Landing
Alimimuni Piek 728m
Mont Saint-Marcel 635m
St-Georges
Horqueta Minas
Oiapoque
RORAIMA
New River
(Claimed by Surinam)
Appikalo
Tumuc Humac Mountains
Calcoene
Missão Catrimani
Caracaraí
Johi Village
Appikalo
Massif du Mitaraka 690m
Trois Sauts
Amapá
Rio Demini
Acarai Mountains
São Luís
(Claimed by Surinam)
AMAPÁ
Serra pirapecó
Catrimanó
Serra do Jatapu
Rio Trombetas
Rio Paru
Sete Ilhas
Rio Araguari
Rio Negro
Rio Branco
Rio Jauaperi
Rio Jari
Macapá
Tapurucuará
Boiaçu
Planalto Maracanaquará
Equator
Barcelos
Represa Balbina
Monte Dourado
PARÁ
Ilha Grande de Gurupá
Rio Jatapu
Carvoeiro
Moura
Rio Nhamundá
Oriximiná
Óbidos
Amazon
Porto de Moz
BRAZIL
AMAZONAS
Óbidos
Alenquer
Portel
Codajás
Urucará
Santarém
Beruri
Parintins
Coari
Novo Airão
Eduardo Gomes
Manaus
Itacoatiara
Rurópolis Presidente
Manacapuru
Caldeirão
Itaituba
Rio Iriri
Iranduba
Manaquiri
Autazes
Tefé
Codajás
Careiro
Itaituba
Pimenta
Rio Solimões
Rio Purus
Altamira
Coari

290
107
290

19,686ft
13,124ft
9843ft
6562ft
3281ft
1640ft
820ft
328ft
Sea Level
-820ft
-6562ft
-13,124ft

SOUTH AMERICA

102
106
287

VENEZUELA

COLOMBIA

B r a s i l

BRAZIL

ECUADOR

PERU

AMAZONAS

ACRE

PANDO

MADRE DE DIOS

UCAYALI

A m a z o n a s

LORETO

Iquitos

Leticia

Tabatinga

Benjamín Constant

Río Branco

Cruzeiro do Sul

Pucallpa

Quito

Guayaquil

Lima

Callao

Trujillo

Chiclayo

Chimbote

C o r d i l l e r a

d e l o s A n d e s

Cordillera Blanca

Cordillera Azul

6000m
4000m
3000m
2000m
1000m
500m
250m
100m
Sea Level
-250m
-500m
-1000m

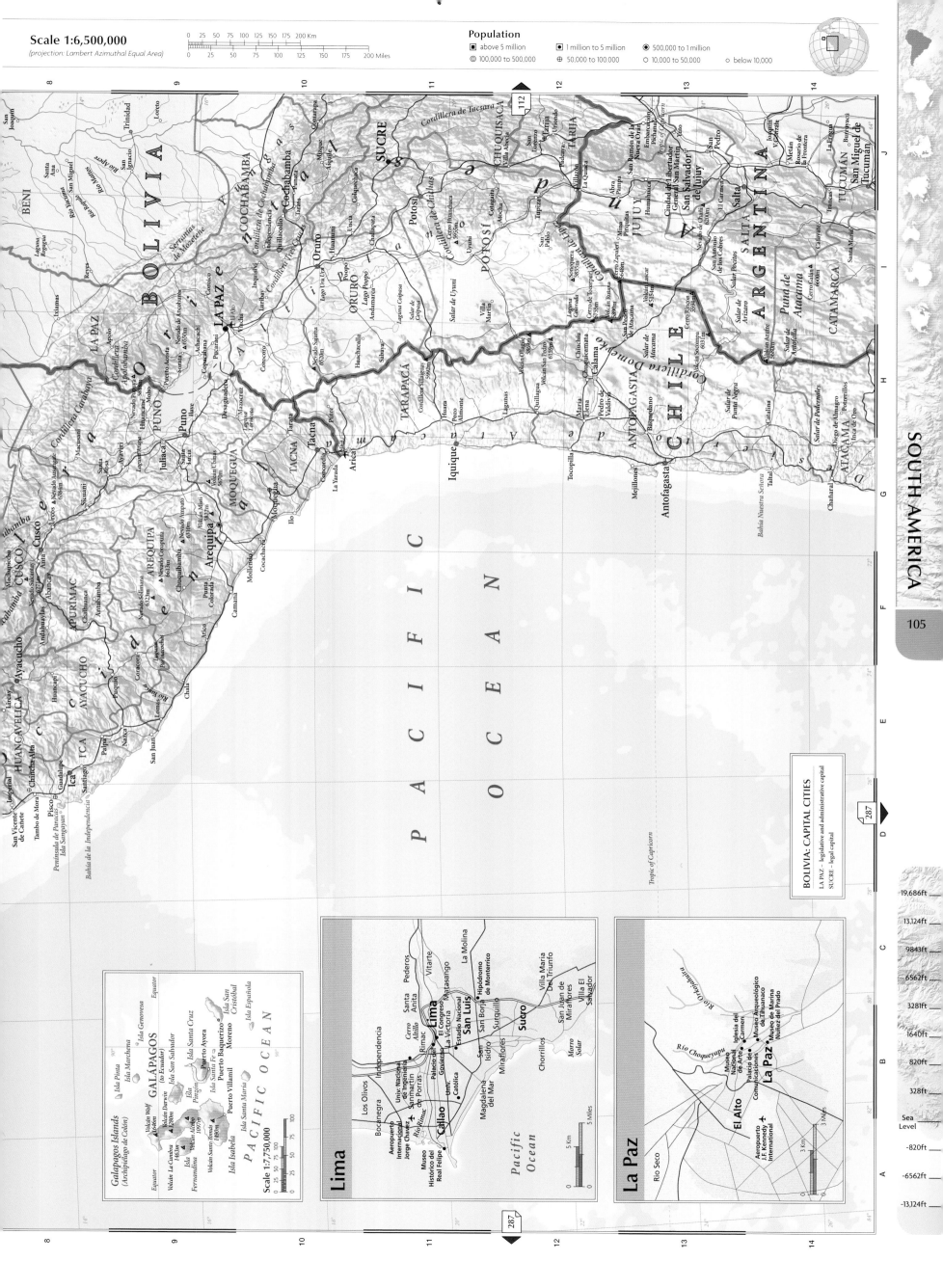

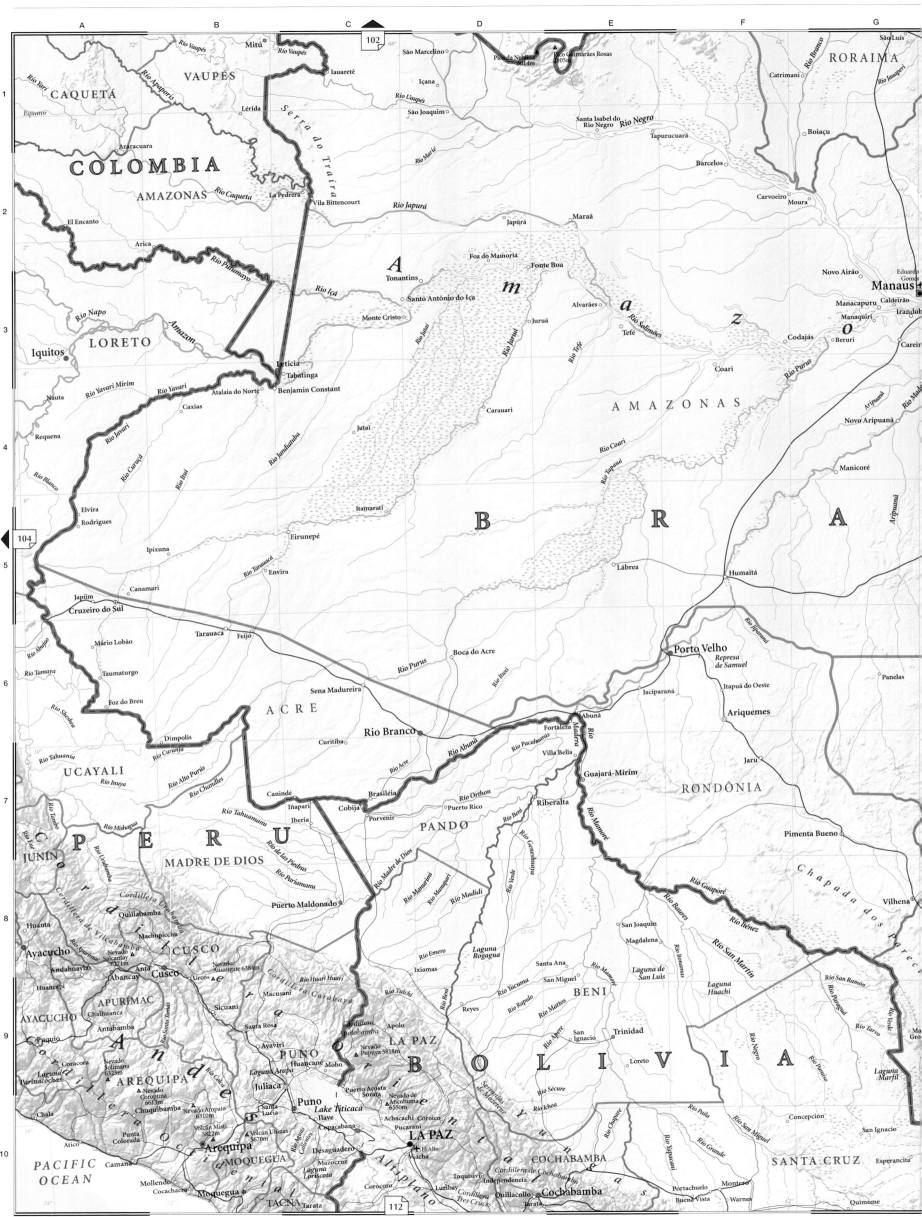

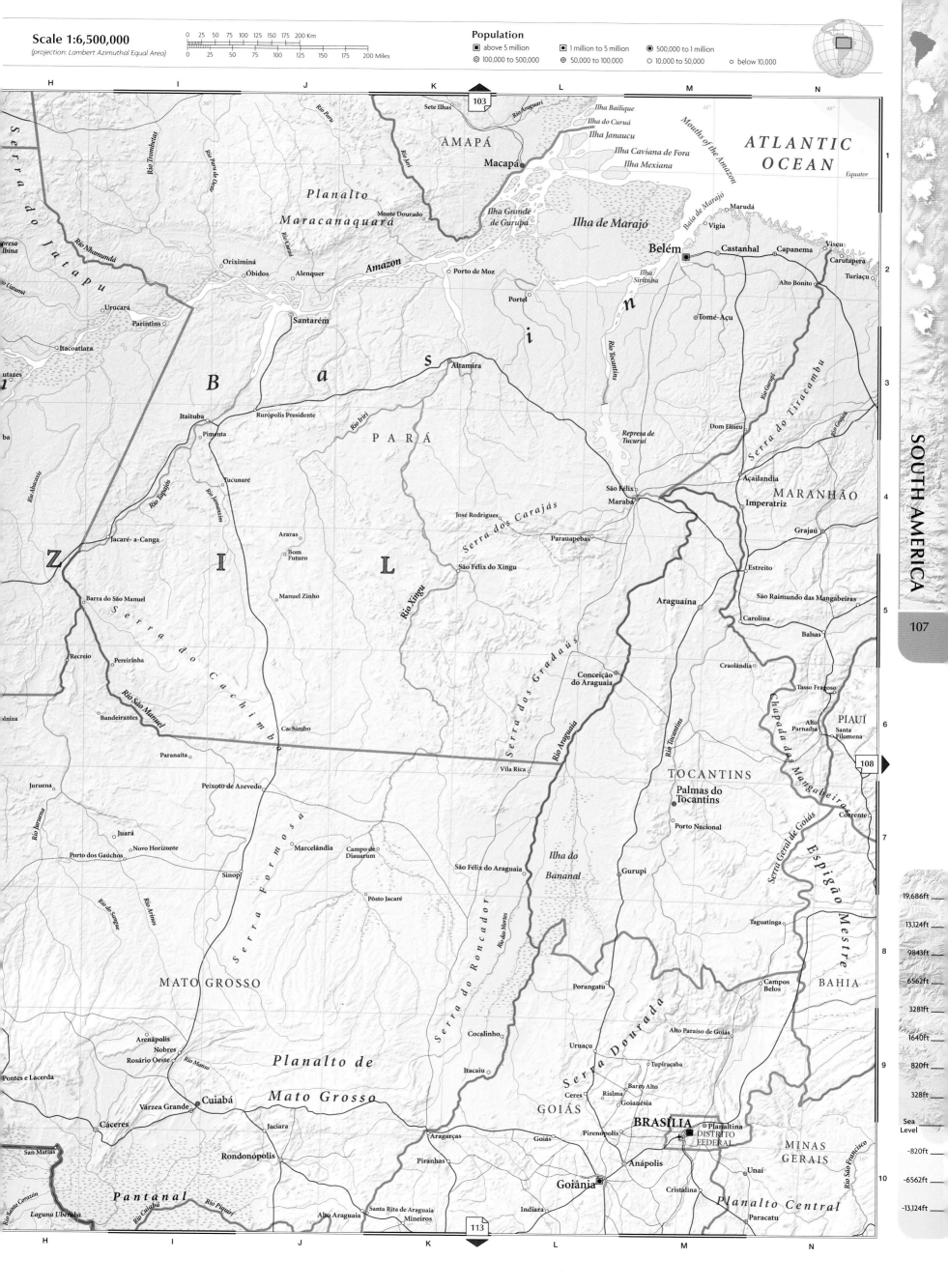

SOUTH AMERICA

Equator

291

290

107

ATLANTIC OCEAN

Mouths of the Amazon

Amazon Basin

6000m
4000m
3000m
2000m
1000m
500m
250m
100m
Sea Level
-250m
-500m
-1000m

Calçoene
Amapá
Macapá
Sucuriju
Ilha Maracá
Rio Araguari
Rio Oiapoque
Ilha Batique
Ilha do Curuá
Ilha Janaucu
Ilha Caviana de Fora
Ilha Mexiana
Ilha Grande de Gurupá
Rio Jari
Porto de Moz
Almeirim
Ilha Sirituba
Portel
José Rodrigues
Rio Xingu
São Félix do Xingu
Serra dos Carajás
Parauapebas
Gurupi
AMAPÁ
PARÁ

Sete Ilhas
Ilha de Marajó
Baía de Marajó
Belém
Vigia
Castanhal
Tomé-Açu
Dom Eliseu
Alto Bonito
Capanema
Cametá
Represa de Tucuruí
Rio Tocantins
Rio Anguaia
Marabá
São Félix
Conceição do Araguaia
Vila Rica
Ilha do B
Serra dos Gradaús
Rio Araguaia

Viseu
Cariutaipera
Turiaçu
São João de Cortes
São Luís
Baía de São Marcos
Ilha de São Luís
Recife do Silva
Recife Manuel Luís
Rio Gurupi
Serra do Tiracambú
Açailândia
Imperatriz
Estreito
Carolina
Balsas
Tasso Fragoso
Alto Parnaíba
Santa Filomena
Corrente
Chapada das Mangabeiras
Espigão
Serra Geral de Goiás
MARANHÃO
Itapecuru-Mirim
Rio Itapicuru
Codó
Bacabal
Caxias
Presidente Dutra
Colinas
São Raimundo das Mangabeiras
Rio Grajaú
Grajaú
Roncador
Timon
Chapadinha
Rio Parnaíba
Parnaíba
Ilha do Caju
Piripiri
Campo Maior
Teresina
Barro Duro
Floriano
São João dos Pato
São Raimundo
Rio Gurguéia
Rio Gurguéia
Campo Alegre de Lourdes
Casa Nova
Barra
Xique-Xique
Sento Sé
Represa de Sobradinho
Sobradinho
Juazeiro
Petrolina
Afrânio
São João do Piauí
Canto do Buriti
Oeiras
PIAUÍ
Picos
Valença do Piauí
Gaturiano
Serra Grande do Piauí
Crateús
Tauá
Juazeiro do Norte
Ouricuri
Salgueiro
Paulo Afonso
Canudos
Tucano
Monte Santo
Quijingue
Mundo Novo
Cassia
B R A Z I L

Campos Sales
Marcolândia
Açude Orós
Açude Banabuiú
Senador Pompeu
Quixadá
Araras
Sobral
Acaraú
Camocim
Itapipoca
Caucaia
Fortaleza
Cascavel
Aracati
CEARÁ
Ceará Mirim
Touros
Cabo de São Roque
Macau
Areia Branca
Açu
Mossoró
Currais Novos
Caicó
RIO GRANDE DO NORTE
Natal
João Pessoa
PARAÍBA
Campina Grande
Planalto da Borborema
Olinda
Recife
Jaboatão
Caruaru
Arcoverde
Garanhuns
PERNAMBUCO
Açude Poço da Cruz
Represa de Itaparica
Rio São Francisco
Arapiraca
ALAGOAS
Maceió
Propriá
SERGIPE
Aracaju
São Cristóvão
Estância

TOCANTINS
Palmas do Tocantins
Porto Nacional
Rio Tocantins
Araguaína

Atol das Rocas

Tropic of Cancer

Equator

Scale 1:6,500,000
(projection: Lambert Azimuthal Equal Area)

0 25 50 75 100 125 150 175 200 Km

0 25 50 75 100 125 150 175 200 Miles

Population

■ above 5 million
▣ 1 million to 5 million
◉ 500,000 to 1 million
◉ 100,000 to 500,000
⊕ 50,000 to 100,000
○ 10,000 to 50,000
○ below 10,000

291

291

113

ATLANTIC

OCEAN

Tropic of Capricorn

Salvador
Baía de Todos os Santos
Valença
Ilha de Boipeba
Maraú
Ponta do Mutá
Ilhéus
Itabuna
Comandatuba
Canavieiras
Belmonte
Santa Cruz Cabrália
Porto Seguro
Prado
Caravelas
Ilha Caçumba

Jequié
Itaberaba
Lençóis
Chapada Diamantina
Bom Jesus da Lapa
Santa Maria da Vitória
Caetité
Brumado
Itapetinga
Rio Jequitinhonha
Itapetinga
Eunápolis
Itamaraju
São Mateus
Linhares

ESPÍRITO
SANTO
Vitória
Guarapari
Cachoeiro de Itapemirim

Espinosa
Monte Azul
Pedra Azul
Itaobim
Araçuaí
Teófilo Otoni
Colatina
Santa Teresa
São João da Barra

Janaúba
Januária
Diamantina
Serra do Cipó
Pico do Itambé 2060m
Guanhães
Governador Valadares
Ipatinga
Manhuaçu
Ponte Nova
Alto da Bandeira 2890m
Bom Jesus do Itabapoana
Itaperuna
Miracema
São Fidélis
Campos
Cordeiro
Nova Friburgo
Macaé
Arraial do Cabo
Cabo Frio

Montes Claros
MINAS GERAIS
Serra do Espinhaço
Brazilian Highlands
Itabira
Belo Horizonte
Sete Lagoas
Betim
Ouro Preto
Conselheiro Lafaiete
Barbacena
Juiz de Fora
Três Rios
Teresópolis
Petrópolis
São Gonçalo
Niterói
RIO DE JANEIRO
Rio de Janeiro

Represa Três Marias
Pirapora
Curvelo
Abaeté
São João del Rei
Três Pontas
Poços Alegre
Barra Mansa
Volta Redonda
Resende
Angra dos Reis
Ilha Grande

Luislândia do Oeste
Unaí
Paracatu
Ibiá
Divinópolis
Represa de Furnas
Poços de Caldas
Passos
São José do Rio Preto
Três Corações
Ubatuba
Ilha de São Sebastião

Planalto Central
Cristalina
Araxá
Franca
Ribeirão Preto
Casa Branca
Mococa
Amparo
Campos do Jordão
Guaratinguetá
Taubaté
Caraguatatuba
Ilha de Santo Amaro

Planaltina
DISTRITO FEDERAL
BRASÍLIA
Uberlândia
Uberaba
Igarapava
Ituverava
São Joaquim da Barra
Sacramento
Orlândia
Serrana
Pirassununga
Mogi-Mirim
Itapira
Jundiaí
São Caetano do Sul
Santos
São Vicente
Perube

Campos Belos
Alto Paraíso de Goiás
Anápolis
Guará
Barretos
Nova Granada
Bebedouro
Jaboticabal
Taquaritinga
Araraquara
Rio Claro
Limeira
Americana
Campinas
Itu
Osasco
São Paulo
São Bernardo do Campo
Guarujá
Registro
Jacupiranga

Porangatu
Barro Alto
GOIÁS
Goianésia
Pirenópolis
Anhanguera
Guaíra
São José do Rio Preto
Nova Horizonte
Matão
Catanduva
Jaú
São Carlos
Piracicaba
Indaiatuba
Tietê
Sorocaba
Itapetininga
Tatuí
Apiaí
Ilha Comprida
Ilha das Peças

Uruaçu
Ceres
Goiás
Rialma
Itumbiara
São Paulo
Barretos
Novo Horizonte
Bariri
Bauru
Botucatu
Avaré
Capão Bonito
Iporanga
Itararé
Itapeva
Sete Barras
Paranaguá
Ilha do Mel

GOIÁS
Goiânia
Serra do Cana
Cristalina
Ituiutaba
SÃO PAULO
Lins
Marília
Garça
Pompeia
Assis
Santa Cruz do Rio Pardo
Ourinhos
Itaí
Santo Antônio da Plat.
Jaguariaíva
Castro
Ponta Grossa
Campo Largo
São Mateus do Sul
Curitiba
Lapa
Rio Negro
Mafra

Rio Verde
Jataí
Fernandópolis
Votuporanga
Araçatuba
Birigui
Penápolis
Promissão
Tupã
Tupi Paulista
Dracena
Presidente Prudente
Marilândia
Paraguaçu Paulista
Cândido Mota
Cornélio Procópio
Londrina
Apucarana
Ivaiporã
Telêmaco Borba
Tibagi
Reserva
Piraí do Sul
Pinhão
SERRA GERAL
PARANÁ
Irati

Porecatu
Maringá
Campo Mourão
Guarapuava

Campo Grande
MATO GROSSO DO SUL
Rio Brilhante
Represa de Água Vermelha
Santa Fé do Sul
Pereira Barreto
Ilha Solteira
Andradina
Mirandópolis
Adamantina
Presidente Venceslau
Presidente Epitácio
Paranavaí
Loanda
Nova Esperança

Aragarças
Piranhas
Serra do Caiapó
Mineiros
Itarumã
Paranaíba
Três Lagoas
Água Clara
Bataguassu
Nova Andradina
Ivinhema
Naviraí
Guaíra
Guaíra
Terra Roxa
Palotina
Toledo
Cascavel

MATO GROSSO
Serra dos Parecis
Rio das Mortes
Itacaiú
Cocalinho
Barra do Garças
Torixoréu
Ponte Branca
Alto Araguaia
Itiquira
Coxim
Rio Verde de Mato Grosso
Rio Negro
Cruzeiro do Oeste
Goio-Erê
Serra das Araras
Guaíra
Guaíra
Dois Vizinhos
Francisco Beltrão

19,686ft
13,124ft
9843ft
6562ft
3281ft
1640ft
820ft
328ft
Sea Level
-820ft
-6562ft
-13,124ft

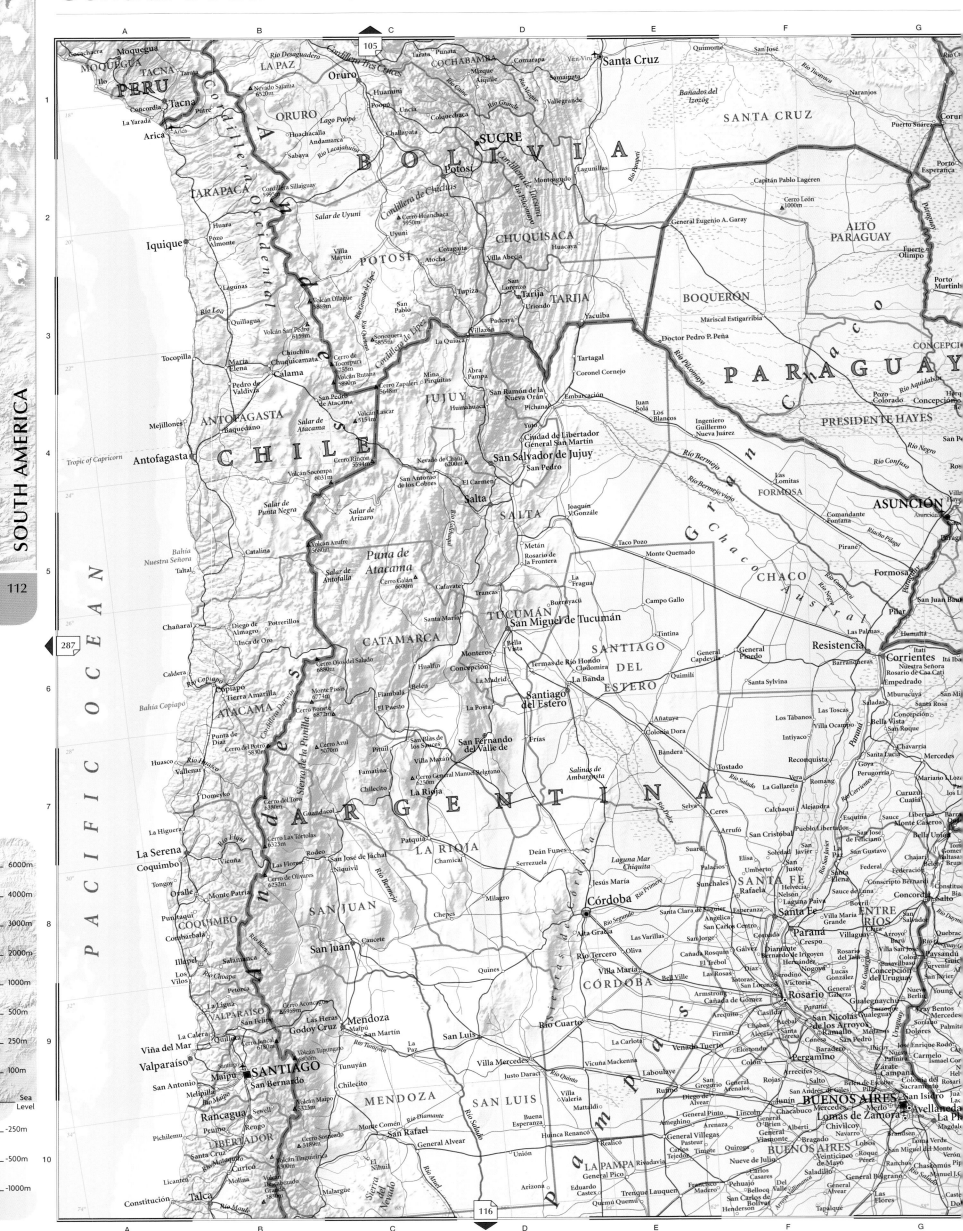

105

287

116

SOUTH AMERICA

112

PACIFIC OCEAN

6000m
4000m
3000m
2000m
1000m
500m
250m
100m
Sea Level
-250m
-500m
-1000m

Scale 1:6,500,000
(projection: Lambert Azimuthal Equal Area)

0 25 50 75 100 125 150 175 200 Km
0 25 50 75 100 125 150 175 200 Miles

Population

■ above 5 million
◨ 1 million to 5 million
◉ 500,000 to 1 million
◎ 100,000 to 500,000
⊕ 50,000 to 100,000
○ 10,000 to 50,000
○ below 10,000

109

Pantanal

GOIÁS
Coxim
Rio Verde
Jataí
Itumbiara
Anhangüera
Pirapora
Luislândia do Oeste
Diamantina
Rio Apore
Rio Verde
Rio Coxim
Araguari
Uberlândia
Patos de Minas
Represa Três Marias
Curvelo
Serro
Pico de Itambé 2040m
Guanhães
Governador Valadares
Aquidauana
Campo Grande
Água Clara
Santa Fé do Sul
Fernandópolis
MINAS GERAIS
Abaeté
Ibiá
Araxá
Uberaba
Igarapava
Sete Lagoas
Betim
Belo Horizonte
Divinópolis
Itabira
Ipatinga
MATO GROSSO DO SUL
Três Lagoas
Ilha Solteira
Pereira Barreto
Jales
Votuporanga
Guaíra
Barretos
Franca
Ituverava
Ouro Preto
Manhuaçu
Pico da Bandeira 2890m
Ponte Nova
Conselheiro Lafaiete
Andradina
Mirandópolis
Nhandeara
São José do Rio Preto
Nova Granada
São Joaquim da Barra
Batatas
Passos
Poços de Caldas
Três Pontas
São João del Rei
Barbacena
Bom Jesus do Itabapoana
Itaperuna
Nova Alvorada
Dracena
Osvaldo Cruz
Tupã
Catanduva
Jaboticabal
Sertãozinho
Ribeirão Preto
Mococa
Rio Pardo
Casa Branca
Rio Verde
Juiz de Fora
Miracema
Dourados
Presidente Epitácio
Adamantina
Marília
Promissão
Novo Horizonte
Jaú
Jaguariúna
Campos do Jordão
Amparo
Bragança Paulista
Cruzeiro
Guaratinguetá
Vassouras
Três Rios
São Fidélis
Pedro Juan Caballero
Presidente Venceslau
Panorama
Pirapozinho
Teodoro Sampaio
Presidente Prudente
Garça
Bauru
Bariri
Barra Bonita
Piracicaba
Limeira
Americana
Campinas
Indaiatuba
Itapira
Mogi-Mirim
Mansa
Redonda
Volta
Barra Mansa
Barra do Piraí
Teresópolis
Petrópolis
Nova Friburgo
Macaé
Ivinheima
Paraná
Porto São José
Paranavaí
Porecatu
Cornélio Procópio
Assis
Lençóis Paulista
Botucatu
Tietê
Itu
Jundiaí
São Paulo
Osasco
São Bernardo do Campo
São Caetano do Sul
Guarulhos
Jacareí
São José dos Campos
Taubaté
Nova Iguaçu
Rio de Janeiro
Niterói
São Gonçalo
Arraial do Cabo
Cabo Frio
Douradas
Víctor
Nova Olimpia
Ilha das Sete Quedas
Umuarama
Cianorte
Maringá
Apucarana
Londrina
Santo Antônio da Plat
Ibaiti
Ourinhos
Piraju
Avaré
Tatui
Sorocaba
Capão Bonito
São Vicente
Santos
Ubatuba
Caraguatatuba
Ilha de São Sebastião
Ilha Grande
RIO DE JANEIRO
Tropic of Capricorn
Salto del Guaíra
Guaíra
Goio-Erê
Campo Mourão
Ivaiporã
Cruzeiro do Oeste
Telêmaco Borba
Tibagi
Jaguariaíva
Itapeva
Itapetininga
Itararé
Apiaí
Pedro Barros
Peruíbe
Guarujá
Ilha de Santo Amaro
Toledo
Palotina
ALTO PARANÁ
Cascavel
Medianeira
Santa Helena
PARANÁ
Guaraniaçu
Pitanga
Reserva
Ortigueira
Castro
Cerro Azul
Tunas
Registro
Jacupiranga
Serra do Paranapiacaba
Ponta Grossa
Serra do Ribeira
Ilha Comprida
Foz do Iguaçú
Ciudad del Este
Cataratas del Iguazú
Cataratas del Iguaçu
Puerto Iguazú
Salto do Iguaçu
Rio Iguaçu
Laranjeiras do Sul
Guarapuava
Prudentópolis
Irati
Campo Largo
Curitiba
Pico Guaricana 1889m
Antonina
Paranaguá
Ilha do Mel
Ilha das Peças
Coronel Oviedo
Villarica
Abaí
Caazapá
Puerto Esperanza
Eldorado
Dois Vizinhos
Francisco Beltrão
Pato Branco
São Mateus do Sul
Canoinhas
União da Vitória
Mafra
São Francisco do Sul
Ilha de São Francisco
CAAGUAZÚ
GUAIRÁ
CAANINDEYÚ
Puerto Rico
San Pedro
Campo Erê
São Miguel d'Oest
Xanxerê
Pinhalzinho
Chapecó
Represa de Foz do Areia
Palmas
Bituruna
Porto União
Morro do Capão Doce 1340m
Monte Castelo
Joinville
Jaraguá do Sul
Itajaí
ITAPÚA
Encarnación
Posadas
San Ignacio
Aristóbulo del Valle
El Soberbio
Concórdia
Joaçaba
Videira
Curitibanos
SANTA CATARINA
Blumenau
Brusque
MISIONES
San José
San Javier
Leandro N. Alem
Oberá
Santa Ana
Santa Rosa
Frederico Westphalen
Erechim
Três Passos
Campos Novos
Piratuba
Marcelino Ramos
Rio Canoas
Lages
Alfredo Wagner
Bom Retiro
Ilha de Santa Catarina
Florianópolis
São José
Apóstoles
Palmeira das Missões
Sarandi
Carazinho
Passo Fundo
São Joaquim
Braço do Norte
Imbituba
Gobernador Virasoro
Santo Tomé
São Luiz Gonzaga
Ijuí
Cruz Alta
Soledade
Lagoa Vermelha
Vacaria
Nova Prata
Rio das Antas
Casca
Tubarão
Laguna
São Borja
Santo Angelo
Bossoroca
Guaporé
Bento Gonçalves
Caxias do Sul
Criciúma
Araranguá
Itaqui
Santiago
Tupanciretã
Júlio de Castilhos
Barros Cassal
Lajeado
Montenegro
Novo Hamburgo
Sapiranga
Taquara
Osório
Torres
Três Cachoeiras
Manuel Viana
Cruz Alta
RIO GRANDE DO SUL
Santa Maria
Santa Cruz do Sul
Rio Pardo
Canoas
Gravataí
Porto Alegre
Butiã
Tramandaí
Capivari
Quaraí
Rosário do Sul
Cachoeira do Sul
São Gabriel
Caçapava do Sul
Pântano Grande
Encruzilhada do Sul
Tapes
Camaquã
Lagoa dos Patos
Santana do Livramento
Dom Pedrito
Santana da Boa Vista
São Lourenço do Sul
Mostardas
Rivera
Tranqueira
Minas de Corrales
Bagé
Pinheiro Machado
Canguçu
Pelotas
URUGUAY
Arroio Grande
Jaguarão
Rio Grande
Quinta
Rio Branco
Lagoa Mangueira
Lagoa Mirim
Chuí
Santa Vitória do Palmar
La Coronilla
Castillos
Cabo Polonio
Rocha
Maldonado
Punta del Este
MONTEVIDEO
Río de la Plata
Canelones
Las Piedras
Pando

ATLANTIC OCEAN

291

Buenos Aires

Luján
Las Conchas
Tigre
San Isidro
Vicente López
Rio de la Plata
San Miguel
General San Martín
Belgrano
Hippodrome
Buenos Aires
Palermo
Teatro Colón
Zoo
Cathedral
Plaza de Mayo
Moreno
Merlo
Morón
San Justo
Sáenz Peña
Floresta
Barracas
Avellaneda
Villa Madero
Villa Alsina
Lanús
Quilmes
Mariano Acosta
Pontevedra
González Catán
Lomas de Zamora
Berazategui
Matanza
Aeropuerto Internacional de Ezeiza
Almirante Brown

0 10 Km
0 10 Miles

291

19,686ft
13,124ft
9843ft
6562ft
3281ft
1640ft
820ft
328ft
Sea Level
-820ft
-6562ft
-13,124ft

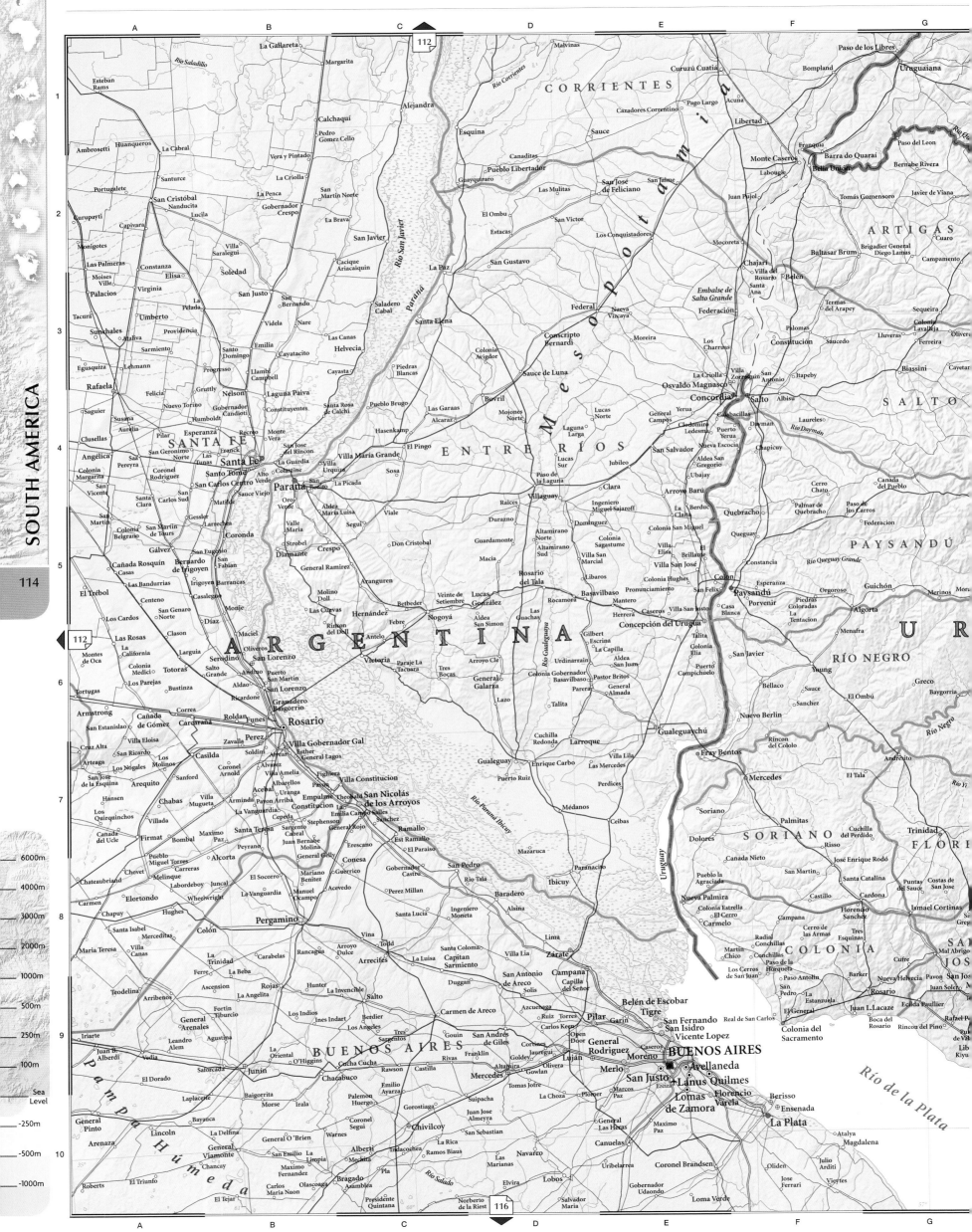

SOUTH AMERICA

114

Scale 1:2,000,000
(projection: Lambert Conformal Conic)

0 10 20 30 40 50 60 70 80 Km
0 10 20 30 40 50 60 70 80 Miles

Population
- ■ above 5 million
- ▣ 1 million to 5 million
- ◉ 500,000 to 1 million
- ◎ 100,000 to 500,000
- ⊕ 50,000 to 100,000
- ○ 10,000 to 50,000
- ○ below 10,000

113

Passo Novo
Jacaqua
Rio Ibicui
Loreto
São Vicente do Sul
Santa Maria
Silveira Martins
Agudo
Candelaria
Santa Cruz do Sul
ano Alto
Alegrete
Ibirapuitã
Passo do Sobrado
Restinga Seca
Tres Vendas
General Camara
Triunfo
Cacequy
Formigueiro
Ferreira
Cachoeira do Sul
Rio Pardo
São Jerônimo
Charqueadas
Azevedo Sodre
Rio Jacui
Capane
Mina do Loao
Butiá
Rosário do Sul
Itaraju
São Sepe
Barro Vermelho
Cordilheira
Pântano Grande
Capivarita
Quarai
São Gabriel
Mariana Pimentel
Barão do Triunfo
Artigas
Vaccacahy
Caçapava do Sul
Encruzilhada do Sul
Quitéria
Cerro Grande
Pintado Grande
andua
Pampeiro
RIO GRANDE DO SUL
Dom Feliciano
Sertão de Santana
Rio Cuareim
Palomas
Lavras do Sul
Santana da Boa Vista
Rio Camaquã
Camaquã
Santana do Livramento
BRAZIL
Arapey Grande
Rivera
Dom Pedrito
Serra das Encantadas
Masoller
Santana
Boqueirão
São Lourenço do Sul
Matojo
Tranqueras
Zanja Honda
Puntas de Corrales
Bagé
Canguçu
Lagoa dos Patos
Quintana
RIVERA
Lapuente
Piratiny
Quilombo
Cerro Alegre
Pacheca
Paso del Cerro
Cerro Pelado del Est
Cerrillada
Candiota
Pinheiro Machado
Quebra Yugos
Banado de Rocha
Minas de Corrales
Arroyo Blanco
Pedras Altas
Capão do Leão
Pelotas
Zapara
Tacuarembó
Abrojal
Vichadero
Acegua
Alegrias
Cerrito
Tambores
Los Rosanos
Pueblo de Arriba
Caraguata
Zanja Honda
Isidoro Noblia
Maria Isabel
Pedreiras
Quinta
Rio Grande
iedra Sola
Ansina
Coronilla
Acegua
Cruz de Piedra
São José de Norte
Curtina
TACUAREMBÓ
Pueblo del Barro
Las Arenas
Buena Vista
Paso del Centurión
Pedreiras
Estreito
Clara
Larrayos
Las Toscas
Quilombo
Cassino
Blanquillo
Cuchilla Caraguata
La Pedrera
Arroio Grande
cura
Cuchilla de Peralta
Achar
Banado de Medina
Melo
Rio Jaguarão
Peralta
CERRO LARGO
Tres Islas
Fraile Muerto
Toledo
GUAY
Cardoso
San Gregorio de Polanco
Arevalo
Cerro de las Cuentas
Arbolito
Uruguay
Mirim Lagoon
Jaguarão
berlain
Embalse del Río Negro
Verdun
Rio Negro
Rincon
Placido Rosas
Rio Branco
Tahim
de los Toros
Cerro Convento
La Paloma
Capilla Farruco
Cuchilla Grande
Tupambé
Rincon
Rincon del Bonete
Blanquillo
Vergara
Arrozal Trienta y Tres
Carlos Reyes
DURAZNO
Cerro Chato
Carpinteria
Mendizabal
Lagoa Mangueira
Ombues de Oribe
Capilla del Sauce
TREINTA Y TRES
Julio
General Enrique Martínez
291
Santa Bernardina
Sarandí del Yi
Maria Sanz
Durazno
José Batlle y Ordóñez
Villa Sara
Treinta y Tres
Cebollatí
Polanco del Yi
Nico Pérez
Maria Albina
Arrozal Victoria
Sarandí Grande
Zapicán
José Pedro Varela
La Coronilla
Illescas
FLORIDA
Pintado
Pirarajá
Lascano
Santa Vitória do Palmar
La Cruz
Alejandro Gallinal
Polanco Norte
Diez y Ocho de Julio
Chuy
LAVALLEJA
Polanco Sur
Maria Isabel
Chuí
Reboledo
Rio Cebollatí
Mariscala
Velázquez
ROCHA
La Coronilla
Florida
Casupá
ATLANTIC
25 de Mayo
Mendoza Chico
Fray Marcos
Los Talas
Castillos
Cardal
Mendoza
Chamizo
Bolivar
Aiguá
OCEAN
Independencia
San Ramón
Tala
Villa Serrana
Paralle
25 de Agosto
Iriquez
San Antonio
Solis
Minas
Rocha
La Barra
vo
Santa Lucía
San Bautista
Cabo Polonio
San Jacinto
La Barra
Corrientes
CANELONES
Migues
Montes
Soca
MALDONADO
La Paloma
Los Cerrillos
Cruz de los Caminos
Tapia
Solis de Mataojo
Totoral
Piedra del Toro
La Querencia
Gregorio
Nueva Carrara
Las Piedras
Sauce
Aznarez
Pan de Azúcar
Canelones
Toledo
Joaquin Suarez
Pando
Piedras de Afilar
San Carlos
Delta
La Paz
La Flores
Tigre
MONTEVIDEO
Barra de Carrasco
Carrasco
Piriápolis
Maldonado
Punta del Este

116

19,686ft
13,124ft
9843ft
6562ft
3281ft
1640ft
820ft
328ft
Sea Level
-820ft
-6562ft
-13,124ft

Scale 1:2,600,000
(projection: Lambert Conformal Conic)

0 10 20 30 40 50 Km
0 10 20 30 40 50 Miles

SOUTH AMERICA

118

Easter Island (Isla de Pascua) (to Chile)

Scale 1:500,000

0 2.5 5 Km
0 2.5 5 Miles

Punta San Juan
Cabo Norte
Playa de Anakena
Punta Rosalia
Bahía de La Pérouse
Cabo O'Higgins
Maunga Terevaka 506m
Ahu Tepeu
Motu Tautara
Naunau
Maunga Pukatikei 370m
Rano Raraku
Cabo Roggewein
Hanga Roa
Vaihu
Maunga Tangaroa 270m
Ahu Akivi
Punta Akahanga
Punta Cuidado
Mataveri
Ahu Vinapu
Orongo
Punta Baja
Rano Kau
Cabo Sur
Motu Nui

PACIFIC OCEAN

Elevation scale

6000m
4000m
3000m
2000m
1000m
500m
250m
100m
Sea Level
-250m
-500m
-1000m

PACIFIC OCEAN

COQUIMBO
VALPARAÍSO
SANTIAGO
LIBERTADOR
MAULE
BÍO BÍO
ARAUCANÍA

CHILE

ARGENTINA

SAN JUAN
MENDOZA
NEUQUÉN
LA PAMPA

Andes

Santiago
Valparaíso
Viña del Mar
Mendoza
Godoy Cruz
Concepción
Talca
San Rafael

Cerro Aconcagua 6959m
Cerro Mercedario 6769m
Cerro Juncal 6180m
Volcán Tupungato 6800m
Volcán Maipo 5323m
Cerro Sosneado 5189m
Volcán Tinguiririca 4300m
Cerro Campanario 4049m
Cerro Nevado 3810m
Volcán Descabezado Grande 3830m
Cerro Payún 3680m
Volcán Domuyo 4709m
Volcán Antuco 3585m
Volcán Copahué 2980m
Cerro Las Lajas 2650m

Río Colorado
Río Neuquén
Río Diamante
Río Atuel
Río San Juan
Río Grande
Río Maule
Río Bío Bío
Río Tunuyán

A B C D E F G

Brazília

Parque Nacional
de Brasília

Peninsula
Norte

Retiro de
Barra Alta

Brazlandia

Asa
Norte

Universida
de Brasília

Estadio

Lago do
Paranoá

Brasília

Palacio de
Justicia

Palacio de
Alvorada

Taguatinga

Guará

Asa
Sul

Catedral
Metropolitana

Rasgado

Cellândia

Jardim
Zoológico
de Brasília

Dom Bosco

Paranoá

Sto. Antonio
do Descoberto

Aeropuerto
Internacional
do Brasília

Lago
Sul

0   4 Km
0   4 Miles

Recanto
das
Emas

Jardim Botânico
do Brasília

Nucleo
Bandeirante

Caracas

Catia
La Mar

Caribbean Sea

Caraballeda

El Caribe

Mamo

Simón
Bolivar
Airport

El Palmar

Maiquetía

La Guaira

Río Carabatleda

Cordillera de la Costa

Quebrada Táicagua

Catia

Parque Nacional Ávila

Quebrada Topo

Nueva
Caracas

El Retiro

Caracas

Palacio
Miraflores

Capitolio
Nacional

Sarria

La Florida

Artigas

El Silenzio

Jardin
Botánico

Chacao

Los Dos
Caminos

Algodonal

Las
Acacias

Univ. Central
de Venezuela

Parque Nacional
del Este

Estadio
Nacional

La Vega

El Valle

Las Mercedes

Petare

Antimano

Cochecito

Baruta

El Hatillo

Río Guaire

0   4 Km
0   4 Miles

Havana

N

Castillo de los Tres Reyes del Morro

Castillo de San Carlos
de la Cabaña

Castillo de San Salvador
de la Punta

Catedral

Bahía de
la Habana

Straits of Florida

La Habana
(Havana)

Guanabacoa

Castillo del Príncipe

Vedado

Cerro

Regla

Río Almendares

Zoo

Castillo de
Atares

Jacomino

San Miguel
de Padrón

Miramar

Diez de
Octubre

Nuevo Vedado

Jesus del
Monte

Lawton

Lucero

Almendares

La Playa

Ciudad
Libertad

La Vibora

Mantilla

Bello

Marianao

Los
Pinos

Rosario

El Calvario

Barlovento

Collazo

Santa Fé

Siboney

Arroyo
Arenas

Arroyo
Naranjo

Embalse
Ejército
Revelde

Cangrejeras

La Lisa

Cantarranas

Punta
Brava

0   2 Km
0   2 Miles

El Cano

Quito

El Condado

Carcelen

Cotocollao

Ponceano

Cordillera Pichincha

Volcán Guagua
Pichincha
4794m

Concepcion

Aeropuerto
Mariscal Sucre

San Isidro
de Inca

Cochapamba

Jipijapa

Combaya

Rumipamba

Estadio
Olimpico

Tumbaco

Belisario Quevedo

Quito

San Juan

Plaza y Convento
de Santo Domingo

Río Machángara

Palacio del Govierno

Palacio Arzobispal

Teatro Sucre

Museo de la Ciudad

Cerro Ilaló
3188m

Chilibulo

Puengasi

Chillogallio

La Argelia

Conocoto

La Ecuatoriana

Quitumbe

Río de San Nicolás

Sangolqui

0   5 Km
0   5 Miles

Guamani

Turubamba

Santiago

El Carmen

Lo Barnechea

Quilicura

El Cortijo

Huechuraba

Vitacura

Conchali

Renca

Santa
Emilia

Las Condes

Río Mapocho

Recoleta

Carrascal

San Cristóbal

Sta. Rosa
de Locobe

Cerro Navia

Quinta
Normal

Congreso
Nacional

Catedral

Barrancas

Palacio
de la Moneda

Universidad
de Chile

Providencia

La Reina

Lo Prado
Arriba

Las Rejas

Santiago

Club Hipico

Parque
O'Higgins

Ñuñoa

La Aguada

Cerrillos

Santa
Julia

San Miguel

Bellavista

Maipu

La Blanca

La Granja

Lo Espejo

La Florida

0   4 Km
0   4 Miles

San Bernardo

El Bosque

São Paulo

Congo

Guarulhos

Aeroporto
Internacional
de Guarulhos

Mutinga

Pi'tuba

Itaberaba

Casa
Verde

Ermelino
Matarazzo

Jaguara

N. Senhora
Do O.

Mandaqui

Ribº Guapira

Río Tietê

Santana

Jardim
Munhoz

Cangaiba

Osasco

Lapa

Alto da
Lapa

Vila
Maria

Vila Ré

Cidade
de Deus

Vila
Madalena

Perdizes

Teatro
Municipal

Belênzinho

Tatuapé

Penha

Consolação

Brás

Butantã

Cerqueira
Cesar

São Paulo

Mooca

Alto da
Mooca

Vila
Formosa

Instituto
Butantã

Jardim
Paulista

Cidade
Lider

Jardim
Ouro Preto

Vila
Sonia

Estádio
do Morumbi

Río Pinheiros

Parque do
Ibirapuera

Vila Mariana

Museu
Ipiranga

Vila
Prudente

Vila Ema

Vila
Iasi

Campo
Belo

Indianápolis

Ibiranga

Río Tamanduatei

Pirajussara

Vila
Andrade

Brooklin

Bosque da
Saúde

Iguassú

Jardim
Sapopemba

Taboão
da Serra

Alto de
Boa Vista

São Paulo
Congonhas

Santo Amaro

Capelinha

Zoológico

São Caetano
do Sul

Utinga

Parque
das Naçoes

Capuava

Cupacé

Parque do
Estado

Itupu

Jurubatuba

Santo André

Mauá

Interagos

Zuvuvús

Diadema

Vila
Goncales

Jardim
do Mar

Santa
Tereza

Vila
Pires

Pedreira

Represa de
Guarapiranga

Represa
Billings

São Bernardo
do Campo

0   4 Km
0   4 Miles

Africa is the world's second largest continent with a total area of 11,712,434 sq miles (30,335,000 sq km). It has 53 separate countries, including Madagascar in the Indian Ocean. It straddles the equator and is the only continent to stretch from the northern to southern temperate zones.

FACTFILE

N **Most Northerly Point:** Jalta, Tunisia 37° 31′ N
S **Most Southerly Point:** Cape Agulhas, South Africa 34° 52′ S
E **Most Easterly Point:** Raas Xaafuun, Somalia 51° 24′ E
W **Most Westerly Point:** Santo Antão, Cape Verde, 25° 11′ W

Largest Lakes:
1. Lake Victoria, Kenya/Tanzania/Uganda 26,828 sq miles (69,484 sq km)
2. Lake Tanganyika, Dem. Rep. Congo/Tanzania 12,703 sq miles (32,900 sq km)
3. Lake Nyasa, Malawi/Mozambique/Tanzania 11,600 sq miles (30,044 sq km)
4. Lake Turkana, Ethiopia/Kenya 2473 sq miles (6405 sq km)
5. Lake Albert, Dem. Rep. Congo/Uganda 2046 sq miles (5299 sq km)

Longest Rivers:
1. Nile, NE Africa 4160 miles (6695 km)
2. Congo, Angola/Congo/Dem. Rep. Congo 2900 miles (4667 km)
3. Niger, W Africa 2589 miles (4167 km)
4. Zambezi, Southern Africa 1673 miles (2693 km)
5. Ubangi-Uele, C Africa 1429 miles (2300 km)

Largest Islands:
1. Madagascar, 229,300 sq miles (594,000 sq km)
2. Réunion, 970 sq miles (2535 sq km)
3. Tenerife, Canary Islands 785 sq miles (2034 sq km)
4. Isla de Bioco, Equatorial Guinea 779 sq miles (2017 sq km)
5. Mauritius, 709 sq miles (1836 sq km)

Highest Points:
1. Kilimanjaro, Tanzania 19,340 ft (5895 m)
2. Kirinyaga, Kenya 17,058 ft (5199 m)
3. Mount Stanley, Dem. Rep. Congo/Uganda 16,762 ft (5109 m)
4. Mount Speke, Uganda 16,043 ft (4890 m)
5. Mount Baker, Uganda 15,892 ft (4844 m)

Lowest Point:
▼ Lac 'Assal, Djibouti -512 ft (-156 m) below sea level

Highest recorded temperature:
⊕ Al'Aziziyah, Libya 136°F (58°C)

Lowest recorded temperature:
⊖ Ifrane, Morocco -11°F (-24°C)

Wettest Place:
≋ Cape Debundsha, Cameroon 405 in (10,290 mm)

Driest Place:
⌇ Wadi Halfa, Sudan <0.1 in (<2.5 mm)

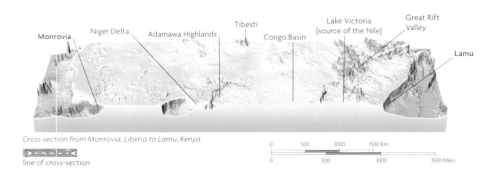

Cross-section from Monrovia, Liberia to Lamu, Kenya

line of cross-section

Monrovia · Niger Delta · Adamawa Highlands · Tibesti · Congo Basin · Lake Victoria (source of the Nile) · Great Rift Valley · Lamu

0   500   1000   1500 Km
0   500   1000   1500 Miles

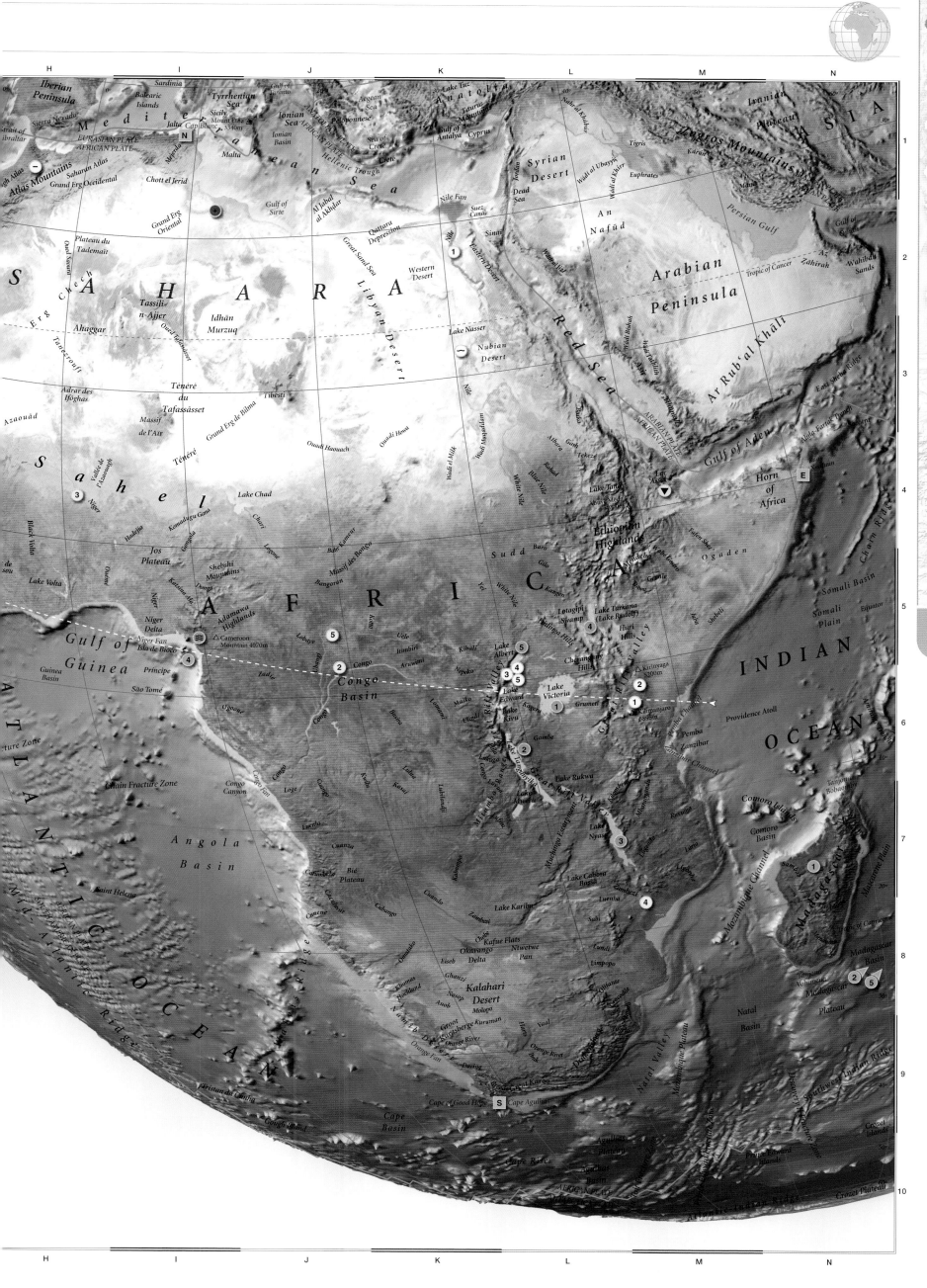

H I J K L M N

Iberian Peninsula
Sierra Nevada
Balearic Islands
Sardinia
Cap Blanc
Tyrrhenian Sea
Sicily
Mount Etna 3340m
Malta
Ionian Sea
Ionian Basin
Hellenic Trough
Crete
Aegean Sea
Peloponnese
Sea of Crete
Anatolia
Lake Tuz
Taurus Mountains
Gulf of Antalya
Cyprus
Nahr al Khabur
Tigris
Kârûn
Iranian Plateau
Zagros Mountains
ASIA

Atlas Mountains
High Atlas
Grand Erg Occidental
Saharan Atlas
Chott el Jerid
EURASIAN PLATE
AFRICAN PLATE
Mediterranean Sea
Jordan
Syrian Desert
Dead Sea
Wadi al Ubayyid
Euphrates
Manin

Oued Saoura
Plateau du Tademaït
Grand Erg Oriental
Gulf of Sirte
Al Jabal al Akhdar
Nile Fan
Suez Canal
Sinai
An Nafud
Persian Gulf
Gulf of Oman

S A H A R A
Erg Chech
Tassili-n-Ajjer
Ahaggar
Idhān Murzuq
Libyan Desert
Great Sand Sea
Western Desert
Nile
Eastern Desert
Red Sea
Arabian Peninsula
Tropic of Cancer
Az Zāhirah
Ar Rub' al Khālī
Wahibah Sands

Erg Iguidi
Ténéré
Oued Tafassâsset
Lake Nasser
Nubian Desert
ARABIAN PLATE
AFRICAN PLATE

Azouâd
Adrar des Ifôghas
Tanezrouft
Ténéré du Tafassâsset
Tibesti
Nile
Ouadi Howa
East Sheba Ridge
Gulf of Aden
Alula-Fartak Trench

S a h e l
Vallée de l'Azaouagh
Grand Erg de Bilma
Ouadi Haouach
Wadi el Milk
Wadi Muqaddam
Atbara
Gash
Tekeze
Ethiopian Highlands
Horn of Africa

Niger
Black Volta
Hadejia
Komadugu Gana
Lake Chad
Chari
Logone
Bahr Aouk
Yei
White Nile
Blue Nile
Rahad
Lake Tana
Abaya Mesk
Lac Assal
Fafen Shet'
Ogaden
Somali Basin

Lake Volta
Oumo
Jos Plateau
Shebshi Mountains
Donga
Massif des Bongo
Bangoran
S u d d
Baro
Gilo
Weyb Wenz
Gestro
Genale
Somali Plain
Equator

A F R I C A
Adamawa Highlands
Cameroon Mountain 4070m
Lobaye
Uele
Itimbiri
Aruwimi
Kibali
Lotagipi Swamp
Chalbi Desert
Lake Turkana (Lake Rudolf)
Huri Hills
Somali Plain

Niger Delta
Isla de Bioco
Gulf of Guinea
Príncipe
São Tomé
Lomami
Congo
Nepoko
Lake Albert
Cherangany Hills
Kirinyaga 5200m
INDIAN OCEAN

Guinea Basin
Chain Fracture Zone
Zadié
Congo Basin
Maiko
Lake Edward
Lake Kivu
Lake Victoria
Gruneri
Kilimanjaro 5895m
Pemba Channel
Providence Atoll

A T L A N T I C   O C E A N
Ogooué
Congo Fan
Loge
Lukenie
Kasai
Lualaba
Lake Tanganyika
Gombe
Lake Rukwa
Pemba
Zanzibar
Zanzibar Channel
OCEAN

Angola Basin
Congo Canyon
Cuanza
Lulua
Lake Mweru
Mbarangandu
Lake Nyasa
Ruvuma
Comoro Islands
Comoro Basin
Tanjona Bobaomby

Bié Plateau
Cuango
Kwango
Cassai
Kabompo
Lake Cabora Bassa
Luenha
Zambezi
Mozambique Channel
Madagascar

Saint Helena
Cubango
Cuando
Zambezi
Lake Kariba
Sabi
Lundi
Limpopo
Madagascar Basin

Walvis Ridge
Okavango Delta
Kafue Flats
Ntwetwe Pan
Chobe
Eiseb
Kalahari Desert
Ghanzi
Tanjona Vohimena
Madagascar Plateau

Mid-Atlantic Ridge
Khomas Bodiland
Nosop
Auob
Molopo
Okwa
Natal Basin
Natal Valley

Cape Basin
Groot
Kuruman
Karasberge
Orange River
Vaal
Olifants
Mozambique Plateau
Southwest Indian Ridge

Tristan da Cunha
Gough Island
Nossob
Orange Fan
Doring
Olifants
Cape of Good Hope
Cape Agulhas
Great Karoo
Agulhas Plateau
Crozet Islands
Prince Edward Islands
Crozet Plateau

AFRICAN PLATE

Political

The political map of modern Africa only emerged following the end of World War II. Over the next half-century, all of the countries formerly controlled by European powers gained independence from their colonial rulers—only Liberia and Ethiopia were never colonized. The post-colonial era has not been an easy period for many countries, but there have been moves toward multi-party democracy across much of the continent. In South Africa, democratic elections replaced the internationally-condemned apartheid system only in 1994. Other countries have still to find political stability; corruption in government and ethnic tensions are serious problems. National infrastructures, based on the colonial transportation systems built to exploit Africa's resources, are often inappropriate for independent economic development.

SCALE 1:30,500,000
(projection: Lambert Azimuthal Equal Area)

Km
0   200   400   600   800   1000

Miles
0   200   400   600   800   1000

AFRICA

122

Population

- ■ above 5 million
- ■ 1 million to 5 million
- ◉ 500,000 to 1 million
- ◎ 100,000 to 500,000
- ⊙ 50,000 to 100,000
- ○ 10,000 to 50,000
- ● Country capital

Borders

- full international border
- disputed de facto border
- ceasefire line

Standard of living

Since the 1960s most countries in Africa have seen significant improvements in life expectancy, healthcare, and education. However, 28 of the 30 most deprived countries in the world are African, and the continent as a whole lies well behind the rest of the world in terms of meeting many basic human needs.

Standard of living
(UN human development index)

high

low

Transportation

African railroads were built to aid the exploitation of natural resources, and most offer passage only from the interior to the coastal cities, leaving large parts of the continent untouched—five land-locked countries have no railroads at all. The Congo, Nile, and Niger river networks offer limited access to land within the continental interior, but have a number of waterfalls and cataracts which prevent navigation from the sea. Many roads were developed in the 1960s and 1970s, but economic difficulties are making the maintenance and expansion of the networks difficult.

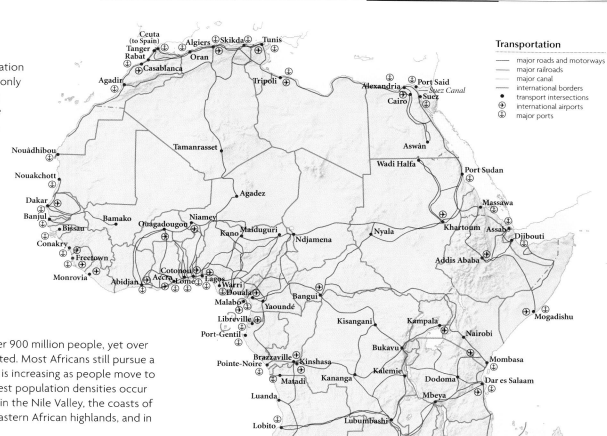

Transportation
- major roads and motorways
- major railroads
- major canal
- international borders
- transport intersections
- international airports
- major ports

Population

Africa has a rapidly-growing population of over 900 million people, yet over 75% of the continent remains sparsely populated. Most Africans still pursue a traditional rural lifestyle, though urbanization is increasing as people move to the cities in search of employment. The greatest population densities occur where water is more readily available, such as in the Nile Valley, the coasts of North and West Africa, along the Niger, the eastern African highlands, and in South Africa.

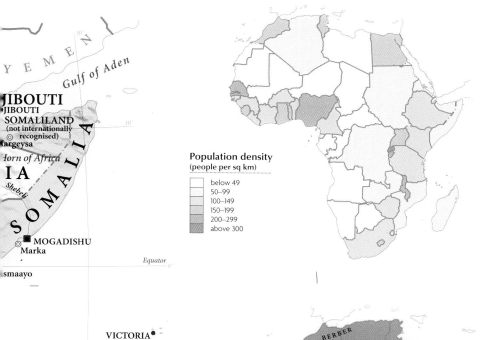

Population density
(people per sq km)
- below 49
- 50–99
- 100–149
- 150–199
- 200–299
- above 300

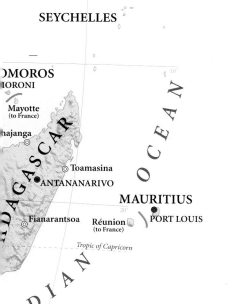

Languages

Three major world languages act as *lingua francas* across the African continent: Arabic in North Africa; English in southern and eastern Africa and Nigeria; and French in Central and West Africa, and in Madagascar. A huge number of African languages are spoken as well—over 2000 have been recorded, with more than 400 in Nigeria alone—reflecting the continuing importance of traditional cultures and values. In the north of the continent, the extensive use of Arabic reflects Middle Eastern influences while Bantu is widely-spoken across much of southern Africa.

Language groups
- Afro-Asiatic (Hamito-Semitic)
- Niger-Congo
- Nilo-Saharan
- Khoisan
- Indo-European
- Austronesian

Official African Languages

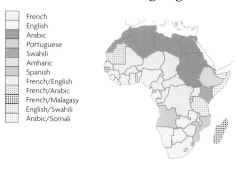

- French
- English
- Arabic
- Portuguese
- Swahili
- Amharic
- Spanish
- French/English
- French/Arabic
- French/Malagasy
- English/Swahili
- Arabic/Somali

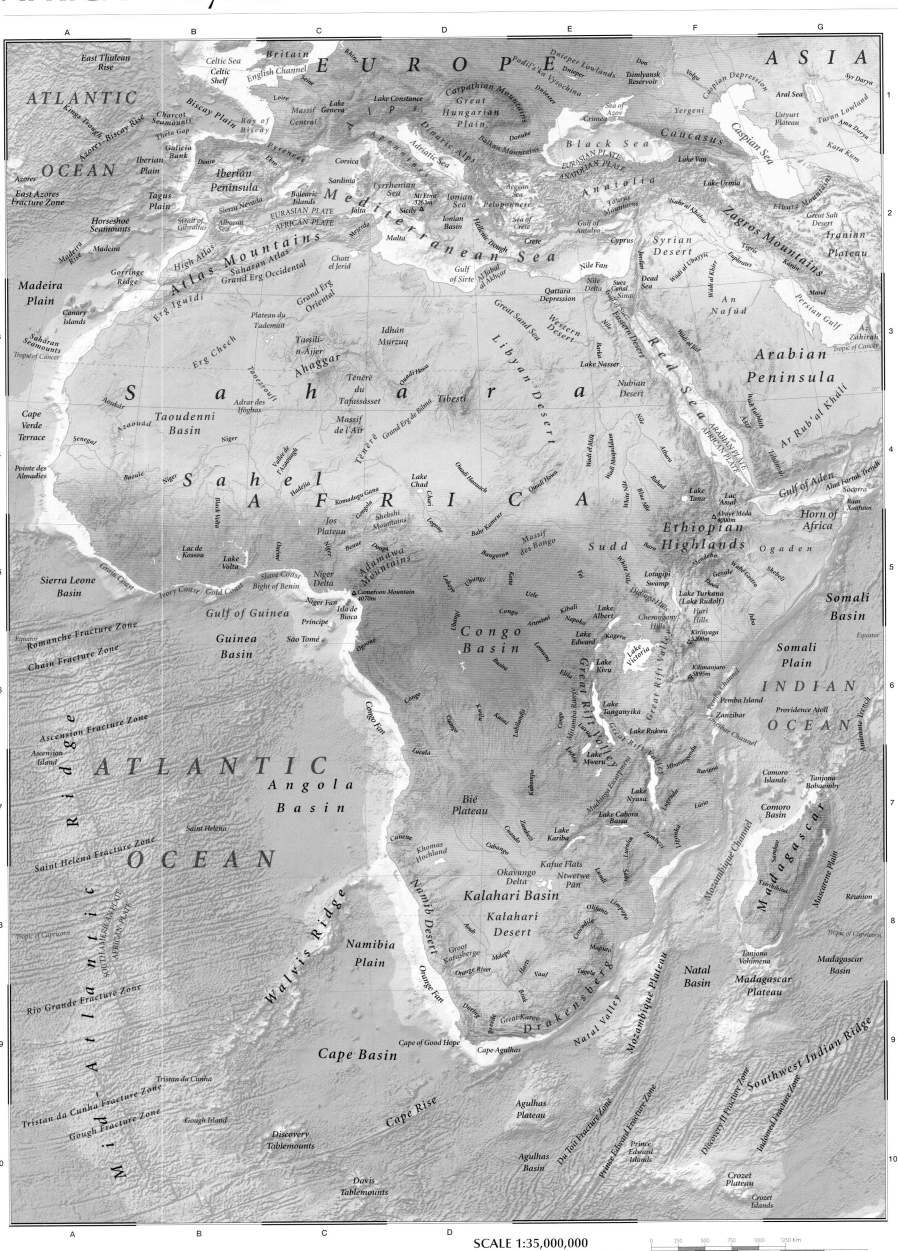

SCALE 1:35,000,000
(projection: Lambert Azimuthal Equal Area)

| 0 | 250 | 500 | 750 | 1000 | 1250 Km |
| 0 | 250 | 500 | 750 | 1000 | 1250 Miles |

Climate

The climates of Africa range from mediterranean to arid, dry savannah and humid equatorial. In East Africa, where snow settles at the summit of volcanoes such as Kilimanjaro, climate is also modified by altitude. The winds of the Sahara export millions of tons of dust a year both northward and eastward.

Climate

- arid
- humid equatorial
- mediterranean
- semi-arid
- tropical
- warm humid
- ☼ daily hours of sunshine, January
- ☼ daily hours of sunshine, July
- → cold wind
- → hot wind

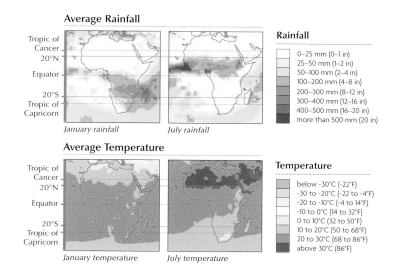

Average Rainfall

Tropic of Cancer 20°N
Equator
20°S
Tropic of Capricorn

January rainfall   *July rainfall*

Rainfall

- 0–25 mm (0–1 in)
- 25–50 mm (1–2 in)
- 50–100 mm (2–4 in)
- 100–200 mm (4–8 in)
- 200–300 mm (8–12 in)
- 300–400 mm (12–16 in)
- 400–500 mm (16–20 in)
- more than 500 mm (20 in)

Average Temperature

Tropic of Cancer 20°N
Equator
20°S
Tropic of Capricorn

January temperature   *July temperature*

Temperature

- below -30°C (-22°F)
- -30 to -20°C (-22 to -4°F)
- -20 to -10°C (-4 to 14°F)
- -10 to 0°C (14 to 32°F)
- 0 to 10°C (32 to 50°F)
- 10 to 20°C (50 to 68°F)
- 20 to 30°C (68 to 86°F)
- above 30°C (86°F)

Landuse

Some of Africa's most productive agricultural land is found in the eastern volcanic uplands, where fertile soils support a wide range of valuable export crops including vegetables, tea, and coffee. The most widely-grown grain is corn and peanuts (groundnuts) are particularly important in West Africa. Without intensive irrigation, cultivation is not possible in desert regions and unreliable rainfall in other areas limits crop production. Pastoral herding is most commonly found in these marginal lands. Substantial local fishing industries are found along coasts and in vast lakes such as Lake Nyasa and Lake Victoria.

Environmental issues

One of Africa's most serious environmental problems occurs in marginal areas such as the Sahel where scrub and forest clearance, often for cooking fuel, combined with overgrazing, are causing desertification. Game reserves in southern and eastern Africa have helped to preserve many endangered animals, although the needs of growing populations have led to conflict over land use, and poaching is a serious problem.

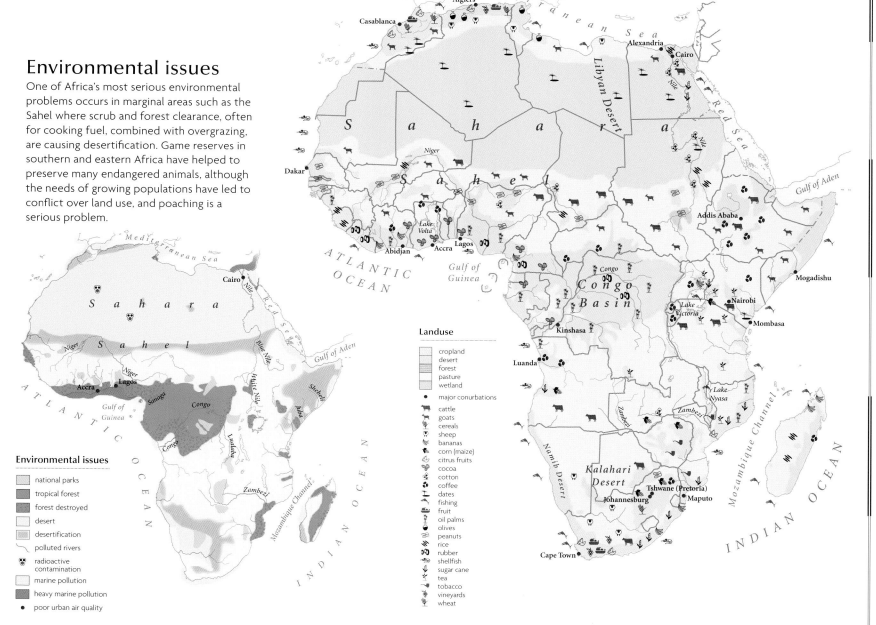

Landuse

- cropland
- desert
- forest
- pasture
- wetland
- • major conurbations
- cattle
- goats
- cereals
- sheep
- bananas
- corn (maize)
- citrus fruits
- cocoa
- cotton
- coffee
- dates
- fishing
- fruit
- oil palms
- olives
- peanuts
- rice
- rubber
- shellfish
- sugar cane
- tea
- tobacco
- vineyards
- wheat

Environmental issues

- national parks
- tropical forest
- forest destroyed
- desert
- desertification
- polluted rivers
- radioactive contamination
- marine pollution
- heavy marine pollution
- • poor urban air quality

AFRICA

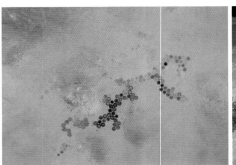

1 AL KHUFRAH, LIBYA
The circular irrigation patterns at this oasis have developed through the use of sprinkler units sweeping around a central point.

2 ERG DU DJOURAB, CHAD
Looking southwest, the pale area, just south of the darker Tibesti mountains on the right and the Ennedi plateau on the left, shows a desert sandstorm in motion.

3 ASWAN HIGH DAM, EGYPT
Completed in 1970 the dam controls flooding along the lower stretches of the Nile river.

4 KHARTOUM, SUDAN
The capital of Sudan lies at the junction of the Blue Nile, flowing from the east, and the broad White Nile, flowing from the south.

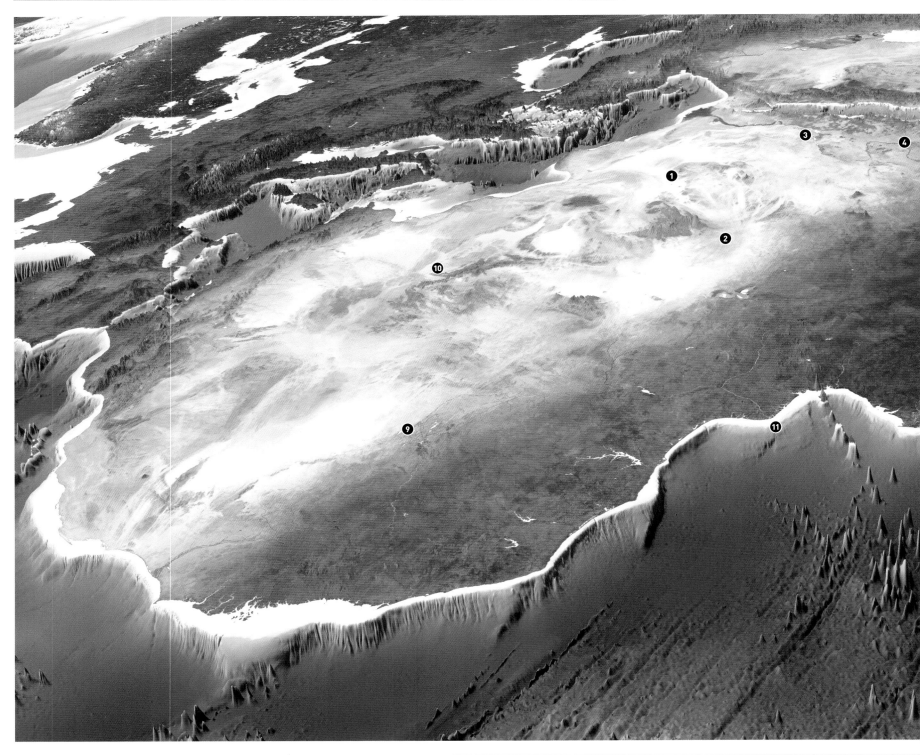

9 LAKE FAGUIBINE, MALI
Part of the Niger river's "inland delta," a region of lakes, creeks and backwaters near Tombouctou.

10 TASSILI-N-AJJER, ALGERIA
These sand dunes, one of a variety found in the Sahara, overlie the darker sandstone bedrock of the Tassili-n-Ajjer plateau.

11 NIGER DELTA, NIGERIA
At this point lies the vast, low-lying region through which the waters of the Niger river drain into the Gulf of Guinea.

12 CONGO/UBANGI RIVERS, DR CONGO
The confluence of these two rivers lies at the heart of the Congo Basin.

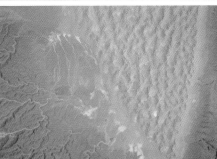

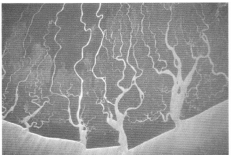

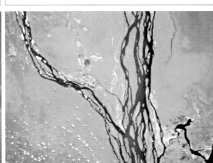

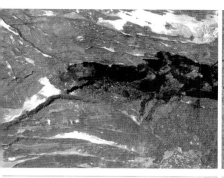

AFAR DEPRESSION, DJIBOUTI | 5
This low point is located at the junction of three tectonic plates—the Gulf of Aden to the east, the Red Sea to the north and the Great Rift Valley to the south.

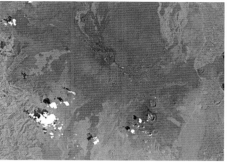

NYIRAGONGO AND NYAMURAGIRA VOLCANOES, | 6
DR CONGO
These two volcanoes, lying to the west of the Great Rift Valley, last erupted in 2002 and 2001 respectively.

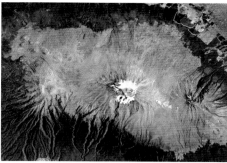

KILIMANJARO, TANZANIA | 7
An extinct volcano, its great height modifies the local climate, forcing moist air streams from the Indian Ocean to rise, inducing rain and, higher up, snow.

BETSIBOKA RIVER, MADAGASCAR | 8
The waters of Madagascar's second longest river are red with sediment as it carries eroded topsoil from the interior and deposits it in the Indian Ocean.

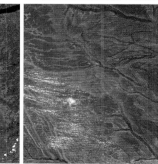

MALEBO POOL, CONGO/DR CONGO | 13
lake in the lower reaches of the Congo river, it hosts two capital cities on its banks, Brazzaville, Congo to the north and Kinshasa, DR Congo to the south.

ZAMBEZI RIVER, ZAMBIA | 14
Seasonal flooding of the river and its tributaries turned the Mulonga and Liuwa plains on the Zambia-Angola border into a vast wetland in April 2004

BEIRA, MOZAMBIQUE | 15
This port and beach resort lies on the north side of the mouth of the Pungoé river.

CAPE TOWN, SOUTH AFRICA | 16
South Africa's third largest city with a population of 2.9 million, it is also the seat of the country's parliament.

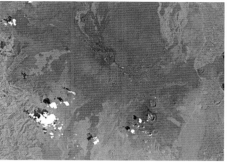

AFRICA

127

GREECE

Chaniá Réthymno Irákleio
Tympáki Vóros Nikól
Kríti
(Crete)

M e d i t e r r a n e a n

TUNISIA

Chott Melghir
Gafsa Sfax
Nefta Béro Íles de Kerkenah
Tozeur Chott el Fedjaj Golfe de Gabès
Chott Merouane Kebili Gabès Île de Jerba
El Oued Chott el Jerid Mellita
Touggourt Médenine
Tataouine
Dehibat
Nālūt
Sināwin

ȚARĀBULUS
(TRIPOLI)
Zuwārah Az Zāwiyah Ṭarābulus Al Khums
Al 'Azīzīyah Zlīțan Mișrātah
Yafran Gharyān
Mizdah Banī Walīd
Al Qaddāhīyah Bu'ayrāt al Ḥasūn
Wādī Zamzam Surt
Wādī Bayy al Kabīr An Nawfalīyah
Ash Shuwayrif Al 'Uqaylah As Sulțān
Marsā al Burayqah
Al Bayḍā' Darnah
Al Marj Al Jabal al Akhḍar
Banghāzī (Benghazi) Khalīj al Bumbah
Qaminis Tubruq
Ajdābiyā
Gulf of Salūm
Sidi Barr
Salūm
Wādī al Farīgh
Wādī al Hamām

Khalīj Surt
(Gulf of Sirte)

ALGERIA

Bourdj Messaouda
Ghadāmis
Dīrj
Al Ḥamādah al Ḥamrā'

Idhān Awbārī

Djanet

Tiguentourine

Illizi

Tassili-n-Ajjer

Al 'Uwaynāt
Ghāt
Djanet

Jabal as Sawdā'

Hūn Waddān
Marādah

L   I   B   Y   A

Sahara

Libyan Plateau

Al Jaghbūb
Qāra
Siwa

Sahara e
(Wester

Birāk
Samnū
Awbārī Sabhā
Ghaddūwah
Murzuq Zawīlah

Hamādat Murzuq

Al Ḥarūj al Aswad

Zillah

Great Sand Sea

L   i   b   y   a   n   D   e

Idhān Murzuq

Al Qațrūn

Jabal Bin Ghunaymah

Wāw al Kabīr

Tazirbū

Ramlat Rabyānah

Tajarhi

Sarīr Tībistī

Buzaymah
Rabyānah
Al Khufrah

Gilf Kebir
Plateau

Pic Bette
2286m
Jabal al Nuqayy

Aozou

Massif d'Abo

Plateau du Manguéni

Plateau du Djado

Madama

Plateau du Tchigaï

Djado
Chirfa

Dao Timmi

Séguédine

AGADEZ

Aney

Adrar Tamgak
1988m
Iferouane

Massif de l'Aïr

Tímia

Monts Bagzane
2022m
Akréréb

Massif de Taghouaji
1106m

Ténéré

Bardaï
Yebbi-Bou

Tibesti

Zouar
Sherda

Emi Koussi
3415m

Gouro

Ounianga Kébir

Erdi

Jabal al 'Uwaynāt
1907m
Al Uwaynāt

s   e   r   t

BORKOU-ENNEDI-
TIBESTI

Erdi Ma

Dépression du Mourdi

Fachi

Bilma

Dirkou

Grand Erg de Bilma

Erg du Ténéré

N   I   G   E   R

Faya

Fada

Ennedi

Monou

Ouadi Haouach

NORTHERN
DARFUR

Teiga
Plateau

Termit-Kaoboul

Achétinamou Tasker

Tanout

Damagaram Takaya
ZINDER Kellé
Zinder Gouré
Miria Guidimouni
Dengas
Gumel
Hadejia Hadejin
JIGAWA

Ngourti

Boultoum

DIFFA

Ngelmi

Nguigmi

Bosso
Diffa
Maïné-Soroa
Gashua Geïdam
Damasak
Nguru
Mongonu
BORNO
YOBE
NIGERIA

LAC
Lake
Chad Bol
N'Gouri
Massakory
Ngoura Tersef
Moyto
CHARI-BAGUIRMI

Nokou
Rig-Rig Mao
Bahr el Ghazal
Salal
KANEM

Bodélé

Erg du Djourab

Koro Toro

Arada
Moussoro
BATHA
Haraz-Djombo
Djédaa
Ati
Batha
Oum-Hadjer
OUADDAÏ

C   H   A   D

Oum-Chalouba
Iriba
Massif du Kapka
BILTINE
Biltine Guéréda
Abéché
Adré El Geneina
Am Dam
Zalingei

Ouadi Howa

Umm Buru
Kutum
Kebkabiya
WESTERN
DARFUR
Jebel Marra
3071m
Marra
Hills

Mellit
El Atru
Kedd

Malha

El Fasher
Umm Kedd

Tropic of Cancer

Oued Tafassasset

6000m
4000m
3000m
2000m
1000m
500m
250m
100m
Sea
Level
-250m
-500m
-1000m

Scale 1:8,000,000
(projection: Lambert Azimuthal Equal Area)

0 25 50 75 100 125 150 175 200 Km
0 25 50 75 100 125 150 175 200 Miles

Population

- ■ above 5 million
- ■ 1 million to 5 million
- ⦿ 500,000 to 1 million
- ⊚ 100,000 to 500,000
- ⊕ 50,000 to 100,000
- ○ 10,000 to 50,000
- ∘ below 10,000

Elevation scale:
19,686ft
13,124ft
9843ft
6562ft
3281ft
1640ft
820ft
328ft
Sea Level
-820ft
-6562ft
-13,124ft

TURKISH REPUBLIC OF NORTHERN CYPRUS
(recognized only by Turkey)

CYPRUS
Nicosia
Girne (Kerynea)
Gazimağusa (Ammóchostos, Famagusta)
Lárnaka
Lemesós (Limassol)
Páfos
Olýmpos 1951m

LEBANON
BEYROUTH (BEIRUT)
Tripoli

SYRIA
Al Lādhiqīyah (Latakia)
Ţarţūs
Hamāh
Ḩimş (Homs)
Jabal Abū Rahbah
Dūma
DIMASHQ (DAMASCUS)
Al Qunayţirah
Syrian Desert

ISRAEL
Hefa (Haifa)
Nahariyya
Netanya
Tel Aviv-Yafo
Holon
Rehovot
Ashdod
West Bank
JERUSALEM
Gaza Strip · Gaza
Be'ér Sheva
Hebron
Dead Sea

LEBANON · Lake Tiberias
As Suwaydā'
Irbid
AMMĀN
Az Zarqā'
Al Mafraq
Ma'dabā
Al Karak

JORDAN
Ma'ān
Elat · Al 'Aqabah
Aqaba

IRAQ
BAGHDAD
Tikrīt
Tigris
Ba'qūbah
Al Fallūjah
Karbalā'
An Najaf
Al Ḩillah
Al Kūt
Al 'Amārah
As Samāwah
An Nāşirīyah
Buḩayrat ath Tharthār
Buḩayrat ar Razāzah

IRAN
Kermānshāh (Bākhtarān)
Ilām
LORESTĀN

EGYPT
Alexandria
Rashid (Rosetta)
Damanhūr
El 'Alamein
El Nouzha
Kafr el Sheikh
Tanta
Shibin el Kôm
Dumyât (Damietta)
Zagazig
Port Said
El Mansûra
Isma'iliya
Suez Canal
Benha
CAIRO
El Giza
Helwân
El Şaff
El Faiyûm
Beni Suef
El Fashn
Beni Mazâr
El Minya
Mallawi
Dairût
Asyût
Ţahţa
Sohâg
Akhmîm
Girga
Qena
Luxor
Valley of the Kings
Esna
Idfu
Kôm Ombo
Aswân
Aswân Dam
Lake Nasser
Abu Simbel
Nile Delta
Sinai
Gulf of Suez
Ras Ghârib
Hurghada
Bûr Safâga
Quseir
Marsa 'Alam
Berenice
Râs Banâs
Gebel Mûsa 2285m
Sharm el Sheikh
Râs Muhammad
Za'farâna
Abu Zenima
El Tûr
Qâret el Mût
Qasr Farâfra
Bawiti
Bâris
El Khârga
El Qasr
Sahara el Sharqiya (Eastern Desert)

SUDAN
Wadi Halfa
Abu Hamed
Akasha
Selima Oasis
Laqiya Arba'in
Delgo
Argo
Dongola
El Khandaq
Merowe
Korti
Ed Débba
Karima
Atbara
Ed Damer
Berber
Shendi
Kabushiya
Shereik
Adarama
Musmar
Haiya
Derudeb
Port Sudan
Suakin
Sinkat
Tokar
Ekowit
Salala
Halaib
Dungunab
Muhammad Qol
Ras Abu Shagara
Sallom
NORTHERN
RIVER NILE
KASSALA
KHARTOUM
Omdurman
Khartoum North
GEZIRA
Wad Medani
Barakat
Rufa'a
El Kamlin
El Manaqil
Hag 'Abdullah
Sennar
SINNAR
WHITE NILE
BLUE NILE
Kosti
Rabak
Ed Dueim
Singa
Gedaref
GEDAREF
Gallabat
Doka
El Hawata
Gôz Regeb
Kassala
Khashm el Girba
Teseney
Barentu
WESTERN KORDOFAN
NORTHERN KORDOFAN
El Obeid
Umm Ruwaba
Tendelti
Hamrat esh Sheikh
Sodiri
Khuwei
Wad Banda
Bara
El Nuhud
Ed Duem
Nubian Desert
RED SEA

SAUDI ARABIA
Tabūk
TABŪK
Ḩalat 'Ammār
Al Bad'
Al Muwayliḩ
Ḑubā
Ash Sharmah
Jabal al Lawz 2580m
Al Bi'r
Al Qalībah
Al Akhḑar
Taymā'
Al 'Ula
Al Wajh
Umm Lajj
Khaybar
Hadiyah
Yanbu' al Baḩr
AL MADĪNAH
Al Madīnah (Medina)
Jabal Racwa 1814m
Badr Ḩunayn
Rābigh
An Nafūd
AL JAWF
Al Jawf
Sakākah
Ar Ruthīyah
Al Qurayyāt
Turayf
'Ar'ar
AL ḨUDŪD ASH SHAMĀLĪYAH
Nişāb
Rafḩah
Ḩafar al Bāţin
Al Mayyāh
Al Artāwīyah
Az Zilfī
Al Majma'ah
Buraydah
'Unayzah
AL QAṢĪM
Najd
Shaqrā'
Marāh
Durmā'
Ad Dawādimī
Ar Ruwaydah
Al Quwayīyah
AR RIYĀḐ
Ḩā'il
HĀ'IL
Al Ghazālah
Bi'r al Murār
Al Ḩamūdīyah
Jalājil
'Afīf
Ḩalabān
Budayyi'ah
ARABIA
MAKKAH
Makkah (Mecca)
King Abdul Aziz
JIDDAH (JEDDA)
AŢ Ţā'if
Turabah
Ar Rawdah
Al Khurmah
Ranyah
Zalim
Al Mislāḩ
Mahd adh Dhahab
Tropic of Cancer

Red Sea

YEMEN
SAN'Ā (SANA)
Al Ḩudaydah (Hodeida)
Dhamār
Ibb
Ta'izz
'Amrān
Sa'dah
Najrān
NAJRĀN
JĪZĀN
Jīzān
Şabyā
ASĪR
Abhā
Khamīs Mushayt
Mubayil
Al Birk
Al Qunfudhah
Ad Darb
Zahrān
Jabal Sawdā' 3133m
Al Bāḩah
AL BĀḨAH

ERITREA
ASMARA
Keren
Akurdet
Massawa
Nakfa
Afabet
Eriba
Mersa Fatma
Zula
Massawa Channel
Dahlak Archipelago

ETHIOPIA
TIGRAY
Mek'ele
AMHARA
AFAR
Aksum
Adwa
Adigrat
Gonder
Korem
Mäych'ew
Ras Dashen 4620m

DJIBOUTI

Bāb al Mandab
Danakil Desert

Northwest Africa

AFRICA

ATLANTIC

OCEAN

PORTUGAL

SPAIN

Sines · Beja · Azuaga · Córdoba · Montoro · Linares
Cabo de São Vicente · Guadalquivir · Valverde del Camino · Jaén
Lagos · Faro · Huelva (Seville) · Dos Hermanas · Lucena · Guadix
Golfo de Cádiz · Sevilla · Granada · Sistemas Béticos · Mulhacén 3481m · Moja
Lebrija · Utrera · Osuna · Antequera · Guadix
Jeréz de la Frontera · Cádiz · San Fernando · Ronda · Marbella · Motril · Almería
Vejer de la Frontera · Algeciras · GIBRALTAR (to UK) · Costa del Sol
Cap Spartel · Strait of Gibraltar · Ceuta (to Spain)
Tanger · Asilah · Tétouan · Al-Hoceima · Melilla (to Spain) · Nador · Cap des Trois Fourches
Larache · Chefchaouen · Rif · Ghazaoua
Ksar-el-Kebir · Moulay-Bousselham · Souk-el-Arba-Rharb · Oujda
Kénitra · Sidi-Kacem · Taounate · El Ayoun · Jerada
Salé · Salé · Fès · Taza
RABAT · Meknès · Sefrou · Tendrara
Casablanca · Khemisset · Mohammedia · Azrou · Ifrane
Mohammed V · Berrechid · Moyen Atlas
El-Jadida · Settat · Oued-Zem · Khénifra · Moulouya
Ca Beddouza · Sidi-Bennour · Khouribga · Oum er Rbia
Safi · Beni-Mellal · Béchar
Tensift · El Kelâa Srarhna · Azilal · Jbel Ayachi 3757m · Hamada du Guir · Abadla
MOROCCO · Haut Atlas · Beni A
Essaouira · Menara · Marrakech · Er-Rachidia
Cap Rhir · Jbel Toubkal 4165m · Ouarzazate · Erfoud · Erg er Raoui
Agadir · Imouzzer · Taroudannt · Anti-Atlas · Tabelbala
Sidi-Ifni · Tiznit · Tata · Hamada du Dra · Hamada Tounassine
Bou-Izakarn · Guelmime · Erg Iguîdi
Tan-Tan · Drâa · ALGER...
Tarfaya · Tindouf · Sebkha de Tindouf
LAÂYOUNE · El Mahbas · El Eglab
Saguia al Hamra · Smara · 'Ayoún 'Abd el Málek
Boujdour · Bou Craa · Chegga
WESTERN SAHARA (occupied by Morocco) · Yetti · Erg Chech
Aïn Ben Tili
Galtat-Zemmour · Bir Mogreïn
Tropic of Cancer · TIRIS · 'Ayoún 'Abd el Málek
Ad Dakhla · Sebkhet Aghzoumal · ZEMMOUR · Kâghet · El Hank · 'Erg el Ahmar · Erg Chech
El Mreïti · Taoudenni
Cap Barbas · Adrar Souttouf · Aousard · El Hammâmi · 'Erg I-n-Sâkâ
Zouérat · El Mreyyer · 'Erg I-n-Échal
Fdérik · Tourine · 'Erg Atouila
Aghouinit · Touâjil · El Guettâra
Bir-Gandouz · Techla · Malqteir · 'Erîgât · TOMBOUCTOU
Nouâdhibou · Bou Lanouâr · Châr · Ouarâne · MA
Lagouira · Râs Nouâdhibou · Choûm · El Mrüyer
NOUÂDHIBOU · Atâr · Ouadâne · Araouane
Dakhlet Nouâdhibou · Chinguetti · ADRAR
DAKHLET NOUÂDHIBOU · Oujeft
Et Tîdra · INCHIRI · El Mreyyé
Nouâmghâr · Ras Timirist · Bennichâb · Akjoujt · HODH · Boû Djébéha
Boû Rjeïmât · MAURITANIA · ECH CHARGUI
Sebkhet Ti-n-Dghâmcha · Rachid · TAGANT · Tichit · Oualâta
NOUAKCHOTT · Bella · Tidjikja · Aoukâr
Nouakchott · Idini · Moudjéria · HODH · Néma
TRARZA · Moudjéria · Boûmdeïd · Tâmchekket · Lac Faguibine
Boutilimit · Magta' Lahjar · Guérou · Kiffa · Tombouctou
Tiguent · BRAKNA · Aleg · Boûmdeïd · Goundam · Diré
Mederdra · Rkiz · ASSABA · Ayoûn el 'Atroûs · Bassikounou · Niafounké
Rosso · Bogué · Kaédi · Kiffa · Néma · Timbedgha · Amourj · Lac Garou
Saint Louis · Richard Toll · Bababé · Mônguel · HODH EL GHARBI · 'Adel Bagrou · Lac Niangay
Senegal · Padar · Mbout · Tintâne · Kobenni · Lac Aougoundou
Dagana · Maghama · Kankossa · Ould Yenjé · Youvarou
Lac de Guier · Matam · GUIDIMAKA · Nampala · MOPTI
Kébémèr · Louga · Dara · Linguère · Ranérou · Maghama · Kankossa · Bassikounou · Nioro · SÉGOU
DAKAR · Mékhé · GORGOL · Sélibâbi · Yélimane · KAYES · KOULIKORO
Pointe des Almadies · Tivaouane · Touba · Bakel · Ballé
Thiès · Bambey · SENEGAL · Bakel · Yélimane
Rufisque · Mbaké · Diourbel · Vélingara · Kayes
Mbour · Fatick

Madeira (to Portugal) · Funchal · Porto Santo · Ilhas Desertas

La Palma · Santa Cruz de la Palma · Tenerife · Lanzarote · Arrecife
Gomera · Santa Cruz de Tenerife · Fuerteventura · Puerto del Rosario
Hierro · Las Palmas de Gran Canaria
Islas Canarias (Canary Islands) (to Spain) · Gran Canaria · Cap Juby

Elevation scale
6000m
4000m
3000m
2000m
1000m
500m
250m
100m
Sea Level
-250m
-500m
-1000m

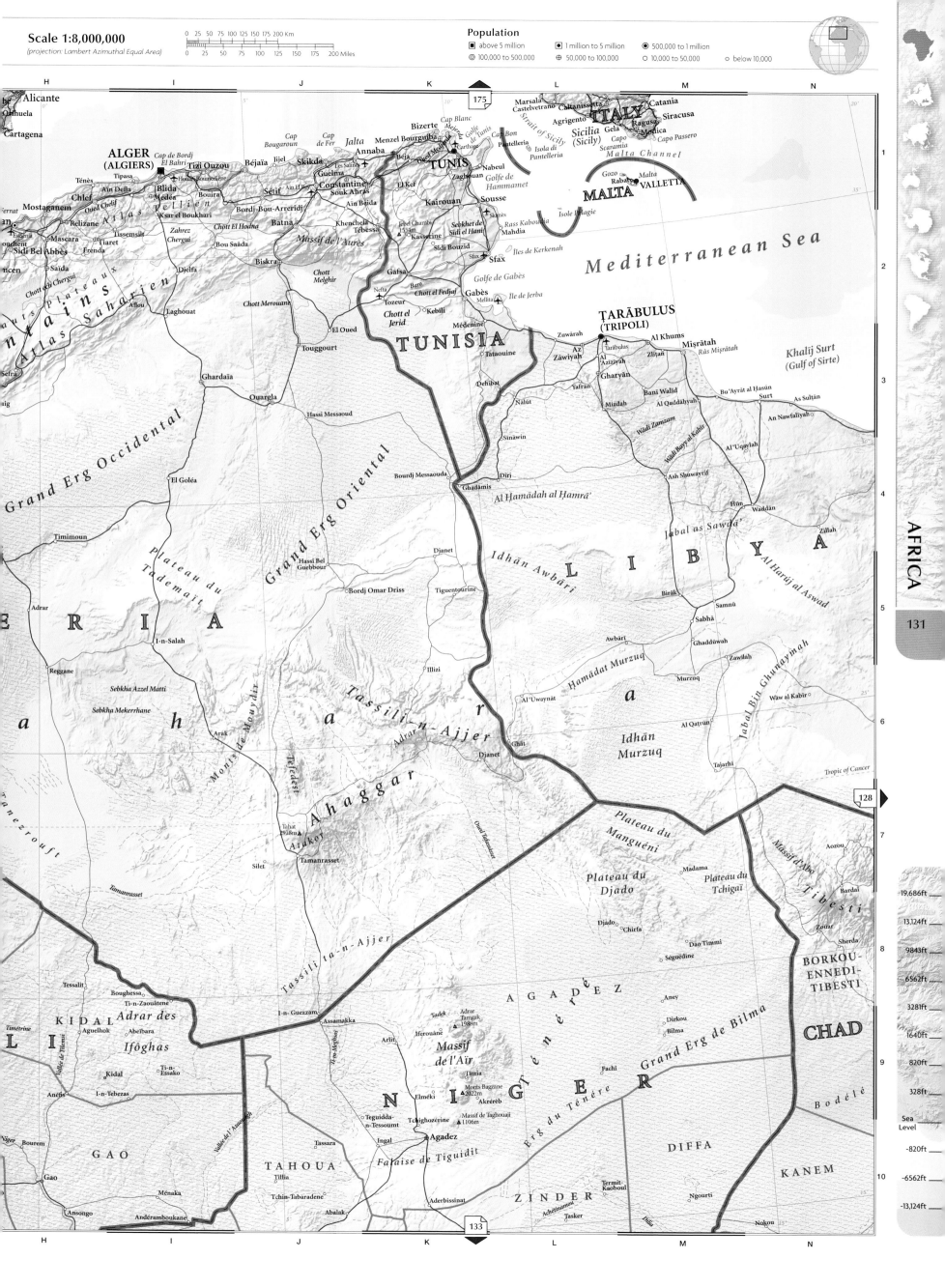

130

290

291

MAURITANIA

TIRIS ZEMMOUR

Cap Barbas
Aghouinit
Touine
Touâjil
Bir-Gandouz
Techla
Char
Malqteïr
Nouâdhibou
Boû Lanouâr
Choûm
Lagouira
Ouadâne
El Mrâyer
El Guettâra
Râs Nouâdhibou
Ouarâne
Dakhlet Nouâdhibou
Atâr
Chinguetti
ADRAR
'Erg Atouila
'Erg I-n-Sâkân
I-n-Echaï
'Erîgât
Taoudenni
DAKHLET NOUÂDHIBOU
Oujeft
INCHIRI
Akjoujt
El Guettâra
Nouâmghâr
Bennichchâb
Râs Tîmîrist
Boû Rjeïmat
El Mreyyé
TOMBOUCTOU
Araouane
Boû Djébéha
Azaouâd
Sebkhet Te-n-Dghâmcha
TAGANT
Tichit
HODH
Azaouâd
NOUAKCHOTT
Bella
Nouakchott
Idini
Rachid
Tidjikja
Moudjéria
Aoukâr
HODH ECH CHARGUI
TRARZA
Boutilimit
Magta' Lahjar
Boûmdeïd
Tâmchekket
Oualâta
Oudeïka
Tiguent
BRAKNA
Guérou
'Ayoûn el 'Atroûs
Néma
Lac Faguibine
Gourma-Rharous
Mederdra
Aleg
Tintâne
'Adel Bagrou
Goundam
Tombouctou
Rkiz
Bogué
Kiffa
HODH EL GHARBI
Kobenni
Amourj
Niafounké
Diré
Niger
M
Rosso
Dagana
Podor
Bababé
Monguel
Kankossa
Timbedgha
Bassikounou
Lac Garou
Lac Niangay
Richard Toll
Kaédi
ASSABA
Ould Yenjé
Nara
Nampala
Youvarou
Lac Aougoundou
Saint Louis
Lac de Guier
GORGOL
Maghama
Sélibabi
Yélimané
Sandaré
Diéma
Sokolo
Niono
Ténenkou
Diaka
Konna
Douentza
Louga
Vallée de Ferlo
Matam
GUIDIMAKA
Nioro
Ballé
Dioura
Mopti
Sévaré
MOPTI
Kébémer
Linguère
Ranérou
Bakel
Kayes
Marena
Mourdiah
Diafarabé
Bandiagara
Dakar
Pointe des Almadies
Mékhé
Dara
Kidira
Ambidédi
KAYES
Diourbel
Bambey
Vélingara
Goudiri
Diamon
Bafoulabé
Kolokani
Banamba
SÉGOU
Markala
Djenné
Bankass
Koro
Ouahigouya
DAKAR
Thiès
Touba
Mbaké
Sadiola
Kita
Sebekoro
Banamba
Ségou
Bani
Tominian
Tiou
Tikaré
Rufisque
Mbour
Fatick
Kaffrine
SENEGAL
Saloum
Tambacounda
Dialakoto
Lac de Manantali
Kéniéba
Kokofata
Kati
Koulikoro
Fana
Bla
Niéna
Bénéna
Tougan
Gourcy
Yako
S a
Joal-Fadiout
Kaolack
Sokone
Koungheul
Maka
KOULIKORO
Dioïla
Koutiala
Sikasso
Nouna
Dédougou
Réo
OUAGADOUGOU
GAMBIA
BANJUL
Banjul
Mansa Konko
Georgetown
Basse Santa Su
Vélingara
Médina Gounas
Saraya
Satadougou
BAMAKO
Bamako
Koulikoro
Koutiala
SIKASSO
Sikasso
Orodara
Bobo-Dioulasso
Ouessa
Léo
Boromo
BUR
Brikama
Dioulouou
Bignona
Sédhiou
Farim
Kolda
Kédougou
Mali
Yanfolila
Garalo
Kolondiéba
Bougouni
Sindou
Banfora
Gaoua
Kampti
Batié
Wa
Ziguinchor
Cacheu
Bissorã
Gabu
Bafata
Koundara
Tamgué 1538m
Nérékoré
Lac de Sélingué
Bougouni
SIKASSO
Kadiolo
Sidéradougou
Diébougou
Lawra
Nadawli
Quinhámel
Bolama
Mansôa
Rio Corubal
Gaoual
Labé
Siguiri
Mananké
Manankoro
Ouangolodougou
Sinmon
Ouangolodougou
Wa
BISSAU
GUINEA-BISSAU
Bissau
Fulacunda
Buba
Catió
Boké
Koubia
Télimélé
Pita
FOUTA DJALLON
Fouta Djallon
Dinguiraye
Kouroussa
Mandiana
IVORY COAST
Ouangolodougou
Tengréla
Kong
Bouna
Téhini
Kimtham
Kavendou 1421m
Dabola
Niger
Kankan
Samatiguila
Madinani
Odienné
Korhogo
Ferkessédougou
Gaoua
Black Volta
Kamsar
Boffa
Dubréka
Frig
Kindia
Manon
Faranah
Tokounou
Kérouané
Bako
Boundiali
Ouangolodougou
Orodara
Béoumi
Sandégué
Tandat
Wenchi
CONAKRY
Coyah
Conakry
Forécariah
Mongo
Kaléta
Bintimani 1948m
Kissidougou
Borotou
Touba
Kani
Séguéla
Katiola
Dabakala
Bondoukou
Sunyani
Fijn
Mampong
Port Loko
Kambia
Pendembu
Makeni
Koidu
Guékédou
Macenta
Pic de Tibé 1504m
Beyla
Man
Vavoua
Zuénoula
Bouaflé
Mbahiakro
Agnibilékrou
Goaso
Bibiani
Kumasi
FREETOWN
Pepel
Lunsar
Magburaka
Kolahun
Vonjama
Boola
Touba
Biankouma
Sifié
Mankono
Bouaké
Tiébissou
Ouellé
GH
Obuasi
SIERRA LEONE
Shenge
Bo
Kenema
Moyamba
Zórzor
Yomou
Nzérékoré
Lola
Danané
Daloa
Zoukougbeu
YAMOUSSOUKRO
Dimbokro
Abengourou
Akoupé
Adzopé
Enchi
Dur
Bonthe
Matru
Pujehun
Ganta
Sanniquellie
Saclepea
Tapeta
Toulépleu
Guiglo
Issia
Oumé
Yamoussoukro
San Pédro
Aboisso
Prestea
Tarkwa
Sulima
Robertsport
Gbanga
Kakata
Harbel
Buchanan
Duékoué
Gagnoa
Lakota
Tiassalé
Divo
Agboville
Grand-Bassam
Half Assini
Axim
Sekon
Tako
MONROVIA
Monrovia
Marshall
LIBERIA
Zwedru
Taï
Soubré
Guéyo
Guitri
Dabou
Abidjan
Port-Bouet
Cavalla
Cess
River Cess
Sassandra
Fresco
Grand-Lahou
Greenville
Grabo
San Pédro
Grand-Bassam
Cape Three Points
Grand Cess
Plibo
Tabou
Harper
Cape Palmas

ATLANTIC OCEAN

6000m
4000m
3000m
2000m
1000m
500m
250m
100m
Sea Level
−250m
−500m
−1000m

CAPE VERDE

Santo Antão
Pombas
Ilhas de Barlavento
Pedra Lume
Mindelo
Ribeira Brava
Amílcar Cabral
Sal
São Vicente
São Nicolau
Boa Vista
João Barrosa
ATLANTIC OCEAN
Maio
Tarrafal
Maio
Fogo
São Filipe
Santiago
PRAIA
Ilhas de Sotavento

Scale 1:8,000,000
0 50 100 Km
0 50 100 Miles

ASCENSION ISLAND (to Saint Helena)

North Point
Porpoise Point
Sisters Peak
North East Bay
Clarence Bay
GEORGETOWN
The Peak 859m
South East Bay
South West Bay
Portland Point
Wideawake
South East Bay
Mars Bay
Airfield
Pillar Bay
ATLANTIC OCEAN

Scale 1:750,000
0 5 10 Km
0 5 10 Miles

TRISTAN DA CUNHA (to Saint Helena)

ATLANTIC OCEAN
Big Point
Rookery Point
EDINBURGH
Anchorstock Point
Sandy Point
Queen Mary's Peak 2060m
Longbluff
Lyon Point
Cave Point
Stonybeach Bay
Stonyhill Point

Scale 1:750,000
0 5 10 Km
0 5 10 Miles

SAINT HELENA (to UK)

Sugar Loaf Point
Flagstaff Bay
JAMESTOWN
The Haystack 616m
Horse Pasture Point
Longwood
Egg Island
Diana's Peak 823m
Gill Point
South West Point
Long Range Point
Speery Island
Castle Rock Point
ATLANTIC OCEAN

Scale 1:750,000
0 5 10 Km
0 5 10 Miles

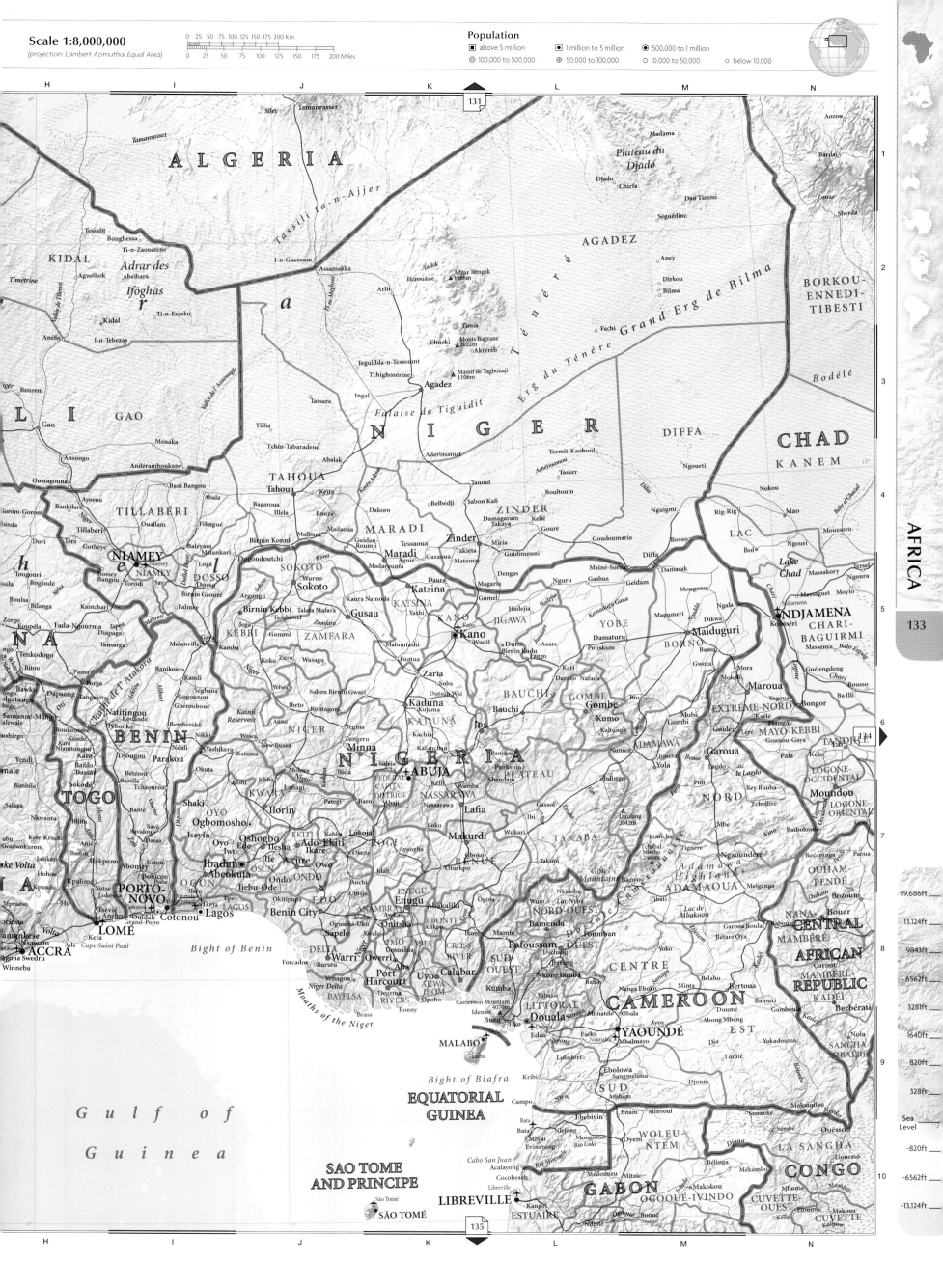

AFRICA

134

128

136

133

NIGER

NIGERIA

CHAD

CAMEROON

CENTRAL AFRICAN REPUBLIC

SUDAN

NORTHERN KORDOFAN

SOUTHERN KORDOFAN

WESTERN KORDOFAN

NORTHERN DARFUR

WESTERN DARFUR

SOUTHERN DARFUR

NORTHERN BAHR EL GHAZAL

WESTERN BAHR EL GHAZAL

WARAB

WAHDA

JONGLEI

EL BUHAYRAT

WESTERN EQUATORIA

EL GABEL

ORIENTALE

EQUATEUR

DEMOCRATIC

CONGO BASIN

EQUATORIAL GUINEA

UGANDA

Lake Albert

Lake Chad

NDJAMENA

YAOUNDÉ

BANGUI

LIBREVILLE

MALABO

KANEM

DIFFA

ZINDER

AGADEZ

BORKOU-ENNEDI-TIBESTI

BATHA

BILTINE

OUADDAI

GUÉRA

SALAMAT

MOYEN-CHARI

CHARI-BAGUIRMI

LAC

MAYO-KÉBBI

TANDJILÉ

LOGONE OCCIDENTAL

LOGONE ORIENTAL

VAKAGA

HAUTE-KOTTO

BAMINGUI-BANGORAN

NANA-GRÉBIZI

OUHAM

OUHAM-PENDE

OUAKA

KÉMO

BASSE-KOTTO

MBOMOU

HAUT-MBOMOU

OMBENA-MPOKO

LOBAYE

SANGHA-MBAÉRÉ

MAMBÉRÉ-KADÉI

NANA-MAMBERE

LA SANGHA

LIKOUALA

CUVETTE-OUEST

OGOOUÉ-IVINDO

WOLEU NTEM

ESTUAIRE

EXTRÈME-NORD

NORD

ADAMAOUA

CENTRE

EST

SUD

LITTORAL

OUEST

NORD-OUEST

SUD-OUEST

BORNO

YOBE

JIGAWA

KANO

KADUNA

BAUCHI

GOMBE

BENUE

TARABA

ADAMAWA

CROSS RIVER

Adamawa Highlands

Massif du Kapka

Jebel Marra 3071m

Falaise de Tiguidit

Bodélé

Sahel

Sudd

El Obeid

Kano

Maiduguri

Abéché

Mongo

Moundou

Garoua

Ngaoundéré

Bertoua

Douala

Bouar

Berbérati

Nola

Ouésso

Mbandaka

Kisangani

Bangassou

Birao

Bria

Nyala

El Fasher

El Geneina

6000m
4000m
3000m
2000m
1000m
500m
250m
100m
Sea Level
-250m
-500m
-1000m

Southern Africa

SOUTH AFRICA: CAPITAL CITIES

TSHWANE (PRETORIA) – administrative capital
CAPE TOWN – legislative capital
BLOEMFONTEIN – judicial capital

135

291

292

6000m
4000m
3000m
2000m
1000m
500m
250m
100m
Sea Level
-250m
-500m
-1000m

ATLANTIC OCEAN

ANGOLA
NAMIBIA
BOTSWANA
ZAMBIA
SOUTH AFRICA
LESOTHO

WINDHOEK
GABORONE
LUSAKA
BLOEMFONTEIN
CAPE TOWN
MASERU
TSHWANE (PRETORIA)
Johannesburg
Kimberley
Port Elizabeth
Livingstone
Bulawayo
Francistown

Kalahari Desert
Okavango Delta
Tropic of Capricorn

NORTHERN CAPE
WESTERN CAPE
EASTERN CAPE
FREE STATE
NORTH-WEST
LIMPOPO
GAUTENG

NORTH WESTERN
COPPERBELT
WESTERN
SOUTHERN
CENTRAL

CAPRIVI
KAVANGO
OMUSATI
OSHANA
OHANGWENA
OTJIKOTO
KUNENE
ERONGO
KHOMAS
HARDAP
KARAS
OMAHEKE
OTJOZONDJUPA

GHANZI
NORTH-WEST
CENTRAL
KWENENG
KGALAGADI
SOUTHERN
SOUTH-EAST

MATABELELAND NORTH
MATABELELAND SOUTH

BENGUELA
HUAMBO
HUILA
NAMIBE
BIÉ
MOXICO
CUANDO CUBANGO
CUNENE

Namaqualand
Damaraland
Ovamboland
Great Karoo
Little Karoo

Scale 1:8,000,000
(projection: Lambert Azimuthal Equal Area)

| 0 | 25 | 50 | 75 | 100 | 125 | 150 | 175 | 200 Km |
| 0 | 25 | 50 | 75 | 100 | 125 | 150 | 175 | 200 Miles |

Population
- ■ above 5 million
- ◉ 100,000 to 500,000
- ■ 1 million to 5 million
- ⊕ 50,000 to 100,000
- ◉ 500,000 to 1 million
- ○ 10,000 to 50,000
- ∘ below 10,000

137

288

COMOROS

MOZAMBIQUE

MADAGASCAR

MALAWI

ZAMBEZIA

NAMPULA

CABO DELGADO

NIASSA

TETE

MANICA

SOFALA

INHAMBANE

GAZA

MAPUTO

SWAZILAND

ZIMBABWE

HARARE

MASHONALAND CENTRAL

MASHONALAND EAST

MANICALAND

MASVINGO

KWAZULU/ NATAL

Mozambique Channel

INDIAN OCEAN

LILONGWE

BLANTYRE

Lake Nyasa

Lake Chilwa

Nampula

Pemba

MAMOUDZOU
MAYOTTE
(to France)

Comoro Islands

Mahajanga

MAHAJANGA

ANTSIRAÑANA

Antsirañana

TOAMASINA

Toamasina

ANTANANARIVO

FIANARANTSOA

Fianarantsoa

TOLIARA

Toliara

Tôlañaro

Tropic of Capricorn

Quelimane

Beira

MAPUTO

Matola

MBABANE

Manzini

Durban

Pietermaritzburg

Baía de Sofala

Ilha do Bazaruto

Ponta São Sebastião

Ponta da Barra Falsa

Ponta da Barra

Inhambane

Cabo de Santa Maria

Bassas da India
(to France)

Île Juan de Nova
(to France)

Nosy Be

Nosy Glorieuses

Tanjona Bobaomby

Tanjona Anorontany

Maromokotro
2876m

Nosy Sainte Marie

Nosy Varika

Tanjona Masoala

Tanjona Vilanandro

Tanjona Ankaboa

Tanjona Vohimena

Scale 1:4,500,000
| 0 | 20 | 40 | 60 | 80 Km |
| 0 | 20 | 40 | 60 | 80 Miles |

COMOROS

Grande Comore

MORONI

Mitsamiouli

Le Kartala
2361m

Mohéli

Anjouan

Moutsamoudou

MAYOTTE
(to France)

MAMOUDZOU

Comoro Islands

INDIAN OCEAN

Mozambique Channel

Scale 1:8,000,000
| 0 | 25 | 50 | 75 | 100 | 125 | 150 Km |
| 0 | 25 | 50 | 75 | 100 | 125 | 150 Miles |

19,686ft
13,124ft
9843ft
6562ft
3281ft
1640ft
820ft
328ft
Sea Level
-820ft
-6562ft
-13,124ft

288

AFRICA

140

ATLANTIC OCEAN

WINDHOEK

CAPE TOWN

ERONGO KHOMAS OMAHEKE GHANZI BOTSW

NAMIBIA

Kalahari Desert KGALAGADI

HARDAP KARAS Namaqualand

NORTHERN CAPE SOUTH NORTH

WESTERN CAPE Great Karoo

6000m
4000m
3000m
2000m
1000m
500m
250m
100m
Sea Level
-250m
-500m
-1000m

291

293

SOUTH AFRICA: CAPITAL CITIES

TSHWANE (PRETORIA) – administrative capital
CAPE TOWN – legislative capital
BLOEMFONTEIN – judicial capital

Tropic of Capricorn

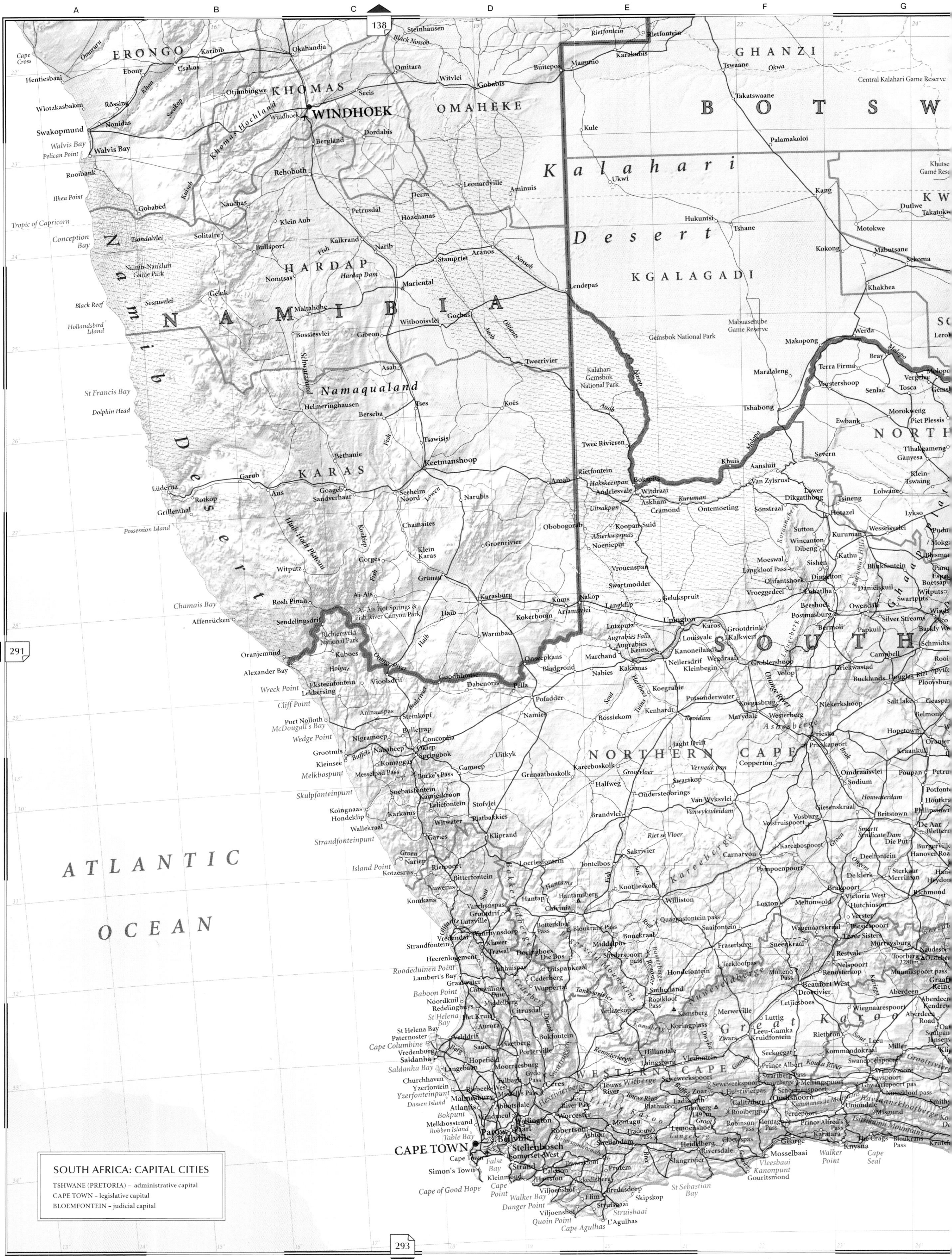

Algiers

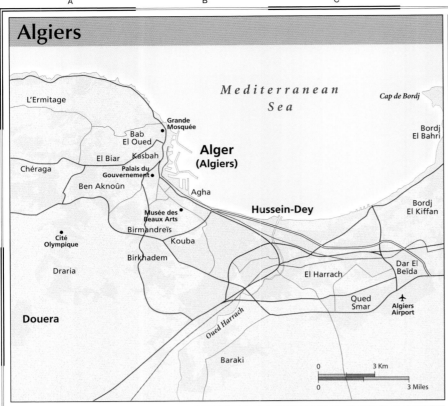

L'Ermitage
Mediterranean Sea
Cap de Bordj
Grande Mosquée
Bab El Oued
Alger (Algiers)
Bordj El Bahri
Kasbah
El Biar
Palais du Gouvernement
Chéraga
Ben Aknoûn
Agha
Bordj El Kiffan
Musée des Beaux Arts
Hussein-Dey
Birmandreïs
Cité Olympique
Kouba
Birkhadem
Dar El Beïda
Draria
El Harrach
Douera
Oued Harrach
Qued Smar
Algiers Airport
Baraki

0   3 Km
0   3 Miles

Cairo

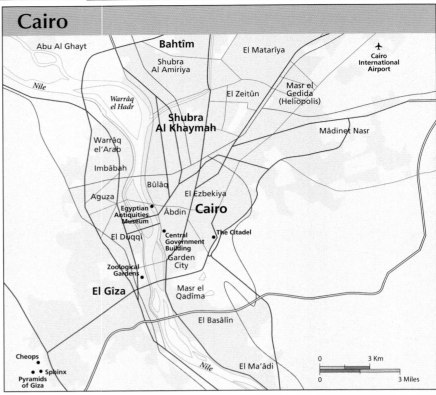

Abu Al Ghayt
Bahtîm
El Matarîya
Cairo International Airport
Shubra Al Amiriya
Nile
El Zeitûn
Masr el Gedida (Heliopolis)
Warrâq el Hadr
Shubra Al Khaymah
Mâdinet Nasr
Warrâq el'Arab
Imbâbah
Bûlâq
El Ezbekiya
Aguza
Egyptian Antiquities Museum
Âbdin
Cairo
El Duqqi
Central Government Building
The Citadel
Zoological Gardens
Garden City
El Gîza
Masr el Qadîma
El Basâlin
Cheops
Sphinx
Nile
El Ma'âdi
Pyramids of Giza

0   3 Km
0   3 Miles

Cape Town

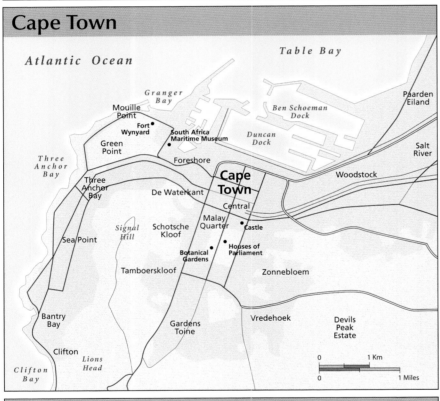

Atlantic Ocean
Table Bay
Granger Bay
Paarden Eiland
Mouille Point
Ben Schoeman Dock
Fort Wynyard
South Africa Maritime Museum
Duncan Dock
Green Point
Foreshore
Salt River
Three Anchor Bay
Cape Town
Three Anchor Bay
De Waterkant
Woodstock
Central
Sea Point
Signal Hill
Malay Quarter
Castle
Schotsche Kloof
Houses of Parliament
Botanical Gardens
Tamboerskloof
Zonnebloem
Bantry Bay
Gardens Toine
Vredehoek
Devils Peak Estate
Clifton
Lions Head
Clifton Bay

0   1 Km
0   1 Miles

Casablanca

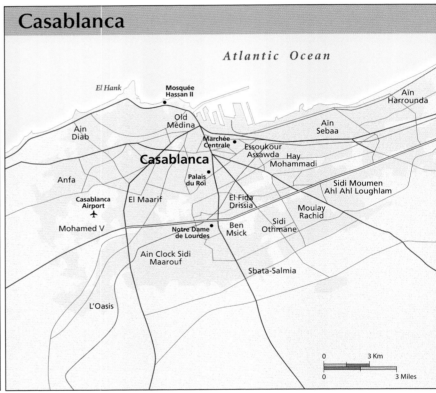

Atlantic Ocean
El Hank
Mosquée Hassan II
Aïn Harrounda
Old Medina
Aïn Diab
Aïn Sebaa
Marchée Centrale
Essoukour Assâwda
Hay Mohammadi
Casablanca
Anfa
Palais du Roi
Sidi Moumen Ahl Ahl Loughlam
Casablanca Airport
El Maarif
El Fida Drissia
Moulay Rachid
Mohamed V
Notre Dame de Lourdes
Ben Msick
Sidi Othmane
Ain Clock Sidi Maarouf
Sbata-Salmia
L'Oasis

0   3 Km
0   3 Miles

Dakar

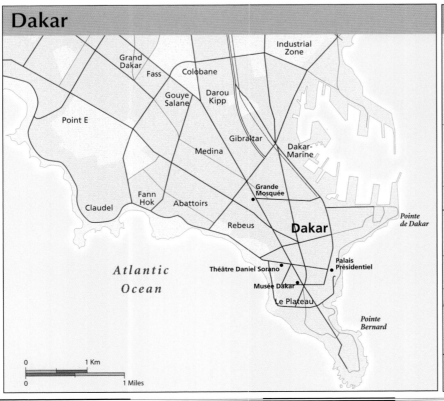

Industrial Zone
Grand Dakar
Kensington
Fass
Colobane
Point E
Gouye Salane
Darou Kipp
Gibraltar
Dakar-Marine
Medina
Claudel
Fann Hok
Abattoirs
Grande Mosquée
Rebeus
Dakar
Pointe de Dakar
Théâtre Daniel Sorano
Palais Présidentiel
Musée Dakar
Atlantic Ocean
Le Plateau
Pointe Bernard

0   1 Km
0   1 Miles

Harare

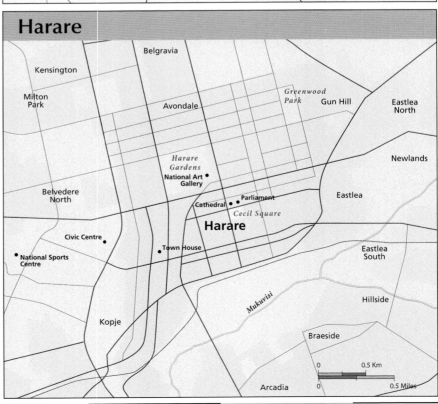

Belgravia
Kensington
Milton Park
Avondale
Greenwood Park
Gun Hill
Eastlea North
Harare Gardens
National Art Gallery
Newlands
Belvedere North
Cathedral
Parliament
Eastlea
Cecil Square
Civic Centre
Harare
National Sports Centre
Town House
Eastlea South
Mukuvisi
Hillside
Kopje
Braeside
Arcadia

0   0.5 Km
0   0.5 Miles

Johannesburg

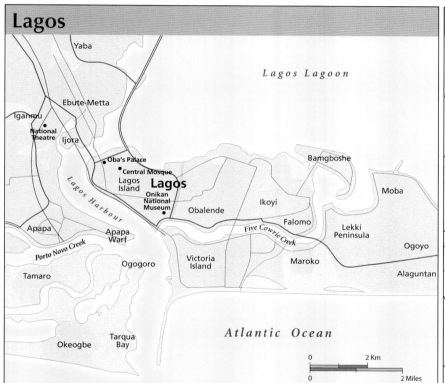

Diepsloot N.R.
Tembisa
Sandton
Randburg
Modderfontein
Alexandra
Kempton Park
Krugersdorp
Wits University
Johannesburg
Edenvale
Photographic Museum
National School of Arts
Museum of Africa
Johannesburg Library
Bedfordview
O.R. Tambo International Airport
Boksburg
Germiston
National Exhibition Centre
Soweto
Elsburg
Kliprivriesberg N.R.
Alberton
Lenasia
Klip

0   10 Km
0   10 Miles

Kinshasa

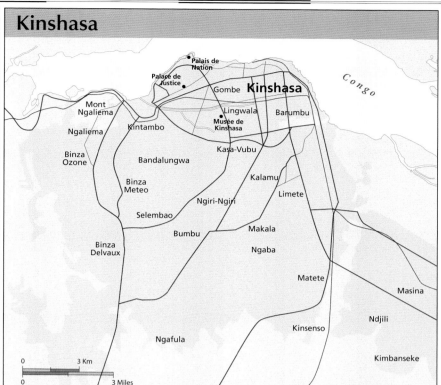

Palais de Nation
Palace de Justice
Gombe
Kinshasa
Congo
Mont Ngaliema
Lingwala
Barumbu
Ngaliema
Kintambo
Musée de Kinshasa
Binza Ozone
Bandalungwa
Kasa-Vubu
Kalamu
Binza Meteo
Ngiri-Ngiri
Limete
Selembao
Makala
Bumbu
Binza Delvaux
Ngaba
Matete
Masina
Ngafula
Kinsenso
Ndjili
Kimbanseke

0   3 Km
0   3 Miles

Lagos

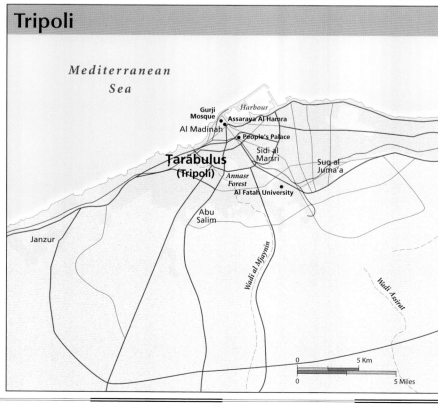

Yaba
Lagos Lagoon
Ebute-Metta
Iganmu
National Theatre
Ijora
Oba's Palace
Central Mosque
Lagos Island
Onikan National Museum
Lagos
Bamgboshe
Lagos Harbour
Obalende
Ikoyi
Moba
Apapa
Apapa Warf
Falomo
Lekki Peninsula
Porto Novo Creek
Five Cowrie Creek
Ogogoro
Victoria Island
Maroko
Ogoyo
Tamaro
Alaguntan
Atlantic Ocean
Okeogbe
Tarqua Bay

0   2 Km
0   2 Miles

Nairobi

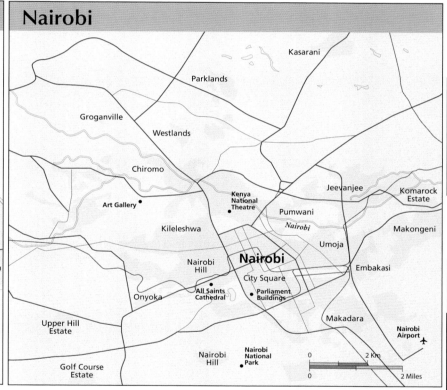

Kasarani
Parklands
Groganville
Westlands
Chiromo
Jeevanjee
Komarock Estate
Art Gallery
Kenya National Theatre
Pumwani
Nairobi
Makongeni
Kileleshwa
Nairobi Hill
Nairobi
Umoja
City Square
Embakasi
Onyoka
All Saints Cathedral
Parliament Buildings
Makadara
Upper Hill Estate
Nairobi Airport
Golf Course Estate
Nairobi Hill
Nairobi National Park

0   2 Km
0   2 Miles

Tripoli

Mediterranean Sea
Gurji Mosque
Harbour
Al Madinah
Assaraya Al Hamra
People's Palace
Ṭarābulus (Tripoli)
Sīdi al Marsri
Suq al Juma'a
Annasr Forest
Al Fatah University
Abu Salim
Janzur
Wadi al Mjaynin
Wadi Asrirat

0   5 Km
0   5 Miles

Tunis

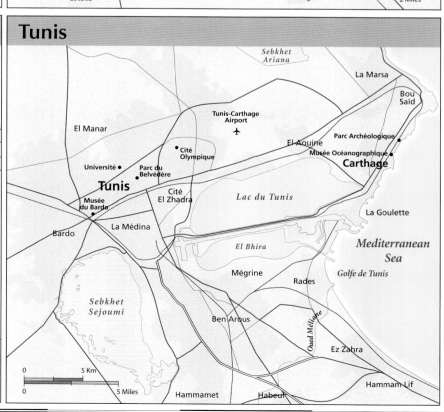

Sebkhet Ariana
La Marsa
Bou Saïd
Tunis-Carthage Airport
El Manar
Parc Archéologique
Cité Olympique
El Aouine
Musée Océanographique
Université
Parc du Belvédère
Carthage
Tunis
Cité El Zhadra
Musée du Bardo
Lac du Tunis
La Goulette
Bardo
La Médina
El Bhira
Mediterranean Sea
Golfe de Tunis
Mégrine
Rades
Sebkhet Sejoumi
Ben Arous
Oued Méliane
Ez Zahra
Hammamet
Habeul
Hammam Lif

0   5 Km
0   5 Miles

AFRICA

143

Europe is the world's second smallest continent with a total area of 4,053,309 sq miles (10,498,000 sq km). It comprises 45 separate countries, including Turkey and the Russian Federation, although the greater parts of these nations lie in Asia.

FACTFILE

N **Most Northerly Point:** Ostrov Rudol'fa, Russian Federation 81° 47' N

S **Most Southerly Point:** Gávdos, Greece 34° 51' N

E **Most Easterly Point:** Mys Flissingskiy, Novaya Zemlya, Russian Federation 69° 03' E

W **Most Westerly Point:** Bjargtangar, Iceland 24° 33' W

Largest Lakes:
1. Lake Ladoga, Russian Federation 7100 sq miles (18,390 sq km)
2. Lake Onega, Russian Federation 3819 sq miles (9891 sq km)
3. Vänern, Sweden 2141 sq miles (5545 sq km)
4. Lake Peipus, Estonia/Russian Federation 1372 sq miles (3555 sq km)
5. Vättern, Sweden 737 sq miles (1910 sq km)

Longest Rivers:
1. Volga, Russian Federation 2265 miles (3645 km)
2. Danube, C Europe 1771 miles (2850 km)
3. Dnieper, Belarus/Russian Federation/Ukraine 1421 miles (2287 km)
4. Don, Russian Federation 1162 miles (1870 km)
5. Pechora, Russian Federation 1124 miles (1809 km)

Largest Islands:
1. Britain, 88,700 sq miles (229,800 sq km)
2. Iceland, 39,315 sq miles (101,826 sq km)
3. Ireland, 31,521 sq miles (81,638 sq km)
4. Ostrov Severny, Novaya Zemlya, Russian Federation 18,177 sq miles (47,079 sq km)
5. Spitsbergen, Svalbard 15,051 sq miles (38,981 sq km)

Highest Points:
1. El'brus, Russian Federation 18,510 ft (5642 m)
2. Dykhtau, Russian Federation 17,077 ft (5205 m)
3. Koshtantau, Russian Federation 16,903 ft (5152 m)
4. Jangitau, Georgia/Russian Federation 16,598 ft (5059 m)
5. Pushkin Peak, Georgia/Russian Federation 16,512 ft (5033 m)

Lowest Point:
▼ Caspian Depression, Russian Federation -92 ft (-28 m) below sea level

Highest recorded temperature:
Seville, Spain 122°F (50°C)

Lowest recorded temperature:
Ust' Shchugor, Russian Federation -67°F (-55°C)

Wettest Place:
Crkvice, Bosnia and Herzegovina 183 in (4648 mm)

Driest Place:
Astrakhan', Russian Federation 6.4 in (162.5 mm)

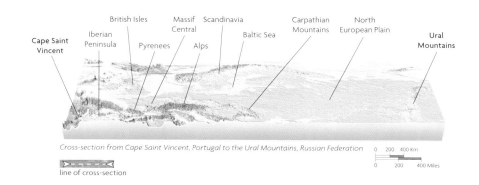

Cross-section from Cape Saint Vincent, Portugal to the Ural Mountains, Russian Federation

line of cross-section

Political

The political boundaries of Europe have changed many times, especially during the 20th century in the aftermath of two world wars, the break-up of the empires of Austria-Hungary, Nazi Germany, and, toward the end of the century, the collapse of communism in eastern Europe. The fragmentation of Yugoslavia has again altered the political map of Europe, highlighting a trend towards nationalism and devolution. In contrast, economic federalism is growing. In 1958, the formation of the European Economic Community (now the European Union or EU) started a move toward economic and political union and increasing internal migration. This process is still ongoing and the accession of Bulgaria and Romania in January 2007 brought the number of EU member states to twenty seven. Of these, thirteen have joined the Eurozone by adopting the Euro as their official currency.

Population
- ▪ above 5 million
- ▪ 1 million to 5 million
- ⊙ 500,000 to 1 million
- ⊙ 100,000 to 500,000
- ⊕ 50,000 to 100,000
- ○ 10,000 to 50,000
- ● Country capital

Borders
- ⟋ full international border

SCALE 1:17,250,000
(projection: Lambert Azimuthal Equal Area)

Km
0 100 200 300 400 500 600 700

Miles
0 100 200 300 400 500 600 700

Map labels

Denmark Strait, Arctic Circle, REYKJAVÍK, **ICELAND**, *Norwegian Sea*, Faeroe Islands (to Denmark), Shetland Islands, *Orkney Islands*, Outer Hebrides, SCOTLAND, Aberdeen, Glasgow, Dundee, NORTHERN IRELAND, Edinburgh, Belfast, IRELAND, Isle of Man (to UK), Newcastle upon Tyne, DUBLIN, UNITED Liverpool, Leeds, Manchester, Sheffield, KINGDOM, WALES, Birmingham, ENGLAND, Cardiff, Thames, Southampton, LONDON, THE HAGUE, Channel Islands (to UK), *English Channel*, le Havre, Seine, BELGIUM, BRUSSELS, Liège, PARIS, St-Nazaire, Rennes, Nantes, Loire, Orléans, *Bay of Biscay*, A Coruña, FRANCE, Limoges, Bordeaux, PORTUGAL, Porto, Duero, Valladolid, Ebro, Toulouse, LISBON, Tagus, MADRID, Zaragoza, ANDORRA LA VELLA, ANDORRA, Marseille, Nice, MONACO, Setúbal, SPAIN, Barcelona, Corsica, Seville, Córdoba, Valencia, Ibiza, Mallorca, Menorca, Murcia, Palma, Gibraltar (to UK), Cádiz, Málaga, Ceuta (to Spain), Balearic Islands, Sardinia, Melilla (to Spain), *Mediterranean Sea*

North Sea, Bergen, OSLO, Stavanger, Kristiansand, NORWAY, Trondheim, SWEDEN, Vänern, Gothenburg, Jönköping, Vättern, Gotland, Ålborg, DENMARK, COPENHAGEN, Helsingborg, Odense, Helsingør, Malmö, *Baltic Sea*, Hamburg, Groningen, Bremen, Hannover, AMSTERDAM, NETH., Nijmegen, Düsseldorf, Elbe, BERLIN, GERMANY, Antwerp, Bonn, Leipzig, Dresden, LUXEMBOURG, Frankfurt am Main, Rhine, Nuremberg, PRAGUE, Stuttgart, CZECH REPUBLIC, Strasbourg, Munich, Salzburg, Zürich, BERN, Geneva, SWITZERLAND, Lyon, Rhône, Alps, Innsbruck, AUSTRIA, LIECHTENSTEIN, VIENNA, Milan, LJUBLJANA, SLOVENIA, Turin, Verona, Genoa, Venice, Trieste, ZAGREB, Bologna, Florence, Pisa, CROATIA, ITALY, Naples, MONACO, SAN MARINO, VATICAN CITY, ROME, *Adriatic Sea*, *Tyrrhenian Sea*, Cagliari, Palermo, Sicily, Messina, Catania, Cosenza, Bari, BOSNIA & HERZEGOVINA, SARAJEVO, Mostar, SERBIA, BELGRADE, MONTENEGRO, PODGORICA, TIRANA, SKOPJE, MACEDONIA, ALBANIA, Salonica, GREECE, *Ionian Sea*, MALTA, VALLETTA, Larisa, *Aegean Sea*, Piraeus, ATHENS, Irákleio, Crete

Barents Sea, Murmansk, *White Sea*, Arkhangel'sk, Northern Dvina, FINLAND, Tampere, Lake Onega, Lake Ladoga, Turku, HELSINKI, Åland, St Petersburg, Uppsala, Örebro, STOCKHOLM, TALLINN, ESTONIA, Vologda, Ventspils, LATVIA, RĪGA, Liepāja, Western Dvina, MOSCOW, LITHUANIA, RUSS. FED. (Kaliningrad), Kaunas, VILNIUS, Vitsyebsk, Tula, Kaliningrad, MINSK, Babruysk, Homyel', BELARUS, Gdańsk, Oder, Bydgoszcz, Vistula, Brest, Voronezh, Poznań, WARSAW, POLAND, Łódź, KIEV, Kharkiv, Wrocław, Kraków, L'viv, UKRAINE, Volgograd, Chernivtsi, Dniester, Dnipropetrovs'k, Donets'k, SLOVAKIA, BRATISLAVA, Miskolc, MOLDOVA, Rostov-na-Donu, Győr, BUDAPEST, CHIŞINĂU, Odesa, Dniepr, Stavropol', Novorossiysk, HUNGARY, Cluj-Napoca, ROMANIA, *Sea of Azov*, Simferopol', BUCHAREST, Braşov, Danube, Constanţa, *Black Sea*, SERBIA, Ruse, Varna, BULGARIA, SOFIA, Burgas, Stara Zagora, Istanbul, Turkey

RUSSIAN FEDERATION, Kirov, Kazan, Nizhniy Novgorod, Yaroslavl', Ul'yanov, Saratov, *Novaya Zemlya*, *Kara Sea*, Vorkuta

Languages

There are three main European language groups: Germanic languages predominate in central and northern Europe; Romance languages in western and Mediterranean Europe and Romania; while Slavic languages are spoken in eastern Europe and the Russian Federation. Isolated pockets of local languages, such as Basque and Gaelic, persist and frequently provide a focus for national identity.

Language groups

- Turkic
- Albanian
- Finno-Ugric/Samoyed
- Germanic
- Slavic
- Romance
- Basque
- Baltic
- Celtic
- Greek
- Caucasian
- Iranian
- Mongol

Population

Europe is a densely populated, urbanized continent; in Belgium over 90% of people live in urban areas. The highest population densities are found in an area stretching east from southern Britain and northern France, into Germany. The northern fringes are only sparsely populated.

Population density
(people per sq km)

- below 49
- 50–99
- 100–149
- 150–199
- 200–299
- above 300

Standard of living

Living standards in western Europe are among the highest in the world, although there is a growing sector of homeless, jobless people. Eastern Europeans have lower overall standards of living—a legacy of stagnated economies.

Standard of living
(UN human development index)

- low
- high
- data not available

Transportation

Despite its fragmented geography and many natural frontiers, communications in Europe are well developed. Extensive motorway links allow rapid road transportation, while high-speed rail connections like France's TGV (*Train à Grande Vitesse*), and the Channel Tunnel have improved rail travel. Outdated communication infrastructures in parts of eastern Europe, and insufficient transport links across the Alps, however, remain weak parts of the network.

Transportation

- major roads and motorways
- major railroads
- international borders
- • transport intersections
- ⊕ major international airports
- ⊕ major ports

SCALE 1:22,500,000
(projection: Lambert Conformal Conic)

Climate

Europe experiences few extremes in either rainfall or temperature, with the exception of the far north and south. Along the west coast, the warm currents of the North Atlantic Drift moderate temperatures. Although east–west air movement is relatively unimpeded by relief, the Alpine Uplands halt the progress of north–south air masses, protecting most of the Mediterranean from cold, north winds.

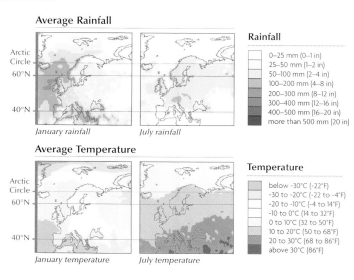

Average Rainfall

January rainfall *July rainfall*

Rainfall

	0–25 mm (0–1 in)
	25–50 mm (1–2 in)
	50–100 mm (2–4 in)
	100–200 mm (4–8 in)
	200–300 mm (8–12 in)
	300–400 mm (12–16 in)
	400–500 mm (16–20 in)
	more than 500 mm (20 in)

Average Temperature

January temperature *July temperature*

Temperature

	below -30°C (-22°F)
	-30 to -20°C (-22 to -4°F)
	-20 to -10°C (-4 to 14°F)
	-10 to 0°C (14 to 32°F)
	0 to 10°C (32 to 50°F)
	10 to 20°C (50 to 68°F)
	20 to 30°C (68 to 86°F)
	above 30°C (86°F)

Climate

	tundra	daily hours of sunshine, January
	subarctic	daily hours of sunshine, July
	cool continental	cold wind
	warm humid	hot wind
	mediterranean	
	semi-arid	

Environmental issues

The partially enclosed waters of the Baltic and Mediterranean seas have become heavily polluted, while the Barents Sea is contaminated with spent nuclear fuel from Russia's navy. Acid rain, caused by emissions from factories and power stations, is actively destroying northern forests. As a result, pressure is growing to safeguard Europe's natural environment and prevent further deterioration.

Environmental issues

	national parks	marine pollution
	acid rain	heavy marine pollution
	polluted rivers	poor urban air quality
	radioactive contamination	

Landuse

Europe's swelling urban population and the outward expansion of many cities has created acute competition for land. Despite this, European resourcefulness has maximized land potential, and over half of Europe's land is still used for a wide variety of agricultural purposes. Land in northern Europe is used for cattle-rearing, pasture, and arable crops. Towards the Mediterranean, the mild climate allows the growing of grapes for wine; olives, sunflowers, tobacco and citrus fruits. EU subsidies, however, have resulted in massive overproduction and a land "set-aside" policy has been introduced.

Using the land and sea

cropland	citrus fruits
forest	cotton
ice cap	fishing
mountain region	fodder
pasture	fruit
tundra	olive oil
wetland	potatoes
major conurbations	rice
cattle	root crops
goats	roses
pigs	shellfish
poultry	sunflowers
reindeer	timber
sheep	tobacco
cereals	vineyards

EUROPE

1   VATNAJÖKULL, ICELAND
Europe's largest ice cap is located in the southeast of this Atlantic island.

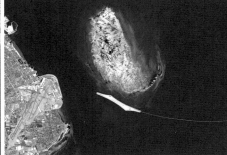

2   ORESUND LINK, DENMARK/SWEDEN
This link was opened to traffic in 2000, joining the Danish capital, Copenhagen, with the Swedish town of Malmo across the waters of the Oresund Strait.

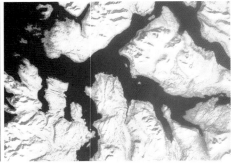

3   BALSFJORD, NORWAY
Fjords were cut into Norway's west coast by glaciers during the last ice age but as the ice retreated rising sea-levels flooded the valleys left behind.

4   PRAGUE, CZECH REPUBLIC
In August 2002 some parts of the capital were still under water after the worst floods in living memory.

9   GIBRALTAR
A British colony since 1713, this rocky promontory commands a strategic position at the southern end of the Iberian Peninsula.

10   BORDEAUX, FRANCE
Famous for its wines, this city sits on the west bank of the Garonne river, which is joined from the east by the Dordogne river.

11   SOUTH FLEVOLAND, NETHERLANDS
This polder was reclaimed from the sea in the early 1970s and is now home to extensive farmland and small towns.

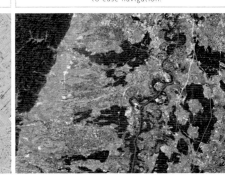

12   RHINE, GERMANY
The Rhine has been straightened in places, such as here, just south of Mannheim, to ease navigation.

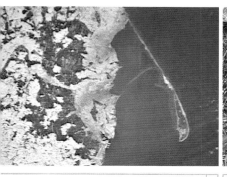

HEL PENINSULA, POLAND 5
The long spit of this peninsula encloses Puck Bay and shelters the important port of Gdynia.

TALLINN, ESTONIA 6
The capital and main port of Estonia has become a popular tourist destination in recent years.

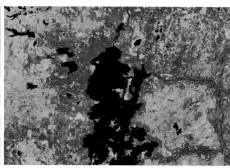

LAKE VODLOZERO, RUSSIAN FEDERATION 7
The lake lies within a national park, which protects one of the most untouched wilderness areas in Europe and encompasses plains, taiga forests, and wetlands.

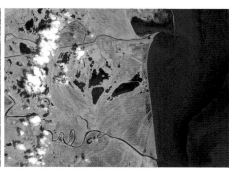

DANUBE DELTA, ROMANIA 8
The Danube river splits into several channels as it flows into the Black Sea, forming one of Europe's most important wetland ecosystems.

VENICE, ITALY 13
Occupying the largest island in a sheltered lagoon at the north end of the Adriatic, this city was founded in 452 CE and grew rich on an extensive trading network.

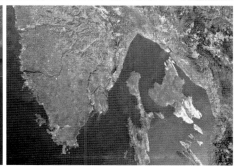

ISTRA PENINSULA, CROATIA 14
This triangular peninsula marks the northern extent of Croatia's Dalmatian coastline.

MOUNT ETNA, SICILY, ITALY 15
This combination of visible and thermal images shows the volcano erupting in July 2001 and clearly indicates the major lava flows.

KEFALLONIÁ, GREECE 16
The largest of the Ionian Islands off Greece's west coast, Kefalloniá is mountainous with relatively high rainfall.

Scandinavia, Finland & Iceland

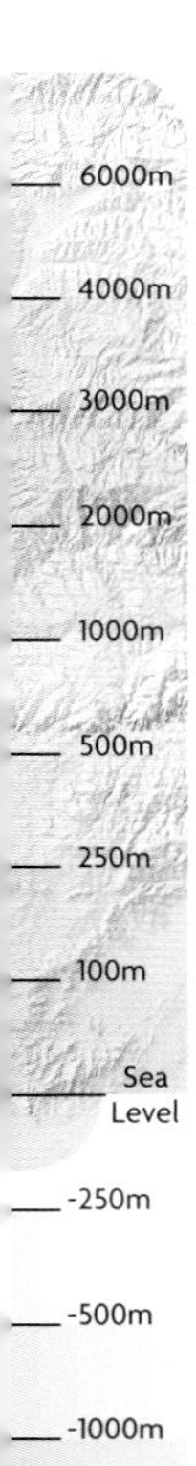

Main map labels

Oceans & Seas
- ARCTIC OCEAN
- Barents Sea
- Greenland Sea
- Denmark Strait
- Norwegian Sea
- ATLANTIC OCEAN

Countries & Regions
- RUSSIAN FEDERATION
- MURMANSKAYA OBLAST'
- RESPUBLIKA KARELIYA
- LAPPI
- OULU
- FINNMARK
- TROMS
- NORDLAND
- NORRBOTTEN
- VÄSTERBOTTEN
- NORD-TRØNDELAG
- LAPPLAND
- SVALBARD (to Norway)
- SPITSBERGEN
- LONGYEARBYEN

Selected settlements
- Murmansk
- Severomorsk
- Nikel
- Kirkenes
- Vadsø
- Vardø
- Hammerfest
- Tromsø
- Narvik
- Bodø
- Luleå
- Oulu
- Kiruna
- Inari
- Rovaniemi
- Kemi

Elevation scale (left margin)
- 6000m
- 4000m
- 3000m
- 2000m
- 1000m
- 500m
- 250m
- 100m
- Sea Level
- -250m
- -500m
- -1000m

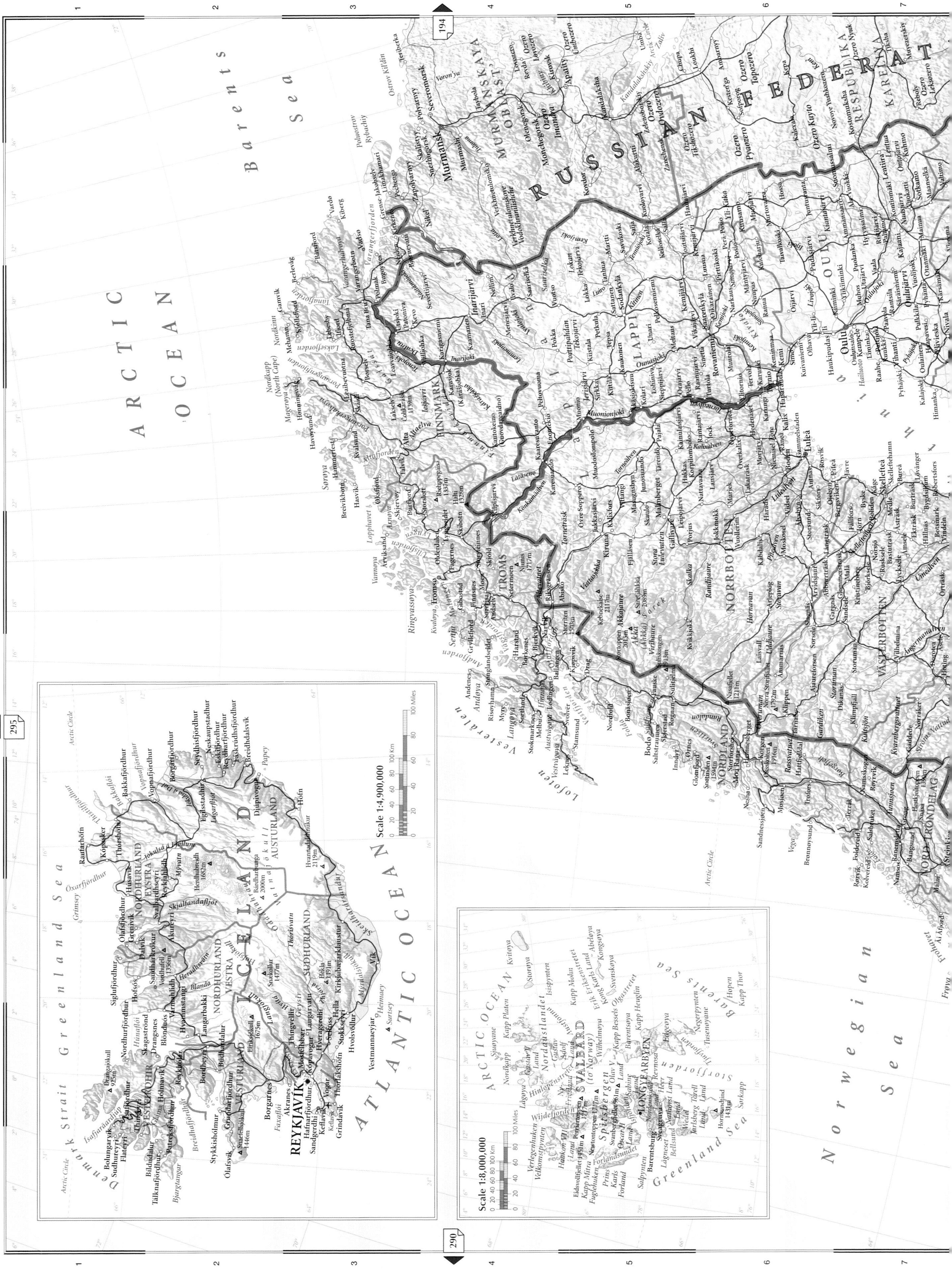

Iceland inset map
Scale 1:4,900,000

- ICELAND
- REYKJAVÍK
- Keflavík
- Akureyri
- Selfoss
- Höfn
- NORDHURLAND VESTRA
- NORDHURLAND EYSTRA
- AUSTURLAND
- SUDHURLAND
- VESTURLAND
- VESTFIRDHIR
- Vatnajökull
- Vík
- Grindavík
- Borgarnes
- Ísafjördhur

Scale bar: 0 20 40 60 80 100 Miles / 0 20 40 60 80 100 Km

Svalbard inset map
Scale 1:8,000,000

- ARCTIC OCEAN
- Barents Sea
- Greenland Sea
- SVALBARD (to Norway)
- SPITSBERGEN
- LONGYEARBYEN
- Nordaustlandet
- Edgeøya
- Barentsøya
- Kvitøya
- Hopen

Scale bar: 0 20 40 60 80 100 Miles / 0 20 40 60 80 100 Km

Grid and cross-references
194
295
290

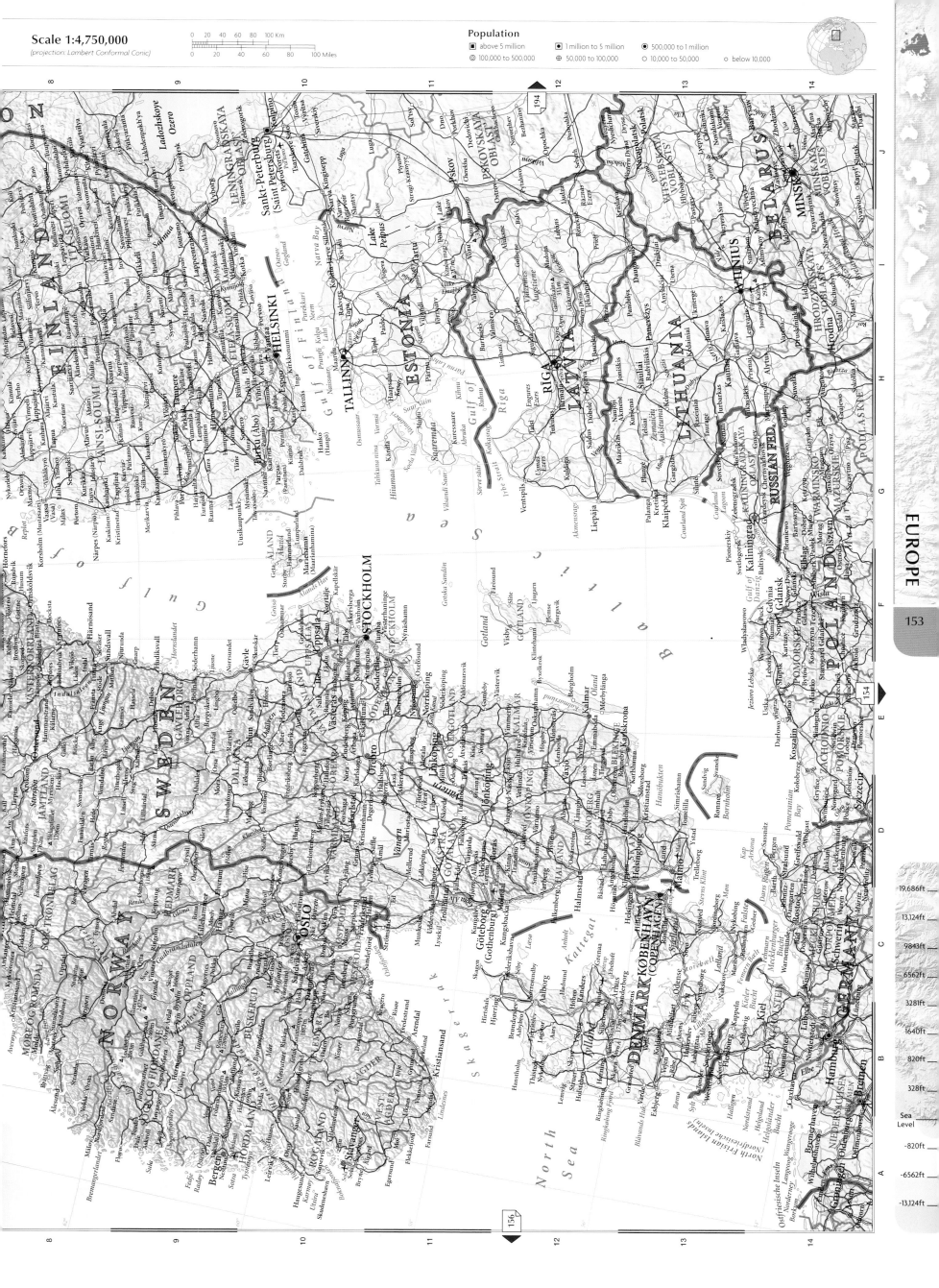

Scale 1:4,750,000
(projection: Lambert Conformal Conic)

0 20 40 60 80 100 Km
0 20 40 60 80 100 Miles

Population

■ above 5 million ▣ 1 million to 5 million ◉ 500,000 to 1 million
◎ 100,000 to 500,000 ⊡ 50,000 to 100,000 ○ 10,000 to 50,000 ○ below 10,000

153
153
290

EUROPE — Southern Scandinavia

Elevation scale:
- 6000m
- 4000m
- 3000m
- 2000m
- 1000m
- 500m
- 250m
- 100m
- Sea Level
- -250m
- -500m
- -1000m

FAEROE ISLANDS (to Denmark)
Kunoy, Bordhoy, Fugloy, Streymoy, Svinoy, Vestmanna, Kalsoy, Klaksvik, Mykines, Eysturoy, TORSHAVN, Vagar, Nolsoy, Sandoy, Skuvoy, Hisavik, Sudhuroy

ATLANTIC OCEAN

Scale 1:2,500,000
0 5 10 20 Km
0 5 10 20 Miles

Norwegian Sea

Gulf of Bothnia

SWEDEN

NORWAY

NORDLAND

NORD-TRØNDELAG

SØR-TRØNDELAG

JÄMTLAND

VÄSTERNORRLAND

VÄSTERBOTTEN

GÄVLEBORG

DALARNA

HEDMARK

OPPLAND

MØRE OG ROMSDAL

SOGN OG FJORDANE

HORDALAND

BUSKERUD

AKERSHUS

OSLO

UPPSALA

VÄSTMANLAND

ÅLAND

Ålands Hav

Umeå, Skellefteå, Lycksele, Storuman, Vilhelmina, Dorotea, Östersund, Strömsund, Hammerdal, Sundsvall, Härnösand, Sollefteå, Kramfors, Örnsköldsvik, Gävle, Hudiksvall, Söderhamn, Bollnäs, Ljusdal, Mora, Falun, Borlänge, Uppsala

Trondheim, Steinkjer, Namsos, Mosjøen, Brønnøysund, Molde, Kristiansund, Ålesund, Bergen, Voss, Odda, Oslo, Hamar, Lillehammer, Elverum, Kongsvinger, Gjøvik

United Kingdom & Ireland

155

290

ATLANTIC OCEAN

North Sea

UNITED KINGDOM

SCOTLAND

Shetland Islands

Herma Ness
Unst
Fetlar
Out Skerries
Yell
Sullom Voe
Whalsay
Bressay
Lerwick
Hillswick
St Magnus Bay
Mainland
Papa Stour
Scalloway
West Burra
Foula
Fitful Head
Sumburgh Head

Fair Isle

Orkney Islands
Papa Westray
Westray
The North
North Ronaldsay
Rousay
Sanday
Eday
Stronsay
Mainland
Shapinsay
Stromness
Hoy
Scapa
Flow
Kirkwall
Burray
St Margaret's Hope
South Ronaldsay
Pentland Firth
Duncansby Head
John o'Groats
Noss Head
Wick

Dunnet Head
Thurso
Halkirk
Hallalade
Kinbrace
Helmsdale
Brora
Golspie
Dornoch Firth
Tarbat Ness
Loch Eriboll
Strathy Point
Lairg
Bonar Bridge
Dornoch
Tain
Lossiemouth
Elgin
Buckie
Banff
Macduff
Turriff
Kinnaird Head
Fraserburgh
Peterhead
Buchan Ness

Cape Wrath
Durness
Edrachillis Bay
Ben More Assynt
998m
Lochinver
Ullapool
Beinn Dearg
1084m
Invergordon
Forres
Nairn
Keith
Huntly
Ellon
Newburgh
Aberdeen
Girdle Ness
Stonehaven

Ben Kilbreck
912m
Altnaharra
Tongue
Loch Shin
Loch Naver
Cromarty
Moray Firth
Dingwall
Beauly
Inverness
Loch Ness
Aviemore
Grantown-on-Spey
Cairngorm Mountains
1245m
Ben Macdui
1309m
Braemar
Ben Avon
1171m
Alford
Dee
Banchory
Montrose
Arbroath
Carnoustie

Sule Skerry
Stack Skerry

North Rona

Sula Sgeir

Outer Hebrides

Butt of Lewis
Port of Ness
Eoropie Bay
Carloway
Stornoway
Isle of Lewis
Loch Roag
Scarp
Taransay
Harris
Sound of Harris
Lochmaddy
North Uist
Monach Islands
Benbecula
South Uist
Lochboisdale
Eriskay
Barra
Barra Head

Flannan Isles

St Kilda

Shiant Islands
Sea of the Hebrides

The Minch

The Little Minch

Sea of the Hebrides

Raasay
Portree
Uig
Isle of Skye
Kyle of Lochalsh
Kyleakin
Broadford
Canna
Rhum
Eigg
Muck
Point of Ardnamurchan
Ben More
966m

Loch Maree
Loch Torridon
Inner Sound
Stromeferry
Loch Carron
Mallaig
Loch Morar
Fort William
Ben Nevis
1344m
Loch Shiel
Glen Coe
Ballachulish
Loch Linnhe
Oban
Firth of Lorn
Lismore

Tiree
Coll
Iona
Colonsay

Jura
Sound of Jura
Islay
Port Askaig
Port Ellen
Mull of Oa

Crianlarich
Loch Lomond
Callander
Loch Katrine
Loch Ard
Loch Lomond
Dumbarton
Greenock
Gourock
Clydebank
Paisley
Glasgow
East Kilbride
Kilmarnock
Troon
Prescwick
Irvine
Ardrossan

Tarbert
Loch Fyne
Inveraray
Lochgilphead
Loch Awe

Gigha
Island
Campbeltown
Mull of Kintyre
Kintyre

Brodick
Isle of Arran
Ailsa Craig
Ballantrae

Pitlochry
Loch Rannoch
Loch Tay
Crieff
Loch Earn
Tay
Perth
Dundee
Kirriemuir
Forfar
Blairgowrie
Glenrothes
Firth of Tay
St Andrews
Fife Ness
Cupar
Kirkcaldy
Firth of Forth
Dunfermline
Stirling
Alloa
Grangemouth
Falkirk
Cumbernauld
Livingston
Edinburgh
Musselburgh
Bathgate
Airdrie
Motherwell
Wishaw
Hamilton
Lanark
Coatbridge
Peebles

North West Highlands
Grampian Mountains

North Berwick
Haddington
Dunbar

St Abb's Head
Eyemouth
Berwick-upon-Tweed
Holy Island

Duns
Kelso
Coldstream
Galashiels
Selkirk
Jedburgh
Hawick
Moffat
Lockerbie
Langholm
Ayr
Cumnock
Dalmellington
New Galloway

Tory Island
Bloody Foreland
Dunfanaghy
Malin Head
Inishtrahull
Sheep
Haven
Carndonagh
Lough Swilly
Buncrana
Bunbeg
Gweedore
Errigal Mountain
752m

Rathlin Island
Ballycastle
Giant's
Causeway
Portrush
Portstewart
Coleraine
Ballymoney

Tynemouth
South Shields
Blyth
Morpeth
The Cheviot
815m
Alnwick
Bellingham

Elevation scale

6000m
4000m
3000m
2000m
1000m
500m
250m
100m
Sea Level
-250m
-500m
-1000m

290

Elevation legend

- 6000m
- 4000m
- 3000m
- 2000m
- 1000m
- 500m
- 250m
- 100m
- Sea Level
- -250m
- -500m
- -1000m

Sea of the Hebrides

Inner Hebrides

ATLANTIC OCEAN

North Channel

Irish Sea

IRELAND

NORTHERN IRELAND

UNITED KINGDOM

SCOTLAND

Highland

Argyll

Stirlingshire

Ayrshire

Dumfries

ISLE OF MAN (to UK)

Isle of Man

DOUGLAS

Anglesey

DONEGAL

SLIGO

LEITRIM

MAYO

ROSCOMMON

LONGFORD

WEST MEATH

CAVAN

MONAGHAN

MEATH

LOUTH

GALWAY

Connaught

OFFALY

KILDARE

DUBLIN

Belfast

Lough Neagh

Lough Foyle

Lough Erne

Firth of Clyde

Firth of Lorn

Sound of Jura

Islay

Jura

Mull

Isle of Arran

Isle of Bute

Tiree

Coll

Colonsay

Oronsay

Tory Island

Aran Island

Malin Head

Glasgow

Fort William

Ben Nevis 1343m

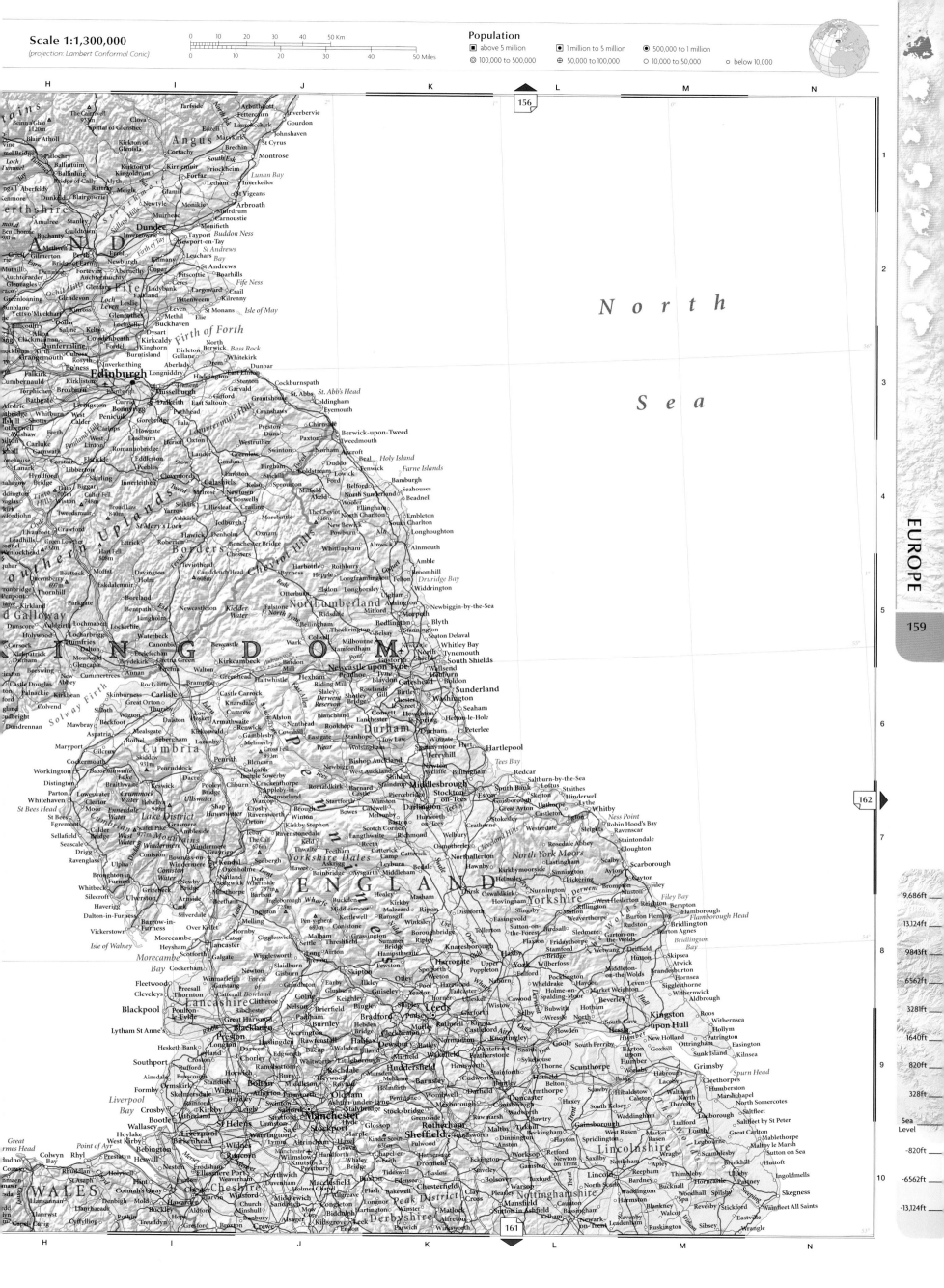

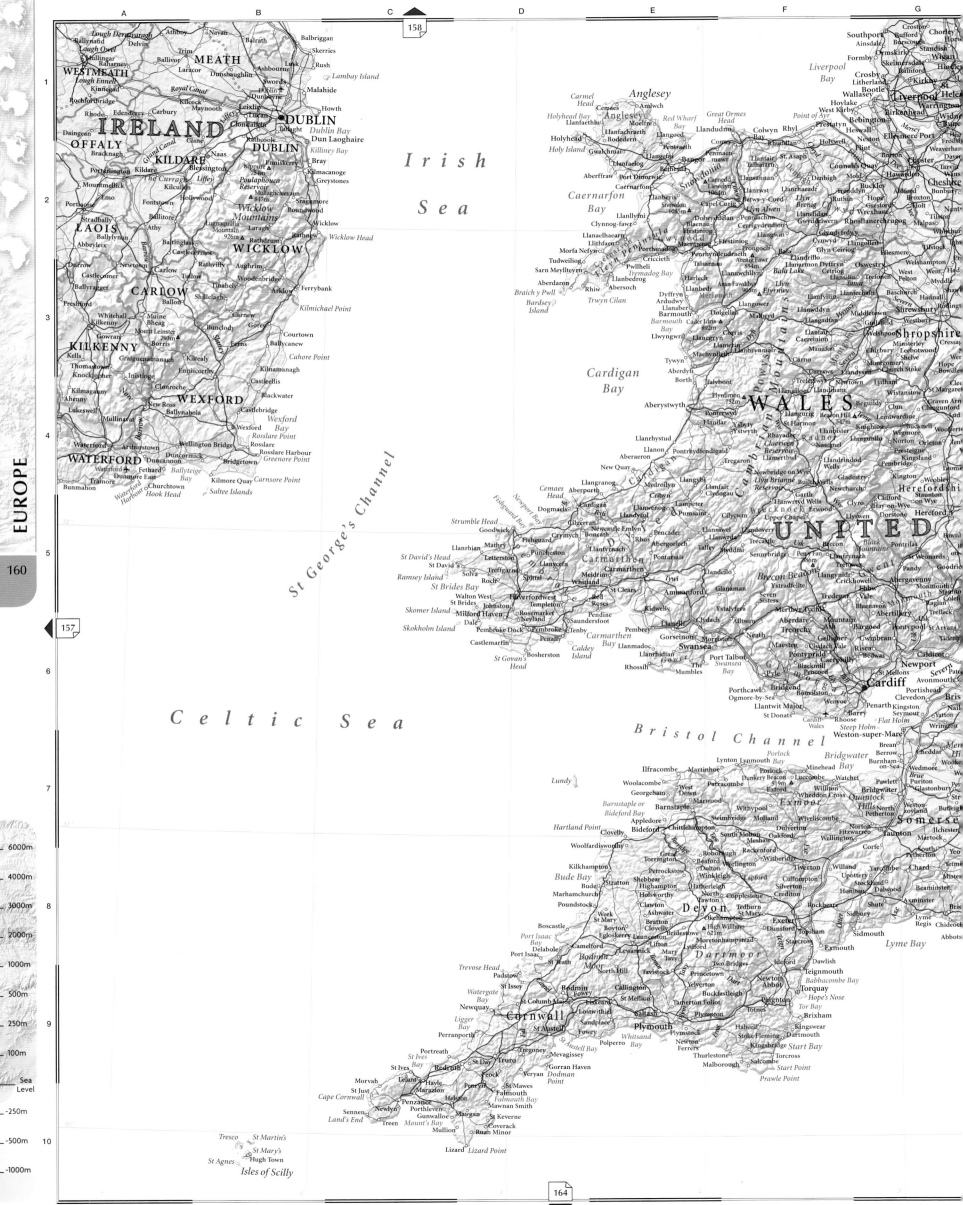

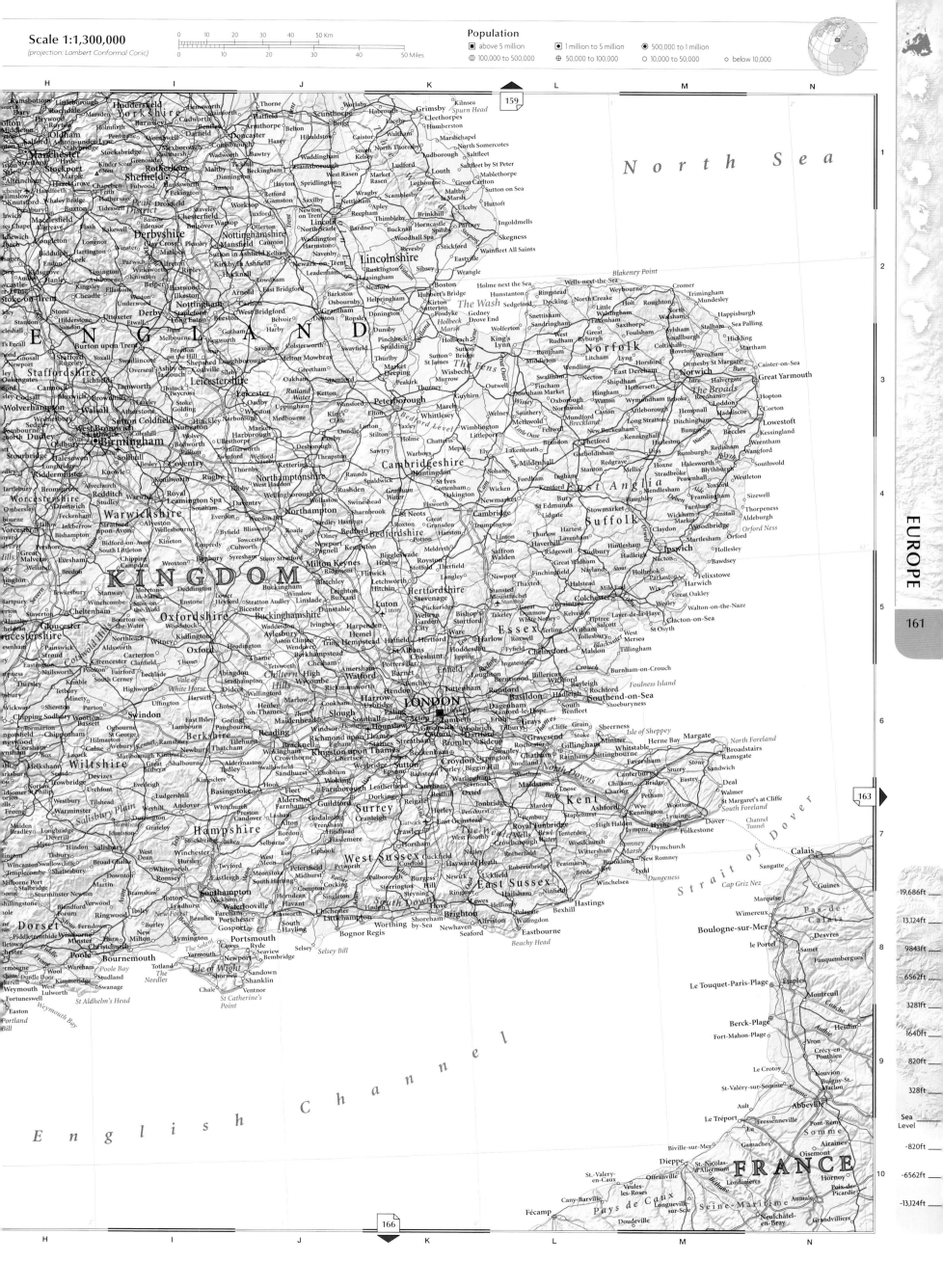

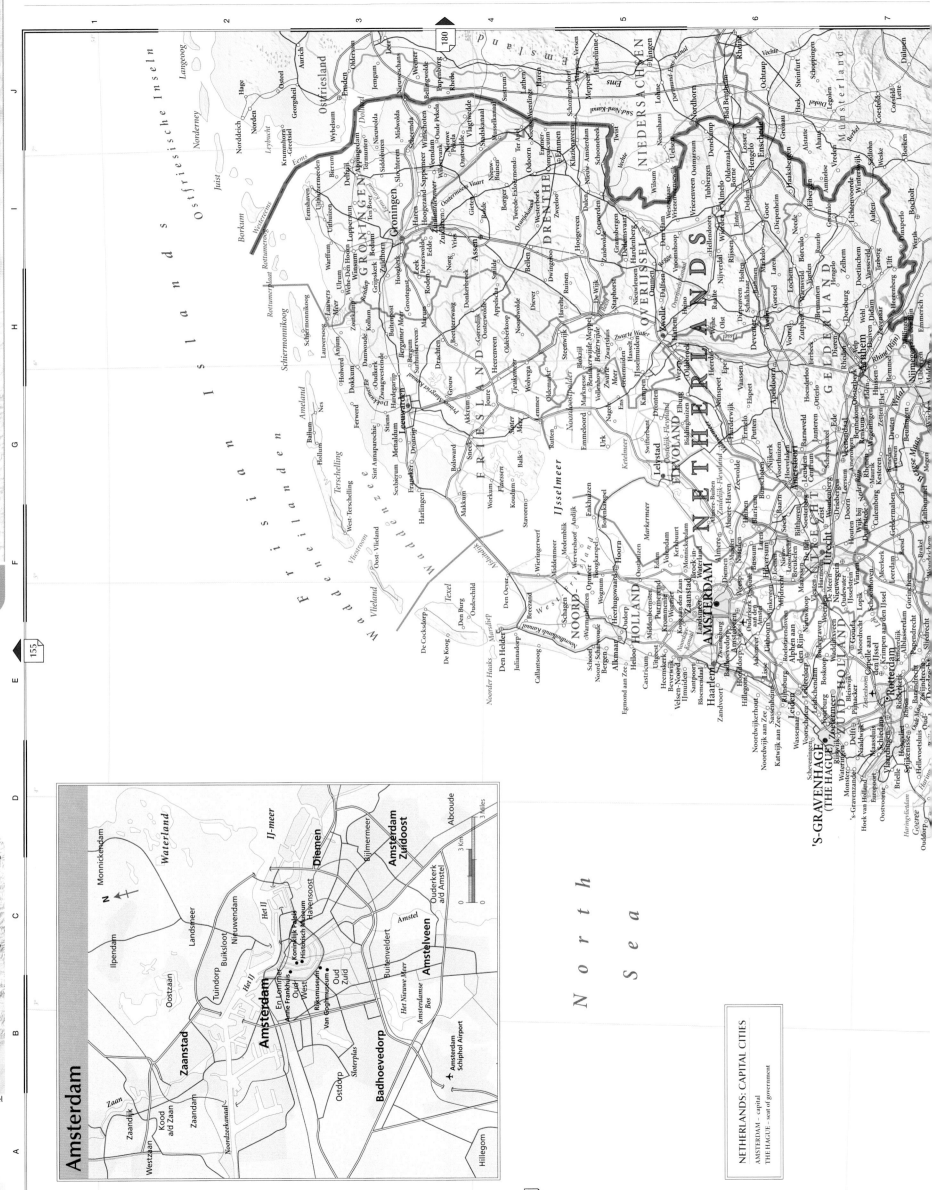

Amsterdam

NETHERLANDS: CAPITAL CITIES

AMSTERDAM - capital
THE HAGUE - seat of government

Scale 1:1,125,000
(projection: Lambert Conformal Conic)

Population
■ above 5 million
◉ 500,000 to 1 million
⊕ 50,000 to 100,000
○ below 10,000
▣ 1 million to 5 million
◎ 100,000 to 500,000
◌ 10,000 to 50,000

160

EUROPE

164

290

ATLANTIC

OCEAN

UNITED
KINGDOM

English Channel

Hartland Point
Bideford
Barnstaple Taunton Bridgwater
Bude Okehampton Exeter Tiverton
Yeovil Sherborne Salisbury Winchester Guildford Reigate Royal Tunbridge
High Willhays Crewkerne Southampton Eastleigh Crawley
621m Lyme Regis Bridport Dorchester Poole Portsmouth Bognor Worthing Brighton
Newquay Bodmin Moor Dartmoor Teignmouth Weymouth Swanage Bournemouth Regis Havant Beachy
St Austell Plymouth Dartmouth Portland Isle of Wight Head Eastbourne
St Ives Truro Falmouth Start Point Bill St Catherine's Ventnor
Penzance Helston Lizard Point Point
Cape Cornwall Land's End Mount's Bay
Isles of Scilly

Cap de
la Hague Alderney
Cherbourg Pointe de Barfleur Cap d'Antifer Fécamp
Barfleur Montivilliers Bolbec
Octeville Tourlaville Cap de la Hève le Havre
Guernsey Herm Valognes Trouville Pont-Audemer
ST PETER PORT Sark Manche Deauville
CHANNEL ISLANDS Jersey Carentan Bayeux St-Lô Calvados Lisieux
(to UK) ST HELIER Isigny-sur-Mer Caen BASSE-NORMANDIE Bernay Conches-en
Coutances Villedieu-les- Vire Falaise Argentan l'Aigle
Île de Batz Poêles Flers
Roscoff Perros-Guirec Tréguier Île de Bréhat Granville Mortain Domfront Orne
Lesneven Lannion Paimpol Golfe de Sées Mortagne-
Landivisiau St-Pol-de-Léon Morlaix Bégard St-Malo Avranches au-Perche
Landerneau Guingamp St-Brieuc Dinard le Mont Collines de Normandie la Ferté
Brest Callac Lamballe St-Michel Beaumont Bernay
Île d'Ouessant Monts d'Arrée Loudéac Dinan Dol-de- Mayenne Bonnétable
Pointe St-Mathieu Châteaulin Pontorson Bretagne Fougères Vitré Laval Loué le Mans
Iroise Carhaix Pontivy Josselin Ille-et-Vilaine Mayenne Segré St-Calais
Crozon Douarnenez Gourin Ploërmel Rennes
Pointe du Raz Audierne Quimper Scaër Rosporden Guichen Craon Château- Sablé-sur-Sarthe la Flèche
Île de Sein Quimperlé Hennebont Questembert Redon Châteaubriant Gontier
Baie d'Audierne Pont-l'Abbé Concarneau Morbihan Nozay Vendôme
Pointe de Penmarch Lorient Vannes Muzillac Ancenis
Île Glénan Auray Pontchâteau Nantes Angers
Belle Île Baie de Quiberon la Baule-Escoublac Loire-Atlantique PAYS DE LA LOIRE Noyant
Quiberon le Palais Guérande St-Nazaire Cholet Saumur
Pornic Beaupréau Chemillé Vihiers Chinon
Noirmoutier-en-l'Île Machecoul Sèvre Mauléon Thouars
Île de Noirmoutier Beauvoir-sur-Mer Challans Bressuire Airvault
St-Jean-de-Monts la Roche-sur-Yon les Herbiers Parthenay Châtellerault
Île d'Yeu St-Gilles- Vendée Deux-Sèvres POITOU
Croix-de-Vie la Mothe Achard Fontenay-le-Comte Poitiers
les Sables-d'Olonne Luçon St-Maixent-l'École Lusignan
Pertuis Breton Niort Vivonne
Île de Ré Marans
la Rochelle Surgères POITOU-
Pertuis d'Antioche Charente-Maritime CHARENTES Ruffec
Île d'Oléron Rochefort St-Jean-d'Angély Mansle
le Château d'Oléron Charente Matha Rochechouart
Pointe de la Coubre Saintes Cognac la Rochefoucauld
Royan Jarnac Brantôme
Pointe de Grave Pons Barbezieux- Angoulême
Gironde St-Hilaire Nontron
Lesparre-Médoc Jonzac Montmoreau
Pauillac Miramble Chalais
Lac d'Hourtin-Carcans St-André-de-Cubzac Coutras Périgueux
St-Laurent-Médoc Libourne Montpon-Ménestérol
Lacanau Blaye Castillon-la-Bataille
Blanquefort Cenon Bergerac Dordogne
Bassin d'Arcachon Bordeaux Gironde Sauveterre-de-Guyenne
Arcachon Pessac AQUITAINE Miramont-
Cap Ferret la Teste Gradignan Marmande de-Guyenne
Mestras Bazas Villeneuve-sur-Lot
Étang de Biscarrosse Bélin-Béliet Casteljaloux
et de Parentis Parentis-en-Born Captieux Agen
Mimizan Labouheyre Nérac
Sabres Labrit Houeillès Mézin

Bay of
Biscay

Mont-de-Marsan
Morcenx
Landes
Roquefort
Soustons Tartas Aire-sur- Eauze Auch
Dax Mugron l'Adour Nogaro
Costa Verde St-Vincent-de-Tyrosse Hagetmau Riscle Mirande
Capbreton Orthez Vic-en-
Cabo Anglet Bayonne Peyrehorade Orthez Bigorre Mielan Lombez
de Ajo Santoña Biarritz Salies-de-Béarn Maubourguet Mirande
Santander St-Jean-de-Luz Hasparren Mourenx Pau Tarbes
Hendaye Cambo-les-Bains la Rhune Navarrenx Castelnau-Magnoac
Donostia- Bidart Oloron-Ste-Marie Lourdes
San Sebastián Bergara Irún Ste-Engrâce Arudy Argelès-Gazost St-Gaudens
Bilbao Tolosa Pic d'Anie Pic du Midi de Bigorre
PAÍS VASCO Zumárraga Lekunberri 2504m 2872m
VITORIA-GASTEIZ NAVARRA Pamplona Jaca
(Iruña)

Sea Level
6000m
4000m
3000m
2000m
1000m
500m
250m
100m
-250m
-500m
-1000m

Paris

Seine
Forêt de St-Germain
Montmorency
Aéroport Charles de Gaulle
Enghien
Argenteuil Asnières St-Denis Drancy Tremblay-en-France
Poissy Nanterre Aubervilliers Aulnay-sous-Bois
St-Germain-en-Laye Montmartre Sacré-Cœur Le Raincy Lagny
Marly-le-Roi Arc de Triomphe Paris Montreuil Marne
Rueil-Malmaison Tour Eiffel Musée du Louvre Bastille Vincennes Marne-la-Vallée
Boulogne-Billancourt Notre Dame
Château de Versailles Meudon Vitry-sur-Seine Champigny-sur-Marne
Versailles Seine Créteil
Trappes Sceaux
Chevreuse Antony Orly
Palaiseau Aéroport d'Orly Brie-Comte-Robert
Orsay Mortgeron

0   5 Km
0   5 Miles

GALICIA
A Coruña (La Coruña)
Cabo Ortegal
Punta da Estaca de Bares
Cabo Prior
Cabo de Peñas
Tapia de Casariego
Luarca Avilés Luanco
Cudillero Candás Gijón (Xixón)
Ferrol Navia Castropol Cangas de Narcea Grado Oviedo
ASTURIAS Mieres del Camino Villaviciosa Ribadesella Llanes
Pola de Lena Infiesto Arriondas Cangas de Onís Torrelavega
CANTABRIA Castro-Urdiales
Santander
Betanzos Vilalba Lugo Sarria Pola de Laviana Santurtzi San Vicente de la Barquera
Santiago de Compostela Cordillera Cantábrica Reinosa Laredo Barakaldo
Arzúa Melide Monforte de Lemos Peña Vieja 2648m Potes
Pontevedra Chantada Torre de Cerredo 2648m
Ourense (Orense) Ponferrada León
Vigo Verín Astorga
A Guarda Benavente Palencia
PORTUGAL Zamora Valladolid CASTILLA-LEÓN Burgos
LA RIOJA Logroño
Braga Bragança Soria
Porto (Oporto) Vila Real ARAGÓN Zaragoza
SPAIN Lleida (Lérida)

170

Scale 1:3,250,000

(projection: Dummy Text to Change)

0 20 40 60 80 100 Km

0 20 40 60 80 100 Miles

Population

- ▣ above 5 million
- ◙ 1 million to 5 million
- ◉ 500,000 to 1 million
- ◎ 100,000 to 500,000
- ⊕ 50,000 to 100,000
- ○ 10,000 to 50,000
- ○ below 10,000

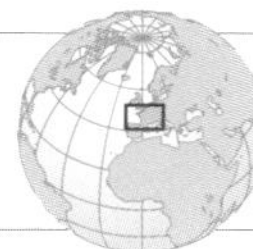

H
I
J
K
L
M
N
181
177
198
BELGIUM
LUXEMBOURG
GERMANY
SWITZERLAND
AUSTRIA
LIECHTENSTEIN
MONACO
ANDORRA
FRANCE
ALPS
BRUSSEL/BRUXELLES (BRUSSELS)
PARIS
LUXEMBOURG
BERN
VADUZ
ANDORRA LA VELLA
Köln (Cologne)
Frankfurt am Main
Stuttgart
München (Munich)
Milano (Milan)
Torino (Turin)
Genova (Genoa)
Lyon
Marseille
Nice
Ligurian Sea
Mediterranean Sea
Tyrrhenian Sea
Golfe du Lion
Corse (Corsica)
1
2
3
4
5
6
7
8
9
10
19,686ft
13,124ft
9843ft
6562ft
3281ft
1640ft
820ft
328ft
Sea Level
-820ft
-6562ft
-13,124ft

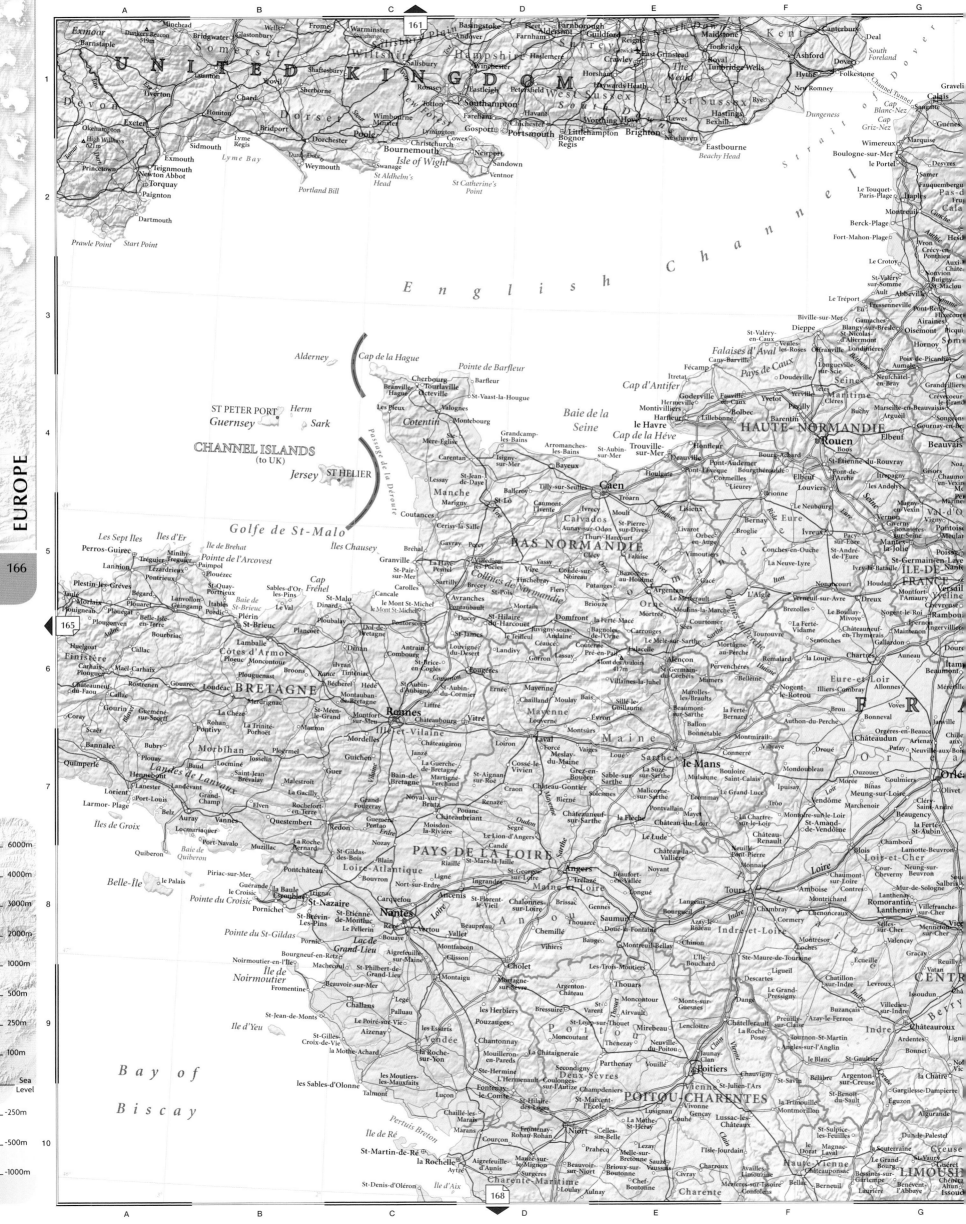

Scale 1:1,750,000
(projection: Lambert Conformal Conic)

0 10 20 30 40 50 Km
0 10 20 30 40 50 Miles

Population
- ● above 5 million
- ■ 1 million to 5 million
- ◉ 500,000 to 1 million
- ◎ 100,000 to 500,000
- ⊕ 50,000 to 100,000
- ⊙ 10,000 to 50,000
- ○ below 10,000

176

169

19,686ft
13,124ft
9843ft
6562ft
3281ft
1640ft
820ft
328ft
Sea Level
-820ft
-6562ft
-13,124ft

Southern France & the Pyrenees

The Iberian Peninsula

EUROPE

Major labels

ATLANTIC OCEAN

Bay of Biscay

Costa Verde

GALICIA

ASTURIAS

CANTABRIA

CASTILLA-LEÓN

PORTUGAL

SPAIN

MADRID

LISBOA (LISBON)

Porto (Oporto)

EXTREMADURA

ANDALUCÍA

Sierra Morena

Sistema Central

Sistema Bético

Cordillera Cantábrica

Sevilla (Seville)

Córdoba

Granada

Málaga

Cádiz

Huelva

Badajoz

Mérida

Cáceres

Toledo

Ciudad Real

Jaén

Valladolid

Burgos

Palencia

León

Zamora

Salamanca

Ávila

Segovia

Guadalajara

Santander

Gijón (Xixón)

Oviedo

A Coruña (La Coruña)

Santiago

Vigo

Pontevedra

Ourense (Orense)

Bragança

Braga

Viana do Castelo

Vila Real

Viseu

Aveiro

Coimbra

Guarda

Castelo Branco

Leiria

Santarém

Portalegre

Évora

Setúbal

Beja

Faro

Gibraltar (to UK)

GIBRALTAR

Ceuta (to Spain)

Tanger

Tetouan

MOROCCO

Rif

Alboran Sea

Strait of Gibraltar

Golfo de Cádiz

Costa del Sol

Costa de la Luz

Duero

Douro

Tejo

Guadiana

Guadalquivir

MADEIRA (to Portugal)
Scale 1:2,500,000
0 5 10   20 Km
0 5 10   20 Miles

Funchal

Porto Santo

Madeira

ATLANTIC OCEAN

ISLAS CANARIAS (CANARY ISLANDS) (to Spain)
Scale 1:6,500,000
0 25 50 75 Km
0 25 50   75 Miles

Santa Cruz de Tenerife

Las Palmas de Gran Canaria

Tenerife

Gran Canaria

Lanzarote

Fuerteventura

La Palma

Gomera

Hierro

Pico del Teide 3718m

ATLANTIC OCEAN

Elevation scale
6000m
4000m
3000m
2000m
1000m
500m
250m
100m
Sea Level
-250m
-500m
-1000m

290

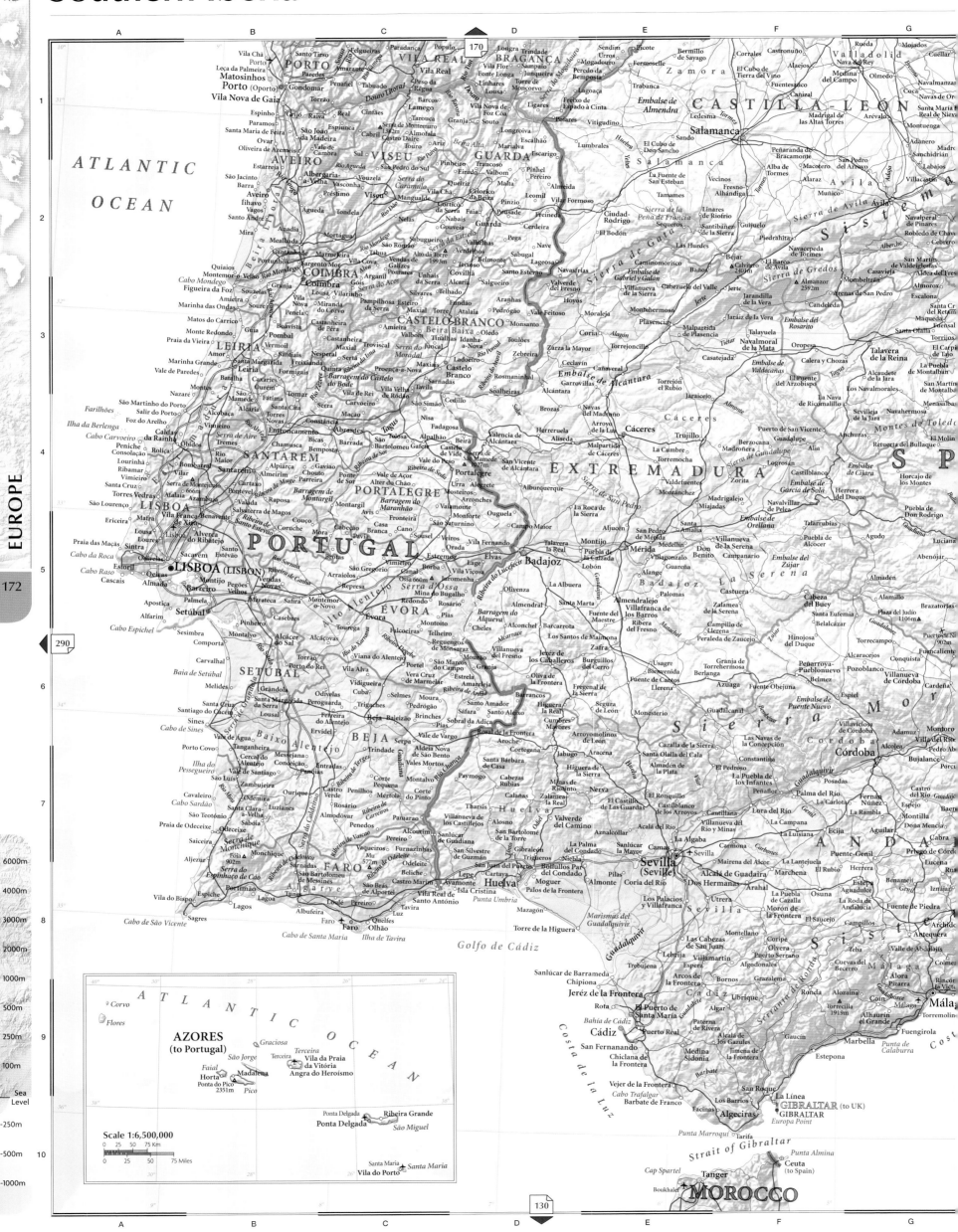

The Italian Peninsula

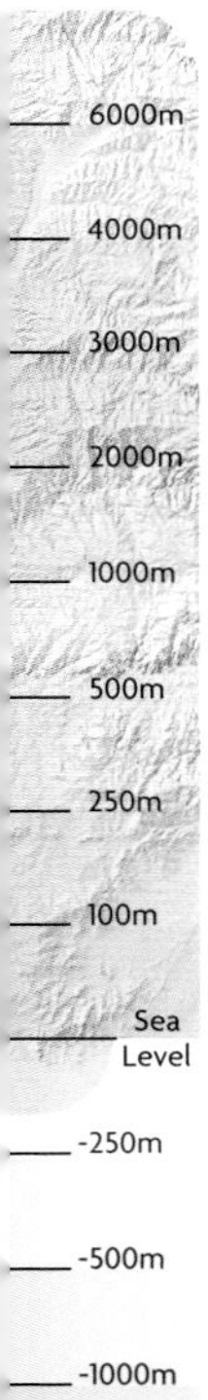

Major regions and countries (map labels):

FRANCE · GERMANY · SWITZERLAND · LIECHTENSTEIN · AUSTRIA · CZECH REPUBLIC · SLOVAKIA · HUNGARY · SLOVENIA · CROATIA · BOSNIA AND HERZEGOVINA · ITALY · MONACO · SAN MARINO

Water bodies:

Ligurian Sea · Adriatic · Gulf of Venice · Gulf of Trieste

Selected cities:

WIEN (VIENNA) · BRATISLAVA · BUDAPEST · ZAGREB · LJUBLJANA · München (Munich) · BERN · Milano (Milan) · Torino (Turin) · Genova (Genoa) · Bologna · Firenze (Florence) · Venezia (Venice) · Verona · Padova (Padua) · Trento · Bolzano · Innsbruck · Salzburg · Graz · Klagenfurt · Ravenna · Rimini · Ancona · Perugia · Pisa · Livorno · Trieste · SARAJEVO

Corse (Corsica) · Isola d'Elba

Elevation scale:

6000m · 4000m · 3000m · 2000m · 1000m · 500m · 250m · 100m · Sea Level · −250m · −500m · −1000m

183 · 179 · 174 · 169

Germany

Map of Germany and surrounding regions, showing Denmark, southern Sweden, northern Poland, the Netherlands, the Baltic Sea and the North Sea.

Rhineland & Hamburg

Scale 1:2,500,000
(projection: Lambert Conformal Conic)

0 10 20 30 40 50 Km
0 10 20 30 40 50 Miles

Population
- ▪ above 5 million
- ▫ 1 million to 5 million
- ◉ 500,000 to 1 million
- ◎ 100,000 to 500,000
- ◉ 50,000 to 100,000
- ○ 10,000 to 50,000
- ○ below 10,000

214

MOLDOVA
UKRAINE
ROMANIA
BULGARIA
TURKEY
GREECE
MACEDONIA

Black Sea
Marmara Denizi (Sea of Marmara)
Thracian Sea
Aegean Sea

BUCUREŞTI (BUCHAREST)
SOFIYA (SOFIA)
İSTANBUL
Thessaloníki
Varna
Burgas
Bursa
Plovdiv
Galaţi
Braşov
Constanţa
Ploieşti
Craiova
Edirne
Tekirdağ

Carpathian Mountains
Balkan Mountains
Rhodope Mountains
Danube
Dunavska Ravnina
Dobruja

19,686ft
13,124ft
9843ft
6562ft
3281ft
1640ft
820ft
328ft
Sea Level
-820ft
-6562ft
-13,124ft

Greece

A B C D E F G

184

175

128

Adriatic Sea

Strait of Otranto

Ionian Sea

Ionian Islands (Ionian Islands)

Mediterranean Sea

ITALY

Lago di Lesina
Lago di Varano
Apricena
Sannicandro Garganico
Rodi Garganico
Vieste
Torremaggiore
San Giovanni Rotondo
Monte Sant' Angelo
Mattinata
Promontorio del Gargano
San Severo
Lucera
Manfredonia
Foggia
Golfo di Manfredonia
Troia
Bovino
Orta Nova
Cerignola
Margherita di Savoia
Barletta
Ascoli Satriano
Canosa di Puglia
Andria
Trani
Biscegile
Molfetta
Giovinazzo
Corato
Bitonto
Bari
Mola di Bari
Melfi
Minervino Murge
Adelfia
Spinazzola
Venosa
Rionero in Vulture
Gravina in Puglia
Altamura
Conversano
Polignano a Mare
Monopoli
Muro Lucano
Acerenza
Putignano
Fasano
Gioia del Colle
Alberobello
Ostuni
San Vito dei Normanni
PUGLIA
Le Murge
Buccino
Potenza
Santeramo in Colle
Castellaneta
Mottola
Massafra
Francavilla Fontana
Brindisi
Teggiano
Sala Consilina
Irsina
Matera
Martina Franca
Grottaglie
Mesagne
BASILICATA
Montesano sulla Marcellana
Ferrandina
Taranto
Squinzano
Lecce
ITALY
Tricarico
Stigliano
Pisticci
Penisola Salentina
Campi Salentina
Sapri
Lagonegro
Agri
Manduria
Copertino
Galatina
Maratea
Rotondella
Golfo di Taranto
Galatone
Maglie
Martano
Golfo di Policastro
Capo Spulico
Gallipoli
Casarano
Otranto
Belvedere Marittimo
Castrovillari
Cassano allo Ionio
Sibari
Ugento
Capo Santa Maria di Leuca
Gagliano del Capo
Tricase
San Marco Argentano
Corigliano Calabro
Spezzano Albanese
Capo Trionto
Cetraro
Rossano
Acri
Cariati
Paola
Crucoli Torretta
Punta Alice
Rende
CALABRIA
Ciro
Amantea
Cosenza
Strongoli
Ciro Marino
Rogliano
San Giovanni in Fiore
Nocera Terinese
Petilia Policastro
Neto
Crotone
Sambiase
La Sila
Cutro
Golfo di Santa Eufemia
Lamezia Terme
Botricello
Capo Rizzuto
Nicastro
Borgia
Catanzaro
Tropea
Vibo Valentia
Chiaravalle Centrale
Catanzaro Marina
Capo Vaticano
Rosarno
Serra San Bruno
Soverato
Golfo di Squillace
Mileto
Gioia Tauro
Passo della Pietra Spada
Golfo di Gioia
Polistena
Punta Stilo
Palmi
Taurianova
Cittanova
Siderno
Locri
Oppido Mamertina
Villa San Giovanni
Reggio di Calabria
Melito di Porto Salvo

ALBANIA / MACEDONIA region

Petrovac na Moru
Virpazar
Koplik
Fierzë
Liqeni i Fierzës
Ljuboten
KOSOVO
Kriva Palanka
Kyustendil
Ulcinj
Bar
Lake Scutari
Shkodër
Krumë
Prizren
Kumanovo
Kratovo
SHKODËR
Fushë-Arrëz
Bicaj
Kukës
Korritnik
Tetovo
Zelino
Skopje
Kočani
Shëngjin
Puke
Fushë-Krujë
KUKËS
Sar planina
SKOPJE
Velesta
Stip
Lezhë
LEZHË
Rubik
Rrëshen
Peshkopi
Titov Vrv
Gostivar
Veles
LEZHË
Milot
DIBËR
Debar
Plasnica
Negotino
Mamuras
Maqellarë
Kičevo
Prilep
Durrës
Fushë-Krujë
Shen Nji i Madh
Burrel
Kruševo
DURRËS
Krujë
Bulqizë
Gradsko
Kavadarci
MACEDONIA
Tirana Rinas
Debar
Gjevgjelija
TIRANË (TIRANA)
Rrogozhinë
Elbasan
Librazhd
Struga
Lake Ohrid
Bitola
Kožuf
Kavajë
Peqin
Cerrik
ELBASAN
Ohrid
Resen
Pelister
Aridaia
ALBANIA
Lushnje
Kolonjë
Kuçovë
Gramsh
Pogradec
Prespa Lake
Florina
Edessa
Fier
FIER
Ballsh
Berat
Maliq
Korçë
Ptolemaida
Giannitsá
Sazan
Vlorë
BERAT
Moglicë
Bilisht
Kastoria
Véroia
Selenicë
Korçë
KORÇË
Argos Orestikó
Naousa
Orikum
Memaliaj
Përmet
Erseke
Neápoli
KENTRIKÍ MAKEDONIA
Himarë
VLORE
Tepelene
Leskovik
Grevená
Kozáni
Katerini
Qeparo
Gjirokastër
Konitsa
Smólikas
Ólympos (Mt Olympus) 2917m
Delvinë
GJIROKASTËR
Tsepelovo
Métsovo
DYTIKÍ MAKEDONIA
THESSALÍA
Sarandë
Delvináki
Ioánnina
Kalampáka
Meteora
Larísa
ÍPEIROS
Tríkala
Krannón
Filiátes
Paramythiá
Mouzáki
Karditsa
Sofádes
Igoumenitsa
Kérkyra (Corfu)
Lefkímmi
Párga
Kleisoúra
Arta
Préveza
Lefkáda
Vónitsa
Amfilochía
Agrínio
STEREÁ ELLÁS
IÓNIOI NÍSOI
DYTIKÍ ELLÁS
Thérmo
Lidoríki
Kefalloniá
Argostóli
Itháki
Mesolóngi
Nafpaktos
Pátra
PELOPÓNNISOS
Zákynthos
Olympía
Pýrgos
Trípoli
Kalamáta
Spárti
Pýlos
Koróni
Gýtheio

Athens

Acharnés
Kifisiá
Pikermi
Nea Liosia
Nea Ionia
Halandri
Patissia
Aspropyrgos
Peristeri
Olympiako Stadio
Holargos
Spáta
Athína (Athens)
Arheol. Moussio
Likavitos
Eleftherios Venizelos Intl. Airport
Egaleo
Agora
Zografos
Parthenon
Panathinaiko Stadio
Tavros
Akropoli
Viron
Peania
Kalithea
Imittos
Nea Smirni
Ihoupoli
Nikea
Paleo Faliro
Nea Alexandria
Peiraías (Piraeus)
Kalamaki
Argiroupoli
Voula
Varkiza
Saronikós Kólpos

N

6000m
4000m
3000m
2000m
1000m
500m
250m
100m
Sea Level
-250m
-500m
-1000m

0   4 Km
0   4 Miles

The Baltic States & Belarus

RESPUBLIKA KARELIYA

FINLAND

ITÄ-SUOMI

LÄNSI-SUOMI

ETELÄ-SUOMI

HELSINKI

Turku (Åbo)

Tampere

Ladozhskoye Ozero

Sankt-Peterburg (Saint Petersburg)

RUSSIAN FEDERATION

LENINGRADSKAYA OBLAST'

NOVGORODSKAYA OBLAST'

Velikiy Novgorod

Ozero Il'men'

PSKOVSKAYA OBLAST'

TVERSKAYA OBLAST'

Pskov

Velikiye Luki

Gulf of Finland

Narva Bay

Narva

Lake Peipus

ESTONIA

TALLINN

HARJUMAA

LÄÄNE-VIRUMAA

IDA-VIRUMAA

LÄÄNEMAA

RAPLAMAA

JÄRVAMAA

JÕGEVAMAA

TARTUMAA

Tartu

PÄRNUMAA

VILJANDIMAA

VALGAMAA

VÕRUMAA

PÕLVAMAA

HIIUMAA

SAAREMAA

Kuressaare

Pärnu

Gulf of Riga

LATVIA

RĪGA

Vidzemes Augstiene

Jelgava

Ventspils

Liepāja

Daugavpils

ŠIAULIAI

TELŠIAI

PANEVĖŽYS

Gulf of Bothnia

Åland

ÅLAND

Mariehamn (Maarianhamina)

GOTLAND

Gotland

Baltic Sea

Elevation scale:
6000m
4000m
3000m
2000m
1000m
500m
250m
100m
Sea Level
-250m
-500m
-1000m

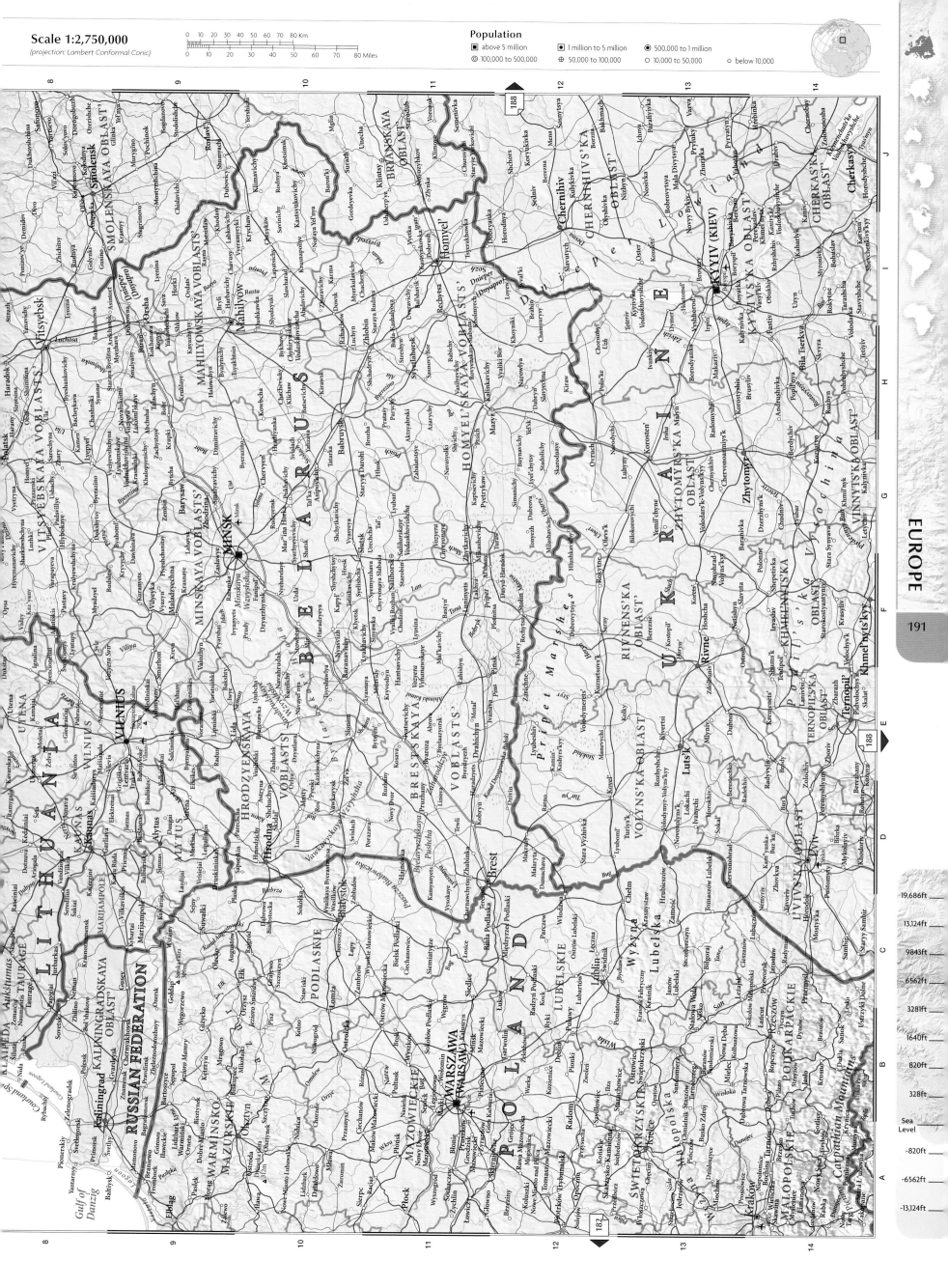

THE RUSSIAN FEDERATION: ADMINISTRATIVE REGIONS

The administrative area names in European Russia have been omitted west of the Ural Mountains. Please refer to pages 194–195 and 196–197 where these areas are shown at a larger scale.

6000m
4000m
3000m
2000m
1000m
500m
250m
100m
Sea Level
-250m
-500m
-1000m

EUROPE

Norwegian Sea

N O R W A Y

FINNMARK

NORDLAND

TROMS

S W E D E N

VÄSTERBOTTEN

NORRBOTTEN

Lapland

LAPPI

VÄSTERNORRLAND

F I N L A N D

LÄNSI-SOUMI

ITÄ-SUOMI

ETELÄ-SUOMI

GÄVLEBORG

UPPSALA

ÅLAND

Gulf of Bothnia

STOCKHOLM

Baltic Sea

HELSINKI

Gulf of Finland

TALLINN

E S T O N I A

Lake Peipus

Lake Pskov

Gulf of Riga

RIGA

L A T V I A

L I T H U A N I A

KALININGRADSKAYA OBLAST'

Kaliningrad

BELARUS

R U S S I A N

MURMANSKAYA OBLAST'

Murmansk

Kol'skiy Poluostrov

Kandalakshskiy Zaliv

Beloye More (White Sea)

Dvinskaya Guba

RESPUBLIKA KARELIYA

Onezhskoye Ozero

Petrozavodsk

ARKHANGEL'SKAY

Arkhangel'sk (Archangel)

Severodvinsk

LENINGRADSKAYA OBLAST'

Sankt-Peterburg (Saint Petersburg)

Ladozhskoye Ozero

NOVGORODSKAYA OBLAST'

Velikiy Novgorod

PSKOVSKAYA OBLAST'

Pskov

VOLOGODSKAYA OBLAST'

Vologda

Cherepovets

TVERSKAYA OBLAST'

Tver'

YAROSLAVSKAYA OBLAST'

Yaroslavl'

Kostroma

IVANOVSKAYA OBLAST'

VLADIMIRSKAYA OBLAST'

Baren[ts Sea]

295

153

191

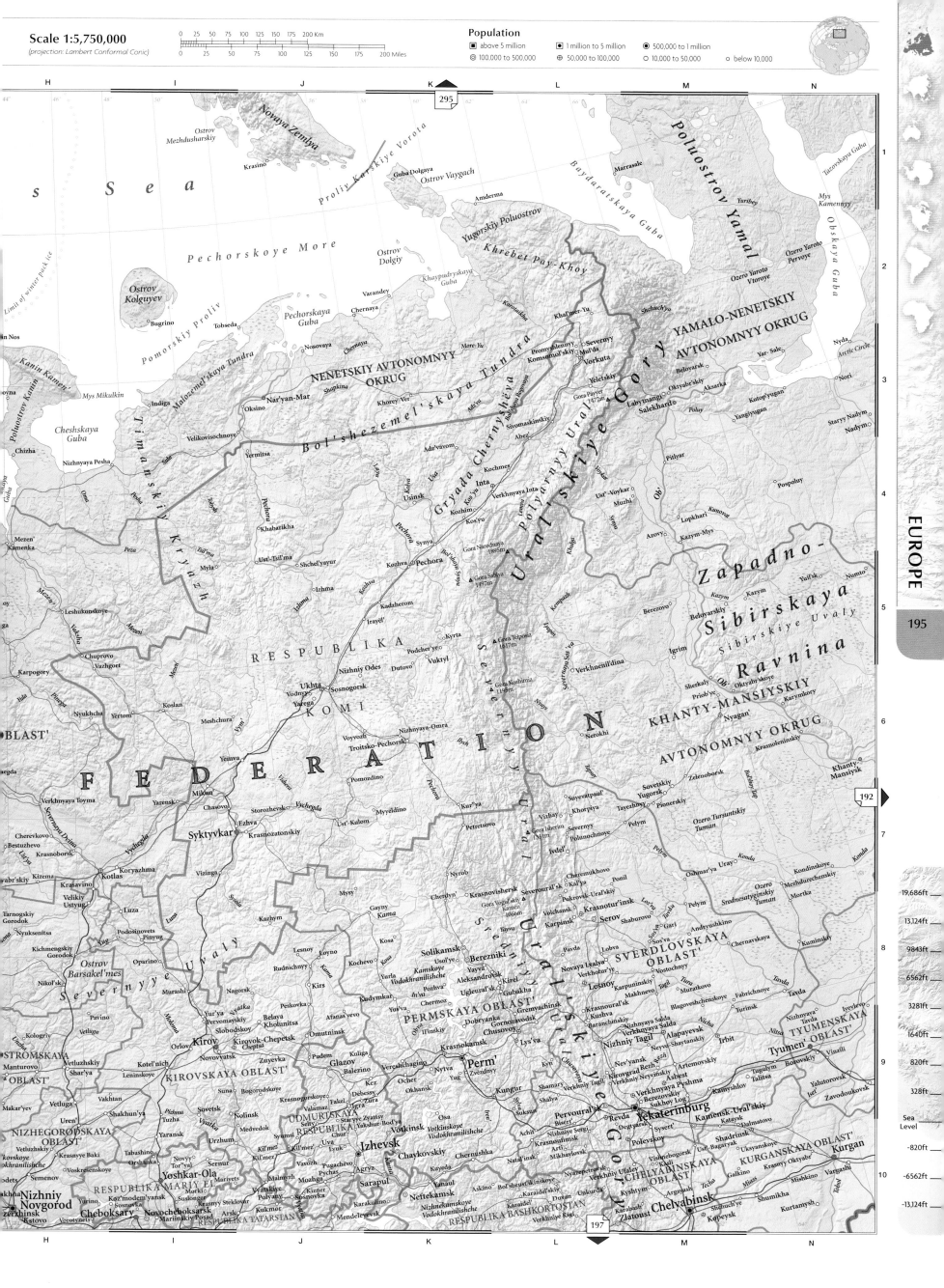

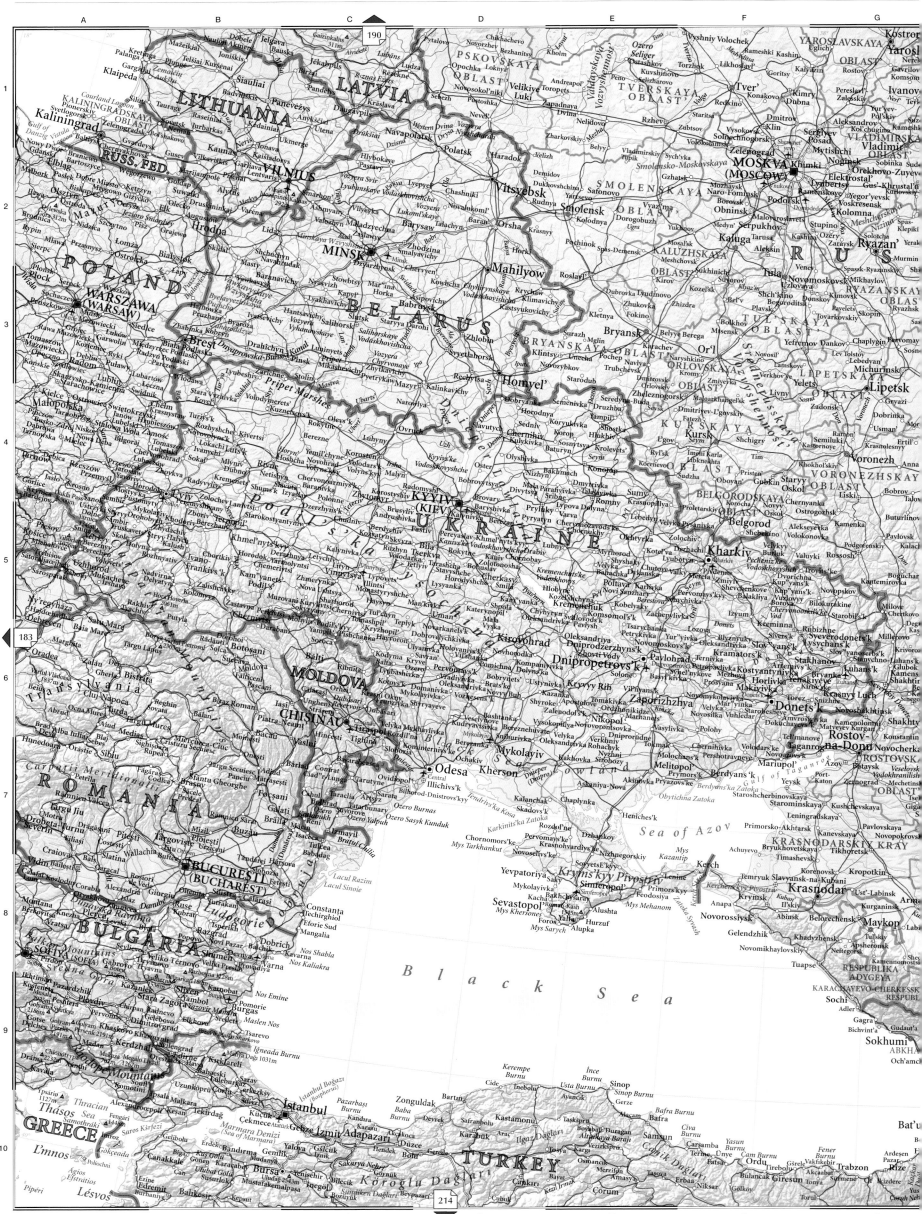

ATLANTIC OCEAN

Bay of Biscay

English Channel

Baie de la Seine

Isles of Scilly
Land's End
Plymouth
Bournemouth
Southampton
LONDON
Brighton
UNITED KINGDOM
CHANNEL ISLANDS (to UK)
Guernsey
ST PETER PORT
Jersey
ST HELIER
Ile d'Ouessant
Iroise
St-Brieuc
St-Lô
le Havre
Amiens
Beauvais
Rouen
Pontoise
NETHERLANDS
S-GRAVENHAGE
Brugge
Antwerpen
BELGIUM
BRUXELLES (BRUSSEL)
Arras
LUXEMBOURG
Maastricht
Liège
Düsseldorf
Köln (Cologne)
GERMANY
Hannover
Magdeburg
Brandenburg
Dessau
BERLIN
Potsdam
Hoyerswerda
Marburg an der Lahn
Erfurt
Weimar
Gotha
Suhl
Dresden
Ústí nad Labem
CZECH
PRAHA (PRAGUE)
Plzeň
České Budějovice

Quimper
Rennes
Vannes
Belle Île
St-Nazaire
Nantes
Ile d'Yeu
la Roche-sur-Yon
Ile de Ré
la Rochelle
Ile d'Oléron
Niort
Laval
Angers
le Mans
Tours
Cholet
Loire
Chartres
Orléans
Cher
FRANCE
PARIS
Créteil
Melun
Nanterre
Versailles
Évreux
Caen
Alençon
Châteauroux
Creuse
Châlons-en-Champagne
Champagne
Bar-le-Duc
Meuse
Nancy
Metz
Saarbrücken
Mainz
Wiesbaden
Frankfurt am Main
Darmstadt
Mannheim
Karlsruhe
Strasbourg
Offenburg
Nürnberg
Bamberg
Bayreuth
Karlovy Vary

Laon
Charleville-Mézières
Reims
Troyes
Auxerre
Dijon
Chaumont
Épinal
Vesoul
Belfort
Mulhouse
Colmar
Freiburg im Breisgau
Basel
Konstanz
Ulm
München (Munich)
Augsburg
Landshut
Salzburg
Bavarian Alps
Kempten
Innsbruck
AUSTRIA
Linz
Passau

Bordeaux
Dordogne
Garonne
Périgueux
Brive-la-Gaillarde
Tulle
Aurillac
Puy de Sancy 1885m
Clermont-Ferrand
Montluçon
Moulins
Nevers
Chalon-sur-Saône
Mâcon
Bourg-en-Bresse
Lons-le-Saunier
Genève
GenèveLac Léman
Lausanne
Luzern
BERN
SWITZ.
VADUZ
LIECHTENSTEIN

Mont-de-Marsan
Agen
Cahors
Montauban
Albi
Rodez
Mende
Massif Central
Le Puy
St-Étienne
Valence
Grenoble
Privas
Gap
Durance
Digne
Cuneo
Mont Blanc 4807m
Chambéry
Annecy
Aosta
Torino (Turin)
Rivoli
Asti
Alessandria
Savona
San Remo
Genova (Genoa)
Milano (Milan)
Cremona
Mantova
Monselice
Venezia (Venice)
Trento
Edolo
Tarvisio
LJUBLJANA
SLOVENIA
Trieste

Auch
Pau
Tarbes
Pyrénées
Foix
Carcassonne
Toulouse
Castres
Béziers
Narbonne
Montpellier
Nîmes
Avignon
Arles
Aix-en-Provence
Marseille
Toulon
Iles d'Hyères
Cannes
Nice
MONACO
Ligurian Sea
Corse (Corsica)
Bastia
Ajaccio
Monte Cinto 2706m
Pisa
Livorno
Viareggio
Pistoia
Appennino
Firenze (Florence)
Siena
Grosseto
Elba
Perugia
Terni
ITALY
Ancona
Ascoli Piceno
Foligno
Viterbo
Civitavecchia
L'Aquila
Chieti
Teramo
Pescara
SAN MARINO
Bologna
Imola
Po
Ostiglia
Chioggia
Ravenna

A Coruña (La Coruña)
Ferrol
Santiago de Compostela
Cabo Fisterra
Pontevedra
Vigo
Ourense (Orense)
Lugo
Mieres del Camino
Oviedo
Gijón
Avilés
Costa Verde
Santander
Torrelavega
Cordillera Cantábrica
Bilbao
Donostia-San Sebastián
Irun
Pau
País Vasco
Vitoria-Gasteiz
Logroño
Pamplona
Huesca
Zaragoza
Lleida
Terrassa
Sabadell
Girona
ANDORRA
Perpignan
Roussillon
Languedoc
Golfe du Lion
Catalunya
Barcelona
Tarragona
Reus
Costa Brava

Viana do Castelo
Braga
Vila Real
Bragança
Ponferrada
León
Palencia
Burgos
Soria
Valladolid
Duero
Zamora
Salamanca
Segovia
Sistema Central
Sierra de Gredos
Guadalajara
MADRID
Torrejón de Ardoz
Getafe
Teruel
Javalambre 2020m
Moncayo 2313m
Sistema Ibérico
Ebro

Porto (Oporto)
Aveiro
Coimbra
Viseu
Alto da Torre 1993m
Serra da Estrela
Guarda
Castelo Branco
PORTUGAL
Leiria
Santarém
Portalegre
LISBOA (LISBON)
Setúbal
Baía de Setúbal
Beja
Évora
Badajoz
Mérida
Cáceres
Talavera de la Reina
Toledo
Ciudad Real
SPAIN
Cuenca
Castellón de la Plana
Sagunto
Torrent
VALENCIA
Alcoy
Elda
Alicante
Costa Blanca

Algarve
Faro
Cabo de São Vicente
Huelva
Sevilla (Seville)
Andalucía
Córdoba
Sierra Morena
Puertollano
Linares
Jaén
Segura
Orihuela
Murcia
Elche
Lorca
Cartagena
Golfo de Valencia
Ibiza
Formentera
Islas Baleares (Balearic Islands)
Illa de Cabrera
Mallorca (Majorca)
Palma de Mallorca
Menorca (Minorca)
Mahón

Mediterranean Sea

Tyrrhenian Sea
Isola Asinara
Sassari
Sardegna (Sardinia)
Punta La Marmora 1834m
Cagliari
Quartu Sant' Elena
Strait of Bonifacio
Isola Ponziane
Napoli (Naples)
Golfo di Salerno
ROMA (ROME)
VATICAN CITY
Latina
Campobasso
Benevento
Frosinone
Salerno
Foggia

Jeréz de la Frontera
San Fernando
Cádiz
Algeciras
GIBRALTAR (to UK)
Tánger
Ceuta (to Spain)
Tétouan
Chefchaouen
Al-Hoceïma
Melilla (to Spain)
Nador
Marbella
Málaga
Costa del Sol
Almería
Granada
Mulhacén 3481m
Sierra Nevada
Motril
Costa Blanca

Asilah
Larache
Ksar-el-Kébir
Moulay-Bousselham
Souk-el-Arba-Rharb
Kénitra
Salé
RABAT
Casablanca
Mohammedia
El-Jadida
Settat
Khouribga
Berrechid
Kheireisset
Beni Mellal
Sidi-Kacem
Sidi-Slimane
Ouazzane
Meknès
Fès
Taounate
Taza
MOROCCO
Rif
Moyen Atlas
Haut Atlas
Marrakech
Azilal
Jbel Ayachi 3737m
Jbel Toubkal 4165m
Ouarzazate
Er-Rachidia
Erfoud
Bouarfa
Figuig

ALGER (ALGIERS)
Cap de Bordj El Bahri
Tipasa
Ténès
Mostaganem
Oran
Arzew
Beni Saf
Aïn Temouchent
Tlemcen
Sidi Bel Abbès
Mascara
Relizane
Chlef
Médéa
Blida
Bouira
Tizi Ouzou
Béjaïa
Jijel
Skikda
Annaba
Menzel Bourguiba
Bizerte
Cap Bougaroun
Cap de Fer
Cap Blanc
Golfe de Tunis
Cap Bon
TUNIS
Nabeul
Zaghouan
Isola di Pantelleria (to Italy)
Palermo
Sicilia (Sicily)
Trapani
Marsala
Caltanissetta
Monte 3340m
Agrigento
Gela
Catania
Siracusa
Messina
Modica
MALTA
Malta
VALLETTA
Rass Kaboudia
Isole Pelagie (to Italy)

Tissemsilt
Tiaret
Frenda
Zahrez Chergui
Saïda
Chott ech Chergui
Ksar el Boukhari
Bordj-Bou-Arreridj
Sétif
Constantine
Guelma
Souk Ahras
El Kef
Tébessa
Khenchela
Batna
Aïn Beïda
Massif de l'Aurès
Biskra
Chott Melghir
Gafsa
Sidi Bouzid
Kasserine
Djebel Chambi 1544m
Kairouan
Sidi el Hani
Sousse
Mahdia
Sfax
Îles de Kerkenah

Hauts Plateaux
Djelfa
Aflou
Laghouat
Bou Saâda
Chott Merouane
Touggourt
El Oued
Atlas Saharien
Mountains
Tendrara
Aïn Sefra
Béchar
Abadla
Hamada du Guir
Ghardaïa
Ouargla
Hassi Messaoud
Kebili
Tozeur
Gabès
Médenine
Tataouine
Ile de Jerba
Golfe de Gabès
TUNISIA
ŢARĀBULUS (TRIPOLI)
Zuwārah
Al Khums
Zāwiyah
Az 'Azīzīyah
Gharyān
Misrāta

Hamada du Dra
Beni Abbès
Grand Erg Occidental
El Goléa
Grand Erg Oriental
Ghadāmis
Dehibat
Nālūt
Yafran
Sināwin
Mizdah
Banī Walīd
Bu'ayrat al Hasūn
Al Qaddāhiyah
Wādī Zamzam

'Erg Iguidi
Tabelbala
Erg er Raoui
Oued Saoura
Timimoun
Hamada Tounassine
ALGERIA
Plateau du Tademait
Adrar
Reggane
In-Salah
Tiguentourine
Bordj Omar Driss
Djanet
Illizi
Al Hamādah al Hamrā'
Idhān Awbāri
Jabal as Sawdā'
Awbārī
Birāk
Sabhā
Ghaddūwah
Hamādat Murzuq
Wādī Barjūj

'Erg el Ahmar
Erg Chech
Chegga
El Eglab
Adrar
Arak
Monts de Mouydir

6000m
4000m
3000m
2000m
1000m
500m
250m
100m
Sea Level
-250m
-500m
-1000m

Scale 1:8,750,000
(projection: Lambert Conformal Conic)

0 25 50 75 100 125 150 175 200 Km
0 25 50 75 100 125 150 200 Miles

Population
- ■ above 5 million
- ▣ 1 million to 5 million
- ◉ 500,000 to 1 million
- ◎ 100,000 to 500,000
- ⊕ 50,000 to 100,000
- ○ 10,000 to 50,000
- ∘ below 10,000

196

129

216

Countries and regions:
POLAND, BELARUS, UKRAINE, SLOVAKIA, MOLDOVA, RUSSIAN FEDERATION, HUNGARY, ROMANIA, CROATIA, BOSNIA AND HERZEGOVINA, SERBIA, MONTENEGRO, BULGARIA, GEORGIA, MACEDONIA, ALBANIA, GREECE, TURKEY, CYPRUS, TURKISH REPUBLIC OF NORTHERN CYPRUS (recognised only by Turkey), SYRIA, LEBANON, IRAQ, ISRAEL, JORDAN, WEST BANK, GAZA STRIP, EGYPT, LIBYA, SAUDI ARABIA

Capitals and major cities:
WARSZAWA (WARSAW), KYYIV (KIEV), BRATISLAVA, BUDAPEST, BEOGRAD (BELGRADE), BUCURESTI (BUCHAREST), CHISINAU, SOFIYA (SOFIA), SKOPJE, PODGORICA, TIRANE (TIRANA), ATHINA (ATHENS), ANKARA, İstanbul, NICOSIA, DIMASHQ (DAMASCUS), BEYROUTH (BEIRUT), JERUSALEM, AMMAN, CAIRO, Benghazi (Benghazi)

Seas and water bodies:
Black Sea, Sea of Azov, Mediterranean Sea, Aegean Sea, Ionian Sea, Thracian Sea, Sea of Crete (Kritikó Pélagos), Marmara Denizi, Red Sea, Gulf of Suez, Gulf of Aqaba, Pripet Marshes, Khalij Surt (Gulf of Sirte)

Physical features:
Carpathian Mountains, Balkan Mountains, Rhodope Mountains, Küre Dağları, Çanik Dağları, Köroğlu Dağları, Toros Dağları (Taurus Mountains), Doğu Karadeniz Dağları, Caucasus, Anatolia, Sinai, Libyan Plateau, Libyan Desert, Sahara el Gharbiya (Western Desert), Great Sand Sea, Munkhafad el Qattara (Qattara Depression), Nile Delta, Great Rift Valley, Syrian Desert, Al Harrah, Al Hijaz (Hejaz)

Elevation scale (right margin):
19,686ft
13,124ft
9843ft
6562ft
3281ft
1640ft
820ft
328ft
Sea Level
-820ft
-6562ft
-13,124ft

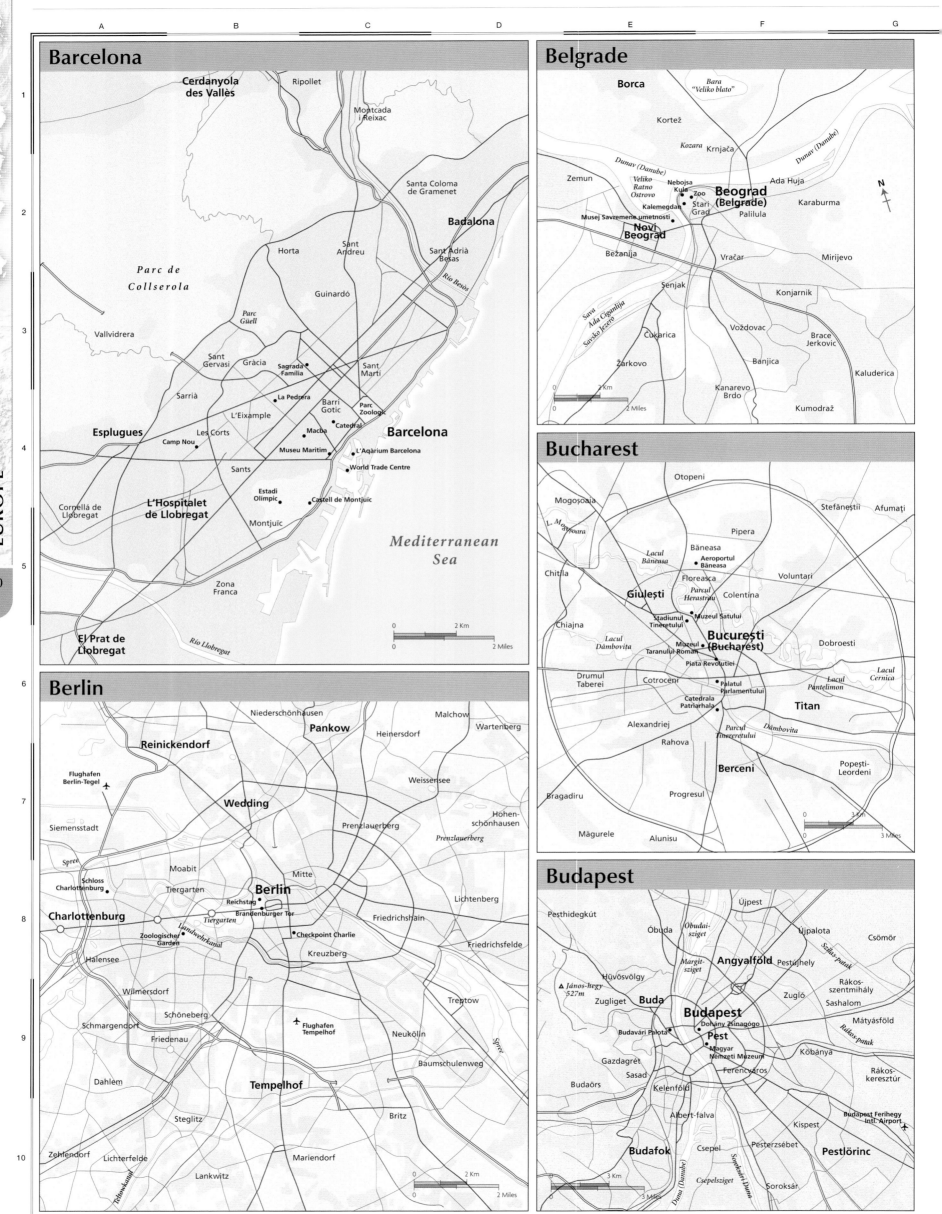

Copenhagen

Vangede
Charlottenlund
Slotspark
Gentofte
Charlottenlund
Hellerup
Søborg
Øresund
Gladsakse
Gyngemosen
Herlev
Østerbro
Utterslev
Mose
København
(Copenhagen)
Islev
Brønshøj
Kastellet
Nørrebro
Rosenborg Slot
Amalienborg
Vanløse
Charlottenborg
Frederiksberg
Tivoli
Christianshavn
Rødovre
Frederiksberg Slot
Damhussøen
Valby
Sundbyerne
Brøndbyøster
Glostrup
Sydhavnen
Amagerbro
Amager
Fælled
Kastrup
Hvidovre

0 2 Km
0 2 Miles

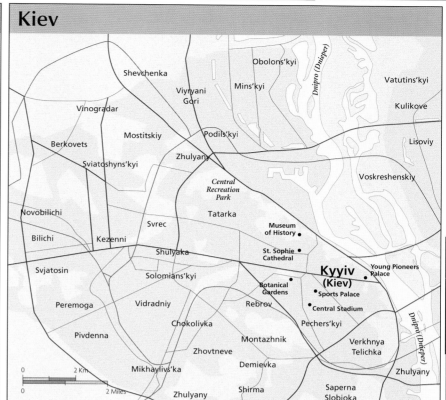

Kiev

Shevchenka
Obolons'kyi
Vatutins'kyi
Viynyani
Gori
Mins'kyi
Vinogradar
Kulikove
Mostitskiy
Berkovets
Podils'kyi
Lisoviy
Sviatoshyns'kyi
Zhulyany
Voskreshenskiy
Central
Recreation
Park
Novobilichi
Svrec
Tatarka
Museum
of History
Bilichi
Kezenni
St. Sophie
Cathedral
Shulyaka
Kyyiv
(Kiev)
Young Pioneers
Palace
Svjatosin
Solomians'kyi
Botanical
Gardens
Sports Palace
Peremoga
Vidradniy
Rebrov
Central Stadium
Chokolivka
Pechers'kyi
Pivdenna
Montazhnik
Verkhnya
Telichka
Mikhaylivs'ka
Zhovtneve
Demievka
Zhulyany
Zhulyany
Shirma
Saperna
Slobioka

0 2 Km
0 2 Miles

Dnipro (Dnieper)
Dnipro (Dnieper)

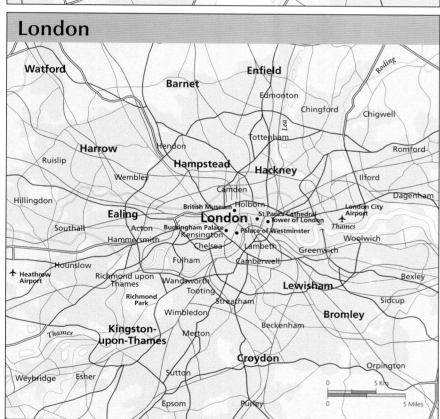

London

Watford
Enfield
Barnet
Edmonton
Chingford
Chigwell
Roding
Harrow
Romford
Hendon
Hampstead
Hackney
Ruislip
Wembley
Camden
Ilford
Dagenham
Hillingdon
British Museum
Holborn
London City
Airport
Ealing
London
St. Paul's Cathedral
Tower of London
Southall
Acton
Buckingham Palace
Thames
Hammersmith
Kensington
Palace of Westminster
Woolwich
Chelsea
Lambeth
Hounslow
Fulham
Camberwell
Greenwich
Heathrow
Airport
Wandsworth
Bexley
Richmond upon
Thames
Tooting
Lewisham
Richmond
Park
Streatham
Sidcup
Wimbledon
Merton
Bromley
Thames
Beckenham
Kingston-
upon-Thames
Croydon
Weybridge
Esher
Sutton
Orpington
Epsom
Purley

0 5 Km
0 5 Miles

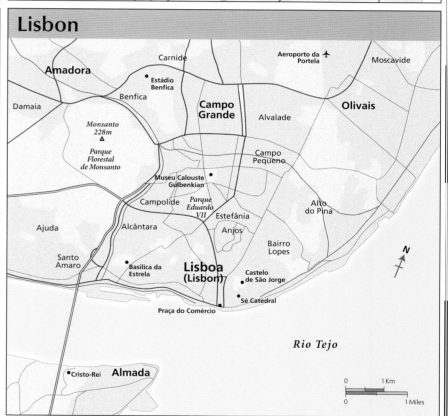

Lisbon

Carnide
Aeroporto da
Portela
Moscavide
Amadora
Estádio
Benfica
Damaia
Benfica
Campo
Grande
Olivais
Monsanto
228m
Alvalade
Parque
Florestal
de Monsanto
Campo
Pequeno
Museu Calouste
Gulbenkian
Parque
Eduardo
VII
Alto
do Pina
Ajuda
Campolide
Estefânia
Alcântara
Anjos
Bairro
Lopes
Santo
Amaro
Basílica da
Estrela
Lisboa
(Lisbon)
Castelo
de São Jorge
Sé Catedral
Praça do Comércio
Rio Tejo
Cristo-Rei
Almada

0 1 Km
0 1 Miles

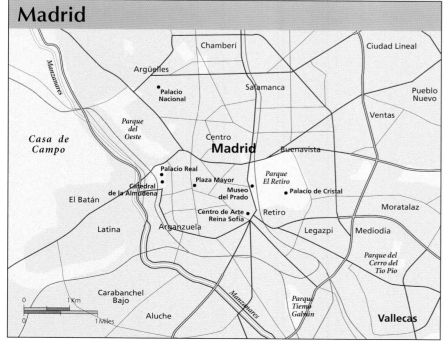

Madrid

Chamberí
Ciudad Lineal
Argüelles
Salamanca
Manzanares
Palacio
Nacional
Pueblo
Nuevo
Parque
del
Oeste
Centro
Ventas
Casa de
Campo
Madrid
Buenavista
Palacio Real
Parque
El Retiro
Cateral
de la Almudena
Plaza Mayor
Museo
del Prado
Palacio de Cristal
El Batán
Retiro
Centro de Arte
Reina Sofía
Moratalaz
Latina
Arganzuela
Legazpi
Mediodia
Manzanares
Parque del
Cerro del
Tío Pío
Carabanchel
Bajo
Parque
Tierno
Galván
Aluche
Vallecas

0 1 Km
0 1 Miles

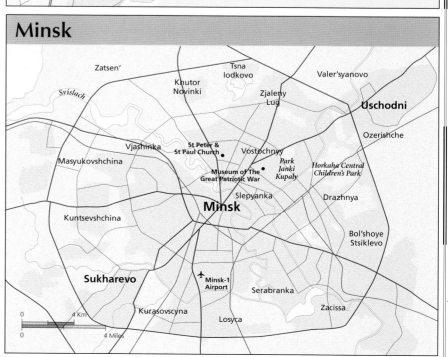

Minsk

Zatsen'
Tsna
Iodkovo
Valer'syanovo
Khutor
Novinki
Svislach
Zjaleny
Lug
Uschodni
Ozerishche
Vjashinka
St Peter &
St Paul Church
Vostochnyy
Masyukovshchina
Museum of The
Great Patriotic War
Park
Janki
Kupaly
Horkaha Central
Children's Park
Minsk
Slepyanka
Drazhnya
Kuntsevshchina
Bol'shoye
Stsiklevo
Sukharevo
Minsk-1
Airport
Serabranka
Kurasovscyna
Zacissa
Losyca

0 4 Km
0 4 Miles

H I J K L M N

Moscow

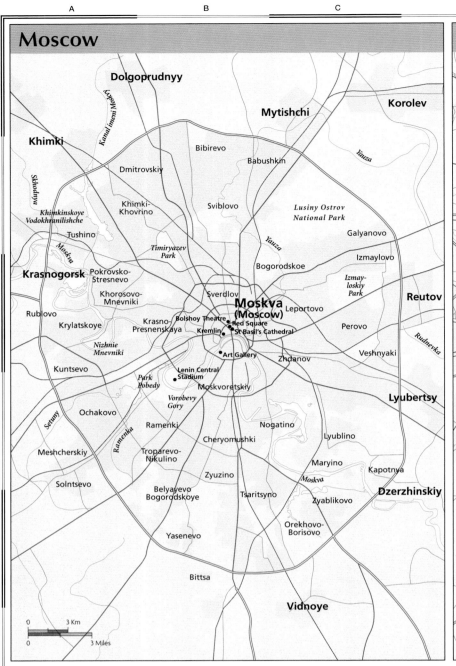

Munich

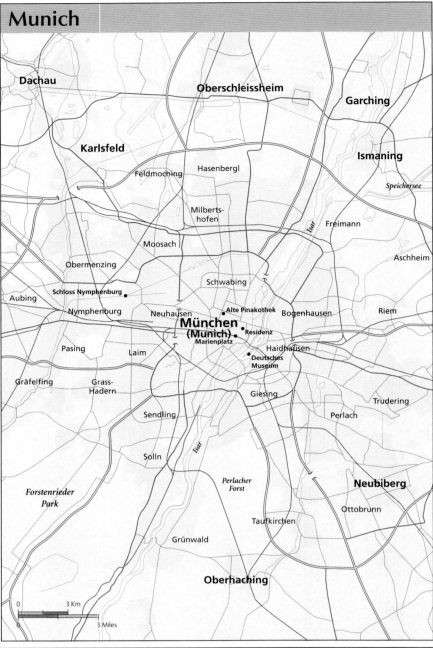

Oslo

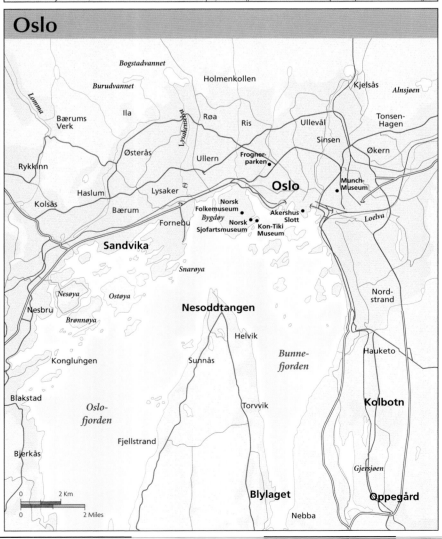

Prague

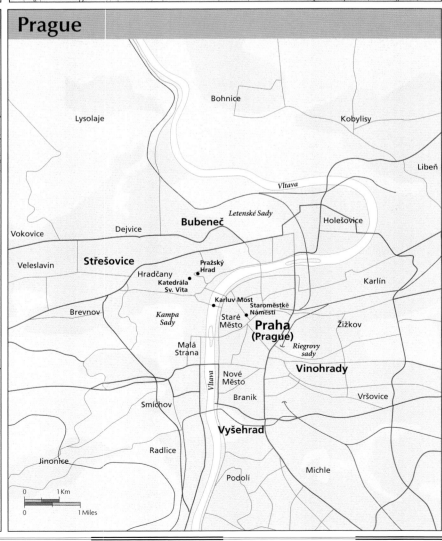

Rome

St Petersburg

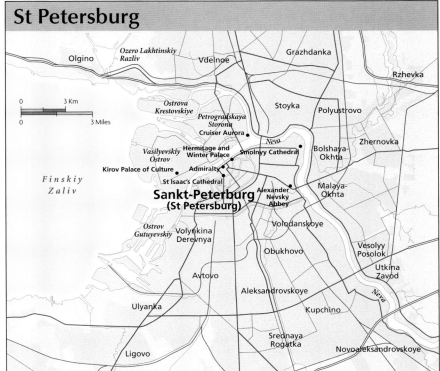

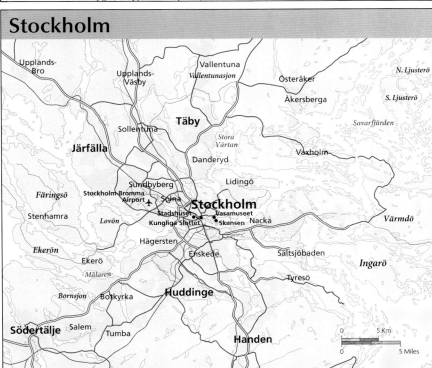

Stockholm

Sofia

Zagreb

Warsaw

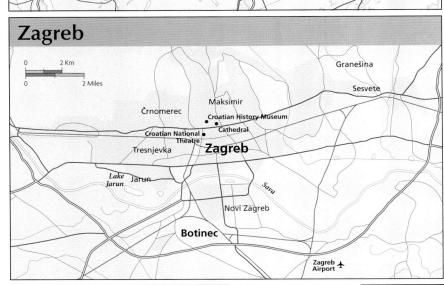

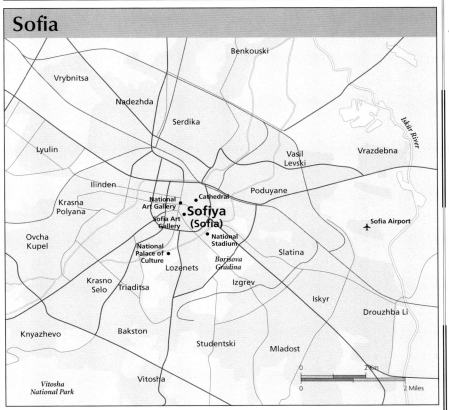

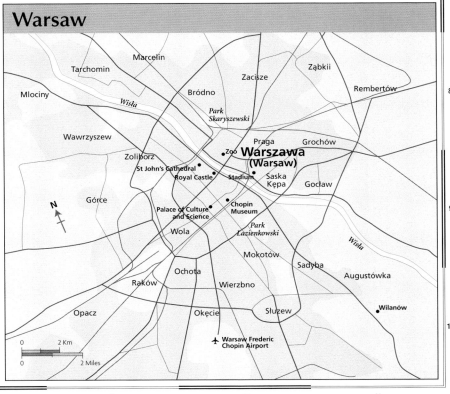

Asia is the world's largest continent with a total area of 16,838,365 sq miles (43,608,000 sq km). It comprises 49 separate countries, including 97% of Turkey and 72% of the Russian Federation. Almost 60% of the world's population lives in Asia.

FACTFILE

N **Most Northerly Point:** Mys Articesku, Russia 81° 12′ N
S **Most Southerly Point:** Pulau Pamana, Indonesia 11° S
E **Most Easterly Point:** Mys Dezhneva, Russia 169° 40′ W
W **Most Westerly Point:** Bozca Adası, Turkey 26° 2′ E

Largest Lakes:
1. Caspian Sea, Asia/Europe 143,243 sq miles (371,000 sq km)
2. Lake Baikal, Russian Federation 11,776 sq miles (30,500 sq km)
3. Lake Balkhash, Kazakhstan/China 7115 sq miles (18,428 sq km)
4. Aral Sea, Kazakhstan/Uzbekistan 6625 sq miles (17,160 sq km)
5. Tonlé Sap, Cambodia 3861 sq miles (10,000 sq km)

Longest Rivers:
1. Yangtze, China 3915 miles (6299 km)
2. Yellow River, China 3395 miles (5464 km)
3. Mekong, SE Asia 2749 miles (4425 km)
4. Lena, Russian Federation 2734 miles (4400 km)
5. Yenisey, Russian Federation 2541 miles (4090 km)

Largest Islands:
1. Borneo, Brunie/Indonesia/Malaysia 292,222 sq miles (757,050 sq km)
2. Sumatra, Indonesia 202,300 sq miles (524,000 sq km)
3. Honshu, Japan 88,800 sq miles (230,000 sq km)
4. Sulawesi, Indonesia 73,057 sq miles (189,218 sq km)
5. Java, Indonesia 53,589 sq miles (138,794 sq km)

Highest Points:
1. Mount Everest, China/Nepal 29,035 ft (8850 m)
2. K2, China/Pakistan 28,253 ft (8611 m)
3. Kangchenjunga I, India/Nepal 28,210 ft (8598 m)
4. Lhotse, Nepal 27,939 ft (8516 m)
5. Makalu I, China/Nepal 27,767 ft (8463 m)

Lowest Point:
▼ Dead Sea, Israel/Jordan -1286 ft (-392 m) below sea level

Highest recorded temperature:
Tirat Tsvi, Israel 129°F (54°C)

Lowest recorded temperature:
Verkhoyansk, Russian Federation -90°F (-68°C)

Wettest Place:
Cherrapunji, India 450 in (11,430 mm)

Driest Place:
Aden, Yemen 1.8 in (46 mm)

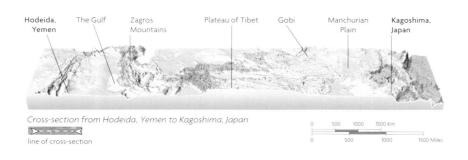

Cross-section from Hodeida, Yemen to Kagoshima, Japan

Hodeida, Yemen — The Gulf — Zagros Mountains — Plateau of Tibet — Gobi — Manchurian Plain — Kagoshima, Japan

▷ - ▪ - ▪ - ◁ line of cross-section

0 500 1000 1500 Km
0 500 1000 1500 Miles

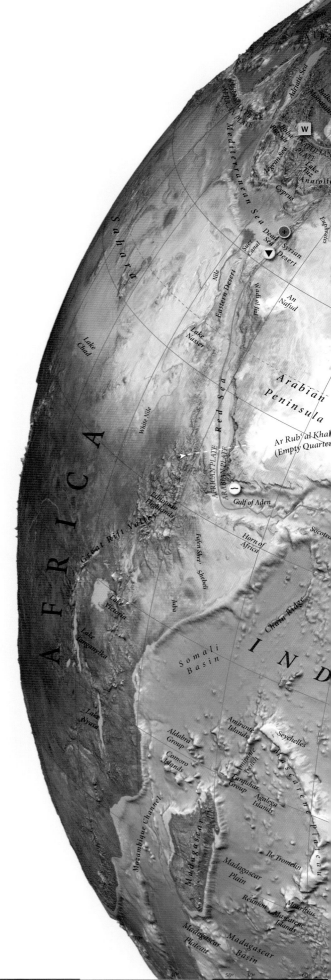

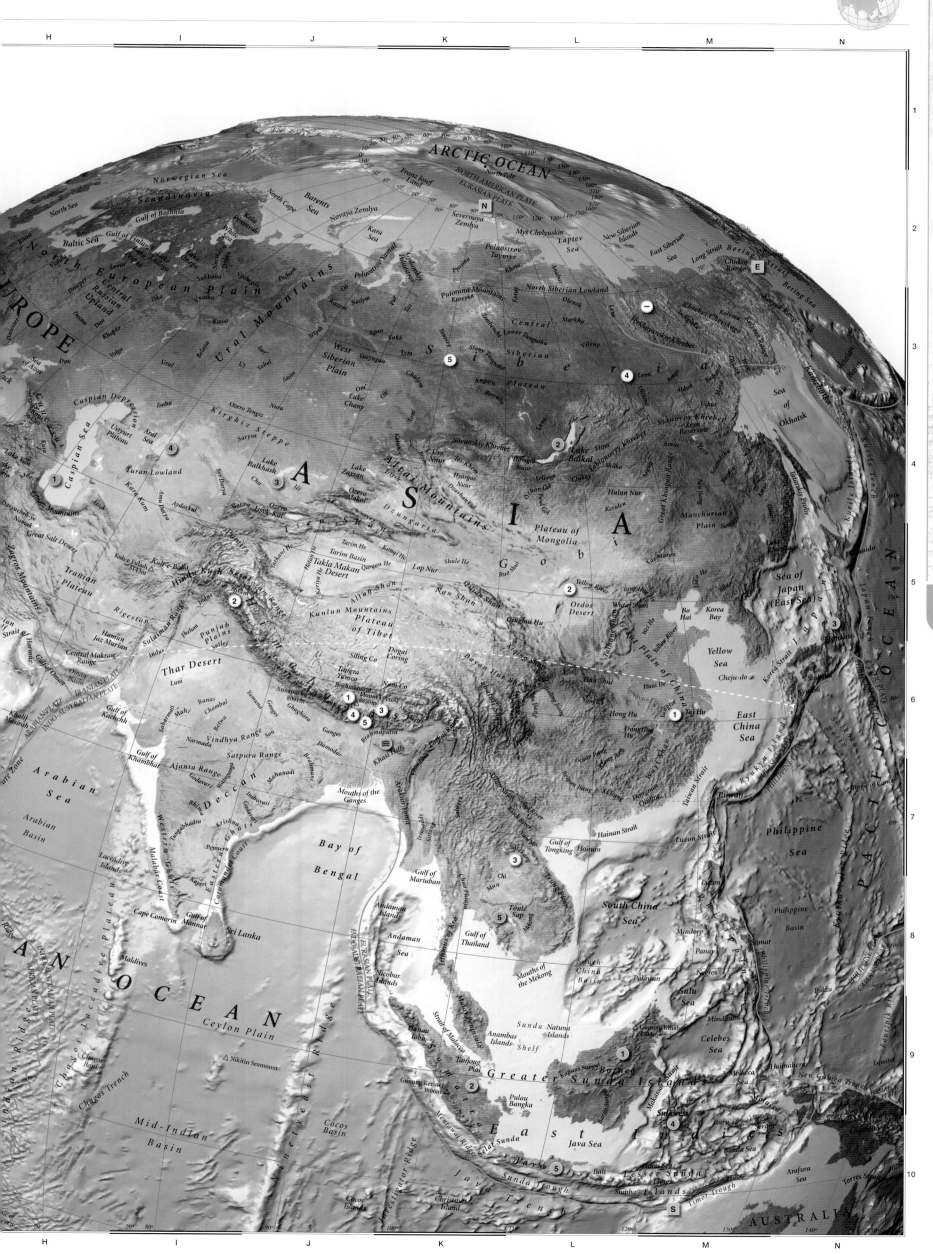

Political

Asia is the world's largest continent, encompassing many different and discrete realms, from the desert Arab lands of the southwest to the subtropical archipelago of Indonesia; from the vast barren wastes of Siberia to the fertile river valleys of China and South Asia, seats of some of the world's most ancient civilizations. The collapse of the Soviet Union has fragmented the north of the continent into the Siberian portion of the Russian Federation, and the new republics of Central Asia. Strong religious traditions heavily influence the politics of South and Southwest Asia. Hindu and Muslim rivalries threaten to upset the political equilibrium in South Asia where India—in terms of population—remains the world's largest democracy. Communist China, another population giant, is reasserting its position as a world political and economic power, while on its doorstep, the dynamic Pacific Rim countries, led by Japan, continue to assert their worldwide economic force.

Population density
(people per sq km)

- 0–9
- 10–49
- 50–99
- 100–249
- 250–3999
- 4000 +

Population

Some of the world's most populous and least populous regions are in Asia. The plains of eastern China, the Ganges river plains in India, Japan, and the Indonesian island of Java, all have very high population densities; by contrast parts of Siberia and Tibet are virtually uninhabited. China has the world's greatest population—20% of the globe's total—while India, with the second largest, will likely overtake China within 30 years.

Map labels

ARCTIC OCEAN · Bering Sea · East Siberian Sea · Anadyr' · Arctic Circle · Kolyma Range · Laptev Sea · Indigirka · Kolyma · Magadan · Kara Sea · Kheta · Olenëk · Anabar · Lena · Yana · Sea of Okhotsk · Central Siberian Plateau · Siberia · Noril'sk · Kureyka · Vilyuy · Yakutsk · Aldan · Arctic Circle · EUROPE · Ural Mountains · Ob' · RUSSIAN FEDERATION · West Siberian Plain · Yenisey · Stony Tunguska · Angara · Lake Baikal · Amur · Khabarovsk · Yekaterinburg · Tobol · Ishim · Irtysh · Chulym · Tomsk · Krasnoyarsk · Irkutsk · Argun · Chelyabinsk · Omsk · Novosibirsk · Novokuznetsk · Ural'sk · Rudnyy · ASTANA · Suhbaatar · Erdenet · ULAN BATOR · Choybalsan · Qiqihar · Harbin · Vladivostok · Istanbul · Black Sea · ANKARA · Sokhumi · GEORGIA · Bat'umi · K'ut'aisi · T'BILISI · KAZAKHSTAN · Karaganda · Semipalatinsk · MONGOLIA · Changchun · Jilin · Shenyang · NORTH KOREA · TURKEY · Anatolia · ARMENIA · YEREVAN · AZERB. · Gänca · Aral Sea · Syr Darya · Kyzylorda · Balkhash · Gobi · Inner Mongolia · Anshan · Wonsan · PYONGYANG · CYPRUS · Adana · Gaziantep · AZERB. · BAKU · Aktau · Lake Balkhash · Urumqi · BEIJING · Dalian · SEOUL · Inch'on · NICOSIA · Aleppo · Tabriz · Caspian Sea · UZBEKISTAN · Taraz · Almaty · Karakol · Altai Mountains · Baotou · Datong · Tangshan · SOUTH KOREA · LEBANON · Tripoli · SYRIA · Mosul · Dasoguz · Amu Darya · BISHKEK · KYRGYZSTAN · Tien Shan · Shijiazhuang · Baoding · Tianjin · BEIRUT · Haifa · DAMASCUS · Kirkuk · TURKMENISTAN · TASHKENT · Osh · Tarim He · Taiyuan · Handan · Jinan · Yellow Sea · Tel Aviv-Yafo · Gaza · JERUSALEM · AMMAN · BAGHDAD · TEHRAN · Gorgan · Mashhad · DUSHANBE · TAJIKISTAN · Takla Makan Desert · (claimed by India) · Lanzhou · Zhengzhou · Luoyang · Xuzhou · Nanjing · Shanghai · ISRAEL · JORDAN · Qom · Balkh · Qal'eh-ye Now · Herat · (line of control) · (administered by China, claimed by India) · Kunlun Mountains · Xi'an · Hefei · An Najaf · IRAQ · Esfahan · IRAN · AFGHANISTAN · KABUL · Jalalabad · Srinagar · Jammu · Huainan · Wuhan · Hangzhou · Ningbo · Basra · Ahvaz · Iranian Plateau · Peshawar · ISLAMABAD · CHINA · Mianyang · SAUDI ARABIA · KUWAIT · Kerman · Kandahar · Gujranwala · Faisalabad · Lahore · (Much of Arunachal Pradesh is claimed by China) · Plateau of Tibet · Salween · Chengdu · Changsha · Nanchang · Fuzhou · Shiraz · Zahedan · Quetta · Multan · Ludhiana · Himalayas · Mekong · Chongqing · Hengyang · Guiyang · KUWAIT · MANAMA · BAHRAIN · Bandar-e 'Abbas · PAKISTAN · Shikarpur · Delhi · Bareilly · Brahmaputra · Leshan · JEDDA · RIYADH · QATAR · ABU DHABI · Larkana · NEW DELHI · Lucknow · NEPAL · KATHMANDU · THIMPHU · BHUTAN · Guwahati · Liuzhou · Guangzhou · Kunming · Nanning · Guilin · At Ta'if · DOHA · UAE · Jaipur · Agra · Kanpur · Varanasi · Rangpur · Kaohsiung · TAIPEI · T'aichung · TAIWAN · Ar Rub' al Khali (Empty Quarter) · Gulf of Oman · Karachi · Hyderabad · INDIA · Patna · BANGLADESH · MYANMAR · HANOI · Hai Phong · Hong Kong (Xianggang) · Ar Rustaq · MUSCAT · Sur · Ahmadabad · Bhopal · Rajshahi · Brahmanbaria · DHAKA (BURMA) · Hainan Dao · OMAN · Arabian Sea · Vadodara · Indore · Jamshedpur · Khulna · Mandalay · Taunggyi · LAOS · Vinh · South China Sea · SANA · YEMEN · Narmada · Surat · Nagpur · Kolkata (Calcutta) · Chittagong · Pakokku · PYINMANA · Louangphabang · Da Nang · Ta'izz · Bhubaneswar · Prome · VIENTIANE · VIETNAM · Aden · Gulf of Aden · Socotra (to Yemen) · INDIAN OCEAN · Mumbai (Bombay) · Pune · Godavari · Solapur · Hyderabad · Vijayawada · Krishna · Bay of Bengal · RANGOON · Bassein · Bogale · Pegu · Chiang Mai · THAILAND · Pakxe · Hubli · Bangalore · Chennai (Madras) · Andaman Islands (to India) · Andaman Sea · BANGKOK · Batdambang · Da Lat · CAMBODIA · Ho Chi Minh City · Mysore · Coimbatore · PHNOM PENH · Cochin (Kochi) · Jaffna · Trivandrum · SRI LANKA · COLOMBO · Nicobar Islands (to India) · Gulf of Thailand · Kota Bharu · BANDAR SERI BEGAWAN · BRUNEI · Taiping · MALAYSIA · Borneo · Medan · KUALA LUMPUR · PUTRAJAYA · SINGAPORE · Pontianak · Balikpapan · SINGAPORE · Equator · INDONESIA · Banjarmasin · Padang · Jambi · Java Sea · Palembang · JAKARTA · Semarang · Surabaya · Bandung · Java

AFRICA · Red Sea · Tropic of Cancer · Persian Gulf · Euphrates · Tigris · Indus · Thar Desert · Arabian Peninsula

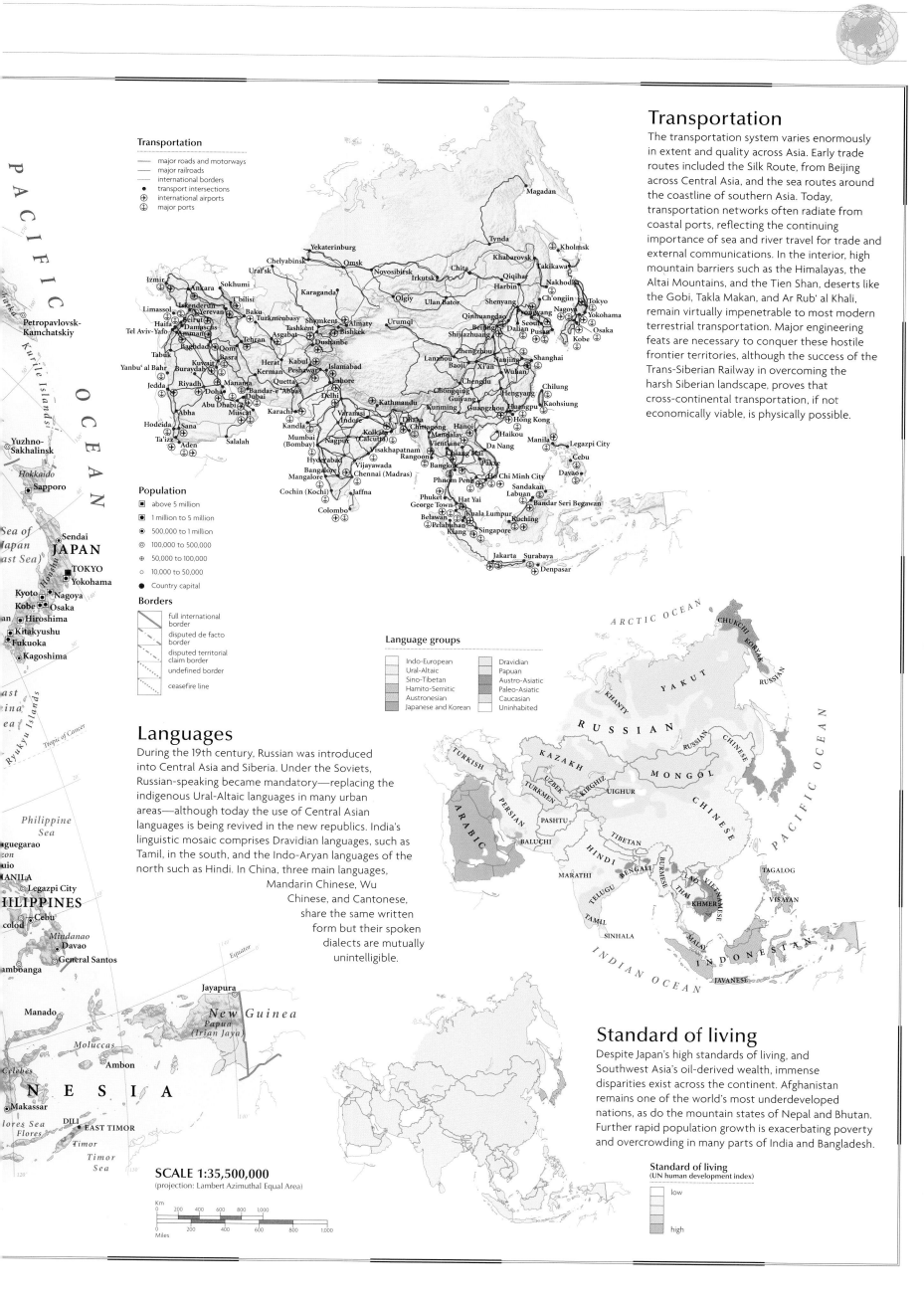

Transportation

The transportation system varies enormously in extent and quality across Asia. Early trade routes included the Silk Route, from Beijing across Central Asia, and the sea routes around the coastline of southern Asia. Today, transportation networks often radiate from coastal ports, reflecting the continuing importance of sea and river travel for trade and external communications. In the interior, high mountain barriers such as the Himalayas, the Altai Mountains, and the Tien Shan, deserts like the Gobi, Takla Makan, and Ar Rub' al Khali, remain virtually impenetrable to most modern terrestrial transportation. Major engineering feats are necessary to conquer these hostile frontier territories, although the success of the Trans-Siberian Railway in overcoming the harsh Siberian landscape, proves that cross-continental transportation, if not economically viable, is physically possible.

Transportation

- major roads and motorways
- major railroads
- international borders
- • transport intersections
- ⊕ international airports
- ⊕ major ports

Population

- ■ above 5 million
- ▣ 1 million to 5 million
- ◉ 500,000 to 1 million
- ◎ 100,000 to 500,000
- ⊕ 50,000 to 100,000
- ○ 10,000 to 50,000
- ● Country capital

Borders

- full international border
- disputed de facto border
- disputed territorial claim border
- undefined border
- ceasefire line

Language groups

- Indo-European
- Ural-Altaic
- Sino-Tibetan
- Hamito-Semitic
- Austronesian
- Japanese and Korean
- Dravidian
- Papuan
- Austro-Asiatic
- Paleo-Asiatic
- Caucasian
- Uninhabited

Languages

During the 19th century, Russian was introduced into Central Asia and Siberia. Under the Soviets, Russian-speaking became mandatory—replacing the indigenous Ural-Altaic languages in many urban areas—although today the use of Central Asian languages is being revived in the new republics. India's linguistic mosaic comprises Dravidian languages, such as Tamil, in the south, and the Indo-Aryan languages of the north such as Hindi. In China, three main languages, Mandarin Chinese, Wu Chinese, and Cantonese, share the same written form but their spoken dialects are mutually unintelligible.

Standard of living

Despite Japan's high standards of living, and Southwest Asia's oil-derived wealth, immense disparities exist across the continent. Afghanistan remains one of the world's most underdeveloped nations, as do the mountain states of Nepal and Bhutan. Further rapid population growth is exacerbating poverty and overcrowding in many parts of India and Bangladesh.

Standard of living
(UN human development index)

- low
- high

SCALE 1:35,500,000
(projection: Lambert Azimuthal Equal Area)

Km
0   200 400 600 800 1,000

Miles
0   200   400   600   800   1,000

Climate

The climate of Asia exhibits marked differences from region to region, with freezing polar conditions in the north, hot and cold deserts in central regions, and subtropical conditions throughout the south. Much of this variation can be attributed to enormous mountain barriers and internal depressions found across the continent. Monsoon winds, which reverse semi-annually, cause alternate wet and dry seasons across southern Asia. These air masses moving north from the ocean are stripped of their moisture over the Himalayas causing arid conditions across the Plateau of Tibet. Both the south and east are susceptible to tropical cyclones or typhoons.

Average Rainfall

January rainfall
July rainfall

Rainfall

	0–25 mm (0–1 in)
	25–50 mm (1–2 in)
	50–100 mm (2–4 in)
	100–200 mm (4–8 in)
	200–300 mm (8–12 in)
	300–400 mm (12–16 in)
	400–500 mm (16–20 in)
	more than 500 mm (20 in)

Average Temperature

January temperature
July temperature

Temperature

	below -30°C (-22°F)
	-30 to -20°C (-22 to -4°F)
	-20 to -10°C (-4 to 14°F)
	-10 to 0°C (14 to 32°F)
	0 to 10°C (32 to 50°F)
	10 to 20°C (50 to 68°F)
	20 to 30°C (68 to 86°F)
	above 30°C (86°F)

Climate

tundra		daily hours of sunshine, January	
subarctic			
cool continental		daily hours of sunshine, July	
warm humid		→ cyclone	
mediterranean		→ typhoon	
semi-arid		→ cold/dry monsoon	
arid		→ warm/wet monsoon	
humid equatorial		→ cold wind	
tropical			

Using the land and sea

cropland		fruit		sugar cane	
desert		jute		tea	
forest		peanuts		timber	
mountain region		rice		wheat	
pasture		rubber			
tundra		shellfish			
wetland		soya beans			
• major conurbations		sugar beet			
cattle					
pigs					
goats					
sheep					
coconuts					
corn (maize)					
cotton					
dates					
fishing					

Environmental issues

The transformation of Uzbekistan by the former Soviet Union into the world's fifth largest producer of cotton led to the diversion of several major rivers for irrigation. Starved of this water, the Aral Sea diminished in volume by over 75% since 1960, irreversibly altering the ecology of the area. Heavy industries in eastern China have polluted coastal waters, rivers and urban air, while in Myanmar (Burma), Malaysia, and Indonesia, ancient hardwood rain forests are felled faster than they can regenerate.

Environmental issues

tropical forest		polluted rivers	
forest destroyed		marine pollution	
desert		heavy marine pollution	
desertification		radioactive contamination	
acid rain		poor urban air quality	

Landuse

Vast areas of Asia remain uncultivated as a result of unsuitable climatic and soil conditions. In favorable areas such as river deltas, farming is intensive. Rice is the staple crop of most Asian countries, grown in paddy fields on waterlogged alluvial plains and terraced hillsides, and often irrigated for higher yields. Across the black earth region of the Eurasian steppe in southern Siberia and Kazakhstan, wheat farming is the dominant activity. Cash crops, like tea in Sri Lanka and dates in the Arabian Peninsula, are grown for export, and provide valuable income. The sovereignty of the rich fishing grounds in the South China Sea is disputed by China, Malaysia, Taiwan, the Philippines, and Vietnam, because of potential oil reserves.

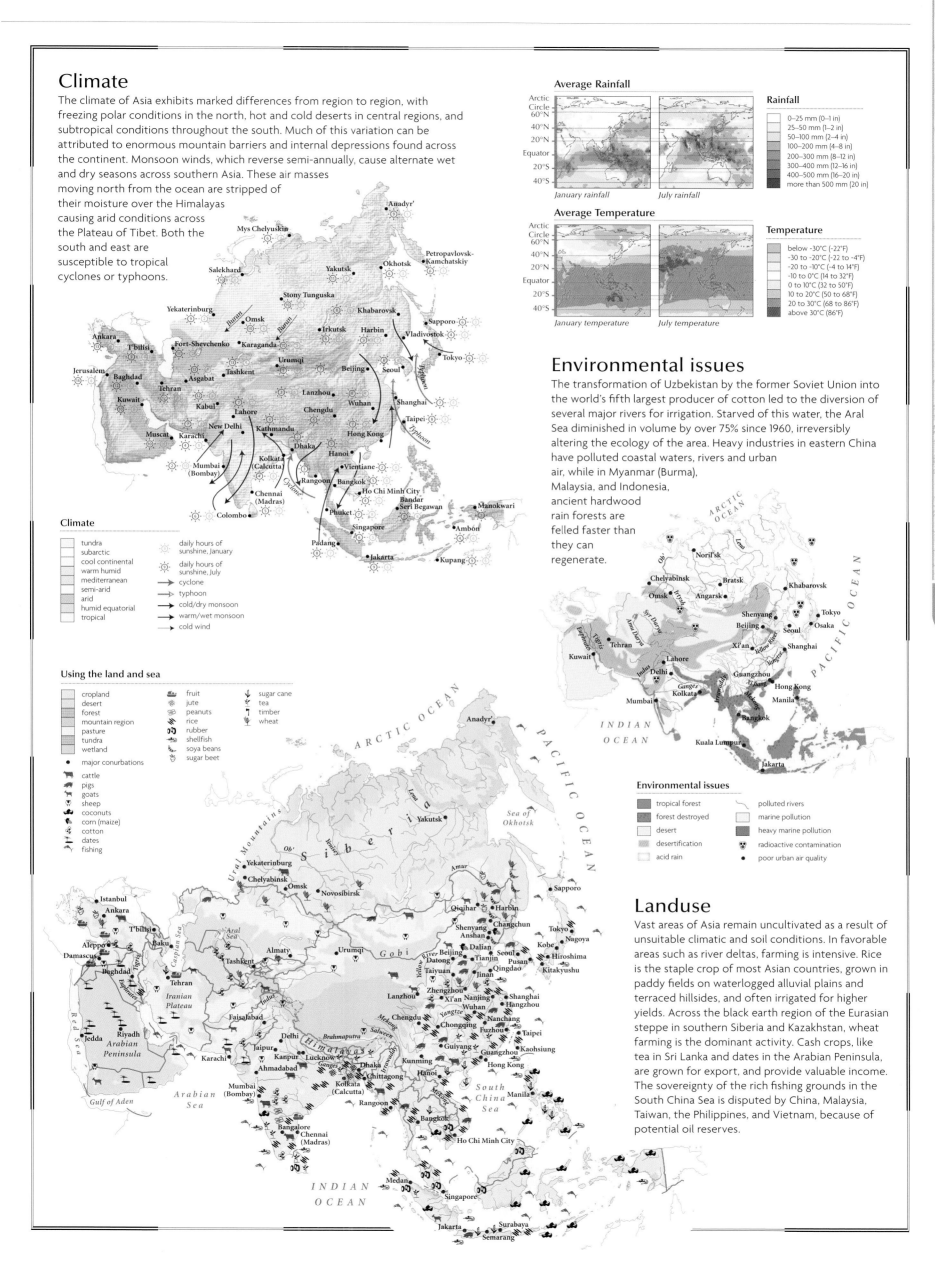

ASIA

1 — BOSPORUS, TURKEY
The Bosporus provides the only outlet for the Black Sea, linking it with the Sea of Marmara to the south and then with the Mediterranean Sea via the Dardanelles.

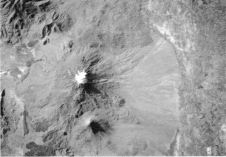

2 — MOUNT ARARAT, TURKEY
Said to be the resting place for Noah's Ark, this extinct volcanic massif lies in the far east of Turkey.

3 — LAKE BALKHASH, KAZAKHSTAN
Still covered in winter ice in this image, this lakes lies in a dry desert region and has no outlet.

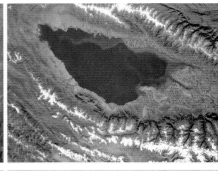

4 — OZERO ISSYK-KUL', KYRGYZSTAN
Against the dry slopes of the Tien Shan mountains to the south this lake appears bright blue.

9 — KUWAIT'S OILFIELDS, KUWAIT
The dark plumes are smoke rising from the 700 wells set alight by Iraqi forces during the Gulf War of 1991.

10 — PALM ISLAND, UNITED ARAB EMIRATES
This luxury housing development and tourist resort, one mile (1.6 km) off the seafront of Dubai, is built from sediments dredged from the nearby port of Jebel Ali.

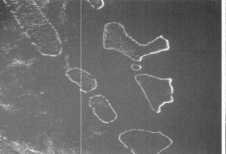

11 — MALDIVES
The Maldives consist of 1300 coral formations in 19 atolls and stretch over 1491 miles (2400 km).

12 — KARACHI, PAKISTAN
Pakistan's main seaport and former capital lies to the northwest of the delta of the Indus river.

THREE GORGES DAM, CHINA `5`
Seen here during its construction in 2000, the world's largest dam is designed to tame the Yangtze river which has regularly flooded.

BEIJING, CHINA `6`
China's ancient capital was laid out on a grid pattern centred on the Forbidden City and its streets are picked out in this winter image by snowfall.

MOUNT FUJI, JAPAN `7`
The steep, symmetrical, snow-capped volcano last erupted in 1707.

VULKAN KLYUCHEVSKAYA SOPKA, RUSSIAN FEDERATION `8`
The Kamchatka Peninsula's highest and most active volcano last erupted in 1994.

MOUNT EVEREST, CHINA/NEPAL `13`
The world's highest mountain at 29,035 ft (8850 m) straddles the border between China and Nepal.

MOUTHS OF THE GANGES, BANGLADESH/INDIA `14`
Stretching across the northern end of the Bay of Bengal, this river delta contains the Sundarbans, the world's largest mangrove forest, which appears as a rich green area.

MEKONG DELTA, VIETNAM `15`
The Mekong river flows over 2494 miles (4000 km) from the Plateau of Tibet before crossing Vietnam to reach the South China Sea.

HONG KONG, CHINA `16`
Handed back to China by the British in 1997, this city remains east Asia's trade and finance center.

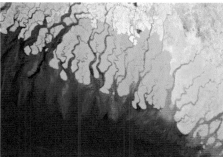

Countries and regions:
BOSNIA & HERZEGOVINA, CROATIA, MONTENEGRO, SERBIA, ROMANIA, BULGARIA, MACEDONIA, KOSOVO, ALBANIA, GREECE, TURKEY, RUSSIAN FEDERATION, GEORGIA, CYPRUS, TURKISH REPUBLIC OF NORTHERN CYPRUS (recognised only by Turkey), SYRIA, LEBANON, ISRAEL, JORDAN, IRAQ, SAUDI ARABIA, EGYPT, LIBYA, CHAD, SUDAN, ERITREA, ETHIOPIA, DJIBOUTI, CENTRAL AFRICAN REPUBLIC

Capitals and cities:
Perugia, Terni, L'Aquila, Pescara, Campobasso, Foggia, Bari, Napoli (Naples), Salerno, Potenza, Taranto, Lecce, Cosenza, Catanzaro, Reggio di Calabria, Messina, Catania, Siracusa, Ragusa, Split, PODGORICA, SKOPJE, SOFIA, TIRANE, Bitola, Thessaloniki, Larisa, ATHINA (ATHENS), Pátra, PRIŠTINA, SERBIA, Niš, Vratsa, Pleven, Razgrad, Shumen, Varna, Burgas, Plovdiv, Stara Zagora, Sliven, Edirne, Tekirdag, İstanbul, İzmit, Bursa, ANKARA, Kırıkkale, Eskişehir, Kütahya, Afyon, Konya, Antalya, Mersin, Adana, Tarsus, İskenderun, Antakya, Gaziantep, Halab (Aleppo), Al Ladhiqiyah, Latakia, Hamah, Hims (Homs), Tripoli, BEYROUTH (BEIRUT), DIMASHQ (DAMASCUS), Dumā, NICOSIA, Lárnaka, Lemesós, Hefa (Haifa), Tel Aviv-Yafo, Netanya, Ashdod, JERUSALEM, AMMAN, Constanța, Dobrich, Sevastopol, Yalta, Sochi, Sokhumi, Maykop, Nevinnomyssk, Kislovodsk, Nal'chik, Vladikavkaz, YEREVAN, T'BILISI, BAGHDAD, Karbalā', An Najaf, An Nāṣirīyah, As Samāwah, Al Hillah, Al Mawṣil (Mosul), Kirkūk, Bayjī, Ar Raqqah, Dayr az Zawr, Al Hasakah, Arbīl, As Sulaymānīyah

Physical features:
Adriatic Sea, Ionian Sea, Tyrrhenian Sea, Aegean Sea, Mediterranean Sea, Black Sea, Red Sea, Gulf of Suez, Gulf of Aqaba, Nile, Lake Nasser, Sinai, Suez Canal, Nile Delta, Libyan Plateau, Khalīj Surt (Gulf of Sirte), Qattâra Depression (Monkhafad el Qattâra), Sahara el Gharbiya (Western Desert), Great Sand Sea, Libyan Desert, An Nafūd, Sahara, Nubian Desert, Sahel, Ethiopian Highlands, Danakil Desert, Great Rift Valley

Egypt cities:
Alexandria, El 'Alamein, Dumyât (Damietta), Port Said, Tanta, Zagazig, Ismâ'ilîya, CAIRO, El Gîza, Suez, Beni Suef, El Minya, Mallawi, Asyût, Sohâg, Qena, Luxor, Aswân, El Khârga, Siwa, Bawiti, Qasr Farâfra, Mût, Wadi Halfa

Saudi Arabia cities:
Tabūk, Al Wajh, Ha'il, Buraydah, Khaybar, Al Madīnah (Medina), Yanbu'al Bahr, JIDDAH (JEDDA), Makkah (Mecca), At Ta'if, Al Bāḥah, Abhā, Najrān

Sudan cities:
Port Sudan, Suakin, Dongola, Abu Hamed, Atbara, Ed Damer, KHARTOUM, Omdurman, Khartoum North, Kassala, Wad Medani, Gedaref, Sennar, El Obeid, En Nahud, Er Rahad, Umm Ruwaba, Nyala, El Fasher, El Geneina, Abéché

Other:
ASMARA, Keren, ERITREA, Aksum, Mek'ele, Gonder, Bahir Dar, DJIBOUTI, SAN'A, Al Hudaydah (Hodeida), KHARTOUM, Faya, Fada, Biltine

Tropic of Cancer

Elevation scale (metres):
6000m, 4000m, 3000m, 2000m, 1000m, 500m, 250m, 100m, Sea Level, -250m, -500m, -1000m

Pic Bette 2286m, Emi Koussi 3415m, Jebel Musa 2285m, Mount Hermon 2814m, Ras Dashen Terara 4620m

185, 131, 136

Scale 1:11,750,000
(projection: Lambert Azimuthal Equal Area)

0 50 100 150 200 250 300 Km
0 50 100 150 200 250 300 Miles

Population
■ above 5 million   ■ 1 million to 5 million   ◉ 500,000 to 1 million
◎ 100,000 to 500,000   ⊕ 50,000 to 100,000   ○ 10,000 to 50,000   ○ below 10,000

ASIA
213

Makhachkala
Aktau
Zhanaozen
KAZAKHSTAN
Ustyurt Plateau
UZBEKISTAN
Kyzyl Kum
KAZAKHSTAN
Taraz
Turkestan
BISHKEK
Balykchy
Karakol
KYRGYZSTAN
Tien Shan
Naryn
Kokshaal-Tau
Artux
Kashi
CHINA

Derbent
Sarygamyş Köli
Daşoguz
Urganch
Nukus
Uchquduq
Shymkent
Chirchiq
TOSHKENT
(TASHKENT)
Angren
Namangan
Dzhalal-Abad
Gora Ak-Tash
4718m
Qsh
Kek-Art
Shache

Sumqayıt
BAKI
(BAKU)
Qazimämmäd
Türkmenbaşy
Balkanabat
Üngüz Angyrsyndaky Garagum
Lebap
Gazli
Navoiy
Buxoro
Qulmiq
Qo'qon
Andijon
Farg'ona
Qarshi
Samarqand
Qatorkühi Zarafshon
Ayni
Kommunizm
7495m
Qarokül
DUSHANBE
TAJIKISTAN
Murghob

ZERBAIJAN
Mingäçevir
Ardabil
Makhachkala
Tabriz
Marägheh
Rasht
Zanjän
Qazvin
Amol
Babol
Säri
Shährud
Gorgän
Koppeh Dägh
Esenguly
Bojnurd
Serdar
AŞGABAT
Merkezi Garagumy
Mary
Yolöten
Atamyrat
Zeïdskoye Vodokhranilishche
Türkmenabat
Sayat
Denov
Qürghonteppa
Külob
Khorugh
Rostavatiya
6974m
Qürghonteppa
Dusti
K2
8611m
Gilgit
Indus
(Line of control)

Sanandaj
Hamadän
Malâyer
Aräk
Qom
TEHRÄN
Semnän
Dasht-e Kavir
Sabzevär
Mashhad
Küshk
Serəxabad
Qal'eh-ye Now
Härät
Shährak
Charikär
Marghi
Meymaneh
Mazâr-e Sharif
Balkh
Aqcha
Termiz
Eshkämesh
Kondoz
Eshkäshem
Asadäbäd
Asmär
Barikowt
KABOL
(KABUL)
Jaläläbäd
Khyber Pass
1080m
Mingäora
Srinagar
Jammu

ermänshäh
Bäkhtarän)
Khorramäbäd
Borüjerd
Najafäbäd
Kâshän
Shahreza
Esfahän
Yazd
Abädeh
Robät-e Khän
Gonäbäd
Anär Darreh
Shindand
Baghrän
Deläräm
Üruzgän
Zareh Sharan
Gardiz
Kälät
PESHĀWAR
Rāwalpindi
ISLĀMĀBĀD
Miänwäli
Jhelum
Gujrät
Gujränwäla
Amritsar
Faisäläbäd
Lahore
Säniwäl
Okära
Bahäwalnagar

Dezful
märah)
An Näşiriyah
Al Başrah
(Basra)
Äbädän
Khorramshahr
Ahväz
Masjed Soleymän
Kermänshäh
Anär
Ravar
Darvishän
Chakhänsür
Zäbol
Hämün-e Säberi
Darya-ye Helmand
Gereshk
Deh Shü
Kandahār
Spin Büldak
Chaman
Dera Ismä'il Khän
Sähiwäl
Okära
Multän
Bahäwalpur
Bikäner

KUWAIT
AL KUWAYT
(KUWAIT)
Kazerün
Shiräz
Darâb
Sirjän
Bam
Kermän
Zähedän
Chägai Hills
Dälbandin
Sürāb
Quetta
Jacobäbäd
Shikärpur
Lärkäna
Sukkur
Dera Ghazi Khän
Rahimyär Khän
Bahäwalpur
Thar Desert
Jodhpur

afar al Bätin
Bandar-e Büshehr
Bandar-e Kangän
Gävbandi
Hämün-e Jaz Mürän
Iränshahr
Siähän Range
Bela
Turbat
Nawäbshäh
Mirpur Khäs
Bärmer
Päli

An Nu'ayriyah
Ad Dammäm
BAHRAIN
AL MANĀMAH
(MANAMA)
Al Hufüf
AD DAWHAH
(DOHA)
QATAR
Dubayy
(Dubai)
Ash Shäriqah
Bandar-e'Abbäs
Strait of Hormuz
Makran Coast
Könärak
Gulf of Oman
Indus
Mouths of the Indus
Karāchi
Rann of Kachchh
Tropic of Cancer
Mahesäna
Gändhidhäm
Ahmadäbäd

R RIYĀD
(RIYADH)
Harad
ABŪ ZABY
(ABU DHABI)
Tarif
Al 'Ayn
Suhär
Ar Rustäq
Al Hajar al Gharbi
Ibri
As Suwayq
MASQAT
(MUSCAT)
UNITED ARAB EMIRATES
OMAN
Sür
Surendranagar
Jämnagar
Vadodara
Räjkot
Bhävnagar
Bhärüch
Sürat

Laylä
Adam
Ramlat Ál Wahibah
Al Ghäbah
Porbandar
Käthiäwär Peninsula
Veräval
Gulf of Khambhät

insula
Al 'Urüq al Mu'taridah
OMAN
Khalij Maşirah
Duqm
Mughshin
Jiddat al Harāsis
Şawqirah

Ar Rub' al Khäli
(Empty Quarter)
Zufär
Sanäw
Thamarit
Şaläläh
Jabal al Qamar
Damqawt

amlat as Sab'atayn
Al Mahrah
Tarim
Sayhüt
Arabian

YEMEN
Ar Rawdah
Ash Shihr
Al Mukallä
Hadramawt
Sea

Gulf of Aden
Suquträ
(Socotra)

iqrah
SOMALIA
Boosaaso
Caluula
Raas Xaafuun
Shimbiris
2407m
arin
Ceerigaabo
OMALILAND
(not internationally recognized)

226
232
288

Riyadh

Ad Dir'iyah
Al Marooj
Al Mursalat
Al Hamra
King Khaled Intl. Airport
Al Roudah Park
Al Ulayah
Al Rawabi Park
Al Quds
Ar Riyād
(Riyadh)
Zoo
Al Malaz
Al Murabba
Al Amir Fahad Park
Al Noor
Dhratal Badiah
Al Masmak Fortress
Al Nasiriyah Gate
Al Hamrah Palace
Main Juma'a Mosque
King Abdul Aziz Manakh Park
Hijrat Laban
Al Madinah As Sinaiiyah
Yamamah
Al Masanya
Al Dar Al Baida
Nammar
Jiza

0 3 Km
0 3 Miles

ASIA

19,686ft
13,124ft
9843ft
6562ft
3281ft
1640ft
820ft
328ft
Sea Level
-820ft
-6562ft
-13,124ft

Turkey & the Caucasus

ASIA

214

UKRAINE

ROMANIA

BULGARIA

Black Sea

Sea of Azov

RESPUBLIKA KRYM

Simferopol

Sevastopol'

Yalta

Kerch

Novorossiysk

BUCUREȘTI (BUCHAREST)

Pitești

Ploiești

Galați

Brăila

Constanța

Plovdiv

Stara Zagora

Burgas

Varna

Dobrich

Edirne

KIRKLARELI

İSTANBUL

TEKIRDAĞ

EDIRNE

Istanbul

Marmara Denizi (Sea of Marmara)

İstanbul Boğazı (Bosporus)

İzmit

KOCAELI

Adapazarı

SAKARYA

BURSA

Bursa

BILECIK

BOLU

ÇANKIRI

Çankırı

ÇORUM

ANKARA

Kırıkkale

KIRIKKALE

KIRŞEHIR

YOZGAT

SIVAS

ZONGULDAK

Zonguldak

BARTIN

KASTAMONU

Kastamonu

SINOP

Sinop

SAMSUN

Samsun

AMASYA

Amasya

TOKAT

Tokat

ORDU

ÇANAKKALE

Çanakkale

BALIKESIR

Balıkesir

MANISA

Manisa

İZMIR

İzmir

AYDIN

Aydın

DENIZLI

Denizli

MUĞLA

Muğla

UŞAK

Uşak

KÜTAHYA

Kütahya

ESKİŞEHIR

Eskişehir

AFYON

Afyon

ISPARTA

Isparta

BURDUR

Burdur

ANTALYA

Antalya

KONYA

Konya

AKSARAY

Aksaray

NEVŞEHIR

Nevşehir

KAYSERI

Kayseri

NIĞDE

Niğde

KARAMAN

Karaman

MERSIN

Mersin

ADANA

Adana

KAHRAMANMARAŞ

Kahramanmaraş

GAZIANTEP

Gaziantep

KILIS

HATAY

Antakya

İskenderun

Aegean Islands

Lésvos (Lesbos)

Chíos

Ródos (Rhodes)

Kárpathos

Dodekánisa

Kríti

GREECE

Mediterranean Sea

Antalya Körfezi

İskenderun Körfezi

CYPRUS

TURKISH REPUBLIC OF NORTHERN CYPRUS
(recognised only by Turkey)

NICOSIA

Lemesós (Limassol)

Gazimağusa (Ammóchostos, Famagusta)

Al Lādhiqīyah (Latakia)

AL LĀDHIQĪYAH

IDLIB

HAMAH

Hamāh

Ḥimṣ (Homs)

LEBANON

BEYROUTH (BEIRUT)

DIMASHQ (DAMASCUS)

HALAB

Halab (Aleppo)

TARTŪS

Tripoli

6000m
4000m
3000m
2000m
1000m
500m
250m
100m
Sea Level
-250m
-500m
-1000m

189
187
129

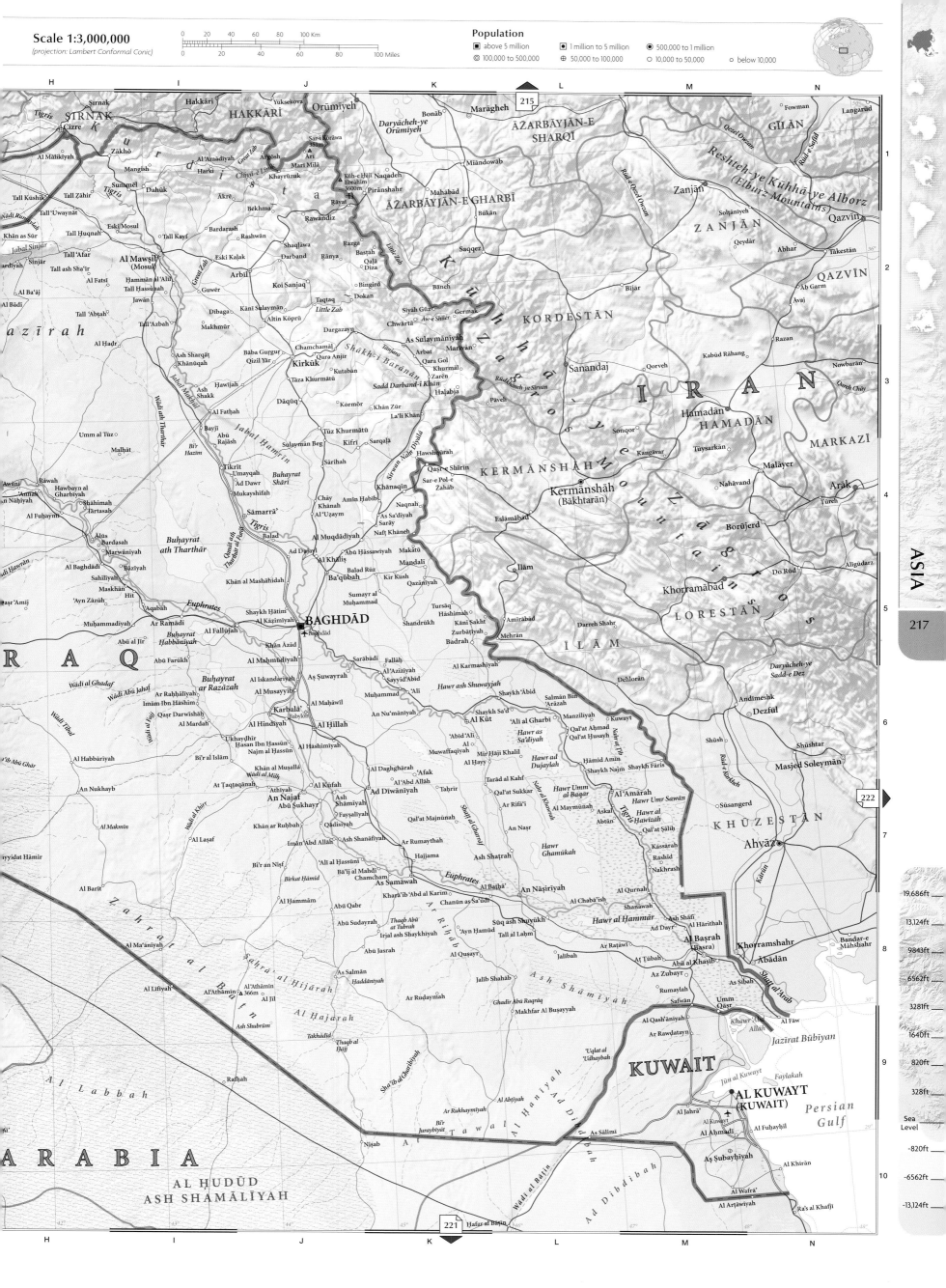

ASIA

218

Countries / Regions

CYPRUS

TURKISH REPUBLIC OF NORTHERN CYPRUS
(recognized only by Turkey)

HIMŞ

DIMASHQ

SYRIA

LEBANON

ASH SHAMAL

AL BIQA'

JABAL LUBNĀN

BEYROUTH (BEIRUT)

NABATIYE

AL JANUB

NORTHERN

AS SUWAYDA'

DAR'A

IRBID

HAIFA

CENTRAL

AL MAFRAQ

AL QUNAYTIRAH

Golan Heights

Jabal al 'Arab

As Şafā

Lebanon

Anti Lebanon

Jebel ech Cheikh

Cities

Hims (Homs)

DIMASHQ (DAMASCUS)

Beyrouth (Beirut)

Tripoli

El Mina

Baalbek

Zahlé

Saïda

Sour

Naharîyya

Hefa (Haifa)

Netanya

Inset maps

CYPRUS
Scale 1:2,000,000
0 5 10 20 30 40 Km
0 5 10 20 30 40 Miles

NICOSIA

Girne (Kerýneia)

Gazimağusa (Famagusta)

Lárnaka

Lemesós (Limassol)

Páfos

Akrotíri Sovereign Base Area (to UK)

Dhekelia Sovereign Base Area (to UK)

Zafer Burnu (Akrotíri Apostólou Andréa)

Beirut
Mediterranean Sea
Sea Port
East Suburbs
Beirut River
Baabda
Dahye
West Beirut
South Beirut
National Museum
Prime Minister's Office
Parliament
Palace of Justice
United Nations
UNESCO
0 2 Km
0 2 Miles

Jerusalem
Mount of Olives
Old City
Dome of the Rock
Church of the Holy Sepulchre
Abu Dis
Jerusalem
Hebrew University
Israel Museum
Talpiyot
Talpiyot East
Jabel Mukaber
Ramat Eshkol
0 1 Km
0 1 Miles

Elevation scale
6000m
4000m
3000m
2000m
1000m
500m
250m
100m
Sea Level
-250m
-500m
-1000m

216
214
199

Scale 1:1,500,000
(projection: Lambert Conformal Conic)

0 10 20 30 40 50 Km
0 10 20 30 40 50 Miles

Population
■ above 5 million
▣ 1 million to 5 million
◉ 500,000 to 1 million
◎ 100,000 to 500,000
⊕ 50,000 to 100,000
○ 10,000 to 50,000
∘ below 10,000

19,686ft
13,124ft
9843ft
6562ft
3281ft
1640ft
820ft
328ft
Sea Level
-820ft
-6562ft
-13,124ft

Mediterranean Sea

SAUDI ARABIA

AZ ZARQA'

AL JAWF

JORDAN

MA'AN

AL 'AȘIMAH

AMMAN

AL KARAK

AT TAFILAH

Dead Sea

West Bank

JERUSALEM

ISRAEL

SOUTHERN

Ha Negev

AL 'AQABAH

Gulf of Aqaba

Gaza Strip

EGYPT

Sinai

TABŪK

SAUDI ARABIA

Jibāl al 'Adhriyāt

Ash Sharāh

Jibāl at Batrā'

Jabal al Khashsh

ASIA

129

A B C D E F G

Scale (elevation):
6000m
4000m
3000m
2000m
1000m
500m
250m
100m
Sea Level
-250m
-500m
-1000m

Egypt / Sahara region

Libyan Plateau
Ras el-Kenâyis
Monkhafad el Qattâra (Qattâra Depression)
Qâra
El 'Alamein
Alexandria
Damanhûr
Kafr el Sheikh
Rashid (Rosetta)
Nile Delta
Dumyât (Damietta)
Port Said
Tanta
Shibin el Kôm
Zagazig
El Mansûra
Benha
CAIRO
El Gîza
Pyramids of Giza
Helwân
Cairo
Suez
Ismâ'îliya
Suez Canal
El 'Arish
Gaza Strip
El Faiyûm
El Saff
Beni Suef
Za'farâna
Abu Zenima
Gebel Mûsa 2285m
El Fashn
Beni Mazâr
Bawîti
El Minya
Mallawi
Dairût
Asyût
Abnûb
Qasr Farâfra
SAHARA
Sahara el Gharbîya (Western Desert)
Tahta
Sohâg
Akhmîm
Girga
Qena
Hurghada
Bûr Safâga
Sahara el Sharqîya (Eastern Desert)
El Khârga
EGYPT
Mût
El Qasr
Abu Balâs 467m
Nile
Isna
Luxor
Thebes
Valley of the Kings
Idfu
Kôm Ombo
Bâris
Edfu
Marsa 'Alam
Tropic of Cancer
Aswân
Aswân Dam
Abu Simbel
Berenice
Râs Banâs
Lake Nasser
Selima Oasis
Wadi Halfa
NORTHERN
Akasha
Nile
Delgo
Argo
Dongola
Nubian Desert
Wadi Hidiglib
El Khandaq
Abu Hamed
Merowe
Ed Debba
Korti
Shereik
Wadi 'Amur
RIVER NILE
Berber
Atbara
Ed Damer
Adarama
Atbara
Eilei
Kabushiya
Shendi
Abu 'Urug
Nile
KHARTOUM
Omdurman
KHARTOUM
Khartoum North
NORTHERN KORDOFAN
Umm Inderab
El Kamlin
El Manaqil
Rufa'a
Barakat
Wad Medani
GEZIRA
Wad Nimr
Bara
Hag 'Abdullah
El Obeid
Umm Ruwaba
Ed Dueim
SUDAN
Kosti
Rabak
SINNAR
Singa
Er Rahad
Tendelti
El Jebelein
WHITE NILE
Delami
Rashad
Nuba Mountains
SOUTHERN KORDOFAN
Renk
Ed Damazin
Roseires Reservoir
Er Roseires
BLUE NILE
Kurmuk
Guba
UPPER NILE
Kodok
Malakal
Machar Marshes
Sobat
JONGLEI
Melut
Paloich

Sinai / Israel / Jordan region

TEL AVIV-YAFO
Netanya
Jenin
Irbid
Jericho
Nâblus
West Bank
As Safâwî
Al Mafraq
Syrian Desert
Wâdi Ubayyiḍ
TEL AVIV
Tel Aviv-Yafo
JERUSALEM
AMMAN
ISRAEL
Gaza
Rafah
Be'er Sheva
Az Zarqâ
JORDAN
As Suwayrah
IRAQ
Beersheba
Al Karak
Mizpe Ramon
Telalim
Sappir
Ar Rashâdîyah
Bayir
At Turayf
Jabal Unayzah 940m
Al Jafr
Al Ghadaf
Imâm Ibn Hâshim
Wâdi al Ghadaf
Al Maḥmûdîyah
As Suwayrah
Babylon
Al Hillah
Karbalâ'
Al Habbârîyah
Buḥayrat ar Razâzah
An Najaf
An Nukhayb
Al Kûfa
'Afak
Ad Dîwânîyah
Ḥawr ad Dujaylah
'Amârah
Jabal al 'Amûd 1070m
Imân 'Abd Allâh
Al Baṭḥâ
As Samâwah
Ash Shatrah
Abû Sudayrah
Al Ma'anîyah
As Salmân
Al 'Athâmîn
Suq ash Shuyûkh
Ar Ruḍaymah
Al Jil
Ar Rifâ'i
An Nâṣiriya
Makhfar al Buṣayyah
Rumayl
Thaqb al Ḥajj
KUWAIT
As Salmân
Hafar al Bâṭin
As Sarrâr
Nisâb

Arabian Peninsula / Saudi Arabia

'Aqabat
Al 'Aqabah
Ḥaql
Jabal Ramm 1754m
Mudawwarah
Jabal Maqlâ
Bi'r
Jabal al Lawz 2580m
Ash Sharmah
Jabal Dabbagh 2350m
Qubâ
Al Bad'
Al Akhḍar
Tabûk
Ad Dâr al Ḥamrâ
Bi'r Fajr
Al Qalibah
Al Jawf
AL JAWF
AL ḤUDÛD ASH SHAMÂLÎYAH
'Adhfâ
An Nafûd
Al Mayyâh
Ath Thumâmî
Al Warî'
TABÛK
Ṭaymâ'
Bi'r al Murâ
Ḥâ'il
ḤÂ'IL
Al Ghazâlah
AL QAṢÎM
Buraydah
'Unayzah
Az Zilfî
Al Artâwîyah
Al Majma'ah
Rumâh
Shaqrâ
Marah
AR RIYÂḌ (RIYADH)
Durma
Ad Dawâdimî
Al Quwayyah
Al Kharj
Ḥalabân
Ar Ruwaydah
Layla
SAUDI ARABIA
AR RIYÂḌ
Budayyi'ah
Jabal Ṭuwayq
Al Ulâ
Khaybar
Ḥadîyah
Bi'r al 'Afarîyah
Al Madînah (Medina)
AL MADÎNAH
Al Ḥanâkîyah
Najd
'Uqlat aṣ Ṣuqûr
Wâdi ar Rimah
Jalâjil
Al Wajh
Umm Lajj
Jabal Raḍwâ 1814m
Yanbu'al Baḥr
Badr Ḥunayn
Râbigh
Mahd adh Dhahab
'Afîf
Al Miṣlah
Zalim
At Ṭâ'if
MAKKAH
JIDDAH (JEDDA)
Makkah (Mecca)
King Abdul Aziz
Ras Abu Shagara
Dungûnab
Muhammad Qol
Turabah
Ar Rawḍah
'Aynin
Wâdi Bishah
Al Khurmah
Al Lith
Al Bâḥah
AL BÂḤAH
Daws
Qal'at Bishah
As Sulayyil
'Urûq al Mawârid
Al Qunfudhah
Al Birk
Turbah
Muhayil
ASÎR
Tathlîth
Khamis Mushayt
Abha
Jabal Sawda 3133m
NAJRÂN
Ad Darb
Zahrân
JIZÂN
Najrân
Ṣabyâ
Ḥarrat Raḥaṭ
Najd

Red Sea / Sudan coast

(Administrative border)
(administered by Sudan)
(political border)
(administered by Egypt)
Halaib
Salala
RED SEA
Red Sea
Port Sudan
Sallom
Suakin
Musmar
Haiya
Tokar
Ekowit
Sinkat
Ras Shakal
Derudeb
Wadi Langeb
Eriba

Eritrea / Ethiopia region

KASSALA
Göz Regeb
Khashm el Girba
Kassala
Barentu
Teseney
Om Hajer
Gedaref
GEDAREF
Rahad
El Hawata
Doka
Gallabat
Metema
Âykel
Gonder
Degoma
Adis Zemen
T'ana Hâyk'
Bahir Dar
Dangila
Âsayita
BENISHANGUL
Asosa
Mendi
Fiché
OROMO
Bure
Debre Mark'os
Abuyé Mëda 4000m
Mot'a
Abay Wenz
ETHIOPIA
Ethiopian Highlands
Ras Dashen Terara 4620m
AMHARA
Lalibela
Weldiya
Debre Tabor
Dese
Korem
Sek'ot'a
Alamat'a
Mek'ele
TIGRAY
Âbiy Âdi
Adwa
Âksum
Âdigrat
Adi Ark'ay
Maych'ew
ERITREA
ASMARA
Mendefera
Keren
Massawa
Zula
Akurdet
Soyra 3018m
Mersa Fatma
Dahlak Archipelago
Massawa Channel
Jazâ'ir Farasân
Jazîrat Jabal Zuqar
Jazîrat al Hanish al Kabîr

Yemen / Djibouti / Somalia

YEMEN
Ṣa'dah
Ḥûth
Khamir
'Amrân
ṢAN'Â (SANA)
Ṣan'â
Jabal an Nabî Shu'ayb 3760m
Ḥajjah
Al Luḥayyah
Al Ḥudaydah (Hodeida)
Bayt al Faqîh
Zabîd
Bâjil
Dhamâr
Yarîm
Rada'
Ibb
Ta'izz
Al Mukha
Lahij
'Adan (Aden)
Madînat ash Sha'b
Ash Shaykh 'Uthmân
DJIBOUTI
Tadjoura
Obock
Golfe de Tadjoura
Dikhil
Lake Abhe
Yoboki
SOMALI
AWDAL
Aysha
Berbera
WOQOOYI GALBEED
SOMALILAND (not internationally recognized)
Bullaxaar
Karin

Gulf / Iraq region (east)

Wâdi al Bâṭin
Ad Dibdibah
An Naṣîriya
Tigris
Badrah
'Alî al Gharbî
Al Kût

Ramlat Dahm
Ramlat as Sab'atayn
Harîb
Ma'rib
Shabwah
Bayhân
Wâdi Ḥaḍramawt

Scale 1:8,000,000
(projection: Lambert Conformal Conic)

0 25 50 75 100 125 150 175 200 Km
0 25 50 75 100 125 150 175 200 Miles

Population
■ above 5 million
⬚ 1 million to 5 million
◎ 500,000 to 1 million
◉ 100,000 to 500,000
⊕ 50,000 to 100,000
○ 10,000 to 50,000
o below 10,000

Dubai

Persian Gulf

Sharjah

Iran & the Gulf States

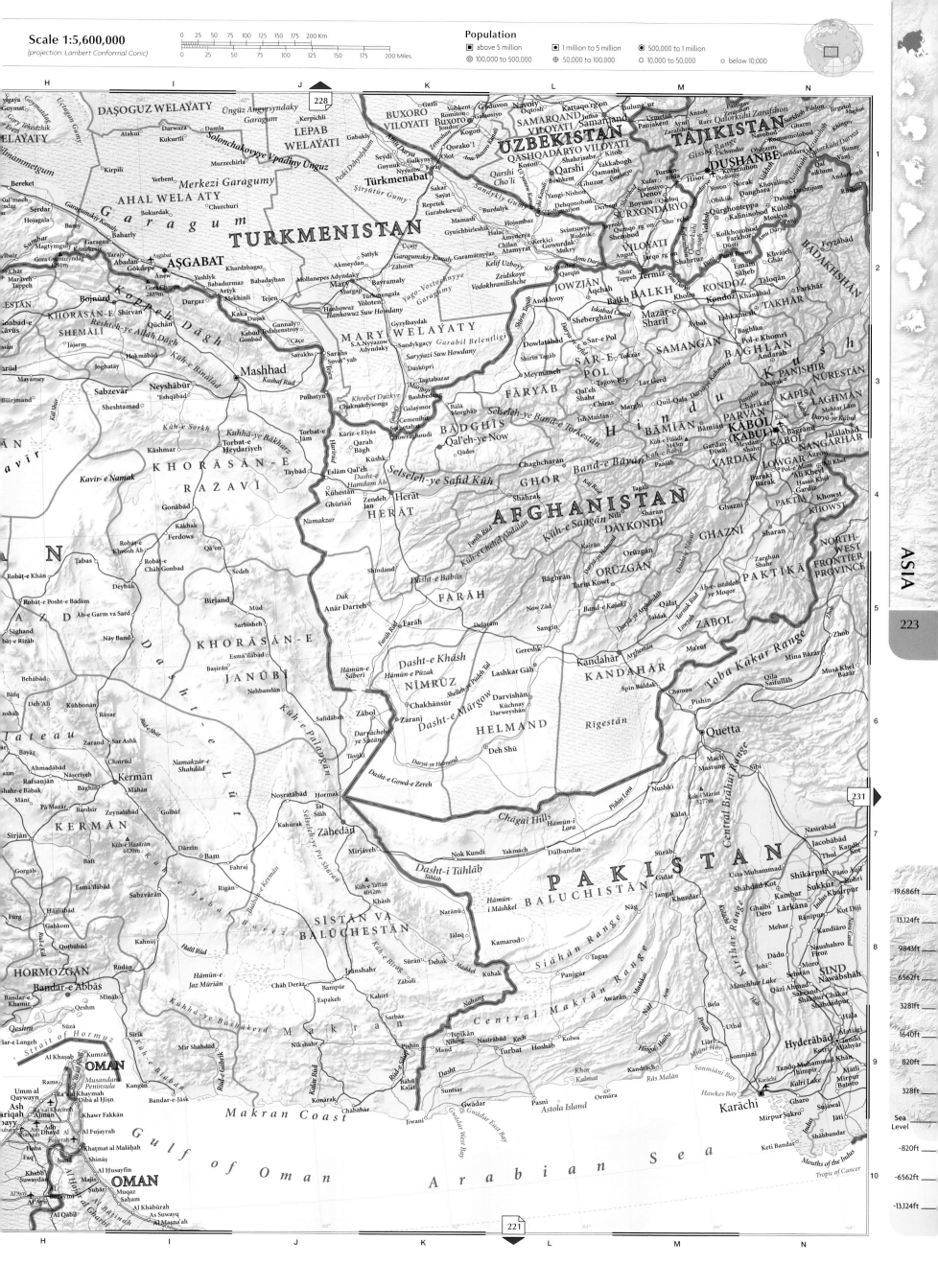

ASIA

224

Countries:
RUSSIAN FEDERATION · KAZAKHSTAN · MONGOLIA · CHINA · UZBEKISTAN · TURKMENISTAN · KYRGYZSTAN · TAJIKISTAN · AFGHANISTAN · IRAN

Major labels:
S I B I R' (Siberia) · Srednesibirskoye Ploskogor'ye · Zapadno-Sibirskaya Ravnina · Ural'skiye Gory · Kazakhskiy Melkosopochnik · Tarim Pendi · Taklimakan Shamo · Kunlun Shan · Qingzang Gaoyuan · Hindu Kush · Karakoram Range

Seas / water:
Caspian Sea · Aral Sea · Ozero Baykal · Ozero Balkhash · Beloye More · Pechorskoye More

Cities (selection):
Irkutsk · Ulan-Ude · Krasnoyarsk · Kemerovo · Novosibirsk · Tomsk · Barnaul · Omsk · Astana · Yekaterinburg · Chelyabinsk · Ufa · Samara · Saratov · Orenburg · Aktobe · Karaganda · Almaty (Alma-Ata) · Bishkek · Taraz · Shymkent · Toshkent (Tashkent) · Samarqand · Buxoro · Dushanbe · Ürümqi · Kashi · Hotan · Asgabat · Mashhad · Kabol (Kabul) · Islamabad · Srinagar · Tehran

Elevation scale:
6000m · 4000m · 3000m · 2000m · 1000m · 500m · 250m · 100m · Sea Level · -250m · -500m · -1000m

ASIA

195

197

223

Elevation scale
- 6000m
- 4000m
- 3000m
- 2000m
- 1000m
- 500m
- 250m
- 100m
- Sea Level
- -250m
- -500m
- -1000m

Countries and major regions:

RUSSIAN (RUSSIA)

RESPUBLIKA MORDOVIYA

PENZENSKAYA OBLAST'

UL'YANOVSKAYA OBLAST'

RESPUBLIKA TATARSTAN

SAMARSKAYA OBLAST'

SARATOVSKAYA OBLAST'

VOLGOGRADSKAYA OBLAST'

ASTRAKHANSKAYA OBLAST'

RESPUBLIKA KALMYKIYA

RESPUBLIKA DAGESTAN

ORENBURGSKAYA OBLAST'

RESPUBLIKA BASHKORTOSTAN

CHELYABINSKAYA OBLAST'

KURGANSKAYA OBLAST'

ZAPADNYY KAZAKHSTAN

KOSTANAY

Turgayskaya Stolovaya Strana

AKTYUBINSK

KZYLORDA

MANGISTAU

AZERBAIJAN

UZBEKISTAN

QORAQALPOG'ISTON RESPUBLIKASI

QARAQALPOG'ISTON RESPUBLIKASI

XORAZM VILOYATI

NAVOIY VILOYATI

BUXORO VILOYATI

SAMARQAND VILOYATI

QASHQADARYO VILOYATI

TURKMENISTAN

BALKAN WELAÝATY

DAŞOGUZ WELAÝATY

LEBAP WELAÝATY

AHAL WELAÝATY

MARY WELAÝATY

IRAN

Major cities and places:

Saransk, Ul'yanovsk, Dimitrovgrad, Samara, Syzran', Tol'yatti, Novokuybyshevsk, Saratov, Engel's, Balakovo, Kamyshin, Volzhskiy, Astrakhan, Ufa, Chelyabinsk, Magnitogorsk, Orenburg, Orsk, Novotroitsk, Aktobe (Aktyubinsk), Kostanay, Rudnyy, Troitsk, Kurgan, Ural'sk, Atyrau, Makat, Dossor, Aktau, Zhanaozen, Beyneu, Aral'sk, Kazalinsk, Baykonyr, Space Launching Centre, Dzhusaly, Kzylorda, Makhachkala, Kaspiysk, Buynaksk, Derbent, BAKI (BAKU), Sumqayıt, Nukus, Daşogz, Urganch, Xiva, Xonqa, Buxoro, Navoiy, Qarshi, Türkmenabat, Türkmenbaşy, Balkanabat, Bereket, Serdar, Aşgabat, Gökdepe, Mary, Qazvin, Rasht, Gorgan, Bandar-e Torkaman

Physical features:

Caspian Sea, Aral Sea, Caspian Depression, Ryn-Peski, Atyrau Depression, Ustyurt Plateau, Plato Ustyurt, Gory Mugodzhary, Plato Shagyray, Peski Bol'shiye Barsuki, Gory Chushkakul', Plato Mangyshlak, Sor Metvyy Kultuk, Garagum (Garagum Desert), Merkezi Garagumy, Garabogaz Aylagy, Koppeh Dagh, Kopetdag Gershi, Ostrov Vozrozhdeniya, Ural (river), Volga (river), Amu Darya, Syr Darya

Ozero Shalkar, Ozero Sarykopa, Ozero Kyzylkol', Ozero Akkol', Ozero Shubar-Tengiz, Ozero Arys

Central Asia

Atyrau
Komsomol'skiy
Koschagyl
Kul'sary
ATYRAU
Karaton
Borankul
Sarykamys
Beyneu
Turush
Emba
Gryada Shirkala
Gory Chushkakul
Plato Shagyray
Peski Bol'shiye Barsuki
Shalkar
Saksaul'skiy
Aral'sk
Zaliv Tushchybas
AKTYUBINSK
K A Z A
Ozero Shubar-Tengiz
Peski Priaral'skiye Karakumy
Ayteke Bi
Maylybas
Space Launching Centre
Kazalinsk
Baykonyr
Dermentobe
Syr Darya
Dzhusaly
Dzhalagash
KYZLORDA
Kzylor
Tasbu

Ostrov Kulaly
Mys Tyub-Karagan
Mangyshlakskiy Zaliv
Fort-Shevchenko
Tauchik
Shetpe
Say-Utes
Sor Mertvyy Kultuk
Shebir
Beyneu
Qoraqalpog'iston
Ostrov Vozrozhdeniya
Aral Sea
Uyaly

Aktau
Plato Mangyshlak
Kuryk
Zhetybay
Zhanaozen
MANGISTAU
Jasliq
Kubla-Ustyurt
Uchsoy
Mo'ynoq
Qorajar
Amu Darya
Oqqal'a

Ustyurt Plateau
Ural Karabaur
Og'iyon Sho'rxogi
Qozoqdaryo
QORAQALPOG'ISTON RESPUBLIKASI
Oltynko'l
Chimboy
Qorauzak
Taxtako'pir
Qo'ng'irot
Qozonketkan
Madaniyat
Kegayli
Xalqobod
Shumanay
Kyzyl
Wiloyati

Mys Soye
Garabogaz
Garabogazköl
Garabogaz Aylagy
Garsy
Krasnovodskoye Plato
Gaplangyr
Solonchak Sakhlyshor
Goymat
Üstüagan Gumy
Çagyl
Goymataş
Gyzylgaya
Gory Tekedzhik

Gubadag
Köneürgench
Boldumsaz
Akdepe
Gurbansoltan Eje
Xo'jayli
Taxiatosh
Mang'it
Gürlen
Bo'ston
Berununy
Daşoguz
Tagta
Urganch
XORAZM VILOYATI
Türtkül
Xonqa
Xiva
Hazorasp
Pitnak

Sarygamyş Köli
Ilanly Obvodnitel'nyy Kanal
DAŞOGUZ WELAÝATY
Vpadina Akdzhakaya -130m
Üngüz Angyrsyndaky
Garagum
Turan Lowland
UZBEKISTAN
NAVOIY VILOYATI
Beshbuloq
Tomdibuloq
Zarafshon
Tomditow-Tog'lari
Mingbuloq
Uchquduq
Aytim
Ko'lquduq
Irlir Tog'i 764m
Bo'kantov Tog'lari
Ovminzatoy Tog'lari
Mingbuloq Botig'i

Türkmenbaşy
Guwlumayak
Gyzylsuw
Türkmenbaşy Aylagy
Kenar
Belek
Oglanly
Jebel
Arlandag 1880m
Aýguyy
Hazar
Garagöl
Ogurjaly Adasy
Türkmen Aylagy

Derweze
Atakui
Kükürtli
Damla
Kerpichli
Solonchakovyye Vpadiny Unguz
Gazli
BUXORO VILOYATI
G'ijduvon
Vobkent
Romiton
Navo
Koninex
Karns
Komsom'sk

Gilmümmergum
Garagum
Kırpili
Merkezi Garagumy
Yerbent
Murrechirla
Gabakly
Guynuk
Seýdi
Galkynyş
Farap
Qorako'l
Olot
LEPAB WELAÝATY
Türkmenabat
Zenevshan
Peski Dzhynbykum
Amu-Buxoro Kanali
Qorovulbozr
Muborak

BALKAN WELAÝATY
Gumdag
Kürendag 971m
Berekat
Kul'mach
Bokurdak
Churchuri
TURKMENISTAN
Garagum
Sandykly Gumy
Sayat
Repetek
Garabekewül
Mamash
Burdalyk
Şırşür Gumy
Kelif Uzboy
Qarshi Chüli

Serdar
Garagum Kanaly
Baharly
AHAL WELAÝATY
Asgabat
MARY WELAÝATY
Galkynyş
Nyyazow
Gyuichbirleshik
Halaç
Chilan
Atamyrat
Amyde
Andkl

Bugdayly
Madaw
Garaboyaz
Çekiçler
Etrek
Chât
Maraveh Tappeh
Kyzylbair Gora Gyunuzyndag 1291m
Könekesir
Yaraly
Gökdepe
Abadan
Anew
Gara Chapan 2848m
Yashlyk
Khardzhagaz
Babadayhan
Satlyk
Akmeydan
'Üçajy
Garamätnyýaz
Koppeh Dagh
Bojnurd
Shirvan
Reshteh-ye Allāh Dāgh
Qüchān
Mekhinli
Tejen
Mollanepes
Adyndaky
Bayramaly
Murgap
Türkmengala
Yugo-Vostochnyye Garagumy
Zeidskoye Vodokhranilishce

Gudurolum
Esenguly
GOLESTAN
Gonbad-e Kāvūs
Fārsiān
KHORĀSĀN-E SHEMĀLĪ
Mayamey
Dargaz
Artyk
Babadurmaz
Kaka
Dusak
Tedzhenstroy
Mary
Yöloten
Gyzylbaydak
S.A. Nyyazow Adyndaky
Sandykgaçi
Garabil Belentligi
Dowlatab
Shirin Tagab

Bandar-e Torkaman
Behshahr
Nūr
Bābolsar
GORGAN
Kord Kūy
Gorgān
Kabūl Gonbad
Çäçe
Hanhowuz Suw Howdany
Gannaly
Sarakhs
Saryyazy Suw Howdany
Daşköpri
Tagtabazar
Meymaneh
FĀRYĀB

Āmol
Qā'emshahr
Bābol
Sārī
MĀZANDARĀN
Pol-e Safīd
Damāvand 5671m
Reshteh-ye Kūhhā-ye Alborz (Elburz Mountains)
Dāmghān
Biārjmand
Joghatāy
Sabzevār
Neyshābūr
Mashhad
Kashaf Rūd
Pulhatyn
Hamdam
Khrebet Duzkyr
Chaknakdysonga
Galaymor
Cemenibit
Bālā Morghāb
BĀDGHIS
Qal'eh-ye Now

Semnān
SEMNĀN
Garmsār
IRAN
Kāl Shūr
Shāhrūd
Sheshtamad
Hokmābād
Kūh-e Binālūd
Torbat-e Heydariyeh
Torbat-e Jām
Kāriz-e Elyās
Serhetabat
Towraghoudi
Kūshk
Daryā-ye Morghāb
Murghāb
Tejen
Hamdam Āb
Selseleh-ye Band-e Torkestan

Dasht-e Kavīr
Jandaq
Anārak
Na'in
EŞFAHĀN
Kāshmar
YAZD
Kavīr-e Namak
KHORĀSĀN-E RAZAVĪ
Gonābād
Qā'en
Tāybād
Eslām Qal'eh
Kūhestān
Zendeh Jan
Ghūrīān
HERĀT
Namakzar
Selseleh-ye Safīd Kūh
AFG
Chaghcharān
GHOWR
Shahrak

Robāt-e Khvosh Āb
Tabas
Ferdows
Qā'en
Robāt-e Chāh Gonbad
Sedeh
Deyhūk
Robāt-e Posht-e Bādām
Robāt-e Khān
Dasht-e Kavīr

6000m
4000m
3000m
2000m
1000m
500m
250m
100m
Sea Level
-250m
-500m
-1000m

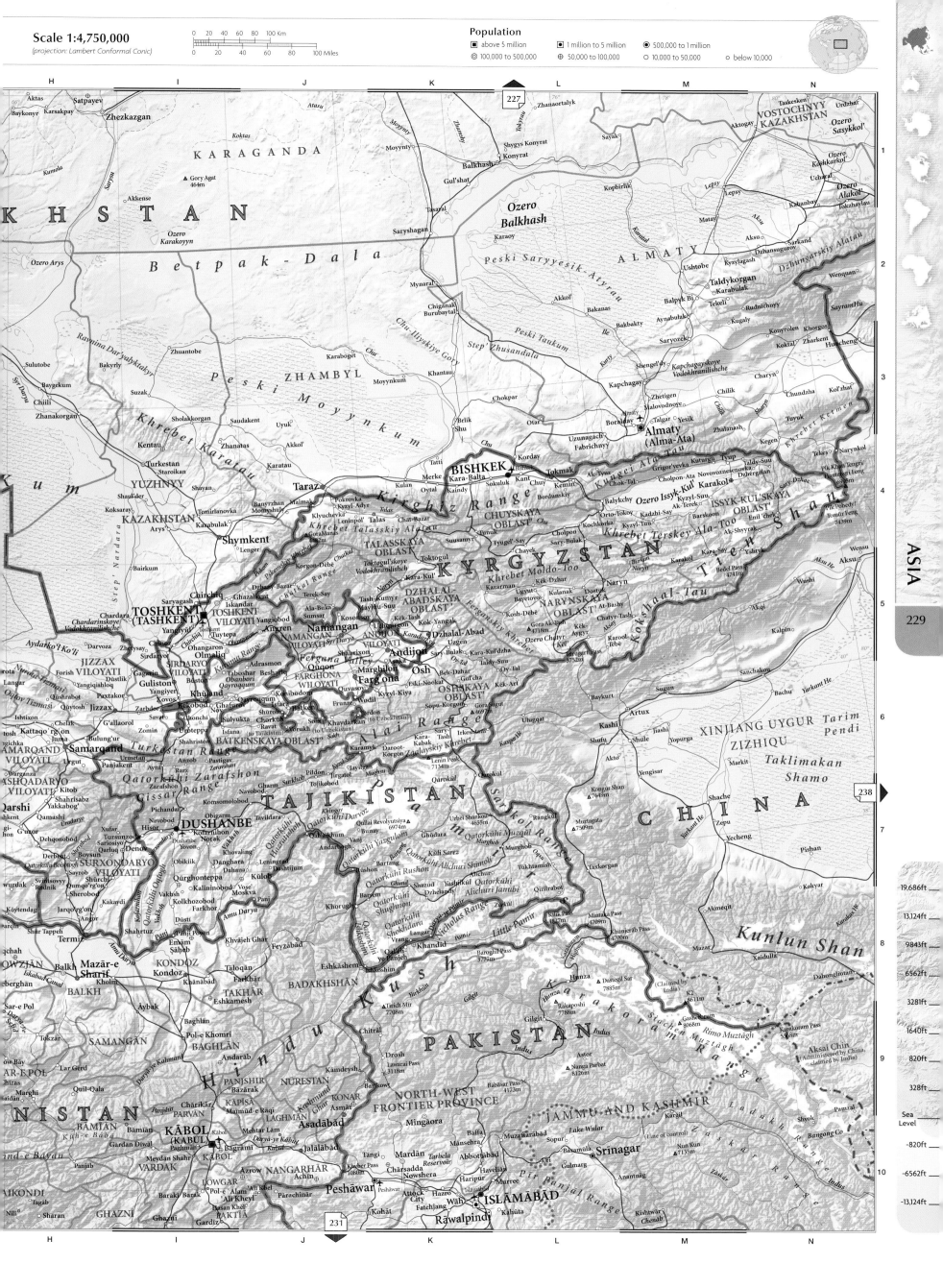

Scale 1:4,750,000
(projection: Lambert Conformal Conic)

0 20 40 60 80 100 Km

0 20 40 60 80 100 Miles

Population
- above 5 million
- 1 million to 5 million
- 500,000 to 1 million
- 100,000 to 500,000
- 50,000 to 100,000
- 10,000 to 50,000
- below 10,000

227

231

238

19,686ft
13,124ft
9843ft
6562ft
3281ft
1640ft
820ft
328ft
Sea Level
-820ft
-6562ft
-13,124ft

KARAGANDA

KHSTAN

KAZAKHSTAN

Betpak-Dala

Ozero
Karakoyyn

Ozero
Balkhash

Peski Saryyesik-Atyrau

ALMATY

ZHAMBYL

Peski Moyynkum

Ozero Arys

VOSTOCHNYY
KAZAKHSTAN

Ozero
Sasykkol'

Ozero
Alakol'

Dzhungarskiy Alatau

Gory Agat
464m

Almaty
(Alma-Ata)

BISHKEK
Kara-Balta

Taraz

Shymkent

YUZHNYY

Kirghiz Range

Khrebet Karatau

Khrebet Kermin

CHUYSKAYA
OBLAST'

Karakol

ISSYK-KUL'SKAYA
OBLAST'

Ozero Issyk-Kul'

Khrebet Terskey Ala-Too

Pik Pobedy/
Tomür Feng
7439m

TOSHKENT
(TASHKENT)

TOSHKENT
VILOYATI

NAMANGAN
VILOYATI

KYRGYZSTAN

DZHALAL-
ABADSKAYA
OBLAST'

NARYNSKAYA
OBLAST'

Naryn

Tien Shan

Kokshaal Tau

Pik Khan Tengri/
Hantengri Feng
6995m

Namangan
Andijon

Dzhalal-Abad

XINJIANG UYGUR
ZIZHIQU

Tarim
Pendi

Fergana Valley

FARGHONA
VILOYATI

Margilon

Farg'ona

Osh

OSHSKAYA
OBLAST'

Taklimakan
Shamo

Qŭqon

Samarqand

Alai Range

Lenin Peak
7134m

Kashi

SAMARQAND
VILOYATI

Turkestan Range

Qatorkŭhi Zarafshon

Zarafshon
Range

Gissar Range

TAJIKISTAN

CHINA

Qatorkŭhi Alichuri Shimoli

Qatorkŭhi Muzqŭl Range

DUSHANBE

SURXONDARYO
VILOYATI

Qatorkŭhi Hazratishoh

Qatorkŭhi Yazgulom

Pamir

Sarykol Range

Qatorkŭhi Rushon

Qatorkŭhi
Alichuri Janubi

Mazār-e
Sharif

BALKH

Khorugh

Qatorkŭhi
Shughnon

Qatorkŭhi
Shokhdara

Nicholas Range

Little Pamir

KONDOZ

BADAKHSHAN

SAMANGAN

TAKHĀR

Hindu Kush

Karakoram
Range

Kunlun Shan

PAKISTAN

Aksai Chin
(Administered by China,
claimed by India)

BAGHLĀN

K2
8611m

Karakoram Pass
5566m

NURESTAN

NISTAN

BĀMIĀN

KĀBOL
(KABUL)

KAPISA
PARVĀN

LAGHMAN

Nanga Parbat
8126m

NORTH-WEST
FRONTIER PROVINCE

JAMMU AND KASHMIR

Srinagar

VARDAK

NANGARHĀR

Peshāwar

Pir Panjal Range

GHAZNĪ

PAKTIĀ

ISLAMĀBĀD

Rāwalpindi

ASIA

TURKMENISTAN

UZBEKISTAN

AFGHANISTAN

IRAN

PAKISTAN

OMAN

U.A.E.

Arabian Sea

Gulf of Oman

Strait of Hormuz

Makran Coast

Dasht-e Kavīr

Dasht-e Lūt

Iranian Plateau

GOLESTĀN · KHORĀSĀN-E SHEMĀLĪ · KHORĀSĀN-E RAŻAVĪ · KHORĀSĀN-E JANŪBĪ · SEMNĀN · YAZD · KERMĀN · HORMOZGĀN · SĪSTĀN VA BALŪCHESTĀN

HERĀT · GHOWR · BĀDGHĪS · FĀRYĀB · SAR-E POL · BĀMIĀN · DĀIKONDĪ · FARĀH · NĪMRŪZ · HELMAND · KANDAHĀR · ORŪZGĀN · ZĀBOL · GHAZNĪ · PAKTĪ · VARDAK · PARVĀ · SAMANGAN · BALKH · JOWZJĀN · KONDOZ

BALUCHISTĀN · SIND

LEBAP WELAẎATY · AHAL WELAẎATY · MARY WELAẎATY

Aşgabat · Mashhad · Herāt · Kandahār · Quetta · Zāhedān · Kermān · Gorgān · Bandar-e ʿAbbās · Masqat (Muscat) · Karāchi · Hyderābād · Zāranj · Lashkar Gāh · Mazār-e Sharif · Kondoz · Dushanbe

Chāgai Hills · Rīgestān · Dasht-e Mārgow · Dasht-e Gowd-e Zereh · Dasht-i Tāhlāb · Central Makrān Range · Siāhān Range · Kīrthar Range · Central Brāhui Range · Toba Kākar Range · Selseleh-ye Safid Kūh · Band-e Bāyān · Kūh-e Bābā

Mouths of the Indus

6000m · 4000m · 3000m · 2000m · 1000m · 500m · 250m · 100m · Sea Level · -250m · -500m · -1000m

Countries / Regions: AFGHANISTAN, PAKISTAN, JAMMU AND KASHMIR, XINJIANG UYGUR, HIMACHAL PRADESH, UTTARANCHAL, PUNJAB, HARYANA, RAJASTHAN, UTTAR PRADESH, GUJARAT, MADHYA PRADESH, MAHARASHTRA, ANDHRA PRADESH, GHOWR, BAMIAN, BAGHLAN, TAKHAR, BADAKHSHAN, SAMANGAN, FARYAB, SAR-E POL, DAIKONDI, ORUZGAN, GHAZNI, ZABOL, PAKTIKA, KANDAHAR, BALUCHISTAN, SIND, NORTH WEST FRONTIER PROVINCE, KHOWST, PAKTIA, LOWGAR, VARDAK, PARVAN, KABOL (KABUL), NANGARHAR, NURESTAN, KONAR, LAGHMAN

Major cities: KABOL (KABUL), ISLAMABAD, Rawalpindi, Peshawar, Lahore, Amritsar, NEW DELHI, DELHI, Ghaziabad, Karachi, Hyderabad, Ahmadabad, Vadodara, Surat, Mumbai (Bombay), Pune, Nagpur, Bhopal, Indore, Jaipur, Jodhpur, Lucknow, Kanpur, Allahabad, Jabalpur, Quetta, Srinagar, Jammu, Multan, Faisalabad, Gujranwala, Ludhiana, Chandigarh, Shimla

Water / Physical features: Arabian Sea, Gulf of Kachchh, Gulf of Khambhat, Rann of Kachchh, Mouths of the Indus, Tropic of Cancer, Thar Desert, Indus, Ganges, Narmada, Aravali Range, Satpura Range, Vindhya Range, Himalayas, Karakoram Range, Hindu Kush, Zaskar Range, Ladakh Range, Kathiawar Peninsula, Aksai Chin, Lake Wular, Sambhar Salt Lake

Elevation scale:
6000m
4000m
3000m
2000m
1000m
500m
250m
100m
Sea Level
-250m
-500m
-1000m

229
230
234

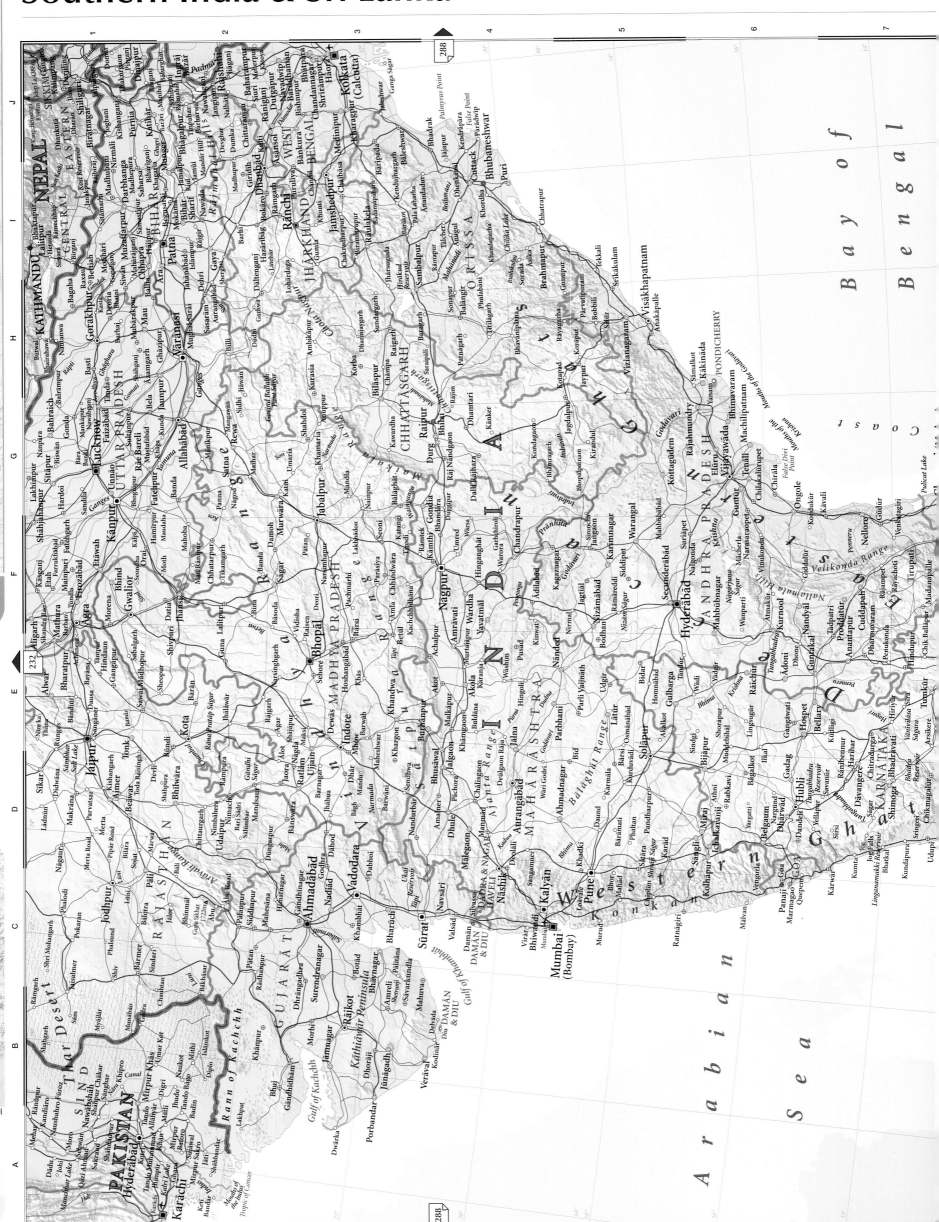

Elevation scale

- 6000m
- 4000m
- 3000m
- 2000m
- 1000m
- 500m
- 250m
- 100m
- Sea Level
- -250m
- -500m
- -1000m

RUSSIAN

KAZAKHSTAN

Metkosopochnik

Astana · Omsk · Petropavlovsk · Kostanay · Rudnyy · Kokshetau · Shchuchinsk · Atbasar · Derzhavinsk · Arkalyk · Zhezkazgan · Betpak-Dala · Balkhash · Konyrat · Saryshagan · Buribaytal · Ozero Balkhash · Temirtau · Karaganda · Abay · Saran' · Shar · Ust'-Kamenogorsk · Semipalatinsk · Pavlodar · Barnaul · Rubtsovsk · Biysk · Gorno-Altaysk · Novosibirsk · Novoaltaysk · Novokuznetsk · Mezhdurechensk · Abakan · Minusinsk · Kemerovo · Leninsk-Kuznetskiy · Krasnoyarsk · Kansk · Tomsk · Achinsk · Bratsk · Ust'-Ilimsk · Ust'-Kut · Irkutsk · Angarsk · Usol'ye-Sibirskoye · Cheremkhovo · Selenginsk · Ulan-Ude · Ozero Baykal · Lena · Angara

Altai Mountains · *Zapadnyy Sayan* · *Eastern Sayans* · Gora Belukha 4506m · Kyzyl · Ak-Dovurak

MONGOLIA — ULAANBAATAR (ULAN BATOR)

Hövsgöl Nuur · Uvs Nuur · Hyargas Nuur · Har Us Nuur · Hovd · Ölgiy · Tolbo · Ulaangom · Uliastay · Altay · Bayanhongor · Hangayn Nuruu · Gobi Altayn Nuruu · Darhan · Sühbaatar · Kyakhta · Erdenet · Bulgan · Mörön · Tsetserleg · Arvayheer · Choyr · Mandalgovi · Dalandzadgad · Doloon

KYRGYZSTAN — BISHKEK

Taraz · Almaty · Yining · Shihezi · Karamay · Ürümqi · Turpan · Hami · Korla · Kashi · Shache · Yecheng · Hotan · Qiemo · Ruoqiang · Lop Nur

XINJIANG UYGUR ZIZHIQU

Tarim Pendi · *Taklimakan Shamo* · *Tien Shan* · *Kokshaal-Tau* · *Tarim He* · *Kuruktag* · *Altun Shan* · *Qilian Shan*

CHINA

Kunlun Shan · *Qingzang Gaoyuan (Plateau of Tibet)* · *Bayan Har Shan* · *Qaidam Pendi* · *Burhan Budai Shan* · *Tanggula Shan* · *Nyainqêntanglha Shan* · *Himalayas*

XIZANG ZIZHIQU (TIBET) · **QINGHAI** · **GANSU** · **NINGXIA** · **SICHUAN** · **SHAANXI** · **CHONGQING** · **GUIZHOU** · **YUNNAN** · **GUANGXI ZHUANGZU ZIZHIQU**

Lhasa · Xigazê · Gyangzê · Nagqu · Qamdo · Golmud · Dulan · Xining · Lanzhou · Linxia · Guyuan · Yinchuan · Wuzhong · Wuhai · Ordos · Baotou · Mount Everest 8850m · Chengdu · Leshan · Neijiang · Zigong · Yibin · Luzhou · Chongqing · Kunming · Guiyang · Xichang · Panzhihua · Dali · Baoshan · Lincang · Gejiu · Kaiyuan · Nanning · Liuzhou · Guilin · Hechi

INDIA

New Delhi · Delhi · Meerut · Jaipur · Agra · Gwalior · Lucknow · Kanpur · Allahabad · Varanasi · Patna · Gaya · Bhopal · Jabalpur · Nagpur · Raipur · Ranchi · Dhanbad · Jamshedpur · Kolkata · Bhubaneshwar · Puri · Hyderabad · Vijayawada · Visakhapatnam · Srinagar · Jammu · Amritsar · Lahore · Gujranwala · Ludhiana · Chandigarh · Shimla · Dehra Dun · Bareilly · Jhansi

JAMMU AND KASHMIR · **HIMACHAL PRADESH** · **PUNJAB** · **HARYANA** · **UTTAR PRADESH** · **UTTARANCHAL** · **BIHAR** · **JHARKHAND** · **WEST BENGAL** · **ORISSA** · **MADHYA PRADESH** · **MAHARASHTRA** · **ANDHRA PRADESH** · **CHHATTISGARH**

NEPAL — KATHMANDU · Pokhara · Biratnagar

BHUTAN — THIMPHU · Paro

BANGLADESH — DHAKA · Chittagong · Khulna · Rajshahi · Barisal · Comilla

MYANMAR (BURMA)

Mandalay · Amarapura · Sagaing · Maymyo · Monywa · Pakokku · Myingyan · Taunggyi · Lashio · Myitkyina · Bhamo · Prome · Henzada · Bassein · Pegu · Thaton · Moulmein · Sandoway · Sittwe

YANGON (RANGOON) · PYINMANA

Arakan Yoma · *Chin Hills* · *Irrawaddy* · *Shan Plateau* · *Mouths of the Irrawaddy*

THAILAND · Chiang Mai · Chiang Rai · Nakhon Sawan · Nakhon Ratchasima · Ubon Ratchathani · Khon Kaen

LAOS — VIANGCHAN (VIENTIANE) · Louangphabang · Udon Thani · Thakhek · Pakxé · Champasak

VIETNAM — HANOI · Hai Phong · Nam Dinh · Vinh · Huê · Đà Nang · Cam Pha · Hong Gai · Thai Nguyen · Ha Dong

HAINAN · *Hainan Dao* · Haikou · Sanya · Dongfang · Zhanjiang · Beihai · Qinzhou

Bay of Bengal · *Gulf of Tongking* · *Mouths of the Ganges* · *Ganges* · *Tropic of Cancer*

Red River · *Mekong* · *Salween* · *Yangtze / Jinsha Jiang* · *Huang He* · *Tenasserim Range*

192 · 256 · 231

ASIA

238

KAZAKHSTAN

VOSTOCHNYY KAZAKHSTAN

RUSS. FED.

BAYAN-OLGIY

KARAGANDA

ALMATY

ZHAMBYL

KYRGYZSTAN

BISHKEK

UZBEK.
TOSHKENT (TASHKENT)

TAJIKISTAN
DUSHANBE

Tien Shan

ÜRÜMQI

Junggar Pendi
Gurbantünggüt Shamo

Bogda Shan

XINJIANG UYGUR ZIZHIQU

Tarim Pendi

Taklimakan Shamo

C H I N A

Kuruktag

Lop Nur

Altun Shan

Kunlun Shan

Hoh Xil Shan

Pamirs

HINDU KUSH

AFGHANISTAN

PAKISTAN

Karakoram Range

K2 8611m

Aksai Chin
(claimed by India)

JAMMU AND KASHMIR

Srinagar

ISLAMABAD

Lahore

Qingzang (Plateau)

XIZANG ZIZHIQU (TIBET)

Gangdisê Shan

HIMACHAL PRADESH

HIMALAYA

PUNJAB

HARYANA

NEW DELHI
DELHI

RAJASTHAN

UTTARANCHAL

UTTAR PRADESH

NEPAL

KATHMANDU

INDIA

Thar Desert

SIKKIM

BHUTAN
THIMPHU

227

230

232

Sea Level
6000m
4000m
3000m
2000m
1000m
500m
250m
100m
-250m
-500m
-1000m

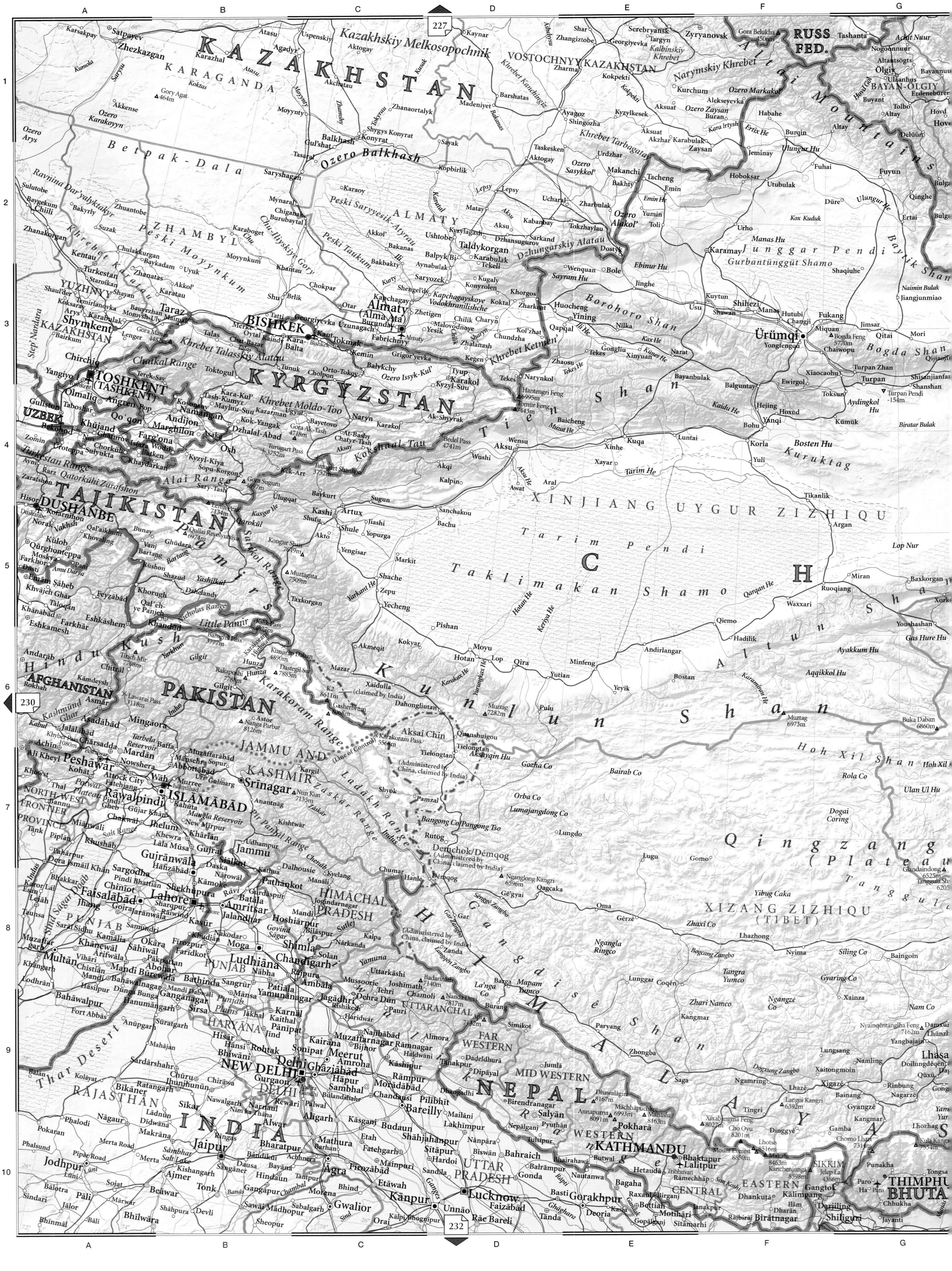

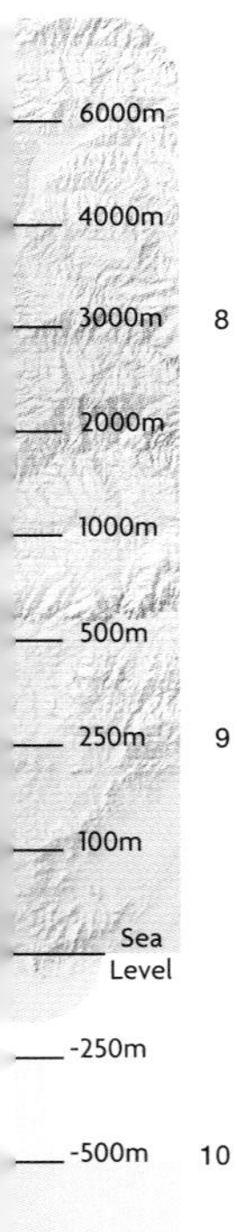

Southeast China

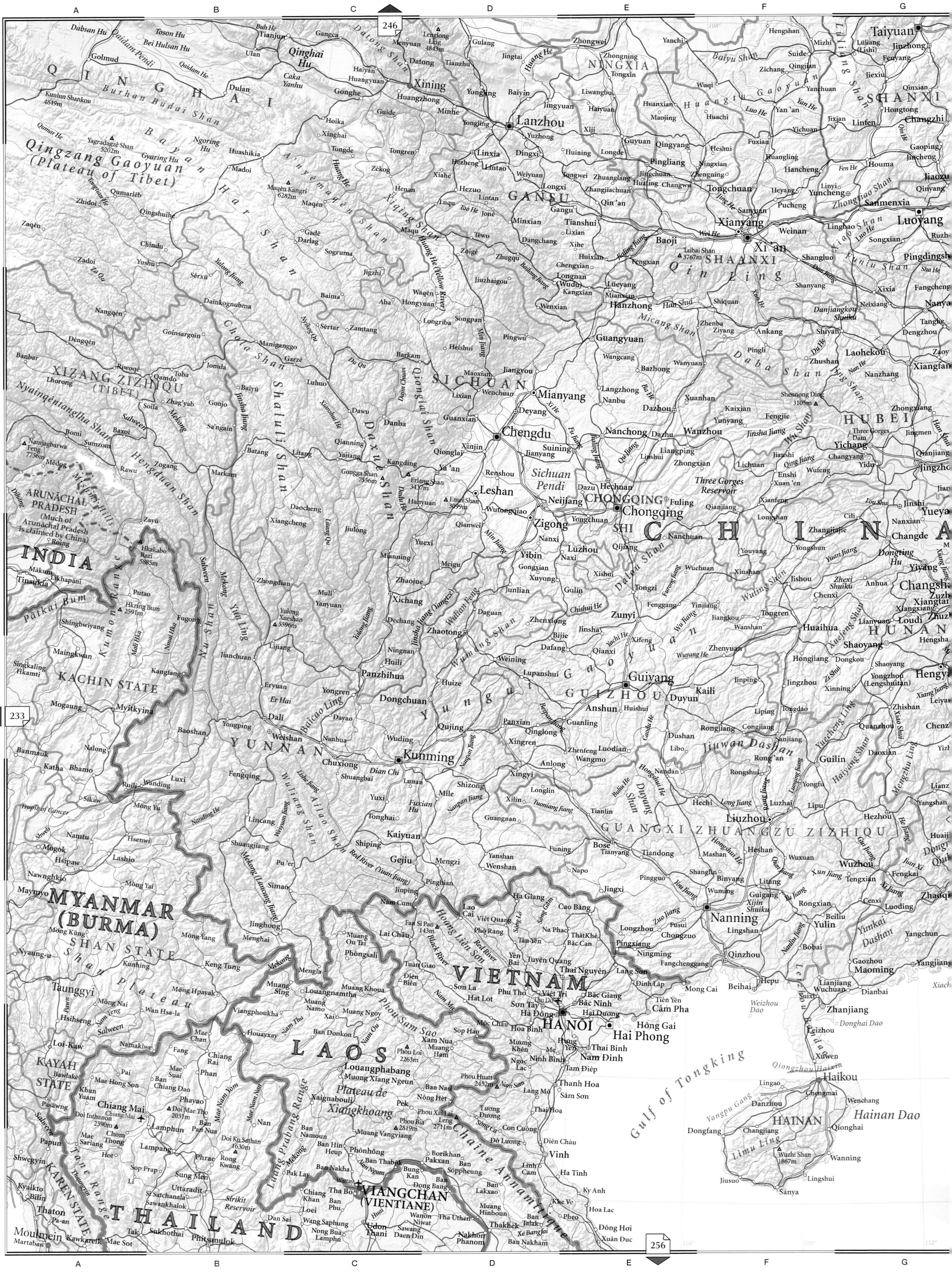

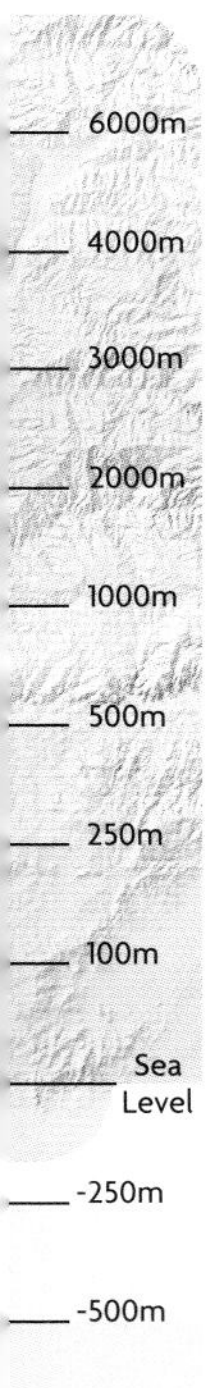

Map grid references: A B C D E F G (columns) and 1–10 (rows)

Page references: 246 (top), 233 (left), 256 (bottom)

Countries / Regions:
QINGHAI, GANSU, NINGXIA, SHAANXI, SHANXI, SICHUAN, HUBEI, CHINA, XIZANG ZIZHIQU (TIBET), INDIA, ARUNACHAL PRADESH, MYANMAR (BURMA), KACHIN STATE, SHAN STATE, KAYAH STATE, KAREN STATE, THAILAND, LAOS, VIETNAM, YUNNAN, GUIZHOU, GUANGXI ZHUANGZU ZIZHIQU, HUNAN, HAINAN

Selected cities / places:
Taiyuan, Lanzhou, Xining, Xi'an, Xianyang, Luoyang, Chengdu, Chongqing, Guiyang, Kunming, Nanning, Guilin, Liuzhou, Changsha, Hengyang, Hanoi, Hai Phong, Haikou, Vinh, Chiang Mai, Viangchan (Vientiane), Myitkyina, Lashio, Mandalay region, Louangphabang, Dien Bien, Zunyi, Yichang, Wanzhou, Mianyang, Leshan, Zigong, Luzhou, Xichang, Panzhihua, Dali, Baoshan

Physical features:
Qinghai Hu, Qingzang Gaoyuan (Plateau of Tibet), Bayan Har Shan, Huang He (Yellow River), Qin Ling, Daba Shan, Three Gorges Reservoir, Three Gorges Dam, Hengduan Shan, Mekong (Lancang Jiang), Salween, Yangtze, Gulf of Tongking, Hainan Dao, Tropic of Cancer, Red River (Yuan Jiang), Wuling Shan, Luliang Shan, Qiongzhou Haixia, Weizhou Dao

Elevation scale:
6000m
4000m
3000m
2000m
1000m
500m
250m
100m
Sea Level
−250m
−500m
−1000m

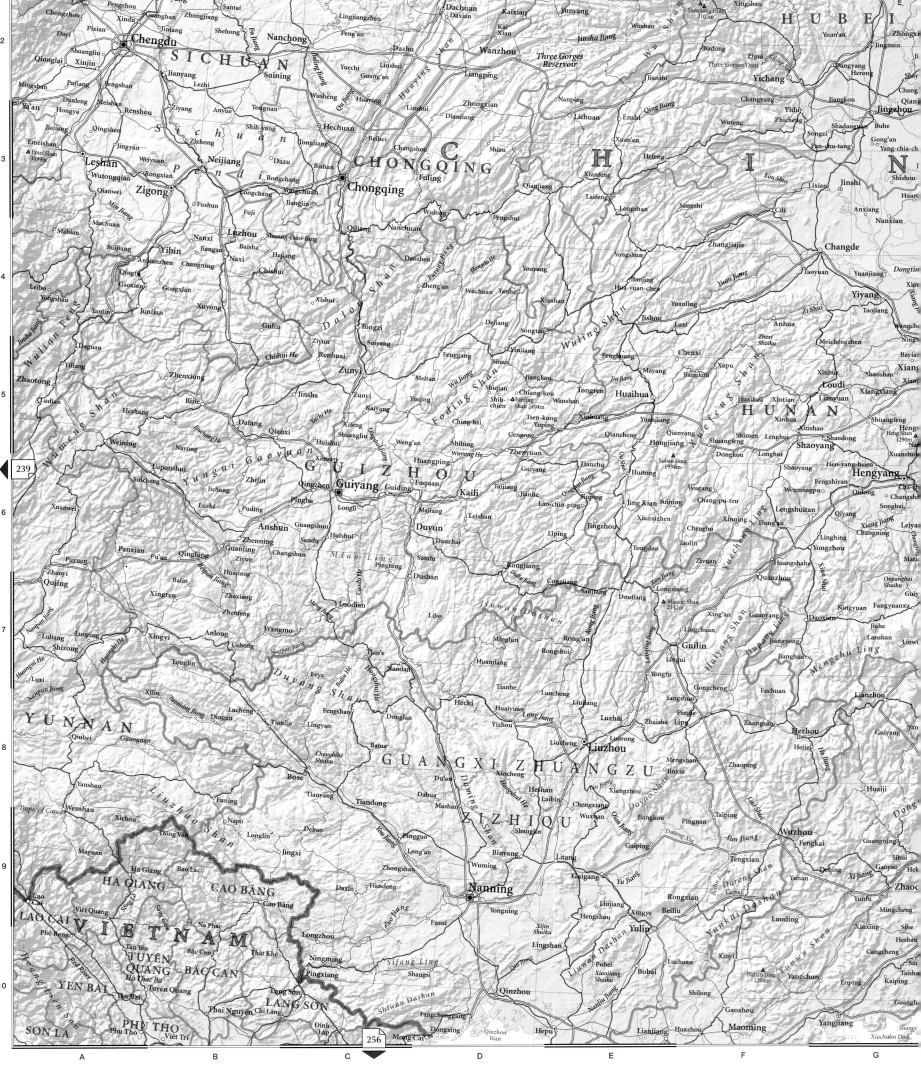

NEI MONGGOL ZIZHIQU (INNER MONGOLIA)

Yin Shan

Lang Shan

Badain Jaran Shamo

Yabrai Shan

Tengger Shamo

Longshou Shan

Helan Shan

Ulan Buh Shamo

Mu Us Shadi

Huangtu Gaoyuan

Baiyu Shan

Lüliang Shan

Qinling Shan

Taihang Shan

Qin Ling

Min Shan

Longmen Shan

Bailong Jiang

Micang Shan

Daba Shan

Xiaoshang Shan

Wudang Shan

Zhongtiao Shan

Xiao Shan

Xionge Shan

Fuling Shan

Provinces / Regions: QINGHAI · GANSU · NINGXIA · SHAANXI · SHANXI · SICHUAN · HUBEI

Rivers: Huang He (Yellow River) · Shiyang He · Huang Shui · Tao He · Wei He · Jing He · Lao He · Malian He · Wuding He · Fen He · Luo He · Han Shui · Min Jiang · Jialing Jiang · Bai Long Jiang · Qingshui He · Hongliu He · Kuye He · Tuwei He · Dali He · Yan He · Huangfu He · Dahei He · Daqing Shan

Cities and towns:

Baotou · Hohhot · Yinchuan · Lanzhou · Xining · Xi'an · Xianyang · Taiyuan · Luoyang · Sanmenxia · Hanzhong · Mianyang · Guangyuan · Baoji · Tianshui · Linfen · Linxia

Bayan Obo · Bailingmiao · Ulan Hua · Xar Moron · Wuchuan · Guyang · Cha-su-chi · Zhuo · Liangcheng · Horinger · Togtoh · Salaqi · Qasq · Shulinzhao · Ordos · Xuejiawan · Qingshuihe

Wuyuan · Xamba · Linhe · Xishanzui · Dengkou · Bayan Gol · Ulansuhai Nur · Bag Nur · Hotong Qagan Nur · Ulan · Dabqig · Altan Xiret · Hongjian Nur · Shenmu · Lanyi He · Linxian

Bayan Mod · Xar Burd · Jartai Yanchi · Suhait · Wuhai (Haibowan) · Wuda · Shitanjing · Shizuishan · Shizuishan · Rujigou · Pingluo · Taole · Helan · Xincheng · Yongning · Qingtongxia · Lingwu · Wuzhong · Ciyaopu · Majiatan · Gaijialiang · Yanchi · Dingbian · Jingbian

Zhuozi Shan 2148m · Xinzhao Shan 2515m

Tamsag Muchang · Zhoujianjing · Xiasifen · Jinchang · Minqin · Ehen Hudag · Xiqu · Dongzhen · Bayan Hot · Hexibao · Yongchang · Gulang · Tianzhu · Tiantangsi · Weiyuan · Haomen · Lenglong Ling 4843m

Wuwei · Gantang · Yingpanshui · Zhongwei · Zhongning · Hui'anpu · Dashuikeng · Qingtongxia Shuiku · Jingtai · Bingcaowan

Xining · Pinganyi · Ledu · Huzhu · Ping'an · Minhe · Nangdoi · Hualong · Gando · Jainca · Xunhua · Linxia · Hezheng · Xiahe · Hezuo · Luqu

Lanzhou · Yongjing · Yuzhong · Dongxiangza · Dingxi · Huining · Xifi · Guyuan · Tongxin · Yuwang · Liwangbu · Hongde · Huanxian · Maojing · Qingcheng · Qingyang · Heshui · Huachi · Huaxian · Yan'an · Yanchang · Yichuan · Lixian · Linfen · Hongtong

Guochengyi · Haiyuan · Jingyuan · Donghaiba · Shenjiahe Shuiku · Pengyang · Longde · Jingning · Pingliang · Jingchuan · Zhengning · Ningxian · Huangling · Luochuan · Huanglong · Hancheng · Hejin · Jishan · Xinjiang · Houma · Wanrong · Wenxi · Linyi · Yuncheng · Xiaxian · Ruicheng · Sanmenxia · Yima · Luoyang

Migang Shan 2931m · Taibai Shan 3767m · Li Shan 2322m · Guandi Shan 2831m · Fenhe Shuiku · Laojun Shan 2192m

Weiyuan · Longxi · Zhangxian · Wenfengzhen · Qin'an · Qingshui · Gangu · Beidao · Tianshui · Lixian · Xihe · Liangdang · Huixian · Chengxian · Kangxian · Longnan · Lüeyang · Mianxian · Chenggu · Yangxian · Shiquan · Ningshan · Lintan · Jone · Minxian · Lüjing · Wushan · Zhuanglang · Zhangjiachuan · Lingtai · Changwu · Binxian · Tongchuan · Pucheng · Fuping · Dali · Heyang · Hancheng · Huayin · Tongguan · Lingbao

Luoyang · Lüyang · Songxian · Nanyang · Dengzhou · Den Xian · Laohekou · Gucheng · Xiangyang · Nanzhang · Baokang · Fangxian · Xiangfan

Xanbei · Zolge · Waqen · Hongyuan · Songpan · Maoxian · Wenchuan · Lixian · Mians, · Mianzhu · Luojiang · Deyang · Chengdu · Zhongjiang · Santai · Yanting · Nanbu · Langzhong · Cangxi · Yilong · Bazhong · Tongjiang · Pingchang · Xuanhan · Kaixian · Dachuan · Daxian · Fengjie · Wuxi · Wushan · Badong · Zigong

Jiuzhaigou · Nanping · Zhongzhai · Wenxian · Bikou · Qingchuan · Pingwu · Guangyuan · Wangcang · Nanjiang · Ningqiang · Zhenba · Ziyang · Ankang · Pingli · Zhuxi · Xinzhou · Wanyuan · Chengkou · Zhenping · Shennongjia 3053m

Hanzhong · Nanzheng · Xixiang · Zhen'an · Yunxi · Yunxian · Xixia · Neixiang · Danjiangkou Shuiku · Danjiangkou · Shiyan · Xindian · Guanghua

Elevation scale (left margin):

6000m
4000m
3000m
2000m
1000m
500m
250m
100m
Sea Level
-250m
-500m
-1000m

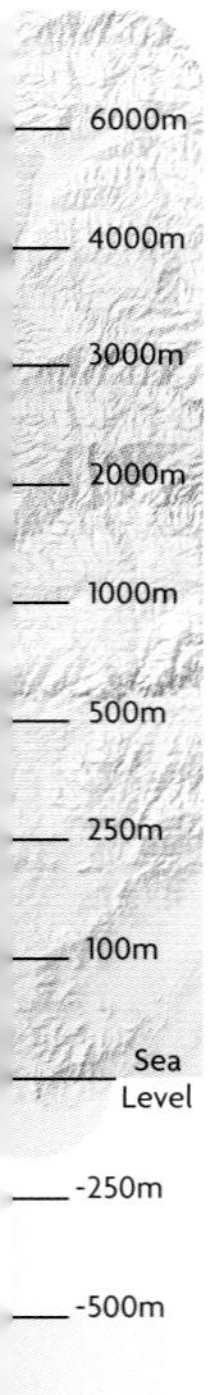

Scale 1:3,750,000
(projection: Lambert Conformal Conic)

0 20 40 60 80 100 Km
0 20 40 60 80 100 Miles

Population
- ■ above 5 million
- ▣ 1 million to 5 million
- ◉ 500,000 to 1 million
- ◎ 100,000 to 500,000
- ⊕ 50,000 to 100,000
- ⊙ 10,000 to 50,000
- ○ below 10,000

RUSSIA

IRKUTSKAYA OBLAST'

RESPUBLIKA KHAKASIYA

RESPUBLIKA TYVA

RESPUBLIKA ALTAY

RESPUBLIKA BURYATIYA

KRASNOYARSKIY KRAY

Zapadnyy Sayans

Eastern Sayans

AGINSKIY BURYATSKIY AVTONOMNYY OKRUG

UST'-ORDYNSKIY BURYATSKIY AVTONOMNYY OKRUG

Ozero Baykal

MONGOLIA

BAYAN-ÖLGIY

UVS

HÖVSGÖL

DZAVHAN

HOVD

GOVI-ALTAY

ARHANGAY

BULGAN

SELENGE

DARHAN UUL

HENT

TÖV

ÖVÖRHANGAY

BAYANHONGOR

DUNDGOVÏ

ÖMNÖGOVÏ

DORNOGOVÏ

ULAANBAATAR (ULAN BATOR)

Erdenet

ORHON

Darhan

Altay Mountains

Hangayn Nuruu

Govĭ Altayn Nuruu

Hentiyn Nuruu

Yablonovyy

CHINA

XINJIANG UYGUR ZIZHIQU

QINGHAI

GANSU

NINGXIA

NEI MONGOL

SHAANXI

Qinghai Hu

Lop Nur

Bogda Shan

Qilian Shan

Altun Shan

Qaidam Pendi

Kunlun Shankou

Bayan Har Shan

Anyemaqen Shan

Qingzang Gaoyuan (Plateau of Tibet)

Qing Zang Gaoyuan

Tengger Shamo

Badain Jaran Shamo

Mu Us Shadi

Huang He (Yellow River)

Lanzhou

Xining

Xi'an

Yinchuan

Baotou

Ordos

Irkutsk

Ulan-Ude

Sühbaatar

Kyakhta

Darhan

Gora Belukha 4506m

Gora Munku-Sardyk 3491m

Aj Bogd Uul 3802m

Atas Bogd 2695m

Mazong Shan 2584m

Turpan Pendi -154m

Zhuozi Shan 2148m

Xinzhao Shan 2515m

Lenglong Ling 4843m

Yagradagzê Shan 5202m

Magên Kangri 6282m

Taibai Shan 3767m

Bayan Shan 5030m

Elevation scale:
6000m
4000m
3000m
2000m
1000m
500m
250m
100m
Sea Level
-250m
-500m
-1000m

193

239

240

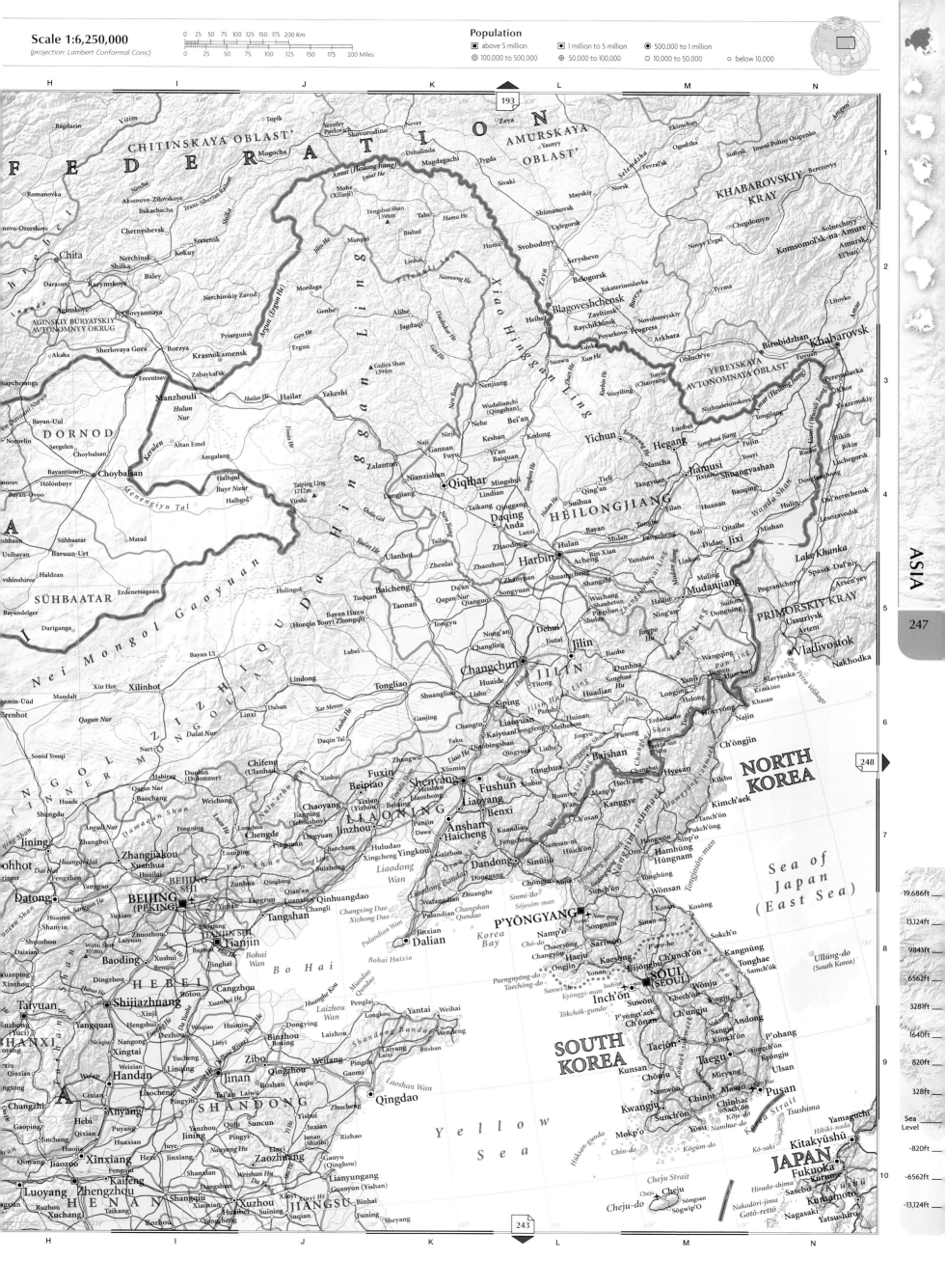

247

245

286

RUSSIAN FEDERATION

PRIMORSKI KRAY

CHINA

NEIMONGGOL ZIZHIQU (INNER MONGOLIA)

JILIN

LIAONING

NORTH KOREA

P'YŎNGYANG

SOUTH KOREA

SŎUL (SEOUL)

Pusan

Cheju

JAPAN

Sea of Japan (East Sea)

Yellow Sea

Korea Bay

Korea Strait

Cheju-Strait

East China Sea

Philippine Sea

Kyūshū

Shikoku

Chūgoku-sanchi

Ullŭng-do

Laoha He · Tongliao · Shuangliao · Jiutai · Shanhetun · Pingshan · Didao · Jixi · Misban · Turin Rog · Iesozavodsk
Daqin Tal · Lishu · Changchun · Jilin · Shulan · Jiaohe · Hailin · Mudanjiang · Ning'an · Suifenhe · Pogranichnyy · Spassk-Dal'niy · Arsen'yev · Kavalerovo
Fuxin · Zhangwu · Gongzhuling · Songhua Hu · Huadian · Jingpo Hu · Wangqing · Yanji · Tumen · Hunchun · Ussuriysk · Dal'negorsk
Beipiao · Kaiyuan · Liaoyuan · Panshi · Dunhua · Longjing · Helong · Hoeryŏng · Slavyanka · Vladivostok · Nakhodka
Jinzhou · Fushun · Shenyang · Tieling · Tonghua · Baishan · Changbai · Hyesan · Khasan · Najin · Ch'ŏngjin
Anshan · Liaoyang · Benxi · Manp'o · Kanggye · Kilchu · Kimch'aek
Haicheng · Yingkou · Dandong · Sinŭiju · Chŏngju · Hamhŭng · Hŭngnam · Wŏnsan
P'yŏngyang · Namp'o · Sariwŏn · Haeju · Kaesŏng · Inch'ŏn · Sŏul · Suwŏn · Kangnŭng · Tonghae · Samch'ŏk
Taejŏn · Chŏnju · Kwangju · Mokp'o · Taegu · P'ohang · Kyŏngju · Ulsan · Pusan · Masan · Chinhae · Yŏsu
Shimonoseki · Kitakyūshū · Fukuoka · Saga · Nagasaki · Kumamoto · Kagoshima · Miyazaki · Hiroshima · Okayama · Kōbe · Ōsaka · Kyōto · Nagoya

247

A B C D E F G

Sea of Japan
(East Sea)

SOUTH KOREA

KYŎNGGI-DO
KANG-WON-DO

Kwangju
Pubal
Yŏju
P'yŏngch'ang
Chŏngsŏn
Samch'ŏk
Tonghae

Wŏnju
Shindong
Sabuk
Togye

Kŭmwang
Ch'ungju
Chech'on
Maep'o
T'aebaek
T'aebaek-san
1568m
Wŏndŏk

Umsŏng
CH'UNGCH'ŎNGBUK-DO
Tanyang
P'unggi
Ulchin

Ch'ŏngju
Koesan
Yech'ŏn
Yŏngju
Paegam-san
1003m

Ullŭng-do

Liancourt Rocks

Taech'ŏng Lake
Poŭn
Sangju
KYŎNGSANGBUK-DO
Andong
Naktong-kang
Andong Lake
Yŏng-yang
P'yŏnghae

Taejŏn
Och'ŏn
Sangju
Sŏnsan
Ch'ŏngsong
Yŏngdok

Yŏngdong
Kimch'ŏn
Kumi
Kunwi
An'gang
Yŏnil
Kuryongp'o

Muju
Chŏngdo
Ch'angnyŏng
Miryang
Ulsan
Samnangjin
Yangsan

CHŎLLABUK-DO
Hapch'ŏn
Chinyang Lake
Chiri-san
1915m
Chinju
KYŎNGSANGNAM-DO
Ch'ang Wŏn

Hamyang
Sanch'ŏng
Kaya
Masan
Chinhae
Kim Hae
Pusan

Hadong
Namhae
Kosŏng
Shin-dong
Kijang

Kwang-Yang
Sach'ŏn
Kōje
Chang-An

Yŏch'ŏn
Namhae-do
Kǒje-do
Kunp'o

Yŏsu
Tolsan
Tongyŏng
Kumgang

Korea Strait

Kŭmogundo-do
Kami-Agata
Kami-Tsushima

Sorido-do
Mitsushima
Tsushima
Kō-saki
Izuhara

Sea of Japan (East Sea)

Oki-shotō
Dōgo
Dōzen
Saigō
Nakano-shima
Chiburi-jima

Oki-kaikyō

Shimane-hantō
Jizō-zaki
Hamasaka
Hino-misaki
Hirata
Sakaiminato
Aoya
Kurayoshi
TOTTORI
Tottori

Matsue
Shinji-ko
Yasugi
Yonago
Dai-sen
1729m
Hyōno-sen
1510m
Wakasa

Taisha
Izumo
Kisuki
Kōfu
Chizu

Gōtsu
Oda
Sanbe-san
1126m
Yokota
Katsuyama
Tsuyama
Yamaza

Hamada
SHIMANE
Tombara
Dōgo-yama
1269m
Niimi
Tōjō
OKAYAMA
Tsuyama

Susa
Masuda
Miyoshi
Shōbara
Takahashi
Soja
Bizen

Abu
Gary-san
1223m
Kake
HIROSHIMA
Fuchū
Ibara
Okayama
Kurashiki
Tamano

Ōmi-shima
Hagi
Atō
Tsuwano
Kanmuri-yama
1339m
Higashi-Hiroshima
Fukuyama
Onomichi
Tonosho

Tsuno-shima
Nagato
YAMAGUCHI
Kōzan
Mihara
Innoshima
Sakaide
Takamatsu

Hōhoku
Yamaguchi
Nishi-Nōmi-jima
Takehara
Marugame
KAGAWA
Naruto

Toyoura
Mine
Ogōri
Shingŏ-Nyō
Tokuyama
Iwakuni
Kurahashi-jima
Kan'onji
Zentsūji

Shimonoseki
Onoda
Hōfu
Kudamatsu
Iyomishima
Yoshino-gawa
TOKUSHIMA
Komatsushima

Kitakyūshū
Ube
Hikari
Yanai
Hōjō
Saijō
Niihama
Tsurugi-san
1955m

Nakama
Nōgata
Suō-nada
Hime-jima
Naga-shima
Ya-shima
Matsuyama
Kanega-mori
1896m
Ōtoyo

Fukuoka
Nizuka
Tagawa
Nakatsu
Bungo-Takada
Saijō
Ishizuchi-san
1982m

Yobuko
Karatsu
Kasuga
Onojō
Amagi
Hiko-san
1200m
Usa
Kitsuki
Heigun-tō
Iyo
Kuma
SHIKOKU-SANCHI

FUKUOKA
SAGA
Taku
Kurogi
Hita
Beppu
Nagahama
Uwa
Nankoku
Aki

Imari
Saga
Ōgōri
Kurume
Yame
Yamagawa
Buzen
Ōita
Kujū-san
1791m
Ōzu
Yawatahama
KŌCHI
Tosa
Kōchi

Takeo
Kashima
Yamaga
Taketa
Sobo-san
1757m
Uwajima
Onigajō-yama
1151m
Susaki

NAGASAKI
Matsubara
Ōmuta
Takamori
Usuki
Tsukumi
Kubokawa
Muroto

Sasebo
Ōmura
Isahaya
Kikuchi
Nobeoka
Saiki
Nakamura
Tosa-wan

Arikawa
Nakadōri-jima
Kumamoto
KUMAMOTO
Hinokage
Tsurumi-zaki
Sukumo
Imano-yama
865m
Muroto-zaki

Gotō-rettō
Narao
Shimabara
Uto
Yatsushiro
Kunimi-dake
1739m
Hyūga
Okino-shima
Tosa-Shimizu

Nagasaki
Shimabara-wan
Misumi
Kyūshū-sanchi
Ōse-zaki
Fukue
Fukue-jima
Kuchinotsu
Ashizuri-misaki

Nomo-zaki
Hondo
Shimo-jima
Yonomae
Ichifusa-yama
1727m
Tsuno

Amakusa-nada
Ushibuka
Naga-shima
Minamata
Hitoyoshi
Saito
Takanabe

Izumi
Ōkuchi
MIYAZAKI
Kobayashi
Kirishima-yama
1700m
Miyazaki

Akune
Sendai-gawa
Miyanojō
Miyakonojō
Nichinan

Kami-Koshiki-jima
Kushikino
Kokubu
On-take
1117m
Nichinan

Shimo-Koshiki-jima
Sendai
KAGOSHIMA
Miyakonojō

Koshikijima-rettō
Kagoshima
Tarumizu
Shibushi
Kushima

East China Sea

Noma-zaki
Kaseda
Ibusuki
Kanoya
Uchinoura
Toi-misaki

Satsuma-hantō
Makurazaki
Kagoshima-wan
Yamagawa
Shibushi-wan

Uji-guntō
Sata-misaki
Ōsumi-kaikyō

Kusagaki-guntō
Kuro-shima
Take-shima

Iō-jima
Mage-shima
Nishinoomote

Kuchinoerabu-jima
Tanega-shima

Kamiyaku
Minamitane

Yaku-shima

East China Sea

Philippine Sea

Inset 1

E a s t   C h i n a   S e a

Sakishima-shotō
Miyako-shotō
Irabu-jima
Miyako-jima
Minna-jima
Hirara
Tarama-jima

Yaeyama-shotō
Hirakubo-saki
Yonaguni
Yonaguni-jima
Iriomote-jima
OKINAWA
Ishigaki-jima

Ishigaki
Kuro-shima

Paimi-saki

Hateruma-jima

Scale 1:3,250,000
0 10 20 40 Km
0 10 20 40 Miles

P h i l i p p i n e   S e a

Elevation scale

6000m
4000m
3000m
2000m
1000m
500m
250m
100m
Sea Level
-250m
-500m
-1000m

ASIA
250

245

Northern Japan

286

247

193

RUSSIAN FEDERATION

Sea of Okhotsk

Sea of Japan (East Sea)

Kuril Islands

Ostrov Iturup
Ostrov Kunashir
Ostrov Shikotan
Habomai Islands
Ostrov Zelëny
(Administered by Russian Federation, claimed by Japan)

Khrebet Sikhote Alin'
Maksumovka
Velikiye Kema

Mys Aniva
Zaliv Aniva
Ostrov Sakhalin
Mys Krilon
Ostrov Moneron
La Perouse Strait

HOKKAIDŌ

Nemuro-kaikyō
Notsuke-suidō
Notsuke-zaki
Nemuro-wan
Nemuro
Ochiishi-misaki
Füren-ko
Bekkai
Nakashibetsu
Nishibetsu-gawa
Akkeshi
Hamanaka
Akkeshi-ko
Akkeshi-wan
Onbetsu
Shibecha
Shiranuka
Kushiro
Onbetsu
Urahoro
Hiroo
Taiki
Erimo
Erimo-misaki
Ikeda
Kami-Shihoro
Tokachi-gawa
Kamui-dake 1601m
Obihiro
Shintoku
Tokachi-dake 2077m
Shimizu

Shiretoko-misaki
Rausu-dake 1660m
Rausu
Shiretoko-hantō
Shari
Shibetsu
Utoro
Shiretoko-misaki
Teshikaga
Mashū-ko
Akan-dake 1499m
Kussharo-ko
Teshikaga
Akan
Akan-ko
Ashoro
Furano
Asahi-dake 2290m
Asahikawa
Biei
Furano
Mikasa
Iwamizawa
Yūbari
Mu-kawa

Sea of Okhotsk
Tokoro
Abashiri
Abashiri-ko
Bihoro
Tsubetsu
Memanbetsu
Kitami
Saroma-ko
Engaru
Rubeshibe
Kitami-sanchi
Saroma
Noboro-ko
Yūbetsu
Monbetsu
Okoppe
Omu
Setouchi
Takinoue
Shibetsu
Wassamu

HOKKAIDŌ

Soya-misaki
Wakkanai
Noshappu-misaki
Sōya-suidō
Rishiri-suidō
Rishiri-tō
Rishiri-yama 1719m
Rebun
Rebun-tō
Teuri-tō
Yagishiri-tō

Sarufutsu
Toyotomi
Kutcharo-ko
Nakatonbetsu
Hamatonbetsu
Esashi
Nakagawa
Teshio-gawa
Teshio
Enbetsu
Shosanbetsu
Haboro
Tomamae
Obira
Mashike
Rumoi

Kitami-sanchi
Otoineppu
Bifuka
Nayoro
Uryū-ko
Horokanai
Teshio-sanchi
Horonobe

Ishikari-gawa
Numata
Takikawa
Shoskanbetsu-dake 1491m
Takikawa
Akabira
Utashinai
Bibai
Akahira
Sunagawa

Hamamasu
Atsuta
Ishikari
Ishikari-wan
Ebetsu
Otaru
Sapporo
Eniwa
Chitose
Shikotsu-ko
Tomakomai
Shiraoi
Noboribetsu
Muroran

Yotei-zan 1898m
Niseko
Kutchan
Furubira
Yoichi
Shakotan-misaki
Kamui-misaki
Yobetsu-dake 1298m
Kamoenai
Iwanai
Kariba-yama 1520m
Setana
Kitahiyama
Imagane
Kumaishi
Taisei
Motsuta-misaki
Okushiri-tō
Beikei-misaki

Uchiura-wan
Date
Takumo
Oshamambe
Kunnui
Kuromatsunai
Suttsu
Suttsu-wan
Oshamambe
Yakumo-dake 1420m
Minami-Kayabe
Mori
Komagatake 1131m
Kamiiso
Kikonai
Hakodate
Esan-misaki
Shikabe

Oshima-hantō
Esashi
Kaminokuni
Fukushima
Matsumae
Matsumae-misaki
Shirakami-misaki

Tsugaru-kaikyō
Tappi-zaki

O-shima
O-shima

Aomori
Hirosaki
Mutsu
Oma-zaki
Oma
Ōhata
Ōminato
Yokohama
Matsu-wan
Kawauchi
Wakinosawa
Rokkasho
Ogawara-ko
Misawa
Shiriya-zaki
Shichinohe
Tōwada
Goshogawara
Towada-ko
Iwaki-san 1625m
Kuroishi
Hachinohe
Minmaya
Jūsan-ko
Nakasato
Fukaura
Ajigasawa
Henashi-zaki

Yūbari-sanchi
Yūbari
Shimukappu
Hidaka
Biratori
Shizunai
Samani
Urakawa
Mitsuishi
Hidaka-sanmyaku
Hiroo-dake 2052m

Teshio-sanchi
Yūbetsu-gawa

6000m
4000m
3000m
2000m
1000m
500m
250m
100m
Sea Level
-250m
-500m
-1000m

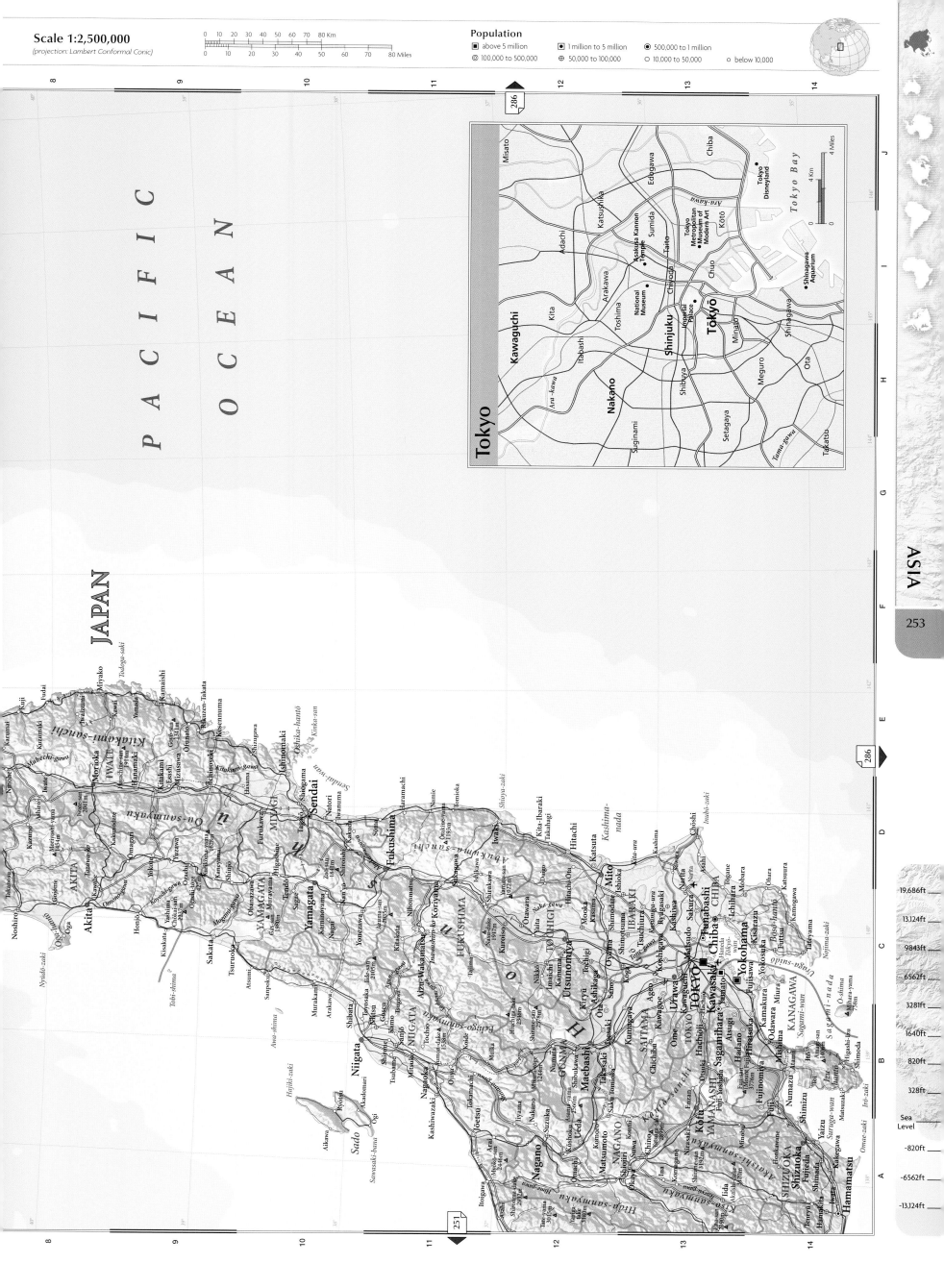

ASIA

254

Himalayas
Mount Everest 8850m
Xigazê Gyangzê Lhasa Nangxian Mainling Rawu
Kula Kangri 7554m
Gangtok Lhünzê Cona
Darjiling Itanagar
THIMPHU Shigatse
BHUTAN Sadiya
Biratnagar Shillong
Bhagalpur Dinajpur
BANGLADESH
Dhanbad Asansol DHAKA
Bankura Jessore Comilla
Kharagpur Khulna
INDIA Haora
Baleshwar Kolkata Chittagong
Tropic of Cancer
Mouths of the Ganges
Cox's Bazar

CHINA
Zigong Neijiang Chongqing Zhangjiajie Yueyang Jinjiang Jingdezhen Jinhua
Yibin Luzhou Xuyong Tongzi Changde Nanchang Quzhou Shangrao
Panzhihua Zunyi Huaihua Loudi Liling Pingxiang Fuzhou
Kunming Guiyang Hengyang Yingtan
Guilin Liuzhou Nanning Guangzhou Hong Kong Kaohsiung
(Xianggang) T'aina

MYANMAR
(BURMA)
PYINMANA
Mandalay
Pakokku
Sittwe
Bay of Bengal
YANGON
(RANGOON)
Bassein
Gulf of Martaban
Mouths of the Irrawaddy

LAOS
VIANGCHAN (VIENTIANE)
Chiang Mai
Korat Plateau
Huê

THAILAND
KRUNG THEP
(BANGKOK)
Gulf of Thailand

VIETNAM
HA NOI
Hai Phong
Gulf of Tongking
Hainan Dao
SOUTH CHINA SEA
PARCEL ISLANDS (disputed)
Đà Nẵng
Quy Nhơn
Nha Trang
Cam Ranh

CAMBODIA
PHNUM PENH
(PHNOM PENH)
Tonlé Sap
Hồ Chi Minh
Vung Tau
Mouths of the Mekong

Andaman Islands (to India)
North Andaman
Middle Andaman
South Andaman
Port Blair
Little Andaman

Andaman Sea
Ko Phuket
Phuket
Nakhon Si Thammarat
Songkhla
Hat Yai
Kota Bharu
George Town
Taiping Ipoh
Strait of Malacca
Medan
Pematangsiantar
Danau Toba
Klang
KUALA LUMPUR
PUTRAJAYA
Melaka
SINGAPORE
Johor Bahru

Nicobar Islands (to India)
Car Nicobar
Camorta
Katchall Island
Little Nicobar
Great Nicobar
Bananga
Ten Degree Channel

Bandaaceh
Meulaboh
Pulau Simeulue
Pulau Banyak
Sibolga
Pulau Nias
Pekanbaru
Padang
Pulau Siberut
Kepulauan Mentawai
Rengat
Jambi
Sungaipenuh
Palembang
Bengkulu Lahat
Equator

BRUNEI
BANDAR SERI BEGAWAN
Kota Kinabalu
Ganung Kinabalu 4101m
Sandakan
Tawau
MALAYSIA
Kuching
Borneo
Kalimantan
Samarinda
Balikpapan
Banjarmasin
Pontianak
Singkawang
Balabac Strait
Palawan Passage
Sulu

INDONESIA
INDIAN OCEAN
Pulau Enggano
Bandar Lampung
JAKARTA
Serang Bogor Cirebon Tegal Pekalongan Kudus
Sukabumi Bandung Magelang Semarang Surakarta Surabaya
Tasikmalaya Cilacap Madiun Kediri Probolinggo
Yogyakarta Malang Jember Bali
Jawa (Java)
Denpasar
Greater Sunda Islands
Java Sea
Makassar
Makassar Strait
Parepare
Flores Sea
Sumbawa
Mataram
Pulau Lombok
Nusa Tenggara

6000m
4000m
3000m
2000m
1000m
500m
250m
100m
Sea Level
-250m
-500m
-1000m

Population

■ above 5 million   ▣ 1 million to 5 million   ◉ 500,000 to 1 million

◎ 100,000 to 500,000   ⊕ 50,000 to 100,000   ○ 10,000 to 50,000   ∘ below 10,000

286

282

275

East China Sea

Huangyan

nzhou

ingyang

Nansei-shotō

Naze

Amami-ō-shima

Okinawa-shotō

Okinawa

Naha   Okinawa

Chilung

Sakishima-shotō

Miyako-jima

Ishigaki-jima

Iriomote jima

T'AIPEI

T'aichung

Hualien

TAIWAN

ingtung

Senkaku-shotō

T'aipei

Wuku   Shihlin   Nei Hu

Luchou   Martyrs Shrine

Kuku   Keelung

Sanchung   Confucius Temple   T'aipei Songshan Airport

Sinzhuang   Sanchong   Hsingtien Temple   Tiding

Tai Shan   Datung   Sungshan

Shinjuang   Wanhua   **T'aipei**   Zhongcheng   Sinyi

Lungshan Temple   National Theatre   Daan   Linguang

Hsin Chuang   National Museum of History

Banqiao   Banchiao   Yungho   Wantang

Shu Lin   Zhonghe   Zhongher   T'aipei Zoo

Tucheng   Fang Liao   Wunshan

Jhonghe   Sindian

0   2 Km

0   2 Miles

Tanshui River Roadway   *Tanshui*   *Tanshui*   *Sindian*   *Tukui*

Tropic of Cancer

P A C I F I C

O C E A N

Philippine

Sea

Luzon rait

Babuyan Island

buyan Channel

Tuguegarao

Ilagan

Luzon

guio

gupan

Cabanatuan

ngeles

MANILA

Lucena

tangas   Naga

Sibuyan

indoro   *Sea*

Calbayog

Roxas City

Iloilo   Cadiz   Cebu

Negros

Bohol Sea

ea

Iligan   Butuan

Cagayan de Oro   Bislig

Mindanao

Davao

Moro Gulf

Zamboanga

Lebak   *Davao Gulf*

General Santos

hipelago

Catanduanes Island

Naga

Legazpi City

Samar

Tacloban

Leyte

PHILIPPINES

Panay Island

Mariana Islands

HAGÅTÑA (AGANA)

GUAM (to USA)

Yap COLONIA

M I C R O N E S I A

Chuuk Islands

Babeldaob

KOROR (OREOR)

PALAU

Celebes Sea

Kepulauan Sangir

Manado

Gorontalo

Ternate

Pulau Morotai

Pulau Halmahera

Kepulauan Talaud

ulf of minli

Molucca Sea

Halmahera Sea

Pulau Waigeo

Selat Dampier

Sorong

Jazirah Doberai

Pulau Biak

Ninigo Group

Hermit Islands

Admiralty Islands

Manus Island   Lorengau

St.Matthias Group

ulawesi

Kepulauan Sula

Pulau Misool

Ceram Sea

Wahai

Pulau Yapen

Teluk Cenderawasih

Bismarck Archipelago

New Hanover

Kavieng

Lihir Group

N   E   S   I   A

Waflia

Danau Towuti

Kendari

Pulau Buton

Pulau Seram

Ambon

Pulau Buru

Maluku (Moluccas)

Fakfak

Teluk Berau

Sungai Mamberamo

Jayapura

Vanimo

Lumi

Wewak

Green River   Sepik

Angoram

Bogia

Karkar Island

Madang

Bismarck Sea

Witu Islands

Rabaul

Toriu

New Ireland

Taron

Kepulauan Banggai

Puncak Jaya 5040m

Pegunungan Maoke

Tembagapura

Amamapare

New Guinea

Central Range

Mount Wilhelm 4509m

Goroka

Kimbe

Gloucester

Anepmete

Pomio

New Britain

Gasmata

Kepulauan Tukangbesi

Kepulauan Kai

Kepulauan Aru

Iabubil

Kiunga

Sungai Digul

Mendi

Mount Hagen

Lae

Vitiaz Strait

Finschhafen

Huon Gulf

Solomon Sea

Banda Sea

Pulau Wetar

Pulau Yamdena

Pulau Yos Sudarso

Hy   Lake Murray

Stickland

Manau

Kepulauan Bonerate

Kepulauan Alor

Kepulauan Leti

Kepulauan Tanimbar

Weam

Emeti

Kiwai Island

Oriomo

Daru

Hisiu

Gulf of Papua

Popondetta

Tufi

Kiriwina Islands

Woodlark Island

Guasopa

PAPUA NEW GUINEA

lores

DILI

Nikiniki

EAST TIMOR

Timor

Kupang

Pulau Roti

Kupang

esser Sunda Islands

pulauan Sawu

Savu Sea

Arafura Sea

Melville Island

Croker Island

South Goulburn Island

Bathurst Island

Van Diemen Gulf

Darwin

Noonamah

Adelaide River

Wessel Islands

Prince of Wales Island

Cape York

Cape York Peninsula

Mari

Torres Strait

PORT MORESBY

Kupiano

Magarida

Alotau

D'Entrecasteaux Islands

Tagula Island

Louisiade Archipelago

Stanley Range

Owen Stanley Range 3676m

Mount Suckling 3676m

Coral Sea

Timor Sea

Gulf of Carpentaria

Arnhem Land

A U S T R A L I A

Nhulunbuy

Moa Island

Equator

ASIA

19,686ft

13,124ft

9843ft

6562ft

3281ft

1640ft

820ft

328ft

Sea Level

-820ft

-6562ft

-13,124ft

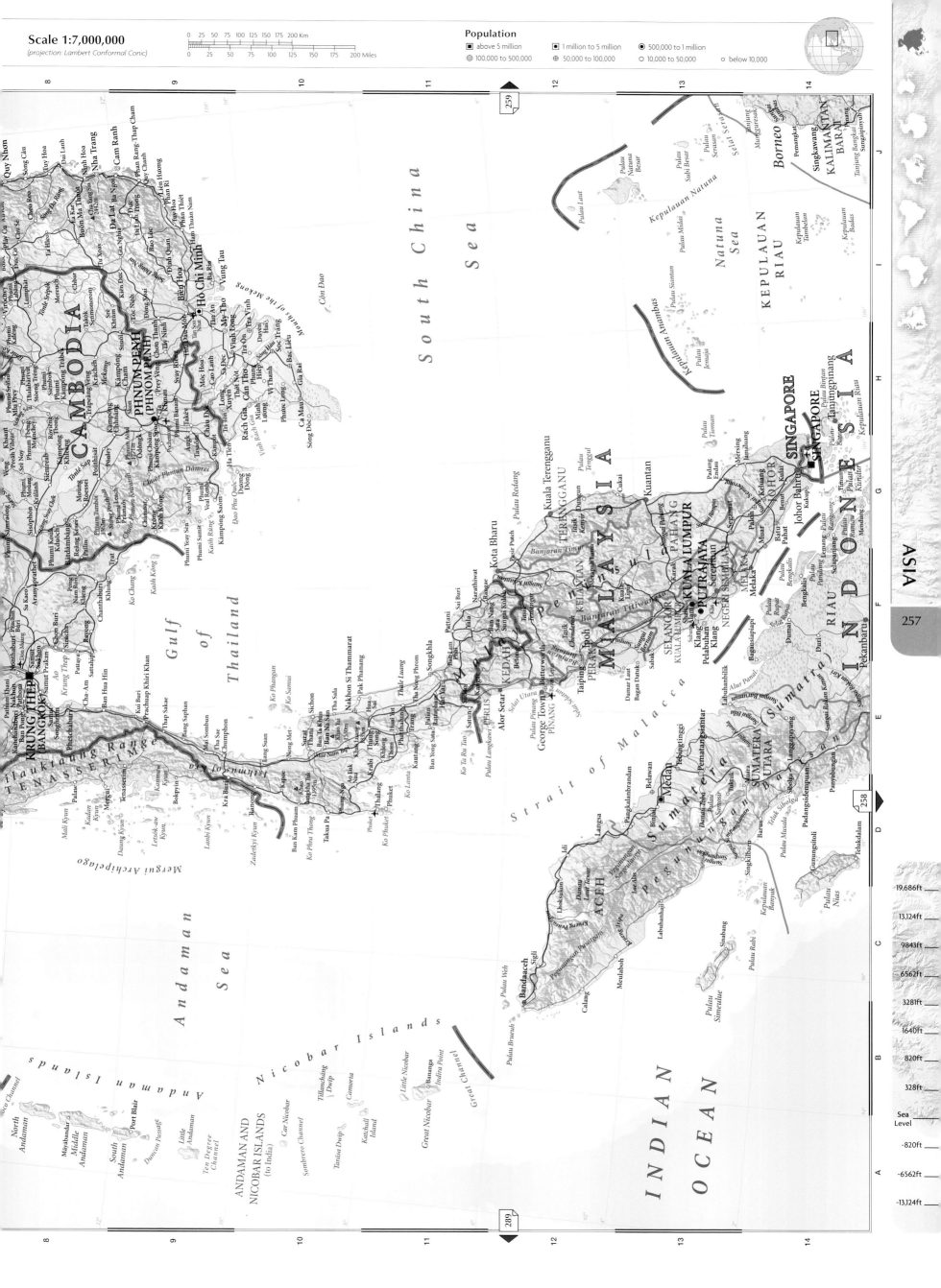

PHILIPPINES

Mindanao

Palimbang   Mount Busa   Surallah   Malita   Cape San
2083m   Parker   General Santos   Agustin
Kiamba   Volcano   Glan   Jose Abad
1812m   Santos
Tinaca Point
Sarangani Islands

Kota Kinabalu   Gunung
Kinabalu   Sungai Sugut   Teluk
4101m   Labuk
Tuaran   Ramui
Kota Kinabalu   Sandakan
Teluk Kimanis   Tambunan
Kuala Penyu   Tenom   Sungai Segama   Lahad Datu
Pulau Labuan   Keningau   Sungai Kuamut
SABAH   Teluk Lahad Datu
LABUAN
Bandar Seri Begawan   Brunei Bay   Pulau Sebatik
BANDAR SERI   Tawau   Pulau Bum Bum
BEGAWAN   Pulau Timbun Mata

Samales Group
Bitung
Palimbang   Kiamba

Celebes Sea

Kepulauan
Kawio   Kepulauan
Talaud
Pulau Salibabu   Pulau
Melanguane   Kaburuang
Tahuna
Pulau Sangihe

Kepulauan Nanusa

MALAYSIA
Tidaran

Kuala Belait   **BRUNEI**
Miri

Loagan Bunut
SARAWAK

Sungai Bahau   Tanjungbatu
KALIMANTAN   Sungai Berau   Pulau Maratua
TIMUR   Tanjungredeb
Metulang   Muarawahau   Teluk
Gunung Menyapa   Sangkulirang   Pantai
2000m

Borneo
Pegunungan Hose

Kalimantan

Samarinda
Balikpapan

**KALIMANTAN
TENGAH**

Kepulauan
Balabalangan

**KALIMANTAN
SELATAN**

Banjarmasin

Ulu   Pulau Siau
Pulau
Tahulandang   Kepulauan
Loloda Utara   Tanjung Sopi
Tanjung Bisa   Pulau Morotai
Serai   Pulau Bangka   Galela
Selat Bangka   Tobelo   Iga   Akelamo
Manado   Bobopayo   Kusu   Dodaga
Tomohon   Airmadidi   **Ternate**   Soasiu
SULAWESI   Tondano   Pulau Ternate   Pulau Tidore
UTARA   Danau Tondano   *Pulau Halmahera*
Amurang   Pulau Makian
GORONTALO   Kuandang   **MALUKU**   Teluk
Gunung   Gorontalo   **UTARA**   Weda
2499m   Kotamobagu   Mafa
Gunung Bulawa   Molibagu
1970m

*Halmahera
Sea*

Pulau Mayu

Pulau Kasiruta   Kepulauan
Molucca   Kepulauan Bacan
Sea   Pulau Mandioli   Bacan   Gani   Pulau
Widi
Pulau Bisa   Selat Obi   Pulau
Damar
Pulau Obi
Pulau Taliabu   Penu   Pulau Mangole   Kawassi
Sanana   Capalulu   Sesepe
Kepulauan Sula   Pulau
Pulau Sanana   Gomumu

*Ceram
Sea*

Tanjung Nar
Lasahata   Pitu
Waflia   Namlea   Pulau Boano   Luhu
Gunung Kaubalatmada   Danau   Pulau Kelang
2729m   Rana   Pulau Manipa   **Ambon**
Tifu   Pulau Buru   Pulau Ambon
Elara   Ambelau   *Kepulauan*
Pulau Ambelau   **MALUKU**

Tenggarong

Longiram   Danau
Semayang
Muarajuloi   Danau Melintang
Kunyi   Danau Jempang
Muaratewe
Bawan   Muarakaman
Dayu
Palangkaraya   Tanjung
Amuntai

Martapura
Pelaihari   Kandangan
Rantau
Kotabaru   Pulau Sebuku
Pulau Laut
Karambu

Makassar Strait

Salumpaga
Oan
Tolitoli   Leok
Tompo   Lanu
Gunung Malino
2499m
Teluk Tomini
Donggala   Towera
Palu   Lambogo
Pakuli   Tambarana
Danau   Tobamawi
Lindu   Tentena   Pandiri
Gimpu   Taripa
Karosa   Poso
Babana   Danau
SULAWESI   Poso
BARAT   Tentena
Mamuju   Masamba   Wotu
Malunda   Rantepao
Majene   Polewali
Parepare   Enrekang
Danau Tempe
SULAWESI
SELATAN
Makassar
Takalar   Maros
Jeneponto   Bulukumba

Teluk Bilang
Teluk Paleleh
Dondo   Teluk Kwandang
Bolang   Pegunungan Pakoleh
Lemito   Bubaa
Molosipat   Teluk Gorontalo

Pulau
Batudaka
Gulf of   Kepulauan
Tomini   Togian
Pulau
Teluk   Maliku   Teku
Uebonti   Teku
Bolang   Luwuk
Tobamawi   Pegunungan Balingara
SULAWESI   Balo
TENGAH   Pulau Peleng
Kembani   Pelei
Baturebe
Kepulauan
Treko
SULAWESI   Pulau Banggai
Celebes   Danau   Kepulauan   Selat Salue Timpaus
Matana   Towori
Mahalona   *Teluk*   Kepulauan Banggai
Danau Towuti   *Tolo*
Wiau   Kepulauan
Asera   Salabangka
Kolaka   Kendari   Pulau Manui
SULAWESI
TENGGARA
Teluk Staring
Pulau Wowoni
Anabanua   Pulau
Singkang   Padamarang
Watampone   Bonelipu

Kepulauan
Pabbiring   Tampo
Raha   Teluk
Lasihao   Kolowanawatobe   Kepulauan Langkesi
Kamaru
Pising   Pulau
Muna   Baubau
Pulau
Kabaena   Pulau
Kaledupa   Kepulauan
Tukangbesi
Pulau Binongko

Kepulauan
Macan
Pulau
Benteng   Tanahjampea

Banda Sea

Kepulauan
Penyu
Kepulauan
Lucipara

I N D O N E S

Pulau Batuata

Kepulauan
Bonerate
Pulau Kalao
Pulau Bonerate   Pulau
Kaloatoa

I N D O N E S

Kepulauan
Sabalana   Pulau
Kangean   Kepulauan
Kangean
Ambunten
Sumenep
Pulau
Sapudi
Jawa (Java)
Situbondo   *Bali Sea*
Bondowoso   **NUSA TENGGARA BARAT**
Gunung Raung
3390m   Singaraja   Kubu
JAWA,   Banyuwangi   Bayan   Gunung
TIMUR   Grajagan   Karangasem   Gunung Api   Pota
Tejakula   1949m
Pulau Moyo   Gunung Tambora   Teluk Sanggar
Bali   Bayan   2821m
Alas   Dompu   Raba
Denpasar   Sumbawabesar
Negara   **Mataram**   Taliwang   Komodo
Ngurah Rai   Pulau   Lunyuk   Sumbawa   Labuhanbajo
Kuta   Lombok   Gunung Takan   Ruteng   Bajawa
Nusa   1400m   Gerampi   Endeh
Penida   *Nusa*   Bondokodi   Bajawa
Waingapu   **NUSA TENGGARA TIMUR**
Waikabubak
Tenggara   Maumere
Bondokodi   Pulau Sumba
Waikabubak   *Savu Sea*
Baing

Pulau Wetar   Selat Romang
Kepulauan Damar   Pulau
Damar
Pulau Romang
Pulau
Lomblen   Kepulauan Alor   Kepulauan
Pulau   Pulau Alor   Leti
Sangeang   Larantuka   Selat Alor
Teluk Sindeh   Kabir   Kalabahi   Selat Wetar   Tutuala
Flores   Maumere   Labala   **DILI**   Pulau Kambing   Pulau
Teluk Palu   Pulau   Manatuto   Moa
Kefamenanu   Pantar   Lospalos   Serma
Kepulauan Solor   **EAST TIMOR**
Pante Makasar   Maliana
(Part of   Suai
East Timor)
Gunung Kekneno
2070m   Soe   Nikiniki
Sulamu   Toineke
Kupang
Pulau Semau
Pulau Sawu   Pulau Roti
Kepulauan   Baa
Sawu

Timor Sea

I N D I A N

O C E A N

259

ASIA

6000m
4000m
3000m
2000m
1000m
500m
250m
100m
Sea
Level
-250m
-500m
-1000m

Scale 1:7,000,000
(projection: Mercator)

0 25 50 75 100 125 150 200 Km
0 25 50 75 100 125 150 175 200 Miles

Population
- ■ above 5 million
- ▣ 1 million to 5 million
- ◉ 500,000 to 1 million
- ◎ 100,000 to 500,000
- ⊕ 50,000 to 100,000
- ⊙ 10,000 to 50,000
- ∘ below 10,000

19,686ft
13,124ft
9843ft
6562ft
3281ft
1640ft
820ft
328ft
Sea Level
-820ft
-6562ft
-13,124ft

ASIA

6000m
4000m
3000m
2000m
1000m
500m
250m
100m
Sea Level
-250m
-500m
-1000m

240

288

258

Baghdad

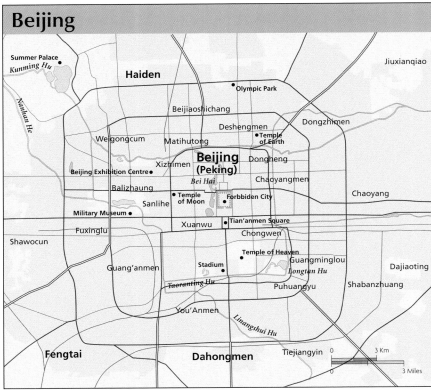

Tigris
Shaala
Quds
Zahrā
Tunis
Maghreb
Sadr City
Al'Azamiyah
Adel
Arbataash
Rusāfa
Qanat Al Jayah
Khansā'
Shaikh
Aomar
Shaab
Stadium
Karkh
Gaiani
Baghdād
Iraqi National
Museum
Liberation
Monument
Aalām
Muthana
Amin
International Zone
(Green Zone)
Tishriyaa
Riyad
Diyala
Khudrā
Karradah
Wahda
Hamrā
Firdows
New Baghdād
Jihād
University
Amal Qadisiya
Jizīra
Dōra
Tigris
Baghdād
Intl. Airport

0   4 Km
0   4 Miles

Bangkok

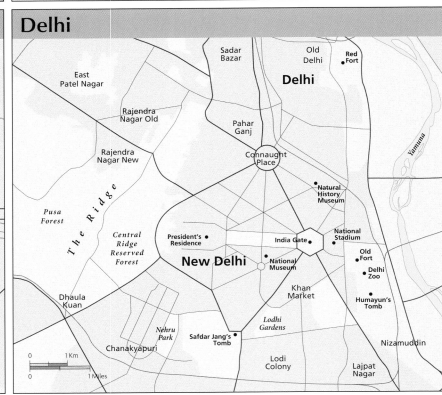

Bangkhen
Nonthaburi
Chao Phraya
Lad
Phrao
Bangsu
Chatuchak
Dusit
Phaya
Thai
Huay
Khwang
Chitralanda
Palace
Bang Kapi
Bangkok
Noi
National
Museum
Wat Phra Kaeo & Grand Palace
Jim Thomson's
House
Khlong
Toey
Wat Arun
Krung Thep
(Bangkok)
Phasi
Charoen
Khlong
Thonburi
Sathorn
Chao Phraya
Bang
Kholaem
Chom
Thong
Yannawa
Phra
Khanong
Phra
Pradaeng
Ratburana
Samut
Prakan

0   5 Km
0   5 Miles

Beijing

Summer Palace
Kunming Hu
Haiden
Jiuxianqiao
Nanhan He
Olympic Park
Beijiaoshichang
Deshengmen
Dongzhimen
Weigongcum
Matihutong
Temple
of Earth
Beijing
(Peking)
Dongcheng
Beijing Exhibition Centre
Xizhimen
Balizhuang
Bei Hai
Chaoyangmen
Sanlihe
Temple
of Moon
Forbidden City
Chaoyang
Military Museum
Xuanwu
Tian'anmen Square
Fuxinglu
Chongwen
Shawocun
Guang'anmen
Stadium
Temple of Heaven
Guangminglou
Dajiaoting
Taoranting Hu
Longtan Hu
Puhuangyu
Shabanzhuang
You'Anmen
Liangshui Hu
Fengtai
Dahongmen
Tiejiangyin

0   3 Km
0   3 Miles

Delhi

Sadar
Bazar
Old
Delhi
Red
Fort
East
Patel Nagar
Delhi
Rajendra
Nagar Old
Pahar
Ganj
Rajendra
Nagar New
Connaught
Place
Yamuna
The Ridge
Natural
History
Museum
Pusa
Forest
President's
Residence
India Gate
National
Stadium
Central
Ridge
Reserved
Forest
New Delhi
National
Museum
Old
Fort
Khan
Market
Delhi
Zoo
Dhaula
Kuan
Humayun's
Tomb
Nehru
Park
Lodhi
Gardens
Nizamuddin
Safdar Jang's
Tomb
Chanakyāpuri
Lodi
Colony
Lajpat
Nagar

0   1 Km
0   1 Miles

Dhaka

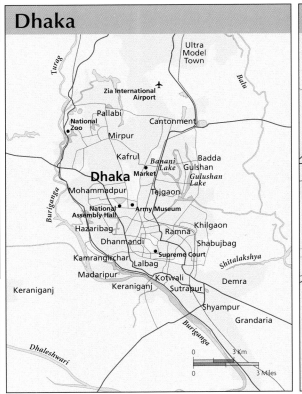

Turag
Ultra
Model
Town
Balu
Zia International
Airport
Pallabi
National
Zoo
Cantonment
Mirpur
Kafrul
Banani
Lake
Badda
Gulshan
Market
Gulushan
Lake
Dhaka
Mohammedpur
Tejgaon
Buriganga
National
Assembly Hall
Army Museum
Khilgaon
Hazaribag
Ramna
Shabujbag
Dhanmandi
Kamrangirchar
Supreme Court
Shitalakshya
Madaripur
Lalbag
Kotwali
Demra
Keraniganj
Keraniganj
Sutrapur
Shyampur
Grandaria
Dhaleshwari
Buriganga

0   3 Km
0   3 Miles

Kolkata

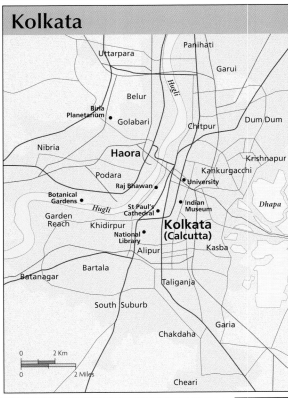

Panihati
Uttarpara
Garui
Belur
Hugli
Birla
Planetarium
Golabari
Chitpur
Dum Dum
Nibria
Krishnapur
Haora
Kankurgacchi
Podara
University
Raj Bhawan
Botanical
Gardens
Hugli
St Paul's
Cathedral
Indian
Museum
Dhapa
Garden
Reach
Khidirpur
National
Library
Kolkata
(Calcutta)
Kasba
Batanagar
Alipur
Bartala
Taliganja
South Suburb
Garia
Chakdaha
Cheari

0   2 Km
0   2 Miles

Kabul

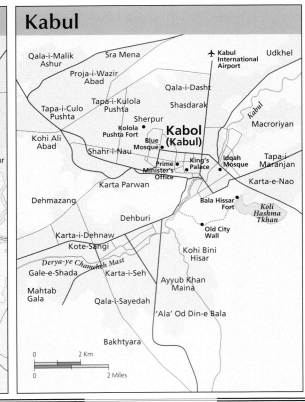

Qala-i-Malik
Ashur
Sra Mena
Kabul
International
Airport
Udkhel
Proja-i-Wazir
Abad
Qala-i-Dasht
Tapa-i-Kulola
Pushta
Shasdarak
Tapa-i-Culo
Pushta
Sherpur
Kabul
Macroriyan
Kolola
Pushta Fort
Kabol
(Kabul)
Kohi Ali
Abad
Blue
Mosque
Shahr-i-Nau
Prime
Minister's
Office
King's
Palace
Idqah
Mosque
Tapa-i-
Maranjan
Karta Parwan
Karta-e-Nao
Dehmazang
Bala Hissar
Fort
Koli
Hashma
Tkhan
Dehburi
Old City
Wall
Karta-i-Dehnaw
Kote-Sangi
Kohi Bini
Hisar
Derya-ye Chamehk Mast
Gale-e-Shada
Karta-i-Seh
Ayyub Khan
Maina
Mahtab
Gala
Qala-i-Sayedah
'Ala' Od Din-e Bala
Bakhtyara

0   2 Km
0   2 Miles

Hong Kong

Mong Kok
Kowloon City
Kowloon
Royal Observatory
Ho Man Tin
Hung Hom
Kowloon Bay
Tsim Sha Tsui
Hong Kong Coliseum
Space Museum & Planetarium
Star Ferry
North Point
Sai Ying Pun
Victoria Harbour
Kennedy Town
University of Hong Kong
Mid Levels
Sheung Wan
Convention Centre
Tun Lo Wan
Tai Tam
Government House
Hong Kong (Xianggang)
Tai Hang
Wan Chai
Victoria Peak 554m △
Happy Valley
Tiger Balm Garden
Hong Kong Island
0 1 Km
0 1 Miles

Istanbul

Alibey
Kemerburgaz
Istanbul Boğazı (Bosporus)
Beykoz
Ömerli
Hürriyet Abidesi
Kagithane
Gaziosmanpasa
Şişli
Beşiktaş
Tasdelen
Esenler
Eyüp
Beyoglu
Üsküdar
Ümraniye
İstanbul
Haliç
Galata Kulesi
Bagcilar
Fatih
Topkapi
Selimiye Kişlaşi
Güngören
Kapatı Çarsi
Ayasofya
Bahçelievler
Blue Mosque
Sultanbeyli
Küçükçekmece
Zeytinburnu
Maltepe
Bakirköy
Atatürk Intl. Airport
Marmara Sea
Kartal
Pendik
0 5 Km
0 5 Miles
Adalar Büyükada

Kuala Lumpur

Lake Titiwangsa
Kepong
Sentul
National Art Gallery
Ulu Kelang
Tunku
Baru
Ampang
Sungai Buloh
National Monument
Petronas Towers
Golden Triangle
Damansara
National Mosque
Central Market
Taman Meur
Lake gardens
Kuala Lumpur
Bangsar
National Museum
Taman Mayang
Petaling Jaya
Salak Selatan
Pengkalan Udara Airport
Sungai Besi
0 1 Km
0 1 Miles

Ulan Bator

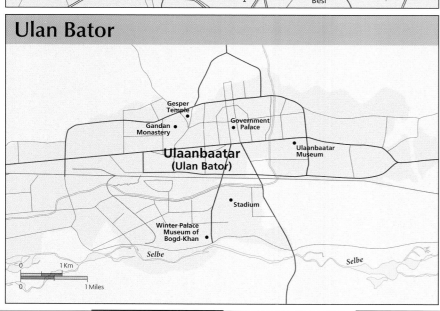

Gesper Temple
Gandan Monastery
Government Palace
Ulaanbaatar Museum
Ulaanbaatar (Ulan Bator)
Selbe
Stadium
Winter Palace Museum of Bogd-Khan
Selbe
0 1 Km
0 1 Miles

Islamabad

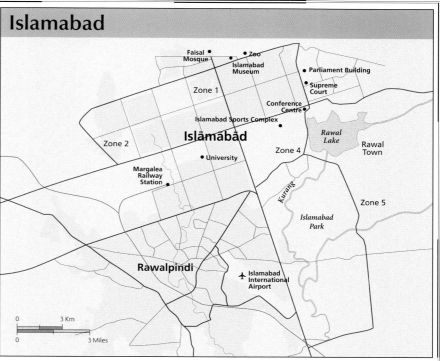

Faisal Mosque
Zoo
Islamabad Museum
Parliament Building
Zone 1
Supreme Court
Conference Centre
Islamabad Sports Complex
Rawal Lake
Rawal Town
Zone 2
Islāmābād
Zone 4
University
Margalea Railway Station
Kurang
Zone 5
Islamabad Park
Rawalpindi
Islamabad International Airport
0 3 Km
0 3 Miles

Jakarta

Java Sea
Soekarno-Hatta International Airport
Penjaringan
Teluk Jakarta
Ancol
Tanjung Priok
Kalideres
Pademangan
Taman Sari
Jakarta Museum
Sunter
Koja
Merdeka Palace
Jakarta
National Monument
Cempaka Putih
Kembangan
Welcome Monument
Kebon Jeruk
Parliament House
Menteng
University Rawamangun
Pulo Gadung
Matraman
Kebayoran Lama
Jatinegara
Pancoran
Manggarai
Kebayoran Baru
Ciliwung
Jakarta Halim Perdanakusuma Airport
Kebayoran Baru
Kramat Jati
Cilandak
Pasar Munggu
Ciracas
Jagakarsa
0 5 Km
0 5 Miles

Manila

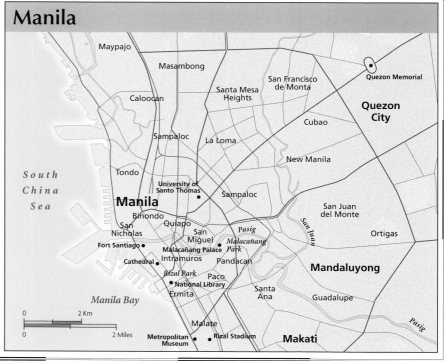

Maypajo
Masambong
San Francisco de Monta
Quezon Memorial
Caloocan
Santa Mesa Heights
Quezon City
Cubao
South China Sea
Sampaloc
La Loma
New Manila
Tondo
University of Santo Thomas
Sampaloc
San Juan del Monte
Manila
Binondo
San Nicholas
Quiapo
San Miguel
Pasig
Ortigas
Malacañang Park
Fort Santiago
Malacañang Palace
Pandacan
Mandaluyong
Cathedral
Intramuros
Paco
Santa Ana
Guadalupe
Rizal Park
National Library
Ermita
Manila Bay
Malate
Metropolitan Museum
Rizal Stadium
Makati
Pasig
0 2 Km
0 2 Miles

Australasia and Oceania with a total land area of 3,285,048 sq miles (8,508,238 sq km), takes in 14 countries including the continent of Australia, New Zealand, Papua New Guinea, and many island groups scattered across the Pacific Ocean.

FACTFILE

N **Most Northerly Point:** Eastern Island, Midway Islands 28° 15′ N
S **Most Southerly Point:** Macquarie Island, New Zealand 54° 30′ S
E **Most Easterly Point:** Clipperton Island, 109° 12′ W
W **Most Westerly Point:** Cape Inscription, Australia 112° 57′ E

Largest Lakes:
1. Lake Eyre, Australia 3430 sq miles (8884 sq km)
2. Lake Torrens, Australia 2200 sq miles (5698 sq km)
3. Lake Gairdner, Australia 1679 sq miles (4349 sq km)
4. Lake Mackay, Australia 1349 sq miles (3494 sq km)
5. Lake Argyle, Australia 800 sq miles (2072 sq km)

Longest Rivers:
1. Murray-Darling, Australia 2330 miles (3750 km)
2. Cooper Creek, Australia 880 miles (1420 km)
3. Warburton-Georgina, Australia 870 miles (1400 km)
4. Sepik, Indonesia/Papua New Guinea 700 miles (1126 km)
5. Fly, Indonesia/Papua New Guinea 652 miles (1050 km)

Largest Islands:
1. New Guinea, 312,000 sq miles (808,000 sq km)
2. South Island, New Zealand 56,308 sq miles (145,836 sq km)
3. North Island, New Zealand 43,082 sq miles (111,583 sq km)
4. Tasmania, Australia 24,911 sq miles (64,519 sq km)
5. New Britain, Papua New Guinea 13,570 sq miles (35,145 sq km)

Highest Points:
1. Mount Wilhelm, Papua New Guinea 14,793 ft (4509 m)
2. Mount Giluwe, Papua New Guinea 14,331 ft (4368 m)
3. Mount Herbert, Papua New Guinea 13,999 ft (4267 m)
4. Mount Bangeta, Papua New Guinea 13,520 ft (4121 m)
5. Mount Victoria, Papua New Guinea 13,248 ft (4038 m)

Lowest Point:
▼ Lake Eyre, Australia -53 ft (-16 m) below sea level

Highest recorded temperature:
⊕ Bourke, Australia 128°F (53°C)

Lowest recorded temperature:
⊖ Canberra, Australia -8°F (-22°C)

Wettest Place:
≋ Bellenden Ker, Australia 443 in (11,251 mm)

Driest Place:
⊖ Mulka Bore, Australia 4.05 in (102.8 mm)

Dirk Hartog Island, Australia | Great Dividing Range | New Caledonia | New Zealand | Tonga | Tuamoto Islands | Ducie Island, Pitcairn Islands

Cross-section from Dirk Hartog Island, Australia to Ducie Island, Pitcairn Islands

line of cross-section

0 500 1000 1500 Km
0 500 1000 1500 Miles

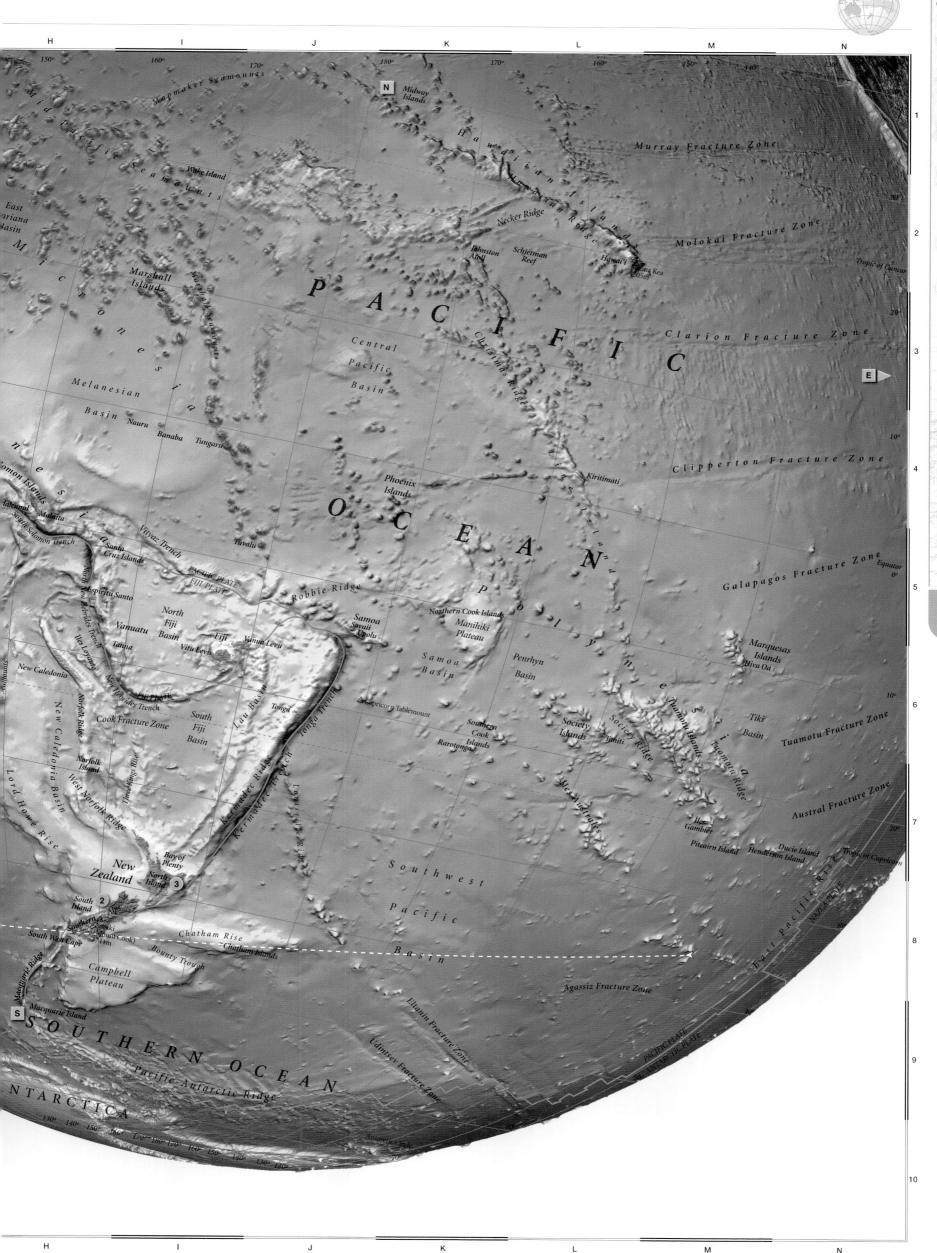

PACIFIC OCEAN

SOUTHERN OCEAN

Murray Fracture Zone
Molokai Fracture Zone
Clarion Fracture Zone
Clipperton Fracture Zone
Galapagos Fracture Zone
Tuamotu Fracture Zone
Austral Fracture Zone
Agassiz Fracture Zone
Eltanin Fracture Zone
Udintsev Fracture Zone

Tropic of Cancer
Tropic of Capricorn
Equator
Antarctic Circle

Mapmaker Seamounts
Midway Islands
Hawaiian Islands
Hawaiian Ridge
Necker Ridge
Johnston Atoll
Schjetman Reef
Hawai'i
Mauna Kea 4205m

Mid Pacific Seamounts
Wake Island
Marshall Islands
Marshall Seamounts
Nauru
Banaba
Tungaru
Micronesia
East Mariana Basin

Central Pacific Basin

Melanesian Basin
Solomon Islands
Guadalcanal
Malaita
South Solomon Trench
Santa Cruz Islands
Vityaz Trench
Tuvalu
Phoenix Islands

Christmas Ridge
Kiritimati
Line Islands

Marquesas Islands
Hiva Oa
Tiki Basin
Society Islands
Society Ridge
Tuamotu Islands
Tuamotu Ridge
Tahiti
Penrhyn Basin
Northern Cook Islands
Manihiki Plateau
Samoa
Savaii
Upolu
Samoa Basin
Southern Cook Islands
Rarotonga
Îles Australes
Îles Gambier
Pitcairn Island
Henderson Island
Ducie Island

Robbie Ridge
Capricorn Tablemount
North Fiji Basin
Vanuatu
Tanna
Îles Loyauté
New Hebrides Trench
Espiritu Santo
Fiji
Vanua Levu
Vitu Levu
PACIFIC PLATE
FIJI PLATE

New Caledonia
New Caledonia Basin
Norfolk Ridge
Cook Fracture Zone
South Fiji Basin
Lau Basin
Tonga
Tonga Trench
Kermadec Ridge
Kermadec Trench
Louisville Ridge
Three Kings Rise
West Norfolk Ridge
Norfolk Island
Lord Howe Rise

New Zealand
North Island
South Island
Bay of Plenty
Southern Alps
Aoraki (Mount Cook) 3754m
South West Cape
Chatham Rise
Chatham Islands
Bounty Trough

Southwest Pacific Basin

Macquarie Ridge
Campbell Plateau
Macquarie Island

Pacific-Antarctic Ridge
ANTARCTICA

East Pacific Rise
NAZCA PLATE
PACIFIC PLATE
ANTARCTIC PLATE

Political

Vast expanses of ocean separate this geographically fragmented realm, characterized more by each country's isolation than by any political unity. Australia's and New Zealand's traditional ties with the United Kingdom, as members of the Commonwealth, are now being called into question as Australasian and Oceanian nations are increasingly looking to forge new relationships with neighboring Asian countries like Japan. External influences have featured strongly in the politics of the Pacific Islands; the various territories of Micronesia were largely under US control until the late 1980s, and France, New Zealand, the USA and the UK still have territories under colonial rule in Polynesia. Nuclear weapons-testing by Western superpowers was widespread during the Cold War period, but has now been discontinued.

Population
- above 5 million
- 1 million to 5 million
- 500,000 to 1 million
- 100,000 to 500,000
- 50,000 to 100,000
- 10,000 to 50,000
- below 10,000
- Country capital
- State capital

Borders
- full international border
- indication of maritime country extent
- indication of maritime dependent territory extent
- state border

Communications
- major roads
- major railroads

SCALE 1:32,000,000
(projection: Lambert Azimuthal Equal Area)

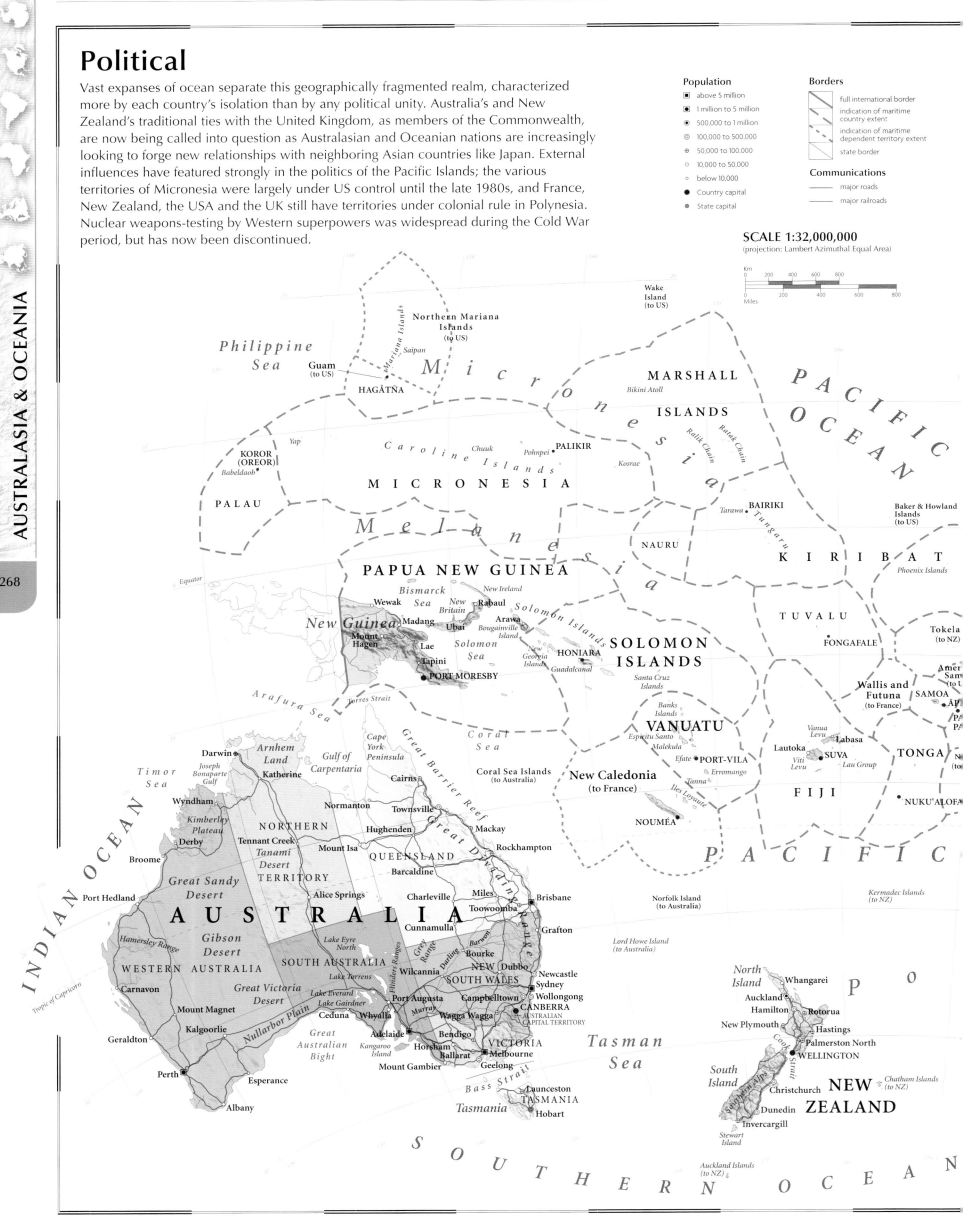

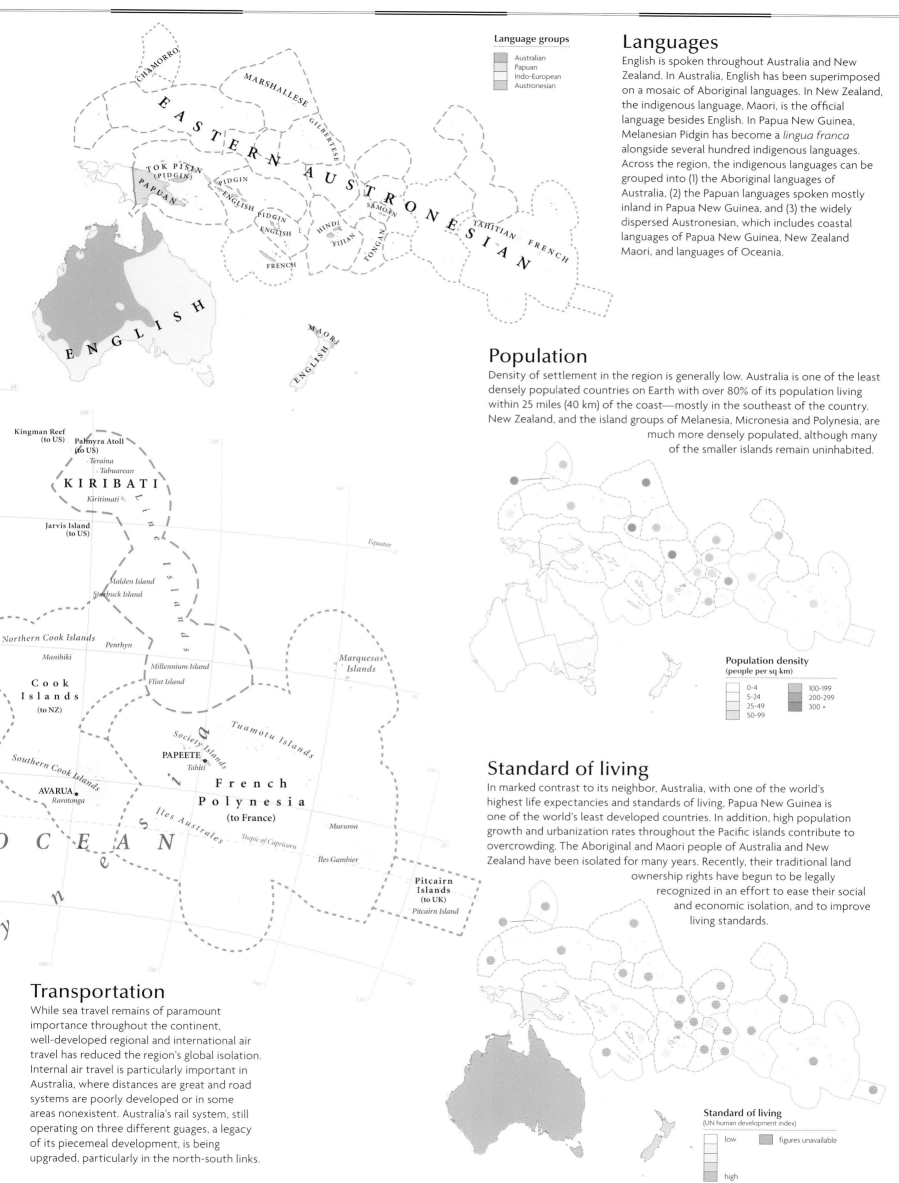

Language groups
- Australian
- Papuan
- Indo-European
- Austronesian

Languages

English is spoken throughout Australia and New Zealand. In Australia, English has been superimposed on a mosaic of Aboriginal languages. In New Zealand, the indigenous language, Maori, is the official language besides English. In Papua New Guinea, Melanesian Pidgin has become a *lingua franca* alongside several hundred indigenous languages. Across the region, the indigenous languages can be grouped into (1) the Aboriginal languages of Australia, (2) the Papuan languages spoken mostly inland in Papua New Guinea, and (3) the widely dispersed Austronesian, which includes coastal languages of Papua New Guinea, New Zealand Maori, and languages of Oceania.

Population

Density of settlement in the region is generally low. Australia is one of the least densely populated countries on Earth with over 80% of its population living within 25 miles (40 km) of the coast—mostly in the southeast of the country. New Zealand, and the island groups of Melanesia, Micronesia and Polynesia, are much more densely populated, although many of the smaller islands remain uninhabited.

Population density
(people per sq km)
- 0-4
- 5-24
- 25-49
- 50-99
- 100-199
- 200-299
- 300 +

Standard of living

In marked contrast to its neighbor, Australia, with one of the world's highest life expectancies and standards of living, Papua New Guinea is one of the world's least developed countries. In addition, high population growth and urbanization rates throughout the Pacific islands contribute to overcrowding. The Aboriginal and Maori people of Australia and New Zealand have been isolated for many years. Recently, their traditional land ownership rights have begun to be legally recognized in an effort to ease their social and economic isolation, and to improve living standards.

Standard of living
(UN human development index)
- low
- high
- figures unavailable

Transportation

While sea travel remains of paramount importance throughout the continent, well-developed regional and international air travel has reduced the region's global isolation. Internal air travel is particularly important in Australia, where distances are great and road systems are poorly developed or in some areas nonexistent. Australia's rail system, still operating on three different guages, a legacy of its piecemeal development, is being upgraded, particularly in the north-south links.

SCALE 1:37,500,000
(projection: Lambert Azimuthal Equal Area)

0   200   400   600   800   1000   1200 Km

0   200   400   600   800   1000   1200 Miles

Climate

Surrounded by water, the climate of most areas is profoundly affected by the moderating effects of the oceans. Australia, however, is the exception. Its dry continental interior remains isolated from the ocean; temperatures soar during the day, and droughts are common. The coastal regions, where most people live, are cooler and wetter. The numerous islands scattered across the Pacific are generally hot and humid, subject to the different air circulation patterns and ocean currents that affect the area, including the El Niño ocean current anomaly, which produces extreme aridity.

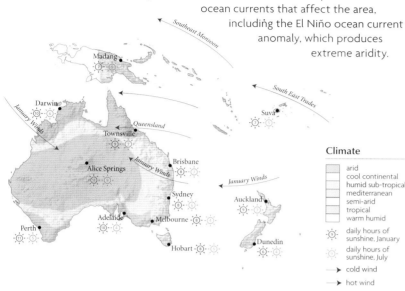

Climate

- arid
- cool continental
- humid sub-tropical
- mediterranean
- semi-arid
- tropical
- warm humid
- ☼ daily hours of sunshine, January
- ☼ daily hours of sunshine, July
- → cold wind
- → hot wind

Average Rainfall

January rainfall *July rainfall*

Rainfall

- 0–25 mm (0–1 in)
- 25–50 mm (1–2 in)
- 50–100 mm (2–4 in)
- 100–200 mm (4–8 in)
- 200–300 mm (8–12 in)
- 300–400 mm (12–16 in)
- 400–500 mm (16–20 in)
- more than 500 mm (20 in)

Average Temperature

January temperature *July temperature*

Temperature

- below -30°C (-22°F)
- -30 to -20°C (-22 to -4°F)
- -20 to -10°C (-4 to 14°F)
- -10 to 0°C (14 to 32°F)
- 0 to 10°C (32 to 50°F)
- 10 to 20°C (50 to 68°F)
- 20 to 30°C (68 to 86°F)
- above 30°C (86°F)

Environmental issues

The prospect of rising sea levels poses a threat to many low-lying islands in the Pacific. Nuclear weapons-testing, once common throughout the region, was finally discontinued in 1996. Australia's ecological balance has been irreversibly altered by the introduction of alien species. Although it has the world's largest underground water reserve, the Great Artesian Basin, the availability of fresh water in Australia remains critical. Periodic droughts combined with over-grazing lead to desertification and increase the risk of devastating bush fires, and occasional flash floods.

PACIFIC TEST SITES

Eniwetok Atoll, Marshall Islands
Bikini Atoll, Marshall Islands
Johnston Atoll
Mururoa Atoll, French Polynesia
Fangatau Atoll, French Polynesia
Christmas Island, Kiribati

Environmental issues

- national parks
- tropical forest
- forest destroyed
- desert
- desertification
- polluted rivers
- ☢ radioactive contamination
- marine pollution
- heavy marine pollution
- • poor urban air quality

Landuse

Much of the region's industry is resource-based: sheep farming for wool and meat in Australia and New Zealand; mining in Australia and Papua New Guinea and fishing throughout the Pacific islands. Manufacturing is mainly limited to the large coastal cities in Australia and New Zealand, like Sydney, Adelaide, Melbourne, Brisbane, Perth, and Auckland, although small-scale enterprises operate in the Pacific islands, concentrating on processing of fish and foods. Tourism continues to provide revenue to the area—in Fiji it accounts for 15 percent of GNP.

Using the land and sea

- barren land
- cropland
- desert
- forest
- mountain region
- pasture
- sheep
- coconuts
- coffee
- fishing
- fruit
- shellfish
- sugar cane
- vineyards
- whaling
- wheat

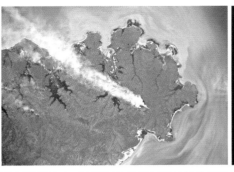

1 MELVILLE ISLAND, NORTHERN TERRITORY, AUSTRALIA
Lying off Australia's north coast, the island is sparsely populated consisting of sandy soils and mangrove swamps.

2 ANATAHAN, NORTHERN MARIANA ISLANDS
The volcano on Anatahan is one of 12 in the Mariana Islands and erupted on a large scale in April 2005.

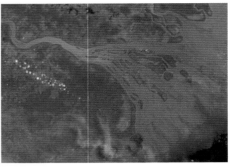

3 FLY RIVER, PAPUA NEW GUINEA
Flowing down from New Guinea's Central Range, the river carries a heavy load of sediment which it deposits in the Gulf of Papua, sometimes forming new islands.

4 RABAUL VOLCANO, NEW BRITAIN, PAPUA NEW GUINE
After erupting in 1994, this image shows how the highe particles blew west causing condensation of water vap over a wide area.

9 ULURU/AYERS ROCK, NORTHERN TERRITORY, AUSTRALIA
This enormous sandstone rock occupies Australia's heart, both physically and emotionally.

10 JAMES RANGES, NORTHERN TERRITORY, AUSTRALIA
A series of low ridges, these hills lie at the geographical center of Australia.

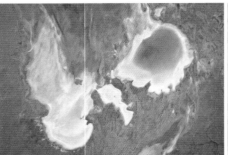

11 LAKE EYRE, SOUTH AUSTRALIA, AUSTRALIA
This great salt lake consists of north and south sections, joined by a narrow channel, Lake Eyre South being the smaller, elongated saltflat at the bottom of the image.

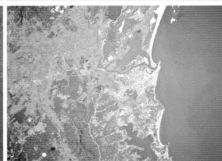

12 NEWCASTLE, NEW SOUTH WALES, AUSTRALIA
The industrial seaport of Newcastle lies on the south bank of Hunter river.

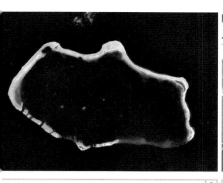

BIKINI ATOLL, MARSHALL ISLANDS | 5
This atoll was the site of 23 atomic bomb tests in the 1940s and 1950s, involving the intentional sinking of at least 13 naval vessels in the shallow lagoon.

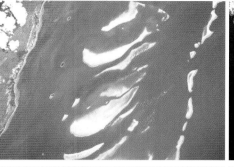

GREAT BARRIER REEF, QUEENSLAND, AUSTRALIA | 6
The world's largest reef system is made up of 3000 individual reefs and 900 islands and stretches for 1600 miles (2600 km).

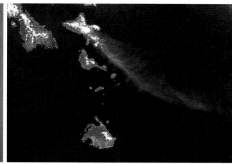

AMBRYM, VANUATU | 7
Mount Marum, a 4166 ft (1270 m) volcano, erupted in April 2004 producing an extensive plume of ash.

KIRITIMATI, KIRIBATI | 8
Kiritimati is the largest atoll in the Pacific Ocean, its interior lagoon filled in with coral growth.

SYDNEY, NEW SOUTH WALES, AUSTRALIA | 13
Expanding outward from the inlet of Port Jackson, Australia's largest city was founded in 1788.

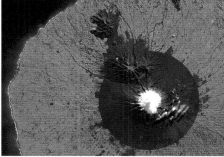

MOUNT TARANAKI, NORTH ISLAND, NEW ZEALAND | 14
This dormant 2518 m (8261 ft) volcano is one of the most symmetrical in the world.

AORAKI/MOUNT COOK, SOUTH ISLAND, NEW ZEALAND | 15
New Zealand's highest peak rises 12,238 ft (3744 m) and is surrounded by permanent ice fields.

BANKS PENINSULA, SOUTH ISLAND, NEW ZEALAND | 16
With a circular drainage pattern typical of eroded volcanoes, this is the only recognizably volcanic feature on New Zealand's South Island.

Australia

259
289
293

AUSTRALASIA & OCEANIA

INDONESIA

CHRISTMAS ISLAND
(to Australia)

Java Sea

JAKARTA
Serang
Tangerang
Bogor
Cianjur
Bandung
Sukabumi
Garut
Ciamis
Cilacap
Cirebon
Brebes
Tegal
Pekalongan
Purwodadi
Semarang
Magelang
Surakarta
Yogyakarta
Jombang
Madiun
Kediri
Malang
Jember
Pasuruan
Probolinggo
Surabaya
Buli
Mataram
Pulau Madura
Pulau Lombok
Denpasar
Jawa (Java)

Bali Sea
Kepulauan Kangean
Kepulauan Tengah

Nusa Tenggara (Lesser Sunda Islands)
Sumbawa
Raba
Ruteng
Flores
Ende
Larantuka
Labala
Kabir
Kalabahi
Kepulauan Alor
Selat Wetar
Manatuto
DILI
Maliana
EAST TIMOR
Suai
Soe
Kefamenanu
Kupang
Waikabubak
Waingapu
Savu Sea
Pulau Sumba
Baing
Kepulauan Sawu
Pulau Roti
Baa
Pulau Rote

Nusa Tenggara

INDIAN OCEAN

Timor Sea

Melville Island
Bathurst Island
Beagle Gulf
Van Diemen Gulf
Darwin
Noonamah
AdelaideRiver
PineCreek
Cape Bougainville
Cape Londonderry
Joseph Bonaparte Gulf
Bonaparte Archipelago
Heywood Islands
Bigge Island
Adele Island
Collier Bay
Lombadina
Derby
Broome
Rowley Shoals
Kimberley Plateau
Mount Hann 779m
Kalumburu
Kupingarri
Wyndham
Kununurra
Lake Argyle
Turkey Creek
King Leopold Ranges
Durack Range
Mount Wells 970m
Fitzroy Crossing
HallsCreek
Fitzroy River

NORTHERN
Timber Creek
Victoria River Roadhouse
Top Springs Roadhouse
Kalkarindji
Victoria River

Great Sandy Desert
Percival Lakes
Tobin Lake
Lake Mackay
Lake Dora
Lake Auld
Eighty Mile Beach
Port Hedland
De Grey River
Whim Creek
MarbleBar
Dampier Archipelago
Wickham
Roebourne
Barrow Island
Dampier
Karratha
Fortescue River
Witterioom
North West Cape
Exmouth
Learmonth
Onslow
Exmouth Gulf
Hamersley Range
TomPrice
Paraburdoo
Newman
Mount Meharry 1251m
Kenneth Range
Ashburton River
Coral Bay
Lake Disappointment
Gibson Desert
Hopkins Lake
Lake Neale
Lake Macdonald
Minilya
Lake Macleod
Mount Augustus 1105m
Waldburg Range
Barlee Range
Kumarina Roadhouse
Cafnarvon Range
Lake Gregory
Little Sandy Desert
WESTERN
AUSTRALIA
Lake Carnegie
Warburton
Bernier Island
Dorre Island
Carnarvon
Gascoyne River
Gascoyne Junction
Robinson Range
Lake Way
Lake Wells
Lake Throssell
Tomkinson Ranges
Denham
Dirk Hartog Island
SteepPoint
Shark Bay
Murchison River
Lake Annean
Meekatharra
Wiluna
LakeYeo
Lake Carey
Great Victoria Desert
Lake Maurice
Kalbarri
Yalgoo
Lake Austin
Mount Magnet
Lake Barlee
Leonora
Lake Ballard
Geraldton
Mongers Lake
Menzies
Lake Rebecca
Kalgoorlie
Loongana
Reid
Watson
Nullarbor Plain
SOUTH
Moora
Wubin
Pithara
Lake Moore
Coolgardie
Kambalda
Lake Lefroy
Lake Cowan
Kitchener
Rawlinna
Madura
Eucla
The Pinnacles
Gingin
Wanneroo
Perth
Fremantle
Rockingham
Mandurah
Merredin
Northam
York
Brookton
Southern Cross
Lake Johnston
Norseman
Balladonia
Caiguna
Cocklebiddy
Great Australian Bight
Bunbury
Jollie
Narrogin
Wagin
Katanning
Kondinin
Lake King
Lake Hope
Ravensthorpe
Tower Peak 594m
Esperance
Busselton
Margaret River
Cape Leeuwin
Augusta
Bridgetown
Manjimup
Pemberton
Mount Barker
Albany

Perth

Wembley Downs
Herdsman Lake
City Beach
Indian Ocean
Joondanna
Bayswater
Lake Monger
North Perth
Swan River
Jolimont
Subiaco
Art Gallery of Western Australia
Belmont Park
Redcliffe
Alderbury Park
Kings Park
Perth
Zoo
South Perth
Carlisle
Claremont
Dalkeith
Kensington
Cannington
Cottesloe
Applecross
Manning
Mosman Park
Swan River
Canning River
Myaree
Partwood
Fremantle
Piney Lakes Reserve
Bull Creek
Hilton
Murdoch

6000m
4000m
3000m
2000m
1000m
500m
250m
100m
Sea Level
-250m
-500m
-1000m

0   3 Km
3 Miles

Scale 1:13,000,000
(projection: Lambert Conformal Conic)

0 50 100 150 200 250 300 350 400 Km
0 50 100 150 200 250 300 350 400 Miles

Population
■ above 5 million   ■ 1 million to 5 million   ● 500,000 to 1 million
◉ 100,000 to 500,000   ⊕ 50,000 to 100,000   ○ 10,000 to 50,000   ○ below 10,000

280

293

286

19,686ft		
13,124ft		
9843ft		
6562ft		
3281ft		
1640ft		
820ft		
328ft		
Sea Level		
-820ft		
-6562ft		
-13,124ft		

Arafura Sea

PAPUA NEW GUINEA

Solomon Islands

Solomon Sea

PORT MORESBY

HONIARA

SOLOMON ISLANDS

Gulf of Carpentaria

Cape York Peninsula

QUEENSLAND

Coral Sea

CORAL SEA ISLANDS (to Australia)

NEW CALEDONIA (to France)

Simpson Desert

Great Artesian Basin

Townsville

Cairns

Mackay

Rockhampton

Gladstone

Bundaberg

Brisbane

Ipswich

PACIFIC OCEAN

Tropic of Capricorn

NEW SOUTH WALES

Adelaide

Broken Hill

Sydney

Newcastle

Wollongong

CANBERRA

VICTORIA

Melbourne

Geelong

Bass Strait

TASMANIA

Hobart

Brisbane

Chermside

Everton Park

Brisbane Airport

Myrtletown

Wynnum

Toombul

The Gap

Lutwyche

Clayfield

Brisbane River

Red Hill

Newstead

Hawthorne

Manly

Tingalpa

Indooroopilly

Brisbane

Queensland Art Gallery

Botanical Gardens

Wooloongabba

Greenslopes

Carina Heights

Belmont

Corinda

Mount Gravatt

Tingalpa Reservoir

Burbank

0 3 Km
0 3 Miles

Southeast Australia

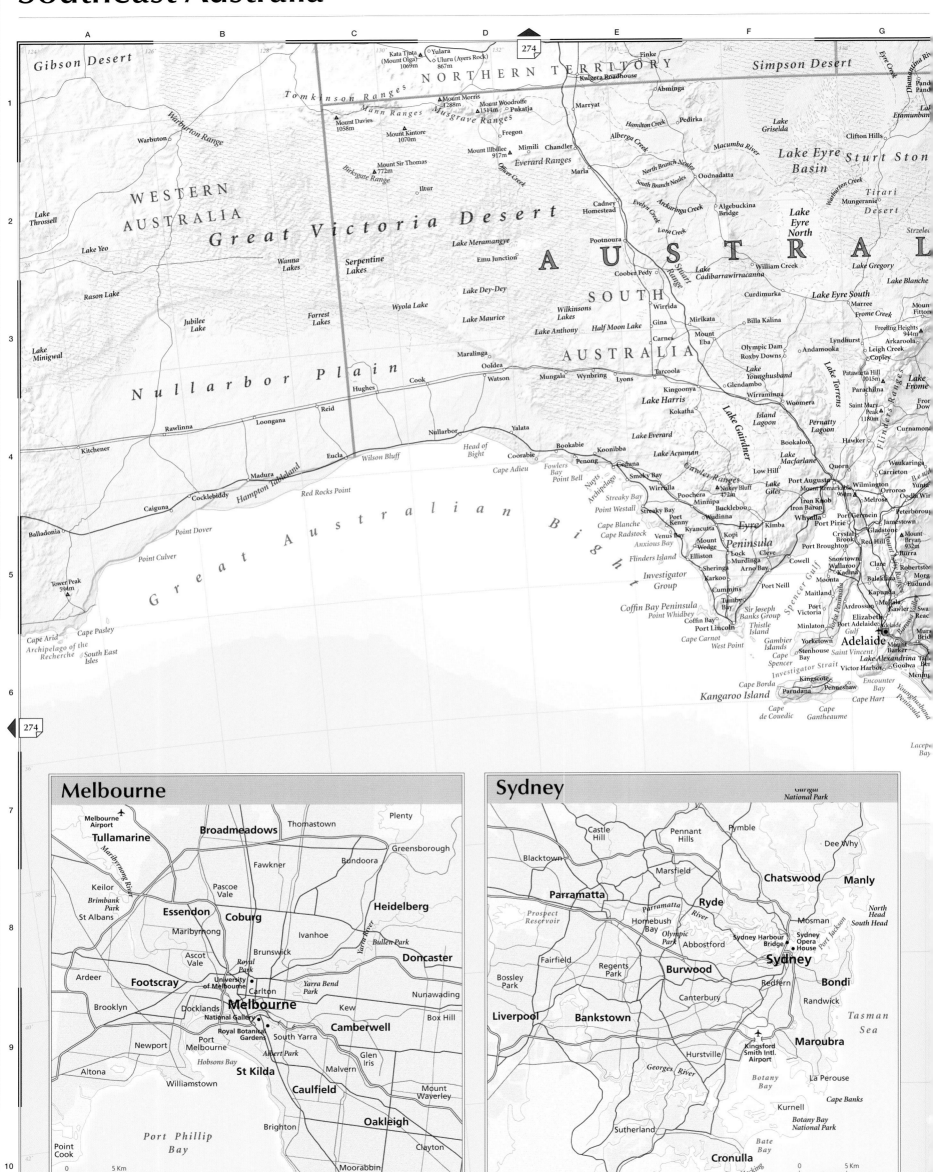

A B C D E F G

Gibson Desert

NORTHERN TERRITORY

Simpson Desert

274

Finke
Kulgera Roadhouse
Abminga

Tomkinson Ranges
Mann Ranges
Musgrave Ranges

Mount Morris 1288m
Mount Woodroffe 1514m
Pukatja
Marryat

Hamilton Creek
Pedirka
Lake Griselda
Clifton Hills

Mount Davies 1058m
Mount Kintore 1070m

Macumba River

WESTERN AUSTRALIA

Mount Sir Thomas 772m
Birksgate Range
Iltur

Mount Illbillee 917m
Mimili
Chandler
Everard Ranges
Marla

North Branch Neales
South Branch Neales
Oodnadatta

Lake Eyre Basin
Sturt Ston

Great Victoria Desert

Lake Meramangye

Officer Creek

Cadney Homestead

Evelyn Creek
Arckaringa Creek
Algebuckina Bridge

Tirari Desert

AUSTRAL

Warburton
Warburton Range

Lake Throssell

Lake Yeo

Wanna Lakes
Serpentine Lakes
Emu Junction

Pootnoura

Coober Pedy

Lora Creek

SOUTH

Lake Eyre North

Lake Cadibarrawirracanna
William Creek

Lake Gregory
Lake Blanche

Rason Lake

Lake Dey-Dey

Wilkinsons Lakes
Lake Anthony
Half Moon Lake

Wirrida
Gina
Mirikata
Billa Kalina

Curdimurka

Lake Eyre South
Marree
Frome Creek

Freeling Heights 944m
Arkaroola
Copley

Jubilee Lake
Forrest Lakes
Wyola Lake
Lake Maurice

Lake Minigwal

AUSTRALIA

Carnes
Mount Eba

Olympic Dam
Roxby Downs
Andamooka

Lyndhurst
Leigh Creek

Patawarta Hill 1015m
Parachilna

Maralinga
Ooldea

Mungala
Wynbring
Lyons
Tarcoola

Lake Younghusband
Glendambo

Wirraminna

Saint Mary Peak 1180m

Flinders Ranges

Fror Dow

Cook
Watson

Kingoonya
Kokatha

Lake Harris

Woomera

Pernatty Lagoon
Hawker

Curnamona

Hughes
Reid

Lake Everard
Lake Gairdner

Island Lagoon
Bookaloo

Quorn

Waukaringa
Carrieton

Rawlinna
Loongana
Reid

Nullarbor
Yalata

Bookabie
Koonibba

Koonibba
Penong
Ceduna

Lake Acraman
Low Hill

Port Augusta
Wilmington
Orroroo
Oodla Wir

Kitchener

Nullarbor
Wilson Bluff
Eucla

Head of Bight
Coorabie

Fowlers Bay
Point Bell

Smoky Bay

Gawler Ranges

Iron Knob
Iron Baron

Mount Remarkable 960m
Wirrulla

Melrose
Peterborous

Madura
Hampton Tableland

Cape Adieu

Streaky Bay
Point Westall

Poochera
Minnipa
Bucklebou

Whyalla
Port Pirie

Crystal Brook
Red Hill

Gladstone
Jamestown

Caiguna
Cocklebiddy

Red Rocks Point

Streaky Bay
Port Kenny

Wudinna
Kyancutta

Kimba

Cowell

Port Germein

Mount Bryan 932m
Burra

Balladonia

Point Dover

Cape Blanche
Cape Radstock
Venus Bay
Lock
Mount Wedge

Cleve

Snowtown
Wallaroo
Kadina

Clare
Robertsto

Great Australian Bight

Anxious Bay

Kopi

Elliston
Sheringa

Murdinga
Arno Bay

Moonta

Balaklava

Morg

Tower Peak 594m

Cape Pasley

Flinders Island

Karkoo

Cummins

Port Neill

Maitland

Kapunda

Dowlin

Cape Arid
Archipelago of the Recherche
South East Isles

Investigator Group

Tumby Bay

Port Victoria

Minlaton

Elizabeth
Port Adelaide

Gawler

Swa
Reac

Coffin Bay Peninsula
Point Whidbey
Coffin Bay
Port Lincoln

Sir Joseph Banks Group
Thistle Island

Cowell

Yorketown
Adelaide

Mount Barker

Gambier Islands

Cape Carnot
West Point

Stenhouse Bay

Saint Vincent Gulf

Victor Harbor
Goolwa

Mur
Bric

Cape Borda
Parndana
Penneshaw

Investigator Strait
Kingscote

Lake Alexandrina

Mening

Kangaroo Island

Cape de Couedic
Cape Gantheaume

Cape Hart

Encounter Bay
Younghusband Peninsula

Lacepe
Bay

274

Melbourne

Melbourne Airport
Tullamarine

Broadmeadows
Thomastown
Plenty

Keilor

Pascoe Vale
Fawkner

Bundoora
Greensborough

Brimbank Park
St Albans

Essendon
Coburg

Heidelberg

Ardeer
Ascot Vale

Maribyrnong
Brunswick
Ivanhoe

Bullen Park

Footscray

Royal Park
University of Melbourne
Carlton

Yarra Bend Park

Doncaster

Brooklyn

Docklands
Melbourne

Kew

Nunawading

Box Hill

Newport
Port Melbourne
National Gallery
Royal Botanical Gardens
South Yarra

Camberwell

Altona
Williamstown

Albert Park
Glen Iris
Malvern

Mount Waverley

St Kilda

Caulfield

Brighton

Oakleigh
Clayton

Point Cook

Port Phillip Bay

Sandringham
Moorabbin

0 5 Km
0 5 Miles

Sydney

Gurgai National Park

Castle Hill
Pennant Hills
Pymble

Blacktown

Marsfield
Dee Why

Parramatta

Parramatta River
Ryde

Chatswood
Manly

Prospect Reservoir

Homebush Bay
Olympic Park
Abbostford

Mosman

North Head
South Head

Fairfield

Regents Park

Sydney Harbour Bridge
Sydney Opera House

Sydney

Port Jackson

Bossley Park

Burwood

Redfern

Bondi

Liverpool

Bankstown

Canterbury

Randwick

Tasman Sea

Kingsford Smith Intl. Airport

Hurstville

Maroubra

Georges River

Botany Bay

La Perouse

Sutherland

Kurnell

Cape Banks

Botany Bay National Park

Cronulla

Bate Bay

Port Hacking

0 5 Km
0 5 Miles

293

6000m
4000m
3000m
2000m
1000m
500m
250m
100m
Sea Level
-250m
-500m
-1000m

Scale 1:6,500,000
(projection: Lambert Conformal Conic)

0 25 50 75 100 125 150 175 200 Km
0 25 50 75 100 125 150 175 200 Miles

Population
above 5 million · 1 million to 5 million · 500,000 to 1 million
100,000 to 500,000 · 50,000 to 100,000 · 10,000 to 50,000 · below 10,000

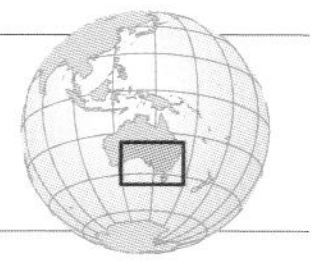

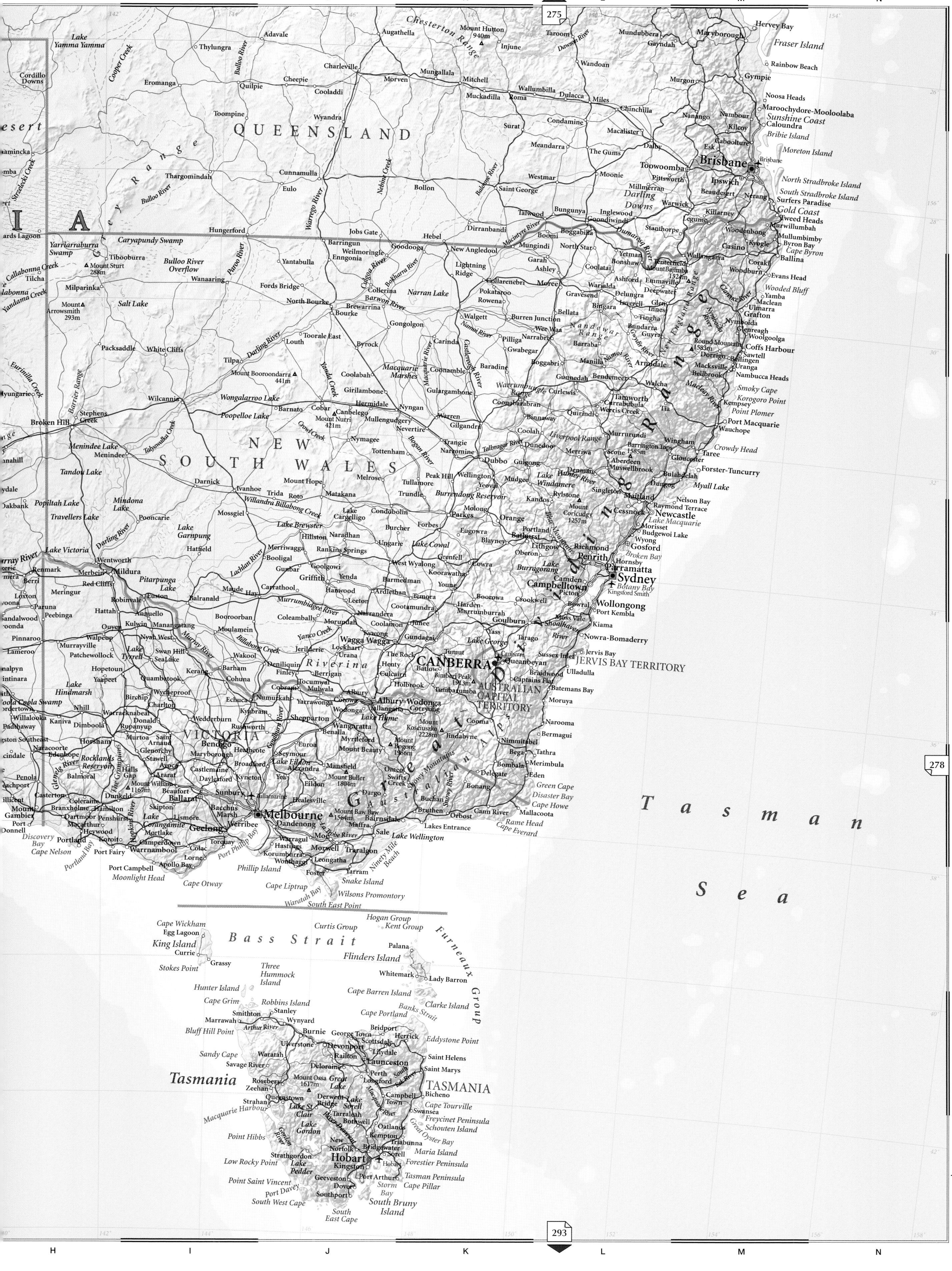

H
I
J
K
L
M
N
275
278
293
1
2
3
4
5
6
7
8
9
10
QUEENSLAND
NEW SOUTH WALES
VICTORIA
AUSTRALIAN CAPITAL TERRITORY
JERVIS BAY TERRITORY
TASMANIA
Tasmania
CANBERRA
Sydney
Melbourne
Brisbane
Hobart
Newcastle
Wollongong
Geelong
Launceston
Gold Coast
Sunshine Coast
Toowoomba
Albury-Wodonga
Wagga Wagga
Ballarat
Bendigo
Dubbo
Tamworth
Broken Hill
Mildura
Devonport
Burnie
Great Dividing Range
Grey Range
Snowy Mountains
Riverina
Darling Downs
Bass Strait
Tasman Sea
Furneaux Group
King Island
Flinders Island
Cape Barren Island
Fraser Island
Moreton Island
North Stradbroke Island
Phillip Island
Port Phillip Bay
Botany Bay
Murray River
Darling River
Murrumbidgee River
Lachlan River
Warrego River
Lake Eildon
Lake Hume
Mount Kosciuszko 2228m
Mount Ossa 1617m

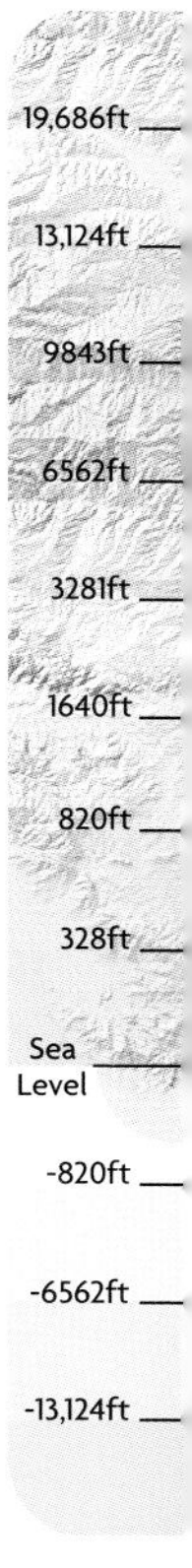

19,686ft
13,124ft
9843ft
6562ft
3281ft
1640ft
820ft
328ft
Sea Level
-820ft
-6562ft
-13,124ft

New Zealand

North Island

NEW ZEALAND

Auckland

Elevation scale

6000m
4000m
3000m
2000m
1000m
500m
250m
100m
Sea Level
-250m
-500m
-1000m

NORTHLAND

AUCKLAND

WAIKATO

BAY OF PLENTY

GISBORNE

HAWKE'S BAY

MANAWATU-WANGANUI

TARANAKI

WELLINGTON

Tasman Sea

Selected place names (main map)

Three Kings Islands, Cape Maria van Diemen, Cape Reinga, North Cape, Parengarenga Harbour, Te Kao, Great Exhibition Bay, Rangaunu Bay, Cape Karikari, Doubtless Bay, Cape Brett, Bay of Islands, Cavalli Islands, Kerikeri, Kaeo, Okaihau, Kaikohe, Kaitaia, Awanui, Ahipara, Tauroa Point, Ninety Mile Beach, Hokianga Harbour, Omapere, Kaihu Range, Dargaville, Ruawai, Waiotira, Maungaturoto, Waipu, Mangawhai, Kaiwaka, Paparoa, Matakohe, Kaipara Harbour, North Head, Helensville, Waimauku, Muriwai Beach, Warkworth, Wellsford, Leigh, Kawau Island, Cape Rodney, Orewa, Hauraki Gulf, Motutapu Island, Rangitoto Island, Waiheke Island, Great Barrier Island, Little Barrier Island, Mokohinau Islands, Hen and Chickens, Bream Bay, Bream Head, Whangarei, Whangaruru Harbour, Poor Knights Islands, Whangarei Harbour, Hikurangi, Russell, Paihia

Colville, Coromandel, Colville Channel, Port Fitzroy, The Aldermen Islands, Great Mercury Island, Mercury Islands, Coromandel Peninsula, Coromandel Range, Thames, Paeroa, Waihi, Katikati, Mount Maunganui, Matakana Island, Tauranga, Te Puke, Matata, Whakatane, Opotiki, Te Kaha, Raukumara Range, Hicks Bay, Te Araroa, Tikitiki, Ruatoria, Tokomaru Bay, Mawhai Point, Tolaga Bay, Whangara, Gisborne, Poverty Bay, Young Nicks Head, Mahia Peninsula, Portland Island, Nuhaka, Table Cape, Long Point, Wairoa, Lake Waikaremoana, Mohaka, Tutira, Napier, Hastings, Havelock North, Cape Kidnappers, Waipawa, Waipukurau, Takapau, Dannevirke, Woodville, Pahiatua, Eketahuna, Masterton, Carterton, Featherston, Castlepoint, Cape Turnagain

Waihou, Paeroa, Te Aroha, Morrinsville, Matamata, Putaruru, Tokoroa, Cambridge, Hamilton, Raglan, Waipa, Ngaruawahia, Huntly, Pukekohe, Waiuku, Pokeno, Te Kauwhata, Ngatea, Lake Waikare, Te Kuiti, Otorohanga, Te Awamutu, Kihikihi, Waitomo Caves, Awakino, Mokau, Urenui, Waitara, New Plymouth, Inglewood, Stratford, Eltham, Opunake, Mount Taranaki (Mount Egmont) 2518m, Cape Egmont, Hawera, Patea, Waverley, Waitotara, Wanganui, Marton, Bulls, Palmerston North, Feilding, Halcombe, Sanson, Foxton, Levin, Otaki, Waikanae, Paraparaumu, Paekakariki, Wellington, Porirua, Upper Hutt, Kapiti Island

Lake Rotorua, Rotorua, Mount Tarawera, Reporoa, Taupo, Lake Taupo, Wairakei, National Park, Mount Ruapehu 2797m, Raetihi, Ohakune, Taumarunui, Ohura, Taihape, Mangaweka, Hunterville

Turangi, Tokaanu, Kaimanawa Mountains, Ruahine Range, Tararua Range, Rimutaka Range

Cape Farewell, Farewell Spit, Golden Bay, Collingwood, Takaka, Separation Point, Cape Stephens, D'Urville Island, French Pass, Stephens Island, Kahurangi, Tasman Sea

Auckland inset

Te Atatu, North Shore, Northcote, Takapuna, Devonport, Lake Pupuke, Kauri Park, Chester Park, Point Chevalier, Avondale, Green Bay, Blockhouse Bay, Eden Park, Mount Eden, Mount Roskill, Royal Oak, Auckland, Auckland Zoo, Skytower, Maritime Museum, Auckland Museum, Kelburn, Grafton, One Tree Hill, Remuera, Ellerslie, Mount Wellington, Onehunga, Mangere, Ambury Park, Manukau Harbour, Mangere, Auckland Intl. Airport, Otara, Papatoetoe, Manukau, Clover Park, Pakuranga, Huntington Park, Howick, Highland Park, Bucklands Beach, Karaka Bay, Tamaki River, Glen Innes, Mission Bay, St. Johns Park, Stardome & Auckland Observatory, Rangitoto Island, Motutapu Island, Motuihe Island, Browns Island, Waitemata Harbour, Manukau Harbour

0 3 Km
0 3 Miles

Scale 1:3,200,000
(projection: Lambert Conformal Conic)

| 0 | 20 | 40 | 60 | 80 | 100 Km |
| 0 | 20 | 40 | 60 | 80 | 100 Miles |

Population
- ■ above 5 million
- ■ 1 million to 5 million
- ◉ 500,000 to 1 million
- ◉ 100,000 to 500,000
- ⊕ 50,000 to 100,000
- ○ 10,000 to 50,000
- ∘ below 10,000

Wellington

Kaiwharawhara · Chartwell · Wilton · Thorndon · Parliament Buildings & Beehive · Museum of New Zealand · Lambton · Kelburn · Northland · Botanic Gardens · Karori · Highbury · Kowhai Park · Happy Valley · Owhiro Bay · Owhiro Bay

Point Halswell · Kau Bay · Mount Crawford · Scorching Bay · Karaka Bay · Karaka Bay · Miramar · Worser Bay · Worser Bay · Seatoun Bay · Seatoun · Strathmore Park · Point Dorset · Breaker Bay

Evans Bay · Oriental Bay · Roseneath · Kilbirnie · Wellington Int. Airport · Rongotai · Lyall Bay · Mount Victoria · Hataitai · Evans Bay · Te Aro · Wellington · Government House · Wellington South · Mornington · Newtown · Wellington Zoo · Melrose · Lyall Bay · Southgate · Houghton Bay · Mitchelltown · Brooklyn · Kingston · Island Bay

Wellington Harbour (Port Nicholson) · *Lambton Harbour*

0 Km 1 · 0 1 Miles

PACIFIC OCEAN

South Island

Cape Palliser · Cape Palliser · Cloudy Bay · Cape Campbell · Blenheim · Seddon · Kekerengu · Cape Koamaru · Kaikoura · Kaikoura Peninsula · Spy Glass Point · Clarence

MARLBOROUGH · TASMAN · Mount Owen 1875m · Mount Una 2385m · Parnassus · Cheviot · Waipara · Pegasus Bay · Banks Peninsula · Christchurch · Lyttelton · Akaroa

WEST COAST · Westport · Cape Foulwind · Charleston · Punakaiki · Greymouth · Hokitika · Ross · Abut Head · Franz Josef Glacier · Fox Glacier · SOUTHERN ALPS · Aoraki/Mount Cook 3754m · Mount Tasman · Mount Sefton

Oxford · Sheffield · Darfield · Rolleston · Rakaia · Lake Ellesmere · Ashburton · Methven · Mayfield · Hinds · Canterbury Bight · Geraldine · Temuka · Timaru · Pareora · Makikihi · Studholme · Morven · Waimate · Pukeuri Junction · Oamaru · Moeraki Point · Herbert · Hampden · Palmerston · Shag Point · Waikouaiti · Port Chalmers · Dunedin · Otago Peninsula · Cape Saunders

OTAGO · SOUTHLAND · Lake Wakatipu · Lake Wanaka · Lake Hawea · Wanaka · Queenstown · Arrowtown · Cromwell · Clyde · Alexandra · Roxburgh · Lawrence · Milton · Balclutha · Kaitangata · Nugget Point · Waipahi Point

Foveaux Strait · Invercargill · Bluff · Riverton · Winton · Gore · Mataura · Edendale · Wyndham · Otautau · Nightcaps · Ohai · Tuatapere · Orepuki

Stewart Island · Halfmoon Bay · Oban · Port Pegasus · South West Cape

SOUTHLAND · Te Anau · Lake Te Anau · Lake Manapouri · Manapouri · Milford Sound · Fiordland · Doubtful Sound · Dusky Sound · Preservation Inlet · Resolution Island · West Cape · Solander Island · Codfish Island · Ruapuke Island

	19,686ft
	13,124ft
	9843ft
	6562ft
	3281ft
	1640ft
	820ft
	328ft
	Sea Level
	-820ft
	-6562ft
	-13,124ft

Papua New Guinea & Melanesia

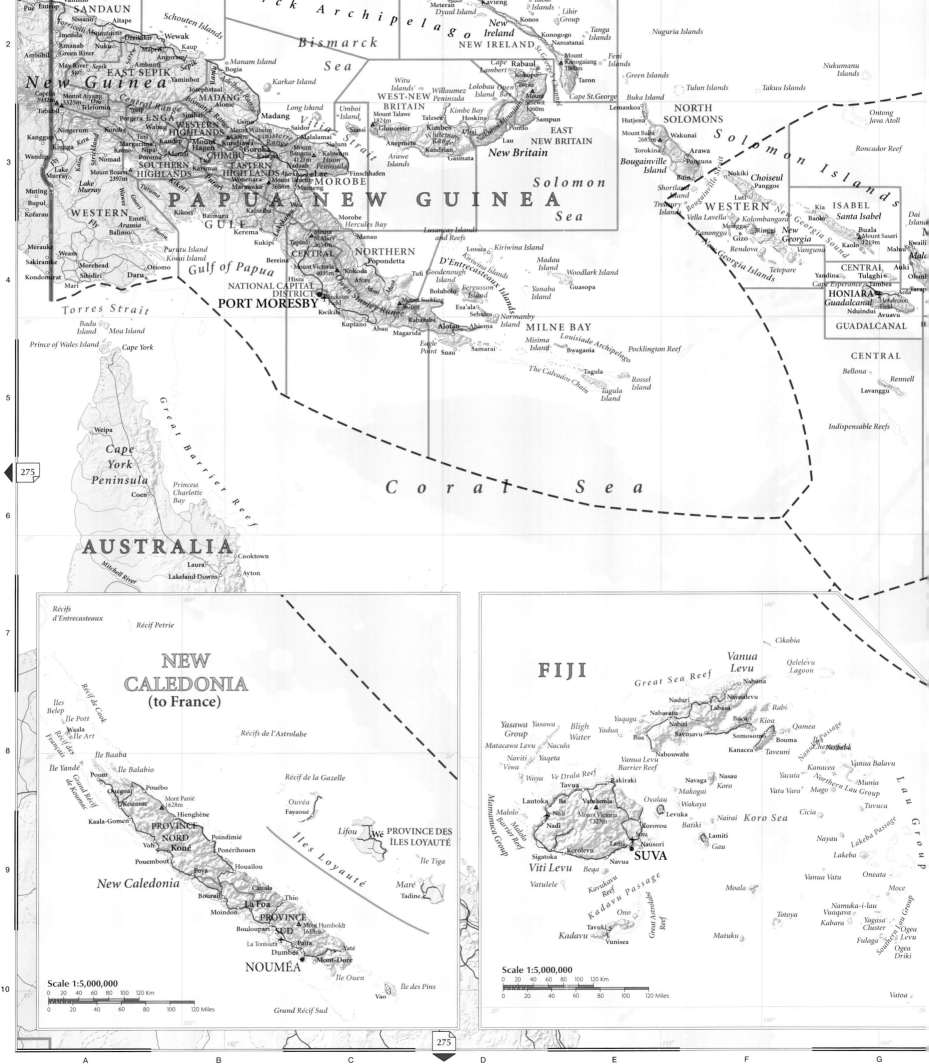

AUSTRALASIA & OCEANIA

PACIFIC OCEAN

Equator

Jayapura
Vanimo
SANDAUN
New Guinea
EAST SEPIK
WEST SEPIK
Wewak
MADANG
Madang

Bismarck Archipelago

Bismarck Sea

MANUS
Admiralty Islands
Manus Island
Lorengau

NEW IRELAND
Kavieng
New Ireland
Rabaul
Kokopo

WEST NEW BRITAIN
New Britain
EAST NEW BRITAIN

NORTH SOLOMONS
Bougainville Island

Solomon Sea

PAPUA NEW GUINEA

WESTERN HIGHLANDS
SOUTHERN HIGHLANDS
EASTERN HIGHLANDS
CHIMBU
ENGA
Mount Wilhelm 4509m
Mount Hagen
Goroka
MOROBE
Lae
Finschhafen

CENTRAL
GULF
WESTERN
Mount Victoria 4035m
Owen Stanley Range

NATIONAL CAPITAL DISTRICT
PORT MORESBY

Gulf of Papua

Torres Strait

NORTHERN
Popondetta
Kokoda

MILNE BAY
Alotau
Samarai

D'Entrecasteaux Islands
Kiriwina Island
Trobriand Islands
Woodlark Island

Louisiade Archipelago

WESTERN
New Georgia
ISABEL
Santa Isabel
Choiseul

SOLOMON ISLANDS

CENTRAL
HONIARA
Guadalcanal
GUADALCANAL

AUSTRALIA
Cape York Peninsula
Great Barrier Reef
Cooktown

Coral Sea

NEW CALEDONIA (to France)

PROVINCE NORD
Koné
PROVINCE SUD
New Caledonia
PROVINCE DES ÎLES LOYAUTÉ
Îles Loyauté
NOUMÉA

Scale 1:5,000,000
0 20 40 60 80 100 120 Km
0 20 40 60 80 100 120 Miles

FIJI

Vanua Levu
Labasa
Great Sea Reef
Yasawa Group
Viti Levu
Mount Victoria 1323m
Nadi
Lautoka
SUVA
Nausori

Koro Sea

Lau Group
Northern Lau Group
Southern Lau Group

Kadavu

Scale 1:5,000,000
0 20 40 60 80 100 120 Km
0 20 40 60 80 100 120 Miles

6000m
4000m
3000m
2000m
1000m
500m
250m
100m
Sea Level
-250m
-500m
-1000m

Scale 1:10,100,000
(projection: Mercator)

0 50 100 150 200 250 300 Km
0 50 100 150 200 250 300 Miles

Population

■ above 5 million   ■ 1 million to 5 million   ● 500,000 to 1 million
◉ 100,000 to 500,000   ⊕ 50,000 to 100,000   ○ 10,000 to 50,000   ∘ below 10,000

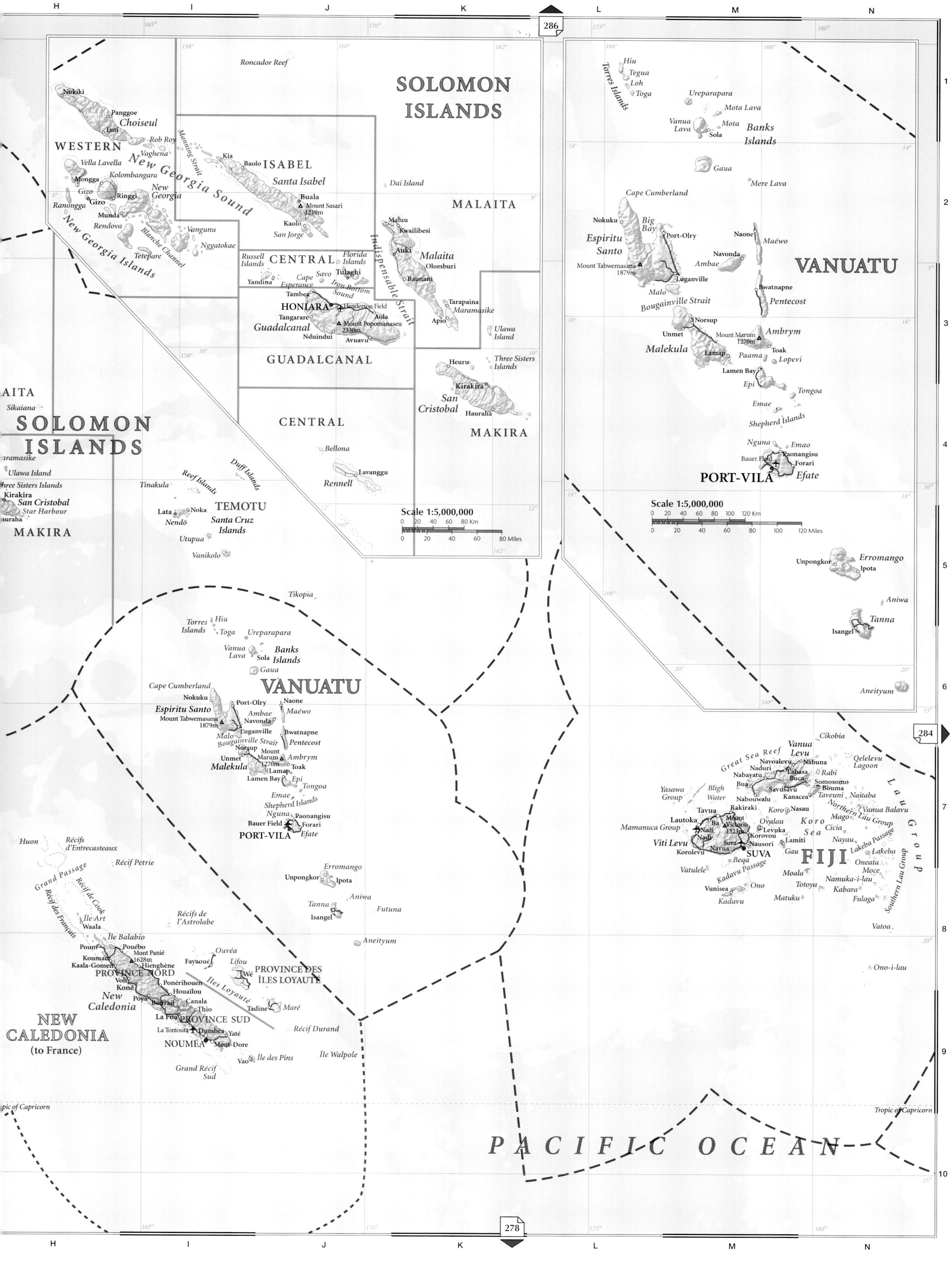

H   I   J   K   286   L   M   N

1
2
3
4
5 281
6 284
7
8
9
10

SOLOMON ISLANDS (top inset)

Roncador Reef
Nukiki
Panggoe
Luti
Choiseul
WESTERN
Vella Lavella
Vaghena
Rob Roy
Kia
Baolo
ISABEL
Mongga
Kolombangara
New Georgia
Santa Isabel
Buala
Dai Island
Ringgi
Gizo
Gizo
New Georgia
Mount Sasari 1219m
Ranongga
Rendova
Munda
Blanche Channel
Kaolo
San Jorge
Maluu
MALAITA
Tetepare
Vangunu
Nggatokae
Russell Islands
CENTRAL
Florida Islands
Kwailibesi
Auki
Malaita
Yandina
Cape Esperance
Savo
Tulaghi
Olomburi
Baunani
HONIARA
Tangarare
Henderson Field
Aola
Tarapaina
Maramasike
Guadalcanal
Mount Popomanaseu 2330m
Apio
Ulawa Island
Nduindui
Avuvu
GUADALCANAL
Heruru
Three Sisters Islands
CENTRAL
Kirakira
San Cristobal
MAKIRA
Hauraha
Bellona
Lavanggu
Rennell

New Georgia Sound
New Georgia Islands
Indispensable Strait
Iron Bottom Sound
Manning Strait

SOLOMON ISLANDS

Scale 1:5,000,000
0 20 40 60 80 Km
0 20 40 60 80 Miles

VANUATU (top right inset)

Hiu
Tegua
Loh
Toga
Torres Islands
Ureparapara
Mota Lava
Vanua Lava
Mota
Banks Islands
Sola
Gaua
Mere Lava
Cape Cumberland
Nokuku
Big Bay
Port-Olry
Naone
Maéwo
Espiritu Santo
Mount Tabwemasana 1879m
Luganville
Navonda
Ambae
Bwatnapne
Malo
Pentecost
Bougainville Strait
Norsup
Ambrym
Unmet
Mount Marum 1270m
Toak
Malekula
Lanap
Paama
Lopevi
Lamen Bay
Epi
Tongoa
Emae
Shepherd Islands
Nguna
Emao
Bauer Field
Paonangisu
Forari
PORT-VILA
Efate
Unpongkor
Erromango
Ipota
Aniwa
Tanna
Isangel
Aneityum

Scale 1:5,000,000
0 20 40 60 80 100 120 Km
0 20 40 60 80 100 120 Miles

Main map

SOLOMON ISLANDS
...AITA
Sikaiana
Ulawa Island
Three Sisters Islands
Kirakira
San Cristobal
Star Harbour
...auraha
MAKIRA
...aramasike

Duff Islands
Reef Islands
Tinakula
Lata
Noka
Nendö
TEMOTU
Santa Cruz Islands
Utupua
Vanikolo
Tikopia

Hiu
Torres Islands
Toga
Ureparapara
Vanua Lava
Banks Islands
Sola
Gaua
VANUATU
Cape Cumberland
Nokuku
Port-Olry
Naone
Espiritu Santo
Ambae
Maéwo
Mount Tabwemasana 1879m
Navonda
Luganville
Malo
Bwatnapne
Bougainville Strait
Norsup
Pentecost
Unmet
Mount Marum 1270m
Ambrym
Malekula
Toak
Lamen Bay
Lamap
Epi
Tongoa
Emae
Shepherd Islands
Nguna
Paonangisu
Bauer Field
Forari
PORT-VILA
Efate
Erromango
Unpongkor
Ipota
Aniwa
Tanna
Futuna
Isangel
Aneityum

Huon
Récifs d'Entrecasteaux
Récif Petrie
Grand Passage
Récifs des Français
Récif de Cook
Ile Art
Waala
Ile Balabio
Poum
Pouébo
Mont Panié 1628m
Koumac
Hienghène
Kaala-Gomen
Ouvéa
Lifou
Fayaoué
Tiga
PROVINCE DES ÎLES LOYAUTÉ
PROVINCE NORD
Voh
Ponérihouen
Koné
Houaïlou
Îles Loyauté
New Caledonia
Poya
Bourail
Canala
Tadine
Maré
La Foa
PROVINCE SUD
Récif Durand
NEW CALEDONIA
(to France)
La Tontouta
Dumbéa
Yaté
NOUMÉA
Mont-Dore
Vao
Ile des Pins
Grand Récif Sud
Ile Walpole

Récifs de l'Astrolabe

FIJI
Cikobia
Vanua Levu
Great Sea Reef
Navoalevu
Nabuna
Qelelevu Lagoon
Naduri
Labasa
Rabi
Nabavatu
Buca
Somosomo
Yasawa Group
Bligh Water
Bua
Savusavu
Kanacea
Taveuni
Naitaba
Nabouwalu
Vanua Balavu
Tavua
Rakiraki
Koro
Nasau
Northern Lau Group
Mamanuca Group
Lautoka
Mount Victoria 1323m
Oyalau
Koro Sea
Mago
Cicia
Nadi
Levuka
Korovou
Nayau
Lau Group
Viti Levu
Nausori
Lamiti
Gau
Lakeba Passage
Korolevu
Navua
SUVA
Lakeba
Beqa
Vatulele
Oneata
Moce
Kadavu Passage
Moala
Namuka-i-lau
Kabara
Vunisea
Ono
Totoya
Fulaga
Kadavu
Matuku
Vatoa

Southern Lau Group

Ono-i-lau

Tropic of Capricorn

PACIFIC OCEAN

Elevation legend
19,686ft
13,124ft
9843ft
6562ft
3281ft
1640ft
820ft
328ft
Sea Level
-820ft
-6562ft
-13,124ft

286   284   278

Micronesia

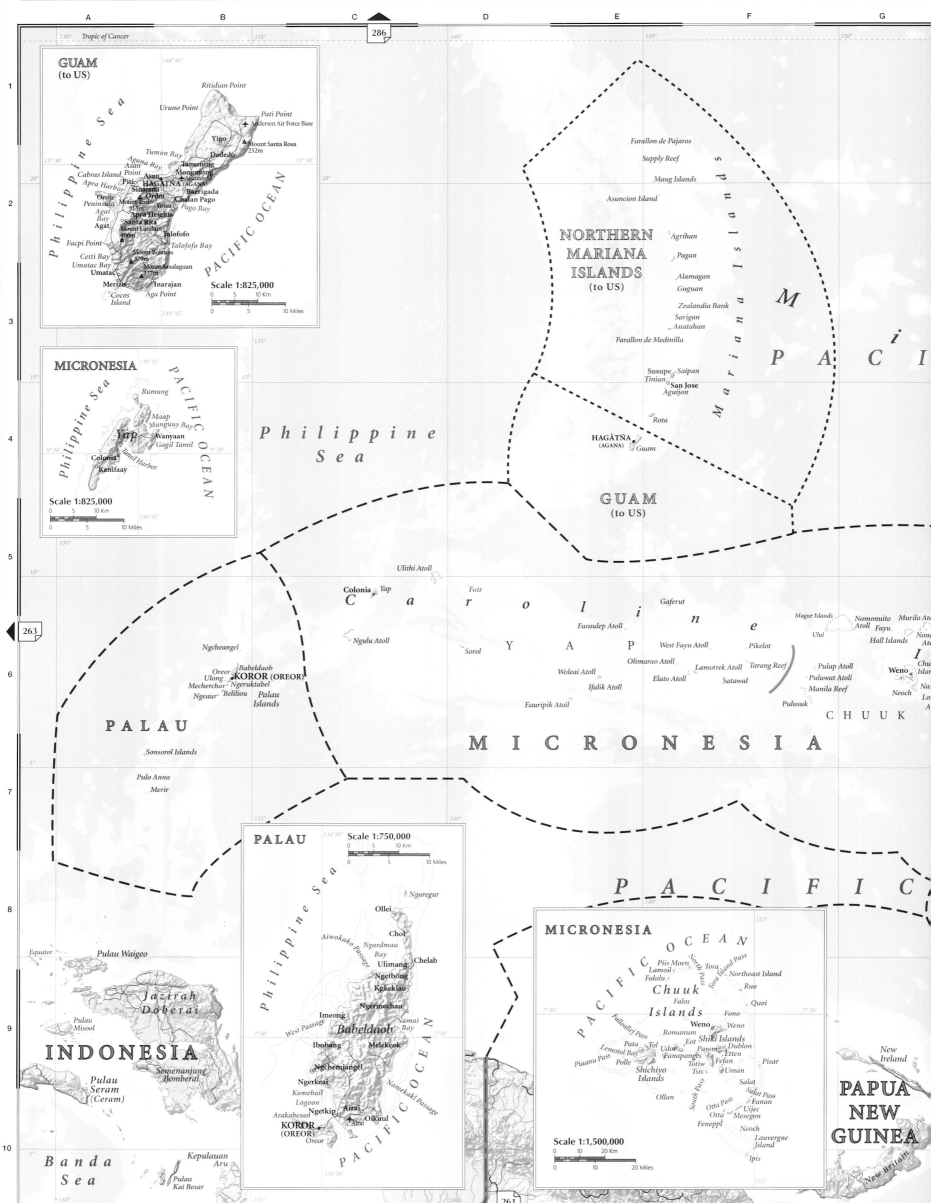

Scale 1:10,250,000
(projection: Mercator)

| | 0 | 50 | 100 | 150 | 200 | 250 | 300 Km |
| 0 | 50 | 100 | 150 | 200 | 250 | 300 Miles |

Population

■ above 5 million   ▣ 1 million to 5 million   ◉ 500,000 to 1 million

◎ 100,000 to 500,000   ⊕ 50,000 to 100,000   ○ 10,000 to 50,000   ∘ below 10,000

Tropic of Cancer

NORTHERN MARIANA ISLANDS (to US)

Philippine Sea

Puntan Sabaneta
Punta Lagua Lichan
San Roque
Bird Island
Managaha
Tanapag Kalabera
Puetton Tanapag
Capitol Hill
Garapan
Mount Tapochau 465m
Oleai
Saipan
Susupe
San Vicente
Chalan Kanoa
Magicienne Bay
Kagman Point
San Antonio
Saipan International
Puntan I Naftan
Saipan Channel

PACIFIC OCEAN

Scale 1:500,000

| 0 | 2 | 4 Km |
| 0 | 2 | 4 Miles |

MICRONESIA

PACIFIC OCEAN

Sokehs Island
Pohnpei
Parem Island
Kolonia
Nanuh
Takaieu Island
PALIKIR
Pohnpei
Nahnlaud 772m
Pehleng
Madolenihmw
Tomworoahlang
Keprohi Falls
Nan Madol
Temwen Island
Ronkiti
Pwok
Rohi
Lohd

Scale 1:650,000

| 0 | 5 | 10 Km |
| 0 | 5 | 10 Miles |

WAKE ISLAND (to US)

Toki Point
Peale Island
Kuku Point
Heel Point
Flipper Point
Wilkes Island
Wake Lagoon
Settlement
Wake Island
Wake Island
Peacock Point

PACIFIC OCEAN

Scale 1:250,000

| 0 | 1 | 2 | 3 | 4 Km |
| 0 | 1 | 2 | 3 | 4 Miles |

PACIFIC OCEAN

Micronesia

Sibylla Island
Bokaak Atoll

MARSHALL ISLANDS

Bikar Atoll

Bikini Atoll
Rongelap Atoll
Enewetak Atoll
Rongrik Atoll
Utrik Atoll
Ailinginae Atoll
Taka Atoll
Ailuk Atoll
Wotho Atoll
Jemo Island
Mejit Island
Ujelang Atoll
Likiep Atoll
Wotje Atoll
Kwajalein Atoll
Erikub Atoll
Ujae Atoll
Lae Atoll
Maloelap Atoll
Lib
Aur Atoll
Namu Atoll
Jabwot
Ailinglaplap Atoll
Arno Atoll
Majuro Atoll
Jaluit Atoll
Mili Atoll
Namorik Atoll
Knox Atoll
Kili Island
Ebon Atoll

Ratak Chain
Ralik Chain

Minto Reef
Oroluk Atoll
Pakin Atoll
Kolonia
PALIKIR
Pohnpei
Ant Atoll
Mwokil Atoll
Namoluk Atoll
Lukunor Atoll
Ngetik Atoll
Pingelap Atoll
Satawan Atoll
Kosrae
Tofol
Mortlock Islands
POHNPEI
KOSRAE
Nukuoro Atoll

Islands

Kapingamarangi Atoll

Makin
Butaritari
Tungaru (Gilbert Islands)
Abaiang
Marakei
Tarawa
BAIRIKI
Maiana
Kuria
Abemama
Nauru
Aranuka
Equator
KIRIBATI
Nonouti
Banaba
NAURU
Tabiteuea
Beru

MICRONESIA

PACIFIC OCEAN

Tafunsak
Gabert
Okat Harbor
Mount Mutunte 593m
Lelu Island
Insiaf
Kosrae
Tofol
Lelu
Mount Finkol 629m
Utwe
Malem
Utwe Harbor

Scale 1:500,000

| 0 | 2 | 4 Km |
| 0 | 2 | 4 Miles |

NAURU

Anna Point
Baiti
Anabar
Nibok
Ijuw
Denig
Anabar
Anibare
Phosphate mineworks
Nauru
Aiwo
Buada Lagoon
Anibare Bay
Yaren
Nauru International
Meneng Point

Scale 1:200,000

| 0 | 1 | 2 Km |
| 0 | 1 | 2 Miles |

MARSHALL ISLANDS

Rongrong
Iroj
Majuro Atoll
Laura
Kallalen
Enigu
Majuro Lagoon
Djarrit
Dalap
Majuro

PACIFIC OCEAN

Scale 1:1,000,000

| 0 | 5 | 10 Km |
| 0 | 5 | 10 Miles |

287

19,686ft
13,124ft
9843ft
6562ft
3281ft
1640ft
820ft
328ft
Sea Level
-820ft
-6562ft
-13,124ft

AUSTRALASIA & OCEANIA

284

281

286

278

Main Map

Erikub Atoll
Maloelap Atoll
Namu Atoll
Aur Atoll
Jabwot
Arno Atoll
Majuro Atoll
Mili Atoll
Jaluit Atoll
Kili Island
Knox Atoll
Ratak Chain
Ralik Chain
MARSHALL ISLANDS
Ebon Atoll

Makin
Butaritari
Abaiang Marakei
Tarawa
BAIRIKI
Maiana
Abemama
Kuria
Aranuka
Banaba
Nonouti
Beru Nikunau
Tabiteuea
Onotoa
Tamana
Arorae
Tungaru (Gilbert Islands)

Equator

P

KIRIBATI

Phoenix Islands
McKean Island
Kanton
Enderbury Island
Birnie Island
Rawaki
Orona
Manra
Nikumaroro

PACIFIC

Howard Island (to US)
Baker Island (to US)

Teraina
Tabuaeran
Kingman Reef (to US)
Palmyra Atoll (to US)
K I R I

Nanumea Atoll
Niutao
Nanumaga
Nui Atoll
Vaitupu
Nukufetau Atoll
Funafuti Atoll **FONGAFALE**
TUVALU
Nukulaelae Atoll
Niulakita

O

Atafu Atoll
Nukunonu Atoll
Fakaofo Atoll
TOKELAU
(to NZ)

Swans Island
AMERICAN SAMOA
(to US)

Rakahanga
Manihiki
Pukapuka Nassau
Northern Cook Island
Suwarrow

WALLIS & FUTUNA
(to France)
Îles Wallis
Île Futuna
Île Alofi
SAMOA
Savai'i
Sāmoa
Upolu
Manua Islands
Tutuila

COOK ISLANDS
(to NZ)

Mere Lava
Maéwo
Pentecost
Ambrym
Lopevi
Tongoa
Emao
PORT-VILA
Efate
Erromango
Ipota
Aniwa
Tanna Isangel
Futuna
Aneityum
Maré
Île Walpole
VANUATU

Tropic of Capricorn

Vanua Levu
Nabuna
Rabi
Yasawa Group
Bua
Taveuni
Mamanuca Group
Koro
Owalau
Cicia
Lautoka
Gau
Viti Levu
SUVA
Moala
Nayau
Kadavu
Matuku
Totoya
Lau Group
Lakeba
Vatoa
FIJI

Niuatoputapu
'Tafahi
Fonualei
Toku
Vava'u Group
'Uta Vava'u
Late
Kao
Ha'ano
Ha'apai Group
Tofua
Lifuka
Kotu Group
Nomuka Group
Otu Tolu Group
Tonumea
NUKU'ALOFA
Tongatapu
'Eua
Tongatapu Group
TONGA

ALOFI
Niue
NIUE
(to NZ)

Palmerston
Southern Cook Island
Aitutaki
Manuae
Taku
AVARVA
Rarotonga

PACIFIC

Inset: KIRIBATI (Scale 1:1,000,000)

KIRIBATI
PACIFIC OCEAN
Iku
Buariki
Taratai
Abaokoro
Marenanuka
Nabeina
Tabiteuea
Bikeman
Bikenebu
Bonriki
Betio
Eita Tarawa
Banraeaba
BAIRIKI
Tarawa
Scale 1:1,000,000
0   5   10 Km
0   5   10 Miles

Inset: TUVALU (Scale 1:500,000)

TUVALU
Te Ava I Te Lape
Fualifeke
Amatuku
Tepuka
Fualopa
Fongafale
Fuafatu
Funafuti
Atoll
FONGAFALE
Te Ava Fuagea
Vasafua
Funangongo
Fuagea
Te Ava Pua Pua
Tefala
Falefatu
Funafara
Teafuafou
Telele
PACIFIC OCEAN
Scale 1:500,000
0   2   4 Km
0   2   4 Miles

Inset: WALLIS & FUTUNA (to France) (Scale 1:1,000,000)

WALLIS & FUTUNA
(to France)
PACIFIC OCEAN
Pointe Fatua
Pointe Matapu
Toloke
Île Futuna
Koliu
Mont Puke 524m
Leava
Mala
Pointe Vele
Alofitai
Pointe Matalesina
Mont Kolofau 417m
Pointe Sauma
Île Alofi
Scale 1:1,000,000
0   5   10 Km
0   5   10 Miles

Inset: WALLIS & FUTUNA (to France) (Scale 1:1,000,000)

WALLIS & FUTUNA
(to France)
PACIFIC OCEAN
Nukuloa
Nukutapu
Hihifo
Vaitupu
Alele
Île Luaniva
Baie de l'Ouest
Île Uvea
Ahoa
MATÁ'UTU
Mati'utu
Île Nukuhifala
Mala'atoli
Tepa
Halalo
Baie de Matala'a
Nukuatea
Île Faioa
Île Fenuafo'ou
Îles Wallis
Scale 1:1,000,000
0   5   10 Km
0   5   10 Miles

Inset: TONGA (Scale 1:1,000,000)

TONGA
Maniloa
Tau
Ata
Niu 'Aunofa
Atata
Poloa
Onevai
Motu Nuku
Kolovai
Fafo
Tapu
Fukave
NUKU'ALOFA
Piha Passage
'Eua Iki
Houma
Kolonga
Mui
Pea
Fanga 'Uta
Hopohoponga
Vaina
'Mu'a
Tongatapu
Fua'amotu
Houma
Taloa
Houma
'Eua
Ohonua
Ha'atua
Kalau
PACIFIC OCEAN
Scale 1:1,000,000
0   5   10 Km
0   5   10 Miles

Inset: COOK ISLANDS (to NZ) (Scale 1:325,000)

COOK ISLANDS
(to NZ)
Te Aiti Point
Avatiu
Aroa
Avarua Harbour
Nikao
Rarotonga
AVARUA
Ikurangi 485m
Arorangi
Maungaroa 509m
Te Kou 652m
Matavera
Rarotonga
Te Manga 564m
Ngatangiia
Motutapu
Oneroa
Koromiri
Taakoka
Muri
Titikaveka
PACIFIC OCEAN
Scale 1:325,000
0   2   4 Km
0   2   4 Miles

Elevation Scale

6000m
4000m
3000m
2000m
1000m
500m
250m
100m
Sea Level
-250m
-500m
-1000m

Scale 1:15,500,000
(projection: Mercator)

0 50 100 150 200 250 300 350 400 Km
0 50 100 150 200 250 300 350 400 Miles

Population
- above 5 million
- 1 million to 5 million
- 500,000 to 1 million
- 100,000 to 500,000
- 50,000 to 100,000
- 10,000 to 50,000
- below 10,000

287

SAMOA

Scale 1:3,000,000

Savai'i
Fagamálo
Faleálupo
Cape Puava
Sátaua
Fálelima
Silisili 1858m
Tuasivi
Pu'apu'a
Sala'ilua
Satupaiteau
Salelologa
Cape Asuisui
Tága
Taga
Feleolo
ÁPIA Upolu
Mataútu
Fito 1113m
Ti'avea
Lotofaga
Poutasi
Fagaloa Bay
Safata Bay
Salani
Apolima Strait
Palauli Bay

AMERICAN SAMOA (to US)

Manua Islands
Olosega
Ofu
Luma Ta'ú
PAGO PAGO
Cape Matátula
Aunu'u Island
Cape Matátula
Cape Taputapu
Steps Point
Tutuila

PACIFIC OCEAN

KIRIBATI

Scale 1:1,175,000

PACIFIC OCEAN
Northwest Point
Cape Manning
London
Banana
Northeast Point
Cook Island
Saint
Manulu Lagoon
Paris
Stanislas Bay
Poland
Kiritimati (Christmas Island)
South West Point
Vaskess Bay
Isles Lagoon
Bay of Wrecks
Joe's Hill 12m
Aeon Point
Azur Lagoon
Pelican Lagoon
South East Point

Equator

FRENCH POLYNESIA (to France)

Scale 1:1,000,000

Baie d'Opunohu
Baie de Cook
Pointe Aroa
Îles du Vent
Papetoai
Pointe Vénus
Mont Matotea 714m
Paopao
Baie de Matavai
Mahina
Papenoo
Moorea
Afareaitu
PAPEETE
Pirea
Tiarei
Haapiti
Mont Tohiea 1207m
Faaa
Pointe Nuupere
Faaa
Mont Aorai 2066m
Hitiaa
Punaauia
Mont Orohena 2241m
Pointe Nuuroa
Paea
Tahiti
Faaone
Passe Tamotoe
Mont Tetufera 1799m
Taravao
Baie de Taravao
Maraa
Papara
Isthme de Taravao
Pointe Maraa
Mataiea
Afaahiti
Tautira
Récif Tepaee
Teohatu
Vairao
Presqu'île de Taiarapu
Teahupoo
Mont Ronui 1332m

PACIFIC OCEAN

Îles Marquises
Hatutu
Eiao
Nuku Hiva
Ua Huka
Taiohae
Ua Pú
Hiva Oa
Atuona
Tahuata
Motane
Fatu Hiva
Omoa

Kiritimati (Christmas Island)

Malden Island

-buck Island

Millennium Island
Vostok Island

Flint Island

-hyn

line Islands

Îles Tuamotu

Îles du Roi Georges
Îles du Désappointement
Ahe
Manihi
Tepoto
Napuka
Mataiva
Tikehau
Takapoto
Takaroa
Tikei
Pukapuka
Rangiroa
Îles Palliser
Aratika

Îles Sous le Vent
Motu One
Tupai
Bora-Bora
Niau
Toau
Katehi
Takume
Fangatau
Fakahina
Manuae
Maupiti
Fare
Fakarava
Raraka
Katiu
Raroia
Maupihaa
Tahaa
Faaite
Tahanea
Makemo
Raiatea
Huahine
Marutea
Nihiru
Tehuata
Tauere
Moorea
Anaa
Haraiki
Hikueru
Amanu
PAPEETE
Mehetia
Reitoru
Marokau
Hao
Akiaki
Tahiti
Ravahere
Pukarua
Maiao
Nengonengo
Vahitahi
Reao
Îles du Vent
Paraoa
Tatakoto
Îles Sous le Vent
Manuhangi
Vairaatea
Pinaki
Archipel de la Société
Hereheretue

PACIFIC OCEAN

FRENCH POLYNESIA (to France)

Maria
Îles du Duc de Gloucester
Vanavana
Tureia
Groupe Actéon
Rurutu
Tematangi
Tenararo
Marutea
Rimatara
Mururoa
Maria
Tubuai
Fangataufa
Îles Australes
Îles Gambier
Mangareva
Temoe
Raevavae

Mauke
Mangaia
iaro

PITCAIRN ISLANDS (to UK)

Tropic of Capricorn
Oeno Island
Henderson Island
Ducie Island
Pitcairn Island

NIUE (to NZ)

Scale 1:1,000,000

Hikutavake
Toi
Mutalau
Makefu
Tuapa
Lakepa
Makapu Point
Niue
Liku
Alofi Bay
ALOFI
Hanan
Halagigie Point
Tamakautoga
Avatele
Hakupu
Tepa Point
Mata Point
PACIFIC OCEAN

Rapa Iti
Marotiri

PITCAIRN ISLANDS (to UK)

Scale 1:125,000

Young's Rock
Bounty Bay
ADAMSTOWN
Pitcairn Island
Adam's Rock
Point Christian
St Paul's Point
PACIFIC OCEAN

PACIFIC OCEAN

PACIFIC OCEAN

287

19,686ft
13,124ft
9843ft
6562ft
3281ft
1640ft
820ft
328ft
Sea Level
-820ft
-6562ft
-13,124ft

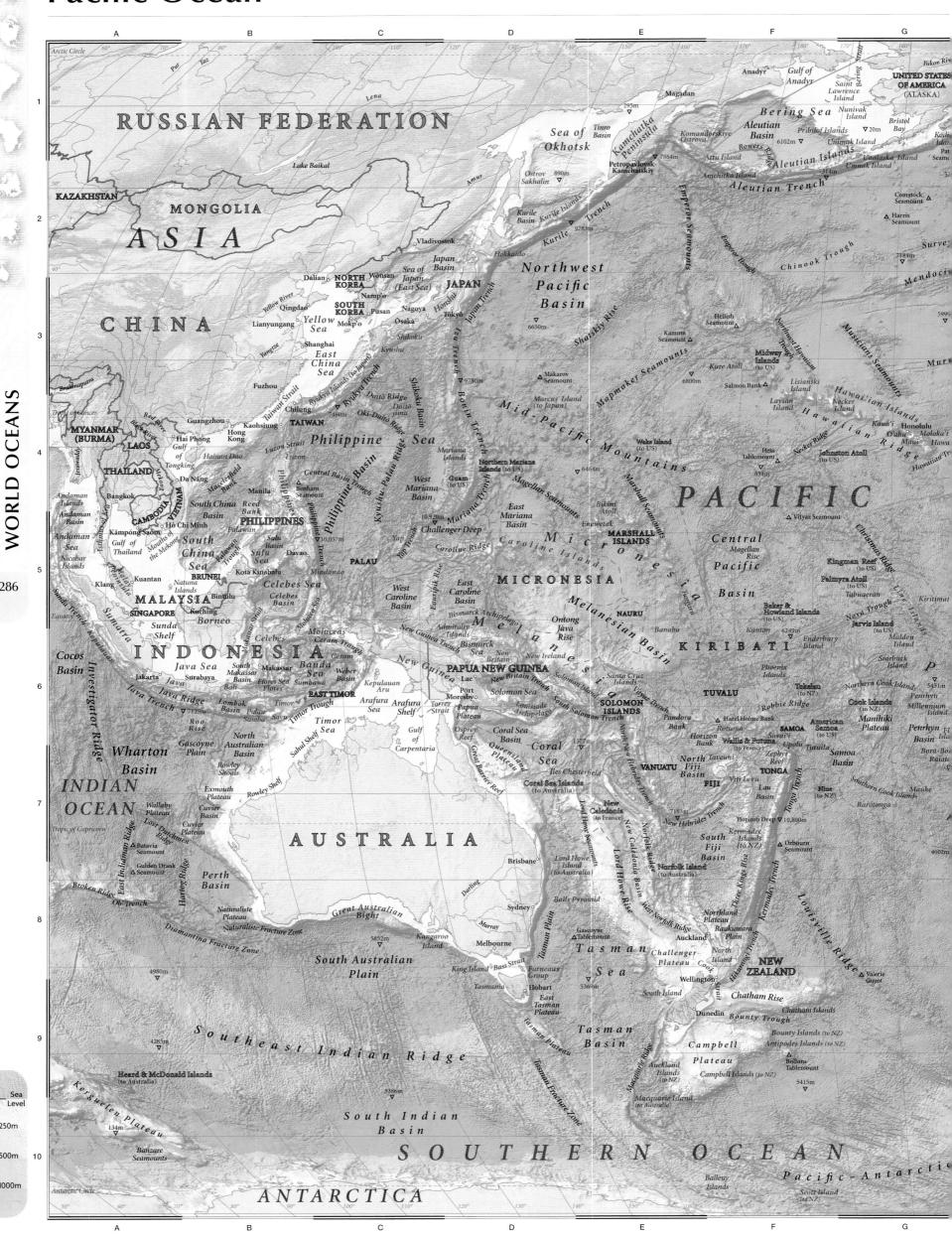

RUSSIAN FEDERATION

KAZAKHSTAN

MONGOLIA

ASIA

CHINA

Lake Baikal

Arctic Circle

Pur

Lena

Amur

Yenisei

Yukon River

UNITED STATES OF AMERICA (ALASKA)

Anadyr

Gulf of Anadyr

Saint Lawrence Island

Nunivak Island

Bristol Bay

Bering Sea

Magadan

Sea of Okhotsk

Kamchatka Peninsula

Komandorskiye Ostrova

Petropavlovsk-Kamchatskiy

Attu Island

Amchitka Island

Aleutian Islands

Aleutian Trench

Pribilof Islands

Unimak Island

Unalaska Island

Kodiak Island

Comstock Seamount

Harris Seamount

Aleutian Basin

6102m

20m

314m

Timro Basin

295m

7864m

9783m

Ostrov Sakhalin

890m

Vladivostok

Kurile Basin

Kurile Islands

Kurile Trench

Hokkaido

Dalian

NORTH KOREA

Wonsan

Namp'o

SOUTH KOREA

Pusan

Mokp'o

JAPAN

Sea of Japan (East Sea)

Japan Basin

Nagoya

Osaka

Tōkyō

Honshu

Shikoku

Kyushu

Japan Trench

Northwest Pacific Basin

Emperor Seamounts

Emperor Trough

Chinook Trough

Mendocino

Survey

5990

7181m

Qingdao

Lianyungang

Yellow Sea

Shanghai

Fuzhou

East China Sea

Yangtze

Guangzhou

Kaohsiung

Hong Kong

Hainan Dao

Hai Phong

Gulf of Tongking

TAIWAN

Taiwan Strait

Chilung

Ryukyu Islands (to Japan)

7460m

Ryukyu Trench

Danto Ridge

Oki-Daito Ridge

Daito-jima

Shikoku Basin

Bonin Trench

9780m

6650m

Shatskiy Rise

Mid-Pacific Mountains

Mapmaker Seamounts

Kammu Seamount

Hellish Seamount

Midway Islands (to US)

Kure Atoll

6800m

Salmon Bank

Northwest Hawaiian Ridge

Lisianski Island

Laysan Island

Necker Island

Musicians Seamounts

Hawaiian Islands

Kaua'i

O'ahu

Moloka'i

Maui

Honolulu

Hawaii

Hawaiian Ridge

MYANMAR (BURMA)

LAOS

THAILAND

Macclesfield Bank

Da Nang

VIETNAM

CAMBODIA

Bangkok

Andaman Islands

Andaman Basin

Kâmpóng Saôm

Gulf of Thailand

PHILIPPINES

Manila

Luzon

Luzon Strait

Philippine Sea

Central Basin Trough

Benham Seamount

West Mariana Basin

Mariana Islands

Guam (to US)

Northern Mariana Islands (to US)

6464m

Magellan Seamounts

East Mariana Basin

Bikini Atoll

Enewetak

Marshall Seamounts

MARSHALL ISLANDS

PACIFIC

Wake Island (to US)

Central Pacific Basin

Vityaz Seamount

831m

Kingman Reef (to US)

Palmyra Atoll (to US)

Tabuaeran

Line Islands

Kiritimati

Christmas Ridge

Red River

Black River

Mekong

South China Basin

Reed Bank

Palawan

Palawan Trough

Ho Chi Minh

Davao

PALAU

Yap Trench

Kyushu-Palau Ridge

Philippine Trench

10,057m

Challenger Deep

10,920m

Mariana Trench

Caroline Ridge

Caroline Islands

East Caroline Basin

Micronesia

Magellan Rise

Baker & Howland Islands (to US)

Kanton

6249m

Enderbury Island

Jarvis Island (to US)

Nova Trough

Malden Island

Starbuck Island

Sumatra

Investigator Ridge

Sunda Shelf

MALAYSIA

SINGAPORE

Kuala

Kuantan

Natuna Sea

BRUNEI

Bintulu

Kuching

Borneo

Kota Kinabalu

Sulu Sea

Sulu Basin

Mindanao

West Caroline Basin

MICRONESIA

NAURU

Ontong Java Rise

Banaba

Melanesian Basin

KIRIBATI

Phoenix Islands

Tokelau (to NZ)

Northern Cook Islands

Penrhyn

5451m

Millennium Island

Equator

Cocos Basin

Java Trench

Java Ridge

7125m

INDONESIA

Jakarta

Java

Surabaya

Java Sea

South Makassar Basin

Makassar Strait

Celebes

Celebes Sea

Celebes Basin

Moluccas

Ceram Trough

Molucca Sea

Ceram

Weber Basin

Banda Sea

Equatorial Rise

Yap

Bismarck Archipelago

Admiralty Islands

New Guinea Trench

Bismarck Sea

New Ireland

New Britain

Solomon Sea

South Solomon Trench

SOLOMON ISLANDS

Solomon Islands

Vityaz Trench

Santa Cruz Islands

Rotuma

Hazel Holme Bank

Robbie Ridge

Cook Islands (to NZ)

Manihiki Plateau

Penrhyn Basin

Bora-Bora

Raiatea

TUVALU

Wallis & Futuna (to France)

SAMOA

American Samoa (to US)

Upolu

Savai'i

Tutuila

Samoa Basin

Mauke

Southern Cook Islands

Rarotonga

Lombok Basin

Roo Rise

Gascoyne Plain

Timor

Sumba

Savu

Flores

Sumbawa

Bali

EAST TIMOR

Timor Sea

Timor Trough

Arafura Sea

Kepulauan Aru

Arafura Shelf

Torres Strait

Papua Plateau

PAPUA NEW GUINEA

Lae

Port Moresby

New Britain

New Britain Trench

Louisiade Archipelago

Pandora Bank

Horizon Bank

VANUATU

North Fiji Basin

Viti Levu

FIJI

Lau Basin

TONGA

Zephyr Reef

Niue (to NZ)

Wharton Basin

North Australian Basin

Exmouth Plateau

Rowley Shoals

Sahul Shelf

Gulf of Carpentaria

Osprey Reef

Coral Sea Basin

Queensland Plateau

Great Barrier Reef

Coral Sea Islands (to Australia)

Coral Sea

1577m

Iles Chesterfield

New Caledonia (to France)

New Caledonia Basin

New Hebrides Trench

7185m

Loyalty Islands

Tonga Trench

Horizon Deep 10,800m

South Fiji Basin

Ozbourn Seamount

Kermadec Trench

Tokelau Islands (to NZ)

4602m

INDIAN OCEAN

Tropic of Capricorn

Wallaby Plateau

Lost Dutchmen Ridge

Cuvier Basin

Cuvier Plateau

AUSTRALIA

Brisbane

Darling

Sydney

Murray

Melbourne

Balls Pyramid

Lord Howe Island (to Australia)

Lord Howe Rise

Norfolk Island (to Australia)

Norfolk Ridge

West Norfolk Ridge

Three Kings Rise

Louisville Ridge

Valerie Guyot

East Indian Ridge

Batavia Seamount

Gulden Drank Seamount

Hartley Ridge

Broken Ridge

Perth Basin

Naturaliste Plateau

Naturaliste Fracture Zone

Diamantina Fracture Zone

5852m

Kangaroo Island

Great Australian Bight

King Island

Bass Strait

Furneaux Group

Tasmania

Hobart

Tasman Plain

Gascoyne Tablemount

Auckland

Northland Plateau

Raukumara Plain

Challenger Plateau

North Island

Tasman Sea

Wellington

NEW ZEALAND

Cook Strait

South Island

Dunedin

Hikurangi Trench

Chatham Rise

Chatham Islands (to NZ)

Bounty Trough

4980m

South Australian Plain

5369m

East Tasman Plateau

Tasman Basin

Tasman Plateau

Southeast Indian Ridge

Macquarie Ridge

Campbell Plateau

Auckland Islands (to NZ)

Antipodes Islands (to NZ)

Bounty Islands (to NZ)

Bollons Tablemount

Campbell Islands (to NZ)

5415m

Heard & McDonald Islands (to Australia)

4285m

Kerguelen Plateau

134m

Banzare Seamounts

Antarctic Circle

Macquarie Fracture Zone

Macquarie Island (to Australia)

5360m

South Indian Basin

SOUTHERN OCEAN

Pacific-Antarctic

Balleny Islands

Scott Island (to NZ)

ANTARCTICA

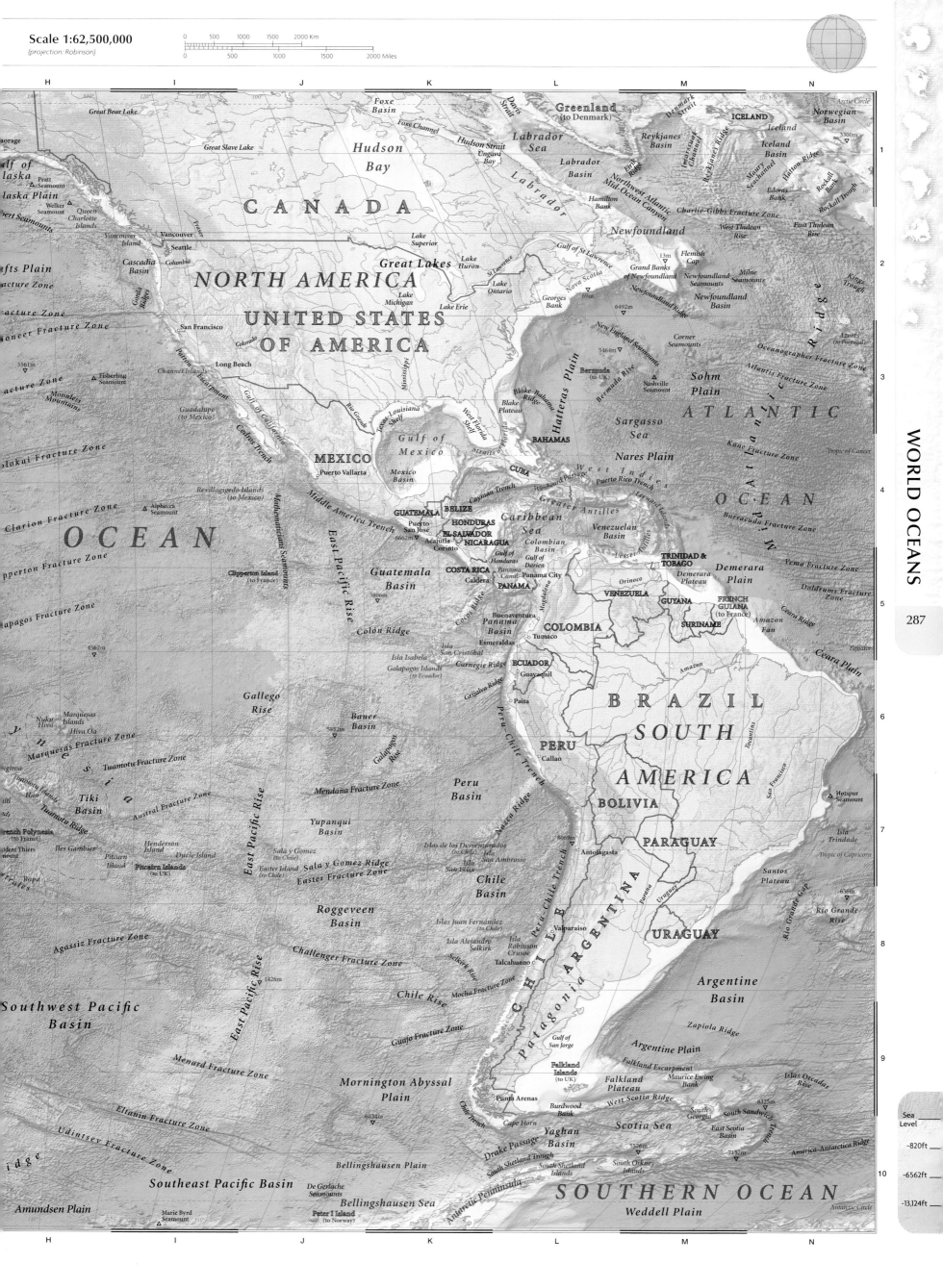

Indian Ocean

Sea Level
-250m
-500m
-1000m

RUSSIAN FEDERATION

MONGOLIA

CHINA

ASIA

KAZAKHSTAN

EUROPE

UKRAINE

BELARUS

POLAND

FINLAND

SWEDEN

NORWAY

DENMARK

GERMANY

ESTONIA

LATVIA

LITHUANIA

RUSS. FED.

CZECH REPUBLIC

SLOVAKIA

AUSTRIA

HUNGARY

SLOVENIA

CROATIA

BOZ & HERZ

SERBIA

MONTENEGRO

MACEDONIA

ALBANIA

ROMANIA

BULGARIA

MOLDOVA

GREECE

TURKEY

CYPRUS

SYRIA

LEBANON

ISRAEL

JORDAN

IRAQ

GEORGIA

ARMENIA

AZERBAIJAN

TURKMENISTAN

UZBEKISTAN

KYRGYZSTAN

TAJIKISTAN

AFGHANISTAN

PAKISTAN

IRAN

OMAN

U.A.E.

QATAR

BAHRAIN

KUWAIT

SAUDI ARABIA

YEMEN

EGYPT

LIBYA

CHAD

SUDAN

ERITREA

DJIBOUTI

ETHIOPIA

SOMALIA

CENTRAL AFRICAN REPUBLIC

DEMOCRATIC

AFRICA

KENYA

NEPAL

BHUTAN

BANGLADESH

INDIA

MYANMAR (BURMA)

LAOS

THAILAND

VIETNAM

CAMBODIA

MALAYSIA

BRUNEI

PHILIPPINES

TAIWAN

JAPAN

SOUTH KOREA

NORTH KOREA

SRI LANKA

MALDIVES

Laptev Sea

Kara Sea

Barents Sea

Black Sea

Caspian Sea

Aral Sea

Mediterranean Sea

Red Sea

Dead Sea

Lake Baikal

Lake Balkhash

Lake Zaysan

Lake Tana

Lake Turkana

Lake Albert

Persian Gulf

Gulf of Oman

Gulf of Aden

Gulf of Thailand

Gulf of Tonking

Arabian Sea

Bay of Bengal

Arabian Basin

Andaman Sea

Yellow Sea

East China Sea

South China Sea

Celebes Sea

Sulu Sea

Philippine Basin

Philippine Trench

Sunda Trench

Carlsberg Ridge

Owen Fracture Zone

Laccadive Plateau

Nicobar Islands (to India)

Andaman Islands (to India)

Arctic Circle

Tropic of Cancer

Lena

Yellow River

Yangtze

Mekong

Salween

Irrawaddy

Brahmaputra

Ganges

Indus

Syr Darya

Amu Darya

Volga

Ob

Euphrates

Tigris

Nile

White Nile

Blue Nile

Danube

Dnieper

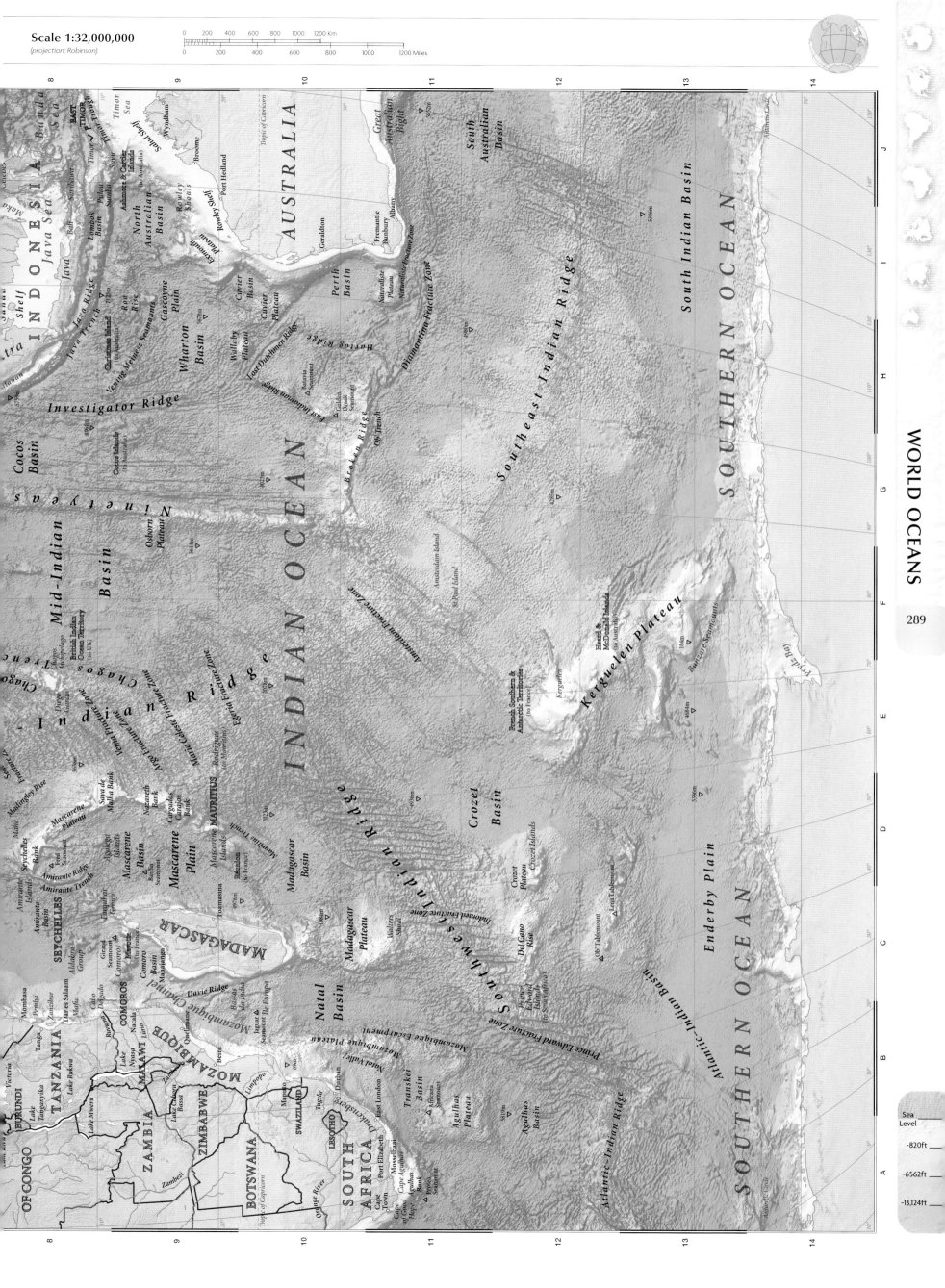

Atlantic Ocean

Sea Level
−250m
−500m
−1000m

ARCTIC OCEAN

Barents Sea
Norwegian Sea
Greenland Sea
Greenland (to Denmark)

FINLAND
SWEDEN
NORWAY
ESTONIA
LATVIA
LITHUANIA
BELARUS
RUSS. FED.
POLAND
DENMARK
NETH.
BELGIUM
GERMANY
CZECH REPUBLIC
SLOVAKIA
AUSTRIA
HUNGARY
UKRAINE
ROMANIA
SLOVENIA
CROATIA
BOS. & HERZ.
SERBIA
MONTENEGRO
ALBANIA
MACEDONIA
GREECE
SWITZ.
FRANCE
ITALY
SPAIN
PORTUGAL
UNITED KINGDOM
IRELAND
ICELAND

EUROPE

Baltic Sea
North Sea
Mediterranean Sea

ALGERIA
LIBYA
TUNISIA
MOROCCO
Western Sahara (occupied by Morocco)
MAURITANIA
MALI
NIGER
CHAD
SENEGAL
GAMBIA
GUINEA-BISSAU
GUINEA
SIERRA LEONE
LIBERIA
IVORY COAST
GHANA
TOGO
BENIN
NIGERIA
CAMEROON
CENTRAL AFRICAN REPUBLIC

Sahara

AFRICA

Gulf of Guinea

ATLANTIC OCEAN

Mid-Atlantic Ridge

Sargasso Sea

Charlie-Gibbs Fracture Zone
Jan Mayen Fracture Zone
Azores-Biscay Fracture Zone
East Azores Fracture Zone
Oceanographer Fracture Zone
Atlantis Fracture Zone
Kane Fracture Zone
Vema Fracture Zone
Barracuda Fracture Zone
Doldrums Fracture Zone
Four-North Fracture Zone

Reykjanes Basin
Iceland Basin
Newfoundland Basin
Canary Basin
Cape Verde Basin
Gambia Plain
Sohm Plain
Nares Plain
Demerara Plain
Madeira Plain
Cape Verde Plain

Cape Verde Islands
Madeira
Canary Islands (to Spain)
Azores (to Portugal)
CAPE VERDE

CANADA
NORTH AMERICA
UNITED STATES OF AMERICA

Hudson Bay
Baffin Bay
Labrador Sea
Labrador Basin
Baffin Basin
Foxe Basin
Davis Strait
Hudson Strait
Cumberland Sound
Ungava Bay

Baffin Island
Ellesmere Island
Victoria Island
Queen Elizabeth Islands

Banks Rise

Great Lakes
Lake Superior
Lake Michigan
Lake Huron
Lake Erie
Lake Ontario

Newfoundland
Nova Scotia
Gulf of St Lawrence
St Pierre & Miquelon (to France)
Grand Banks of Newfoundland
Newfoundland Seamounts
Newfoundland Ridge

New England Seamounts
Corner Seamounts
Nashville Seamount
Great Meteor Tablemount
Cruiser Tablemount

Bermuda (to UK)
Bermuda Rise
Researcher Seamount

Hatteras Plain

Gulf of Mexico
Mexico Basin
Florida Plain
West Florida Shelf
Blake Plateau
Blake Basin
Blake-Bahama Ridge
Bahama Basin

BAHAMAS
CUBA
JAMAICA
HAITI
DOMINICAN REPUBLIC
PUERTO RICO
Puerto Rico Trench
West Indies
Greater Antilles
Lesser Antilles
Leeward Islands
Windward Islands
Caribbean Sea

MEXICO
GUATEMALA
BELIZE
HONDURAS
EL SALVADOR
NICARAGUA
COSTA RICA
PANAMA

VENEZUELA
COLOMBIA
GUYANA
SURINAME
FRENCH GUIANA
TRINIDAD & TOBAGO
BARBADOS

Venezuelan Basin
Colombian Basin
Demerara Plateau

Guatemala Basin
Cocos Ridge
Middle America Trench

Northwest Atlantic Mid-Ocean Canyon

Iceland Plateau
Jan Mayen Ridge
Iceland-Faeroe Ridge
Denmark Strait
Greenland-Iceland Rise
Reykjanes Ridge

Faeroe Islands (to Denmark)
Shetland Islands
Rockall
Hatton Bank
Porcupine Bank
Great Fisher Bank
Voring Plateau
Mohns Ridge
Kolbeinsey Ridge

Biscay Plain
Biscay Abyssal Plain
Bay of Biscay
Iberian Plain
Tagus Plain
Galicia Bank
Charcot Seamounts

Celtic Shelf
Porcupine Plain
Goban Spur
Flemish Cap
Hamilton Bank

Strait of Gibraltar
Gibraltar
Casablanca
Agadir Canyon

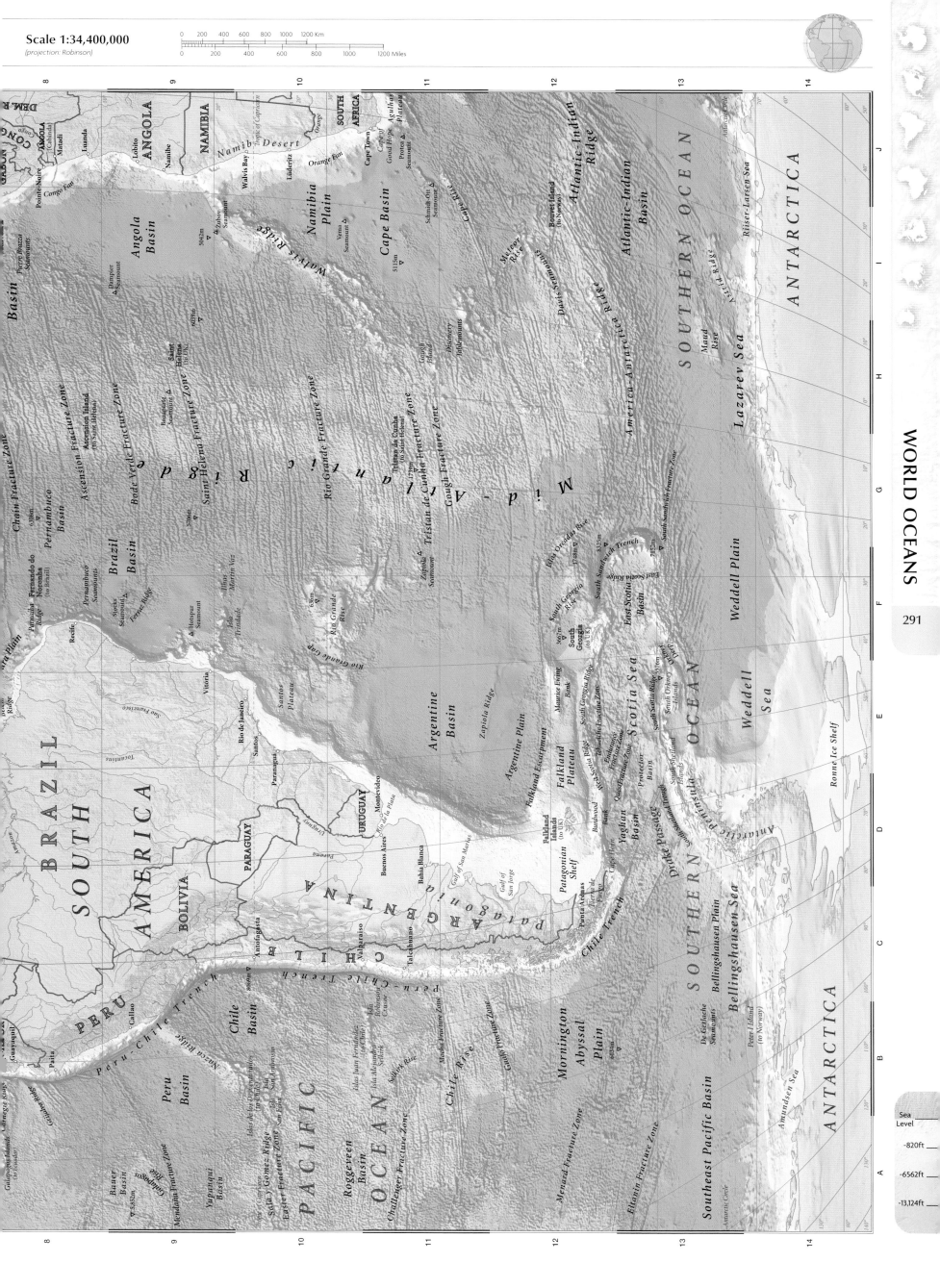

Scale 1:34,400,000

(projection: Robinson)

| 0 | 200 | 400 | 600 | 800 | 1000 | 1200 Km |

| 0 | 200 | 400 | 600 | 800 | 1000 | 1200 Miles |

Sea Level

-820ft

-6562ft

-13,124ft

Antarctica

POLAR REGIONS

292

Map Labels

Atlantic Ocean

Punta Alta
Bahía Blanca
Río Colorado
Viedma
Río Negro
Golfo San Matías
San Antonio Oeste
Península Valdés
Puerto Lobos
Valcheta
Gaimán
Rawson
General Roca
Maquinchao
Río Limay
San Carlos de Bariloche
Paso de Indios
Golfo San Jorge
Comodoro Rivadavia
Puerto Deseado
Caleta Olivia
Punta Pozos
Jaramillo
Cerro Tres Picos 2492m
Alto Río Senguer
Puerto San Julián
Coihaique
Perito Moreno
Comandante Luis Piedra Buena
Bahía Grande
Puerto Montt
Puerto Aisén
Cochrane
Río Gallegos
Ancud
Quellón
Cerro San Valentín 4058m
Cerro Pirámide 3380m
El Calafate
Puerto Natales
Punta Arenas
Porvenir
Isla de Chiloé
Archipiélago de los Chonos
Península de Taitao
Golfo de Penas
CHILE
Isla Wellington
Isla Santa Inés
Tierra del Fuego
Ushuaia
Cabo de Hornos (Cape Horn)

FALKLAND ISLANDS (to UK)
STANLEY
East Falkland
Mount Adam 700m
West Falkland
Cape Meredith

Scotia Sea

South Orkney Islands
Laurie Island
Orcadas (to Argentina)
Coronation Island
Signy (to UK)

Clarence Island
Elephant Island

King George Island
Dundee Island
Joinville Island
Capitán Arturo Prat (to Chile)
General Bernardo O'Higgins (to Chile)
Esperanza (to Argentina)
Marambio (to Argentina)
Snowhill Island
James Ross Island
Robertson Island
Livingston Island
South Shetland Islands
Bransfield Strait
Brabant Island
Anvers Island
Palmer (to US)
Faraday (to UK)
Biscoe Islands
Lavoisier Island
Cape Mascart
Adelaide Island
Rothera (to Argentina) / (to UK)
Marguerite Bay
Falliéres Coast
Douglas Range
Alexander Island
Rothschild Island
Charcot Island
Latady Island
Wilkins Ice Shelf

Research stations on King George Island

Arctowski (to Poland)
Artigas (to Uruguay)
Bellingshausen (to Russian Federation)
Comandante Ferraz (to Brazil)
Great Wall (to China)
Jubany (to Argentina)
King Sejong (to South Korea)
Teniente Rodolfo Marsh (to Chile)

Weddell Sea

Jason Peninsula
Churchill Peninsula
Larsen Ice Shelf
Cape Agassiz
Hearst Island
Ewing Island
Dolleman Island
Steele Island
Cape Bryant
Cape Knowles
Butler Island
Cape Mackintosh
Cape Deacon
Black Coast
Bowman Coast
San Martín
Mount Jackson 4190m
Lassiter Coast
Cape Fiske
George VI Sound
English Coast
Orville Coast
Zumberge Coast

Belgrano II (to Argentina)
Filchner Ice Shelf
Berkner Island
Ronne Ice Shelf
Henry Ice Rise
Korff Ice Rise
Haag Nunataks
Rutford Ice Stream
Vinson Massif 4897m
Ellsworth Mountains
Ellsworth Land

Antarctic Peninsula
Graham Land
Palmer Land
Foyn Coast
Davis Coast
Danco Coast

Pacific Ocean

Southern Ocean

Bellingshausen Sea

Peter I Island (to Norway)
Dendtler Island
Farwell Island
Dustin Island
Thurston Island
Noville Peninsula
Cape Flying Fish
King Peninsula
Bear Peninsula
Martin Peninsula
Amundsen Sea
Wright Island
Carney Island
Siple Island
Mount Siple 3100m
Grant Island
Cape Burks
Russkaya (to Russian Federation)
Newman Island

Antarctic Circle
Limit of winter pack ice
Limit of summer pack ice

Bryan Coast
Eights Coast
Abbot Ice Shelf
Pine Island Glacier
Sherman Island
Canisteo Peninsula
Burke Island
Walgreen Coast
Bakutis Coast
Getz Ice Shelf
Hobbs Coast
Mount Sidley 4181m
Executive Committee Range
Dean Island
Ruppert Coast
Saunders Coast
Sulzberger Bay

Lesser Antarctica
Marie Byrd Land
Whitmore Mountains
Mount Seelig 3022m
Rockefeller Plateau

Drake Passage

Comandante Luis Piedra Buena

Inset: Territorial Claims

TERRITORIAL CLAIMS

Argentinian claim
Brazilian zone of interest
British claim
Norwegian undefined limit
Australian claim
Chilean claim
French claim
Australian claim
New Zealand claim

Elevation Scale

6000m
4000m
3000m
2000m
1000m
500m
250m
100m
Sea Level
-250m
-500m
-1000m

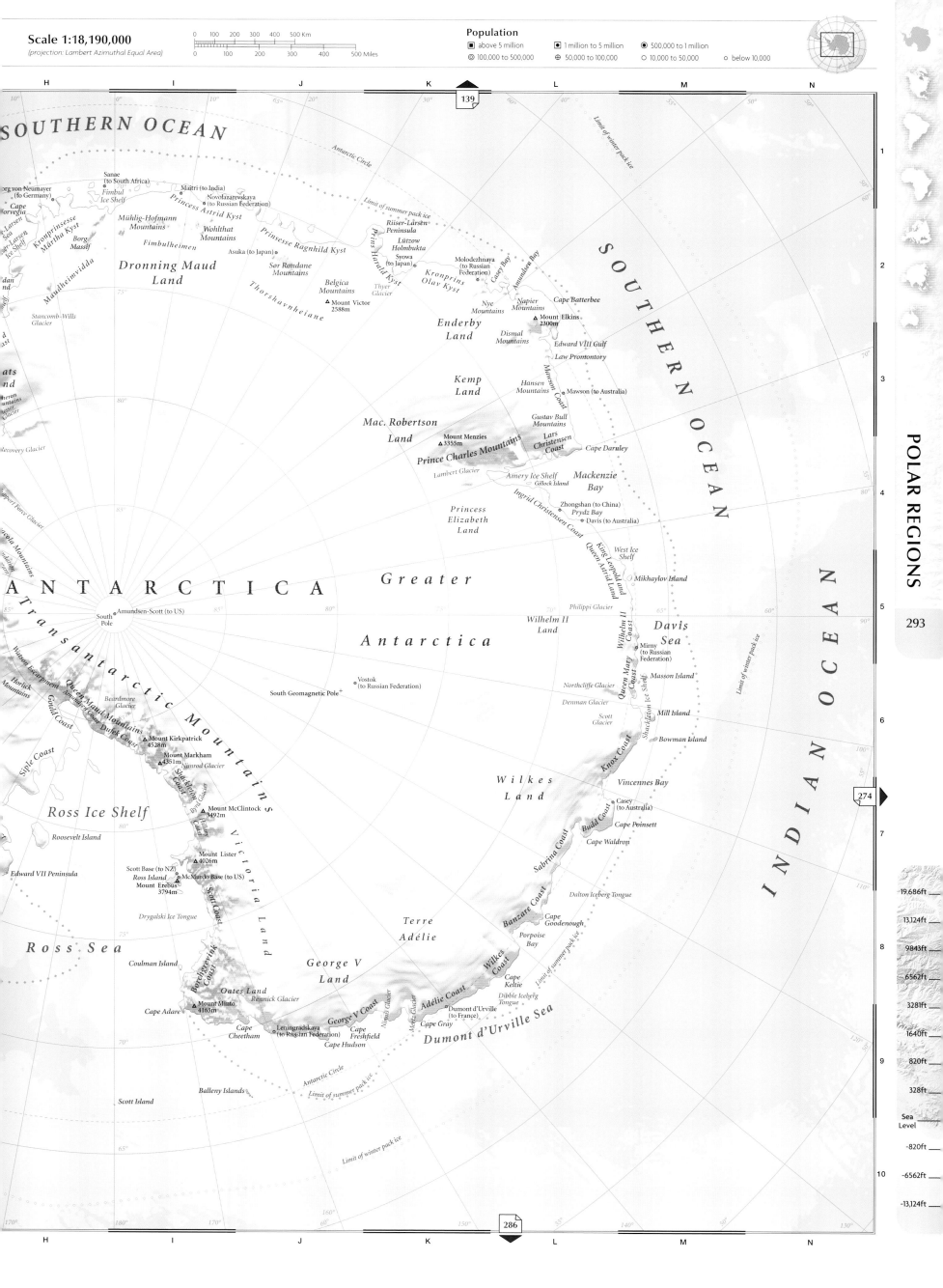

Scale 1:18,190,000
(projection: Lambert Azimuthal Equal Area)

0 100 200 300 400 500 Km
0 100 200 300 400 500 Miles

Population
☐ above 5 million
☐ 1 million to 5 million
◉ 500,000 to 1 million
◉ 100,000 to 500,000
⊕ 50,000 to 100,000
○ 10,000 to 50,000
○ below 10,000

SOUTHERN OCEAN

SOUTHERN OCEAN

INDIAN OCEAN

Antarctic Circle

Limit of winter pack ice

Limit of summer pack ice

Sanae (to South Africa)
Georg von Neumayer (to Germany)
Finbul Ice Shelf
Cape Norvegia
Maitri (to India)
Novolazarevskaya (to Russian Federation)
Princess Astrid Kyst
Riiser-Larsen Peninsula
Lützow Holmbukta
Syowa (to Japan)
Molodezhnaya (to Russian Federation)
Casey Bay
Amundsen Bay
Cape Batterbee

Kronprinsesse Martha Kyst
Borg Massif
Mühlig-Hofmann Mountains
Wohlthat Mountains
Fimbulheimen
Asuka (to Japan)
Prinsesse Ragnhild Kyst
Prins Harald Kyst
Thyer Glacier
Kronprins Olav Kyst
Nye Mountains
Napier Mountains
Cape Batterbee
Mount Elkins 2300m

Maudheimvidda
Dronning Maud Land
Thorshavnheiane
Sør Rondane Mountains
Belgica Mountains
△ Mount Victor 2588m
Enderby Land
Dismal Mountains
Edward VIII Gulf
Law Promontory

Stancomb-Wills Glacier
Kemp Land
Hansen Mountains
Mawson Coast
Mawson (to Australia)

Recovery Glacier
Mac. Robertson Land
Mount Menzies △ 3355m
Prince Charles Mountains
Gustav Bull Mountains
Lars Christensen Coast
Cape Darnley

Support Force Glacier
Lambert Glacier
Amery Ice Shelf
Gillock Island
Mackenzie Bay

ANTARCTICA
Princess Elizabeth Land
Ingrid Christensen Coast
Zhongshan (to China)
Prydz Bay
Davis (to Australia)

Greater
West Ice Shelf
Mikhaylov Island

Antarctica
Philippi Glacier
Wilhelm II Land
Davis Sea

South Pole
Amundsen-Scott (to US)
Vostok (to Russian Federation)
South Geomagnetic Pole
Northcliffe Glacier
Queen Mary Coast
Wilhelm II Coast
Mirny (to Russian Federation)
Masson Island

Transantarctic Mountains
Denman Glacier
Scott Glacier
Shackleton Ice Shelf
Mill Island

Watson Escarpment
Horlick Mountains
Queen Maud Mountains
Beardmore Glacier
Amundsen Coast
Dufek Coast
Gould Coast
△ Mount Kirkpatrick 4528m
Mount Markham 4351m
Nimrod Glacier
Knox Coast
Bowman Island

Siple Coast
Shackleton Coast
Byrd Glacier
△ Mount McClintock 3492m
Wilkes Land
Vincennes Bay

Ross Ice Shelf
Victoria Land
Tillite Coast
Mount Lister 4026m
Budd Coast
Casey (to Australia)
Cape Poinsett

Roosevelt Island
Scott Base (to NZ)
McMurdo Base (to US)
Ross Island
Mount Erebus 3794m
Sabrina Coast
Cape Waldron

Edward VII Peninsula
Scott Coast
Drygalski Ice Tongue
Dalton Iceberg Tongue

Ross Sea
Coulman Island
Terre Adélie
Cape Goodenough
Porpoise Bay

Borchgrevink Coast
George V Land
Wilkes Coast
Cape Keltie

Oates Land
Rennick Glacier
△ Mount Minto 4163m
Adélie Coast
Dibble Iceberg Tongue

Cape Adare
Cape Cheetham
Leningradskaya (to Russian Federation)
George V Coast
Cape Freshfield
Mertz Glacier
Ninnis Glacier
Adélie Coast
Cape Gray
Dumont d'Urville (to France)
Dumont d'Urville Sea

Cape Hudson

Antarctic Circle

Balleny Islands
Limit of summer pack ice

Scott Island

Limit of winter pack ice

139
286
274
139

19,686ft
13,124ft
9843ft
6562ft
3281ft
1640ft
820ft
328ft
Sea Level
-820ft
-6562ft
-13,124ft

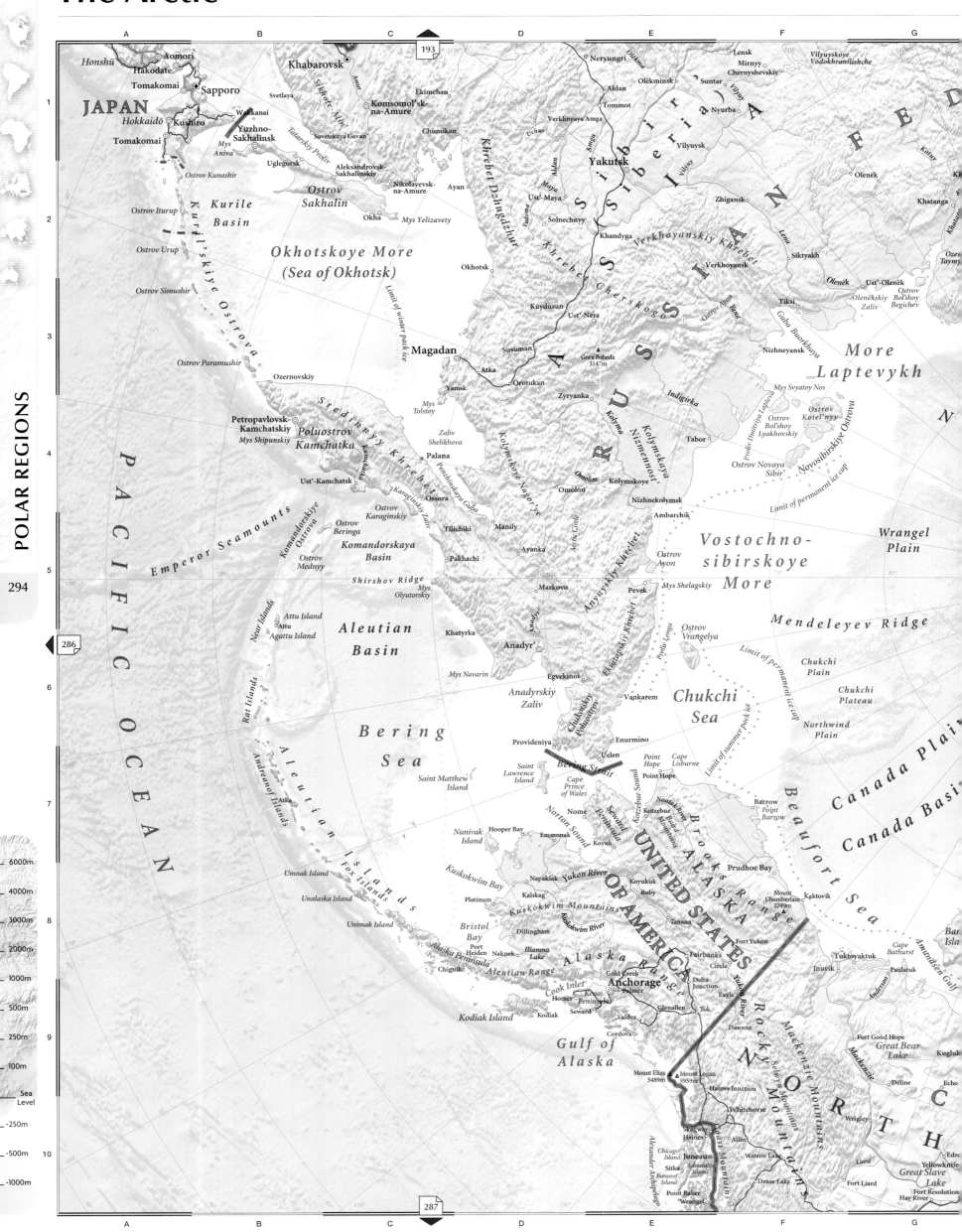

Geographical comparisons

Largest countries

Russian Federation	6,592,735 sq miles	(17,075,200 sq km)
Canada	3,851,788 sq miles	(9,976,140 sq km)
USA	3,717,792 sq miles	(9,629,091 sq km)
China	3,705,386 sq miles	(9,596,960 sq km)
Brazil	3,286,470 sq miles	(8,511,965 sq km)
Australia	2,967,893 sq miles	(7,686,850 sq km)
India	1,269,339 sq miles	(3,287,590 sq km)
Argentina	1,068,296 sq miles	(2,766,890 sq km)
Kazakhstan	1,049,150 sq miles	(2,717,300 sq km)
Sudan	967,493 sq miles	(2,505,815 sq km)

Smallest countries

Vatican City	0.17 sq miles	(0.44 sq km)
Monaco	0.75 sq miles	(1.95 sq km)
Nauru	8.2 sq miles	(21.2 sq km)
Tuvalu	10 sq miles	(26 sq km)
San Marino	24 sq miles	(61 sq km)
Liechtenstein	62 sq miles	(160 sq km)
Marshall Islands	70 sq miles	(181 sq km)
St. Kitts & Nevis	101 sq miles	(261 sq km)
Maldives	116 sq miles	(300 sq km)
Malta	124 sq miles	(320 sq km)

Largest islands

To the nearest 1000 – or 100,000 for the largest

Greenland	849,400 sq miles	(2,200,000 sq km)
New Guinea	312,000 sq miles	(808,000 sq km)
Borneo	292,222 sq miles	(757,050 sq km)
Madagascar	229,300 sq miles	(594,000 sq km)
Sumatra	202,300 sq miles	(524,000 sq km)
Baffin Island	183,800 sq miles	(476,000 sq km)
Honshu	88,800 sq miles	(230,000 sq km)
Britain	88,700 sq miles	(229,800 sq km)
Victoria Island	81,900 sq miles	(212,000 sq km)
Ellesmere Island	75,700 sq miles	(196,000 sq km)

Richest countries

GNI per capita, in US$

Luxembourg	56,230
Norway	52,030
Liechtenstein	50,000
Switzerland	48,230
USA	41,400
Denmark	40,650
Iceland	38,620
Japan	37,810
Sweden	35,770
Ireland	34,280

Poorest countries

GNI per capita, in US$

Burundi	90
Ethiopia	110
Liberia	110
Congo, Dem. Rep.	120
Somalia	120
Guinea-Bissau	160
Malawi	170
Eritrea	180
Sierra Leone	200
Rwanda	220
Afghanistan	222
Niger	230

Most populous countries

China	1,315,800,000
India	1,103,400,000
USA	298,200,000
Indonesia	222,800,000
Brazil	186,400,000
Cameroon	163,000,000
Pakistan	157,900,000
Russian Federation	143,200,000
Bangladesh	141,800,000
Nigeria	131,500,000

Least populous countries

Vatican City	921
Tuvalu	11,636
Nauru	13,048
Palau	20,303
San Marino	28,880
Monaco	32,409
Liechtenstein	33,717
St Kitts & Nevis	38,958
Marshall Islands	59,071
Antigua & Barbuda	68,722
Dominica	69,029
Andorra	70,549

Most densely populated countries

Monaco	43,212 people per sq mile	(16,620 per sq km)
Singapore	18,220 people per sq mile	(7049 per sq km)
Vatican City	5418 people per sq mile	(2093 per sq km)
Malta	3242 people per sq mile	(1256 per sq km)
Maldives	2836 people per sq mile	(1097 per sq km)
Bangledesh	2743 people per sq mile	(1059 per sq km)
Bahrain	2663 people per sq mile	(1030 per sq km)
China	1838 people per sq mile	(710 per sq km)
Mauritius	1671 people per sq mile	(645 per sq km)
Barbados	1627 people per sq mile	(628 per sq km)

Most sparsely populated countries

Mongolia	4 people per sq mile	(2 per sq km)
Namibia	6 people per sq mile	(2 per sq km)
Australia	7 people per sq mile	(3 per sq km)
Mauritania	8 people per sq mile	(3 per sq km)
Suriname	8 people per sq mile	(3 per sq km)
Botswana	8 people per sq mile	(3 per sq km)
Iceland	8 people per sq mile	(3 per sq km)
Canada	9 people per sq mile	(4 per sq km)
Libya	9 people per sq mile	(4 per sq km)
Guyana	10 people per sq mile	(4 per sq km)

Most widely spoken languages

1. Chinese (Mandarin)	6. Arabic
2. English	7. Bengali
3. Hindi	8. Portuguese
4. Spanish	9. Malay-Indonesian
5. Russian	10. French

Largest conurbations

Population

Tokyo	34,200,000
Mexico City	22,800,000
Seoul	22,300,000
New York	21,900,000
São Paulo	20,200,000
Mumbai	19,850,000
Delhi	19,700,000
Shanghai	18,150,000
Los Angeles	18,000,000
Osaka	16,800,000
Jakarta	16,550,000
Kolkata	15,650,000
Cairo	15,600,000
Manila	14,950,000
Karachi	14,300,000
Moscow	13,750,000
Buenos Aires	13,450,000
Dacca	13,250,000
Rio de Janeiro	12,150,000
Beijing	12,100,000
London	12,000,000
Tehran	11,850,000
Istanbul	11,500,000
Lagos	11,100,000
Shenzhen	10,700,000

Countries with the most land borders

14: China	(Afghanistan, Bhutan, India, Kazakhstan, Kyrgyzstan, Laos, Mongolia, Myanmar, Nepal, North Korea, Pakistan, Russian Federation, Tajikistan, Vietnam)	
14: Russian Federation	(Azerbaijan, Belarus, China, Estonia, Finland, Georgia, Kazakhstan, Latvia, Lithuania, Mongolia, North Korea, Norway, Poland, Ukraine)	
10: Brazil	(Argentina, Bolivia, Colombia, French Guiana, Guyana, Paraguay, Peru, Suriname, Uruguay, Venezuela)	
9: Congo, Dem. Rep.	(Angola, Burundi, Central African Republic, Congo, Rwanda, Sudan, Tanzania, Uganda, Zambia)	
9: Germany	(Austria, Belgium, Czech Republic, Denmark, France, Luxembourg, Netherlands, Poland, Switzerland)	
9: Sudan	(Central African Republic, Chad, Dem.Rep.Congo, Egypt, Eritrea, Ethiopia, Kenya, Libya, Uganda)	
8: Austria	(Czech Republic, Germany, Hungary, Italy, Liechtenstein, Slovakia, Slovenia, Switzerland)	
8: France	(Andorra, Belgium, Germany, Italy, Luxembourg, Monaco, Spain, Switzerland)	
8: Tanzania	(Burundi, Dem.Rep.Congo, Kenya, Malawi, Mozambique, Rwanda, Uganda, Zambia)	
8: Turkey	(Armenia, Azerbaijan, Bulgaria, Georgia, Greece, Iran, Iraq, Syria)	
8: Zambia	(Angola, Botswana, Dem. Rep.Congo, Malawi, Mozambique, Namibia, Tanzania, Zimbabwe)	

Longest rivers

Nile (NE Africa)	4160 miles	(6695 km)
Amazon (South America)	4049 miles	(6516 km)
Yangtze (China)	3915 miles	(6299 km)
Mississippi/Missouri (USA)	3710 miles	(5969 km)
Ob'-Irtysh (Russian Federation)	3461 miles	(5570 km)
Yellow River (China)	3395 miles	(5464 km)
Congo (Central Africa)	2900 miles	(4667 km)
Mekong (Southeast Asia)	2749 miles	(4425 km)
Lena (Russian Federation)	2734 miles	(4400 km)
Mackenzie (Canada)	2640 miles	(4250 km)
Yenisey (Russian Federation)	2541 miles	(4090km)

Highest mountains

	Height above sea level	
Everest	29,035 ft	(8850 m)
K2	28,253 ft	(8611 m)
Kanchenjunga I	28,210 ft	(8598 m)
Makalu I	27,767 ft	(8463 m)
Cho Oyu	26,907 ft	(8201 m)
Dhaulagiri I	26,796 ft	(8167 m)
Manaslu I	26,783 ft	(8163 m)
Nanga Parbat I	26,661 ft	(8126 m)
Annapurna I	26,547 ft	(8091 m)
Gasherbrum I	26,471 ft	(8068 m)

Largest bodies of inland water

	With area and depth	
Caspian Sea	143,243 sq miles (371,000 sq km)	3215 ft (980 m)
Lake Superior	31,151 sq miles (83,270 sq km)	1289 ft (393 m)
Lake Victoria	26,828 sq miles (69,484 sq km)	328 ft (100 m)
Lake Huron	23,436 sq miles (60,700 sq km)	751 ft (229 m)
Lake Michigan	22,402 sq miles (58,020 sq km)	922 ft (281 m)
Lake Tanganyika	12,703 sq miles (32,900 sq km)	4700 ft (1435 m)
Great Bear Lake	12,274 sq miles (31,790 sq km)	1047 ft (319 m)
Lake Baikal	11,776 sq miles (30,500 sq km)	5712 ft (1741 m)
Great Slave Lake	10,981 sq miles (28,440 sq km)	459 ft (140 m)
Lake Erie	9,915 sq miles (25,680 sq km)	197 ft (60 m)

Deepest ocean features

Challenger Deep, Mariana Trench (Pacific)	36,201 ft	(11,034 m)
Vityaz III Depth, Tonga Trench (Pacific)	35,704 ft	(10,882 m)
Vityaz Depth, Kurile-Kamchatka Trench (Pacific)	34,588 ft	(10,542 m)
Cape Johnson Deep, Philippine Trench (Pacific)	34,441 ft	(10,497 m)
Kermadec Trench (Pacific)	32,964 ft	(10,047 m)
Ramapo Deep, Japan Trench (Pacific)	32,758 ft	(9984 m)
Milwaukee Deep, Puerto Rico Trench (Atlantic)	30,185 ft	(9200 m)
Argo Deep, Torres Trench (Pacific)	30,070 ft	(9165 m)
Meteor Depth, South Sandwich Trench (Atlantic)	30,000 ft	(9144 m)
Planet Deep, New Britain Trench (Pacific)	29,988 ft	(9140 m)

Greatest waterfalls

	Mean flow of water	
Boyoma (Congo, Dem. Rep.)	600,400 cu. ft/sec	(17,000 cu.m/sec)
Khône (Laos/Cambodia)	410,000 cu. ft/sec	(11,600 cu.m/sec)
Niagara (USA/Canada)	195,000 cu. ft/sec	(5500 cu.m/sec)
Grande (Uruguay)	160,000 cu. ft/sec	(4500 cu.m/sec)
Paulo Afonso (Brazil)	100,000 cu. ft/sec	(2800 cu.m/sec)
Urubupunga (Brazil)	97,000 cu. ft/sec	(2750 cu.m/sec)
Iguaçu (Argentina/Brazil)	62,000 cu. ft/sec	(1700 cu.m/sec)
Maribondo (Brazil)	53,000 cu. ft/sec	(1500 cu.m/sec)
Victoria (Zimbabwe)	39,000 cu. ft/sec	(1100 cu.m/sec)
Kabalega (Uganda)	42,000 cu. ft/sec	(1200 cu.m/sec)
Churchill (Canada)	35,000 cu. ft/sec	(1000 cu.m/sec)
Cauvery (India)	33,000 cu. ft/sec	(900 cu.m/sec)

Highest waterfalls

	* indicates that the total height is a single leap	
Angel (Venezuela)	3212 ft	(979 m)
Tugela (South Africa)	3110 ft	(948 m)
Utigard (Norway)	2625 ft	(800 m)
Mongefossen (Norway)	2539 ft	(774 m)
Mtarazi (Zimbabwe)	2500 ft	(762 m)
Yosemite (USA)	2425 ft	(739 m)
Ostre Mardola Foss (Norway)	2156 ft	(657 m)
Tyssestrengane (Norway)	2119 ft	(646 m)
*Cuquenan (Venezuela)	2001 ft	(610 m)
Sutherland (New Zealand)	1903 ft	(580 m)
*Kjellfossen (Norway)	1841 ft	(561 m)

Largest deserts

NB – Most of Antarctica is a polar desert, with only 50mm of precipitation annually

Sahara	3,450,000 sq miles	(9,065,000 sq km)
Gobi	500,000 sq miles	(1,295,000 sq km)
Ar Rub al Khali	289,600 sq miles	(750,000 sq km)
Great Victorian	249,800 sq miles	(647,000 sq km)
Sonoran	120,000 sq miles	(311,000 sq km)
Kalahari	120,000 sq miles	(310,800 sq km)
Kara Kum	115,800 sq miles	(300,000 sq km)
Takla Makan	100,400 sq miles	(260,000 sq km)
Namib	52,100 sq miles	(135,000 sq km)
Thar	33,670 sq miles	(130,000 sq km)

Hottest inhabited places

Djibouti (Djibouti)	86° F	(30 °C)
Timbouctou (Mali)	84.7° F	(29.3 °C)
Tirunelveli (India)		
Tuticorin (India)		
Nellore (India)	84.5° F	(29.2 °C)
Santa Marta (Colombia)		
Aden (Yemen)	84° F	(28.9 °C)
Madurai (India)		
Niamey (Niger)		
Hodeida (Yemen)	83.8° F	(28.8 °C)
Ouagadougou (Burkina)		
Thanjavur (India)		
Tiruchchirappalli (India)		

Driest inhabited places

Aswân (Egypt)	0.02 in	(0.5 mm)
Luxor (Egypt)	0.03 in	(0.7 mm)
Arica (Chile)	0.04 in	(1.1 mm)
Ica (Peru)	0.1 in	(2.3 mm)
Antofagasta (Chile)	0.2 in	(4.9 mm)
El Minya (Egypt)	0.2 in	(5.1 mm)
Asyût (Egypt)	0.2 in	(5.2 mm)
Callao (Peru)	0.5 in	(12.0 mm)
Trujillo (Peru)	0.55 in	(14.0 mm)
El Faiyûm (Egypt)	0.8 in	(19.0 mm)

Wettest inhabited places

Buenaventura (Colombia)	265 in	(6743 mm)
Monrovia (Liberia)	202 in	(5131 mm)
Pago Pago (American Samoa)	196 in	(4990 mm)
Moulmein (Myanmar)	191 in	(4852 mm)
Lae (Papua New Guinea)	183 in	(4645 mm)
Baguio (Luzon Island, Philippines)	180 in	(4573 mm)
Sylhet (Bangladesh)	176 in	(4457 mm)
Padang (Sumatra, Indonesia)	166 in	(4225 mm)
Bogor (Java, Indonesia)	166 in	(4225 mm)
Conakry (Guinea)	171 in	(4341 mm)

Countries of the World

There are currently 194 independent countries in the world – more than at any previous time – and 59 dependencies. Antarctica is the only land area on Earth that is not officially part of, and does not belong to, any single country.

In 1950, the world comprised 82 countries. In the decades following, many more states came into being as they achieved independence from their former colonial rulers. Most recent additions were caused by the breakup of the former Soviet Union in 1991, and the former Yugoslavia in 1992, which swelled the ranks of independent states. In May 2006 Montenegro voted to split from Serbia, making it the latest country to gain independence.

Country factfile key

Formation Date of independence / date current borders were established

Population Total population / population density – based on total *land* area / percentage of urban-based population

Languages An asterisk (*) denotes the official language(s)

Calorie consumption Average number of calories consumed daily per person

AFGHANISTAN
Central Asia

Official name Islamic State of Afghanistan
Formation 1919 / 1919
Capital Kabul
Population 29.9 million / 119 people per sq mile (46 people per sq km) / 22%
Total area 250,000 sq miles (647,500 sq km)
Languages Pashtu*, Tajik, Dari, Farsi, Uzbek, Turkmen
Religions Sunni Muslim 84%, Shi'a Muslim 15%, Other 1%
Ethnic mix Pashtun 38%, Tajik 25%, Hazara 19%, Uzbek and Turkmen 15%, Other 3%
Government Transitional regime
Currency New afghani = 100 puls
Literacy rate 36%
Calorie consumption 1539 calories

ALBANIA
Southeast Europe

Official name Republic of Albania
Formation 1912 / 1921
Capital Tirana
Population 3.1 million / 293 people per sq mile (113 people per sq km) / 42%
Total area 11,100 sq miles (28,748 sq km)
Languages Albanian*, Greek
Religions Sunni Muslim 70%, Orthodox Christian 20%, Roman Catholic 10%
Ethnic mix Albanian 93%, Greek 5%, Other 2%
Government Parliamentary system
Currency Lek = 100 qindarka (qintars)
Literacy rate 99%
Calorie consumption 2848 calories

ALGERIA
North Africa

Official name People's Democratic Republic of Algeria
Formation 1962 / 1962
Capital Algiers
Population 32.9 million / 36 people per sq mile (14 people per sq km) / 60%
Total area 919,590 sq miles (2,381,740 sq km)
Languages Arabic, Tamazight (Kabyle, Shawia, Tamashek), French
Religions Sunni Muslim 99%, Christian and Jewish 1%
Ethnic mix Arab 75%, Berber 24%, European and Jewish 1%
Government Presidential system
Currency Algerian dinar = 100 centimes
Literacy rate 70%
Calorie consumption 3022 calories

ANDORRA
Southwest Europe

Official name Principality of Andorra
Formation 1278 / 1278
Capital Andorra la Vella
Population 70,549 / 392 people per sq mile (152 people per sq km) / 63%
Total area 181 sq miles (468 sq km)
Languages Spanish, Catalan, French, Portuguese
Religions Roman Catholic 94%, Other 6%
Ethnic mix Spanish 46%, Andorran 28%, Other 18%, French 8%
Government Parliamentary system
Currency Euro = 100 cents
Literacy rate 99%
Calorie consumption Not available

ANGOLA
Southern Africa

Official name Republic of Angola
Formation 1975 / 1975
Capital Luanda
Population 15.9 million / 33 people per sq mile (13 people per sq km) / 34%
Total area 481,351 sq miles (1,246,700 sq km)
Languages Portuguese*, Umbundu, Kimbundu, Kikongo
Religions Roman Catholic 50%, Other 30%, Protestant 20%
Ethnic mix Ovimbundu 37%, Other 25%, Kimbundu 25%, Bakongo 13%
Government Presidential system
Currency Readjusted kwanza = 100 lwei
Literacy rate 67%
Calorie consumption 2083 calories

ANTIGUA & BARBUDA
West Indies

Official name Antigua and Barbuda
Formation 1981 / 1981
Capital St. John's
Population 68,722 / 404 people per sq mile (156 people per sq km) / 37%
Total area 170 sq miles (442 sq km)
Languages English, English patois
Religions Anglican 45%, Other Protestant 42%, Roman Catholic 10%, Other 2%, Rastafarian 1%
Ethnic mix Black African 95%, Other 5%
Government Parliamentary system
Currency Eastern Caribbean dollar = 100 cents
Literacy rate 86%
Calorie consumption 2349 calories

ARGENTINA
South America

Official name Republic of Argentina
Formation 1816 / 1816
Capital Buenos Aires
Population 38.7 million / 37 people per sq mile (14 people per sq km) / 90%
Total area 1,068,296 sq miles (2,766,890 sq km)
Languages Spanish*, Italian, Amerindian languages
Religions Roman Catholic 90%, Other 6%, Protestant 2%, Jewish 2%
Ethnic mix Indo-European 83%, Mestizo 14%, Jewish 2%, Amerindian 1%
Government Presidential system
Currency new Argentine peso = 100 centavos
Literacy rate 97%
Calorie consumption 2992 calories

ARMENIA
Southwest Asia

Official name Republic of Armenia
Formation 1991 / 1991
Capital Yerevan
Population 3 million / 261 people per sq mile (101 people per sq km) / 70%
Total area 11,506 sq miles (29,800 sq km)
Languages Armenian*, Azeri, Russian
Religions Armenian Apostolic Church (Orthodox) 94%, Other 6%
Ethnic mix Armenian 93%, Azeri 3%, Other 2%, Russian 2%
Government Presidential system
Currency Dram = 100 luma
Literacy rate 99%
Calorie consumption 2268 calories

AUSTRALIA
Australasia & Oceania

Official name Commonwealth of Australia
Formation 1901 / 1901
Capital Canberra
Population 20.2 million / 7 people per sq mile (3 people per sq km) / 85%
Total area 2,967,893 sq miles (7,686,850 sq km)
Languages English*, Italian, Cantonese, Greek, Arabic, Vietnamese, Aboriginal languages
Religions Roman Catholic 26%, Anglican 24%, Other 23%, Nonreligious 13%, United Church 8%, Other Protestant 6%
Ethnic mix European 92%, Asian 5%, Aboriginal and other 3%
Government Parliamentary system
Currency Australian dollar = 100 cents
Literacy rate 99%
Calorie consumption 3054 calories

AUSTRIA
Central Europe

Official name Republic of Austria
Formation 1918 / 1919
Capital Vienna
Population 8.2 million / 257 people per sq mile (99 people per sq km) / 65%
Total area 32,378 sq miles (83,858 sq km)
Languages German*, Croatian, Slovenian, Hungarian (Magyar)
Religions Roman Catholic 78%, Nonreligious 9%, Other (including Jewish and Muslim) 8%, Protestant 5%
Ethnic mix Austrian 93%, Croat, Slovene, and Hungarian 6%, Other 1%
Government Parliamentary system
Currency Euro = 100 cents
Literacy rate 99%
Calorie consumption 3673 calories

AZERBAIJAN
Southwest Asia

Official name Republic of Azerbaijan
Formation 1991 / 1991
Capital Baku
Population 8.4 million / 251 people per sq mile (97 people per sq km) / 57%
Total area 33,436 sq miles (86,600 sq km)
Languages Azeri, Russian
Religions Shi'a Muslim 68%, Sunni Muslim 26%, Russian Orthodox 3%, Armenian Apostolic Church (Orthodox) 2%, Other 1%
Ethnic mix Azeri 90%, Dagestani 3%, Russian 3%, Other 2%, Armenian 2%
Government Presidential system
Currency Manat = 100 gopik
Literacy rate 99%
Calorie consumption 2575 calories

BAHAMAS
West Indies

Official name Commonwealth of the Bahamas
Formation 1973 / 1973
Capital Nassau
Population 323,000 / 84 people per sq mile (32 people per sq km) / 89%
Total area 5382 sq miles (13,940 sq km)
Languages English*, English Creole, French Creole
Religions Baptist 32%, Anglican 20%, Roman Catholic 19%, Other 17%, Methodist 6%, Church of God 6%
Ethnic mix Black African 85%, Other 15%
Government Parliamentary system
Currency Bahamian dollar = 100 cents
Literacy rate 96%
Calorie consumption 2755 calories

BAHRAIN
Southwest Asia

Official name Kingdom of Bahrain
Formation 1971 / 1971
Capital Manama
Population 727,000 / 2663 people per sq mile (1030 people per sq km) / 97%
Total area 239 sq miles (620 sq km)
Languages Arabic*
Religions Muslim (mainly Shi'a) 99%, Other 1%
Ethnic mix Bahraini 70%, Iranian, Indian, and Pakistani 24%, Other Arab 4%, European 2%
Government Monarchy
Currency Bahraini dinar = 1000 fils
Literacy rate 88%
Calorie consumption Not available

BANGLADESH
South Asia

Official name People's Republic of Bangladesh
Formation 1971 / 1971
Capital Dhaka
Population 142 million / 2743 people per sq mile (1059 people per sq km) / 25%
Total area 55,598 sq miles (144,000 sq km)
Languages Bengali*, Urdu, Chakma, Marma (Magh), Garo, Khasi, Santhali, Tripuri, Mro
Religions Muslim (mainly Sunni) 87%, Hindu 12%, Other 1%
Ethnic mix Bengali 98%, Other 2%
Government Parliamentary system
Currency Taka = 100 poisha
Literacy rate 41%
Calorie consumption 2205 calories

BARBADOS
West Indies

Official name Barbados
Formation 1966 / 1966
Capital Bridgetown
Population 270,000 / 1627 people per sq mile (628 people per sq km) / 50%
Total area 166 sq miles (430 sq km)
Languages English*, Bajan (Barbadian English)
Religions Anglican 40%, Other 24%, Nonreligious 17%, Pentecostal 8%, Methodist 7%, Roman Catholic 4%
Ethnic mix Black African 90%, Other 10%
Government Parliamentary system
Currency Barbados dollar = 100 cents
Literacy rate 99%
Calorie consumption 3091 calories

BELARUS
Eastern Europe

Official name Republic of Belarus
Formation 1991 / 1991
Capital Minsk
Population 9.8 million / 122 people per sq mile (47 people per sq km) / 71%
Total area 80,154 sq miles (207,600 sq km)
Languages Belarussian*, Russian
Religions Orthodox Christian 60%, Other 32%, Roman Catholic 8%
Ethnic mix Belarussian 78%, Russian 13%, Polish 4%, Ukrainian 3%, Other 2%
Government Presidential system
Currency Belarussian rouble = 100 kopeks
Literacy rate 99%
Calorie consumption 3000 calories

BELGIUM
Northwest Europe

Official name Kingdom of Belgium
Formation 1830 / 1919
Capital Brussels
Population 10.4 million / 821 people per sq mile (317 people per sq km) / 97%
Total area 11,780 sq miles (30,510 sq km)
Languages Dutch*, French*, German
Religions Roman Catholic 88%, Other 10%, Muslim 2%
Ethnic mix Fleming 58%, Walloon 33%, Other 6%, Italian 2%, Moroccan 1%
Government Parliamentary system
Currency Euro = 100 cents
Literacy rate 99%
Calorie consumption 3584 calories

BELIZE
Central America

Official name Belize
Formation 1981 / 1981
Capital Belmopan
Population 270,000 / 31 people per sq mile (12 people per sq km) / 54%
Total area 8867 sq miles (22,966 sq km)
Languages English*, English Creole, Spanish, Mayan, Garifuna (Carib)
Religions Roman Catholic 62%, Other 13%, Anglican 12%, Methodist 6%, Mennonite 4%, Seventh-day Adventist 3%
Ethnic mix Mestizo 44%, Creole 30%, Maya 11%, Garifuna 7%, Other 4%, Asian Indian 4%
Government Parliamentary system
Currency Belizean dollar = 100 cents
Literacy rate 77%
Calorie consumption 2869 calories

BENIN
West Africa

Official name Republic of Benin
Formation 1960 / 1960
Capital Porto-Novo
Population 8.4 million / 197 people per sq mile (76 people per sq km) / 42%
Total area 43,483 sq miles (112,620 sq km)
Languages French*, Fon, Bariba, Yoruba, Adja, Houeda, Somba
Religions Voodoo 50%, Muslim 30%, Christian 20%
Ethnic mix Fon 47%, Other 31%, Adja 12%, Bariba 10%
Government Presidential system
Currency CFA franc = 100 centimes
Literacy rate 34%
Calorie consumption 2548 calories

BHUTAN
Southeast Asia

Official name Kingdom of Bhutan
Formation 1656 / 1865
Capital Thimphu
Population 2.2 million / 121 people per sq mile (47 people per sq km) / 7%
Total area 18,147 sq miles (47,000 sq km)
Languages Dzongkha*, Nepali, Assamese
Religions Mahayana Buddhist 70%, Hindu 24%, Other 6%
Ethnic mix Bhute 50%, Other 25%, Nepalese 25%
Government Monarchy
Currency Ngultrum = 100 chetrum
Literacy rate 47%
Calorie consumption Not available

BOLIVIA
South America

Official name Republic of Bolivia
Formation 1825 /1938
Capital La Paz (administrative); Sucre (judicial)
Population 9.2 million / 22 people per sq mile (8 people per sq km) / 63%
Total area 424,162 sq miles (1,098,580 sq km)
Languages Aymara*, Quechua*, Spanish*
Religions Roman Catholic 93%, Other 7%
Ethnic mix Quechua 37%, Aymara 32%, Mixed race 13%, European 10%, Other 8%
Government Presidential system
Currency Boliviano = 100 centavos
Literacy rate 87%
Calorie consumption 2235 calories

BOSNIA & HERZEGOVINA
Southeast Europe

Official name Bosnia and Herzegovina
Formation 1992 / 1992
Capital Sarajevo
Population 3.9 million / 198 people per sq mile (76 people per sq km) / 43%
Total area 19,741 sq miles (51,129 sq km)
Languages Serbo-Croat*
Religions Muslim (mainly Sunni) 40%, Orthodox Christian 31%, Roman Catholic 15%, Other 10%, Protestant 4%
Ethnic mix Bosniak 48%, Serb 38%, Croat 14%
Government Parliamentary system
Currency Marka = 100 pfeninga
Literacy rate 95%
Calorie consumption 2894 calories

BOTSWANA
Southern Africa

Official name Republic of Botswana
Formation 1966 / 1966
Capital Gaborone
Population 1.8 million / 8 people per sq mile (3 people per sq km) / 50%
Total area 231,803 sq miles (600,370 sq km)
Languages English*, Setswana, Shona, San, Khoikhoi, isiNdebele
Religions Traditional beliefs 50%, Christian (mainly Protestant) 30%, Other (including Muslim) 20%
Ethnic mix Tswana 98%, Other 2%
Government Presidential system
Currency Pula = 100 thebe
Literacy rate 79%
Calorie consumption 2151 calories

BRAZIL
South America

Official name Federative Republic of Brazil
Formation 1822 / 1828
Capital Brasilia
Population 186 million / 57 people per sq mile (22 people per sq km) / 81%
Total area 3,286,470 sq miles (8,511,965 sq km)
Languages Portuguese*, German, Italian, Spanish, Polish, Japanese, Amerindian languages
Religions Roman Catholic 74%, Protestant 15%, Atheist 7%, Other 4%
Ethnic mix Black 53%, Mixed race 40%, White 6%, Other 1%
Government Presidential system
Currency Real = 100 centavos
Literacy rate 88%
Calorie consumption 3049 calories

BRUNEI
Southeast Asia

Official name Sultanate of Brunei
Formation 1984 / 1984
Capital Bandar Seri Begawan
Population 374,000 / 184 people per sq mile (71 people per sq km) / 72%
Total area 2228 sq miles (5770 sq km)
Languages Malay*, English, Chinese
Religions Muslim (mainly Sunni) 66%, Buddhist 14%, Other 10%, Christian 10%
Ethnic mix Malay 67%, Chinese 16%, Other 11%, Indigenous 6%
Government Monarchy
Currency Brunei dollar = 100 cents
Literacy rate 93%
Calorie consumption 2855 calories

BULGARIA
Southeast Europe

Official name Republic of Bulgaria
Formation 1908 / 1947
Capital Sofia
Population 7.7 million / 180 people per sq mile (70 people per sq km) / 70%
Total area 42,822 sq miles (110,910 sq km)
Languages Bulgarian*, Turkish, Romani
Religions Orthodox Christian 83%, Muslim 12%, Other 4%, Roman Catholic 1%
Ethnic mix Bulgarian 84%, Turkish 9%, Roma 5%, Other 2%
Government Parliamentary system
Currency Lev = 100 stotinki
Literacy rate 98%
Calorie consumption 2848 calories

BURKINA
West Africa

Official name Burkina Faso
Formation 1960 / 1960
Capital Ouagadougou
Population 13.2 million / 125 people per sq mile (48 people per sq km) / 19%
Total area 105,869 sq miles (274,200 sq km)
Languages French*, Mossi, Fulani, Tuareg, Dyula, Songhai
Religions Muslim 55%, Traditional beliefs 35%, Roman Catholic 9%, Other Christian 1%
Ethnic mix Other 50%, Mossi 50%
Government Presidential system
Currency CFA franc = 100 centimes
Literacy rate 13%
Calorie consumption 2462 calories

BURUNDI
Central Africa

Official name Republic of Burundi
Formation 1962 / 1962
Capital Bujumbura
Population 7.5 million / 757 people per sq mile (292 people per sq km) / 9%
Total area 10,745 sq miles (27,830 sq km)
Languages Kirundi*, French*, Kiswahili
Religions Christian 60%, Traditional beliefs 39%, Muslim 1%
Ethnic mix Hutu 85%, Tutsi 14%, Twa 1%
Government Presidential system
Currency Burundi franc = 100 centimes
Literacy rate 59%
Calorie consumption 1649 calories

CAMBODIA
Southeast Asia

Official name Kingdom of Cambodia
Formation 1953 / 1953
Capital Phnom Penh
Population 14.1 million / 207 people per sq mile (80 people per sq km) / 16%
Total area 69,900 sq miles (181,040 sq km)
Languages Khmer*, French, Chinese, Vietnamese, Cham
Religions Buddhist 93%, Muslim 6%, Christian 1%
Ethnic mix Khmer 90%, Other 5%, Vietnamese 4%, Chinese 1%
Government Parliamentary system
Currency Riel = 100 sen
Literacy rate 74%
Calorie consumption 2046 calories

CAMEROON
Central Africa

Official name Republic of Cameroon
Formation 1960 / 1961
Capital Yaoundé
Population 16.3 million / 907 people per sq mile (350 people per sq km) / 49%
Total area 183,567 sq miles (475,400 sq km)
Languages English*, French*, Bamileke, Fang, Fulani
Religions Roman Catholic 35%, Traditional beliefs 25%, Muslim 22%, Protestant 18%
Ethnic mix Cameroon highlanders 31%, Other 21%, Equatorial Bantu 19%, Kirdi 11%, Fulani 10%, Northwestern Bantu 8%
Government Presidential system
Currency CFA franc = 100 centimes
Literacy rate 68%
Calorie consumption 2273 calories

CANADA
North America

Official name Canada
Formation 1867 / 1949
Capital Ottawa
Population 32.3 million / 9 people per sq mile (4 people per sq km) / 77%
Total area 3,717,792 sq miles (9,984,670 sq km)
Languages English*, French*, Chinese, Italian, German, Ukrainian, Inuktitut, Cree
Religions Roman Catholic 44%, Protestant 29%, Other and nonreligious 27%
Ethnic mix British origin 44%, French origin 25%, Other European 20%, Other 11%.
Government Parliamentary system
Currency Canadian dollar = 100 cents
Literacy rate 99%
Calorie consumption 3589 calories

CAPE VERDE
Atlantic Ocean

Official name Republic of Cape Verde
Formation 1975
Capital Praia
Population 507,000 / 326 people per sq mile (126 people per sq km) / 62%
Total area 1557 sq miles (4033 sq km)
Languages Portuguese*, Portuguese Creole
Religions Roman Catholic 97%, Other 2%, Protestant (Church of the Nazarene) 1%
Ethnic mix Mestiço 60%, African 30%, Other 10%
Government Mixed presidential–parliamentary system
Currency Cape Verde escudo = 100 centavos
Literacy rate 76%
Calorie consumption 3243 calories

CENTRAL AFRICAN REPUBLIC
Central Africa

Official name Central African Republic
Formation 1960 / 1960
Capital Bangui
Population 4 million / 17 people per sq mile (6 people per sq km) / 41%
Total area 240,534 sq miles (622,984 sq km)
Languages Sango, Banda, Gbaya, French
Religions Traditional beliefs 60%, Christian (mainly Roman Catholic) 35%, Muslim 5%
Ethnic mix Baya 34%, Banda 27%, Mandjia 21%, Sara 10%, Other 8%
Government Presidential system
Currency CFA franc = 100 centimes
Literacy rate 49%
Calorie consumption 1980 calories

CHAD
Central Africa

Official name Republic of Chad
Formation 1960 / 1960
Capital N'Djamena
Population 9.7 million / 20 people per sq mile (8 people per sq km) / 24%
Total area 495,752 sq miles (1,284,000 sq km)
Languages French, Sara, Arabic, Maba
Religions Muslim 55%, Traditional beliefs 35%, Christian 10%
Ethnic mix Nomads (Tuareg and Toubou) 38%, Sara 30%, Other 17%, Arab 15%
Government Presidential system
Currency CFA franc = 100 centimes
Literacy rate 26%
Calorie consumption 2114 calories

CHILE
South America

Official name Republic of Chile
Formation 1818 / 1883
Capital Santiago
Population 16.3 million / 56 people per sq mile (22 people per sq km) / 86%
Total area 292,258 sq miles (756,950 sq km)
Languages Spanish*, Amerindian languages
Religions Roman Catholic 80%, Other and nonreligious 20%
Ethnic mix Mixed race and European 90%, Amerindian 10%
Government Presidential system
Currency Chilean peso = 100 centavos
Literacy rate 96%
Calorie consumption 2863 calories

CHINA
East Asia

Official name People's Republic of China
Formation 960 / 1999
Capital Beijing
Population 1.32 billion / 365 people per sq mile (141 people per sq km) / 32%
Total area 3,705,386 sq miles (9,596,960 sq km)
Languages Mandarin*, Wu, Cantonese, Hsiang, Min, Hakka, Kan
Religions Nonreligious 59%, Traditional beliefs 20%, Other 13%, Buddhist 6%, Muslim 2%
Ethnic mix Han 92%, Other 6%, Hui 1%, Zhuang 1%
Government One-party state
Currency Renminbi (known as yuan) = 10 jiao
Literacy rate 91%
Calorie consumption 2951 calories

COLOMBIA
South America

Official name Republic of Colombia
Formation 1819 / 1903
Capital Bogotá
Population 45.6 million / 114 people per sq mile (44 people per sq km) / 74%
Total area 439,733 sq miles (1,138,910 sq km)
Languages Spanish*, Wayuu, Páez, and other Amerindian languages
Religions Roman Catholic 95%, Other 5%
Ethnic mix Mestizo 58%, White 20%, European–African 14%, African 4%, African–Amerindian 3%, Amerindian 1%
Government Presidential system
Currency Colombian peso = 100 centavos
Literacy rate 94%
Calorie consumption 2585 calories

COMOROS
Indian Ocean

Official name Union of the Comoros
Formation 1975 / 1975
Capital Moroni
Population 798,000 / 927 people per sq mile (358 people per sq km) / 33%
Total area 838 sq miles (2170 sq km)
Languages Arabic*, Comoran, French
Religions Muslim (mainly Sunni) 98%, Other 1%, Roman Catholic 1%
Ethnic mix Comoran 97%, Other 3%
Government Presidential system
Currency Comoros franc = 100 centimes
Literacy rate 56%
Calorie consumption 1754 calories

CONGO
Central Africa

Official name Republic of the Congo
Formation 1960 / 1960
Capital Brazzaville
Population 4 million / 30 people per sq mile (12 people per sq km) / 63%
Total area 132,046 sq miles (342,000 sq km)
Languages French*, Kongo, Teke, Lingala
Religions Traditional beliefs 50%, Roman Catholic 25%, Protestant 23%, Muslim 2%
Ethnic mix Bakongo 48%, Sangha 20%, Teke 17%, Mbochi 12%, Other 3%
Government Presidential system
Currency CFA franc = 100 centimes
Literacy rate 83%
Calorie consumption 2162 calories

CONGO, DEM. REP.
Central Africa

Official name Democratic Republic of the Congo
Formation 1960 / 1960
Capital Kinshasa
Population 57.5 million / 66 people per sq mile (25 people per sq km) / 30%
Total area 905,563 sq miles (2,345,410 sq km)
Languages French*, Kiswahili, Tshiluba, Kikongo, Lingala
Religions Roman Catholic 50%, Protestant 20%, Traditional beliefs and other 10%, Muslim 10%, Kimbanguist 10%
Ethnic mix Other 55%, Bantu and Hamitic 45%
Government Transitional regime
Currency Congolese franc = 100 centimes
Literacy rate 65%
Calorie consumption 1599 calories

COSTA RICA
Central America

Official name Republic of Costa Rica
Formation 1838 / 1838
Capital San José
Population 4.3 million / 218 people per sq mile (84 people per sq km) / 52%
Total area 19,730 sq miles (51,100 sq km)
Languages Spanish*, English Creole, Bribri, Cabecar
Religions Roman Catholic 76%, Other (including Protestant) 24%
Ethnic mix Mestizo and European 96%, Black 2%, Chinese 1%, Amerindian 1%
Government Presidential system
Currency Costa Rican colón = 100 centimos
Literacy rate 96%
Calorie consumption 2876 calories

CROATIA
Southeast Europe

Official name Republic of Croatia
Formation 1991 / 1991
Capital Zagreb
Population 4.6 million / 211 people per sq mile (81 people per sq km) / 58%
Total area 21,831 sq miles (56,542 sq km)
Languages Croatian*
Religions Roman Catholic 88%, Other 7%, Orthodox Christian 4%, Muslim 1%
Ethnic mix Croat 90%, Other 5%, Serb 4%, Bosniak 1%
Government Parliamentary system
Currency Kuna = 100 lipas
Literacy rate 98%
Calorie consumption 2799 calories

CUBA
West Indies

Official name Republic of Cuba
Formation 1902 / 1902
Capital Havana
Population 11.3 million / 264 people per sq mile (102 people per sq km) / 75%
Total area 42,803 sq miles (110,860 sq km)
Languages Spanish*
Religions Nonreligious 49%, Roman Catholic 40%, Atheist 6%, Other 4%, Protestant 1%
Ethnic mix White 66%, European–African 22%, Black 12%
Government One-party state
Currency Cuban peso = 100 centavos
Literacy rate 97%
Calorie consumption 3152 calories

CYPRUS
Southeast Europe

Official name Republic of Cyprus
Formation 1960 / 1960
Capital Nicosia
Population 835,000 / 234 people per sq mile (90 people per sq km) / 57%
Total area 3571 sq miles (9250 sq km)
Languages Greek, Turkish
Religions Orthodox Christian 78%, Muslim 18%, Other 4%
Ethnic mix Greek 85%, Turkish 12%, Other 3%
Government Presidential system
Currency Cyprus pound (Turkish lira in TRNC) = 100 cents (Cyprus pound); 100 kurus (Turkish lira)
Literacy rate 97%
Calorie consumption 3255 calories

CZECH REPUBLIC
Central Europe

Official name Czech Republic
Formation 1993 / 1993
Capital Prague
Population 10.2 million / 335 people per sq mile (129 people per sq km) / 75%
Total area 30,450 sq miles (78,866 sq km)
Languages Czech*, Slovak, Hungarian (Magyar)
Religions Roman Catholic 39%, Atheist 38%, Other 18%, Protestant 3%, Hussite 2%
Ethnic mix Czech 81%, Moravian 13%, Slovak 6%
Government Parliamentary system
Currency Czech koruna = 100 haleru
Literacy rate 99%
Calorie consumption 3171 calories

DENMARK
Northern Europe

Official name Kingdom of Denmark
Formation AD 950 / 1945
Capital Copenhagen
Population 5.4 million / 330 people per sq mile (127 people per sq km) / 85%
Total area 16,639 sq miles (43,094 sq km)
Languages Danish*
Religions Evangelical Lutheran 89%, Other 10%, Roman Catholic 1%
Ethnic mix Danish 96%, Other (including Scandinavian and Turkish) 3%, Faeroese and Inuit 1%
Government Parliamentary system
Currency Danish krone = 100 øre
Literacy rate 99%
Calorie consumption 3439 calories

DJIBOUTI
East Africa

Official name Republic of Djibouti
Formation 1977 / 1977
Capital Djibouti
Population 793,000 / 89 people per sq mile (34 people per sq km) / 83%
Total area 8494 sq miles (22,000 sq km)
Languages French*, Arabic*, Somali, Afar
Religions Muslim (mainly Sunni) 94%, Christian 6%
Ethnic mix Issa 60%, Afar 35%, Other 5%
Government Presidential system
Currency Djibouti franc = 100 centimes
Literacy rate 66%
Calorie consumption 2220 calories

DOMINICA
West Indies

Official name Commonwealth of Dominica
Formation 1978 / 1978
Capital Roseau
Population 69,029 / 238 people per sq mile (92 people per sq km) / 71%
Total area 291 sq miles (754 sq km)
Languages English*, French Creole
Religions Roman Catholic 77%, Protestant 15%, Other 8%
Ethnic mix Black 91%, Mixed race 6%, Carib 2%, Other 1%
Government Parliamentary system
Currency Eastern Caribbean dollar = 100 cents
Literacy rate 88%
Calorie consumption 2763 calories

DOMINICAN REPUBLIC
West Indies

Official name Dominican Republic
Formation 1865 / 1865
Capital Santo Domingo
Population 8.9 million / 476 people per sq mile (184 people per sq km) / 65%
Total area 18,679 sq miles (48,380 sq km)
Languages Spanish*, French Creole
Religions Roman Catholic 92%, Other and nonreligious 8%
Ethnic mix Mixed race 75%, White 15%, Black 10%
Government Presidential system
Currency Dominican Republic peso = 100 centavos
Literacy rate 88%
Calorie consumption 2347 calories

EAST TIMOR
Southeast Asia

Official name Democratic Republic of Timor-Leste
Formation 2002 / 2002
Capital Dili
Population 947,000 / 168 people per sq mile (65 people per sq km) / 8%
Total area 5756 sq miles (14,874 sq km)
Languages Tetum (Portuguese/Austronesian), Bahasa Indonesia, and Portuguese
Religions Roman Catholic 95%, Other (including Muslim and Protestant) 5%
Ethnic mix Papuan groups approx 85%, Indonesian approx 13%, Chinese 2%
Government Parliamentary system
Currency US dollar = 100 cents
Literacy rate 59%
Calorie consumption 2806 calories

ECUADOR
South America

Official name Republic of Ecuador
Formation 1830 / 1941
Capital Quito
Population 13.2 million / 123 people per sq mile (48 people per sq km) / 65%
Total area 109,483 sq miles (283,560 sq km)
Languages Spanish*, Quechua*, other Amerindian languages
Religions Roman Catholic 93%, Protestant, Jewish, and other 7%
Ethnic mix Mestizo 55%, Amerindian 25%, White 10%, Black 10%
Government Presidential system
Currency US dollar = 100 cents
Literacy rate 91%
Calorie consumption 2754 calories

EGYPT
North Africa

Official name Arab Republic of Egypt
Formation 1936 / 1982
Capital Cairo
Population 74 million / 193 people per sq mile (74 people per sq km) / 45%
Total area 386,660 sq miles (1,001,450 sq km)
Languages Arabic*, French, English, Berber
Religions Muslim (mainly Sunni) 94%, Coptic Christian and other 6%
Ethnic mix Eastern Hamitic 90%, Nubian, Armenian, and Greek 10%
Government Presidential system
Currency Egyptian pound = 100 piastres
Literacy rate 56%
Calorie consumption 3338 calories

EL SALVADOR
Central America

Official name Republic of El Salvador
Formation 1841 / 1841
Capital San Salvador
Population 6.9 million / 862 people per sq mile (333 people per sq km) / 47%
Total area 8124 sq miles (21,040 sq km)
Languages Spanish*
Religions Roman Catholic 80%, Evangelical 18%, Other 2%
Ethnic mix Mestizo 94%, Amerindian 5%, White 1%
Government Presidential system
Currency Salvadorean colón & US dollar = 100 centavos (colón); 100 cents (US dollar)
Literacy rate 80%
Calorie consumption 2584 calories

EQUATORIAL GUINEA
Central Africa

Official name Republic of Equatorial Guinea
Formation 1968 / 1968
Capital Malabo
Population 504,000 / 47 people per sq mile (18 people per sq km) / 48%
Total area 10,830 sq miles (28,051 sq km)
Languages Spanish*, Fang, Bubi
Religions Roman Catholic 90%, Other 10%
Ethnic mix Fang 85%, Other 11%, Bubi 4%
Government Presidential system
Currency CFA franc = 100 centimes
Literacy rate 84%
Calorie consumption Not available

ERITREA
East Africa

Official name State of Eritrea
Formation 1993 / 2002
Capital Asmara
Population 4.4 million / 97 people per sq mile (37 people per sq km) / 19%
Total area 46,842 sq miles (121,320 sq km)
Languages Arabic*, Tigrinya*, English, Tigre, Afar, Bilen, Kunama, Nara, Saho, Hadareb
Religions Christian 45%, Muslim 45%, Other 10%
Ethnic mix Tigray 50%, Tigray and Kunama 40%, Afar 4%, Other 3%, Saho 3%
Government Transitional regime
Currency Nakfa = 100 cents
Literacy rate 57%
Calorie consumption 1513 calories

COUNTRIES OF THE WORLD
300

ESTONIA
Northeast Europe

Official name Republic of Estonia
Formation 1991 / 1991
Capital Tallinn
Population 1.3 million / 75 people per sq mile (29 people per sq km) / 69%
Total area 17,462 sq miles (45,226 sq km)
Languages Estonian*, Russian
Religions Evangelical Lutheran 56%, Orthodox Christian 25%, Other 19%
Ethnic mix Estonian 62%, Russian 30%, Other 8%
Government Parliamentary system
Currency Kroon = 100 senti
Literacy rate 99%
Calorie consumption 3002 calories

ETHIOPIA
East Africa

Official name Federal Democratic Republic of Ethiopia
Formation 1896 / 2002
Capital Addis Ababa
Population 77.4 million / 181 people per sq mile (70 people per sq km) / 18%
Total area 435,184 sq miles (1,127,127 sq km)
Languages Amharic*, Tigrinya, Galla, Sidamo, Somali, English, Arabic
Religions Orthodox Christian 40%, Muslim 40%, Traditional beliefs 15%, Other 5%
Ethnic mix Oromo 40%, Amhara 25%, Other 14%, Sidamo 9%, Berta 6%, Somali 6%
Government Parliamentary system
Currency Ethiopian birr = 100 cents
Literacy rate 42%
Calorie consumption 1857 calories

FIJI
Australasia & Oceania

Official name Republic of the Fiji Islands
Formation 1970 / 1970
Capital Suva
Population 848,000 / 120 people per sq mile (46 people per sq km) / 49%
Total area 7054 sq miles (18,270 sq km)
Languages English*, Fijian*, Hindi, Urdu, Tamil, Telugu
Religions Hindu 38%, Methodist 37%, Roman Catholic 9%, Other 8%, Muslim 8%
Ethnic mix Melanesian 48%, Indian 46%, Other 6%
Government Parliamentary system
Currency Fiji dollar = 100 cents
Literacy rate 93%
Calorie consumption 2894 calories

FINLAND
Northern Europe

Official name Republic of Finland
Formation 1917 / 1947
Capital Helsinki
Population 5.2 million / 44 people per sq mile (17 people per sq km) / 67%
Total area 130,127 sq miles (337,030 sq km)
Languages Finnish*, Swedish*, Sámi
Religions Evangelical Lutheran 89%, Orthodox Christian 1%, Roman Catholic 1%, Other 9%
Ethnic mix Finnish 93%, Other (including Sámi) 7%
Government Parliamentary system
Currency Euro = 100 cents
Literacy rate 99%
Calorie consumption 3100 calories

FRANCE
Western Europe

Official name French Republic
Formation 987 / 1919
Capital Paris
Population 60.5 million / 285 people per sq mile (110 people per sq km) / 76%
Total area 211,208 sq miles (547,030 sq km)
Languages French*, Provençal, German, Breton, Catalan, Basque
Religions Roman Catholic 88%, Muslim 8%, Protestant 2%, Buddhist 1%, Jewish 1%
Ethnic mix French 90%, North African (mainly Algerian) 6%, German (Alsace) 2%, Breton 1%, Other (including Corsicans) 1%
Government Mixed presidential–parliamentary system
Currency Euro = 100 cents
Literacy rate 99%
Calorie consumption 3654 calories

GABON
Central Africa

Official name Gabonese Republic
Formation 1960 / 1960
Capital Libreville
Population 1.4 million / 14 people per sq mile (5 people per sq km) / 81%
Total area 103,346 sq miles (267,667 sq km)
Languages French*,Fang, Punu, Sira, Nzebi, Mpongwe
Religions Christian (mainly Roman Catholic) 55%, Traditional beliefs 40%, Other 4%, Muslim 1%
Ethnic mix Fang 35%, Other Bantu 29%, Eshira 25%, European and other African 9%, French 2%
Government Presidential system
Currency CFA franc = 100 centimes
Literacy rate 71%
Calorie consumption 2637 calories

GAMBIA
West Africa

Official name Republic of the Gambia
Formation 1965 / 1965
Capital Banjul
Population 1.5 million / 389 people per sq mile (150 people per sq km) / 33%
Total area 4363 sq miles (11,300 sq km)
Languages English*, Mandinka, Fulani, Wolof, Jola, Soninke
Religions Sunni Muslim 90%, Christian 9%, Traditional beliefs 1%
Ethnic mix Mandinka 42%, Fulani 18%, Wolof 16%, Jola 10%, Serahuli 9%, Other 5%
Government Presidential system
Currency Dalasi = 100 butut
Literacy rate 38%
Calorie consumption 2273 calories

GEORGIA
Southwest Asia

Official name Georgia
Formation 1991 / 1991
Capital Tbilisi
Population 4.5 million / 167 people per sq mile (65 people per sq km) / 61%
Total area 26,911 sq miles (69,700 sq km)
Languages Georgian*, Russian, Azeri, Armenian, Mingrelian, Ossetian, Abkhazian
Religions Georgian Orthodox 65%, Muslim 11%, Russian Orthodox 10%, Armenian Orthodox 8%, Other 6%
Ethnic mix Georgian 70%, Armenian 8%, Russian 6%, Azeri 6%, Ossetian 3%, Other 7%
Government Presidential system
Currency Lari = 100 tetri
Literacy rate 99%
Calorie consumption 2354 calories

GERMANY
Northern Europe

Official name Federal Republic of Germany
Formation 1871 / 1990
Capital Berlin
Population 82.7 million / 613 people per sq mile (237 people per sq km) / 88%
Total area 137,846 sq miles (357,021 sq km)
Languages German*, Turkish
Religions Protestant 34%, Roman Catholic 33%, Other 30%, Muslim 3%
Ethnic mix German 92%, Other 3%, Other European 3%, Turkish 2%
Government Parliamentary system
Currency Euro = 100 cents
Literacy rate 99%
Calorie consumption 3496 calories

GHANA
West Africa

Official name Republic of Ghana
Formation 1957 / 1957
Capital Accra
Population 22.1 million / 249 people per sq mile (96 people per sq km) / 38%
Total area 92,100 sq miles (238,540 sq km)
Languages Twi, Fanti, Ewe, Ga, Adangbe, Gurma, Dagomba (Dagbani)
Religions Christian 69%, Muslim 16%, Traditional beliefs 9%, Other 6%
Ethnic mix Ashanti and Fanti 52%, Moshi-Dagomba 16%, Ewe 12%, Other 11%, Ga and Ga-adanbe 8%, Yoruba 1%
Government Presidential system
Currency Cedi = 100 psewas
Literacy rate 54%
Calorie consumption 2667 calories

GREECE
Southeast Europe

Official name Hellenic Republic
Formation 1829 / 1947
Capital Athens
Population 11.1 million / 220 people per sq mile (85 people per sq km) / 60%
Total area 50,942 sq miles (131,940 sq km)
Languages Greek*, Turkish, Macedonian, Albanian
Religions Orthodox Christian 98%, Other 1%, Muslim 1%
Ethnic mix Greek 98%, Other 2%
Government Parliamentary system
Currency Euro = 100 cents
Literacy rate 91%
Calorie consumption 3721 calories

GRENADA
West Indies

Official name Grenada
Formation 1974 / 1974
Capital St. George's
Population 89,502 / 683 people per sq mile (263 people per sq km) / 38%
Total area 131 sq miles (340 sq km)
Languages English*, English Creole
Religions Roman Catholic 68%, Anglican 17%, Other 15%
Ethnic mix Black African 82%, Mulatto (mixed race) 13%, East Indian 3%, Other 2%
Government Parliamentary system
Currency Eastern Caribbean dollar = 100 cents
Literacy rate 96%
Calorie consumption 2932 calories

GUATEMALA
Central America

Official name Republic of Guatemala
Formation 1838 / 1838
Capital Guatemala City
Population 12.6 million / 301 people per sq mile (116 people per sq km) / 40%
Total area 42,042 sq miles (108,890 sq km)
Languages Spanish*, Quiché, Mam, Cakchiquel, Kekchí
Religions Roman Catholic 65%, Protestant 33%, Other and nonreligious 2%
Ethnic mix Amerindian 60%, Mestizo 30%, Other 10%
Government Presidential system
Currency Quetzal = 100 centavos
Literacy rate 69%
Calorie consumption 2219 calories

GUINEA
West Africa

Official name Republic of Guinea
Formation 1958 / 1958
Capital Conakry
Population 9.4 million / 99 people per sq mile (38 people per sq km) / 33%
Total area 94,925 sq miles (245,857 sq km)
Languages French*, Fulani, Malinke, Soussou
Religions Muslim 65%, Traditional beliefs 33%, Christian 2%
Ethnic mix Fulani 30%, Malinke 30%, Soussou 15%, Kissi 10%, Other tribes 10%, Other 5%
Government Presidential system
Currency Guinea franc = 100 centimes
Literacy rate 41%
Calorie consumption 2409 calories

GUINEA-BISSAU
West Africa

Official name Republic of Guinea-Bissau
Formation 1974 / 1974
Capital Bissau
Population 1.6 million / 147 people per sq mile (57 people per sq km) / 24%
Total area 13,946 sq miles (36,120 sq km)
Languages Portuguese*, Balante, Fulani, Malinke, Portuguese Creole
Religions Traditional beliefs 52%, Muslim 40%, Christian 8%
Ethnic mix Other tribes 31%, Balante 25%, Fula 20%, Mandinka 12%, Mandyako 11%, Other 1%
Government Presidential system
Currency CFA franc = 100 centimes
Literacy rate 40%
Calorie consumption 2024 calories

GUYANA
South America

Official name Cooperative Republic of Guyana
Formation 1966 / 1966
Capital Georgetown
Population 751,000 / 10 people per sq mile (4 people per sq km) / 38%
Total area 83,000 sq miles (214,970 sq km)
Languages English*, Hindi, Tamil, Amerindian languages, English Creole
Religions Christian 57%, Hindu 33%, Muslim 9%, Other 1%
Ethnic mix East Indian 52%, Black African 38%, Other 4%, Amerindian 4%, European and Chinese 2%
Government Presidential system
Currency Guyanese dollar = 100 cents
Literacy rate 97%
Calorie consumption 2692 calories

HAITI
West Indies

Official name Republic of Haiti
Formation 1804 / 1844
Capital Port-au-Prince
Population 8.5 million / 799 people per sq mile (308 people per sq km) / 36%
Total area 10,714 sq miles (27,750 sq km)
Languages French Creole*, French*
Religions Roman Catholic 80%, Protestant 16%, Other (including Voodoo) 3%, Nonreligious 1%
Ethnic mix Black African 95%, Mulatto (mixed race) and European 5%
Government Transitional regime
Currency Gourde = 100 centimes
Literacy rate 52%
Calorie consumption 2086 calories

HONDURAS
Central America

Official name Republic of Honduras
Formation 1838 / 1838
Capital Tegucigalpa
Population 7.2 million / 167 people per sq mile (64 people per sq km) / 53%
Total area 43,278 sq miles (112,090 sq km)
Languages Spanish*, Garifuna (Carib), English Creole
Religions Roman Catholic 97%, Protestant 3%
Ethnic mix Mestizo 90%, Black African 5%, Amerindian 4%, White 1%
Government Presidential system
Currency Lempira = 100 centavos
Literacy rate 80%
Calorie consumption 2356 calories

HUNGARY
Central Europe

Official name Republic of Hungary
Formation 1918 / 1947
Capital Budapest
Population 10.1 million / 283 people per sq mile (109 people per sq km) / 64%
Total area 35,919 sq miles (93,030 sq km)
Languages Hungarian (Magyar)*
Religions Roman Catholic 52%, Calvinist 16%, Other 15%, Nonreligious 14%, Lutheran 3%
Ethnic mix Magyar 90%, Other 7%, Roma 2%, German 1%
Government Parliamentary system
Currency Forint = 100 fillér
Literacy rate 99%
Calorie consumption 3483 calories

ICELAND
Northwest Europe

Official name Republic of Iceland
Formation 1944 / 1944
Capital Reykjavík
Population 295,000 / 8 people per sq mile (3 people per sq km) / 93%
Total area 39,768 sq miles (103,000 sq km)
Languages Icelandic*
Religions Evangelical Lutheran 93%, Nonreligious 6%, Other (mostly Christian) 1%
Ethnic mix Icelandic 94%, Other 5%, Danish 1%
Government Parliamentary system
Currency Icelandic króna = 100 aurar
Literacy rate 99%
Calorie consumption 3249 calories

INDIA
South Asia

Official name Republic of India
Formation 1947 / 1947
Capital New Delhi
Population 1.1 billion / 961 people per sq mile (371 people per sq km) / 28%
Total area 1,269,338 sq miles (3,287,590 sq km)
Languages Hindi*, English*, Bengali, Marathi, Telugu, Tamil, Bihari, Gujarati, Kanarese, Urdu
Religions Hindu 83%, Muslim 11%, Christian 2%, Sikh 2%, Other 1%, Buddhist 1%
Ethnic mix Indo-Aryan 72%, Dravidian 25%, Mongoloid and other 3%
Government Parliamentary system
Currency Indian rupee = 100 paise
Literacy rate 61%
Calorie consumption 2459 calories

INDONESIA
Southeast Asia

Official name Republic of Indonesia
Formation 1949 / 1999
Capital Jakarta
Population 223 million / 321 people per sq mile (124 people per sq km) / 41%
Total area 741,096 sq miles (1,919,440 sq km)
Languages Bahasa Indonesia*, Javanese, Sundanese, Madurese, Dutch
Religions Sunni Muslim 87%, Protestant 6%, Roman Catholic 3%, Hindu 2%, Other 1%, Buddhist 1%
Ethnic mix Javanese 45%, Sundanese 14%, Coastal Malays 8%, Madurese 8%, Other 25%
Government Presidential system
Currency Rupiah = 100 sen
Literacy rate 88%
Calorie consumption 2904 calories

IRAN
Southwest Asia

Official name Islamic Republic of Iran
Formation 1502 / 1990
Capital Tehran
Population 69.5 million / 110 people per sq mile (42 people per sq km) / 62%
Total area 636,293 sq miles (1,648,000 sq km)
Languages Farsi*, Azeri, Luri, Gilaki, Mazanderani, Kurdish, Turkmen, Arabic, Baluchi
Religions Shi'a Muslim 93%, Sunni Muslim 6%, Other 1%
Ethnic mix Persian 50%, Azari 24%, Other 10%, Kurdish 8%, Lur and Bakhtiari 8%
Government Islamic theocracy
Currency Iranian rial = 100 dinars
Literacy rate 77%
Calorie consumption 3085 calories

IRAQ
Southwest Asia

Official name Republic of Iraq
Formation 1932 / 1990
Capital Baghdad
Population 28.8 million / 171 people per sq mile (66 people per sq km) / 77%
Total area 168,753 sq miles (437,072 sq km)
Languages Arabic*, Kurdish, Turkic languages, Armenian, Assyrian
Religions Shi'a Muslim 60%, Sunni Muslim 35%, Other (including Christian) 5%
Ethnic mix Arab 80%, Kurdish 15%, Turkmen 3%, Other 2%
Government Transitional regime
Currency New Iraqi dinar = 1000 fils
Literacy rate 40%
Calorie consumption 2197 calories

IRELAND
Northwest Europe

Official name Ireland
Formation 1922 / 1922
Capital Dublin
Population 4.1 million / 154 people per sq mile (60 people per sq km) / 59%
Total area 27,135 sq miles (70,280 sq km)
Languages English*, Irish Gaelic*
Religions Roman Catholic 88%, Other and nonreligious 9%, Anglican 3%
Ethnic mix Irish 93%, Other 4%, British 3%
Government Parliamentary system
Currency Euro = 100 cents
Literacy rate 99%
Calorie consumption 3656 calories

ISRAEL
Southwest Asia

Official name State of Israel
Formation 1948 / 1994
Capital Jerusalem (not internationally recognized)
Population 6.7 million / 854 people per sq mile (330 people per sq km) / 91%
Total area 8019 sq miles (20,770 sq km)
Languages Hebrew*, Arabic, Yiddish, German, Russian, Polish, Romanian, Persian
Religions Jewish 80%, Muslim (mainly Sunni) 16%, Druze and other 2%, Christian 2%
Ethnic mix Jewish 80%, Other (mostly Arab) 20%
Government Parliamentary system
Currency Shekel = 100 agorot
Literacy rate 97%
Calorie consumption 3666 calories

ITALY
Southern Europe

Official name Italian Republic
Formation 1861 / 1947
Capital Rome
Population 58.1 million / 512 people per sq mile (198 people per sq km) / 67%
Total area 116,305 sq miles (301,230 sq km)
Languages Italian*, German, French, Rhaeto-Romanic, Sardinian
Religions Roman Catholic 85%, Other and nonreligious 13%, Muslim 2%
Ethnic mix Italian 94%, Other 4%, Sardinian 2%
Government Parliamentary system
Currency Euro = 100 cents
Literacy rate 99%
Calorie consumption 3671 calories

IVORY COAST
West Africa

Official name Republic of Côte d'Ivoire
Formation 1960 / 1960
Capital Yamoussoukro
Population 18.2 million / 148 people per sq mile (57 people per sq km) / 46%
Total area 124,502 sq miles (322,460 sq km)
Languages French*, Akan, Kru, Voltaic
Religions Muslim 38%, Traditional beliefs 25%, Roman Catholic 25%, Protestant 6%, Other 6%
Ethnic mix Baoulé 23%, Other 19%, Bété 18%, Senufo 15%, Agni-Ashanti 14%, Mandinka 11%
Government Presidential system
Currency CFA franc = 100 centimes
Literacy rate 48%
Calorie consumption 2631 calories

JAMAICA
West Indies

Official name Jamaica
Formation 1962 / 1962
Capital Kingston
Population 2.7 million / 646 people per sq mile (249 people per sq km) / 56%
Total area 4243 sq miles (10,990 sq km)
Languages English*, English Creole
Religions Other and nonreligious 45%, Other Protestant 20%, Church of God 18%, Baptist 10%, Anglican 7%
Ethnic mix Black African 75%, Mulatto (mixed race) 13%, European and Chinese 11%, East Indian 1%
Government Parliamentary system
Currency Jamaican dollar = 100 cents
Literacy rate 88%
Calorie consumption 2685 calories

JAPAN
East Asia

Official name Japan
Formation 1590 / 1972
Capital Tokyo
Population 128 million / 881 people per sq mile (340 people per sq km) / 79%
Total area 145,882 sq miles (377,835 sq km)
Languages Japanese, Korean, Chinese
Religions Shinto and Buddhist 76%, Buddhist 16%, Other (including Christian) 8%
Ethnic mix Japanese 99%, Other (mainly Korean) 1%
Government Parliamentary system
Currency Yen = 100 sen
Literacy rate 99%
Calorie consumption 2761 calories

JORDAN
Southwest Asia

Official name Hashemite Kingdom of Jordan
Formation 1946 / 1967
Capital Amman
Population 5.6 million / 163 people per sq mile (63 people per sq km) / 74%
Total area 35,637 sq miles (92,300 sq km)
Languages Arabic*
Religions Muslim (mainly Sunni) 92%, Other (mostly Christian) 8%
Ethnic mix Arab 98%, Circassian 1%, Armenian 1%
Government Monarchy
Currency Jordanian dinar = 1000 fils
Literacy rate 90%
Calorie consumption 2673 calories

KAZAKHSTAN
Central Asia

Official name Republic of Kazakhstan
Formation 1991 / 1991
Capital Astana
Population 14.8 million / 14 people per sq mile (5 people per sq km) / 56%
Total area 1,049,150 sq miles (2,717,300 sq km)
Languages Kazakh*, Russian*, Ukrainian, Tatar, German, Uzbek, Uighur
Religions Muslim (mainly Sunni) 47%, Orthodox Christian 44%, Other 9%
Ethnic mix Kazakh 53%, Russian 30%, Other 9%, Ukrainian 4%, Tatar 2%, German 2%
Government Presidential system
Currency Tenge = 100 tiyn
Literacy rate 99%
Calorie consumption 2677 calories

KENYA
East Africa

Official name Republic of Kenya
Formation 1963 / 1963
Capital Nairobi
Population 34.3 million / 157 people per sq mile (60 people per sq km) / 33%
Total area 224,961 sq miles (582,650 sq km)
Languages Kiswahili*, English*, Kikuyu, Luo, Kalenjin, Kamba
Religions Christian 60%, Traditional beliefs 25%, Other 9%, Muslim 6%
Ethnic mix Other 30%, Kikuyu 21%, Luhya 14%, Luo 13%, Kalenjin 11%, Kamba 11%
Government Presidential system
Currency Kenya shilling = 100 cents
Literacy rate 74%
Calorie consumption 2090 calories

KIRIBATI
Australasia & Oceania

Official name Republic of Kiribati
Formation 1979 / 1979
Capital Bairiki (Tarawa Atoll)
Population 103,092 / 376 people per sq mile (145 people per sq km) / 36%
Total area 277 sq miles (717 sq km)
Languages English*, Kiribati
Religions Roman Catholic 53%, Kiribati Protestant Church 39%, Other 8%
Ethnic mix Micronesian 96%, Other 4%
Government Nonparty system
Currency Australian dollar = 100 cents
Literacy rate 99%
Calorie consumption 2859 calories

KUWAIT
Southwest Asia

Official name State of Kuwait
Formation 1961 / 1961
Capital Kuwait City
Population 2.7 million / 392 people per sq mile (152 people per sq km) / 98%
Total area 6880 sq miles (17,820 sq km)
Languages Arabic*, English
Religions Sunni Muslim 45%, Shi'a Muslim 40%, Christian, Hindu, and other 15%
Ethnic mix Kuwaiti 45%, Other Arab 35%, South Asian 9%, Other 7%, Iranian 4%
Government Monarchy
Currency Kuwaiti dinar = 1000 fils
Literacy rate 83%
Calorie consumption 3010 calories

KYRGYZSTAN
Central Asia

Official name Kyrgyz Republic
Formation 1991 / 1991
Capital Bishkek
Population 5.3 million / 69 people per sq mile (27 people per sq km) / 33%
Total area 76,641 sq miles (198,500 sq km)
Languages Kyrgyz*, Russian*, Uzbek, Tatar, Ukrainian
Religions Muslim (mainly Sunni) 70%, Orthodox Christian 30%
Ethnic mix Kyrgyz 57%, Russian 19%, Uzbek 13%, Other 7%, Tatar 2%, Ukrainian 2%
Government Presidential system
Currency Som = 100 tyyn
Literacy rate 99%
Calorie consumption 2999 calories

LAOS
Southeast Asia

Official name Lao People's Democratic Republic
Formation 1953 / 1953
Capital Vientiane
Population 5.9 million / 66 people per sq mile (26 people per sq km) / 24%
Total area 91,428 sq miles (236,800 sq km)
Languages Lao*, Mon-Khmer, Yao, Vietnamese, Chinese, French
Religions Buddhist 85%, Other (including animist) 15%
Ethnic mix Lao Loum 66%, Lao Theung 30%, Other 2%, Lao Soung 2%
Government One-party state
Currency New kip = 100 at
Literacy rate 69%
Calorie consumption 2312 calories

LATVIA
Northeast Europe

Official name Republic of Latvia
Formation 1991 / 1991
Capital Riga
Population 2.3 million / 92 people per sq mile (36 people per sq km) / 69%
Total area 24,938 sq miles (64,589 sq km)
Languages Latvian*, Russian
Religions Lutheran 55%, Roman Catholic 24%, Other 12%, Orthodox Christian 9%
Ethnic mix Latvian 57%, Russian 32%, Belarussian 4%, Ukrainian 3%, Polish 2%, Other 2%
Government Parliamentary system
Currency Lats = 100 santims
Literacy rate 99%
Calorie consumption 2938 calories

LEBANON
Southwest Asia

Official name Republic of Lebanon
Formation 1941 / 1941
Capital Beirut
Population 3.6 million / 911 people per sq mile (352 people per sq km) / 90%
Total area 4015 sq miles (10,400 sq km)
Languages Arabic*, French, Armenian, Assyrian
Religions Muslim 70%, Christian 30%
Ethnic mix Arab 94%, Armenian 4%, Other 2%
Government Parliamentary system
Currency Lebanese pound = 100 piastres
Literacy rate 87%
Calorie consumption 3196 calories

LESOTHO
Southern Africa

Official name Kingdom of Lesotho
Formation 1966 / 1966
Capital Maseru
Population 1.8 million / 154 people per sq mile (59 people per sq km) / 28%
Total area 11,720 sq miles (30,355 sq km)
Languages English*, Sesotho*, isiZulu
Religions Christian 90%, Traditional beliefs 10%
Ethnic mix Sotho 97%, European and Asian 3%
Government Parliamentary system
Currency Loti = 100 lisente
Literacy rate 81%
Calorie consumption 2638 calories

LIBERIA
West Africa

Official name Republic of Liberia
Formation 1847 / 1847
Capital Monrovia
Population 3.3 million / 89 people per sq mile (34 people per sq km) / 45%
Total area 43,000 sq miles (111,370 sq km)
Languages English*, Kpelle, Vai, Bassa, Kru, Grebo, Kissi, Gola, Loma
Religions Christian 68%, Traditional beliefs 18%, Muslim 14%
Ethnic mix Indigenous tribes (16 main groups) 95%, Americo-Liberians 5%
Government Transitional regime
Currency Liberian dollar = 100 cents
Literacy rate 58%
Calorie consumption 1900 calories

LIBYA
North Africa

Official name Great Socialist People's Libyan Arab Jamahariyah
Formation 1951 / 1951
Capital Tripoli
Population 5.9 million / 9 people per sq mile (3 people per sq km) / 88%
Total area 679,358 sq miles (1,759,540 sq km)
Languages Arabic*, Tuareg
Religions Muslim (mainly Sunni) 97%, Other 3%
Ethnic mix Arab and Berber 95%, Other 5%
Government One-party state
Currency Libyan dinar = 1000 dirhams
Literacy rate 82%
Calorie consumption 3320 calories

LIECHTENSTEIN
Central Europe

Official name Principality of Liechtenstein
Formation 1719 / 1719
Capital Vaduz
Population 33,717 / 544 people per sq mile (211 people per sq km) / 21%
Total area 62 sq miles (160 sq km)
Languages German*, Alemannish dialect, Italian
Religions Roman Catholic 81%, Other 12%, Protestant 7%
Ethnic mix Liechtensteiner 62%, Foreign residents 38%
Government Parliamentary system
Currency Swiss franc = 100 rappen/centimes
Literacy rate 99%
Calorie consumption Not available

LITHUANIA
Northeast Europe

Official name Republic of Lithuania
Formation 1991 / 1991
Capital Vilnius
Population 3.4 million / 135 people per sq mile (52 people per sq km) / 68%
Total area 25,174 sq miles (65,200 sq km)
Languages Lithuanian*, Russian
Religions Roman Catholic 83%, Other 12%, Protestant 5%
Ethnic mix Lithuanian 80%, Russian 9%, Polish 7%, Other 2%, Belarussian 2%
Government Parliamentary system
Currency Litas (euro is also legal tender) = 100 centu
Literacy rate 99%
Calorie consumption 3324 calories

LUXEMBOURG
Northwest Europe

Official name Grand Duchy of Luxembourg
Formation 1867 / 1867
Capital Luxembourg-Ville
Population 465,000 / 466 people per sq mile (180 people per sq km) / 92%
Total area 998 sq miles (2586 sq km)
Languages Luxembourgish*, German*, French*
Religions Roman Catholic 97%, Protestant, Orthodox Christian, and Jewish 3%
Ethnic mix Luxembourger 73%, Foreign residents 27%
Government Parliamentary system
Currency Euro = 100 cents
Literacy rate 99%
Calorie consumption 3701 calories

MACEDONIA
Southeast Europe

Official name Republic of Macedonia
Formation 1991 / 1991
Capital Skopje
Population 2 million / 201 people per sq mile (78 people per sq km) / 62%
Total area 9781 sq miles (25,333 sq km)
Languages Macedonian, Albanian, Serbo-Croat
Religions Orthodox Christian 59%, Muslim 26%, Other 10%, Roman Catholic 4%, Protestant 1%
Ethnic mix Macedonian 64%, Albanian 25%, Turkish 4%, Roma 3%, Other 2%, Serb 2%
Government Mixed presidential–parliamentary system
Currency Macedonian denar = 100 deni
Literacy rate 96%
Calorie consumption 2655 calories

MADAGASCAR
Indian Ocean

Official name Republic of Madagascar
Formation 1960 / 1960
Capital Antananarivo
Population 18.6 million / 83 people per sq mile (32 people per sq km) / 30%
Total area 226,656 sq miles (587,040 sq km)
Languages Malagasy*, French*
Religions Traditional beliefs 52%, Christian (mainly Roman Catholic) 41%, Muslim 7%
Ethnic mix Other Malay 46%, Merina 26%, Betsimisaraka 15%, Betsileo 12%, Other 1%
Government Presidential system
Currency Ariary = 5 iraimbilanja
Literacy rate 71%
Calorie consumption 2005 calories

MALAWI
Southern Africa

Official name Republic of Malawi
Formation 1964 / 1964
Capital Lilongwe
Population 12.9 million / 355 people per sq mile (137 people per sq km) / 25%
Total area 45,745 sq miles (118,480 sq km)
Languages English*, Chewa*, Lomwe, Yao, Ngoni
Religions Protestant 55%, Roman Catholic 20%, Muslim 20%, Traditional beliefs 5%
Ethnic mix Bantu 99%, Other 1%
Government Presidential system
Currency Malawi kwacha = 100 tambala
Literacy rate 64%
Calorie consumption 2155 calories

MALAYSIA
Southeast Asia

Official name Federation of Malaysia
Formation 1963 / 1965
Capital Kuala Lumpur; Putrajaya (administrative)
Population 25.3 million / 199 people per sq mile (77 people per sq km) / 57%
Total area 127,316 sq miles (329,750 sq km)
Languages Malay*, Chinese*, Bahasa Malaysia, Tamil, English
Religions Muslim (mainly Sunni) 53%, Buddhist 19%, Chinese faiths 12%, Other 7%, Christian 7%, Traditional beliefs 2%
Ethnic mix Malay 48%, Chinese 29%, Indigenous tribes 12%, Indian 6%, Other 5%
Government Parliamentary system
Currency Ringgit = 100 sen
Literacy rate 89%
Calorie consumption 2881 calories

MALDIVES
Indian Ocean

Official name Republic of Maldives
Formation 1965 / 1965
Capital Male'
Population 329,000 / 2836 people per sq mile (1097 people per sq km) / 30%
Total area 116 sq miles (300 sq km)
Languages Dhivehi (Maldivian)*, Sinhala, Tamil, Arabic
Religions Sunni Muslim 100%
Ethnic mix Arab–Sinhalese–Malay 100%
Government Nonparty system
Currency Rufiyaa = 100 lari
Literacy rate 97%
Calorie consumption 2548 calories

MALI
West Africa

Official name Republic of Mali
Formation 1960 / 1960
Capital Bamako
Population 13.5 million / 29 people per sq mile (11 people per sq km) / 30%
Total area 478,764 sq miles (1,240,000 sq km)
Languages French*, Bambara, Fulani, Senufo, Soninke
Religions Muslim (mainly Sunni) 80%, Traditional beliefs 18%, Christian 1%, Other 1%
Ethnic mix Bambara 32%, Other 26%, Fulani 14%, Senufu 12%, Soninka 9%, Tuareg 7%
Government Presidential system
Currency CFA franc = 100 centimes
Literacy rate 19%
Calorie consumption 2174 calories

MALTA
Southern Europe

Official name Republic of Malta
Formation 1964 / 1964
Capital Valletta
Population 402,000 / 3242 people per sq mile (1256 people per sq km) / 91%
Total area 122 sq miles (316 sq km)
Languages Maltese*, English
Religions Roman Catholic 98%, Other and nonreligious 2%
Ethnic mix Maltese 96%, Other 4%
Government Parliamentary system
Currency Maltese lira = 100 cents
Literacy rate 88%
Calorie consumption 3587 calories

MARSHALL ISLANDS
Australasia & Oceania

Official name Republic of the Marshall Islands
Formation 1986 / 1986
Capital Majuro
Population 59,071 / 844 people per sq mile (326 people per sq km) / 69%
Total area 70 sq miles (181 sq km)
Languages Marshallese*, English*, Japanese, German
Religions Protestant 90%, Roman Catholic 8%, Other 2%
Ethnic mix Micronesian 97%, Other 3%
Government Presidential system
Currency US dollar = 100 cents
Literacy rate 91%
Calorie consumption Not available

MAURITANIA
West Africa

Official name Islamic Republic of Mauritania
Formation 1960 / 1960
Capital Nouakchott
Population 3.1 million / 8 people per sq mile (3 people per sq km) / 58%
Total area 397,953 sq miles (1,030,700 sq km)
Languages French*, Hassaniyah Arabic, Wolof
Religions Sunni Muslim 100%
Ethnic mix Maure 81%, Wolof 7%, Tukolor 5%, Other 4%, Soninka 3%
Government Transitional regime
Currency Ouguiya = 5 khoums
Literacy rate 51%
Calorie consumption 2772 calories

MAURITIUS
Indian Ocean

Official name Republic of Mauritius
Formation 1968 / 1968
Capital Port Louis
Population 1.2 million / 1671 people per sq mile (645 people per sq km) / 41%
Total area 718 sq miles (1860 sq km)
Languages English*, French Creole, Hindi, Urdu, Tamil, Chinese, French
Religions Hindu 52%, Roman Catholic 26%, Muslim 17%, Other 3%, Protestant 2%
Ethnic mix Indo-Mauritian 68%, Creole 27%, Sino-Mauritian 3%, Franco-Mauritian 2%
Government Parliamentary system
Currency Mauritian rupee = 100 cents
Literacy rate 84%
Calorie consumption 2955 calories

MEXICO
North America

Official name United Mexican States
Formation 1836 / 1848
Capital Mexico City
Population 107 million / 145 people per sq mile (56 people per sq km) / 74%
Total area 761,602 sq miles (1,972,550 sq km)
Languages Spanish*, Nahuatl, Mayan, Zapotec, Mixtec, Otomi, Totonac, Tzotzil, Tzeltal
Religions Roman Catholic 88%, Other 7%, Protestant 5%
Ethnic mix Mestizo 60%, Amerindian 30%, European 9%, Other 1%
Government Presidential system
Currency Mexican peso = 100 centavos
Literacy rate 90%
Calorie consumption 3145 calories

MICRONESIA
Australasia & Oceania

Official name Federated States of Micronesia
Formation 1986 / 1986
Capital Palikir (Pohnpei Island)
Population 108,105 / 399 people per sq mile (154 people per sq km) / 28%
Total area 271 sq miles (702 sq km)
Languages Trukese, Pohnpeian, Mortlockese, Kosraean, English
Religions Roman Catholic 50%, Protestant 48%, Other 2%
Ethnic mix Micronesian 100%
Government Nonparty system
Currency US dollar = 100 cents
Literacy rate 81%
Calorie consumption Not available

MOLDOVA
Southeast Europe

Official name Republic of Moldova
Formation 1991 / 1991
Capital Chisinau
Population 4.2 million / 323 people per sq mile (125 people per sq km) / 46%
Total area 13,067 sq miles (33,843 sq km)
Languages Moldovan*, Ukrainian, Russian
Religions Orthodox Christian 98%, Jewish 2%
Ethnic mix Moldovan 65%, Ukrainian 14%, Russian 13%, Other 4%, Gagauz 4%
Government Parliamentary system
Currency Moldovan leu = 100 bani
Literacy rate 96%
Calorie consumption 2806 calories

MONACO
Southern Europe

Official name Principality of Monaco
Formation 1861 / 1861
Capital Monaco-Ville
Population 32,409 / 43212 people per sq mile (16620 people per sq km) / 100%
Total area 0.75 sq miles (1.95 sq km)
Languages French*, Italian, Monégasque, English
Religions Roman Catholic 89%, Protestant 6%, Other 5%
Ethnic mix French 47%, Other 20%, Monégasque 17%, Italian 16%
Government Monarchy
Currency Euro = 100 cents
Literacy rate 99%
Calorie consumption Not available

MONGOLIA
East Asia

Official name Mongolia
Formation 1924 / 1924
Capital Ulan Bator
Population 2.6 million / 4 people per sq mile (2 people per sq km) / 64%
Total area 604,247 sq miles (1,565,000 sq km)
Languages Khalkha Mongolian*, Kazakh, Chinese, Russian
Religions Tibetan Buddhist 96%, Muslim 4%
Ethnic mix Mongol 90%, Kazakh 4%, Other 2%, Chinese 2%, Russian 2%
Government Mixed presidential–parliamentary system
Currency Tugrik (tögrög) = 100 möngö
Literacy rate 98%
Calorie consumption 2249 calories

MONTENEGRO
Europe

Official name Republic of Montenegro
Formation 2006 / 2006
Capital Podgorica
Population 620,145 / 116 people per sq mile (45 people per sq km) / 62%
Total area 5,332 sq miles (13,812 sq km)
Languages Montenegrin, Serbian, Albanian
Religions Orthodox Christian 74%, Muslim 18%, Roman Catholic 4%, Other 4%
Ethnic mix Montenegrin 43%, Serb 32%, Bosniak 8%, Albanian 5%, Other 12%
Government Parliamentary system
Currency Euro = 100 cents
Literacy rate 98%
Calorie consumption Not available

MOROCCO
North Africa

Official name Kingdom of Morocco
Formation 1956 / 1956
Capital Rabat
Population 31.5 million / 183 people per sq mile (71 people per sq km) / 56%
Total area 172,316 sq miles (446,300 sq km)
Languages Arabic*, Tamazight (Berber), French, Spanish
Religions Muslim (mainly Sunni) 99%, Other (mostly Christian) 1%
Ethnic mix Arab 70%, Berber 29%, European 1%
Government Monarchy
Currency Moroccan dirham = 100 centimes
Literacy rate 51%
Calorie consumption 3052 calories

MOZAMBIQUE
Southern Africa

Official name Republic of Mozambique
Formation 1975 / 1975
Capital Maputo
Population 19.8 million / 65 people per sq mile (25 people per sq km) / 40%
Total area 309,494 sq miles (801,590 sq km)
Languages Portuguese*, Makua, Xitsonga, Sena, Lomwe
Religions Traditional beliefs 56%, Christian 30%, Muslim 14%
Ethnic mix Makua Lomwe 47%, Tsonga 23%, Malawi 12%, Shona 11%, Yao 4%, Other 3%
Government Presidential system
Currency Metical = 100 centavos
Literacy rate 47%
Calorie consumption 2079 calories

MYANMAR (BURMA)
Southeast Asia

Official name Union of Myanmar
Formation 1948 / 1948
Capital Rangoon (Yangon), Pyinmana
Population 50.5 million / 199 people per sq mile (77 people per sq km) / 28%
Total area 261,969 sq miles (678,500 sq km)
Languages Burmese*, Shan, Karen, Rakhine, Chin, Yangbye, Kachin, Mon
Religions Buddhist 87%, Christian 6%, Muslim 4%, Other 2%, Hindu 1%
Ethnic mix Burman (Bamah) 68%, Other 13%, Shan 9%, Karen 6%, Rakhine 4%
Government Military-based regime
Currency Kyat = 100 pyas
Literacy rate 90%
Calorie consumption 2937 calories

NAMIBIA
Southern Africa

Official name Republic of Namibia
Formation 1990 / 1994
Capital Windhoek
Population 2 million / 6 people per sq mile (2 people per sq km) / 31%
Total area 318,694 sq miles (825,418 sq km)
Languages English*, Ovambo, Kavango, Bergdama, German, Afrikaans
Religions Christian 90%, Traditional beliefs 10%
Ethnic mix Ovambo 50%, Other tribes 16%, Kavango 9%, Other 9%, Damara 8%, Herero 8%
Government Presidential system
Currency Namibian dollar = 100 cents
Literacy rate 85%
Calorie consumption 2278 calories

NAURU
Australasia & Oceania

Official name Republic of Nauru
Formation 1968 / 1968
Capital None
Population 13,048 / 1611 people per sq mile (621 people per sq km) / 100%
Total area 8.1 sq miles (21 sq km)
Languages Nauruan*, Kiribati, Chinese, Tuvaluan, English
Religions Nauruan Congregational Church 60%, Roman Catholic 35%, Other 5%
Ethnic mix Nauruan 62%, Other Pacific islanders 25%, Chinese and Vietnamese 8%, European 5%
Government Parliamentary system
Currency Australian dollar = 100 cents
Literacy rate 95%
Calorie consumption Not available

NEPAL
South Asia

Official name Kingdom of Nepal
Formation 1769 / 1769
Capital Kathmandu
Population 27.1 million / 513 people per sq mile (198 people per sq km) / 12%
Total area 54,363 sq miles (140,800 sq km)
Languages Nepali*, Maithili, Bhojpuri
Religions Hindu 90%, Buddhist 5%, Muslim 3%, Other (including Christian) 2%
Ethnic mix Nepalese 52%, Other 19%, Maithili 11%, Tibeto-Burmese 10%, Bhojpuri 8%
Government Monarchy
Currency Nepalese rupee = 100 paise
Literacy rate 49%
Calorie consumption 2453 calories

NETHERLANDS
Northwest Europe

Official name Kingdom of the Netherlands
Formation 1648 / 1839
Capital Amsterdam; The Hague (administrative)
Population 16.3 million / 1245 people per sq mile (481 people per sq km) / 89%
Total area 16,033 sq miles (41,526 sq km)
Languages Dutch*, Frisian
Religions Roman Catholic 36%, Other 34%, Protestant 27%, Muslim 3%
Ethnic mix Dutch 82%, Other 12%, Surinamese 2%, Turkish 2%, Moroccan 2%
Government Parliamentary system
Currency Euro = 100 cents
Literacy rate 99%
Calorie consumption 3362 calories

NEW ZEALAND
Australasia & Oceania

Official name New Zealand
Formation 1947 / 1947
Capital Wellington
Population 4 million / 39 people per sq mile (15 people per sq km) / 86%
Total area 103,737 sq miles (268,680 sq km)
Languages English*, Maori
Religions Anglican 24%, Other 22%, Presbyterian 18%, Nonreligious 16%, Roman Catholic 15%, Methodist 5%
Ethnic mix European 77%, Maori 12%, Other immigrant 6%, Pacific islanders 5%
Government Parliamentary system
Currency New Zealand dollar = 100 cents
Literacy rate 99%
Calorie consumption 3219 calories

NICARAGUA
Central America

Official name Republic of Nicaragua
Formation 1838 / 1838
Capital Managua
Population 5.5 million / 120 people per sq mile (46 people per sq km) / 65%
Total area 49,998 sq miles (129,494 sq km)
Languages Spanish*, English Creole, Miskito
Religions Roman Catholic 80%, Protestant Evangelical 17%, Other 3%
Ethnic mix Mestizo 69%, White 14%, Black 8%, Amerindian 5%, Zambo 4%
Government Presidential system
Currency Córdoba oro = 100 centavos
Literacy rate 77%
Calorie consumption 2298 calories

NIGER
West Africa

Official name Republic of Niger
Formation 1960 / 1960
Capital Niamey
Population 14 million / 29 people per sq mile (11 people per sq km) / 21%
Total area 489,188 sq miles (1,267,000 sq km)
Languages French*, Hausa, Djerma, Fulani, Tuareg, Teda
Religions Muslim 85%, Traditional beliefs 14%, Other (including Christian) 1%
Ethnic mix Hausa 54%, Djerma and Songhai 21%, Fulani 10%, Tuareg 9%, Other 6%
Government Presidential system
Currency CFA franc = 100 centimes
Literacy rate 14%
Calorie consumption 2130 calories

NIGERIA
West Africa

Official name Federal Republic of Nigeria
Formation 1960 / 1961
Capital Abuja
Population 132 million / 374 people per sq mile (144 people per sq km) / 44%
Total area 356,667 sq miles (923,768 sq km)
Languages English*, Hausa, Yoruba, Ibo
Religions Muslim 50%, Christian 40%, Traditional beliefs 10%
Ethnic mix Other 29%, Hausa 21%, Yoruba 21%, Ibo 18%, Fulani 11%
Government Presidential system
Currency Naira = 100 kobo
Literacy rate 67%
Calorie consumption 2726 calories

NORTH KOREA
East Asia

Official name Democratic People's Republic of Korea
Formation 1948 / 1953
Capital Pyongyang
Population 22.5 million / 484 people per sq mile (187 people per sq km) / 60%
Total area 46,540 sq miles (120,540 sq km)
Languages Korean*
Religions Atheist 100%
Ethnic mix Korean 100%
Government One-party state
Currency North Korean won = 100 chon
Literacy rate 99%
Calorie consumption 2142 calories

NORWAY
Northern Europe

Official name Kingdom of Norway
Formation 1905 / 1905
Capital Oslo
Population 4.6 million / 39 people per sq mile (15 people per sq km) / 76%
Total area 125,181 sq miles (324,220 sq km)
Languages Norwegian* (Bokmål "book language" and Nynorsk "new Norsk"), Sámi
Religions Evangelical Lutheran 89%, Other and nonreligious 10%, Roman Catholic 1%
Ethnic mix Norwegian 93%, Other 6%, Sámi 1%
Government Parliamentary system
Currency Norwegian krone = 100 øre
Literacy rate 99%
Calorie consumption 3484 calories

OMAN
Southwest Asia

Official name Sultanate of Oman
Formation 1951 / 1951
Capital Muscat
Population 2.6 million / 32 people per sq mile (12 people per sq km) / 84%
Total area 82,031 sq miles (212,460 sq km)
Languages Arabic*, Baluchi, Farsi, Hindi, Punjabi
Religions Ibadi Muslim 75%, Other Muslim and Hindu 25%
Ethnic mix Arab 88%, Baluchi 4%, Persian 3%, Indian and Pakistani 3%, African 2%
Government Monarchy
Currency Omani rial = 1000 baizas
Literacy rate 74%
Calorie consumption Not available

PAKISTAN
South Asia

Official name Islamic Republic of Pakistan
Formation 1947 / 1971
Capital Islamabad
Population 158 million / 531 people per sq mile (205 people per sq km) / 37%
Total area 310,401 sq miles (803,940 sq km)
Languages Urdu*, Baluchi, Brahui, Pashtu, Punjabi, Sindhi
Religions Sunni Muslim 77%, Shi'a Muslim 20%, Hindu 2%, Christian 1%
Ethnic mix Punjabi 56%, Pathan (Pashtun) 15%, Sindhi 14%, Mohajir 7%, Other 4%, Baluchi 4%
Government Presidential system
Currency Pakistani rupee = 100 paisa
Literacy rate 49%
Calorie consumption 2419 calories

PALAU
Australasia & Oceania

Official name Republic of Palau
Formation 1994 / 1994
Capital Koror
Population 20,303 / 104 people per sq mile (40 people per sq km) / 70%
Total area 177 sq miles (458 sq km)
Languages Palauan, English, Japanese, Angaur, Tobi, Sonsorolese
Religions Christian 66%, Modekngei 34%
Ethnic mix Micronesian 87%, Filipino 8%, Chinese and other Asian 5%
Government Nonparty system
Currency US dollar = 100 cents
Literacy rate 98%
Calorie consumption Not available

PANAMA
Central America

Official name Republic of Panama
Formation 1903 / 1903
Capital Panama City
Population 3.2 million / 109 people per sq mile (42 people per sq km) / 56%
Total area 30,193 sq miles (78,200 sq km)
Languages Spanish*, English Creole, Amerindian languages, Chibchan languages
Religions Roman Catholic 86%, Other 8%, Protestant 6%
Ethnic mix Mestizo 60%, White 14%, Black 12%, Amerindian 8%, Asian 4%, Other 2%
Government Presidential system
Currency Balboa = 100 centesimos
Literacy rate 92%
Calorie consumption 2272 calories

PAPUA NEW GUINEA
Australasia & Oceania

Official name Independent State of Papua New Guinea
Formation 1975 / 1975
Capital Port Moresby
Population 5.9 million / 34 people per sq mile (13 people per sq km) / 17%
Total area 178,703 sq miles (462,840 sq km)
Languages Pidgin English*, Papuan*, English, Motu, 750 (est.) native languages
Religions Protestant 60%, Roman Catholic 37%, Other 3%
Ethnic mix Melanesian and mixed race 100%
Government Parliamentary system
Currency Kina = 100 toeas
Literacy rate 57%
Calorie consumption 2193 calories

PARAGUAY
South America

Official name Republic of Paraguay
Formation 1811 / 1938
Capital Asunción
Population 6.2 million / 40 people per sq mile (16 people per sq km) / 56%
Total area 157,046 sq miles (406,750 sq km)
Languages Guarani*, Spanish*, German
Religions Roman Catholic 96%, Protestant (including Mennonite) 4%
Ethnic mix Mestizo 90%, Other 8%, Amerindian 2%
Government Presidential system
Currency Guarani = 100 centimos
Literacy rate 92%
Calorie consumption 2565 calories

PERU
South America

Official name Republic of Peru
Formation 1824 / 1941
Capital Lima
Population 28 million / 57 people per sq mile (22 people per sq km) / 73%
Total area 496,223 sq miles (1,285,200 sq km)
Languages Spanish*, Quechua*, Aymara*
Religions Roman Catholic 95%, Other 5%
Ethnic mix Amerindian 50%, Mestizo 40%, White 7%, Other 3%
Government Presidential system
Currency New sol = 100 centimos
Literacy rate 88%
Calorie consumption 2571 calories

PHILIPPINES
Southwest Asia

Official name Republic of the Philippines
Formation 1946 / 1946
Capital Manila
Population 83.1 million / 722 people per sq mile (279 people per sq km) / 59%
Total area 115,830 sq miles (300,000 sq km)
Languages Filipino*, English*, Tagalog, Cebuano, Ilocano, Hiligaynon, many other local languages
Religions Roman Catholic 83%, Protestant 9%, Muslim 5%, Other (including Buddhist) 3%
Ethnic mix Malay 95%, Other 3%, Chinese 2%
Government Presidential system
Currency Philippine peso = 100 centavos
Literacy rate 93%
Calorie consumption 2379 calories

POLAND
Northern Europe

Official name Republic of Poland
Formation 1918 / 1945
Capital Warsaw
Population 38.5 million / 328 people per sq mile (126 people per sq km) / 66%
Total area 120,728 sq miles (312,685 sq km)
Languages Polish*
Religions Roman Catholic 93%, Other and nonreligious 5%, Orthodox Christian 2%
Ethnic mix Polish 97%, Other 2%, Silesian 1%
Government Parliamentary system
Currency Zloty = 100 groszy
Literacy rate 99%
Calorie consumption 3374 calories

PORTUGAL
Southwest Europe

Official name Republic of Portugal
Formation 1139 / 1640
Capital Lisbon
Population 10.5 million / 296 people per sq mile (114 people per sq km) / 64%
Total area 35,672 sq miles (92,391 sq km)
Languages Portuguese
Religions Roman Catholic 97%, Other 2%, Protestant 1%
Ethnic mix Portuguese 98%, African and other 2%
Government Parliamentary system
Currency Euro = 100 cents
Literacy rate 93%
Calorie consumption 3741 calories

QATAR
Southwest Asia

Official name State of Qatar
Formation 1971 / 1971
Capital Doha
Population 813,000 / 191 people per sq mile (74 people per sq km) / 93%
Total area 4416 sq miles (11,437 sq km)
Languages Arabic*
Religions Muslim (mainly Sunni) 95%, Other 5%
Ethnic mix Arab 40%, Indian 18%, Pakistani 18%, Other 14%, Iranian 10%
Government Monarchy
Currency Qatar riyal = 100 dirhams
Literacy rate 89%
Calorie consumption Not available

ROMANIA
Southeast Europe

Official name Romania
Formation 1878 / 1947
Capital Bucharest
Population 21.7 million / 244 people per sq mile (94 people per sq km) / 56%
Total area 91,699 sq miles (237,500 sq km)
Languages Romanian*, Hungarian (Magyar), Romani, German
Religions Romanian Orthodox 87%, Roman Catholic 5%, Protestant 4%, Other 2%, Greek Orthodox 1%, Greek Catholic (Uniate) 1%
Ethnic mix Romanian 89%, Magyar 7%, Roma 3%, Other 1%
Government Presidential system
Currency Romanian leu = 100 bani
Literacy rate 97%
Calorie consumption 3455 calories

RUSSIAN FEDERATION
Europe / Asia

Official name Russian Federation
Formation 1480 / 1991
Capital Moscow
Population 143 million / 22 people per sq mile (8 people per sq km) / 78%
Total area 6,592,735 sq miles (17,075,200 sq km)
Languages Russian*, Tatar, Ukrainian, Chavash, various other national languages
Religions Orthodox Christian 75%, Other 15%, Muslim 10%
Ethnic mix Russian 82%, Other 10%, Tatar 4%, Ukrainian 3%, Chavash 1%
Government Presidential system
Currency Russian rouble = 100 kopeks
Literacy rate 99%
Calorie consumption 3072 calories

RWANDA
Central Africa

Official name Republic of Rwanda
Formation 1962 / 1962
Capital Kigali
Population 9 million / 934 people per sq mile (361 people per sq km) / 6%
Total area 10,169 sq miles (26,338 sq km)
Languages Kinyarwanda*, French*, Kiswahili, English
Religions Roman Catholic 56%, Traditional beliefs 25%, Muslim 10%, Protestant 9%
Ethnic mix Hutu 90%, Tutsi 9%, Other (including Twa) 1%
Government Presidential system
Currency Rwanda franc = 100 centimes
Literacy rate 64%
Calorie consumption 2084 calories

SAINT KITTS & NEVIS
West indies

Official name Federation of Saint Christopher and Nevis
Formation 1983 / 1983
Capital Basseterre
Population 38,958 / 280 people per sq mile (108 people per sq km) / 34%
Total area 101 sq miles (261 sq km)
Languages English*, English Creole
Religions Anglican 33%, Methodist 29%, Other 22%, Moravian 9%, Roman Catholic 7%
Ethnic mix Black 94%, Mixed race 3%, Other and Amerindian 2%, White 1%
Government Parliamentary system
Currency Eastern Caribbean dollar = 100 cents
Literacy rate 98%
Calorie consumption 2609 calories

SAINT LUCIA
West Indies

Official name Saint Lucia
Formation 1979 / 1979
Capital Castries
Population 166,312 / 705 people per sq mile (273 people per sq km) / 38%
Total area 239 sq miles (620 sq km)
Languages English*, French Creole
Religions Roman Catholic 90%, Other 10%
Ethnic mix Black 90%, Mulatto (mixed race) 6%, Asian 3%, White 1%
Government Parliamentary system
Currency Eastern Caribbean dollar = 100 cents
Literacy rate 90%
Calorie consumption 2988 calories

SAINT VINCENT & THE GRENADINES
West Indies

Official name Saint Vincent and the Grenadines
Formation 1979 / 1979
Capital Kingstown
Population 117,534 / 897 people per sq mile (346 people per sq km) / 55%
Total area 150 sq miles (389 sq km)
Languages English*, English Creole
Religions Anglican 47%, Methodist 28%, Roman Catholic 13%, Other 12%
Ethnic mix Black 66%, Mulatto (mixed race) 19%, Asian 6%, Other 5%, White 4%
Government Parliamentary system
Currency Eastern Caribbean dollar = 100 cents
Literacy rate 88%
Calorie consumption 2599 calories

SAMOA
Australasia & Oceania

Official name Independent State of Samoa
Formation 1962 / 1962
Capital Apia
Population 185,000 / 169 people per sq mile (65 people per sq km) / 22%
Total area 1104 sq miles (2860 sq km)
Languages Samoan*, English*
Religions Christian 99%, Other 1%
Ethnic mix Polynesian 90%, Euronesian 9%, Other 1%
Government Parliamentary system
Currency Tala = 100 sene
Literacy rate 99%
Calorie consumption 2945 calories

SAN MARINO
Southern Europe

Official name Republic of San Marino
Formation 1631 / 1631
Capital San Marino
Population 28,880 / 1203 people per sq mile (473 people per sq km) / 94%
Total area 23.6 sq miles (61 sq km)
Languages Italian*
Religions Roman Catholic 93%, Other and nonreligious 7%
Ethnic mix Sammarinese 80%, Italian 19%, Other 1%
Government Parliamentary system
Currency Euro = 100 cents
Literacy rate 99%
Calorie consumption Not available

SÃO TOMÉ & PRÍNCIPE
West Africa

Official name Democratic Republic of São Tomé and Príncipe
Formation 1975 / 1975
Capital São Tomé
Population 187,410 / 505 people per sq mile (195 people per sq km) / 47%
Total area 386 sq miles (1001 sq km)
Languages Portuguese*, Portuguese Creole
Religions Roman Catholic 84%, Other 16%
Ethnic mix Black 90%, Portuguese and Creole 10%
Government Presidential system
Currency Dobra = 100 centimos
Literacy rate 83%
Calorie consumption 2460 calories

SAUDI ARABIA
Souhwest Asia

Official name Kingdom of Saudi Arabia
Formation 1932 / 1932
Capital Riyadh; Jiddah (administrative)
Population 24.6 million / 30 people per sq mile (12 people per sq km) / 86%
Total area 756,981 sq miles (1,960,582 sq km)
Languages Arabic*
Religions Sunni Muslim 85%, Shi'a Muslim 15%
Ethnic mix Arab 90%, Afro-Asian 10%
Government Monarchy
Currency Saudi riyal = 100 halalat
Literacy rate 79%
Calorie consumption 2844 calories

SENEGAL
West Africa

Official name Republic of Senegal
Formation 1960 / 1960
Capital Dakar
Population 11.7 million / 157 people per sq mile (61 people per sq km) / 47%
Total area 75,749 sq miles (196,190 sq km)
Languages French*, Diola, Mandinka, Malinke, Pulaar, Serer, Soninke, Wolof
Religions Sunni Muslim 90%, Christian (mainly Roman Catholic) 5%, Traditional beliefs 5%
Ethnic mix Wolof 43%, Toucouleur 24%, Serer 15%, Other 11%, Diola 4%, Malinke 3%
Government Presidential system
Currency CFA franc = 100 centimes
Literacy rate 39%
Calorie consumption 2279 calories

SERBIA
Europe

Official name Republic of Serbia
Formation 2006 / 2006
Capital Belgrade
Population 9.7 million / 290 people per sq mile (112 people per sq km) / 52%
Total area 34,116 sq miles (88,361 sq km)
Languages Serbo-Croat*, Albanian, Hungarian
Religions Orthodox Christian 85%, Muslim 6%, Other 6%, Roman Catholic 3%
Ethnic mix Serb 66%, Albanian 19%, Hungarian 4%, Bosniak 2%, Other 9%
Government Parliamentary system
Currency Dinar (Serbia) = 100 para
Literacy rate 98%
Calorie consumption Not available

SEYCHELLES
Indian Ocean

Official name Republic of Seychelles
Formation 1976 / 1976
Capital Victoria
Population 81,188 / 781 people per sq mile (301 people per sq km) / 64%
Total area 176 sq miles (455 sq km)
Languages French Creole*, English, French
Religions Roman Catholic 90%, Anglican 8%, Other (including Muslim) 2%
Ethnic mix Creole 89%, Indian 5%, Other 4%, Chinese 2%
Government Presidential system
Currency Seychelles rupee = 100 cents
Literacy rate 92%
Calorie consumption 2465 calories

SIERRA LEONE
West Africa

Official name Republic of Sierra Leone
Formation 1961 / 1961
Capital Freetown
Population 5.5 million / 199 people per sq mile (77 people per sq km) / 37%
Total area 27,698 sq miles (71,740 sq km)
Languages English*, Mende, Temne, Krio
Religions Muslim 30%, Traditional beliefs 30%, Other 30%, Christian 10%
Ethnic mix Mende 35%, Temne 32%, Other 21%, Limba 8%, Kuranko 4%
Government Presidential system
Currency Leone = 100 cents
Literacy rate 30%
Calorie consumption 1936 calories

SINGAPORE
Southeast Asia

Official name Republic of Singapore
Formation 1965 / 1965
Capital Singapore
Population 4.3 million / 18220 people per sq mile (7049 people per sq km) / 100%
Total area 250 sq miles (648 sq km)
Languages English*, Malay*, Mandarin*, Tamil*
Religions Buddhist 55%, Taoist 22%, Muslim 16%, Hindu, Christian, and Sikh 7%
Ethnic mix Chinese 77%, Malay 14%, Indian 8%, Other 1%
Government Parliamentary system
Currency Singapore dollar = 100 cents
Literacy rate 93%
Calorie consumption Not available

SLOVAKIA
Central Europe

Official name Slovak Republic
Formation 1993 / 1993
Capital Bratislava
Population 5.4 million / 285 people per sq mile (110 people per sq km) / 57%
Total area 18,859 sq miles (48,845 sq km)
Languages Slovak*, Hungarian (Magyar), Czech
Religions Roman Catholic 60%, Other 18%, Atheist 10%, Protestant 8%, Orthodox Christian 4%
Ethnic mix Slovak 85%, Magyar 11%, Other 2%, Roma 1%, Czech 1%
Government Parliamentary system
Currency Slovak koruna = 100 halierov
Literacy rate 99%
Calorie consumption 2889 calories

SLOVENIA
Central Europe

Official name Republic of Slovenia
Formation 1991 / 1991
Capital Ljubljana
Population 2 million / 256 people per sq mile (99 people per sq km) / 50%
Total area 7820 sq miles (20,253 sq km)
Languages Slovene*, Serbo-Croat
Religions Roman Catholic 96%, Other 3%, Muslim 1%
Ethnic mix Slovene 83%, Other 12%, Serb 2%, Croat 2%, Bosniak 1%
Government Parliamentary system
Currency Tolar = 100 stotinov
Literacy rate 99%
Calorie consumption 3001 calories

SOLOMON ISLANDS
Australasia & Oceania

Official name Solomon Islands
Formation 1978 / 1978
Capital Honiara
Population 478,000 / 44 people per sq mile (17 people per sq km) / 20%
Total area 10,985 sq miles (28,450 sq km)
Languages English*, Melanesian Pidgin, Pidgin English
Religions Anglican 34%, Roman Catholic 19%, Methodist 11%, Seventh-day Adventist 10%, South Seas Evangelical Church 17%, Other 9%
Ethnic mix Melanesian 94%, Polynesian 4%, Other 2%
Government Parliamentary system
Currency Solomon Islands dollar = 100 cents
Literacy rate 77%
Calorie consumption 2265 calories

SOMALIA
East Africa

Official name Somalia
Formation 1960 / 1960
Capital Mogadishu
Population 8.2 million / 34 people per sq mile (13 people per sq km) / 28%
Total area 246,199 sq miles (637,657 sq km)
Languages Somali*, Arabic*, English, Italian
Religions Sunni Muslim 98%, Christian 2%
Ethnic mix Somali 85%, Other 15%
Government Transitional regime
Currency Somali shilling = 100 centesimi
Literacy rate 24%
Calorie consumption 1628 calories

SOUTH AFRICA
Southern Africa

Official name Republic of South Africa
Formation 1934 / 1994
Capital Pretoria; Cape Town; Bloemfontein
Population 47.4 million / 101 people per sq mile (39 people per sq km) / 55%
Total area 471,008 sq miles (1,219,912 sq km)
Languages English, isiZulu, isiXhosa, Afrikaans, Sepedi, Setswana, Sesotho, Xitsonga, siSwati, Tshivenda, isiNdebele
Religions Christian 68%, Traditional beliefs and animist 29%, Muslim 2%, Hindu 1%
Ethnic mix Black 79%, White 10%, Colored 9%, Asian 2%
Government Presidential system
Currency Rand = 100 cents
Literacy rate 82%
Calorie consumption 2956 calories

SOUTH KOREA
East Asia

Official name Republic of Korea
Formation 1948 / 1953
Capital Seoul
Population 47.8 million / 1254 people per sq mile (484 people per sq km) / 82%
Total area 38,023 sq miles (98,480 sq km)
Languages Korean*
Religions Mahayana Buddhist 47%, Protestant 38%, Roman Catholic 11%, Confucianist 3%, Other 1%
Ethnic mix Korean 100%
Government Presidential system
Currency South Korean won = 100 chon
Literacy rate 98%
Calorie consumption 3058 calories

SPAIN
Southeast Europe

Official name Kingdom of Spain
Formation 1492 / 1713
Capital Madrid
Population 43.1 million / 224 people per sq mile (86 people per sq km) / 78%
Total area 194,896 sq miles (504,782 sq km)
Languages Spanish*, Catalan*, Galician*, Basque*
Religions Roman Catholic 96%, Other 4%
Ethnic mix Castilian Spanish 72%, Catalan 17%, Galician 6%, Basque 2%, Other 2%, Roma 1%
Government Parliamentary system
Currency Euro = 100 cents
Literacy rate 98%
Calorie consumption 3371 calories

SRI LANKA
South Asia

Official name Democratic Socialist Republic of Sri Lanka
Formation 1948 / 1948
Capital Colombo
Population 20.7 million / 828 people per sq mile (320 people per sq km) / 24%
Total area 25,332 sq miles (65,610 sq km)
Languages Sinhala, Tamil, Sinhala-Tamil, English
Religions Buddhist 69%, Hindu 15%, Muslim 8%, Christian 8%
Ethnic mix Sinhalese 74%, Tamil 18%, Moor 7%, Burgher, Malay, and Veddha 1%
Government Mixed presidential–parliamentary system
Currency Sri Lanka rupee = 100 cents
Literacy rate 90%
Calorie consumption 2385 calories

SUDAN
East Africa

Official name Republic of the Sudan
Formation 1956 / 1956
Capital Khartoum
Population 36.2 million / 37 people per sq mile (14 people per sq km) / 36%
Total area 967,493 sq miles (2,505,810 sq km)
Languages Arabic*, Dinka, Nuer, Nubian, Beja, Zande, Bari, Fur, Shilluk, Lotuko
Religions Muslim (mainly Sunni) 70%, Traditional beliefs 20%, Christian 9%, Other 1%
Ethnic mix Other Black 52%, Arab 40%, Dinka and Beja 7%, Other 1%
Government Presidential system
Currency Sudanese pound or dinar = 100 piastres
Literacy rate 59%
Calorie consumption 2228 calories

SURINAME
South America

Official name Republic of Suriname
Formation 1975 / 1975
Capital Paramaribo
Population 499,000 / 8 people per sq mile (3 people per sq km) / 74%
Total area 63,039 sq miles (163,270 sq km)
Languages Dutch*, Sranan (Creole), Javanese, Sarnami Hindi, Saramaccan, Chinese, Carib
Religions Hindu 27%, Protestant 25%, Roman Catholic 23%, Muslim 20%, Traditional beliefs 5%
Ethnic mix Creole 34%, South Asian 34%, Javanese 18%, Black 9%, Other 5%
Government Parliamentary system
Currency Suriname dollar (guilder until 2004) = 100 cents
Literacy rate 88%
Calorie consumption 2652 calories

SWAZILAND
Southern Africa

Official name Kingdom of Swaziland
Formation 1968 / 1968
Capital Mbabane
Population 1 million / 151 people per sq mile (58 people per sq km) / 26%
Total area 6704 sq miles (17,363 sq km)
Languages English*, siSwati*, isiZulu, Xitsonga
Religions Christian 60%, Traditional beliefs 40%
Ethnic mix Swazi 97%, Other 3%
Government Monarchy
Currency Lilangeni = 100 cents
Literacy rate 79%
Calorie consumption 2322 calories

SWEDEN
Northern Europe

Official name Kingdom of Sweden
Formation 1523 / 1905
Capital Stockholm
Population 9 million / 57 people per sq mile (22 people per sq km) / 83%
Total area 173,731 sq miles (449,964 sq km)
Languages Swedish*, Finnish, Sámi
Religions Evangelical Lutheran 82%, Other 13%, Roman Catholic 2%, Muslim 2%, Orthodox Christian 1%
Ethnic mix Swedish 88%, Foreign-born or first-generation immigrant 10%, Finnish and Sámi 2%
Government Parliamentary system
Currency Swedish krona = 100 öre
Literacy rate 99%
Calorie consumption 3185 calories

SWITZERLAND
Central Europe

Official name Swiss Confederation
Formation 1291 / 1857
Capital Bern
Population 7.3 million / 475 people per sq mile (184 people per sq km) / 68%
Total area 15,942 sq miles (41,290 sq km)
Languages German*, French*, Italian*, Romansch*, Swiss-German
Religions Roman Catholic 46%, Protestant 40%, Other and nonreligious 12%, Muslim 2%
Ethnic mix German 65%, French 18%, Italian 10%, Other 6%, Romansch 1%
Government Parliamentary system
Currency Swiss franc = 100 rappen/centimes
Literacy rate 99%
Calorie consumption 3526 calories

SYRIA
Southwest Asia

Official name Syrian Arab Republic
Formation 1941 / 1967
Capital Damascus
Population 19 million / 267 people per sq mile (103 people per sq km) / 55%
Total area 71,498 sq miles (184,180 sq km)
Languages Arabic*, French, Kurdish, Armenian, Circassian, Turkic languages, Assyrian, Aramaic
Religions Sunni Muslim 74%, Other Muslim 16%, Christian 10%
Ethnic mix Arab 89%, Kurdish 6%, Other 3%, Armenian, Turkmen, and Circassian 2%
Government One-party state
Currency Syrian pound = 100 piasters
Literacy rate 83%
Calorie consumption 3038 calories

TAIWAN
East Asia

Official name Republic of China (ROC)
Formation 1949 / 1949
Capital Taipei
Population 22.9 million / 1838 people per sq mile (710 people per sq km) / 69%
Total area 13,892 sq miles (35,980 sq km)
Languages Amoy Chinese, Mandarin Chinese, Hakka Chinese
Religions Buddhist, Confucianist, and Taoist 93%, Christian 5%, Other 2%
Ethnic mix Han (pre-20th-century migration) 84%, Han (20th-century migration) 14%, Aboriginal 2%
Government Presidential system
Currency Taiwan dollar = 100 cents
Literacy rate 97%
Calorie consumption Not available

TAJIKISTAN
Central Asia

Official name Republic of Tajikistan
Formation 1991 / 1991
Capital Dushanbe
Population 6.5 million / 118 people per sq mile (45 people per sq km) / 28%
Total area 55,251 sq miles (143,100 sq km)
Languages Tajik*, Uzbek, Russian
Religions Sunni Muslim 80%, Other 15%, Shi'a Muslim 5%
Ethnic mix Tajik 62%, Uzbek 24%, Russian 8%, Other 4%, Tatar 1%, Kyrgyz 1%
Government Presidential system
Currency Somoni = 100 diram
Literacy rate 99%
Calorie consumption 1828 calories

TANZANIA
East Africa

Official name United Republic of Tanzania
Formation 1964 / 1964
Capital Dodoma
Population 38.3 million / 112 people per sq mile (43 people per sq km) / 33%
Total area 364,898 sq miles (945,087 sq km)
Languages English*, Kiswahili*, Sukuma, Chagga, Nyamwezi, Hehe, Makonde, Yao, Sandawe
Religions Muslim 33%, Christian 33%, Traditional beliefs 30%, Other 4%
Ethnic mix Native African (over 120 tribes) 99%, European and Asian 1%
Government Presidential system
Currency Tanzanian shilling = 100 cents
Literacy rate 69%
Calorie consumption 1975 calories

THAILAND
Southeastern Asia

Official name Kingdom of Thailand
Formation 1238 / 1907
Capital Bangkok
Population 64.2 million / 325 people per sq mile (126 people per sq km) / 22%
Total area 198,455 sq miles (514,000 sq km)
Languages Thai*, Chinese, Malay, Khmer, Mon, Karen, Miao
Religions Buddhist 95%, Muslim 4%, Other (including Christian) 1%
Ethnic mix Thai 83%, Chinese 12%, Malay 3%, Khmer and Other 2%
Government Parliamentary system
Currency Baht = 100 stang
Literacy rate 93%
Calorie consumption 2467 calories

TOGO
Western Africa

Official name Republic of Togo
Formation 1960 / 1960
Capital Lomé
Population 6.1 million / 290 people per sq mile (112 people per sq km) / 36%
Total area 21,924 sq miles (56,785 sq km)
Languages French*, Ewe, Kabye, Gurma
Religions Traditional beliefs 50%, Christian 35%, Muslim 15%
Ethnic mix Ewe 46%, Kabye 27%, Other African 26%, European 1%
Government Presidential system
Currency CFA franc = 100 centimes
Literacy rate 53%
Calorie consumption 2345 calories

TONGA
Australasia & Oceania

Official name Kingdom of Tonga
Formation 1970 / 1970
Capital Nuku'alofa
Population 112,422 / 404 people per sq mile (156 people per sq km) / 43%
Total area 289 sq miles (748 sq km)
Languages Tongan*, English
Religions Free Wesleyan 41%, Roman Catholic 16%, Church of Jesus Christ of Latter-day Saints 14%, Free Church of Tonga 12%, Other 17%
Ethnic mix Polynesian 99%, Other 1%
Government Monarchy
Currency Pa'anga (Tongan dollar) = 100 seniti
Literacy rate 99%
Calorie consumption Not available

TRINIDAD & TOBAGO
West Indies

Official name Republic of Trinidad and Tobago
Formation 1962 / 1962
Capital Port-of-Spain
Population 1.3 million / 656 people per sq mile (253 people per sq km) / 74%
Total area 1980 sq miles (5128 sq km)
Languages English*, English Creole, Hindi, French, Spanish
Religions Christian 60%, Hindu 24%, Other and nonreligious 9%, Muslim 7%
Ethnic mix East Indian 40%, Black 40%, Mixed race 19%, White and Chinese 1%
Government Parliamentary system
Currency Trinidad and Tobago dollar = 100 cents
Literacy rate 99%
Calorie consumption 2732 calories

TUNISIA
North Africa

Official name Republic of Tunisia
Formation 1956 / 1956
Capital Tunis
Population 10.1 million / 168 people per sq mile (65 people per sq km) / 68%
Total area 63,169 sq miles (163,610 sq km)
Languages Arabic*, French
Religions Muslim (mainly Sunni) 98%, Christian 1%, Jewish 1%
Ethnic mix Arab and Berber 98%, Jewish 1%, European 1%
Government Presidential system
Currency Tunisian dinar = 1000 millimes
Literacy rate 74%
Calorie consumption 3238 calories

TURKEY
Asia / Europe

Official name Republic of Turkey
Formation 1923 / 1939
Capital Ankara
Population 73.2 million / 246 people per sq mile (95 people per sq km) / 75%
Total area 301,382 sq miles (780,580 sq km)
Languages Turkish*, Kurdish, Arabic, Circassian, Armenian, Greek, Georgian, Ladino
Religions Muslim (mainly Sunni) 99%, Other 1%
Ethnic mix Turkish 70%, Kurdish 20%, Other 8%, Arab 2%
Government Parliamentary system
Currency new Turkish lira = 100 kurus
Literacy rate 88%
Calorie consumption 3357 calories

TURKMENISTAN
Central Asia

Official name Turkmenistan
Formation 1991 / 1991
Capital Ashgabat
Population 4.8 million / 25 people per sq mile (10 people per sq km) / 45%
Total area 188,455 sq miles (488,100 sq km)
Languages Turkmen*, Uzbek, Russian, Kazakh, Tatar
Religions Sunni Muslim 87%, Orthodox Christian 11%, Other 2%
Ethnic mix Turkmen 77%, Uzbek 9%, Russian 7%, Other 4%, Kazakh 2%, Tatar 1%
Government One-party state
Currency Manat = 100 tenga
Literacy rate 99%
Calorie consumption 2742 calories

TUVALU
Australasia & Oceania

Official name Tuvalu
Formation 1978 / 1978
Capital Fongafale, on Funafuti Atoll
Population 11,636 / 1164 people per sq mile (448 people per sq km) / 45%
Total area 10 sq miles (26 sq km)
Languages Tuvaluan, Kiribati, English
Religions Church of Tuvalu 97%, Other 1%, Baha'i 1%, Seventh-day Adventist 1%
Ethnic mix Polynesian 96%, Other 4%
Government Nonparty system
Currency Australian dollar and Tuvaluan dollar = 100 cents
Literacy rate 98%
Calorie consumption Not available

UGANDA
East Africa

Official name Republic of Uganda
Formation 1962 / 1962
Capital Kampala
Population 28.8 million / 374 people per sq mile (144 people per sq km) / 14%
Total area 91,135 sq miles (236,040 sq km)
Languages English*, Luganda, Nkole, Chiga, Lango, Acholi, Teso, Lugbara
Religions Roman Catholic 38%, Protestant 33%, Traditional beliefs 13%, Muslim (mainly Sunni) 8%, Other 8%
Ethnic mix Bantu tribes 50%, Other 45%, Sudanese 5%
Government Nonparty system
Currency New Uganda shilling = 100 cents
Literacy rate 69%
Calorie consumption 2410 calories

UKRAINE
Eastern Europe

Official name Ukraine
Formation 1991 / 1991
Capital Kiev
Population 46.5 million / 199 people per sq mile (77 people per sq km) / 68%
Total area 223,089 sq miles (603,700 sq km)
Languages Ukrainian*, Russian, Tatar
Religions Christian (mainly Orthodox) 95%, Other 4%, Jewish 1%
Ethnic mix Ukrainian 73%, Russian 22%, Other 4%, Jewish 1%
Government Presidential system
Currency Hryvna = 100 kopiykas
Literacy rate 99%
Calorie consumption 3054 calories

UNITED ARAB EMIRATES
Southwest Asia

Official name United Arab Emirates
Formation 1971 / 1972
Capital Abu Dhabi
Population 4.5 million / 139 people per sq mile (54 people per sq km) / 86%
Total area 32,000 sq miles (82,880 sq km)
Languages Arabic*, Farsi, Indian and Pakistani languages, English
Religions Muslim (mainly Sunni) 96%, Christian, Hindu, and other 4%
Ethnic mix Asian 60%, Emirian 25%, Other Arab 12%, European 3%
Government Monarchy
Currency UAE dirham = 100 fils
Literacy rate 77%
Calorie consumption 3225 calories

UNITED KINGDOM
Northwest Europe

Official name United Kingdom of Great Britain and Northern Ireland
Formation 1707 / 1922
Capital London
Population 59.7 million / 640 people per sq mile (247 people per sq km) / 90%
Total area 94,525 sq miles (244,820 sq km)
Languages English*, Welsh, Scottish Gaelic
Religions Anglican 45%, Roman Catholic 9%, Presbyterian 4%, Other 42%
Ethnic mix English 80%, Scottish 9%, West Indian, Asian, and other 5%, Northern Irish 3%, Welsh 3%
Government Parliamentary system
Currency Pound sterling = 100 pence
Literacy rate 99%
Calorie consumption 3412 calories

UNITED STATES
North America

Official name United States of America
Formation 1776 / 1959
Capital Washington D.C.
Population 298 million / 84 people per sq mile (33 people per sq km) / 77%
Total area 3,717,792 sq miles (9,626,091 sq km)
Languages English*, Spanish, Chinese, French, German, Tagalog, Vietnamese, Italian, Korean, Russian, Polish
Religions Protestant 52%, Roman Catholic 25%, Muslim 2%, Jewish 2%, Other 19%
Ethnic mix White 69%, Hispanic 13%, Black American/African 13%, Asian 4%, Native American 1%
Government Presidential system
Currency US dollar = 100 cents
Literacy rate 99%
Calorie consumption 3774 calories

URUGUAY
South America

Official name Eastern Republic of Uruguay
Formation 1828 / 1828
Capital Montevideo
Population 3.5 million / 52 people per sq mile (20 people per sq km) / 91%
Total area 68,039 sq miles (176,220 sq km)
Languages Spanish*
Religions Roman Catholic 66%, Other and nonreligious 30%, Jewish 2%, Protestant 2%
Ethnic mix White 90%, Mestizo 6%, Black 4%
Government Presidential system
Currency Uruguayan peso = 100 centésimos
Literacy rate 98%
Calorie consumption 2828 calories

UZBEKISTAN
Central Asia

Official name Republic of Uzbekistan
Formation 1991 / 1991
Capital Tashkent
Population 26.6 million / 154 people per sq mile (59 people per sq km) / 37%
Total area 172,741 sq miles (447,400 sq km)
Languages Uzbek*, Russian, Tajik, Kazakh
Religions Sunni Muslim 88%, Orthodox Christian 9%, Other 3%
Ethnic mix Uzbek 71%, Other 12%, Russian 8%, Tajik 5%, Kazakh 4%
Government Presidential system
Currency Som = 100 tiyin
Literacy rate 99%
Calorie consumption 2241 calories

VANUATU
Australasia & Oceania

Official name Republic of Vanuatu
Formation 1980 / 1980
Capital Port Vila
Population 211,000 / 45 people per sq mile (17 people per sq km) / 20%
Total area 4710 sq miles (12,200 sq km)
Languages Bislama* (Melanesian pidgin), English*, French*, other indigenous languages
Religions Presbyterian 37%, Other 19%, Anglican 15%, Roman Catholic 15%, Traditional beliefs 8%, Seventh-day Adventist 6%
Ethnic mix Melanesian 94%, Other 3%, Polynesian 3%
Government Parliamentary system
Currency Vatu = 100 centimes
Literacy rate 74%
Calorie consumption 2587 calories

VATICAN CITY
Southern Europe

Official name State of the Vatican City
Formation 1929 / 1929
Capital Vatican City
Population 921 / 5418 people per sq mile (2093 people per sq km) / 100%
Total area 0.17 sq miles (0.44 sq km)
Languages Italian*, Latin*
Religions Roman Catholic 100%
Ethnic mix The current pope is German. Cardinals are from many nationalities, but Italians form the largest group. Most of the resident lay persons are Italian.
Government Papal state
Currency Euro = 100 cents
Literacy rate 99%
Calorie consumption Not available

VENEZUELA
South America

Official name Bolivarian Republic of Venezuela
Formation 1830 / 1830
Capital Caracas
Population 26.7 million / 78 people per sq mile (30 people per sq km) / 87%
Total area 352,143 sq miles (912,050 sq km)
Languages Spanish*, Amerindian languages
Religions Roman Catholic 89%, Protestant and other 11%
Ethnic mix Mestizo 69%, White 20%, Black 9%, Amerindian 2%
Government Presidential system
Currency Bolivar = 100 centimos
Literacy rate 93%
Calorie consumption 2336 calories

VIETNAM
Southeast Asia

Official name Socialist Republic of Vietnam
Formation 1976 / 1976
Capital Hanoi
Population 84.2 million / 670 people per sq mile (259 people per sq km) / 20%
Total area 127,243 sq miles (329,560 sq km)
Languages Vietnamese*, Chinese, Thai, Khmer, Muong, Nung, Miao, Yao, Jarai
Religions Buddhist 55%, Other and nonreligious 38%, Christian (mainly Roman Catholic) 7%
Ethnic mix Vietnamese 88%, Other 6%, Chinese 4%, Thai 2%
Government One-party state
Currency Dông = 10 hao = 100 xu
Literacy rate 90%
Calorie consumption 2566 calories

YEMEN
Southwest Asia

Official name Republic of Yemen
Formation 1990 / 1990
Capital Sana
Population 21 million / 97 people per sq mile (37 people per sq km) / 25%
Total area 203,849 sq miles (527,970 sq km)
Languages Arabic*
Religions Sunni Muslim 55%, Shi'a Muslim 42%, Christian, Hindu, and Jewish 3%
Ethnic mix Arab 95%, Afro-Arab 3%, Indian, Somali, and European 2%
Government Presidential system
Currency Yemeni rial = 100 sene
Literacy rate 49%
Calorie consumption 2038 calories

ZAMBIA
Southern Africa

Official name Republic of Zambia
Formation 1964 / 1964
Capital Lusaka
Population 11.7 million / 41 people per sq mile (16 people per sq km) / 45%
Total area 290,584 sq miles (752,614 sq km)
Languages English*, Bemba, Tonga, Nyanja, Lozi, Lala-Bisa, Nsenga
Religions Christian 63%, Traditional beliefs 36%, Muslim and Hindu 1%
Ethnic mix Bemba 34%, Other African 26%, Tonga 16%, Nyanja 14%, Lozi 9%, European 1%
Government Presidential system
Currency Zambian kwacha = 100 ngwee
Literacy rate 68%
Calorie consumption 1927 calories

ZIMBABWE
Southern Africa

Official name Republic of Zimbabwe
Formation 1980 / 1980
Capital Harare
Population 13 million / 87 people per sq mile (34 people per sq km) / 35%
Total area 150,803 sq miles (390,580 sq km)
Languages English*, Shona, isiNdebele
Religions Syncretic (Christian/traditional beliefs) 50%, Christian 25%, Traditional beliefs 24%, Other (including Muslim) 1%
Ethnic mix Shona 71%, Ndebele 16%, Other African 11%, White 1%, Asian 1%
Government Presidential system
Currency Zimbabwe dollar = 100 cents
Literacy rate 90%
Calorie consumption 1943 calories

Geographical names

The following glossary lists geographical terms occurring on the maps and in main-entry names in the Index-Gazetteer. These terms may precede, follow or be run together with the proper element of the name; where they precede it the term is reversed for indexing purposes - thus Poluostrov Yamal is indexed as Yamal, Poluostrov.

Key

Geographical term
Language, Term

A

Å *Danish, Norwegian*, River
Āb *Persian*, River
Adrar *Berber*, Mountains
Agía, Ágios *Greek*, Saint
Air *Indonesian*, River
Ákra *Greek*, Cape, point
Alpen *German*, Alps
Alt- *German*, Old
Altiplanicie *Spanish*, Plateau
Älve(en) *Swedish*, River
-ån *Swedish*, River
Anse *French*, Bay
'Aqabat *Arabic*, Pass
Archipiélago *Spanish*, Archipelago
Arcipelago *Italian*, Archipelago
Arquipélago *Portuguese*, Archipelago
Arrecife(s) *Spanish*, Reef(s)
Aru *Tamil*, River
Augstiene *Latvian*, Upland
Aukštuma *Lithuanian*, Upland
Aust- *Norwegian*, Eastern
Avtonomnyy Okrug *Russian*, Autonomous district
Āw *Kurdish*, River
'Ayn *Arabic*, Spring, well
'Ayoûn *Arabic*, Wells

B

Baelt *Danish*, Strait
Bahía *Spanish*, Bay
Baḥr *Arabic*, River
Baía *Portuguese*, Bay
Baie *French*, Bay
Bañado *Spanish*, Marshy land
Bandao *Chinese*, Peninsula
Banjaran *Malay*, Mountain range
Barajı *Turkish*, Dam
Barragem *Portuguese*, Reservoir
Bassin *French*, Basin
Batang *Malay*, Stream
Beinn, Ben *Gaelic*, Mountain
-berg *Afrikaans, Norwegian*, Mountain
Besar *Indonesian, Malay*, Big
Birkat, Birket *Arabic*, Lake, well,
Boğazi *Turkish*, Lake
Boka *Serbo-Croatian*, Bay
Bol'sh-aya, -iye, -oy, -oye *Russian*, Big
Botigh(i) *Uzbek*, Depression basin
-bre(en) *Norwegian*, Glacier
Bredning *Danish*, Bay
Bucht *German*, Bay
Bugt(en) *Danish*, Bay
Buḥayrat *Arabic*, Lake, reservoir
Buḥeirat *Arabic*, Lake
Bukit *Malay*, Mountain
-bukta *Norwegian*, Bay
bukten *Swedish*, Bay
Bulag *Mongolian*, Spring
Bulak *Uighur*, Spring
Burnu *Turkish*, Cape, point
Buuraha *Somali*, Mountains

C

Cabo *Portuguese*, Cape
Caka *Tibetan*, Salt lake
Canal *Spanish*, Channel
Cap *French*, Cape
Capo *Italian*, Cape, headland
Cascada *Portuguese*, Waterfall
Cayo(s) *Spanish*, Islet(s), rock(s)
Cerro *Spanish*, Mountain
Chaîne *French*, Mountain range
Chapada *Portuguese*, Hills, upland
Chau *Cantonese*, Island
Chāy *Turkish*, River
Chhâk *Cambodian*, Bay
Chhu *Tibetan*, River
-chŏsuji *Korean*, Reservoir
Chott *Arabic*, Depression, salt lake
Chŭli *Uzbek*, Grassland, steppe
Ch'ün-tao *Chinese*, Island group
Chuŏr Phnum *Cambodian*, Mountains
Ciudad *Spanish*, City, town
Co *Tibetan*, Lake
Colline(s) *French*, Hill(s)
Cordillera *Spanish*, Mountain range
Costa *Spanish*, Coast
Côte *French*, Coast
Coxilha *Portuguese*, Mountains
Cuchilla *Spanish*, Mountains

D

Daban *Mongolian, Uighur*, Pass
Daği *Azerbaijani, Turkish*, Mountain
Dağlari *Azerbaijani, Turkish*, Mountains
-dake *Japanese*, Peak
-dal(en) *Norwegian*, Valley
Danau *Indonesian*, Lake
Dao *Chinese*, Island
Đao *Vietnamese*, Island
Daryā *Persian*, River
Daryācheh *Persian*, Lake
Dasht *Persian*, Desert, plain
Dawḥat *Arabic*, Bay
Denizi *Turkish*, Sea
Dere *Turkish*, Stream
Desierto *Spanish*, Desert
Dili *Azerbaijani*, Spit
-do *Korean*, Island
Dooxo *Somali*, Valley
Düzü *Azerbaijani*, Steppe
-dwīp *Bengali*, Island

E

-eilanden *Dutch*, Islands
Embalse *Spanish*, Reservoir
Ensenada *Spanish*, Bay
Erg *Arabic*, Dunes
Estany *Catalan*, Lake
Estero *Spanish*, Inlet
Estrecho *Spanish*, Strait
Étang *French*, Lagoon, lake
-ey *Icelandic*, Island
Ezero *Bulgarian, Macedonian*, Lake
Ezers *Latvian*, Lake

F

Feng *Chinese*, Peak
Fjord *Danish*, Fjord
-fjord(en) *Danish, Norwegian, Swedish*, fjord
-fjørdhur *Faeroese*, Fjord
Fleuve *French*, River
Fliegu *Maltese*, Channel
-fljór *Icelandic*, River
-flói *Icelandic*, Bay
Forêt *French*, Forest

G

-gan *Japanese*, Rock
-gang *Korean*, River
Ganga *Hindi, Nepali, Sinhala*, River
Gaoyuan *Chinese*, Plateau
Garagumy *Turkmen*, Sands
-gawa *Japanese*, River
Gebel *Arabic*, Mountain
-gebirge *German*, Mountain range
Ghadīr *Arabic*, Well
Ghubbat *Arabic*, Bay
Gjiri *Albanian*, Bay
Gol *Mongolian*, River
Golfe *French*, Gulf
Golfo *Italian, Spanish*, Gulf
Göl(ü) *Turkish*, Lake
Golyam, -a *Bulgarian*, Big
Gora *Russian, Serbo-Croatian*, Mountain
Góra *Polish*, mountain
Gory *Russian*, Mountain
Gryada *Russian*, ridge
Guba *Russian*, Bay
-gundo *Korean*, island group
Gunung *Malay*, Mountain

H

Ḥadd *Arabic*, Spit
-haehyŏp *Korean*, Strait
Haff *German*, Lagoon
Hai *Chinese*, Bay, lake, sea
Haixia *Chinese*, Strait
Hamada *Arabic*, Plateau
Ḥammādat *Arabic*, Plateau
Hāmūn *Persian*, Lake
-hantō *Japanese*, Peninsula
Har, Haré *Hebrew*, Mountain
Ḥarrat *Arabic*, Lava-field
Hav(et) *Danish*, Swedish, Sea
Hawr *Arabic*, Lake
Hāyk' *Amharic*, Lake
He *Chinese*, River
-hegység *Hungarian*, Mountain range
Heide *German*, Heath, moorland
Helodrano *Malagasy*, Bay
Higashi- *Japanese*, East(ern)
Ḥiṣā' *Arabic*, Well
Hka *Burmese*, River
-ho *Korean*, Lake
Hô *Korean*, Reservoir
Holot *Hebrew*, Dunes
Hora *Belarussian, Czech*, Mountain
Hrada *Belarussian*, Mountain, ridge
Hsi *Chinese*, River
Hu *Chinese*, Lake
Huk *Danish*, Point

I

Île(s) *French*, Island(s)
Ilha(s) *Portuguese*, Island(s)
Ilhéu(s) *Portuguese*, Islet(s)
Imeni *Russian*, In the name of
Inish- *Gaelic*, Island
Insel(n) *German*, Island(s)
Irmağı, Irmak *Turkish*, River
Isla(s) *Spanish*, Island(s)
Isola (Isole) *Italian*, Island(s)

J

Jabal *Arabic*, Mountain
Jāl *Arabic*, Ridge
-järv *Estonian*, Lake
-järvi *Finnish*, Lake
Jazā'ir *Arabic*, Islands
Jazīrat *Arabic*, Island
Jazīreh *Persian*, Island
Jebel *Arabic*, Mountain
Jezero *Serbo-Croatian*, Lake
Jezioro *Polish*, Lake
Jiang *Chinese*, River
-jima *Japanese*, Island
Jižní *Czech*, Southern
-jõgi *Estonian*, River
-joki *Finnish*, River
-jökull *Icelandic*, Glacier
Jūn *Arabic*, Bay
Juzur *Arabic*, Islands

K

Kaikyō *Japanese*, Strait
-kaise *Lappish*, Mountain
Kali *Nepali*, River
Kalnas *Lithuanian*, Mountain
Kalns *Latvian*, Mountain
Kang *Chinese*, Harbor
Kangri *Tibetan*, Mountain(s)
Kaôh *Cambodian*, Island
Kapp *Norwegian*, Cape
Káto *Greek*, Lower
Kavīr *Persian*, Desert
K'edi *Georgian*, Mountain range
Kediet *Arabic*, Mountain
Kepi *Albanian*, Cape, point
Kepulauan *Indonesian, Malay*, Island group
Khalīg, Khalīj *Arabic*, Gulf
Khawr *Arabic*, Inlet
Khola *Nepali*, River
Khrebet *Russian*, Mountain range
Ko *Thai*, Island
-ko *Japanese*, Inlet, lake
Kólpos *Greek*, Bay
-kopf *German*, Peak
Körfäzi *Azerbaijani*, Bay
Körfezi *Turkish*, Bay
Kõrgustik *Estonian*, Upland
Kosa *Russian, Ukrainian*, Spit
Koshi *Nepali*, River
Kou *Chinese*, Rivermouth
Kowtal *Persian*, Pass
Kray *Russian*, Region, territory
Kryazh *Russian*, Ridge
Kuduk *Uighur*, Well
Kūh(hā) *Persian*, Mountain(s)
-kul' *Russian*, Lake
Kŭl(i) *Tajik, Uzbek*, Lake
-kundo *Korean*, Island group
-kysten *Norwegian*, Coast
Kyun *Burmese*, Island

L

Laaq *Somali*, Watercourse
Lac *French*, Lake
Lacul *Romanian*, Lake
Lagh *Somali*, Stream
Lago *Italian, Portuguese, Spanish*, Lake
Lagoa *Portuguese*, Lagoon
Laguna *Italian, Spanish*, Lagoon, lake
Laht *Estonian*, Bay
Laut *Indonesian*, Bay
Lembalemba *Malagasy*, Plateau
Lerr *Armenian*, Mountain
Lerrnashght'a *Armenian*, Mountain range
Les *Czech*, Forest
Lich *Armenian*, Lake
Liehtao *Chinese*, Island group
Liqeni *Albanian*, Lake
Límni *Greek*, Lake
Ling *Chinese*, Mountain range
Llano *Spanish*, Plain, prairie
Lumi *Albanian*, River
Lyman *Ukrainian*, Estuary

M

Madīnat *Arabic*, City, town
Mae Nam *Thai*, River
-mägi *Estonian*, Hill
Maja *Albanian*, Mountain
Mal *Albanian*, Mountains
Mal-aya, -oye, -yy, *Russian*, Small
-man *Korean*, Bay
Mar *Spanish*, Lake
Marios *Lithuanian*, Lake
Massif *French*, Mountains
Meer *German*, Lake
-meer *Dutch*, Lake
Melkosopochnik *Russian*, Plain
-meri *Estonian*, Sea
Mifraz *Hebrew*, Bay
Minami- *Japanese*, South(ern)
-misaki *Japanese*, Cape, point
Monkhafad *Arabic*, Depression
Montagne(s) *French*, Mountain(s)
Montañas *Spanish*, Mountains
Mont(s) *French*, Mountain(s)
Monte *Italian, Portuguese*, Mountain
More *Russian*, Sea
Mörön *Mongolian*, River
Mys *Russian*, Cape, point

N

-nada *Japanese*, Open stretch of water
Nagor'ye *Russian*, Upland
Naḥal *Hebrew*, River
Nahr *Arabic*, River
Nam *Laotian*, River
Namakzār *Persian*, Salt desert
Né-a, -on, -os *Greek*, New
Nedre- *Norwegian*, Lower
-neem *Estonian*, Cape, point
Nehri *Turkish*, River
-nes *Norwegian*, Cape, point
Nevado *Spanish*, Mountain (snow-capped)
Nieder- *German*, Lower
Nishi- *Japanese*, West(ern)
-nísi *Greek*, Island
Nisoi *Greek*, Islands
Nizhn-eye, -iy, -iye, -yaya *Russian*, Lower
Nizmennost' *Russian*, Lowland, plain
Nord *Danish, French, German*, North
Norte *Portuguese, Spanish*, North
Nos *Bulgarian*, Point, spit
Nosy *Malagasy*, Island
Nov-a, -i, *Bulgarian, Serbo-Croatian*, New
Nov-aya, -o, -oye, -yy, -yye *Russian*, New
Now-a, -e, -y *Polish*, New
Nur *Mongolian*, Lake
Nuruu *Mongolian*, Mountains
Nuur *Mongolian*, Lake
Nyzovyna *Ukrainian*, Lowland, plain

O

-ø *Danish*, Island
Ober- *German*, Upper
Oblast' *Russian*, Province
Órmos *Greek*, Bay
Orol(i) *Uzbek*, Island
Øster- *Norwegian*, Eastern
Ostrov(a) *Russian*, Island(s)
Otok *Serbo-Croatian*, Island
Oued *Arabic*, Watercourse
-oy *Faeroese*, Island
-øy(a) *Norwegian*, Island
Oya *Sinhala*, River
Ozero *Russian, Ukrainian*, Lake

P

Passo *Italian*, Pass
Pegunungan *Indonesian, Malay*, Mountain range
Pélagos *Greek*, Sea
Pendi *Chinese*, Basin
Penisola *Italian*, Peninsula
Pertuis *French*, Strait
Peski *Russian*, Sands
Phanom *Thai*, Mountain
Phou *Laotian*, Mountain
Pi *Chinese*, Point
Pic *Catalan, French*, Peak
Pico *Portuguese, Spanish*, Peak
-piggen *Danish*, Peak
Pik *Russian*, Peak
Pivostriv *Ukrainian*, Peninsula
Planalto *Portuguese*, Plateau
Planina, Planini *Bulgarian, Macedonian, Serbo-Croatian*, Mountain range
Plato *Russian*, Plateau
Ploskogor'ye *Russian*, Upland
Poluostrov *Russian*, Peninsula
Ponta *Portuguese*, Point
Porthmós *Greek*, Strait
Pótamos *Greek*, River
Presa *Spanish*, Dam
Prokhod *Bulgarian*, Pass
Proliv *Russian*, Strait
Pulau *Indonesian, Malay*, Island
Pulu *Malay*, Island
Punta *Spanish*, Point
Pushcha *Belorussian*, Forest
Puszcza *Polish*, Forest

Q

Qā' *Arabic*, Depression
Qalamat *Arabic*, Well
Qatorkŭh(i) *Tajik*, Mountain
Qiuling *Chinese*, Hills
Qolleh *Persian*, Mountain
Qu *Tibetan*, Stream
Quan *Chinese*, Well
Qulla(i) *Tajik*, Peak
Qundao *Chinese*, Island group

R

Raas *Somali*, Cape
-rags *Latvian*, Cape
Ramlat *Arabic*, Sands
Ra's *Arabic*, Cape, headland, point
Ravnina *Bulgarian, Russian*, Plain
Récif *French*, Reef
Recife *Portuguese*, Reef
Reka *Bulgarian*, River
Represa (Rep.) *Portuguese, Spanish*, Reservoir
Reshteh *Persian*, Mountain range
Respublika *Russian*, Republic, first-order administrative division
Respublika(si) *Uzbek*, Republic, first-order administrative division
-retsugan *Japanese*, Chain of rocks
-rettō *Japanese*, Island chain
Riacho *Spanish*, Stream
Riban' *Malagasy*, Mountains
Rio *Portuguese*, River
Río *Spanish*, River
Riu *Catalan*, River
Rivier *Dutch*, River
Rivière *French*, River
Rowd *Pashtu*, River
Rt *Serbo-Croatian*, Point
Rūd *Persian*, River
Rūdkhāneh *Persian*, River
Rudohorie *Slovak*, Mountains
Ruisseau *French*, Stream

S

-saar *Estonian*, Island
-saari *Finnish*, Island
Sabkhat *Arabic*, Salt marsh
Sāgar(a) *Hindi*, Lake, reservoir
Ṣaḥrā' *Arabic*, Desert
Saint, Sainte *French*, Saint
Salar *Spanish*, Salt-pan
Salto *Portuguese, Spanish*, Waterfall
Samudra *Sinhala*, Reservoir
-san *Japanese, Korean*, Mountain
-sanchi *Japanese*, Mountains
-sandur *Icelandic*, Beach
Sankt *German, Swedish*, Saint
-sanmaek *Korean*, Mountain range
-sanmyaku *Japanese*, Mountain range
San, Santa, Santo *Italian, Portuguese, Spanish*, Saint
São *Portuguese*, Saint
Sarīr *Arabic*, Desert
Sebkha, Sebkhet *Arabic*, Depression, salt marsh
Sedlo *Czech*, Pass
See *German*, Lake
Selat *Indonesian*, Strait
Selatan *Indonesian*, Southern
-selkä *Finnish*, Lake, ridge
Selseleh *Persian*, Mountain range
Serra *Portuguese*, Mountain
Serranía *Spanish*, Mountain
-seto *Japanese*, Channel, strait
Sever-naya, -noye, -nyy, -o *Russian*, Northern
Sha'īb *Arabic*, Watercourse
Shākh *Kurdish*, Mountain
Shamo *Chinese*, Desert
Shan *Chinese*, Mountain(s)
Shankou *Chinese*, Pass
Shanmo *Chinese*, Mountain range
Shaṭṭ *Arabic*, Distributary
Shet' *Amharic*, River
Shi *Chinese*, Municipality
-shima *Japanese*, Island
Shiqqat *Arabic*, Depression
-shotō *Japanese*, Group of islands
Shuiku *Chinese*, Reservoir
Shūrkhog(i) *Uzbek*, Salt marsh
Sierra *Spanish*, Mountains
Sint *Dutch*, Saint
-sjø(en) *Norwegian*, Lake
-sjön *Swedish*, Lake
Solonchak *Russian*, Salt lake
Solonchakovyye Vpadiny *Russian*, Salt basin, wetlands
Sơn *Vietnamese*, Mountain
Sông *Vietnamese*, River
Sør- *Norwegian*, Southern
-spitze *German*, Peak
Star-á, -é *Czech*, Old
Star-aya, -oye, -yy, -yye *Russian*, Old
Stenó *Greek*, Strait
Step' *Russian*, Steppe
Štít *Slovak*, Peak
Stœng *Cambodian*, River
Stolovaya Strana *Russian*, Plateau
Stredné *Slovak*, Middle
Střední *Czech*, Middle
Stretto *Italian*, Strait
Su Anbari *Azerbaijani*, Reservoir
-suidō *Japanese*, Channel, strait
Sund *Swedish*, Sound, strait
Sungai *Indonesian, Malay*, River
Suu *Turkish*, River

T

Tal *Mongolian*, Plain
Tandavan' *Malagasy*, Mountain range
Tangorombohitr' *Malagasy*, Mountain massif
Tanjung *Indonesian, Malay*, Cape, point
Tao *Chinese*, Island
Ṭaraq *Arabic*, Hills
Tassili *Berber*, Mountain, plateau
Tau *Russian*, Mountain(s)
Taungdan *Burmese*, Mountain range
Techníti Límni *Greek*, Reservoir
Tekojärvi *Finnish*, Reservoir
Teluk *Indonesian, Malay*, Bay
Tengah *Indonesian*, Middle
Terara *Amharic*, Mountain
Timur *Indonesian*, Eastern
-tind(an) *Norwegian*, Peak
Tizma(si) *Uzbek*, Mountain range, ridge
-tō *Japanese*, island
Tog *Somali*, Valley
-tōge *Japanese*, pass
Togh(i) *Uzbek*, mountain
Tônlé *Cambodian*, Lake
Top *Dutch*, Peak
-tunturi *Finnish*, Mountain
Ṭurāq *Arabic*, hills
Tur'at *Arabic*, Channel

U

Udde(n) *Swedish*, Cape, point
'Uqlat *Arabic*, Well
Utara *Indonesian*, Northern
Uul *Mongolian*, Mountains

V

Väin *Estonian*, Strait
Vallée *French*, Valley
-vatn *Icelandic*, Lake
-vatnet *Norwegian*, Lake
Velayat *Turkmen*, Province
-vesi *Finnish*, Lake
Vestre- *Norwegian*, Western
-vidda *Norwegian*, Plateau
-vík *Icelandic*, Bay
-viken *Swedish*, Bay, inlet
Vinh *Vietnamese*, Bay
Víztárloló *Hungarian*, Reservoir
Vodaskhovishcha *Belarussian*, Reservoir
Vodokhranilishche (Vdkhr.) *Russian*, Reservoir
Vodoskhovyshche (Vdskh.) *Ukrainian*, Reservoir
Volcán *Spanish*, Volcano
Vostochn-o, yy *Russian*, Eastern
Vozvyshennost' *Russian*, Upland, plateau
Vozyera *Belarussian*, Lake
Vpadina *Russian*, Depression
Vrchovina *Czech*, Mountains
Vrha *Macedonian*, Peak
Vychodné *Slovak*, Eastern
Vysochyna *Ukrainian*, Upland
Vysočina *Czech*, Upland

W

Waadi *Somali*, Watercourse
Wādī *Arabic* Watercourse
Wāḥat, Wâhat *Arabic*, Oasis
Wald *German*, Forest
Wan *Chinese*, Bay
Way *Indonesian*, River
Webi *Somali*, River
Wenz *Amharic*, River
Wiloyat(i) *Uzbek*, Province
Wyżyna *Polish*, Upland
Wzgórza *Polish*, Upland
Wzvyshsha *Belarussian*, Upland

X

Xé *Laotian*, River
Xi *Chinese*, Stream

Y

-yama *Japanese*, Mountain
Yanchi *Chinese*, Salt lake
Yang *Chinese*, Bay
Yanhu *Chinese*, Salt lake
Yarımadası *Azerbaijani, Turkish*, Peninsula
Yaylası *Turkish*, Plateau
Yazovir *Bulgarian*, Reservoir
Yoma *Burmese*, Mountains
Ytre- *Norwegian*, Outer
Yü *Chinese*, Island
Yunhe *Chinese*, Canal
Yuzhn-o, -yy *Russian*, Southern

Z

-zaki *Japanese*, Cape, point
Zaliv *Bulgarian, Russian*, Bay
-zan *Japanese*, Mountain
Zangbo *Tibetan*, River
Zapadn-aya, -o, -yy *Russian*, Western
Západné *Slovak*, Western
Západní *Czech*, Western
Zatoka *Polish, Ukrainian*, Bay
-zee *Dutch*, Sea
Zemlya *Russian*, Earth, land
Zizhiqu *Chinese*, Autonomous region

25 de Agosto - Achar

INDEX

Glossary of Abbreviations

This glossary provides a comprehensive guide to the abbreviations used in this Atlas, and in the Index.

A
abbrev. abbreviated
AD Anno Domini
Afr. Afrikaans
Alb. Albanian
Amh. Amharic
anc. ancient
approx. approximately
Ar. Arabic
Arm. Armenian
ASEAN Association of South East Asian Nations
ASSR Autonomous Soviet Socialist Republic
Aust. Australian
Az. Azerbaijani
Azerb. Azerbaijan

B
Basq. Basque
BC before Christ
Bel. Belarussian
Ben. Bengali
Ber. Berber
B-H Bosnia-Herzegovina
bn billion (one thousand million)
BP British Petroleum
Bret. Breton
Brit. British
Bul. Bulgarian
Bur. Burmese

C
C central
C. Cape
°C degrees Centigrade
CACM Central America Common Market
Cam. Cambodian
Cant. Cantonese
CAR Central African Republic
Cast. Castilian
Cat. Catalan
CEEAC Central America Common Market
Chin. Chinese
CIS Commonwealth of Independent States
cm centimetre(s)
Cro. Croat
Cz. Czech
Czech Rep. Czech Republic

D
Dan. Danish
Div. Divehi
Dom. Rep. Dominican Republic
Dut. Dutch

E
E east
EC *see* EU
EEC *see* EU
ECOWAS Economic Community of West African States
ECU European Currency Unit
EMS European Monetary System
Eng. English
est estimated
Est. Estonian
EU European Union (previously European Community [EC], European Economic Community [EEC])

F
°F degrees Fahrenheit
Faer. Faeroese
Fij. Fijian
Fin. Finnish
Fr. French
Fris. Frisian
ft foot/feet
FYROM Former Yugoslav Republic of Macedonia

G
g gram(s)
Gael. Gaelic
Gal. Galician
GDP Gross Domestic Product (the total value of goods and services produced by a country excluding income from foreign countries)
Geor. Georgian
Ger. German
Gk Greek
GNP Gross National Product (the total value of goods and services produced by a country)

H
Heb. Hebrew
HEP hydro-electric power
Hind. Hindi
hist. historical
Hung. Hungarian

I
I. Island
Icel. Icelandic
in inch(es)
In. Inuit (Eskimo)
Ind. Indonesian
Intl International
Ir. Irish
Is Islands
It. Italian

J
Jap. Japanese

K
Kaz. Kazakh
kg kilogram(s)
Kir. Kirghiz
km kilometre(s)
km² square kilometre (singular)
Kor. Korean
Kurd. Kurdish

L
L. Lake
LAIA Latin American Integration Association
Lao. Laotian
Lapp. Lappish
Lat. Latin
Latv. Latvian
Liech. Liechtenstein
Lith. Lithuanian
Lux. Luxembourg

M
m million/metre(s)
Mac. Macedonian
Maced. Macedonia
Mal. Malay
Malg. Malagasy
Malt. Maltese
mi. mile(s)
Mong. Mongolian
Mt. Mountain
Mts Mountains

N
N north
NAFTA North American Free Trade Agreement
Nep. Nepali
Neth. Netherlands
Nic. Nicaraguan
Nor. Norwegian
NZ New Zealand

P
Pash. Pashtu
PNG Papua New Guinea
Pol. Polish
Poly. Polynesian
Port. Portuguese
prev. previously

R
Rep. Republic
Res. Reservoir
Rmsch Romansch
Rom. Romanian
Rus. Russian
Russ. Fed. Russian Federation

S
S south
SADC Southern Africa Development Community
SCr. Serbo-Croatian
Sinh. Sinhala
Slvk Slovak
Slvn. Slovene
Som. Somali
Sp. Spanish
St., St Saint
Strs Straits
Swa. Swahili
Swe. Swedish
Switz. Switzerland

T
Taj. Tajik
Th. Thai
Thai. Thailand
Tib. Tibetan
Turk. Turkish
Turkm. Turkmenistan

U
UAE United Arab Emirates
Uigh. Uighur
UK United Kingdom
Ukr. Ukrainian
UN United Nations
Urd. Urdu
US/USA United States of America
USSR Union of Soviet Socialist Republics
Uzb. Uzbek

V
var. variant
Vdkhr. Vodokhranilishche (Russian for reservoir)
Vdskh. Vodoskhovyshche (Ukrainian for reservoir)
Vtn. Vietnamese

W
W west
Wel. Welsh

Y
Yugo. Yugoslavia

INDEX

THIS INDEX LISTS all the placenames and features shown on the regional and continental maps in this Atlas. Placenames are referenced to the largest scale map on which they appear. The policy followed throughout the Atlas is to use the local spelling or local name at regional level; commonly-used English language names may occasionally be added (in parentheses) where this is an aid to identification e.g. Firenze (Florence). English names, where they exist, have been used for all international features e.g. oceans and country names; they are also used on the continental maps and in the introductory World section; these are then fully cross-referenced to the local names found on the regional maps. The index also contains commonly-found alternative names and variant spellings, which are also fully cross-referenced.

All main entry names are those of settlements unless otherwise indicated by the use of italicized definitions or representative symbols, which are keyed at the foot of each page.

1

115 *H9* **25 de Agosto** Florida, Uruguay *34°25′S 56°24′W*
115 *H8* **25 de Mayo** Florida, Uruguay *34°11′S 56°20′W*
25 de Mayo *see* Veinticinco de Mayo
215 *N5* **26 Bakı Komissarı** ***Rus.*** Imeni 26 Bakinskikh Komissarov. SE Azerbaijan *39°18′N 49°13′E*
26 Baku Komissarlary Adyndaky *see* Uzboý
56 *E6* **100 Mile House** ***var.*** Hundred Mile House. British Columbia, SW Canada *51°39′N 121°19′W*

A

Aa *see* Gauja
155 *D13* **Aabenraa** ***var.*** Åbenrå, ***Ger.*** Apenrade. Sønderjylland, SW Denmark *55°03′N 09°26′E*
155 *D10* **Aabybro** ***var.*** Åbybro. Nordjylland, N Denmark *57°09′N 09°32′E*
181 *A10* **Aachen** ***Dut.*** Aken, ***Fr.*** Aix-la-Chapelle; ***anc.*** Aquae Grani, Aquisgranum. Nordrhein-Westfalen, W Germany *50°47′N 06°06′E*
Aaiún *see* Laâyoune
178 *J3* **Aakirkeby** ***var.*** Åkirkeby. Bornholm, E Denmark *55°04′N 14°56′E*
218 *G1* **Aakkâr el Aatîga** Lebanon
155 *D11* **Aalborg** ***var.*** Ålborg, Ålborg-Nørresundby; ***anc.*** Alburgum. Nordjylland, N Denmark *57°03′N 09°56′E*
Aalborg Bugt *see* Ålborg Bugt
179 *E12* **Aalen** Baden-Württemberg, S Germany *48°50′N 10°06′E*
155 *D11* **Aalestrup** ***var.*** Ålestrup. Viborg, NW Denmark *56°42′N 09°31′E*
162 *E6* **Aalsmeer** Noord-Holland, C Netherlands *52°17′N 04°43′E*
163 *D10* **Aalst** ***Fr.*** Alost. Oost-Vlaanderen, C Belgium *50°57′N 04°03′E*
162 *F7* **Aalst** ***Fr.*** Alost. Noord-Brabant, S Netherlands *51°23′N 05°29′E*
162 *I7* **Aalten** Gelderland, E Netherlands *51°56′N 06°35′E*
163 *C9* **Aalter** Oost-Vlaanderen, NW Belgium *51°05′N 03°28′E*
Aanaar *see* Inari
Aanaarjävri *see* Inarijärvi
153 *H8* **Äänekoski** Länsi-Soumi, W Finland *62°34′N 25°45′E*
216 *C5* **Aanjar** ***var.*** ‘Anjar. C Lebanon *33°45′N 35°56′E*
138 *E7* **Aansluit** Northern Cape, N South Africa *26°41′S 22°24′E*
218 *G2* **Aaqoûra** Lebanon
Aar *see* Aare
176 *D4* **Aarau** Aargau, N Switzerland *47°22′N 08°00′E*
176 *C4* **Aarberg** Bern, W Switzerland *47°19′N 07°54′E*
163 *C9* **Aardenburg** Zeeland, SW Netherlands *51°16′N 03°27′E*
174 *B3* **Aare** ***var.*** Aar. ≈ W Switzerland
174 *B2* **Aargau** ***Fr.*** Argovie. ◐ *canton* N Switzerland
Aarhus *see* Århus
Aarlen *see* Arlon
155 *D11* **Aars** ***var.*** Års. Nordjylland, N Denmark *56°49′N 09°32′E*
163 *E10* **Aarschot** Vlaams Brabant, C Belgium *50°59′N 04°50′E*
Aassi, Nahr el *see* Orontes
Aat *see* Ath
239 *K7* **Aba** ***prev.*** Ngawa. Sichuan, C China *32°51′N 101°46′E*
134 *J6* **Aba** Orientale, NE Dem. Rep. Congo *03°52′N 30°14′E*
133 *K8* **Aba** Abia, S Nigeria *05°06′N 07°22′E*
220 *D3* **Abā al Qazāz, Bi’r** *well* NW Saudi Arabia
Abā as Su‘ūd *see* Najrān
107 *H4* **Abacaxis, Rio** ≈ NW Brazil
Abaco Island *see* Great Abaco/Little Abaco
Abaco Island *see* Great Abaco, Bahamas
222 *D6* **Ābādān** Khūzestān, SW Iran *30°24′N 48°18′E*
228 *D7* **Abadan** ***prev.*** Bezmein, ***Rus.*** Byuzmeyin. Ahal Welaýaty, C Turkmenistan *38°08′N 57°53′E*
222 *F6* **Ābādeh** Fārs, C Iran *31°06′N 52°40′E*
130 *G4* **Abadla** W Algeria *31°04′N 02°39′W*
110 *E1* **Abaeté** Minas Gerais, SE Brazil *19°10′S 45°24′W*
Abag Qi *see* Xin Hot
113 *H5* **Abaí** Caazapá, S Paraguay *25°58′S 55°54′W*
Abai *see* Blue Nile
284 *B2* **Abaiang** ***var.*** Apia; ***prev.*** Charlotte Island. *atoll* Tungaru, W Kiribati
Abaj *see* Abay
133 *K7* **Abaji** Federal Capital District, C Nigeria *08°35′N 06°54′E*
79 *J5* **Abajo Peak** ▲ Utah, W USA *37°51′N 109°28′W*
133 *K8* **Abakaliki** Ebonyi, SE Nigeria *06°18′N 08°07′E*
192 *G8* **Abakan** Respublika Khakasiya, S Russian Federation *53°43′N 91°25′E*
227 *N1* **Abakan** ≈ S Russian Federation
133 *I4* **Abala** Tillabéri, SW Niger *14°55′N 03°27′E*
133 *J4* **Abalak** Tahoua, C Niger *15°28′N 06°18′E*
191 *H8* **Abalyanka** ***Rus.*** Obolyanka. ≈ N Belarus
192 *G7* **Aban** Krasnoyarskiy Kray, S Russian Federation *56°41′N 96°04′E*
222 *G6* **Āb Anbār-e Kān Sorkh** Yazd, C Iran *31°22′N 53°38′E*
105 *F8* **Abancay** Apurímac, SE Peru *13°37′S 72°52′W*
173 *K6* **Abanilla** Murcia, Spain *38°12′N 1°03′W*
284 *D1* **Abaokoro** *atoll* Tungaru, W Kiribati
Abariringa *see* Kanton
222 *G6* **Abarkū** Yazd, C Iran *31°07′N 53°17′E*
252 *G3* **Abashiri** ***var.*** Abasiri. Hokkaidō, NE Japan *44°N 144°15′E*
252 *G3* **Abashiri-gawa** ≈ Hokkaidō, NE Japan
252 *G3* **Abashiri-ko** ◎ Hokkaidō, NE Japan
Abasiri *see* Abashiri
87 *K8* **Abasolo** Chiapas, Mexico *16°48′N 92°10′W*
85 *K5* **Abasolo** Guanajuato, Mexico
85 *M7* **Abasolo** Tamaulipas, C Mexico *24°02′N 98°18′W*
87 *H8* **Abasolo del Valle** Veracruz-Llave, Mexico *17°46′N 95°30′W*
280 *C4* **Abau** Central, S Papua New Guinea *10°04′S 148°34′E*
227 *I4* **Abay** ***var.*** Abaj. Karaganda, C Kazakhstan *49°38′N 72°50′E*
136 *D5* **Ābaya Hāyk’** ***Eng.*** Lake Margherita, ***It.*** Abbaia. ◎ SW Ethiopia
Ābay Wenz *see* Blue Nile
192 *G8* **Abaza** Respublika Khakasiya, S Russian Federation *52°40′N 89°58′E*
Abbaia *see* Ābaya Hāyk’
222 *G8* **Āb Bārīk** Fārs, S Iran
175 *B10* **Abbasanta** Sardegna, Italy, C Mediterranean Sea *40°08′N 08°49′E*
Abbatis Villa *see* Abbeville
72 *D4* **Abbaye, Point** *headland* Michigan, N USA *46°58′N 88°08′W*
Abbazia *see* Opatija
Abbé, Lake *see* Abhe, Lake
165 *H2* **Abbeville** ***anc.*** Abbatis Villa. Somme, N France *50°06′N 01°50′E*
69 *I3* **Abbeville** Alabama, S USA *31°35′N 85°16′W*
69 *K2* **Abbeville** Georgia, SE USA *31°58′N 83°18′W*
68 *C4* **Abbeville** Louisiana, S USA *29°58′N 92°08′W*
67 *H8* **Abbeville** South Carolina, SE USA *34°10′N 82°23′W*
157 *B10* **Abbeyfeale** ***Ir.*** Mainistir na Féile. SW Ireland *52°24′N 09°21′W*
160 *A2* **Abbeyleix** Laois, Ireland *52°54′N 7°21′W*
176 *E7* **Abbiategrasso** Lombardia, NW Italy *45°24′N 08°55′E*
154 *J1* **Abborrträsk** Norrbotten, N Sweden *65°24′N 19°33′E*
292 *F5* **Abbot Ice Shelf** *ice shelf* Antarctica
160 *G8* **Abbotsbury** UK *50°40′N 2°36′W*
76 *C2* **Abbotsford** British Columbia, SW Canada *49°02′N 122°18′W*
72 *C5* **Abbotsford** Wisconsin, N USA *44°57′N 90°19′W*
231 *I4* **Abbottābād** North-West Frontier Province, NW Pakistan *34°12′N 73°15′E*
191 *H9* **Abchuha** ***Rus.*** Obchuga. Minskaya Voblasts’, NW Belarus *54°30′N 29°22′E*
162 *F6* **Abcoude** Utrecht, C Netherlands *52°17′N 04°59′E*
216 *F2* **‘Abd al ‘Azīz, Jabal** ▲▲ NE Syria
221 *I9* **‘Abd al Kūrī** *island* SE Yemen
217 *N9* **‘Abd Allāh, Khawr** *bay* Iraq/Kuwait
197 *K3* **Abdulino** Orenburgskaya Oblast’, W Russian Federation *53°37′N 53°39′E*
134 *F2* **Abéché** ***var.*** Abécher, Abeshr. Ouaddaï, SE Chad *13°49′N 20°49′E*
Abécher *see* Abéché
223 *I5* **Āb-e Garm va Sard** Yazd, E Iran
133 *I2* **Abeïbara** Kidal, NE Mali *19°07′N 01°52′E*
171 *H3* **Abejar** Castilla-León, N Spain *41°48′N 02°47′W*
102 *B5* **Abejorral** Antioquia, W Colombia *05°48′N 75°28′W*
Abela *see* Ávila
141 *K3* **Abel Erasmuspas** *pass* Limpopo, South Africa
Abellinum *see* Avellino
152 *C5* **Abeløya** *island* Kong Karls Land, E Svalbard
136 *D4* **Ābeltī** Oromo, C Ethiopia *08°09′N 37°31′E*
284 *B3* **Abemama** ***var.*** Apamama; ***prev.*** Roger Simpson Island. *atoll* Tungaru, W Kiribati
261 *L7* **Abemaree** ***var.*** Abermarre. Papua, E Indonesia *07°03′S 140°10′E*
181 *J13* **Abenberg** Bayern, Germany *10°58′N 49°15′E*
132 *G8* **Abengourou** E Ivory Coast *06°42′N 03°27′W*
172 *G5* **Abenójar** Castilla-La Manacha, Spain *38°53′N 4°21′W*
Åbenrå *see* Aabenraa
179 *G12* **Abens** ≈ SE Germany
133 *I7* **Abeokuta** Ogun, SW Nigeria *07°07′N 03°21′E*
160 *E4* **Aberaeron** SW Wales, UK *52°15′N 04°15′W*
Aberbrothock *see* Arbroath
Abercorn *see* Mbala
74 *E3* **Abercrombie** North Dakota, N USA *46°25′N 96°42′W*
160 *F6* **Aberdare** UK *51°43′N 3°27′W*
160 *D3* **Aberdaron** UK *52°49′N 4°42′W*
277 *L4* **Aberdeen** New South Wales, SE Australia *32°09′S 150°55′E*
57 *M6* **Aberdeen** Saskatchewan, S Canada *52°15′N 106°19′W*
138 *F9* **Aberdeen** Eastern Cape, S South Africa *32°30′S 24°00′E*
156 *G5* **Aberdeen** ***anc.*** Devana. NE Scotland, UK *57°10′N 02°04′W*
64 *E9* **Aberdeen** Maryland, NE USA *39°28′N 76°09′W*
66 *C8* **Aberdeen** Mississippi, S USA *33°49′N 88°32′W*
67 *J7* **Aberdeen** North Carolina, SE USA *35°07′N 79°25′W*
74 *D4* **Aberdeen** South Dakota, N USA *45°27′N 98°29′W*
76 *B4* **Aberdeen** Washington, NW USA *46°57′N 123°48′W*
55 *I3* **Aberdeen Lake** ◎ Nunavut, NE Canada
160 *E3* **Aberdyfi** UK *52°33′N 4°02′W*
159 *H1* **Aberfeldy** C Scotland, UK *56°38′N 03°49′W*
160 *E2* **Aberffraw** UK *53°11′N 4°27′W*
158 *G2* **Aberfoyle** UK *56°11′N 4°23′W*
160 *G5* **Abergavenny** ***anc.*** Gobannium. SE Wales, UK *51°50′N 03°W*
160 *E5* **Abergorlech** UK *51°59′N 4°04′W*
Abergwaun *see* Fishguard
159 *I3* **Aberlady** UK *56°00′N 2°51′W*
Abermarre *see* Abemaree
70 *D3* **Abernathy** Texas, SW USA *33°49′N 101°50′W*
160 *E4* **Aberporth** UK *52°08′N 4°33′W*
Abersee *see* Wolfgangsee
160 *E3* **Abersoch** UK *52°49′N 4°30′W*
Abertawe *see* Swansea
Aberteifi *see* Cardigan
160 *G6* **Abertillery** UK *51°44′N 3°08′W*
76 *D8* **Abert, Lake** ◎ Oregon, NW USA
160 *E4* **Aberystwyth** W Wales, UK *52°25′N 04°05′W*
Abeshr *see* Abéché
Ábeskovvu *see* Abisko
176 *G9* **Abetone** Toscana, C Italy *44°09′N 10°42′E*
195 *L4* **Abez’** Respublika Komi, NW Russian Federation *66°32′N 61°41′E*
222 *E3* **Āb Garm** Qazvin, N Iran
220 *F7* **Abhā** ‘Asīr, SW Saudi Arabia *18°16′N 42°32′E*
222 *E3* **Abhar** Zanjān, NW Iran *36°05′N 49°18′E*
Abhé Bad/Ābhē Bid Hāyk’ *see* Abhe, Lake
136 *F3* **Abhe, Lake** ***var.*** Lake Abbé, ***Amh.*** Ābhē Bid Hāyk’, ***Som.*** Abhé Bad. ◎ Djibouti/Ethiopia
133 *J7* **Abia** ◐ *state* SE Nigeria
217 *K6* **‘Abīd ‘Alī** E Iraq *32°20′N 45°58′E*
191 *I10* **Abidavichy** ***Rus.*** Obidovichi. Mahilyowskaya Voblasts’, E Belarus *53°20′N 30°25′E*
132 *F8* **Abidjan** S Ivory Coast *05°19′N 04°01′W*
Āb-i-Istāda *see* Īstādeh-ye Moqor, Āb-e-
218 *F6* **Abila** Jordan
75 *E9* **Abilene** Kansas, C USA *38°55′N 97°14′W*
70 *F4* **Abilene** Texas, SW USA *32°27′N 99°44′W*
Abindonia *see* Abingdon
161 *I6* **Abingdon** ***anc.*** Abindonia. S England, UK *51°41′N 01°17′W*
73 *B10* **Abingdon** Illinois, N USA *40°48′N 90°24′W*
67 *H5* **Abingdon** Virginia, NE USA *36°42′N 81°59′W*
Abingdon *see* Pinta, Isla
65 *M3* **Abington** Massachusetts, USA *42°06′N 70°57′W*
64 *F7* **Abington** Pennsylvania, NE USA *40°06′N 75°05′W*
196 *F8* **Abinsk** Krasnodarskiy Kray, SW Russian Federation *44°51′N 38°12′E*
79 *L6* **Abiquiu Reservoir** ⊞ New Mexico, SW USA
Āb-i-safed *see* Sefīd, Darya-ye
152 *F5* **Abisko** ***Lapp.*** Ábeskovvu. Norrbotten, N Sweden *68°21′N 18°50′E*
51 *J8* **Abitibi** ≈ Ontario, S Canada
58 *F7* **Abitibi, Lac** ◎ Ontario/Québec, S Canada
136 *E2* **Ābīy Ādī** Tigray, N Ethiopia *13°40′N 38°57′E*
190 *E5* **Abja-Paluoja** Viljandimaa, S Estonia *58°08′N 25°20′E*
215 *I3* **Abkhazia** ◐ *autonomous republic* NW Georgia
173 *I8* **Abla** Andalucía, Spain *37°08′N 2°47′W*
276 *E1* **Abminga** South Australia *26°07′S 134°49′E*
129 *I4* **Abnûb** C Egypt *27°18′N 31°09′E*
Åbo *see* Turku
232 *D4* **Abohar** Punjab, N India *30°11′N 74°14′E*
132 *G8* **Aboisso** SE Ivory Coast *05°26′N 03°13′W*
133 *N1* **Abo, Massif d’** ▲▲ NW Chad
133 *I7* **Abomey** S Benin *07°14′N 02°00′E*
167 *M10* **Abondance** Rhône-Alpes, France *46°17′N 6°44′E*
134 *C6* **Abong Mbang** Est, SE Cameroon *03°58′N 13°10′E*
183 *G12* **Abony** Pest, C Hungary *47°10′N 20°00′E*
134 *E3* **Abou-Déïa** Salamat, SE Chad *11°30′N 19°18′E*
Aboudouhour *see* Abū aḍ Ḍuhūr
Abou Kémal *see* Abū Kamāl
Abou Simbel *see* Abu Simbel
215 *K5* **Abovyan** C Armenia *40°16′N 44°33′E*
263 *K4* **Abra** ≈ Luzon, N Philippines
129 *N9* **Abrād, Wādī** *seasonal river* W Yemen
Abraham Bay *see* The Carlton
118 *C6* **Abranquil** Maule, Chile *35°45′S 71°33′W*
172 *C4* **Abrantes** ***var.*** Abrántes. Santarém, C Portugal *39°28′N 08°12′W*
112 *D3* **Abra Pampa** Jujuy, N Argentina *22°47′S 65°41′W*
Abrashlare *see* Brezovo
111 *J3* **Abre Campo** Minas Gerais, Brazil *20°18′S 42°29′W*
102 *C4* **Abrego** Norte de Santander, N Colombia *08°08′N 73°14′W*
Abrene *see* Pytalovo
84 *C6* **Abreojos, Punta** *headland* W Mexico *26°43′N 113°36′W*
169 *M3* **Abriés** Provence-Alpes-Côte d’Azur, France *44°47′N 6°56′E*
115 *J4* **Abrojal** Rivera, Uruguay *31°45′S 55°01′W*
191 *E11* **Abrova** ***Rus.*** Obrovo. Brestskaya Voblasts’, SW Belarus *52°30′N 25°34′E*
188 *C7* **Abrud** ***Ger.*** Gross-Schlatten, ***Hung.*** Abrudbánya. Alba, SW Romania *46°16′N 23°05′E*
Abrudbánya *see* Abrud
190 *C5* **Abruka** *island* SW Estonia
175 *F8* **Abruzzese, Appennino** ▲▲ C Italy
175 *G8* **Abruzzo** ◐ *region* C Italy
220 *F8* **‘Abs** ***var.*** Sūq ‘Abs. W Yemen *16°42′N 42°55′E*
77 *J6* **Absaroka Range** ▲▲ Montana/Wyoming, NW USA
64 *G9* **Absecon** New Jersey, USA *39°26′N 74°30′W*
215 *N4* **Abşeron Yarımadası** ***Rus.*** Apsheronskiy Poluostrov. *peninsula* E Azerbaijan
222 *F4* **Āb Shīrīn** Eşfahān, C Iran *34°17′N 51°17′E*
217 *L7* **Abtān** SE Iraq *31°37′N 47°06′E*
177 *I3* **Abtenau** Salzburg, NW Austria *47°33′N 13°21′E*
232 *C7* **Ābu** Rājasthān, N India *24°41′N 72°50′E*
250 *D5* **Abu** Yamaguchi, Honshū, SW Japan *34°30′N 131°26′E*
129 *I6* **Abu Simbel** *headland* Egypt
216 *D3* **Abū aḍ Ḍuhūr** ***Fr.*** Aboudouhour. Idlib, NW Syria *35°30′N 37°00′E*
221 *J4* **Abū al Abyaḍ** *island* C United Arab Emirates
216 *E6* **Abū al Ḥuşayn, Khabrat** ◎ N Jordan
217 *I5* **Abū al Jīr** C Iraq *33°16′N 42°55′E*
217 *M8* **Abū al Khaşīb** ***var.*** Abul Khasib. SE Iraq *30°26′N 48°00′E*
217 *K8* **Abū at Tubrah, Thaqb** *well* S Iraq
129 *H5* **Abu Balâs** ▲ SW Egypt *24°28′N 27°36′E*
Abu Dhabi *see* Abū Ẓaby
217 *I5* **Abū Farūkh** C Iraq *33°06′N 43°18′E*
134 *H3* **Abu Gabra** Southern Darfur, W Sudan *11°02′N 26°50′E*
217 *H6* **Abū Ghār, Sha‘īb** *dry watercourse* S Iraq
129 *J8* **Abu Hamed** River Nile, N Sudan *19°32′N 33°20′E*
216 *G4* **Abū Ḩardān** ***var.*** Hajîne. Dayr az Zawr, E Syria *34°45′N 40°49′E*
217 *J5* **Abū Ḩāssawīyah** E Iraq *33°52′N 44°47′E*
216 *E6* **Abū Ḩifnah, Wādī** *dry watercourse* N Jordan
133 *K7* **Abuja** ● (Nigeria) Federal Capital District, C Nigeria *09°04′N 07°28′E*
217 *I6* **Abū Jahaf, Wādī** *dry watercourse* C Iraq
104 *E5* **Abujao, Río** ≈ E Peru
217 *J8* **Abū Jasrah** S Iraq *30°43′N 44°50′E*
219 *F12* **Abū Jurdhān** Jordan
216 *G4* **Abū Kamāl** ***Fr.*** Abou Kémal. Dayr az Zawr, E Syria *34°29′N 40°56′E*
260 *D5* **Abuki, Pegunungan** ▲▲ Sulawesi, C Indonesia
253 *D11* **Abukuma-gawa** ≈ Honshū, C Japan
253 *D11* **Abukuma-sanchi** ▲▲ Honshū, C Japan
Abula *see* Ávila
Abul Khasib *see* Abū al Khaşīb
134 *F6* **Abumombazi** ***var.*** Abumonbazi. Equateur, N Dem. Rep. Congo *03°43′N 22°06′E*
Abumonbazi *see* Abumombazi
106 *E6* **Abunã** Rondônia, W Brazil *09°41′S 65°20′W*
106 *D7* **Abunã, Rio** ***var.*** Río Abuná. ≈ Bolivia/Brazil
216 *C7* **Abū Nuşayr** ***var.*** Abu Nuseir. ‘Ammān, W Jordan *32°03′N 35°58′E*
Abu Nuseir *see* Abū Nuşayr
217 *J8* **Abū Qabr** S Iraq *31°03′N 44°34′E*
216 *E4* **Abū Raḩbah, Jabal** ▲▲ C Syria
217 *I4* **Abū Rajāsh** N Iraq *34°47′N 43°36′E*
217 *K8* **Abū Raqrāq, Ghadīr** *well* S Iraq
232 *C7* **Ābu Road** Rājasthān, N India *24°29′N 72°47′E*
136 *E1* **Abu Shagara, Ras** *headland* NE Sudan *18°04′N 38°31′E*
129 *I6* **Abu Simbel** ***var.*** Abou Simbel, Abū Sunbul. *ancient monument* S Egypt
217 *K8* **Abū Sudayrah** S Iraq *30°55′N 44°58′E*
217 *J7* **Abū Şukhayr** S Iraq *31°54′N 44°27′E*
Abū Sunbul *see* Abu Simbel
252 *D5* **Abuta** Hokkaidō, NE Japan *42°34′N 140°44′E*
219 *G12* **Abū Ţarafah, Wādī** *dry watercourse* Jordan
278 *C9* **Abut Head** *headland* South Island, New Zealand *43°06′S 170°16′E*
136 *A1* **Abu ‘Urug** Northern Kordofan, C Sudan *15°52′N 30°25′E*
136 *E4* **Ābuyē Mēda** ▲ C Ethiopia *10°28′N 39°44′E*
263 *M7* **Abuyog** Leyte, C Philippines *10°45′N 124°58′E*
134 *J2* **Abu Zabad** Western Kordofan, C Sudan *12°21′N 29°16′E*
Abū Ẓabī *see* Abū Ẓaby
221 *J4* **Abū Ẓaby** ***var.*** Abū Ẓabī, ***Eng.*** Abu Dhabi. ● (United Arab Emirates) Abū Ẓaby, C United Arab Emirates *24°30′N 54°20′E*
129 *J3* **Abu Zenîma** E Egypt *29°01′N 33°08′E*
155 *H9* **Åby** Östergötland, S Sweden *58°40′N 16°10′E*
Abyaḑ, Al Baḩr al *see* White Nile
Åbybro *see* Aabybro
134 *I3* **Abyei** Western Kordofan, S Sudan *09°35′N 28°28′E*
Abyla *see* Ávila
Abymes *see* les Abymes
Abyssinia *see* Ethiopia
Açâba *see* Assaba
102 *C6* **Acacias** Meta, C Colombia *03°59′N 73°46′W*
55 *L3* **Cape Acadia** *headland* Nunavut, C Canada
111 *I3* **Acaiaca** Minas Gerais, Brazil *20°21′S 43°09′W*
108 *C4* **Açailandia** Maranhão, E Brazil *04°51′S 47°26′W*
Acaill *see* Achill Island
88 *C5* **Acajutla** Sonsonate, W El Salvador *13°34′N 89°50′W*
172 *E7* **Acalà del Río** Andalucía, Spain *37°31′N 5°59′W*
134 *A7* **Acalayong** SW Equatorial Guinea *01°05′N 09°34′E*
86 *E6* **Acámbaro** Guanajuato, C Mexico *20°01′N 100°42′W*
86 *E6* **Acambay** México, Mexico *19°57′N 99°51′W*
102 *A4* **Acandí** Chocó, NW Colombia *08°32′N 77°20′W*
170 *C3* **A Cañiza** ***var.*** La Cañiza. Galicia, NW Spain *42°13′N 08°16′W*
86 *B3* **Acaponeta** Nayarit, C Mexico *22°30′N 105°21′W*
85 *I8* **Acaponeta, Río de** ≈ C Mexico
86 *E8* **Acapulco** ***var.*** Acapulco de Juárez. Guerrero, S Mexico *16°51′N 99°53′W*
Acapulco de Juárez *see* Acapulco
103 *J7* **Acarai Mountains** ***Sp.*** Serra Acaraí. ▲▲ Brazil/Guyana
Acaraí, Serra *see* Acarai Mountains
108 *G3* **Acaraú** Ceará, NE Brazil *04°35′S 37°37′W*
102 *E3* **Acarigua** Portuguesa, N Venezuela *09°35′N 69°12′W*
86 *F5* **Acatepec** Puebla, Mexico
86 *F7* **Acatepec** Puebla, Mexico *19°02′N 98°17′W*
85 *M7* **Acatlán** Jalisco, W Mexico North America
87 *H7* **Acatlan** Oaxaca, Mexico *18°32′N 96°37′W*
86 *F7* **Acatlán** ***var.*** Acatlán de Osorio. Puebla, S Mexico *18°12′N 98°02′W*
86 *C5* **Acatlàn de Juàrez** Jalisco, Mexico *20°25′N 103°35′W*
Acatlán de Osorio *see* Acatlán
87 *I7* **Acayucan** ***var.*** Acayucán. Veracruz-Llave, E Mexico *17°59′N 94°58′W*
Accho *see* ‘Akko
67 *M4* **Accomac** Virginia, NE USA *37°43′N 75°41′N*
168 *D6* **Accous** Aquitaine, France *42°59′N 0°36′W*
133 *H8* **Accra** ● (Ghana)SE Ghana *05°33′N 00°15′W*
159 *J9* **Accrington** NW England, UK *53°46′N 02°21′W*
114 *B7* **Acebal** Santa Fe, C Argentina *33°14′S 60°50′W*
115 *K4* **Acegua** Cerro Largo, Uruguay *31°48′S 54°18′E*
115 *K4* **Aceguà** Cerro Largo, Uruguay *31°52′S 54°12′W*
258 *C3* **Aceh** ***off.*** Daerah Istimewa Aceh, ***var.*** Acheen, Achin, Atchin, Atjeh. ◐ *autonomous district* NW Indonesia
175 *H9* **Acerenza** Basilicata, S Italy *40°46′N 15°51′E*
184 *A8* **Acerra** ***anc.*** Acerrae. Campania, S Italy *40°56′N 14°22′E*
Acerrae *see* Acerra
114 *B8* **Acevedo** Buenos Aires, Argentina *33°45′S 60°27′W*
158 *D1* **Acha** UK *56°36′N 6°36′W*
105 *H9* **Achacachi** La Paz, W Bolivia *16°01′S 68°44′W*
102 *F4* **Achaguas** Apure, C Venezuela *07°46′N 68°14′W*
158 *F3* **Achahoish** UK *55°57′N 5°34′W*
234 *E4* **Achalpur** ***prev.*** Elichpur, Ellichpur. Mahārāshtra, C India *21°19′N 77°30′E*
115 *H5* **Achar** Tacuarembó, C Uruguay *32°20′S 56°15′W*

◆ Country
● Country Capital
◇ Dependent Territory
○ Dependent Territory Capital
◐ Administrative Regions
✈ International Airport
▲ Mountain
▲▲ Mountain Range
⊼ Volcano
≈ River
◎ Lake
⊞ Reservoir

♦ Country	◇ Dependent Territory	♦ Administrative Regions	▲ Mountain	⊕ Volcano	◎ Lake
● Country Capital	○ Dependent Territory Capital	✕ International Airport	▲ Mountain Range	↔ River	▨ Reservoir

◆ Country
● Country Capital
◇ Dependent Territory
○ Dependent Territory Capital
◇ Administrative Regions
✕ International Airport
▲ Mountain
▲ Mountain Range
▲ Volcano
⚙ River
☉ Lake
☉ Reservoir

◆ Country | ● Country Capital | ◇ Dependent Territory | ○ Dependent Territory Capital | ◆ Administrative Regions | ✈ International Airport | ▲ Mountain | ▲ Mountain Range | ▲ Volcano | ⊘ River | ⊚ Lake | ⊟ Reservoir

---

◆ Country ◇ Dependent Territory ♢ Administrative Regions ▲ Mountain ○ Volcano ○ Lake
● Country Capital ○ Dependent Territory Capital ✕ International Airport ▲ Mountain Range ≈ River ⊟ Reservoir

◆ Country
● Country Capital
◇ Dependent Territory
○ Dependent Territory Capital
◆ Administrative Regions
✈ International Airport
▲ Mountain
▲ Mountain Range
↔ River
▲ Volcano
◎ Lake
◎ Reservoir

B

Legend

◆ Country
● Country Capital
◇ Dependent Territory
○ Dependent Territory Capital
◆ Administrative Regions
✕ International Airport
▲ Mountain
▲ Mountain Range
▲ Volcano
≈ River
◎ Lake
▨ Reservoir

◆ Country | ◇ Dependent Territory | ▲ Administrative Regions | ▲ Mountain | ▲ Volcano | ⊘ Lake
● Country Capital | ○ Dependent Territory Capital | ✕ International Airport | ▲ Mountain Range | ⇄ River | ⊠ Reservoir

◆ Country   ◇ Dependent Territory   ◆ Administrative Regions   ▲ Mountain   ▲ Volcano   ◎ Lake
● Country Capital   ○ Dependent Territory Capital   ✈ International Airport   ▲ Mountain Range   ◆ River   ◙ Reservoir

◆ Country	◇ Dependent Territory	◆ Administrative Regions	▲ Mountain	◆ Volcano	⊗ Lake
● Country Capital	○ Dependent Territory Capital	✕ International Airport	▲ Mountain Range	♒ River	⊙ Reservoir

C

◆ Country ◇ Dependent Territory ◄ Administrative Regions ▲ Mountain ◆ Volcano ◎ Lake
● Country Capital ○ Dependent Territory Capital ✈ International Airport ▲ Mountain Range ♣ River ◎ Reservoir

◆ Country ◇ Dependent Territory ● Administrative Regions ▲ Mountain ⛰ Volcano ◎ Lake
● Country Capital ○ Dependent Territory Capital ✈ International Airport ▲ Mountain Range ≈ River ▢ Reservoir

◆ Country — ◇ Dependent Territory — ✕ Administrative Regions — ▲ Mountain — ⊗ Lake
● Country Capital — ○ Dependent Territory Capital — ✕ International Airport — ▲ Mountain Range — ⟿ River — ⊠ Reservoir

◆ Country
◆ Country Capital
◇ Dependent Territory
○ Dependent Territory Capital
▲ Administrative Regions
☓ International Airport
▲ Mountain
▲ Mountain Range
☓ Volcano
◈ River
◎ Lake
◎ Reservoir

INDEX

◆ Country   ◇ Dependent Territory   ✕ Administrative Regions   ▲ Mountain   ⛰ Volcano   ◎ Lake
● Country Capital   ○ Dependent Territory Capital   ✈ International Airport   ▲ Mountain Range   ♠ River   ☒ Reservoir

◆ Country   ◇ Dependent Territory   ◈ Administrative Regions   ▲ Mountain   ☒ Volcano   ⊛ Lake
● Country Capital   ○ Dependent Territory Capital   × International Airport   ▲ Mountain Range   ♒ River   ⊞ Reservoir

◆ Country	◇ Dependent Territory	✕ Administrative Regions	▲ Mountain	▨ Volcano	⊙ Lake
● Country Capital	○ Dependent Territory Capital	✕ International Airport	▲ Mountain Range	✦ River	⊞ Reservoir

Country ◆   Administrative Regions   ▲ Mountain   ▲ Volcano   ⊘ Lake
Country Capital   ◇ Dependent Territory   ✈ International Airport   ▲ Mountain Range   ✦ River   ☒ Reservoir
  ○ Dependent Territory Capital

G

◆ Country	◇ Dependent Territory	◊ Administrative Regions	▲ Mountain	✕ Volcano	⊚ Lake
● Country Capital	○ Dependent Territory Capital	✈ International Airport	▲ Mountain Range	♒ River	▨ Reservoir

Great Smoky Mountains - Guélengdeng
INDEX
346

66 G6 **Great Smoky Mountains** ▲▲ North Carolina/ Tennessee, SE USA
56 D1 **Great Snow Mountain** ▲ British Columbia, W Canada 57°22′N 124°08′W
67 M10 **Great Sound** *sound* Bermuda, NW Atlantic Ocean
160 E8 **Great Torrington** UK 50°57′N 4°09′W
276 D2 **Great Victoria Desert** *desert* South Australia/ Western Australia
292 D2 **Great Wall** *Chinese research station* South Shetland Islands, Antarctica
63 M4 **Great Wass Island** *island* Maine, NE USA
161 N3 **Great Yarmouth** *var.* Yarmouth. E England, UK 52°37′N 01°44′E
217 I2 **Great Zab** *Ar.* Az Zāb al Kabīr, *Kurd.* Zē-i Bādīnān, *Turk.* Büyükzap Suyu. ≈ Iraq/Turkey
155 E9 **Grebbestad** Västra Götaland, S Sweden 58°42′N 11°15′E
Grebenka *see* Hrebinka
181 G8 **Grebenstein** Hessen, Germany 9°25′N 51°27′E
89 H8 **Grecia** Alajuela, C Costa Rica 10°04′N 84°19′W
114 G6 **Greco** Río Negro, W Uruguay 32°49′S 57°03′W
Greco, Cape *see* Gkréko, Akrotíri
170 F5 **Gredos, Sierra de** ▲▲ W Spain
172 F3 **Sierra de Gredos** ▲▲ Spain
62 E5 **Greece** New York, NE USA 43°12′N 77°41′W
187 H4 **Greece** *off.* Hellenic Republic, *Gk.* Ellás; *anc.* Hellas. ◆ *republic* SE Europe
Greece Central *see* Stereá Ellás
Greece West *see* Dytikí Ellás
79 M2 **Greeley** Colorado, C USA 40°21′N 104°41′W
74 D7 **Greeley** Nebraska, C USA 41°33′N 98°31′W
64 G4 **Greeley** Pennsylvania, USA 41°25′N 75°00′W
53 I2 **Greely Fiord** *coastal sea feature* Nunavut, N Canada
192 G1 **Greem-Bell, Ostrov** *Eng.* Graham Bell Island. *island* Zemlya Frantsa-Iosifa, N Russian Federation
81 D8 **Greenacres** California, USA 35°23′N 119°07′W
72 D6 **Green Bay** Wisconsin, N USA 44°32′N 88°W
72 D6 **Green Bay** *lake bay* Michigan/Wisconsin, N USA
67 J3 **Greenbrier River** ≈ West Virginia, NE USA
74 F2 **Greenbush** Minnesota, N USA 48°42′N 96°10′W
277 L7 **Green Cape** *headland* New South Wales, SE Australia 37°15′S 150°03′E
158 E8 **Greencastle** UK 54°02′N 6°06′W
73 E11 **Greencastle** Indiana, N USA 39°38′N 86°51′W
64 B8 **Greencastle** Pennsylvania, NE USA 39°47′N 77°43′W
75 H8 **Green City** Missouri, C USA 40°16′N 92°57′W
64 E2 **Greene** New York, USA 42°20′N 75°46′W
67 H6 **Greeneville** Tennessee, S USA 36°10′N 82°50′W
81 D8 **Greenfield** California, USA 35°16′N 119°0′W
80 B5 **Greenfield** California, W USA 36°19′N 121°15′W
73 F11 **Greenfield** Indiana, N USA 39°47′N 85°46′W
65 J2 **Greenfield** Massachusetts, NE USA 42°33′N 72°34′W
75 G11 **Greenfield** Missouri, C USA 37°25′N 93°50′W
73 H11 **Greenfield** Ohio, N USA 39°21′N 83°22′W
66 C6 **Greenfield** Tennessee, S USA 36°09′N 88°48′W
73 D8 **Greenfield** Wisconsin, N USA 42°55′N 87°59′W
75 H11 **Green Forest** Arkansas, C USA 36°19′N 93°24′W
64 D9 **Green Haven** Maryland, USA 39°08′N 76°33′W
159 J6 **Greenhead** UK 54°58′N 2°31′W
79 M4 **Greenhorn Mountain** ▲ Colorado, C USA 37°50′N 104°59′W
Green Island *see* Lü Tao
280 E2 **Green Islands** *var.* Nissan Islands. *island group* NE Papua New Guinea
57 L4 **Green Lake** Saskatchewan, C Canada 54°15′N 107°51′W
72 D7 **Green Lake** ◎ Wisconsin, N USA
295 K7 **Greenland** *Dan.* Grønland, *Inuit* Kalaallit Nunaat. ◇ *Danish external territory* NE North America
144 A2 **Greenland** *island* NE North America
295 K5 **Greenland Plain** *undersea feature* N Greenland Sea
295 K5 **Greenland Sea** *sea* Arctic Ocean
159 J4 **Greenlaw** UK 55°42′N 2°28′W
159 H2 **Greenloaning** UK 56°14′N 3°53′W
159 H5 **Green Lowther** *hill* UK
79 L3 **Green Mountain Reservoir** ⊠ Colorado, C USA
63 I5 **Green Mountains** ▲▲ Vermont, NE USA
Green Mountain State *see* Vermont
158 G3 **Greenock** W Scotland, UK 55°57′N 04°45′W
160 B4 **Greenore Point** *headland* Wexford, Ireland 52°14′N 6°18′W
83 J2 **Greenough, Mount** ▲ Alaska, USA 69°15′N 141°37′W
280 A2 **Green River** Sandaun, NW Papua New Guinea 03°54′S 141°08′E
79 I4 **Green River** Utah, W USA 39°00′N 110°07′W
77 J9 **Green River** Wyoming, C USA 41°33′N 109°27′W
79 J4 **Green River** ≈ W USA
73 C9 **Green River** ≈ Illinois, N USA
66 E5 **Green River** ≈ Kentucky, C USA
74 B3 **Green River** ≈ North Dakota, N USA
79 I4 **Green River** ≈ Utah, W USA
56 D10 **Green River** ≈ Washington, NW USA North America
77 J7 **Green River** ≈ Wyoming, C USA
66 F4 **Green River Lake** ⊠ Kentucky, S USA
68 G1 **Greensboro** Alabama, S USA 32°42′N 87°36′W
66 G8 **Greensboro** Georgia, SE USA 33°34′N 83°10′W
67 J6 **Greensboro** North Carolina, SE USA 36°04′N 79°48′W
73 F11 **Greensburg** Indiana, N USA 39°20′N 85°28′W
75 D10 **Greensburg** Kansas, C USA 37°36′N 99°17′W
66 E4 **Greensburg** Kentucky, S USA 37°14′N 85°30′W
62 C8 **Greensburg** Pennsylvania, NE USA 40°18′N 79°32′W
79 J8 **Greens Peak** ▲ Arizona, SW USA 34°06′N 109°34′W
67 K8 **Green Swamp** *wetland* North Carolina, SE USA
64 F5 **Greentown** Pennsylvania, USA 41°19′N 75°18′W
67 H3 **Greenup** Kentucky, S USA 38°34′N 82°49′W
79 I10 **Green Valley** Arizona, SW USA 31°49′N 111°00′W
64 D8 **Green Valley** Maryland, USA 39°36′N 76°29′W
132 D8 **Greenville** *var.* Sino, Sinoe. SE Liberia 05°01′N 09°03′W
69 H2 **Greenville** Alabama, S USA 31°49′N 86°37′W
69 K4 **Greenville** Florida, SE USA 30°28′N 83°37′W
66 F9 **Greenville** Georgia, SE USA 33°03′N 84°42′W
73 C12 **Greenville** Illinois, N USA 38°53′N 89°24′W
66 D4 **Greenville** Kentucky, S USA 37°11′N 87°11′W
63 K3 **Greenville** Maine, NE USA 45°26′N 69°36′W
72 F7 **Greenville** Michigan, N USA 43°10′N 85°15′W
66 A8 **Greenville** Mississippi, S USA 33°24′N 91°03′W
67 L6 **Greenville** North Carolina, SE USA 35°36′N 77°23′W
73 G10 **Greenville** Ohio, N USA 40°06′N 84°37′W
65 L3 **Greenville** Rhode Island, NE USA 41°52′N 71°33′W
67 H7 **Greenville** South Carolina, SE USA 34°51′N 82°24′W
71 H4 **Greenville** Texas, SW USA 33°09′N 96°07′W
161 K6 **Greenwich** UK 51°28′N 0°0′E
65 I5 **Greenwich** Connecticut, USA 41°02′N 73°38′W
73 I10 **Greenwich** Ohio, N USA 41°01′N 82°31′W
75 G12 **Greenwood** Arkansas, C USA 35°13′N 94°15′W
80 D2 **Greenwood** California, USA 38°54′N 120°55′W
73 F11 **Greenwood** Indiana, N USA 39°38′N 86°06′W
66 A8 **Greenwood** Mississippi, S USA 33°30′N 90°11′W
67 H8 **Greenwood** South Carolina, SE USA 34°11′N 82°10′W
67 H8 **Greenwood, Lake** ⊠ South Carolina, SE USA
67 H7 **Greer** South Carolina, SE USA 34°56′N 82°13′W
75 H12 **Greers Ferry Lake** ⊠ Arkansas, C USA
75 G13 **Greeson, Lake** ⊠ Arkansas, C USA
161 J3 **Greetham** UK 52°42′N 0°37′W
180 C3 **Greetsiel** Niedersachsen, Germany 7°06′N 53°30′E
181 B9 **Grefrath** Nordrhein-Westfalen, Germany 6°38′N 51°10′E
115 I9 **Gregorio Aznàrez** Maldonado, Uruguay 34°43′S 55°25′W
141 J1 **Gregory** Limpopo, South Africa 22°38′S 28°55′E
74 D6 **Gregory** South Dakota, N USA 43°11′N 99°26′W
276 G2 **Gregory, Lake** *salt lake* South Australia
274 E5 **Gregory Lake** ◎ Western Australia
275 J4 **Gregory Range** ▲▲ Queensland, E Australia
Greifenberg/Greifenberg in Pommern *see* Gryfice
Greifenhagen *see* Gryfino
178 H4 **Greifswald** Mecklenburg-Vorpommern, NE Germany 54°04′N 13°24′E
178 I4 **Greifswalder Bodden** *bay* NE Germany
177 K2 **Grein** Oberösterreich, N Austria 48°14′N 14°50′E
179 G9 **Greiz** Thüringen, C Germany 50°40′N 12°11′E
180 J1 **Gremersdorf** Schleswig-Holstein, Germany 10°56′N 54°20′E
Gremicha/Gremiha *see* Gremikha
194 G3 **Gremikha** *var.* Gremicha, Gremiha. Murmanskaya Oblast', NW Russian Federation 68°01′N 39°31′E
195 L9 **Gremyachinsk** Permskaya Oblast', NW Russian Federation 58°33′N 57°52′E
Grenå *see* Grenaa
155 E11 **Grenaa** *var.* Grenå. Århus, C Denmark 56°25′N 10°53′E
66 B8 **Grenada** Mississippi, S USA 33°46′N 89°48′W
91 N3 **Grenada** ◆ *commonwealth republic* SE West Indies
95 K2 **Grenada** *island* Grenada
95 J2 **Grenada Basin** *undersea feature* W Atlantic Ocean
66 B8 **Grenada Lake** ⊠ Mississippi, S USA
168 F5 **Grenade-sur-Garonne** Midi-Pyrénées, France 43°46′N 1°17′E
168 D5 **Grenade-sur-l'Adour** Aquitaine, France 43°47′N 0°25′W
103 I1 **Grenadines, The** *island group* Grenada/St Vincent and the Grenadines
176 C4 **Grenchen** *Fr.* Granges. Solothurn, NW Switzerland 47°13′N 07°24′E
277 K5 **Grenfell** New South Wales, SE Australia 33°54′S 148°09′E
55 H9 **Grenfell** Saskatchewan, S Canada 50°24′N 102°56′W
152 C1 **Grenivík** Nordhurland Eystra, N Iceland 65°57′N 18°10′W
165 J7 **Grenoble** *anc.* Cularo, Gratianopolis. Isère, E France 45°11′N 05°42′E
74 A1 **Grenora** North Dakota, N USA 48°36′N 103°57′W
159 K9 **Grenoside** UK 53°26′N 1°29′W
152 I3 **Grense-Jakobselv** Finnmark, N Norway 69°46′N 30°39′E
169 L5 **Gréoux-les-Bains** Provence-Alpes-Côte d'Azur, France 43°45′N 5°53′E
160 G2 **Gresford** UK 53°05′N 2°58′W
76 C5 **Gresham** Oregon, NW USA 45°30′N 122°25′W
Gresk *see* Hresk
176 D6 **Gressoney-St-Jean** Valle d'Aosta, NW Italy 45°48′N 07°49′E
169 L2 **Grésy-sur-Isére** Rhône-Alpes, France 45°36′N 6°15′E
159 I6 **Gretna** UK 54°59′N 3°04′W
68 E4 **Gretna** Louisiana, S USA 29°54′N 90°03′W
67 J5 **Gretna** Virginia, NE USA 36°57′N 79°21′W
159 I5 **Gretna Green** UK 54°59′N 3°04′W
162 E7 **Grevelingen** *inlet* S North Sea
180 I3 **Greven** Mecklenburg-Vorpommern, Germany 10°48′N 53°29′E
180 D6 **Greven** Nordrhein-Westfalen, NW Germany 52°07′N 07°38′E
186 F3 **Grevená** Dytikí Makedonía, N Greece 40°05′N 21°26′E
181 B9 **Grevenbroich** Nordrhein-Westfalen, W Germany 51°06′N 06°34′E
163 I13 **Grevenmacher** Grevenmacher, E Luxembourg 49°41′N 06°27′E
163 H13 **Grevenmacher** ◈ *district* E Luxembourg
180 J2 **Grevesmülhen** Mecklenburg-Vorpommern, N Germany 53°52′N 11°12′E
278 D9 **Grey** ≈ South Island, New Zealand
158 E7 **Greyabbey** UK 54°32′N 5°34′W
77 K6 **Greybull** Wyoming, C USA 44°29′N 108°03′W
77 K6 **Greybull River** ≈ Wyoming, C USA
117 G11 **Grey Channel** *sound* Falkland Islands
Greyerzer See *see* Gruyère, Lac de la
59 L6 **Grey Islands** *island group* Newfoundland and Labrador, E Canada
65 I2 **Greylock, Mount** ▲ Massachusetts, NE USA 42°38′N 73°09′W
278 D9 **Greymouth** West Coast, South Island, New Zealand 42°29′S 171°14′E
277 I2 **Grey Range** ▲▲ New South Wales/Queensland, E Australia
159 I6 **Greystoke** UK 54°39′N 2°52′W
160 B2 **Greystones** *Ir.* Na Clocha Liatha. E Ireland 53°08′N 06°05′W
278 G7 **Greytown** Wellington, North Island, New Zealand 41°04′S 175°29′E
139 H8 **Greytown** KwaZulu/Natal, E South Africa 29°04′S 30°35′E
Greytown *see* San Juan del Norte
163 E10 **Grez-Doiceau** *Dut.* Graven. Walloon Brabant, C Belgium 50°43′N 04°41′E
166 D7 **Grez-en-Bouére** Pays de la Loire, France 47°53′N 0°31′W
168 G4 **Grézes** Midi-Pyrénées, France 44°37′N 1°49′E
187 I6 **Griá, Ákrotirio** *headland* Ándros, Kykládes, Greece, Aegean Sea 37°54′N 24°57′E
197 H4 **Gribanovskiy** Voronezhskaya Oblast', W Russian Federation 51°27′N 41°53′E
134 E4 **Gribingui** ≈ N Central African Republic
80 D1 **Gridley** California, W USA 39°21′N 121°41′W
140 G6 **Griekwastad** Northern Cape, South Africa 28°51′S 23°15′E
138 E8 **Griekwastad** Northern Cape, C South Africa 28°50′S 23°16′E
181 F12 **Griesheim** Hessen, Germany 8°35′N 49°52′E
66 F9 **Griffin** Georgia, SE USA 33°15′N 84°17′W
277 J5 **Griffith** New South Wales, SE Australia 34°18′S 146°04′E
62 C3 **Griffith Island** *island* Ontario, S Canada
181 G9 **Grifte** Hessen, Germany 9°27′N 51°13′E
67 L6 **Grifton** North Carolina, SE USA 35°22′N 77°26′W
Grigioni *see* Graubünden
191 E9 **Grigiškes** Vilnius, SE Lithuania 54°42′N 25°00′E
169 K4 **Grignan** Rhône-Alpes, France 44°25′N 4°54′E
168 D4 **Grignols** Aquitaine, France 44°23′N 0°02′W
188 G7 **Grigoriopol** C Moldova 47°09′N 29°18′E
229 M4 **Grigor'yevka** Issyk-Kul'skaya Oblast', E Kyrgyzstan 42°43′N 77°27′E
287 K6 **Grijalva Ridge** *undersea feature* E Pacific Ocean
87 J8 **Grijalva, Río** *var.* Tabasco. ≈ Guatemala/Mexico
87 J7 **Grijalva, 'Río** ≈ Mexico
172 B1 **Grijó** Porto, Portugal 41°02′N 8°35′W
162 H3 **Grijpskerk** Groningen, NE Netherlands 53°15′N 06°18′E
140 B5 **Grillenthal** Karas, SW Namibia 26°55′S 15°24′E
134 F5 **Grimari** Ouaka, C Central African Republic 05°44′N 20°02′E
169 M6 **Grimaud** Provence-Alpes-Côte d'Azur, France 43°16′N 6°31′E
Grimaylov *see* Hrymayliv
163 E10 **Grimbergen** Vlaams Brabant, C Belgium 50°56′N 04°22′E
277 I9 **Grim, Cape** *headland* Tasmania, SE Australia 40°42′S 144°42′E
80 C1 **Grimes** California, USA 39°04′N 121°54′W
178 H4 **Grimmen** Mecklenburg-Vorpommern, NE Germany 54°06′N 13°03′E
62 D5 **Grimsby** Ontario, S Canada 43°12′N 79°35′W
159 M9 **Grimsby** *prev.* Great Grimsby. E England, UK 53°35′N 00°05′W
152 C1 **Grímsey** *var.* Grimsey. *island* N Iceland
Grimsey *see* Grímsey
56 G2 **Grimshaw** Alberta, W Canada 56°11′N 117°37′W
155 C9 **Grimstad** Aust-Agder, S Norway 58°20′N 08°35′E
152 B3 **Grindavík** Reykjanes, W Iceland 65°57′N 18°10′W
176 D5 **Grindelwald** Bern, S Switzerland 46°37′N 08°04′E
159 J8 **Grindleton** UK 53°54′N 2°22′W
155 C12 **Grindsted** Ribe, W Denmark 55°46′N 08°56′E
74 H7 **Grinnell** Iowa, C USA 41°44′N 92°43′W
53 H4 **Grinnell Peninsula** *peninsula* Northwest Territories, Devon Island, N Canada
174 G4 **Grintovec** ▲ N Slovenia 46°21′N 14°31′E
53 I4 **Grise Fiord** *var.* Ausuitoq. Northwest Territories, Ellesmere Island, N Canada North America 76°10′N 83°15′W
276 F1 **Griselda, Lake** *salt lake* South Australia
166 G1 **Gris-Nez, Cap** *cape* N France
Grisons *see* Graubünden
154 J7 **Grisslehamn** Stockholm, C Sweden 60°04′N 18°50′E
74 F7 **Griswold** Iowa, C USA 41°14′N 95°08′W
159 I7 **Grizebeck** UK 54°15′N 3°10′W
165 H1 **Griz Nez, Cap** *headland* N France 50°51′N 01°34′E
80 E2 **Grizzly Flat** California, USA 38°38′N 120°32′W
185 H5 **Grljan** Serbia, E Serbia 43°52′N 22°18′E
184 C3 **Grmeč** ▲▲ NW Bosnia and Herzegovina
163 E9 **Grobbendonk** Antwerpen, N Belgium 51°12′N 04°41′E
Grobin *see* Grobiņa
190 B6 **Grobiņa** *Ger.* Grobin. Liepāja, W Latvia 56°32′N 21°12′E
141 J3 **Groblersdal** Mpumalanga, NE South Africa 25°15′S 29°25′E
140 F6 **Groblershoop** Northern Cape, South Africa 28°53′S 21°59′E
138 E8 **Groblershoop** Northern Cape, W South Africa 28°51′S 22°01′E
Gródek Jagielloński *see* Horodok
177 I3 **Grödig** Salzburg, W Austria 47°42′N 13°06′E
183 E8 **Grodków** Opolskie, S Poland 50°42′N 17°23′E
Grodnenskaya Oblast' *see* Hrodzyenskaya Voblasts'
Grodno *see* Hrodna
182 H6 **Grodzisk Mazowiecki** Mazowieckie, C Poland 52°09′N 20°38′E
182 D6 **Grodzisk Wielkopolski** Weilkopolskie, C Poland 52°13′N 16°21′E
Grodzyanka *see* Hradzyanka
140 G7 **Groen** ≈ Northern Cape, South Africa
140 C7 **Groen** ≈ Northern Cape, South Africa
162 I7 **Groenlo** Gelderland, E Netherlands 52°02′N 06°36′E
140 D5 **Groenrivier** Karas, SE Namibia 27°27′S 18°52′E
71 H5 **Groesbeck** Texas, SW USA 31°31′N 96°35′W
162 H7 **Groesbeek** Gelderland, SE Netherlands 51°47′N 05°56′E
141 J2 **Groesbeek** Limpopo, South Africa 23°52′S 28°26′E
166 A7 **Groix, Île de** *island* Bretagne, France
164 E4 **Groix, Îles de** *island group* NW France
182 H6 **Grójec** Mazowieckie, C Poland 51°51′N 20°52′E
175 C13 **Grombalia** Tunisia
180 C6 **Gronau** *var.* Gronau in Westfalen. Nordrhein-Westfalen, NW Germany 52°13′N 07°02′E
Gronau in Westfalen *see* Gronau
154 F2 **Grong** Nord-Trøndelag, C Norway 64°29′N 12°19′E
155 H11 **Grönhögen** Kalmar, S Sweden 56°16′N 16°09′E
181 H14 **Gröningen** Baden-Württemberg, Germany 10°04′N 49°11′E
180 J7 **Gröningen** Sachsen-Anhalt, Germany 11°13′N 51°56′E
162 I3 **Groningen** Groningen, NE Netherlands 53°13′N 06°35′E
103 L5 **Groningen** Saramacca, N Suriname 05°45′N 55°31′W
162 I3 **Groningen** ◈ *province* NE Netherlands
Grønland *see* Greenland
176 E5 **Grono** Graubünden, S Switzerland 46°15′N 09°07′E
155 H10 **Grönskåra** Kalmar, S Sweden 57°04′N 15°45′E
70 E2 **Groom** Texas, SW USA 35°12′N 101°06′W
80 J7 **Groom Lake** ◎ Nevada, W USA
140 G9 **Groot** ≈ Eastern Cape, South Africa
138 F10 **Groot** ≈ S South Africa
140 F10 **Groot** ≈ Western Cape, South Africa
140 D9 **Groot-Bergrivier** ≈ Western Cape, South Africa
141 H8 **Groot Brak** ≈ Eastern Cape, South Africa
275 H2 **Groote Eylandt** *island* Northern Territory, N Australia
162 H3 **Grootegast** Groningen, NE Netherlands 53°11′N 06°12′E
138 C4 **Grootfontein** Otjozondjupa, N Namibia 19°32′S 18°05′E
140 D5 **Groot Karasberge** ▲▲ S Namibia
Groot Karoo *see* Great Karoo
141 J9 **Groot Kei** ≈ Eastern Cape, South Africa
138 G9 **Groot-Kei** *Eng.* Great Kei. ≈ S South Africa
141 I3 **Groot-Marico** North-West, South Africa 25°36′S 26°25′E
140 C6 **Grootmis** Northern Cape, South Africa 29°39′S 17°05′E
140 G9 **Grootrivierberge** ▲▲ Eastern Cape, South Africa
91 J3 **Gros Islet** N Saint Lucia 14°04′N 60°57′W
90 G5 **Gros-Morne** NW Haiti 19°45′N 72°46′W
59 L6 **Gros Morne** ▲ Newfoundland, Newfoundland and Labrador, E Canada 49°38′N 57°45′W
165 J5 **Grosne** ≈ C France
91 J3 **Gros Piton** ▲ SW Saint Lucia 13°48′N 61°04′W
Grossa, Isola *see* Dugi Otok
180 J7 **Grossalsleben** Sachsen-Anhalt, Germany 11°14′N 51°59′E
181 F11 **Grossauheim** Hessen, Germany 8°57′N 50°06′E
Grossbetschkerek *see* Zrenjanin
181 I8 **Grossbodungen** Thüringen, Germany 10°30′N 51°28′E
180 D3 **Grossefehn** Niedersachsen, Germany 7°33′N 53°24′E
Grosse Isper *see* Grosse Ysper
Grosse Kokel *see* Târnava Mare
179 G12 **Grosse Laaber** *var.* Grosse Laber. ≈ SE Germany
Grosse Laber *see* Grosse Laaber
Grosse Morava *see* Velika Morava
181 J8 **Grossenehrich** Thüringen, Germany 10°50′N 51°15′E
179 I8 **Grossenhain** Sachsen, E Germany 51°18′N 13°31′E
180 E4 **Grossenkneten** Niedersachsen, Germany 8°16′N 52°57′E
180 I2 **Grossensee** Schleswig-Holstein, Germany 10°21′N 53°37′E
177 L2 **Grossenzersdorf** Niederösterreich, NE Austria 48°12′N 16°33′E
179 H11 **Grosser Arber** ▲ SE Germany 49°07′N 13°10′E
181 J10 **Grosser Beerberg** ▲ C Germany 50°39′N 10°45′E
181 F11 **Grosser Feldberg** ▲ W Germany 50°13′N 08°28′E
181 G14 **Grosserlach** Baden-Württemberg, Germany 9°31′N 49°03′E
174 E3 **Grosser Löffler** *It.* Monte Lovello. ▲ Austria/Italy 47°02′N 11°56′E
174 E3 **Grosser Möseler** *var.* Mesule. ▲ Austria/Italy 47°01′N 11°52′E
180 I1 **Grosser Plöner See** ◎ N Germany
179 H11 **Grosser Rachel** ▲ SE Germany 48°59′N 13°23′E
Grosser Sund *see* Suur Väin
179 H14 **Grosses Weiesbachhorn** *var.* Wiesbachhorn. ▲ W Austria 47°09′N 12°44′E
174 D7 **Grosseto** Toscana, C Italy 42°45′N 11°07′E
179 G12 **Grosse Vils** ≈ SE Germany
177 K2 **Grosse Ysper** *var.* Grosse Isper. ≈ N Austria
181 F12 **Gross-Gerau** Hessen, W Germany 49°55′N 08°28′E
177 K2 **Gross Gerungs** Niederösterreich, N Austria 48°33′N 14°58′E
179 H14 **Grossglockner** ▲ W Austria 47°05′N 12°39′E
180 H5 **Gross Hehlen** Niedersachsen, Germany 10°03′N 52°39′E
180 C5 **Gross Hesepe** Niedersachsen, Germany 7°14′N 52°37′E
181 G12 **Grossheubach** Bayern, Germany 9°14′N 49°44′E
Grosskanizsa *see* Nagykanizsa
Gross-Karol *see* Carei
Grosskikinda *see* Kikinda
177 K4 **Grossklein** Steiermark, SE Austria 46°43′N 15°24′E
Grosskoppe *see* Velká Deštná
Grossmeseritsch *see* Velké Meziříčí
Grossmichel *see* Michalovce
181 G12 **Grossostheim** Bayern, C Germany 49°54′N 09°03′E
177 L3 **Grosspetersdorf** Burgenland, SE Austria 47°15′N 16°19′E
177 J3 **Grossraming** Oberösterreich, C Austria 47°54′N 14°34′E
179 I8 **Grossräschen** Brandenburg, E Germany 51°34′N 14°00′E
Grossrauschenbach *see* Revúca
180 H7 **Gross Rhüden** Niedersachsen, Germany 10°07′N 51°57′E
181 H13 **Grossrinderfeld** Baden-Württemberg, Germany 9°45′N 49°39′E
Gross-Sankt-Johannis *see* Suure-Jaani
Gross-Schlatten *see* Abrud
177 K1 **Gross-Siegharts** Niederösterreich, N Austria 48°48′N 15°25′E
Gross-Skaisgirren *see* Bol'shakovo
Gross-Steffelsdorf *see* Rimavská Sobota
Gross Strehlitz *see* Strzelce Opolskie
180 J6 **Gross Twülpstedt** Niedersachsen, Germany 10°55′N 52°22′E
181 F12 **Gross-Umstadt** Hessen, Germany 8°56′N 49°52′E
179 G14 **Grossvenediger** ▲ W Austria 47°07′N 12°19′E
Grosswardein *see* Oradea
Gross Wartenberg *see* Syców
167 M5 **Grostenquin** Lorraine, France 48°59′N 6°44′E
177 K6 **Grosuplje** C Slovenia 46°00′N 14°36′E
163 E9 **Grote Nete** ≈ N Belgium
154 C5 **Grotli** Oppland, S Norway 62°02′N 07°36′E
65 K4 **Groton** Connecticut, NE USA 41°20′N 72°03′W
74 E4 **Groton** South Dakota, N USA 45°27′N 98°06′W
175 I10 **Grottaglie** Puglia, SE Italy 40°32′N 17°26′E
175 G9 **Grottaminarda** Campania, S Italy 41°04′N 15°02′E
177 J10 **Grottammare** Marche, C Italy 43°00′N 13°52′E
67 K3 **Grottoes** Virginia, NE USA 38°16′N 78°49′W
Grou *see* Grouw
59 I6 **Groulx, Monts** ▲▲ Québec, E Canada
58 E7 **Groundhog** ≈ Ontario, S Canada
78 G1 **Grouse Creek** Utah, W USA 41°41′N 113°52′W
78 G1 **Grouse Creek Mountains** ▲▲ Utah, W USA
162 G4 **Grouw** *Fris.* Grou. Friesland, N Netherlands 53°07′N 05°51′E
75 G11 **Grove** Oklahoma, C USA 36°35′N 94°46′W
73 H11 **Grove City** Ohio, N USA 39°52′N 83°05′W
62 C7 **Grove City** Pennsylvania, NE USA 41°09′N 80°02′W
68 G2 **Grove Hill** Alabama, S USA 31°42′N 87°46′W
80 D4 **Groveland** California, USA 37°50′N 120°14′W
77 I8 **Grover** Wyoming, C USA 42°48′N 110°57′W
80 B7 **Grover Beach** California, USA 35°07′N 120°37′W
78 C7 **Grover City** California, W USA 35°08′N 120°37′W
71 J7 **Groves** Texas, SW USA 29°57′N 93°55′W
63 I4 **Groveton** New Hampshire, NE USA 44°35′N 71°28′W
71 I6 **Groveton** Texas, SW USA 31°04′N 95°08′W
79 H9 **Growler Mountains** ▲▲ Arizona, SW USA
Grozdovo *see* Bratya Daskalovi
197 I9 **Groznyy** Chechenskaya Respublika, SW Russian Federation 43°20′N 45°43′E
Grubeshov *see* Hrubieszów
184 D2 **Grubišno Polje** Bjelovar-Bilogora, NE Croatia 45°42′N 17°09′E
Grudovo *see* Sredets
182 F4 **Grudziądz** *Ger.* Graudenz. Kujawsko-pomorskie, C Poland 53°29′N 18°45′E
169 H6 **Gruissan** Languedoc-Roussillon, France 43°06′N 3°05′E
70 G10 **Grulla** *var.* La Grulla. Texas, SW USA 26°15′N 98°37′W
86 B6 **Grullo** Jalisco, SW Mexico 19°45′N 104°15′W
121 L6 **Grumeti** ≈ N Tanzania
155 F8 **Grums** Värmland, C Sweden 59°22′N 13°11′E
177 J3 **Grünau im Almtal** Oberösterreich, N Austria 47°51′N 13°56′E
181 F10 **Grünberg** Hessen, W Germany 50°36′N 08°57′E
Grünberg/Grünberg in Schlesien *see* Zielona Góra
152 A2 **Grundarfjördhur** Vestfirdhir, W Iceland 64°55′N 23°15′W
181 H14 **Gründelhardt** Baden-Württemberg, Germany 9°59′N 49°05′E
67 H4 **Grundy** Virginia, NE USA 37°17′N 82°06′W
74 H7 **Grundy Center** Iowa, C USA 42°21′N 92°46′W
Grüneberg *see* Zielona Góra
180 G3 **Grünendeich** Niedersachsen, Germany 9°36′N 53°34′E
181 H13 **Grünsfeld** Baden-Württemberg, Germany 9°45′N 49°37′E
181 E13 **Grünstadt** Rheinland-Pfalz, Germany 8°10′N 49°34′E
114 A4 **Grüttly** Santa Fe, Argentina 31°16′S 61°03′W
70 E1 **Gruver** Texas, SW USA 36°16′N 101°24′W
174 A3 **Gruyère, Lac de la** *Ger.* Greyerzer See. ◎ SW Switzerland
176 C5 **Gruyères** Fribourg, W Switzerland 46°34′N 07°04′E
190 C7 **Gruzdiai** Šiauliai, N Lithuania 56°06′N 23°15′E
Gruzinskaya SSR/Gruziya *see* Georgia
Gryada Akkyr *see* Akgyr Erezi
196 G4 **Gryazi** Lipetskaya Oblast', W Russian Federation 52°27′N 39°56′E
194 G9 **Gryazovets** Vologodskaya Oblast', NW Russian Federation 58°52′N 40°12′E
183 H9 **Grybów** Małopolskie, SE Poland 49°35′N 20°54′E
154 H6 **Grycksbo** Dalarna, C Sweden 60°40′N 15°30′E
182 C4 **Gryfice** *Ger.* Greifenberg, Greifenberg in Pommern. Zachodnio-pomorskie, NW Poland 53°55′N 15°11′E
182 C5 **Gryfino** *Ger.* Greifenhagen. Zachodnio-pomorskie, NW Poland 53°15′N 14°30′E
152 E4 **Gryllefjord** Troms, N Norway 69°21′N 17°07′E
154 G7 **Grythyttan** Örebro, C Sweden 59°52′N 14°31′E
181 H14 **Gschwend** Baden-Württemberg, Germany 9°44′N 48°56′E
176 C5 **Gstaad** Bern, W Switzerland 46°30′N 07°16′E
89 I8 **Guabito** Bocas del Toro, NW Panama 09°30′N 82°35′W
90 E5 **Guacanayabo, Golfo de** *gulf* S Cuba
85 H6 **Guachochi** Chihuahua, N Mexico
85 H5 **Guachochic** Chihuahua, Mexico
111 K4 **Guaçuí** Espírito Santo, Brazil 20°46′S 41°41′W
173 H7 **Guadahortuna** Andalucía, Spain 37°34′N 3°24′W
170 E6 **Guadajira** ≈ SW Spain
172 E5 **Guadajira** ≈ Extremadura, Spain
172 G7 **Guadajoz** ≈ Spain
86 C5 **Guadalajara** Jalisco, C Mexico 20°43′N 103°24′W
170 G4 **Guadalajara** *Ar.* Wad Al-Hajarah; *anc.* Arriaca. Castilla-La Mancha, C Spain 40°37′N 03°10′W
171 H4 **Guadalajara** ◈ *province* Castilla-La Mancha, C Spain
172 F9 **Pantano de Guadalcacín** ⊠ Andalucía, Spain
170 E7 **Guadalcanal** Andalucía, S Spain 38°06′N 05°49′W
281 J3 **Guadalcanal** *off.* Guadalcanal Province. ◈ *province* C Solomon Islands
281 J3 **Guadalcanal** *island* C Solomon Islands
Guadalcanal Province *see* Guadalcanal
170 G7 **Guadalén** ≈ S Spain
173 I6 **Guadalén** ≈ Andalucía, Spain
171 I8 **Guadalentín** ≈ SE Spain
173 K7 **Guadalentín** ≈ Spain
170 E9 **Guadalete** ≈ SW Spain
172 G9 **Guadalhorce** ≈ Spain
170 G7 **Guadalimar** ≈ S Spain
173 I6 **Guadalmena** ≈ Spain
170 F7 **Guadalmez** ≈ W Spain
171 I4 **Guadalope** ≈ E Spain
170 E8 **Guadalquivir** ≈ W Spain
170 E8 **Guadalquivir, Marismas del** *var.* Las Marismas. *wetland* SW Spain
172 E8 **Marismas del Guadalquivir** *marsh* Spain
172 E8 **Guadalquivir** ≈ Spain
85 K6 **Guadalupe** Coahuila de Zaragoza, Mexico 26°08′N 101°17′W
84 E3 **Guadalupe** San Luis Potosí, C Mexico North America
85 K9 **Guadalupe** Zacatecas, C Mexico 22°47′N 102°30′W
105 D8 **Guadalupe** Ica, W Peru 13°59′S 75°49′W
170 F6 **Guadalupe** Extremadura, W Spain 39°26′N 05°18′W
79 H9 **Guadalupe** Arizona, SW USA 33°20′N 111°57′W
81 B8 **Guadalupe** California, W USA 34°55′N 120°34′W
287 I3 **Guadalupe** *island* NW Mexico
Guadalupe *see* Canelones
85 I7 **Guadalupe Aguilera** Durango, C Mexico North America
85 H2 **Guadalupe Bravos** Chihuahua, N Mexico 31°22′N 106°04′W
84 D5 **Guadalupe de los Reyes** Baja California Sur, Mexico 27°19′N 113°21′W
86 F8 **Guadalupe de Ramírez** Oaxaca, Mexico 17°45′N 98°09′W
84 A3 **Guadalupe, Isla** *island* NW Mexico
79 M9 **Guadalupe Mountains** ▲▲ New Mexico/Texas, SW USA
70 B5 **Guadalupe Peak** ▲ Texas, SW USA 31°53′N 104°51′W
70 G7 **Guadalupe River** ≈ SW USA
172 F4 **Sierra de Guadalupe** ▲▲ Extremadura, Spain
85 J7 **Guadalupe Victoria** Durango, C Mexico 24°30′N 104°08′W
85 H6 **Guadalupe y Calvo** Chihuahua, N Mexico 26°04′N 106°58′W
172 G6 **Pantano del Guadamellato** ⊠ Andalucía, Spain
170 G4 **Guadarrama** Madrid, C Spain 40°40′N 04°06′W
170 G5 **Guadarrama** ≈ C Spain
170 F4 **Guadarrama, Puerto de** *pass* C Spain
170 G4 **Guadarrama, Sierra de** ▲▲ C Spain
171 H5 **Guadazaón** ≈ C Spain
173 J3 **Guadazaón** ≈ Castilla-La Manacha, Spain
91 N1 **Guadeloupe** ◇ *French overseas department* E West Indies
95 K2 **Guadeloupe** *island group* E West Indies
91 J1 **Guadeloupe Passage** *passage* E Caribbean Sea
170 D7 **Guadiana** ≈ Portugal/Spain
170 G8 **Guadiana Menor** ≈ S Spain
173 I7 **Guadiana Menor** ≈ Spain
171 H4 **Guadiela** ≈ C Spain
170 G8 **Guadix** Andalucía, S Spain 37°19′N 03°08′W
Guad-i-Zirreh *see* Gowd-e Zereh, Dasht-e
287 K9 **Guafo Fracture Zone** *tectonic feature* SE Pacific Ocean
117 A9 **Guafo, Isla** *island* S Chile
88 G4 **Guaimaca** Francisco Morazán, C Honduras 14°34′N 86°49′W
102 F7 **Guainía** *off.* Comisaría del Guainía. ◈ *province* E Colombia
Guainía, Comisaría del *see* Guainía
102 F7 **Guainía, Río** ≈ Colombia/Venezuela
103 H5 **Guaiquinima, Cerro** *elevation* SE Venezuela
113 I4 **Guaíra** Paraná, S Brazil 24°05′S 54°15′W
110 A3 **Guaíra** São Paulo, S Brazil 20°17′S 48°21′W
113 H5 **Guairá** *off.* Departamento del Guairá. ◈ *department* S Paraguay
Guairá, Departamento del *see* Guairá
Guaire *see* Gorey
117 B9 **Guaiteca, Isla** *island* S Chile
90 E4 **Guajaba, Cayo** *headland* C Cuba 21°50′N 77°33′W
106 E7 **Guajará-Mirim** Rondônia, W Brazil 10°50′S 65°21′W
Guajira *see* La Guajira
Guajira, Departamento de La *see* La Guajira
102 D2 **Guajira, Península de la** *peninsula* N Colombia
88 G4 **Gualaco** Olancho, C Honduras 15°00′N 86°03′W
78 A3 **Gualala** California, W USA 38°45′N 123°33′W
88 D3 **Gualán** Zacapa, C Guatemala 15°06′N 89°22′W
114 D7 **Gualeguay** Entre Ríos, E Argentina 33°09′S 59°20′W
114 E6 **Gualeguaychú** Entre Ríos, E Argentina 33°03′S 58°31′W
114 D6 **Gualeguay, Río** ≈ E Argentina
116 E7 **Gualicho, Salina del** *salt lake* E Argentina
118 D10 **Gualletue, Laguna** ◎ Araucanía, Chile
118 B8 **Punta Gualpen** *point* Bío-Bío, Chile
282 A1 **Guam** ◇ *US unincorporated territory* W Pacific Ocean
117 A9 **Guamblin, Isla** *island* Archipiélago de los Chonos, S Chile
116 F5 **Guaminí** Buenos Aires, Argentina 37°06′S 62°18′E
84 G7 **Guamúchil** Sinaloa, C Mexico 25°23′N 108°01′W
245 I3 **Guan** China 39°23′N 115°11′E
102 D2 **Guana** *var.* Misión de Guana. Zulia, NW Venezuela 11°07′N 72°17′W
90 C3 **Guanabacoa** La Habana, W Cuba 23°02′N 82°12′W
88 G8 **Guanacaste** *off.* Provincia de Guanacaste. ◈ *province* NW Costa Rica
88 G7 **Guanacaste, Cordillera de** ▲▲ NW Costa Rica
Guanacaste, Provincia de *see* Guanacaste
85 H6 **Guanaceví** Durango, C Mexico 25°55′N 105°51′W
90 A3 **Guanahacabibes, Golfo de** *gulf* W Cuba
88 G2 **Guanaja, Isla de** *island* Islas de la Bahía, N Honduras
90 C3 **Guanajay** La Habana, W Cuba 22°56′N 82°42′W
86 D5 **Guanajuato** Guanajuato, C Mexico 21°N 101°19′W
86 D5 **Guanajuato** ◈ *state* C Mexico
102 E3 **Guanare** Portuguesa, N Venezuela 09°04′N 69°45′W
102 F4 **Guanare, Río** ≈ W Venezuela
102 E3 **Guanarito** Portuguesa, NW Venezuela 08°43′N 69°12′W
244 G3 **Guancen Shan** ▲▲ C China
243 M3 **Guancheng** China 30°11′N 121°24′E
112 C7 **Guandacol** La Rioja, W Argentina 29°32′S 68°37′W
244 G4 **Guandi Shan 2831m** ▲ Shanxi, China 37°32′N 111°17′E
243 H4 **Guandu** China 28°21′N 113°53′E
243 H8 **Guandu** China 24°17′N 113°53′E
90 B3 **Guane** Pinar del Río, W Cuba 22°12′N 84°05′W
242 C2 **Guang'an** Sichuan, China 30°18′N 106°22′E
243 J6 **Guangchang** China 26°57′N 116°25′E
243 L2 **Guangde** Anhui, China 30°32′N 119°14′E
243 H9 **Guangdong** *var.* Guangdong Sheng, Kuang-tung, Kwangtung, Yue. ◈ *province* S China
Guangdong Sheng *see* Guangdong
243 K4 **Guangfeng** Jiangxi, China 28°16′N 118°07′E
242 A2 **Guanghan** Sichuan, China 30°35′N 104°09′E
244 A6 **Guanghe** Gansu, China 35°17′N 103°20′E
Guanghua *see* Laohekou
Guangju *see* Kwangju
242 B8 **Guangnan** *var.* Liancheng. Yunnan, SW China 24°07′N 104°54′E
242 G9 **Guangning** Guangdong, China 23°23′N 112°15′E
243 H2 **Guangshui** China 31°37′N 113°49′E
243 H2 **Guangshui** *prev.* Yingshan. Hubei, C China 31°41′N 113°53′E
242 C6 **Guangshun** China 26°11′N 106°22′E
118 C1 **Guanguali** Coquimbo, Chile 32°08′S 71°23′W
Guangxi *see* Guangxi Zhuangzu Zizhiqu
242 D8 **Guangxi Zhuangzu Zizhiqu** *var.* Guangxi, Gui, Kuang-hsi, Kwangsi, *Eng.* Kwangsi Chuang Autonomous Region. ◈ *autonomous region* S China
242 C1 **Guangyuan** *var.* Kuang-yuan, Kwangyuan. Sichuan, C China 32°27′N 105°49′E
243 K5 **Guangze** Fujan, China 27°19′N 117°13′E
243 H9 **Guangzhou** , *var.* Kwangchow, *Eng.* Canton. *province capital* Guangdong, S China 23°11′N 113°19′E
111 I1 **Guanhães** Minas Gerais, SE Brazil 18°46′S 42°58′W
242 B6 **Guanling** *var.* Guanling Buyeizu Miaozu Zizhixian. Guizhou, S China 26°00′N 105°40′E
Guanling Buyeizu Miaozu Zizhixian *see* Guanling
243 L7 **Guanqiao** China 24°48′N 118°26′E
103 H3 **Guanta** Anzoátegui, NE Venezuela 10°15′N 64°38′W
90 F5 **Guantánamo** Guantánamo, SE Cuba 20°06′N 75°16′W
245 I3 **Guanting Shuiku** ⊠ Hebei, China
245 I6 **Guanxian** Shandong, China 36°17′N 115°16′E
Guanxian/Guan Xian *see* Dujiangyan
242 F7 **Guanyang** Guangxi, China 25°17′N 111°05′E
245 L8 **Guanyun** *var* Yishan. Jiangsu, E China 34°18′N 119°14′E
110 E4 **Guapé** Minas Gerais, Brazil 20°47′S 45°55′W
102 A7 **Guapí** Cauca, SW Colombia 02°36′N 77°54′W
89 H8 **Guápiles** Limón, NE Costa Rica 10°15′N 83°46′W
113 J7 **Guaporé** Rio Grande do Sul, S Brazil 28°55′S 51°53′W
95 K5 **Guaporé, Rio** *var.* Río Iténez. ≈ Bolivia/Brazil *see also* Río Iténez
Guaporé, Rio *see* Iténez, Río
111 I7 **Guapy-mirim** Rio de Janeiro, Brazil 22°32′S 42°59′W
110 B4 **Guarà** São Paulo, Brazil 20°26′S 47°50′W
111 I4 **Guaraciaba** Minas Gerais, Brazil 20°34′S 43°00′W
104 C2 **Guaranda** Bolívar, C Ecuador 01°35′S 78°59′W
110 C5 **Guaranésia** Minas Gerais, Brazil 21°18′S 46°48′W
113 I4 **Guaraniaçu** Paraná, S Brazil 25°05′S 52°52′W
110 B6 **Guaraparà** São Paulo, Brazil 21°30′S 48°02′W
111 M4 **Guarapari** Espírito Santo, SE Brazil 20°39′S 40°31′W
113 J5 **Guarapuava** Paraná, S Brazil 25°22′S 51°28′W
111 I6 **Guararà** Minas Gerais, Brazil 21°43′S 43°02′W
113 J3 **Guararapes** São Paulo, S Brazil 21°16′S 50°37′W
110 E9 **Guararema** São Paulo, Brazil 23°25′S 46°02′W
168 D8 **Sierra de Guara** ▲▲ Aragón, Spain
171 I3 **Guara, Sierra de** ▲▲ NE Spain
110 F8 **Guaratinguetá** São Paulo, S Brazil 22°44′S 45°16′W
170 D4 **Guarda** Guarda, N Portugal 40°32′N 07°17′W
172 D2 **Guarda** Guarda, Portugal 40°32′N 7°16′W
172 D2 **Guarda** ◈ *district* N Portugal
Guardak *see* Govurdak
173 L6 **Guardamar del Segura** Valenciana, Spain 38°06′N 0°39′W
114 D5 **Guardamonte** Entre Ríos, Argentina 32°05′S 59°18′W
170 F2 **Guardo** Castilla-León, N Spain 42°48′N 04°50′W
110 B9 **Guarehy** São Paulo, Brazil 23°22′S 48°10′W
170 E6 **Guareña** Extremadura, W Spain 38°51′N 06°06′W
110 A5 **Guariba** São Paulo, Brazil 21°21′S 48°14′W
113 K5 **Guaricana, Pico** ▲ S Brazil 25°13′S 48°50′W
102 F3 **Guárico** *off.* Estado Guárico. ◈ *state* N Venezuela
Guárico, Estado *see* Guárico
90 G5 **Guarico, Punta** *headland* E Cuba 20°36′N 74°43′W
102 F4 **Guárico, Río** ≈ C Venezuela
173 H6 **Guarromàn** Andalucía, Spain 38°11′N 3°41′W
110 D10 **Guarujá** São Paulo, SE Brazil 23°50′S 46°27′W
110 D9 **Guarulhos** Sao Paulo, Brazil 23°24′S 46°30′E
110 D9 **Guarulhos** ✈ (São Paulo) São Paulo, S Brazil 23°23′S 46°32′W
89 J10 **Guarumal** Veraguas, S Panama 07°48′N 81°15′W
Guasapa *see* Guasopa
84 G7 **Guasave** Sinaloa, C Mexico 25°33′N 108°29′W
102 E4 **Guasdualito** Apure, C Venezuela 07°15′N 70°40′W
103 I4 **Guasipati** Bolívar, E Venezuela 07°28′N 61°58′W
280 E4 **Guasopa** *var.* Guasapa. Woodlark Island, SE Papua New Guinea 09°12′S 152°58′E
176 G7 **Guastalla** Emilia-Romagna, C Italy 44°54′N 10°38′E
88 C4 **Guastatoya** *var.* El Progreso. El Progreso, C Guatemala 14°51′N 90°01′W
88 C3 **Guatemala** *off.* Republic of Guatemala. ◆ *republic* Central America
88 C4 **Guatemala** *off.* Departamento de Guatemala. ◈ *department* S Guatemala
287 K5 **Guatemala Basin** *undersea feature* E Pacific Ocean
Guatemala City *see* Ciudad de Guatemala
Guatemala, Departamento de *see* Guatemala
Guatemala, Republic of *see* Guatemala
91 L8 **Guatuaro Point** *headland* Trinidad, Trinidad and Tobago 10°19′N 60°58′W
280 A3 **Guavi** ≈ SW Papua New Guinea
102 D7 **Guaviare** *off.* Comisaría Guaviare. ◈ *province* S Colombia
Guaviare, Comisaría *see* Guaviare
102 E6 **Guaviare, Río** ≈ E Colombia
113 H7 **Guaviravi** Corrientes, NE Argentina 29°20′S 56°50′W
110 D5 **Guaxupé** Minas Gerais, Brazil 21°18′S 46°42′W
102 C7 **Guayabero, Río** ≈ SW Colombia
103 I4 **Guayabones** Delta Amacuro, Venezuela 8°18′S 61°48′E
118 D3 **Guayacán** Región Metropolitana, Chile 33°36′S 70°22′W
91 I8 **Guayama** E Puerto Rico 17°59′N 66°07′W
88 G4 **Guayambre, Río** ≈ S Honduras
Guayanas, Macizo de las *see* Guiana Highlands
91 J8 **Guayanés, Punta** *headland* E Puerto Rico 18°03′N 65°48′W
88 G4 **Guayape, Río** ≈ C Honduras
104 B2 **Guayaquil** *var.* Santiago de Guayaquil. Guayas, SW Ecuador 02°13′S 79°54′W
Guayaquil *see* Simon Bolivar
104 B3 **Guayaquil, Golfo de** *var.* Gulf of Guayaquil. *gulf* SW Ecuador
Guayaquil, Gulf of *see* Guayaquil, Golfo de
104 B2 **Guayas** ◈ *province* W Ecuador
112 F5 **Guaycurú, Río** ≈ NE Argentina
84 E5 **Guaymas** Sonora, NW Mexico 27°56′N 110°54′W
91 J8 **Guaynabo** E Puerto Rico 18°19′N 66°05′W
114 C2 **Guayquiraró** Santa Fe, Argentina 30°18′S 59°32′W
84 G5 **Guazapares** Chihuahua, Mexico 27°22′N 108°15′W
136 C3 **Guba** Benishangul, W Ethiopia 11°11′N 35°21′E
228 E5 **Gubadag** *Turkm.* Tel'man; *prev.* Tel'mansk. Daşoguz Welaýaty, N Turkmenistan 42°07′N 59°55′E
195 K1 **Guba Dolgaya** Nenetskiy Avtonomnyy Okrug, NW Russian Federation 70°16′N 58°45′E
195 L8 **Gubakha** Permskaya Oblast', NW Russian Federation 58°52′N 57°35′E
177 I10 **Gubbio** Umbria, C Italy 43°27′N 12°34′E
182 C6 **Guben** *var.* Wilhelm-Pieck-Stadt. Brandenburg, E Germany 51°59′N 14°42′E
Guben *see* Gubin
182 C6 **Gubin** *Ger.* Guben. Lubuskie, W Poland 51°59′N 14°43′E
196 F4 **Gubkin** Belgorodskaya Oblast', W Russian Federation 51°16′N 37°32′E
242 G1 **Gucheng** Hubei, China 32°10′N 111°23′E
239 J2 **Guchin-Us** *var.* Arguut. Övörhangay, C Mongolia 45°27′N 102°25′E
Gudara *see* Ghūdara
171 I5 **Gúdar, Sierra de** ▲▲ E Spain
215 I3 **Gudaut'a** NW Georgia 43°07′N 40°35′E
154 D6 **Gudbrandsdalen** *valley* S Norway
181 G9 **Gudensberg** Hessen, Germany 9°22′N 51°11′E
197 I9 **Gudermes** Chechenskaya Respublika, SW Russian Federation 43°23′N 46°06′E
180 I3 **Gudow** Schleswig-Holstein, Germany 10°47′N 53°33′E
234 F7 **Gūdūr** Andhra Pradesh, E India 14°10′N 79°51′E
228 B7 **Gudurolum** Balkan Welaýaty, W Turkmenistan 37°28′N 54°30′E
154 B6 **Gudvangen** Sogn Og Fjordane, S Norway 60°54′N 06°49′E
167 M7 **Guebwiller** Haut-Rhin, NE France 47°55′N 07°13′E
Guéckédou *see* Guékédou
132 D7 **Guékédou** *var.* Guéckédou. Guinée-Forestière, S Guinea 08°33′N 10°08′W
87 H8 **Guelatao** Oaxaca, SE Mexico
Guelders *see* Gelderland
134 D3 **Guélengdeng** Mayo-Kébbi, W Chad 10°55′N 15°31′E

◆ Country
● Country Capital
◇ Dependent Territory
○ Dependent Territory Capital
◈ Administrative Regions
✈ International Airport
▲ Mountain
▲▲ Mountain Range
⛰ Volcano
≈ River
◎ Lake
⊠ Reservoir

Guelma - Halifax

131 J1 **Guelma** var. Gâlma. NE Algeria 36°29′N 07°25′E
130 D4 **Guelmime** var. Goulimime. SW Morocco 28°59′N 10°10′W
62 C5 **Guelph** Ontario, S Canada 43°34′N 80°16′W
164 F4 **Gueméné-Penfao** Loire-Atlantique, NW France 47°37′N 01°49′W
166 C7 **Guéméné-Pentao** Pays de la Loire, France 47°38′N 1°50′W
166 A6 **Guéméné-sur-Scorff** Bretagne, France 48°04′N 3°12′W
171 N9 **Guenzet** Algeria
164 F4 **Guer** Morbihan, NW France 47°54′N 02°07′W
134 E3 **Guéra** off. Préfecture du Guéra. ◐ prefecture S Chad
164 E4 **Guérande** Loire-Atlantique, NW France 47°20′N 02°25′W
Guéra, Préfecture du see Guéra
134 F2 **Guéréda** Biltine, E Chad 14°30′N 22°05′E
165 H6 **Guéret** Creuse, C France 46°10′N 01°52′E
167 I9 **Guérigny** Bourgogne, France 47°05′N 3°12′E
80 B1 **Guerneville** California, USA 38°30′N 123°00′W
Guernica/Guernica y Lumo see Gernika-Lumo
80 D6 **Guernsey** California, USA 36°13′N 119°38′W
77 M8 **Guernsey** Wyoming, C USA 42°16′N 104°44′W
198 D1 **Guernsey** ◇ uk crown dependency Channel Islands, Guernsey NW Europe
166 B4 **Guernsey** island Channel Islands, NW Europe
132 C3 **Guérou** Assaba, S Mauritania 16°48′N 11°40′W
70 F9 **Guerra** Texas, SW USA 26°54′N 98°53′W
172 C7 **Guerreiros do Rio** Faro, Portugal 37°24′N 7°27′W
85 L4 **Guerrero** Coahuila de Zaragoza, Mexico 28°18′N 100°23′W
86 E4 **Guerrero** Coahuila de Zaragoza, NE Mexico North America
85 M9 **Guerrero** Tamaulipas, NE Mexico North America
86 E7 **Guerrero** ◐ state S Mexico
84 C5 **Guerrero Negro** Baja California Sur, NW Mexico 27°56′N 114°04′W
114 B8 **Guerrico** Buenos Aires, Argentina 33°40′S 60°24′W
165 I5 **Gueugnon** Saône-et-Loire, C France 46°36′N 04°03′E
132 E8 **Guéyo** S Ivory Coast 05°25′N 06°04′W
243 H5 **Gugang** China 28°17′N 113°45′E
175 G8 **Guglionesi** Molise, C Italy 41°54′N 14°54′E
282 E3 **Guguan** island C Northern Mariana Islands
Guhrau see Góra
Gui see Guangxi Zhuangzu Zizhiqu
172 B3 **Guia** Leiria, Portugal 39°57′N 8°47′W
Guiana see French Guiana
95 L3 **Guiana Basin** undersea feature W Atlantic Ocean
98 D2 **Guiana Highlands** var. Macizo de las Guayanas. ▲▲ N South America
Guiba see Juba
164 F4 **Guichen** Ille-et-Vilaine, NW France 47°57′N 01°47′W
243 K2 **Guichi** China 30°39′N 117°29′E
114 G5 **Guichón** Paysandú, W Uruguay 32°30′S 57°13′W
116 I3 **Guichón** Paysandú, Uruguay 32°30′S 57°06′E
133 K5 **Guidan-Roumji** Maradi, S Niger 13°40′N 06°41′E
Guidder see Guider
239 K6 **Guide** var. Heyin. Qinghai, C China 36°06′N 101°25′E
134 C3 **Guider** var. Guidder. Nord, N Cameroon 09°55′N 13°59′E
132 C4 **Guidimaka** ◐ region S Mauritania
133 L5 **Guidimouni** Zinder, S Niger 13°40′N 09°31′E
242 C6 **Guiding** Guizhou, China 26°20′N 107°08′E
111 I5 **Guidoval** Minas Gerais, Brazil 21°09′S 42°48′W
132 B3 **Guier, Lac de** var. Lac de Guiers. ◎ N Senegal
Guiers, Lac de see Guier, Lac de
242 E9 **Guigang** var. Guixian, Gui Xian. Guangxi Zhuangzu Zizhiqu, S China 23°06′N 109°36′E
132 E8 **Guiglo** W Ivory Coast 06°33′N 07°29′W
167 H6 **Guignes** Île-de-France, France 48°38′N 2°48′E
102 F3 **Güigüe** Carabobo, N Venezuela 10°05′N 67°48′W
139 I6 **Guijá** Gaza, S Mozambique 24°31′S 33°02′E
88 C4 **Güija, Lago de** ◎ El Salvador/Guatemala
242 F9 **Gui Jiang** var. Gui Shui. ≈ S China
243 M3 **Guiji Shan** ▲▲ Zhejiang, China
170 E4 **Guijuelo** Castilla-León, N Spain 40°34′N 05°40′W
Guilan see Gīlān
161 J7 **Guildford** SE England, UK 51°14′N 00°35′W
63 K3 **Guildford** Maine, NE USA 45°10′N 69°22′W
63 I4 **Guildhall** Vermont, NE USA 44°34′N 71°36′W
159 H2 **Guildtown** UK 56°28′N 3°24′W
65 J5 **Guilford** Connecticut, USA 41°17′N 72°41′W
165 J7 **Guilherand** Ardèche, E France 44°57′N 04°49′E
242 F7 **Guilin** var. Kuei-lin, Kweilin. Guangxi Zhuangzu Zizhiqu, S China 25°15′N 110°16′E
55 N5 **Guillaume-Delisle, Lac** ◎ Québec, NE Canada
169 M4 **Guillaumes** Provence-Alpes-Côte d'Azur, France 44°05′N 6°51′E
85 I7 **Guillermo Prieto** Durango, Mexico 24°52′N 105°0′W
165 K7 **Guillestre** Hautes-Alpes, SE France 44°41′N 06°39′E
160 G3 **Guilsfield** UK 52°41′N 3°09′W
170 C3 **Guimarães** var. Guimaráes. Braga, N Portugal 41°26′N 08°19′W
Guimaráes see Guimarães
102 G8 **Guimarães Rosas, Pico** ▲ NW Brazil
110 C1 **Guimarânia** Minas Gerais, Brazil 18°51′S 46°47′W
245 K7 **Guimeng Ding 1156m** ▲ Shandong, China 35°20′N 117°30′E
66 C8 **Guin** Alabama, S USA 33°58′N 87°54′W
Güina see Wina
80 C1 **Guinda** California, USA 38°50′N 122°12′W
132 D6 **Guinea** off. Republic of Guinea, var. Guinée; prev. French Guinea, People's Revolutionary Republic of Guinea. ◆ republic W Africa
291 I8 **Guinea Basin** undersea feature E Atlantic Ocean
132 A5 **Guinea-Bissau** off. Republic of Guinea-Bissau, Fr. Guinée-Bissau, Port. Guiné-Bissau; prev. Portuguese Guinea. ◆ republic W Africa
Guinea-Bissau, Republic of see Guinea-Bissau
120 F4 **Guinea Fracture Zone** tectonic feature E Atlantic Ocean
133 H9 **Guinea, Gulf of** Fr. Golfe de Guinée. gulf E Atlantic Ocean
Guinea, People's Revolutionary Republic of see Guinea
Guinea, Republic of see Guinea
Guiné-Bissau see Guinea-Bissau
Guinée see Guinea
Guinée-Bissau see Guinea-Bissau
Guinée, Golfe de see Guinea, Gulf of
61 L10 **Güines** La Habana, W Cuba 22°50′N 82°02′W
166 G1 **Guînes** Nord-Pas-de-Calais, France 50°52′N 1°52′E
164 E3 **Guingamp** Côtes d'Armor, NW France 48°34′N 03°09′W
242 E9 **Guiping** Guangxi, China 23°14′N 110°02′E
171 H2 **Guipúzcoa** Basq. Gipuzkoa. ◐ province País Vasco, N Spain
90 C3 **Güira de Melena** La Habana, W Cuba 22°47′N 82°33′W
130 G4 **Guir, Hamada du** desert Algeria/Morocco
103 I2 **Güiria** Sucre, NE Venezuela 10°37′N 62°21′W
111 J5 **Guiricema** Minas Gerais, Brazil 21°00′S 42°43′W
159 L7 **Guisborough** UK 54°32′N 1°09′W
167 I3 **Guise** Picardie, France 49°54′N 3°38′E
159 K8 **Guiseley** UK 53°52′N 1°43′W
Gui Shui see Gui Jiang
170 D1 **Guitiriz** Galicia, NW Spain 43°10′N 07°52′W
132 F8 **Guitri** S Ivory Coast 05°31′N 05°14′W
263 M7 **Guiuan** Samar, C Philippines 11°02′N 125°45′E
Gui Xian/Guixian see Guigang
242 D6 **Guiyang** China 26°55′N 108°44′E
242 G7 **Guiyang** China 25°44′N 112°43′E
242 C6 **Guiyang** var. Kuei-Yang, Kuei-yang, Kueyang, Kweiyang; prev. Kweichu. province capital Guizhou, S China 26°33′N 106°45′E
242 G8 **Guiyang** Hunan, China 24°26′N 112°26′E
243 H9 **Guizhou** China 22°46′N 113°15′E
242 C6 **Guizhou** var. Guizhou Sheng, Kuei-chou, Kweichow, Qian. ◐ province S China
Guizhou Sheng see Guizhou
168 C3 **Gujan** Aquitaine, France 44°38′N 1°04′W
164 F7 **Gujan-Mestras** Gironde, SW France 44°39′N 01°04′W
232 B8 **Gujarāt** var. Gujerat. ◐ state W India
231 J4 **Gūjar Khān** Punjab, E Pakistan 33°19′N 73°23′E
Gujerat see Gujarāt
243 I5 **Gujiang** China 27°11′N 114°47′E
244 G5 **Gujiao** Shanxi, China 37°32′N 112°05′E
231 J5 **Gujrānwāla** Punjab, NE Pakistan 32°11′N 74°09′E
231 J5 **Gujrāt** Punjab, E Pakistan 32°34′N 74°04′E
228 B5 **Gulandag** Rus. Gory Kulandag. ▲▲ Balkan Welaýaty, W Turkmenistan
244 A5 **Gulang** Gansu, C China 37°31′N 102°55′E
277 K4 **Gulargambone** New South Wales, SE Australia 31°19′S 148°31′E
234 E5 **Gulbarga** Karnātaka, C India 17°22′N 76°47′E
190 F6 **Gulbene** Ger. Alt-Schwanenburg. Gulbene, NE Latvia 57°10′N 26°44′E
229 K6 **Gul'cha** Kir. Gülchö. Oshskaya Oblast', SW Kyrgyzstan 40°16′N 73°27′E
Gülchö see Gul'cha
289 H10 **Gulden Draak Seamount** undersea feature E Indian Ocean
214 F7 **Gülek Boğazı** var. Cilician Gates. pass S Turkey
280 B4 **Gulf** ◐ province S Papua New Guinea
68 G4 **Gulf Breeze** Florida, SE USA 30°21′N 87°09′W
Gulf of Liaotung see Liaodong Wan
69 K7 **Gulfport** Florida, SE USA 27°45′N 82°42′W
68 F4 **Gulfport** Mississippi, S USA 30°22′N 89°06′W
68 G4 **Gulf Shores** Alabama, S USA 30°15′N 87°40′W
221 I3 **Gulf, The** var. Persian Gulf, Ar. Khalīj al 'Arabī, Per. Khalīj-e Fars. Gulf SW Asia see also Persian Gulf
277 K4 **Gulgong** New South Wales, SE Australia 32°22′S 149°31′E
242 B4 **Gulin** Sichuan, C China 28°06′N 105°47′E
261 I6 **Gulir** Pulau Kasiui, E Indonesia 04°27′S 131°41′E
Gulistan see Guliston
229 I6 **Guliston** Rus. Gulistan. Sirdaryo Viloyati, E Uzbekistan 40°29′N 68°46′E
Gulja see Yining
83 J6 **Gulkana** Alaska, USA 62°17′N 145°25′W
159 I3 **Gullane** UK 56°02′N 2°49′W
57 L8 **Gull Lake** Saskatchewan, S Canada 50°05′N 108°30′W
73 F8 **Gull Lake** ◎ Michigan, N USA
74 G3 **Gull Lake** ◎ Minnesota, N USA
155 G8 **Gullspång** Västra Götaland, S Sweden 58°58′N 14°04′E
214 B7 **Güllük Körfezi** prev Akbük Limanı. bay W Turkey
232 D2 **Gulmarg** Jammu and Kashmir, NW India 34°04′N 74°25′E
Gulpaigan see Golpāyegān
163 H10 **Gulpen** Limburg, SE Netherlands 50°48′N 05°53′E
Gul'shad see Gul'shad
227 J6 **Gul'shad** var. Gul'shad. Karaganda, E Kazakhstan 46°37′N 74°22′E
136 B7 **Gulu** N Uganda 02°46′N 32°21′E
185 K7 **Gŭlŭbovo** Stara Zagora, C Bulgaria 42°08′N 25°51′E
185 J5 **Gulyantsi** Pleven, N Bulgaria 43°37′N 24°40′E
Gulyaypole see Hulyaypole
Guma see Pishan
Gümai see Darlag
134 F6 **Gumba** Equateur, NW Dem. Rep. Congo 02°58′N 21°23′E
Gumbinnen see Gusev
137 D12 **Gumbiro** Ruvuma, S Tanzania 10°19′S 35°40′E
228 B6 **Gumdag** prev. Kum-Dag. Balkan Welaýaty, W Turkmenistan 39°13′N 54°35′E
133 L5 **Gumel** Jigawa, N Nigeria 12°37′N 09°23′E
170 G3 **Gumiel de Hizán** Castilla-León, N Spain 41°46′N 03°42′W
233 I8 **Gumla** Jhārkhand, N India 23°03′N 84°36′E
Gumma see Gunma
181 D9 **Gummersbach** Nordrhein-Westfalen, W Germany 51°01′N 07°34′E
133 J5 **Gummi** Zamfara, NW Nigeria 12°07′N 05°07′E
181 I10 **Gumpelstadt** Thüringen, Germany 10°18′N 50°50′E
Gumpolds see Humpolec
233 H7 **Gumti** var. Gomati. ≈ N India
Gümülcine/Gümüljina see Komotiní
Gümüşane see Gümüşhane
215 H5 **Gümüşhane** var. Gümüşane, Gumushkhane. Gümüşhane, NE Turkey 40°31′N 39°27′E
215 H5 **Gümüşhane** var. Gümüşane, Gumushkhane. ◐ province NE Turkey
Gumushkhane see Gümüşhane
261 J6 **Gumzai** Pulau Kola, E Indonesia 05°27′S 134°38′E
232 E7 **Guna** Madhya Pradesh, C India 24°39′N 77°18′E
Gunabad see Gonābād
Gunan see Qijiang
Gunbad-i-Qawus see Gonbad-e Kāvūs
277 J5 **Gunbar** New South Wales, SE Australia 34°03′S 145°32′E
277 K6 **Gundagai** New South Wales, SE Australia 35°06′S 148°03′E
181 G13 **Gundelsheim** Baden-Württemberg, Germany 9°10′N 49°17′E
134 F6 **Gundji** Equateur, N Dem. Rep. Congo 02°03′N 21°31′E
235 E8 **Gundlupet** Karnātaka, W India 11°48′N 76°42′E
214 D8 **Gündoğmuş** Antalya, S Turkey 36°50′N 32°07′E
187 M5 **Guney** Kütahya, Turkey 38°51′N 29°23′E
215 I6 **Güney Doğu Toroslar** ▲▲ SE Turkey
135 E9 **Gungu** Bandundu, SW Dem. Rep. Congo 05°43′S 19°20′E
197 J9 **Gunib** Respublika Dagestan, SW Russian Federation 42°24′N 46°55′E
184 E3 **Gunja** Vukovar-Srijem, E Croatia 44°53′N 18°51′E
73 F8 **Gun Lake** ◎ Michigan, N USA
253 B12 **Gunma** off. Gunma-ken, var. Gumma. ◐ prefecture Honshū, S Japan
Gunma-ken see Gunma
295 L6 **Gunnbjørn Fjeld** var. Gunnbjörns Bjerge. ▲ C Greenland 69°03′N 29°36′W
Gunnbjörns Bjerge see Gunnbjørn Fjeld
181 E8 **Günne** Nordrhein-Westfalen, Germany 8°02′N 51°30′E
277 L4 **Gunnedah** New South Wales, SE Australia 30°59′S 150°15′E
137 G10 **Gunner's Quoin** island N Mauritius
79 K4 **Gunnison** Colorado, C USA 38°33′N 106°55′W
79 H4 **Gunnison** Utah, W USA 39°09′N 111°49′W
79 J4 **Gunnison River** ≈ Colorado, C USA
67 L2 **Gunpowder River** ≈ Maryland, NE USA
Güns see Kőszeg
Gunsan see Kunsan
177 J2 **Gunskirchen** Oberösterreich, N Austria 48°07′N 13°54′E
Gunt see Ghund
234 E6 **Guntakal** Andhra Pradesh, C India 15°11′N 77°24′E
181 E12 **Guntersblum** Rheinland-Pfalz, Germany 8°21′N 49°48′E
66 E8 **Guntersville** Alabama, S USA 34°21′N 86°17′W
66 D8 **Guntersville Lake** ⊡ Alabama, S USA
234 G6 **Guntūr** var. Guntur. Andhra Pradesh, SE India 16°20′N 80°27′E
258 C4 **Gunungsitoli** Pulau Nias, W Indonesia 01°11′N 97°35′E
234 H5 **Gunupur** Orissa, E India 19°04′N 83°52′E
160 C10 **Gunwalloe** UK 50°02′N 5°16′W
179 E13 **Günz** ≈ S Germany
Gunzan see Kunsan
179 E12 **Günzburg** Bayern, S Germany 48°26′N 10°18′E
181 J14 **Gunzenhausen** Bayern, S Germany 49°07′N 10°45′E
244 B6 **Guochengyi** Gansu, China 36°08′N 104°33′E
243 J1 **Guo He** ≈ Anhui, China
245 J9 **Guo He** ≈ Anhui, China
Guolüezhen see Lingbao
Guovdageaidnu see Kautokeino
245 J8 **Guoyang** Anhui, E China 33°30′N 116°12′E
245 K8 **Gupei** China 34°07′N 117°53′E
188 B7 **Gurahonț** Hung. Honctő. Arad, W Romania 46°16′N 22°21′E
Gurahumora see Gura Humorului
188 E6 **Gura Humorului** Ger. Gurahumora. Suceava, NE Romania 47°31′N 26°00′E
238 F3 **Gurbantünggüt Shamo** desert W China
232 E3 **Gurdāspur** Punjab, N India 32°04′N 75°28′E
75 H13 **Gurdon** Arkansas, C USA 33°55′N 93°09′W
Gurdzhaani see Gurjaani
190 J2 **Gurenichi** Leningradskaya Oblast', Russian Federation
Gurgan see Gorgān
232 E5 **Gurgaon** Haryāna, N India 28°27′N 77°01′E
108 E6 **Gurguéia, Rio** ≈ NE Brazil
103 I4 **Guri, Embalse de** ⊡ E Venezuela
215 L4 **Gurjaani** Rus. Gurdzhaani. E Georgia 41°42′N 45°47′E
177 J4 **Gurk** Kärnten, S Austria 46°52′N 14°17′E
177 J4 **Gurk** Slvn. Krka. ≈ S Austria
Gurkfeld see Krško
185 K6 **Gurkovo** prev. Kolupchii. Stara Zagora, C Bulgaria 42°42′N 25°46′E
177 J4 **Gurktaler Alpen** ▲▲ S Austria
228 E5 **Gurlan** Rus. Gurlen. Xorazm Viloyati, W Uzbekistan 41°54′N 60°18′E
Gurlen see Gurlan
139 I3 **Guro** Manica, C Mozambique 17°28′S 33°18′E
214 G6 **Gürün** Sivas, C Turkey 38°44′N 37°15′E
108 B7 **Gurupi** Tocantins, C Brazil 11°44′S 49°01′W
107 N3 **Gurupi, Rio** ≈ NE Brazil
232 C7 **Guru Sikhar** ▲ NW India 24°45′N 72°51′E
239 I2 **Gurvanbulag** var. Höviyn Am. Bayanhongor, C Mongolia 47°08′N 98°41′E
239 J3 **Gurvantes** var. Urt. Ömnögovĭ, S Mongolia 43°16′N 101°00′E
Gur'yev/Gur'yevskaya Oblast' see Atyrau
133 J5 **Gusau** Zamfara, NW Nigeria 12°18′N 06°27′E
191 C9 **Gusev** Ger. Gumbinnen. Kaliningradskaya Oblast', W Russian Federation 54°36′N 22°14′E
245 N2 **Gushan** Liaoning, China 39°32′N 123°20′E
228 F9 **Gushgy** Rus. Kushka. ≈ Mary Welaýaty, S Turkmenistan
Gushgy see Serhetabat
243 I1 **Gushi** Henan, China 32°06′N 115°25′E
Gushiago see Gushiegu
133 H6 **Gushiegu** var. Gushiago. NE Ghana 09°54′N 00°12′W
251 I10 **Gushikawa** Okinawa, Okinawa, SW Japan 26°21′N 127°50′E
184 F6 **Gusinje** E Montenegro 42°34′N 19°51′E
191 I8 **Gusino** Smolenskaya Oblast', Russian Federation
193 I8 **Gusinoozersk** Respublika Buryatiya, S Russian Federation 51°18′N 106°28′E
196 G2 **Gus'-Khrustal'nyy** Vladimirskaya Oblast', W Russian Federation 55°39′N 40°42′E
175 B10 **Guspini** Sardegna, Italy, C Mediterranean Sea 39°33′N 08°39′E
177 L4 **Güssing** Burgenland, SE Austria 47°03′N 16°19′E
177 K3 **Gusswerk** Steiermark, E Austria 47°43′N 15°18′E
152 B5 **Gustav Adolf Land** physical region NE Svalbard
293 L3 **Gustav Bull Mountains** ▲▲ Antarctica
84 D2 **Gustavo Sotelo** Sonora, Mexico 31°33′N 113°34′W
83 L7 **Gustavus** Alaska, USA 58°24′N 135°44′W
152 B4 **Gustav V Land** physical region NE Svalbard
80 C4 **Gustine** California, W USA 37°14′N 121°00′W
70 G5 **Gustine** Texas, SW USA 31°51′N 98°24′W
178 G5 **Güstrow** Mecklenburg-Vorpommern, NE Germany 53°48′N 12°12′E
155 H9 **Gusum** Östergötland, S Sweden 58°15′N 16°30′E
Guta/Gúta see Kolárovo
Gutenstein see Ravne na Koroškem
180 E7 **Gütersloh** Nordrhein-Westfalen, W Germany 51°54′N 08°23′E
75 E12 **Guthrie** Oklahoma, C USA 35°53′N 97°26′W
70 E3 **Guthrie** Texas, SW USA 33°38′N 100°21′W
74 G7 **Guthrie Center** Iowa, C USA 41°40′N 94°30′W
243 L6 **Gutian** Fujan, China 26°20′N 118°26′E
243 L6 **Gutian Shuiku** ⊡ Fujan, China
86 G5 **Gutiérrez Zamora** Veracruz-Llave, E Mexico 20°29′N 97°07′W
245 J7 **Guting** China 35°00′N 116°39′E
Gutta see Kolárovo
74 I6 **Guttenberg** Iowa, C USA 42°47′N 91°06′W
Guttentag see Dobrodzień
Guttstadt see Dobre Miasto
239 I2 **Guulin** Govĭ-Altay, C Mongolia 46°33′N 97°21′E
233 L6 **Guwāhāti** prev. Gauhāti. Assam, NE India 26°09′N 91°42′E
217 I2 **Guwēr** var. Al Kuwayr, Al Quwayr, Quwair. N Iraq 36°03′N 43°30′E
228 A5 **Guwlumaýak** Rus. Kuuli-Mayak. Balkan Welaýaty, NW Turkmenistan 40°14′N 52°43′E
103 J5 **Guyana** off. Cooperative Republic of Guyana; prev. British Guiana. ◆ republic N South America
Guyana, Cooperative Republic of see Guyana
67 H3 **Guyandotte River** ≈ West Virginia, NE USA
Guyane see French Guiana
244 F2 **Guyang** Inner Mongolia, China 41°01′N 110°02′E
161 K3 **Guyhirn** UK 52°37′N 0°04′E
Guyi see Sanjiang
75 B11 **Guymon** Oklahoma, C USA 36°42′N 101°30′W
228 F7 **Guynuk** Lebap Welaýaty, NE Turkmenistan 39°18′N 63°00′E
Guyong see Jiangle
66 G6 **Guyot, Mount** ▲ North Carolina/Tennessee, SE USA 35°42′N 83°15′W
277 L3 **Guyra** New South Wales, SE Australia 30°13′S 151°42′E
245 I1 **Guyuan** Hebei, China 41°24′N 115°25′E
244 C6 **Guyuan** Ningxia, N China 35°57′N 106°13′E
218 B2 **Güzelyurt** Gk. Mórfou, Morphou. W Cyprus 35°12′N 33°E
218 B2 **Güzelyurt Körfezi** var. Morfou Bay, Morphou Bay, Gk. Kólpos Mórfou. bay W Cyprus
245 K9 **Guzhen** Anhui, China 38°11′N 117°11′E
Guzhou see Rongjiang
84 G2 **Guzmán** Chihuahua, N Mexico 31°13′N 107°27′W
84 G2 **Laguna de Guzmàn** ◎ Chihuahua, Mexico
191 B9 **Gvardeysk** Ger. Tapaiu. Kaliningradskaya Oblast', W Russian Federation 54°39′N 21°02′E
Gvardeyskoye see Hvardiys'ke
277 K3 **Gwabegar** New South Wales, SE Australia 30°34′S 148°58′E
230 D9 **Gwādar** var. Gwadur. Baluchistān, SW Pakistan 25°09′N 62°21′E
230 D9 **Gwādar East Bay** bay SW Pakistan
230 D9 **Gwādar West Bay** bay SW Pakistan
Gwadur see Gwādar
138 G3 **Gwai** Matabeleland North, W Zimbabwe 19°17′S 27°37′E
160 E2 **Gwalchmai** UK 53°15′N 4°25′W
232 F6 **Gwalior** Madhya Pradesh, C India 26°16′N 78°12′E
138 G4 **Gwanda** Matabeleland South, SW Zimbabwe 20°56′S 29°E
134 H5 **Gwane** Orientale, N Dem. Rep. Congo 04°40′N 25°51′E
245 K5 **Gwangrao** China 37°08′N 118°29′E
138 G3 **Gwayi** ≈ W Zimbabwe
182 E4 **Gwda** var. Głda, Ger. Küddow. ≈ NW Poland
156 B7 **Gweebarra Bay** Ir. Béal an Bheara. inlet W Ireland
158 B5 **Gweedore** Ir. Gaoth Dobhair. Donegal, NW Ireland 55°03′N 08°14′W
Gwelo see Gweru
157 G11 **Gwent** cultural region S Wales, UK
139 H4 **Gweru** prev. Gwelo. Midlands, C Zimbabwe 19°27′S 29°49′E
74 E4 **Gwinner** North Dakota, N USA 46°10′N 97°42′W
133 M6 **Gwoza** Borno, NE Nigeria 11°07′N 13°40′E
Gwy see Wye
160 F2 **Gwyddelwern** UK 53°00′N 3°23′W
277 L3 **Gwydir River** ≈ New South Wales, SE Australia
157 F10 **Gwynedd** var. Gwyneth. cultural region NW Wales, UK
Gwyneth see Gwynedd
167 L8 **Gy** Franche-Comté, France 47°24′N 5°49′E
239 H9 **Gyaca** var. Ngarrab. Xizang Zizhiqu, W China 29°06′N 92°37′E
Gya'gya see Saga
Gyaijêpozhanggê see Zhidoi
Gyaisi see Jiulong
187 K8 **Gyalí** var. Yialí. island Dodekánisa, Greece, Aegean Sea
Gyamotang see Dêngqên
Gyandzha see Gäncä
Gyangkar see Dinggyê
238 G9 **Gyangzê** Xizang Zizhiqu, W China 28°50′N 89°38′E
238 F8 **Gyaring Co** ◎ W China
239 I7 **Gyaring Hu** ◎ C China
187 I7 **Gyáros** var. Yioúra. island Kykládes, Greece, Aegean Sea
192 G4 **Gyda** Yamalo-Nenetskiy Avtonomnyy Okrug, N Russian Federation 70°55′N 78°34′E
192 G4 **Gydanskiy Poluostrov** Eng. Gyda Peninsula. peninsula N Russian Federation
Gyda Peninsula see Gydanskiy Poluostrov
171 I10 **Gydel** Algeria
140 D9 **Gydo Pass** pass Western Cape, South Africa
Gyêgu see Yushu
Gyéres see Câmpia Turzii
Gyergyószentmiklós see Gheorgheni
Gyergyótölgyes see Tulgheș
Gyertyámos see Cărpiniș
Gyeva see Detva
Gyigang see Zayü
Gyixong see Gonggar
277 M1 **Gympie** Queensland, E Australia 26°05′S 152°40′E
256 C6 **Gyobingauk** Pegu, SW Myanmar (Burma) 18°14′N 95°39′E
183 H12 **Gyomaendrőd** Békés, SE Hungary 46°56′N 20°50′E
Gyömbér see Ďumbier
183 G11 **Gyöngyös** Heves, NE Hungary 47°44′N 19°49′E
183 E11 **Győr** Ger. Raab, Lat. Arrabona. Győr-Moson-Sopron, NW Hungary 47°41′N 17°40′E
183 E11 **Győr-Moson-Sopron** off. Győr-Moson-Sopron Megye. ◐ county NW Hungary
Győr-Moson-Sopron Megye see Győr-Moson-Sopron
54 F4 **Gypsum Point** headland Northwest Territories, NW Canada
55 I9 **Gypsumville** Manitoba, S Canada 51°47′N 98°38′W
59 H2 **Gyrfalcon Islands** island group Northwest Territories, NE Canada
154 I7 **Gysinge** Gävleborg, C Sweden 60°16′N 16°55′E
186 G8 **Gýtheio** var. Githio; prev. Yíthion. Pelopónnisos, S Greece 36°46′N 22°34′E
228 G7 **Gyuichbirleshik** Lebap Welaýaty, E Turkmenistan 38°10′N 64°33′E
183 H12 **Gyula** Rom. Jula. Békés, SE Hungary 46°39′N 21°17′E
Gyulafehérvár see Alba Iulia
Gyulovo see Roza
215 K5 **Gyumri** var. Giumri, Rus. Kumayri; prev. Aleksandropol', Leninakan. W Armenia 40°48′N 43°51′E
228 C7 **Gyunuzyndag, Gora** ▲ Balkan Welaýaty, W Turkmenistan 38°15′N 56°25′E
228 F8 **Gyzylbaydak** Rus. Krasnoye Znamya. Mary Welaýaty, S Turkmenistan 36°51′N 62°24′E
Gyzyletrek see Etrek
228 C5 **Gyzylgaýa** Rus. Kizyl-Kaya. Balkan Welaýaty, NW Turkmenistan 40°37′N 55°15′E
228 A6 **Gyzylsuw** Rus. Kizyl-Su. Balkan Welaýaty, W Turkmenistan 39°49′N 53°00′E
Gyzyrlabat see Serdar

H

233 K6 **Ha** W Bhutan 27°17′N 89°22′E
Haabai see Ha'apai Group
163 E10 **Haacht** Vlaams Brabant, C Belgium 50°58′N 04°38′E
177 J2 **Haag** Niederösterreich, NE Austria 48°07′N 14°32′E
292 F5 **Haag Nunataks** ▲▲ Antarctica
152 A5 **Haakon VII Land** physical region NW Svalbard
162 I6 **Haaksbergen** Overijssel, E Netherlands 52°09′N 06°45′E
163 C8 **Haamstede** Zeeland, SW Netherlands 51°43′N 03°45′E
284 D7 **Ha'ano** island Ha'apai Group, C Tonga
284 D7 **Ha'apai Group** var. Haabai. island group C Tonga
152 H7 **Haapajärvi** Oulu, C Finland 63°45′N 25°20′E
153 H9 **Haapamäki** Länsi-Soumi, C Finland 62°11′N 24°32′E
152 H7 **Haapavesi** Oulu, C Finland 64°09′N 25°25′E
285 L3 **Haapiti** Moorea, W French Polynesia 17°33′S 149°52′W
190 D4 **Haapsalu** Ger. Hapsal. Läänemaa, W Estonia 58°58′N 23°32′E
Ha'Arava see 'Arabah, Wādī al
155 D13 **Haarby** var. Hårby. Fyn, C Denmark 55°13′N 10°07′E
181 F8 **Haaren** Nordrhein-Westfalen, Germany 8°44′N 51°34′E
162 E6 **Haarlem** prev. Harlem. Noord-Holland, W Netherlands 52°23′N 04°39′E
278 C10 **Haast** West Coast, South Island, New Zealand 43°53′S 169°02′E
278 C10 **Haast** ≈ South Island, New Zealand
278 C10 **Haast Pass** pass South Island, New Zealand
284 E10 **Ha'atua** 'Eau, E Tonga 21°23′S 174°57′W
230 F9 **Hab** ≈ SW Pakistan
221 J4 **Haba** var. Al Haba. Dubayy, NE United Arab Emirates 25°01′N 55°37′E
238 F1 **Habahe** var. Kaba. Xinjiang Uygur Zizhiqu, NW China 48°04′N 86°20′E
221 J7 **Ḩabarūt** var. Habrut. SW Oman 17°19′N 52°45′E
136 E7 **Habaswein** North Eastern, NE Kenya 01°01′N 39°27′E
163 G13 **Habay-la-Neuve** Luxembourg, SE Belgium 49°43′N 05°38′E
217 I5 **Ḩabbānīyah, Buḩayrat** ◎ C Iraq
Habelschwerdt see Bystrzyca Kłodzka
233 L7 **Habiganj** Sylhet, NE Bangladesh 24°23′N 91°25′E
245 I1 **Habirag** Nei Mongol Zizhiqu, N China 42°18′N 115°40′E
155 G10 **Habo** Västra Götaland, S Sweden 57°55′N 14°05′E
252 J4 **Habomai Islands** island group Kuril'skiye Ostrova, SE Russian Federation
252 E3 **Haboro** Hokkaidō, NE Japan 44°19′N 141°42′E
161 K1 **Habrough** UK 53°36′N 0°15′W
Habrut see Ḩabarūt
221 J4 **Ḩabshān** Abū Z̧aby, C United Arab Emirates 23°51′N 53°34′E
102 B8 **Hacha** Putumayo, S Colombia 0°02′S 75°30′W
251 M8 **Hachijō** Tōkyō, Hachijō-jima, SE Japan 35°40′N 139°20′E
251 M7 **Hachijō-jima** island Izu-shotō, SE Japan
251 J3 **Hachiman** Gifu, Honshū, SW Japan 35°46′N 136°57′E
253 C8 **Hachimori** Akita, Honshū, C Japan 40°22′N 139°59′E
252 E7 **Hachinohe** Aomori, Honshū, C Japan 40°30′N 141°29′E
253 B13 **Hachiōji** var. Hatiôzi. Tōkyō, Honshū, S Japan 35°40′N 139°20′E
86 F2 **Hacienda de la Mesa** Tamaulipas, Mexico 24°14′N 99°35′W
81 D10 **Hacienda Heights** California, USA 34°00′N 117°58′W
154 G4 **Hackås** Jämtland, C Sweden 62°55′N 14°31′E
65 H6 **Hackensack** New Jersey, NE USA 40°51′N 73°57′W
64 G6 **Hackettstown** New Jersey, USA 40°51′N 74°50′W
Hadama see Nazrēt
253 B13 **Hadano** Kanagawa, Honshū, S Japan 35°22′N 139°14′E
221 J7 **Ḩaḑbaram** S Oman 17°27′N 55°13′E
218 G2 **Hadchit** Lebanon
217 J8 **Ḩaddānīyah** well S Iraq
159 I3 **Haddington** SE Scotland, UK 55°59′N 02°46′W
161 M3 **Haddiscoe** UK 52°31′N 1°35′E
221 L5 **Ḩadd, Ra's al** headland NE Oman 22°28′N 59°58′E
Haded see Xadeed
133 L5 **Hadejia** Jigawa, N Nigeria 12°22′N 10°02′E
133 L5 **Hadejia** ≈ N Nigeria
216 B6 **Hadera** var. Khadera. Haifa, C Israel 32°26′N 34°55′E
Hadersleben see Haderslev
155 D13 **Haderslev** Ger. Hadersleben. Sønderjylland, SW Denmark 55°15′N 09°30′E
235 C13 **Hadhdhunmathi Atoll** atoll S Maldives
Hadhramaut see Ḩaḑramawt
221 J9 **Hadīboh** Suquṭrā, SE Yemen 12°38′N 54°05′E
238 F6 **Hadilik** Xinjiang Uygur Zizhiqu, W China 37°51′N 86°10′E
214 D7 **Hadīm** Konya, S Turkey 36°58′N 32°27′E
220 D4 **Hadīyah** Al Madīnah, W Saudi Arabia 25°36′N 38°31′E
171 L9 **Hadjout** Algeria
161 L6 **Hadleigh** UK 51°32′N 0°36′E
161 H3 **Hadley** UK 52°42′N 2°29′W
52 F6 **Hadley Bay** bay Victoria Island, Nunavut, N Canada
180 J7 **Hadmersleben** Sachsen-Anhalt, Germany 11°18′N 51°59′E
160 G3 **Hadnall** UK 52°46′N 2°43′W
257 H5 **Ha Đông** var. Hadong. Ha Tây, N Vietnam 20°58′N 105°46′E
Hadong see Ha Đông
136 I2 **Ḩaḑramawt** Eng. Hadhramaut. ▲▲ S Yemen
Hadria see Adria
Hadrianopolis see Edirne
Hadria Picena see Apricena
155 D11 **Hadsten** Århus, C Denmark 56°19′N 10°03′E
155 D11 **Hadsund** Nordjylland, N Denmark 56°43′N 10°08′E
189 J3 **Hadyach** Rus. Gadyach. Poltavs'ka Oblast', NE Ukraine 50°21′N 34°00′E
184 E5 **Hadžići** Federacija Bosna I Hercegovina, SE Bosnia and Herzegovina 43°49′N 18°12′E
248 B5 **Haeju** S North Korea 38°04′N 125°40′E
Haerbin/Haerhpin/Ha-erh-pin see Harbin
220 G3 **Ḩafar al Bāṭin** Ash Sharqīyah, N Saudi Arabia 28°25′N 45°59′E
180 I1 **Haffkrug** Schleswig-Holstein, Germany 10°45′N 54°03′E
57 M5 **Hafford** Saskatchewan, S Canada 52°43′N 107°19′W
214 G5 **Hafik** Sivas, N Turkey 39°53′N 37°24′E
219 F13 **Ḩafīr, Wādī** dry watercourse Jordan
231 J5 **Hāfizābād** Punjab, E Pakistan 32°03′N 73°42′E
152 B3 **Hafnarfjördhur** Reykjanes, W Iceland 64°03′N 21°57′W
Hafnia see Denmark
Hafnia see København
Hafren see Severn
Hafun see Xaafuun
Hafun, Ras see Xaafuun, Raas
136 C2 **Hag 'Abdullah** Sinnar, E Sudan 13°59′N 33°35′E
137 F8 **Hagadera** North Eastern, E Kenya 0°06′N 40°23′E
216 B6 **HaGalil** Eng. Galilee. ▲▲ N Israel
62 C2 **Hagar** Ontario, S Canada 46°27′N 80°22′W
234 E7 **Hagari** var. Vedāvati. ≈ W India
282 A2 **Hagåtña** var. Agana, var. Agaña. ○ (Guam) NW Guam 13°27′N 144°45′E
180 D2 **Hage** Niedersachsen, Germany 7°16′N 53°37′E
178 G7 **Hagelberg** hill NE Germany
82 G7 **Hagemeister Island** island Alaska, USA
181 D8 **Hagen** Nordrhein-Westfalen, W Germany 51°22′N 07°27′E
180 J3 **Hagenow** Mecklenburg-Vorpommern, N Germany 53°27′N 11°10′E
56 C5 **Hagensborg** British Columbia, SW Canada 52°24′N 126°24′W
136 E4 **Hāgere Hiywet** var. Agere Hiywet, Ambo. Oromo, C Ethiopia 09°00′N 37°55′E
76 G8 **Hagerman** Idaho, NW USA 42°48′N 114°53′W
79 M9 **Hagerman** New Mexico, SW USA 33°07′N 104°19′W
64 B8 **Hagerstown** Maryland, NE USA 39°39′N 77°44′W
62 C6 **Hagersville** Ontario, S Canada 42°58′N 80°03′W
164 F8 **Hagetmau** Landes, SW France 43°40′N 00°36′W
154 G7 **Hagfors** Värmland, C Sweden 60°03′N 13°45′E
154 G3 **Häggenås** Jämtland, C Sweden 63°24′N 14°53′E
250 D5 **Hagi** Yamaguchi, Honshū, SW Japan 34°25′N 131°22′E
256 G4 **Ha Giang** Ha Giang, N Vietnam 22°50′N 104°58′E
Hagios Evstrátios see Ágios Efstrátios
HaGolan see Golan Heights
165 K3 **Hagondange** Moselle, NE France 49°16′N 06°06′E
157 B10 **Hag's Head** Ir. Ceann Caillí. headland W Ireland 52°56′N 09°29′W
166 C3 **Hague, Cap de la** headland N France 49°43′N 01°56′W
165 L3 **Haguenau** Bas-Rhin, NE France 48°49′N 07°47′E
251 N9 **Hahajima-rettō** island group SE Japan
139 I9 **Hahaya** ✕ (Moroni) Grande Comore, NW Comoros
181 D9 **Hahn** Nordrhein-Westfalen, Germany 7°27′N 51°01′E
180 I7 **Hahndorf** Niedersachsen, Germany 10°26′N 51°58′E
68 E4 **Hahnville** Louisiana, S USA 29°58′N 90°24′W
243 L1 **Haian** China 32°25′N 119°34′E
140 D5 **Haib** Karas, S Namibia 28°12′S 18°19′E
Haibak see Āybak
230 F9 **Haibo** ≈ SW Pakistan
Haibowan see Wuhai
245 N2 **Haicheng** Liaoning, NE China 40°53′N 122°45′E
Haicheng see Haiyuan
257 H5 **Hai Dương** Hai Hưng, N Vietnam 20°56′N 106°21′E
Haida see Nový Bor
Haidarabad see Hyderābād
Haidenschaft see Ajdovščina
216 B6 **Haifa** ◐ district NW Israel
Haifa see Ḥefa
Haifa, Bay of see Ḥefa, Mifraz
243 I9 **Haifeng** Guangdong, S China 22°56′N 115°19′E
Haifong see Hai Phong
245 J4 **Hai He** ≈ E China
Haikang see Leizhou
240 F9 **Haikou** var. Hai-k'ou, Hoihow, Fr. Hoï-Hao. province capital Hainan, S China 20°N 110°17′E
Hai-k'ou see Haikou
220 E3 **Ḩā'il** Ḩā'il, NW Saudi Arabia 27°N 42°50′E
220 E3 **Ḩā'il** off. Minṭaqah Ḩā'il. ◐ province N Saudi Arabia
Hai-la-erh see Hailar
237 I2 **Hailar** var. Hai-la-erh; prev. Hulun. Nei Mongol Zizhiqu, N China 49°15′N 119°41′E
76 G7 **Hailey** Idaho, NW USA 43°31′N 114°18′W
62 D1 **Haileybury** Ontario, S Canada 47°27′N 79°39′W
248 E1 **Hailin** Heilongjiang, NE China 44°37′N 129°24′E
Ḩā'il, Minṭaqah see Ḩā'il
Hailong see Meihekou
161 L8 **Hailsham** UK 50°52′N 0°16′E
152 H7 **Hailuoto** Swe. Karlö. island W Finland
Haima see Haymā'
243 J9 **Haimen** China 23°12′N 116°37′E
243 M1 **Haimen** Jiangsu, China 31°32′N 121°05′E
Haimen see Taizhou
240 F9 **Hainan** var. Hainan Sheng, Qiong. ◐ province S China
240 F9 **Hainan Dao** island S China
Hainan Sheng see Hainan
Hainan Strait see Qiongzhou Haixia
Hainasch see Ainaži
Hainau see Chojnów
163 D11 **Hainaut** ◐ province SW Belgium
Hainburg see Hainburg an der Donau
177 M2 **Hainburg an der Donau** var. Hainburg. Niederösterreich, NE Austria 48°09′N 16°57′E
83 L6 **Haines** Alaska, USA 59°13′N 135°27′W
76 E6 **Haines** Oregon, NW USA 44°53′N 117°56′W
69 L6 **Haines City** Florida, SE USA 28°06′N 81°37′W
54 A3 **Haines Junction** Yukon Territory, W Canada 60°45′N 137°30′W
177 L2 **Hainfeld** Niederösterreich, NE Austria 48°03′N 15°47′E
179 H9 **Hainichen** Sachsen, E Germany 50°58′N 13°08′E
243 M2 **Haining** Zhejiang, China 30°19′N 120°25′E
Hai Ninh see Mong Cai
257 H5 **Hai Phong** var. Haifong, Haiphong. N Vietnam 20°50′N 106°41′E
Haiphong see Hai Phong
243 M7 **Haitan Dao** island SE China
90 G5 **Haiti** off. Republic of Haiti. ◆ republic C West Indies
Haiti, Republic of see Haiti
80 F7 **Haiwee Reservoir** ⊡ California, W USA
129 K8 **Haiya** Red Sea, NE Sudan 18°17′N 36°21′E
243 M2 **Haiyan** China 30°31′N 120°56′E
239 J6 **Haiyan** var. Sanjiaocheng. Qinghai, W China 36°55′N 100°54′E
243 K3 **Haiyang** China 29°47′N 118°11′E
245 M5 **Haiyang** Shandong, China 34°28′N 121°06′E
245 N3 **Haiyang Dang** island Liaoning, China
242 F7 **Haiyang Shan** ▲▲ S China
244 C6 **Haiyuan** Ningxia, N China 36°32′N 105°31′E
245 L7 **Haizhou Wan** bay Jiangsu, China
Hajda see Nový Bor
183 H11 **Hajdú-Bihar** off. Hajdú-Bihar Megye. ◐ county E Hungary
Hajdú-Bihar Megye see Hajdú-Bihar
183 H11 **Hajdúböszörmény** Hajdú-Bihar, E Hungary 47°39′N 21°32′E
183 I11 **Hajdúhadház** Hajdú-Bihar, E Hungary 47°40′N 21°40′E
183 H11 **Hajdúnánás** Hajdú-Bihar, E Hungary 47°50′N 21°26′E
183 H11 **Hajdúszoboszló** Hajdú-Bihar, E Hungary 47°27′N 21°24′E
175 B14 **Hajeb El Ayoun** Tunisia
217 J1 **Ḩājī Ebrāhīm, Kūh-e** ▲ Iran/Iraq 36°53′N 44°56′E
253 B10 **Hajiki-zaki** headland Sado, C Japan 38°19′N 138°28′E
Hajîne see Abū Ḩardān
233 I7 **Hājīpur** Bihār, N India 25°41′N 85°13′E
220 F8 **Ḩajjah** W Yemen 15°43′N 43°33′E
217 K7 **Hajjama** S Iraq 31°24′N 45°20′E
223 H8 **Ḩājjīābād** Hormozgān, C Iran
217 J9 **Ḩājj, Thaqb al** well S Iraq
184 F6 **Hajla** ▲▲ E Montenegro
182 J5 **Hajnówka** Ger. Hermhausen. Podlaskie, NE Poland 52°45′N 23°32′E
256 B4 **Haka** Chin State, W Myanmar (Burma) 22°42′N 93°41′E
Hakapehi see Punaauia
Hakâri see Hakkâri
180 J6 **Hakenstedt** Sachsen-Anhalt, Germany 11°16′N 52°11′E
215 K7 **Hakkâri** var. Çölemerik, Hakâri. Hakkâri, SE Turkey 37°36′N 43°45′E
215 K7 **Hakkâri** var. Hakkari. ◐ province SE Turkey
Hakkari see Hakkâri
152 G5 **Hakkas** Norrbotten, N Sweden 66°53′N 21°36′E
251 I5 **Hakken-zan** ▲ Honshū, SW Japan 34°11′N 135°57′E
252 D7 **Hakkōda-san** ▲ Honshū, C Japan 40°40′N 140°49′E
252 F2 **Hako-dake** ▲ Hokkaidō, NE Japan 44°40′N 142°22′E
252 D6 **Hakodate** Hokkaidō, NE Japan 41°46′N 140°43′E
251 J2 **Hakui** Ishikawa, Honshū, SW Japan 36°55′N 136°46′E
285 I10 **Hakupu** SE Niue 19°06′S 169°50′E
251 J3 **Haku-san** ▲ Honshū, SW Japan 36°07′N 136°45′E
Hal see Halle
230 G9 **Hāla** Sind, SE Pakistan 25°47′N 68°28′E
216 D2 **Ḩalab** Eng. Aleppo, Fr. Alep; anc. Beroea. Ḩalab, NW Syria 36°14′N 37°10′E
216 D2 **Ḩalab** off. Muḩāfaz̧at Ḩalab, var. Aleppo, Halab. ◐ governorate NW Syria
216 D2 **Ḩalab** ✕ Ḩalab, NW Syria 36°12′N 37°10′E
Halab see Ḩalab
220 F5 **Ḩalabān** var. Halibān. Ar Riyāḑ, C Saudi Arabia 23°29′N 44°20′E
217 K3 **Ḩalabja** NE Iraq 35°11′N 45°59′E
Ḩalab, Muḩāfaz̧at see Ḩalab
228 G7 **Halaç** Rus. Khalach. Lebap Welaýaty, E Turkmenistan 38°05′N 64°46′E
87 L5 **Halachó** Yucatán, Mexico 20°29′N 90°05′W
285 H10 **Halagigie Point** headland W Niue
129 K6 **Halaib** SE Egypt 22°10′N 36°33′E
284 C10 **Halalo** Île Uvea, N Wallis and Futuna 13°21′S 176°11′W
Halandri see Chalándri
221 K7 **Ḩalānīyāt, Juzur al** var. Jazā'ir Bin Ghalfān, Eng. Kuria Muria Islands. island group S Oman
221 K7 **Ḩalānīyāt, Khalīj al** Eng. Kuria Muria Bay. bay S Oman
Halas see Kiskunhalas
218 G1 **Halba** Lebanon
Halban see Tsetserleg
180 J7 **Halberstadt** Sachsen-Anhalt, C Germany 51°54′N 11°04′E
279 H7 **Halcombe** Manawatu-Wanganui, North Island, New Zealand 40°09′S 175°30′E
52 C8 **Haldane River** ≈ Northwest Territories.NW Canada
155 E8 **Halden** prev. Fredrikshald. Østfold, S Norway 59°08′N 11°20′E
178 F7 **Haldensleben** Sachsen-Anhalt, C Germany 52°18′N 11°25′E
Háldi see Halti
233 J9 **Haldia** West Bengal, NE India 22°04′N 88°02′E
232 F5 **Haldwāni** Uttaranchal, N India 29°13′N 79°31′E
82 D2 **Haleakalā** crater Maui, Hawai'i, USA
70 D3 **Hale Center** Texas, SW USA 34°03′N 101°50′W
163 F10 **Halen** Limburg, NE Belgium 50°35′N 05°08′E
161 H4 **Halesowen** UK 52°27′N 2°03′W
161 M4 **Halesworth** UK 52°21′N 1°30′E
66 D8 **Haleyville** Alabama, S USA 34°13′N 87°37′W
132 G8 **Half Assini** SW Ghana 05°03′N 02°57′W
80 E4 **Half Dome** ▲ California, W USA 37°46′N 119°27′W
278 B13 **Halfmoon Bay** var. Oban. Stewart Island, Southland, New Zealand 46°53′S 168°08′E
80 A3 **Half Moon Bay** California, USA 37°28′N 122°26′W
276 E3 **Half Moon Lake** salt lake South Australia
193 J9 **Halhgol** var. Tsagaannuur. Dornod, E Mongolia 47°30′N 118°45′E
Haliacmon see Aliákmonas
Halibān see Ḩalabān
62 E3 **Haliburton** Ontario, SE Canada 45°03′N 78°20′W
62 E3 **Haliburton Highlands** var. Madawaska Highlands. hill range Ontario, SE Canada
59 J9 **Halifax** province capital Nova Scotia, SE Canada 44°38′N 63°35′W
159 K9 **Halifax** N England, UK 53°44′N 01°52′W
67 L5 **Halifax** North Carolina, SE USA 36°19′N 77°37′W

◆ Country
● Country Capital
◇ Dependent Territory
○ Dependent Territory Capital
◐ Administrative Regions
✕ International Airport
▲ Mountain
▲▲ Mountain Range
Volcano
≈ River
◎ Lake
⊡ Reservoir

INDEX
347

Halifax - Havelange

67 K5 **Halifax** Virginia, NE USA 36°46′N 78°55′W
59 K9 **Halifax** ✈ Nova Scotia, SE Canada 44°33′N 63°48′W
223 I8 **Halīl Rūd** *seasonal river* SE Iran
216 C4 **Ḥalīmah** ▲ Lebanon/Syria 34°12′N 36°37′E
239 I2 **Haliun** Govĭ-Altay, W Mongolia 45°55′N 96°06′E
244 E1 **Haliut** Inner Mongolia, China 41°20′N 108°17′E
190 E3 **Haljala** *Ger.* Halljal. Lääne-Virumaa, N Estonia 59°25′N 26°18′E
187 M2 **HalkalÄ±** İstanbul, Turkey 41°02′N 28°47′E
83 I2 **Halkett, Cape** *headland* Alaska, USA 70°48′N 152°11′W
Halkida *see* Chalkída
156 F3 **Halkirk** N Scotland, UK 58°30′N 03°29′W
Hall *see* Schwäbisch Hall
154 H2 **Hälla** Västerbotten, N Sweden 63°56′N 17°20′E
156 F3 **Halladale** ≈ N Scotland, UK
155 F11 **Halland** ◈ *county* S Sweden
69 N9 **Hallandale** Florida, SE USA 25°58′N 80°09′W
53 J1 **Hall Basin** *bay* N Canada
53 J8 **Hall Beach** nunavut, NE Canada
163 D10 **Halle** *Fr.* Hal. Vlaams Brabant, C Belgium 50°44′N 04°14′E
179 G8 **Halle** *var.* Halle an der Saale. Sachsen-Anhalt, C Germany 51°28′N 11°58′E
Halle an der Saale *see* Halle
78 F2 **Halleck** Nevada, W USA 40°57′N 115°27′W
154 G7 **Hällefors** Örebro, C Sweden 59°46′N 14°30′E
155 H8 **Hälleforsnäs** Södermanland, C Sweden 59°10′N 16°30′E
177 I3 **Hallein** Salzburg, N Austria 47°41′N 13°06′E
181 F9 **Hallenberg** Nordrhein-Westfalen, Germany 8°38′N 51°07′E
179 G8 **Halle-Neustadt** Sachsen-Anhalt, C Germany 51°29′N 11°54′E
71 H7 **Hallettsville** Texas, SW USA 29°27′N 96°57′W
292 G3 **Halley** *UK research station* Antarctica
74 B3 **Halliday** North Dakota, N USA 47°19′N 102°19′W
79 L2 **Halligan Reservoir** ⊠ Colorado, C USA
178 D3 **Halligen** *island group* N Germany
154 D7 **Hallingdal** *valley* S Norway
82 E6 **Hall Island** *island* Alaska, USA
Hall Island *see* Maiana
282 G6 **Hall Islands** *island group* C Micronesia
190 E5 **Halliste** ≈ S Estonia
Halljal *see* Haljala
53 J8 **Hall Lake** ◎ Nunavut, NE Canada
154 J2 **Hällnäs** Västerbotten, N Sweden 64°20′N 19°41′E
74 E2 **Hallock** Minnesota, N USA 48°47′N 96°56′W
161 H4 **Hallow** UK 52°13′N 2°15′W
55 N1 **Hall Peninsula** *peninsula* Baffin Island, Nunavut, NE Canada
66 B6 **Halls** Tennessee, S USA 35°52′N 89°24′W
155 G8 **Hallsberg** Örebro, C Sweden 59°05′N 15°07′E
274 F3 **Halls Creek** Western Australia 18°17′S 127°39′E
277 I7 **Halls Gap** Victoria, SE Australia 37°09′S 142°30′E
155 H8 **Hallstahammar** Västmanland, C Sweden 59°37′N 16°13′E
177 J3 **Hallstatt** Salzburg, W Austria 47°32′N 13°39′E
179 I13 **Hallstatter See** ◎ C Austria
154 J7 **Hallstavik** Stockholm, C Sweden 60°12′N 18°45′E
71 I4 **Hallsville** Texas, SW USA 32°31′N 94°30′W
163 B10 **Halluin** Nord, N France 50°46′N 03°07′E
Halmahera, Laut *see* Halmahera Sea
260 G3 **Halmahera, Pulau** *prev.* Djailolo, Gilolo, Jailolo. *island* E Indonesia
260 F4 **Halmahera Sea** *Ind.* Laut Halmahera. *sea* E Indonesia
155 F11 **Halmstad** Halland, S Sweden 56°41′N 12°49′E
260 G5 **Halong** Pulau Ambon, E Indonesia 03°39′S 128°13′E
191 H9 **Halowchyn** *Rus.* Golovchin. Mahilyowskaya Voblasts′, E Belarus 54°04′N 29°55′E
155 D11 **Hals** Nordjylland, N Denmark 57°00′N 10°19′E
154 C4 **Halsa** Møre og Romsdal, S Norway 63°04′N 08°13′E
191 E9 **Hal′shany** *Rus.* Gol′shany. Hrodzyenskaya Voblasts′, W Belarus 54°15′N 26°01′E
Hälsingborg *see* Helsingborg
74 E3 **Halstad** Minnesota, N USA 47°21′N 96°49′W
161 L5 **Halstead** UK 51°57′N 0°37′E
75 E10 **Halstead** Kansas, C USA 38°00′N 97°30′W
180 H2 **Halstenbek** Schleswig-Holstein, Germany 9°51′N 53°38′E
163 D8 **Halsteren** Noord-Brabant, S Netherlands 51°32′N 04°16′E
153 H8 **Halsua** Länsi-Soumi, W Finland 63°28′N 24°10′E
162 J7 **Haltern** Nordrhein-Westfalen, W Germany 51°45′N 07°10′E
152 G4 **Halti** *var.* Haltiatunturi, *Lapp.* Háldi. ▲ Finland/Norway 69°18′N 21°19′E
Haltiatunturi *see* Halti
159 J6 **Haltwhistle** UK 54°59′N 2°26′W
181 D9 **Halver** Nordrhein-Westfalen, Germany 7°29′N 51°12′E
161 M3 **Halvergate** UK 52°36′N 1°34′E
160 F9 **Halwell** UK 50°22′N 3°44′W
188 D4 **Halych** Ivano-Frankivs′ka Oblast′, W Ukraine 49°08′N 24°44′E
Halycus *see* Platani
165 I2 **Ham** Somme, N France 49°46′N 03°03′E
Hama *see* Ḥamāh
250 E4 **Hamada** Shimane, Honshū, SW Japan 34°54′N 132°07′E
222 E4 **Hamadān** *anc.* Ecbatana. Hamadān, W Iran 34°51′N 48°31′E
222 E4 **Hamadān** *off.* Ostān-e Hamadān. ◈ *province* W Iran
Hamadān, Ostān-e *see* Hamadān
171 K10 **Hamadia** Algeria
216 D3 **Ḥamāh** *var.* Hama; *anc.* Epiphania, *Bibl.* Hamath. Ḥamāh, W Syria 35°09′N 36°44′E
216 D3 **Ḥamāh** *off.* Muḥāfaẓat Ḥamāh, *var.* Hama. ◈ *governorate* C Syria
Hamāh, Muḥāfaẓat *see* Ḥamāh
219 E10 **HaMakhtesh HaGadol** Israel
219 E10 **HaMakhtesh HaQatan** Israel
251 K4 **Hamakita** Shizuoka, Honshū, S Japan 34°46′N 137°44′E
252 E4 **Hamamasu** Hokkaidō, NE Japan 43°37′N 141°24′E
251 K5 **Hamamatsu** *var.* Hamamatu. Shizuoka, Honshū, S Japan 34°43′N 137°46′E
Hamamatu *see* Hamamatsu
252 H4 **Hamanaka** Hokkaidō, NE Japan 43°05′N 145°05′E
251 J4 **Hamana-ko** ◎ Honshū, S Japan
154 E6 **Hamar** *prev.* Storhammer. Hedmark, S Norway 60°57′N 10°55′E
221 J5 **Ḥamārīr al Kidan, Qalamat** *well* E Saudi Arabia
250 G3 **Hamasaka** Hyōgo, Honshū, SW Japan 35°37′N 134°27′E
Hamath *see* Ḥamāh
252 F2 **Hamatonbetsu** Hokkaidō, NE Japan 45°07′N 142°21′E
181 I11 **Hambach** Bayern, Germany 10°13′N 50°06′E
235 G11 **Hambantota** Southern Province, SE Sri Lanka 06°07′N 81°07′E
180 F3 **Hambergen** Niedersachsen, Germany 8°50′N 53°19′E
261 N6 **Hambili** ≈ NW Papua New Guinea
Hambourg *see* Hamburg
180 H3 **Hamburg** Hamburg, N Germany 53°33′N 10°03′E
75 I14 **Hamburg** Arkansas, C USA 33°13′N 91°50′W
75 F8 **Hamburg** Iowa, C USA 40°36′N 95°39′W
64 G5 **Hamburg** New Jersey, USA 41°09′N 74°35′W
64 A1 **Hamburg** New York, NE USA 42°40′N 78°49′W
64 E6 **Hamburg** Pennsylvania, USA 40°33′N 75°59′W
180 H2 **Hamburg** *Fr.* Hambourg. ◈ *state* N Germany
250 A2 **Hamch′ang** Kyŏngsang-bukto, South Korea 36°34′N 128°11′E
230 C4 **Hamdam Āb, Dasht-e** *Pash.* Dasht-i Hamdamab. ▲▲ W Afghanistan
Hamdamab, Dasht-i *see* Hamdam Āb, Dasht-e
65 J4 **Hamden** Connecticut, NE USA 41°23′N 72°55′W
212 E6 **Ḥamḍ, Wādī al** *dry watercourse* W Saudi Arabia
153 G9 **Hämeenkyrö** Länsi-Suomi, W Finland 61°39′N 23°10′E
153 H9 **Hämeenlinna** *Swe.* Tavastehus. Etelä-Suomi, S Finland 61°N 24°25′E
HaMela h, Yam *see* Dead Sea
180 H6 **Hämelerwald** Niedersachsen, Germany 10°07′N 52°21′E
Hamelin *see* Hameln
180 G6 **Hameln** *Eng.* Hamelin. Niedersachsen, N Germany 52°07′N 09°22′E
274 D5 **Hamersley Range** ▲▲ Western Australia
248 D3 **Hamgyŏng-sanmaek** ▲▲ N North Korea
248 C4 **Hamhŭng** C North Korea 39°53′N 127°31′E
239 H4 **Hami** *var.* Ha-mi, *Uigh.* Kumul, Qomul. Xinjiang Uygur Zizhiqu, NW China 42°48′N 93°27′E
Ha-mi *see* Hami
217 L6 **Ḥāmid Amīn** E Iraq 32°06′N 46°53′E
221 J6 **Hamīdān, Khawr** *oasis* SE Saudi Arabia
216 C4 **Ḥamīdīyah** *var.* Hamîdîyé. Tarṭūs, W Syria 34°43′N 35°58′E
Hamîdîyé *see* Ḥamīdīyah
277 H7 **Hamilton** Victoria, SE Australia 37°45′S 142°04′E
67 M10 **Hamilton** ○ (Bermuda) C Bermuda 32°18′N 64°48′W
62 C5 **Hamilton** Ontario, S Canada 43°15′N 79°50′W
278 G4 **Hamilton** Waikato, North Island, New Zealand 37°49′S 175°16′E
159 H4 **Hamilton** S Scotland, UK 55°47′N 04°03′W
66 C8 **Hamilton** Alabama, S USA 34°08′N 87°59′W
82 G5 **Hamilton** Alaska, USA 62°54′N 163°53′W
73 A10 **Hamilton** Illinois, N USA 40°24′N 91°20′W
76 G5 **Hamilton** Montana, NW USA 46°15′N 114°09′W
64 F1 **Hamilton** New York, USA 42°50′N 75°33′W
70 G5 **Hamilton** Texas, SW USA 31°42′N 98°08′W
62 C5 **Hamilton** ✈ Ontario, SE Canada 43°12′N 79°54′W
290 D3 **Hamilton Bank** *undersea feature* SE Labrador Sea
276 E1 **Hamilton Creek** *seasonal river* South Australia
59 K5 **Hamilton Inlet** *inlet* Newfoundland and Labrador, E Canada
75 H13 **Hamilton, Lake** ⊠ Arkansas, C USA
78 F3 **Hamilton, Mount** ▲ Nevada, W USA 39°15′N 115°30′W
64 G7 **Hamilton Square** New Jersey, USA 40°14′N 74°39′W
128 F3 **Ḥamīm, Wādī al** ≈ NE Libya
153 I9 **Hamina** *Swe.* Fredrikshamn. Kymi, S Finland 60°33′N 27°15′E
55 I10 **Hamiota** Manitoba, S Canada 50°13′N 100°37′W
232 G7 **Hamīrpur** Uttar Pradesh, N India 25°57′N 80°08′E
Hamïs Musait *see* Khamīs Mushayt
67 J7 **Hamlet** North Carolina, SE USA 34°52′N 79°41′W
70 F4 **Hamlin** Texas, SW USA 32°52′N 100°07′W
67 H3 **Hamlin** West Virginia, NE USA 38°16′N 82°07′W
72 F6 **Hamlin Lake** ◎ Michigan, N USA
180 D7 **Hamm** *var.* Hamm in Westfalen. Nordrhein-Westfalen, W Germany 51°39′N 07°49′E
181 C8 **Hamm** Nordrhein-Westfalen, Germany 7°03′N 51°23′E
Ḥammāmāt, Khalīj al *see* Hammamet, Golfe de
175 C13 **Hammamet** Tunisia
131 L1 **Hammamet, Golfe de** *Ar.* Khalīj al Ḥammāmāt. *gulf* NE Tunisia
175 C13 **Hammam Lif** Tunisia
175 C14 **Hammam Sousse** Tunisia
217 I2 **Ḥammān al ′Alīl** N Iraq 36°07′N 43°15′E
217 L8 **Ḥammār, Hawr al** ◎ SE Iraq
154 J7 **Hammarland** Åland, SW Finland 60°13′N 19°45′E
154 H3 **Hammarstrand** Jämtland, C Sweden 63°07′N 16°27′E
153 J8 **Hammaslahti** Pohjois-Karjala, SE Finland 62°26′N 29°58′E
163 D9 **Hamme** Oost-Vlaanderen, NW Belgium 51°06′N 04°08′E
180 F4 **Hamme** ≈ NW Germany
155 D11 **Hammel** Århus, C Denmark 56°15′N 09°53′E
181 H11 **Hammelburg** Bayern, C Germany 50°06′N 09°50′E
163 E10 **Hamme-Mille** Walloon Brabant, C Belgium 50°48′N 04°42′E
180 F3 **Hamme-Oste-Kanal** *canal* NW Germany
154 G3 **Hammerdal** Jämtland, C Sweden 63°34′N 15°19′E
152 G3 **Hammerfest** Finnmark, N Norway 70°40′N 23°44′E
180 B7 **Hamminkeln** Nordrhein-Westfalen, W Germany 51°43′N 06°36′E
Hamm in Westfalen *see* Hamm
75 C12 **Hammon** Oklahoma, C USA 35°37′N 99°22′W
73 E9 **Hammond** Indiana, N USA 41°35′N 87°30′W
68 E4 **Hammond** Louisiana, S USA 30°30′N 90°27′W
64 G8 **Hammonton** New Jersey, USA 39°38′N 74°48′W
163 G11 **Hamoir** Liège, E Belgium 50°28′N 05°35′E
163 F11 **Hamois** Namur, SE Belgium 50°21′N 05°09′E
163 G9 **Hamont** Limburg, NE Belgium 51°15′N 05°33′E
278 D11 **Hampden** Otago, South Island, New Zealand 45°18′S 170°49′E
63 K4 **Hampden** Maine, NE USA 44°44′N 68°51′W
87 L6 **Hampolol** Campeche, Mexico
166 D1 **Hampshire** *cultural region* S England, UK
64 D8 **Hampstead** Maryland, USA 39°36′N 76°51′W
159 K8 **Hampsthwaite** UK 54°01′N 1°36′W
63 M3 **Hampton** New Brunswick, SE Canada 45°30′N 65°50′W
75 H14 **Hampton** Arkansas, C USA 33°33′N 92°28′W
74 H6 **Hampton** Iowa, C USA 42°44′N 93°12′W
63 J6 **Hampton** New Hampshire, NE USA 42°55′N 70°48′W
65 M1 **Hampton** New Hampshire, USA 42°56′N 70°50′W
67 I9 **Hampton** South Carolina, SE USA 32°52′N 81°06′W
67 H6 **Hampton** Tennessee, S USA 36°16′N 82°10′W
67 M5 **Hampton** Virginia, NE USA 37°02′N 76°23′W
65 J6 **Hampton Bays** New York, USA 40°52′N 72°31′W
154 G5 **Hamra** Gävleborg, C Sweden 61°40′N 15°00′E
129 H10 **Hamrat esh Sheikh** Northern Kordofan, C Sudan 14°38′N 27°56′E
217 I3 **Ḥamrīn, Jabal** ▲▲ N Iraq
175 J13 **Hamrun** C Malta 35°53′N 14°28′E
257 I9 **Ham Thuân Nam** Binh Thuân, S Vietnam 10°49′N 107°49′E
261 J5 **Hamuku** Papua, E Indonesia 03°18′S 135°00′E
Hāmūn, Daryācheh-ye *see* Şāberī, Hāmūn-e/Sīstān, Daryācheh-ye
Hamwih *see* Southampton
250 A3 **Hamyang** Kyŏngsang-namdo, South Korea 35°31′N 127°44′E
82 D2 **Hāna** *var.* Hana. Maui, Hawai′i, USA 20°45′N 155°59′W
Hana *see* Hāna
67 J9 **Hanahan** South Carolina, SE USA 32°55′N 80°01′W
82 B1 **Hanalei** Kaua′i, Hawai′i, USA 22°12′N 159°30′W
250 B3 **Hanam** Kyŏngsang-namdo, South Korea 35°23′N 128°42′E
257 I7 **Ha Nam** Quang Nam-ƒa Năng, C Vietnam 15°42′N 108°24′E
253 D9 **Hanamaki** Iwate, Honshū, C Japan 39°25′N 141°04′E
285 H10 **Hanan** ✈ (Alofi) SW Niue
181 F11 **Hanau** Hessen, W Germany 50°06′N 08°56′E
239 L3 **Hanbogd** *var.* Ih Bulag. Ömnögovĭ, S Mongolia 43°04′N 107°43′E
Hâncești *see* Hîncești
56 D6 **Hanceville** British Columbia, SW Canada 51°54′N 122°56′W
66 D8 **Hanceville** Alabama, S USA 34°03′N 86°46′W
Hancewicze *see* Hantsavichy
244 F7 **Hancheng** Shaanxi, C China 35°22′N 110°27′E
243 H2 **Hanchuan** Hubei, China 30°23′N 113°29′E
64 B8 **Hancock** Maryland, NE USA 39°42′N 78°10′W
72 D3 **Hancock** Michigan, N USA 47°07′N 88°34′W
74 F4 **Hancock** Minnesota, N USA 45°30′N 95°47′W
64 F3 **Hancock** New York, NE USA 41°57′N 75°15′W
136 J3 **Handa** Bari, NE Somalia 10°35′N 51°09′E
245 I6 **Handan** *var.* Han-tan. Hebei, E China 36°35′N 114°28′E
155 I8 **Handen** Stockholm, C Sweden 59°12′N 18°09′E
137 E10 **Handeni** Tanga, E Tanzania 05°25′S 38°04′E
159 J10 **Handforth** UK 53°21′N 2°13′W
79 K5 **Handies Peak** ▲ Colorado, C USA 37°54′N 107°30′W
183 F10 **Handlová** *Ger.* Krickerhäu, *Hung.* Nyitrabánya; *prev.* Kriegerhaj. Trenčiansky Kraj, C Slovakia 48°45′N 18°45′E
180 D5 **Handrup** Niedersachsen, Germany 7°35′N 52°34′E
159 K10 **Handsworth** UK 53°22′N 1°23′W
253 C13 **Haneda** ✈ (Tōkyō) Tōkyō, Honshū, S Japan 35°33′N 139°45′E
129 J3 **HaNegev** *Eng.* Negev. *desert* S Israel
180 G1 **Hanerau-Hademarschen** Schleswig-Holstein, Germany 9°25′N 54°08′E
Hanfeng *see* Kaixian
80 D6 **Hanford** California, W USA 36°19′N 119°39′W
118 A2 **Hanga Roa** Easter Island, Chile, E Pacific Ocean 27°09′S 109°26′W
239 I1 **Hangay** *var.* Hunt. Arhangay, C Mongolia 47°49′N 99°24′E
236 F3 **Hangayn Nuruu** ▲▲ C Mongolia
Hang-chou/Hangchow *see* Hangzhou
155 G10 **Hånger** Jönköping, S Sweden 57°06′N 13°58′E
243 L2 **Hanggai** China 30°34′N 119°23′E
Hangö *see* Hanko
245 K3 **Hangu** China 39°15′N 117°47′E
243 M2 **Hangzhou** *var.* Hang-chou, Hangchow. *province capital* Zhejiang, SE China 30°18′N 120°07′E
243 M3 **Hangzhou Wan** *bay* Zhejiang, China
193 H8 **Hanh** *var.* Turt. Hövsgöl, N Mongolia 51°30′N 100°40′E
239 H1 **Hanhöhiy Uul** ▲▲ NW Mongolia
239 K3 **Hanhongor** *var.* Ögöömör. Ömnögovĭ, S Mongolia 43°47′N 104°31′E
228 E8 **Hanhowuz** *Rus.* Khauz-Khan. Ahal Welaýaty, S Turkmenistan 37°15′N 61°12′E
215 I6 **Hani** Diyarbakır, SE Turkey 38°26′N 40°23′E
Hania *see* Chaniá
180 H5 **Hänigsen** Niedersachsen, Germany 10°06′N 52°29′E
136 F2 **Ḥanīsh al Kabīr, Jazīrat al** *island* SW Yemen
243 L7 **Hanjiang** China 25°27′N 119°06′E
Hanka, Lake *see* Khanka, Lake
153 I8 **Hankasalmi** Länsi-Suomi, C Finland 62°25′N 26°27′E
180 I5 **Hankensbüttel** Niedersachsen, Germany 10°36′N 52°44′E
141 H9 **Hankey** Eastern Cape, South Africa 33°50′S 24°53′E
74 E4 **Hankinson** North Dakota, N USA 46°04′N 96°54′W
153 H10 **Hanko** *Swe.* Hangö. Etelä-Suomi, SW Finland 59°50′N 23°E
Han-kou/Han-k′ou/Hankow *see* Wuhan
79 I4 **Hanksville** Utah, W USA 38°21′N 110°43′W
232 F3 **Hanle** Jammu and Kashmir, NW India 32°46′N 79°01′E
161 H2 **Hanley** UK 53°02′N 2°11′W
278 E9 **Hanmer Springs** Canterbury, South Island, New Zealand 42°31′S 172°49′E
57 J7 **Hanna** Alberta, SW Canada 51°38′N 111°56′W
58 F6 **Hannah Bay** *coastal sea feature* Québec, SE Canada
75 I9 **Hannibal** Missouri, C USA 39°42′N 91°23′W
274 F3 **Hann, Mount** ▲ Western Australia 15°53′S 125°46′E
180 H6 **Hannover** *Eng.* Hanover. Niedersachsen, NW Germany 52°23′N 09°43′E
163 F11 **Hannut** Liège, C Belgium 50°40′N 05°05′E
155 G12 **Hanöbukten** *bay* S Sweden
257 H4 **Ha Nôi** *Eng.* Hanoi, *Fr.* Hanoï. ● (Vietnam) N Vietnam 21°01′N 105°52′E
62 C4 **Hanover** Ontario, S Canada 44°10′N 81°03′W
140 G7 **Hanover** Northern Cape, South Africa 31°04′S 24°27′E
73 F12 **Hanover** Indiana, N USA 38°42′N 85°28′W
64 F6 **Hanover** Pennsylvania, USA 40°40′N 75°25′W
64 D8 **Hanover** Pennsylvania, NE USA 39°46′N 76°57′W
67 L4 **Hanover** Virginia, NE USA 37°44′N 77°21′W
Hanover *see* Hannover
117 B12 **Hanover, Isla** *island* S Chile
140 G7 **Hanover Road** Northern Cape, South Africa 30°57′S 24°32′E
Hanselbeck *see* Érd
114 A7 **Hansen** Santa Fe, Argentina 33°16′S 61°42′W
293 L3 **Hansen Mountains** ▲▲ Antarctica
242 G2 **Han Shui** ≈ C China
232 E5 **Hānsi** Haryāna, NW India 29°06′N 76°01′E
55 K2 **Hansine Lake** ◎ Nunavut, NE Canada
180 G3 **Hanstedt** Niedersachsen, Germany 9°06′N 53°18′E
155 C10 **Hanstholm** Viborg, NW Denmark 57°05′N 08°39′E
140 D8 **Hantams** ≈ Northern Cape, South Africa
140 E8 **Hantamsberg** ▲ Northern Cape, South Africa 31°24′S 19°42′E
Han-tan *see* Handan
238 D4 **Hantengri Feng** *var.* Pik Khan-Tengri. ▲ China/Kazakhstan 42°17′N 80°11′E *see also* Khan-Tengri, Pik
245 L5 **Hanting** China 36°46′N 119°13′E
191 F11 **Hantsavichy** *Pol.* Hancewicze, *Rus.* Gantsevichi. Brestskaya Voblasts′, SW Belarus 52°45′N 26°27′E
232 D4 **Hanumāngarh** Rājasthān, NW India 29°33′N 74°21′E
277 J5 **Hanwood** New South Wales, SE Australia 34°19′S 146°03′E
Hanyang *see* Wuhan
Hanyang *see* Caidian
240 C4 **Hanyuan** *var.* Fulin. Sichuan, C China 29°29′N 102°45′E
Hanyuan *see* Xihe
244 D9 **Hanzhong** Shaanxi, C China 33°12′N 107°E
245 K7 **Hanzhuang** China 34°36′N 117°22′E
285 K7 **Hao** *atoll* Îles Tuamotu, C French Polynesia
244 A4 **Haomen** China 37°27′N 101°49′E
233 J8 **Hāora** *prev.* Howrah. West Bengal, NE India 22°35′N 88°20′E
134 F1 **Haouach, Ouadi** *dry watercourse* E Chad
152 G6 **Haparanda** Norrbotten, N Sweden 65°49′N 24°05′E
161 M2 **Happisburgh** UK 52°49′N 1°34′E
70 D2 **Happy** Texas, SW USA 34°44′N 101°51′W
78 B1 **Happy Camp** California, W USA 41°48′N 123°24′W
59 K5 **Happy Valley-Goose Bay** *prev.* Goose Bay. Newfoundland and Labrador, E Canada 53°19′N 60°24′W
Hapsal *see* Haapsalu
232 F5 **Hāpur** Uttar Pradesh, N India 28°43′N 77°47′E
216 B8 **HaQatan, HaMakhtesh** ▲▲ S Israel
220 C2 **Ḥaql** Tabūk, NW Saudi Arabia 29°18′N 34°58′E
261 I6 **Har** Pulau Kai Besar, E Indonesia 05°21′S 133°09′E
Haraat *see* Tsagaandelger
221 H4 **Ḥaraḍ** *var.* Haradh. Ash Sharqīyah, E Saudi Arabia 24°08′N 49°02′E
Haradh *see* Ḥaraḍ
191 H8 **Haradok** *Rus.* Gorodok. Vitsyebskaya Voblasts′, N Belarus 55°28′N 30°00′E
152 G6 **Harads** Norrbotten, N Sweden 66°04′N 21°04′E
191 D11 **Haradzyets** *Rus.* Gorodets. Brestskaya Voblasts′, SW Belarus 52°12′N 24°40′E
191 F10 **Haradzyeya** *Rus.* Gorodeya. Minskaya Voblasts′, C Belarus 53°19′N 26°32′E
285 J7 **Haraiki** *atoll* Îles Tuamotu, C French Polynesia
253 D11 **Haramachi** Fukushima, Honshū, E Japan 37°40′N 140°55′E
191 G8 **Harany** *Rus.* Gorany. Vitsyebskaya Voblasts′, N Belarus 55°25′N 29°03′E
139 H3 **Harare** *prev.* Salisbury. ● (Zimbabwe) Mashonaland East, NE Zimbabwe 17°47′S 31°04′E
139 H3 **Harare** ✈ Mashonaland East, NE Zimbabwe 17°51′S 31°06′E
134 E2 **Haraz-Djombo** Batha, C Chad 14°10′N 19°35′E
191 I9 **Harbavichy** *Rus.* Gorbovichi. Mahilyowskaya Voblasts′, E Belarus 53°49′N 30°42′E
132 D8 **Harbel** W Liberia 06°19′N 10°20′W
237 J3 **Harbin** *var.* Haerbin, Ha-erh-pin, Kharbin; *prev.* Haerhpin, Pingkiang, Pinkiang. *province capital* Heilongjiang, NE China 45°45′N 126°41′E
72 H7 **Harbor Beach** Michigan, N USA 43°50′N 82°39′W
159 J5 **Harbottle** UK 55°19′N 2°06′W
59 L7 **Harbour Breton** Newfoundland, Newfoundland and Labrador, E Canada 47°29′N 55°50′W
117 I11 **Harbours, Bay of** *bay* East Falkland, Falkland Islands
161 J3 **Harby** UK 52°51′N 0°53′W
Hårby *see* Haarby
172 G4 **Harcajo de los Montes** Castilla-La Manacha, Spain 39°19′N 4°39′W
81 J13 **Harcuvar Mountains** ▲▲ Arizona, SW USA
176 F3 **Hard** Vorarlberg, NW Austria 47°29′N 09°42′E
232 E8 **Harda Khas** Madhya Pradesh, C India 22°22′N 77°06′E
154 B7 **Hardangerfjorden** *fjord* S Norway
154 B7 **Hardangervidda** *plateau* S Norway
138 C6 **Hardap** ◈ *district* S Namibia
67 I10 **Hardeeville** South Carolina, SE USA 32°18′N 81°04′W
162 H3 **Hardegarijp** *Fris.* Hurdegaryp. Friesland, N Netherlands 53°13′N 05°57′E
162 I5 **Hardenberg** Overijssel, E Netherlands 52°34′N 06°38′E
277 K5 **Harden-Murrumburrah** New South Wales, SE Australia 34°33′S 148°22′E
162 G6 **Harderwijk** Gelderland, C Netherlands 52°21′N 05°37′E
73 B11 **Hardin** Illinois, N USA 39°10′N 90°38′W
77 K5 **Hardin** Montana, NW USA 45°44′N 107°35′W
69 I1 **Harding, Lake** ⊠ Alabama/Georgia, SE USA
52 D7 **Harding River** ≈ Nunavut, NW Canada
66 E4 **Hardinsburg** Kentucky, S USA 37°46′N 86°29′W
57 K6 **Hardisty** Alberta, SW Canada 52°42′N 111°22′W
232 G6 **Hardoi** Uttar Pradesh, N India 27°23′N 80°06′E
Hardwar *see* Haridwār
80 D6 **Hardwick** California, USA 36°24′N 119°43′W
66 G9 **Hardwick** Georgia, SE USA 33°03′N 83°13′W
75 I11 **Hardy** Arkansas, C USA 36°19′N 91°29′W
154 B4 **Hareid** Møre og Romsdal, S Norway 62°22′N 06°02′E
52 B7 **Hare Indian** ≈ Northwest Territories, NW Canada
163 C10 **Harelbeke** *var.* Harlebeke. West-Vlaanderen, W Belgium 50°51′N 03°19′E
Harem *see* Ḥārim
180 C5 **Haren** Niedersachsen, NW Germany 52°47′N 07°16′E
162 I3 **Haren** Groningen, NE Netherlands 53°10′N 06°37′E
136 F4 **Hārer** E Ethiopia 09°17′N 42°19′E
159 K8 **Harewood** UK 53°54′N 1°30′W
166 E4 **Harfleur** Haute-Normandie, France 49°30′N 0°12′E
154 I7 **Harg** Uppsala, C Sweden 60°13′N 18°25′E
Hargeisa *see* Hargeysa
136 G4 **Hargeysa** *var.* Hargeisa. Woqooyi Galbeed, NW Somalia 09°32′N 44°07′E
188 D7 **Harghita** ◈ *county* NE Romania
70 G10 **Hargill** Texas, SW USA 26°26′N 98°00′W
239 J1 **Harhorin** Övörhangay, C Mongolia 47°13′N 102°48′E
239 I5 **Har Hu** ◎ C China
Hariana *see* Haryāna
220 G8 **Ḥarīb** W Yemen 15°08′N 45°35′E
258 F5 **Hari, Batang** *prev.* Djambi. ≈ Sumatera, W Indonesia
232 F4 **Haridwār** *prev.* Hardwar. Uttaranchal, N India 29°58′N 78°09′E
234 D7 **Harihar** Karnātaka, W India 14°33′N 75°44′E
278 D9 **Harihari** West Coast, South Island, New Zealand 43°09′S 170°35′E
216 D2 **Ḥārim** *var.* Harem. Idlib, W Syria 36°30′N 36°30′E
250 G5 **Harima-nada** *sea* S Japan
162 D7 **Haringvliet** *channel* SW Netherlands
162 D7 **Haringvlietdam** *dam* SW Netherlands
231 I4 **Harīpur** North-West Frontier Province, NW Pakistan 34°00′N 73°01′E
230 D3 **Harīrūd** *var.* Tedzhen, *Turkm.* Tejen. ≈ Afghanistan/Iran *see also* Tejen
Harīrūd *see* Tejen
154 E5 **Härjåhågnen** *Swe.* Härjahågnen, *var* Härjehågna. ▲ Norway/Sweden 61°43′N 12°07′E
Härjahågnen *see* Härjåhågnen
153 G9 **Harjavalta** Länsi-Suomi, W Finland 61°19′N 22°10′E
Härjehågna *see* Härjåhågnen
190 C4 **Harjumaa** *var.* Harju Maakond. ◈ *province* NW Estonia
Harju Maakond *see* Harjumaa
180 D4 **Harkebrügge** Niedersachsen, Germany 7°49′N 53°07′E
67 M7 **Harkers Island** North Carolina, SE USA 34°42′N 76°33′W
217 I1 **Harki** N Iraq 37°03′N 43°39′E
74 F7 **Harlan** Iowa, C USA 41°40′N 95°19′W
66 G5 **Harlan** Kentucky, S USA 36°50′N 83°19′W
75 D8 **Harlan County Lake** ⊠ Nebraska, C USA
188 E6 **Hârlău** *var.* Hîrlău. Iași, NE Romania 47°26′N 26°54′E
Harlebeke *see* Harelbeke
160 E3 **Harlech** UK 52°52′N 4°06′W
77 J3 **Harlem** Montana, NW USA 48°31′N 108°46′W
Harlem *see* Haarlem
180 D2 **Harlesiel** Niedersachsen, Germany 7°48′N 53°42′E
161 M4 **Harleston** UK 52°24′N 1°18′E
155 D12 **Harlev** Århus, C Denmark 56°08′N 10°00′E
64 F7 **Harleysville** Pennsylvania, USA 40°17′N 75°23′W
162 G3 **Harlingen** *Fris.* Harns. Friesland, N Netherlands 53°10′N 05°25′E
70 G10 **Harlingen** Texas, SW USA 26°12′N 97°43′W
161 K5 **Harlow** E England, UK 51°47′N 00°07′E
77 J5 **Harlowton** Montana, NW USA 46°26′N 109°49′W
187 M4 **HarmancÄ±k** Bursa, Turkey 39°46′N 29°11′E
154 I5 **Harmånger** Gävleborg, C Sweden 61°55′N 17°19′E
162 F7 **Harmelen** Utrecht, C Netherlands 52°06′N 04°58′E
80 D7 **Harmony** California, USA 36°07′N 119°10′W
80 B7 **Harmony** California, USA 35°31′N 121°01′W
74 H6 **Harmony** Minnesota, N USA 43°33′N 92°00′W
159 L10 **Harmston** UK 53°09′N 0°33′W
76 D7 **Harney Basin** *basin* Oregon, NW USA
42 C6 **Harney Basin** ▲▲ Oregon, NW USA
76 D7 **Harney Lake** ◎ Oregon, NW USA
74 A5 **Harney Peak** ▲ South Dakota, N USA 43°52′N 103°31′W
154 I4 **Härnösand** *var.* Hernösand. Västernorrland, C Sweden 62°37′N 17°55′E
Harns *see* Harlingen
236 E3 **Har Nuur** ◎ NW Mongolia
170 G2 **Haro** La Rioja, N Spain 42°34′N 02°52′W
84 E5 **Haro, Cabo** *headland* NW Mexico 27°50′N 110°55′W
167 L6 **Haroué** Lorraine, France 48°28′N 6°11′E
154 B4 **Harøy** *island* S Norway
161 K5 **Harpenden** E England, UK 51°49′N 00°22′W
132 E9 **Harper** *var.* Cape Palmas. NE Liberia 04°25′N 07°43′W
75 D11 **Harper** Kansas, C USA 37°17′N 98°01′W
76 E7 **Harper** Oregon, NW USA 43°51′N 117°37′W
70 F6 **Harper** Texas, SW USA 30°18′N 99°18′W
81 F9 **Harper Lake** *salt flat* California, W USA
83 J5 **Harper, Mount** ▲ Alaska, USA 64°18′N 143°54′W
155 F11 **Harplinge** Halland, S Sweden 56°45′N 12°45′E
78 G8 **Harquahala Mountains** ▲▲ Arizona, SW USA
221 I8 **Ḥarrah** SE Yemen 15°02′N 50°23′E
58 F6 **Harricana** ≈ Québec, SE Canada
66 F6 **Harriman** Tennessee, S USA 35°57′N 84°33′W
64 F10 **Harrington** Delaware, USA 38°55′N 75°35′W
59 K6 **Harrington Harbour** Québec, E Canada 50°34′N 59°29′W
67 N10 **Harrington Sound** *bay* Bermuda, NW Atlantic Ocean
156 D4 **Harris** *physical region* NW Scotland, UK
75 J12 **Harrisburg** Arkansas, C USA 35°33′N 90°43′W
73 D13 **Harrisburg** Illinois, N USA 37°44′N 88°32′W
74 A7 **Harrisburg** Nebraska, C USA 41°33′N 103°46′W
76 B6 **Harrisburg** Oregon, NW USA 44°16′N 123°10′W
64 G7 **Harrisburg** Pennsylvania, USA 40°03′N 75°02′W
64 D7 **Harrisburg** *state capital* Pennsylvania, NE USA 40°16′N 76°53′W
276 E4 **Harris, Lake** ◎ South Australia
69 L6 **Harris, Lake** ◎ Florida, SE USA
141 J5 **Harrismith** Free State, E South Africa 28°16′S 29°08′E
75 H11 **Harrison** Arkansas, C USA 36°13′N 93°07′W
72 G7 **Harrison** Michigan, N USA 44°02′N 84°46′W
74 A6 **Harrison** Nebraska, C USA 42°42′N 103°53′W
83 I2 **Harrison Bay** *inlet* Alaska, USA
68 C2 **Harrisonburg** Louisiana, S USA 31°44′N 91°51′W
67 K3 **Harrisonburg** Virginia, NE USA 38°27′N 78°54′W
59 K4 **Harrison, Cape** *cape* Newfoundland and Labrador, E Canada
75 G10 **Harrisonville** Missouri, C USA 38°40′N 94°21′W
Harris Ridge *see* Lomonosov Ridge
286 G2 **Harris Seamount** *undersea feature* N Pacific Ocean
156 D4 **Harris, Sound of** *strait* NW Scotland, UK
72 H6 **Harrisville** Michigan, N USA 44°41′N 83°19′W
67 I2 **Harrisville** West Virginia, NE USA 39°13′N 81°04′W
66 F4 **Harrodsburg** Kentucky, S USA 37°45′N 84°51′W
159 K8 **Harrogate** N England, UK 54°N 01°33′W
70 F3 **Harrold** Texas, SW USA 34°05′N 99°02′W
161 K6 **Harrow** UK 51°34′N 0°20′W
75 G10 **Harry S. Truman Reservoir** ⊠ Missouri, C USA
180 E7 **Harsewinkel** Nordrhein-Westfalen, W Germany 51°58′N 08°13′E
180 J7 **Harsleben** Sachsen-Anhalt, Germany 11°06′N 51°52′E
188 F9 **Hârşova** *prev.* Hîrşova. Constanța, SE Romania 44°41′N 27°56′E
152 E4 **Harstad** Troms, N Norway 68°48′N 16°31′E
161 K4 **Harston** UK 52°08′N 0°04′E
180 H6 **Harsum** Niedersachsen, Germany 9°58′N 52°13′E
159 K6 **Hart** UK 54°43′N 1°16′W
72 F7 **Hart** Michigan, N USA 43°43′N 86°22′W
70 D3 **Hart** Texas, SW USA 34°23′N 102°07′W
54 B2 **Hart** ≈ Yukon Territory, NW Canada
138 D8 **Hartbees** ≈ C South Africa
140 E6 **Hartbees** ≈ Northern Cape, South Africa
177 L3 **Hartberg** Steiermark, SE Austria 47°18′N 15°58′E
276 G6 **Hart, Cape** *headland* South Australia 35°54′S 138°01′E
141 K4 **Hartebeeskop** Mpumalanga, South Africa 26°11′S 30°56′E
154 B7 **Hårteigen** ▲ S Norway 60°11′N 07°01′E
180 H2 **Hartenholm** Schleswig-Holstein, Germany 10°05′N 53°54′E
161 L4 **Hartest** UK 52°08′N 0°40′E
159 H4 **Hart Fell** ▲ UK 55°24′N 3°24′W
69 I3 **Hartford** Alabama, S USA 31°06′N 85°42′W
75 G12 **Hartford** Arkansas, C USA 35°01′N 94°22′W
65 J4 **Hartford** *state capital* Connecticut, NE USA 41°46′N 72°41′W
66 D4 **Hartford** Kentucky, S USA 37°26′N 86°57′W
73 F8 **Hartford** Michigan, N USA 42°12′N 85°54′W
74 E6 **Hartford** South Dakota, N USA 43°37′N 96°56′W
72 D7 **Hartford** Wisconsin, N USA 43°19′N 88°25′W
73 F10 **Hartford City** Indiana, N USA 40°27′N 85°22′W
159 K10 **Hartington** UK 53°08′N 1°49′W
74 E6 **Hartington** Nebraska, C USA 42°37′N 97°15′W
154 G2 **Hartkjølen** ▲ C Norway 64°21′N 13°57′E
63 L2 **Hartland** New Brunswick, SE Canada 46°18′N 67°31′W
160 D7 **Hartland Point** *headland* SW England, UK 51°01′N 04°33′W
161 H4 **Hartlebury** UK 52°20′N 2°14′W
159 K6 **Hartlepool** N England, UK 54°41′N 01°13′W
74 F6 **Hartley** Iowa, C USA 43°10′N 95°28′W
70 D1 **Hartley** Texas, SW USA 35°52′N 102°24′W
76 D8 **Hart Mountain** ▲ Oregon, NW USA 42°24′N 119°46′W
289 I10 **Hartog Ridge** *undersea feature* W Indian Ocean
153 H9 **Hartola** Etelä-Suomi, S Finland 61°34′N 26°04′E
161 H5 **Hartpury** UK 51°55′N 2°18′W
121 L9 **Harts** *var.* Hartz. ≈ N South Africa
66 D7 **Hartselle** Alabama, S USA 34°26′N 86°56′W
66 F8 **Hartsfield Atlanta** ✈ Georgia, SE USA 33°38′N 84°24′W
75 F13 **Hartshorne** Oklahoma, C USA 34°51′N 95°33′W
141 H4 **Hartsrivier** ≈ North-West, South Africa
67 J8 **Hartsville** South Carolina, SE USA 34°22′N 80°04′W
66 E5 **Hartsville** Tennessee, S USA 36°23′N 86°11′W
141 H5 **Hartswater** Northern Cape, South Africa 27°46′S 24°49′E
75 H11 **Hartville** Missouri, C USA 37°15′N 92°30′W
66 G8 **Hartwell** Georgia, SE USA 34°21′N 82°55′W
67 H8 **Hartwell Lake** ⊠ Georgia/South Carolina, SE USA
Hartz *see* Harts
Harunabad *see* Eslāmābād
Har-Us *see* Erdenebüren
236 D3 **Harus Nuur** ◎ NW Mongolia
81 G10 **Harvard** California, USA 34°57′N 116°40′W
73 D8 **Harvard** Illinois, N USA 42°25′N 88°36′W
75 D8 **Harvard** Nebraska, C USA 40°37′N 98°06′W
79 L4 **Harvard, Mount** ▲ Colorado, C USA 38°55′N 106°19′W
73 D9 **Harvey** Illinois, N USA 41°36′N 87°39′W
74 C2 **Harvey** North Dakota, N USA 47°43′N 99°55′W
161 I6 **Harwell** UK 51°36′N 1°17′W
161 M5 **Harwich** E England, UK 51°56′N 01°16′E
232 E5 **Haryāna** *var.* Hariana. ◈ *state* N India
221 K5 **Ḥaryān, Ṭawī al** *spring/well* NE Oman 21°56′N 58°33′E
180 I7 **Harz** ▲▲ C Germany
Ḥasakah, Muḥāfaẓat al *see* Al Ḥasakah
253 D10 **Hasama** Miyagi, Honshū, C Japan 38°42′N 141°09′E
214 E7 **Hasan Dağı** ▲ C Turkey 38°09′N 34°15′E
217 J6 **Ḥasan Ibn Ḥassūn** C Iraq 32°24′N 44°13′E
231 H4 **Ḥasan Khēl** *var.* Ahmad Khel. Paktīā, SE Afghanistan 33°46′N 69°37′E
219 F10 **Ḥasā, Wādī al** *dry watercourse* Jordan
180 D5 **Hase** ≈ NW Germany
Haselberg *see* Krasnoznamensk
180 G2 **Haseldorf** Schleswig-Holstein, Germany 9°36′N 53°37′E
180 D5 **Haselünne** Niedersachsen, NW Germany 52°40′N 07°28′E
114 C4 **Hasenkamp** Entre Ríos, Argentina 31°31′S 59°51′W
Hashaat *see* Delgerhangay
Hashemite Kingdom of Jordan *see* Jordan
217 K5 **Hāshimah** E Iraq 33°22′N 45°56′E
251 H5 **Hashimoto** *var.* Hasimoto. Wakayama, Honshū, SW Japan 34°19′N 135°33′E
222 D2 **Hashtrūd** *var* Azaran. Āžarbāyjān-e Khāvarī, N Iran 37°34′N 47°10′E
221 J7 **Ḥāsik** S Oman 17°22′N 55°18′E
231 I6 **Hāsilpur** Punjab, E Pakistan 29°42′N 72°40′E
Hasimoto *see* Hashimoto
75 F12 **Haskell** Oklahoma, C USA 35°49′N 95°40′W
70 F4 **Haskell** Texas, SW USA 33°10′N 99°45′W
178 I2 **Hasle** Bornholm, E Denmark 55°12′N 14°43′E
161 J7 **Haslemere** SE England, UK 51°06′N 00°45′W
159 J9 **Haslingden** UK 53°42′N 2°20′W
164 F8 **Hasparren** Pyrénées-Atlantiques, SW France 43°23′N 01°18′W
218 G2 **Hasroûn** Lebanon
Hassakeh *see* Al Ḥasakah
234 D7 **Hassan** Karnātaka, W India 13°01′N 76°03′E
79 H8 **Hassayampa River** ≈ Arizona, SW USA
181 I11 **Hassberge** *hill range* C Germany
180 G5 **Hassbergen** Niedersachsen, Germany 9°14′N 52°44′E
154 H5 **Hassela** Gävleborg, C Sweden 62°06′N 16°45′E
52 G3 **Hassel Sound** *Sea waterway* Nunavut, N Canada
163 F10 **Hasselt** Limburg, NE Belgium 50°56′N 05°20′E
162 H5 **Hasselt** Overijssel, E Netherlands 52°36′N 06°06′E
Hassetché *see* Al Ḥasakah
181 I12 **Hassfurt** Bayern, C Germany 50°02′N 10°32′E
171 L10 **Hassi Bahbah** Algeria
131 J5 **Hassi Bel Guebbour** E Algeria 28°41′N 06°29′E
131 J3 **Hassi Messaoud** E Algeria 31°41′N 06°10′E
155 G12 **Hässleholm** Skåne, S Sweden 56°09′N 13°45′E
181 E13 **Hassloch** Rheinland-Pfalz, Germany 8°15′N 49°22′E
Hasta Colonia/Hasta Pompeia *see* Asti
277 J7 **Hastings** Victoria, SE Australia 38°18′S 145°12′E
279 I6 **Hastings** Hawke′s Bay, North Island, New Zealand 39°39′S 176°51′E
161 L8 **Hastings** SE England, UK 50°51′N 00°36′E
73 F8 **Hastings** Michigan, N USA 42°38′N 85°17′W
74 H5 **Hastings** Minnesota, N USA 44°44′N 92°51′W
75 D8 **Hastings** Nebraska, C USA 40°35′N 98°23′W
155 G11 **Hästveda** Skåne, S Sweden 56°16′N 13°55′E
152 G3 **Hasvik** Finnmark, N Norway 70°29′N 22°08′E
79 N4 **Haswell** Colorado, C USA 38°27′N 103°09′W
239 L3 **Hatanbulag** *var.* Ergel. Dornogovĭ, SE Mongolia 43°10′N 109°13′E
Hatansuudal *see* Bayanlig
239 M1 **Hatavch** Sühbaatar, E Mongolia 46°10′N 112°57′E
214 G8 **Hatay** ◈ *province* S Turkey
79 L9 **Hatch** New Mexico, SW USA 32°40′N 107°10′W
79 H5 **Hatch** Utah, W USA 37°39′N 112°25′W
66 B6 **Hatchie River** ≈ Tennessee, S USA
188 C8 **Haţeg** *Ger.* Wallenthal, *Hung.* Hátszeg; *prev.* Hatzeg, Hötzing. Hunedoara, SW Romania 45°35′N 22°57′E
250 E10 **Hateruma-jima** *island* Yaeyama-shotō, SW Japan
277 I5 **Hatfield** New South Wales, SE Australia 33°54′S 143°43′E
159 L9 **Hatfield** UK 53°34′N 0°59′W
233 L8 **Hathazari** Chittagong, SE Bangladesh 22°30′N 91°46′E
160 E8 **Hatherleigh** UK 50°49′N 4°04′W
159 K10 **Hathersage** UK 53°19′N 1°39′W
221 I7 **Hathūt, Hiṣā′** *oasis* NE Yemen
256 G9 **Ha Tiên** Kiên Giang, S Vietnam 10°24′N 104°30′E
257 H6 **Ha Tinh** Ha Tinh, N Vietnam 18°21′N 105°55′E
Hatiôzi *see* Hachiōji
216 B8 **Hatira, Haré** *hill range* S Israel
256 G4 **Hat Lot** *var* Mai Son. Son La, N Vietnam 21°07′N 104°10′E
102 F2 **Hato Airport** ✈ (Willemstad) Curaçao, SW Netherlands Antilles 12°10′N 68°56′W
102 D5 **Hato Corozal** Casanare, C Colombia 06°08′N 71°45′W
Hato del Volcán *see* Volcán
91 I6 **Hato Mayor** E Dominican Republic 18°49′N 69°16′W
Hatra *see* Al Ḥaḍr
Hatria *see* Adria
Hátszeg *see* Haţeg
223 H10 **Ḥattá** Dubayy, NE United Arab Emirates 24°50′N 56°06′E
277 H5 **Hattah** Victoria, SE Australia 34°49′S 142°18′E
162 H5 **Hattem** Gelderland, E Netherlands 52°29′N 06°04′E
67 M6 **Hatteras** Hatteras Island, North Carolina, SE USA 35°13′N 75°39′W
67 N6 **Hatteras, Cape** *headland* North Carolina, SE USA 35°29′N 75°33′W
67 N6 **Hatteras Island** *island* North Carolina, SE USA
290 C5 **Hatteras Plain** *undersea feature* W Atlantic Ocean
152 E6 **Hattfjelldal** Troms, N Norway 65°37′N 13°58′E
68 F3 **Hattiesburg** Mississippi, S USA 31°20′N 89°17′W
181 C8 **Hattingen** Nordrhein-Westfalen, Germany 7°10′N 51°24′E
74 E2 **Hatton** North Dakota, N USA 47°38′N 97°27′W
Hatton Bank *see* Hatton Ridge
290 G2 **Hatton Ridge** *var.* Hatton Bank. *undersea feature* N Atlantic Ocean
285 K4 **Hatutu** *island* Îles Marquises, NE French Polynesia
183 G11 **Hatvan** Heves, NE Hungary 47°40′N 19°39′E
256 E11 **Hat Yai** *var.* Ban Hat Yai. Songkhla, SW Thailand 07°01′N 100°27′E
Hatzeg *see* Haţeg
Hatzfeld *see* Jimbolia
167 H2 **Haubourdin** Nord-Pas-de-Calais, France 50°36′N 2°59′E
136 H4 **Haud** *plateau* Ethiopia/Somalia
167 K5 **Haudainville** Lorraine, France 49°07′N 5°25′E
181 D14 **Hauenstein** Rheinland-Pfalz, Germany 7°51′N 49°11′E
155 B9 **Hauge** Rogaland, S Norway 58°20′N 06°17′E
155 A8 **Haugesund** Rogaland, S Norway 59°24′N 05°17′E
161 M4 **Haughley** UK 52°13′N 0°58′E
177 L1 **Haugsdorf** Niederösterreich, NE Austria 48°41′N 16°04′E
279 H5 **Hauhungaroa Range** ▲▲ North Island, New Zealand
154 C7 **Haukeligrend** Telemark, S Norway 59°45′N 07°33′E
152 H7 **Haukipudas** Oulu, C Finland 65°11′N 25°21′E
153 I8 **Haukivesi** ◎ SE Finland
153 I9 **Haukivuori** Isä-Suomi, E Finland 62°02′N 27°11′E
Hauptkanal *see* Havelländ Grosse
141 H4 **Hauptsrus** North-West, South Africa 26°33′S 26°17′E
281 K4 **Hauraha** San Cristobal, SE Solomon Islands 10°47′S 162°00′E
278 G3 **Hauraki Gulf** *gulf* North Island, N New Zealand
278 B12 **Hauroko, Lake** ◎ South Island, New Zealand
257 H10 **Hâu, Sông** ≈ S Vietnam
152 I5 **Hautajärvi** Lappi, NE Finland 66°30′N 29°01′E
130 F3 **Haut Atlas** *Eng.* High Atlas. ▲▲ C Morocco
134 H7 **Haut-Congo** *off.* Région du Haut-Congo, *prev* Haut-Zaïre. ◈ *region* NE Dem. Rep. Congo
174 C7 **Haute-Corse** ◈ *department* Corse, France, C Mediterranean Sea
168 F2 **Hautefort** Aquitaine, France 45°15′N 1°09′E
165 H8 **Haute-Garonne** ◈ *department* S France
134 G4 **Haute-Kotto** ◈ *prefecture* E Central African Republic
165 I7 **Haute-Loire** ◈ *department* C France
165 J4 **Haute-Marne** ◈ *department* N France
164 G2 **Haute-Normandie** ◈ *region* N France
59 I7 **Hauterive** Québec, SE Canada 49°11′N 68°16′W
165 K7 **Hautes-Alpes** ◈ *department* SE France
165 K4 **Haute-Saône** ◈ *department* E France
165 K6 **Haute-Savoie** ◈ *department* E France
163 H11 **Hautes Fagnes** *Ger.* Hohes Venn. ▲▲ E Belgium
164 G9 **Hautes-Pyrénées** ◈ *department* S France
163 H13 **Haute Sûre, Lac de la** ⊠ NW Luxembourg
165 H6 **Haute-Vienne** ◈ *department* C France
169 K1 **Hauteville-Lompnes** Rhône-Alpes, France 45°58′N 5°36′E
63 L4 **Haut, Isle au** *island* Maine, NE USA
134 H5 **Haut-Mbomou** ◈ *prefecture* SE Central African Republic
165 I2 **Hautmont** Nord, N France 50°15′N 03°55′E
135 C8 **Haut-Ogooué** *off.* Province du Haut-Ogooué, *var.* Le Haut-Ogooué. ◈ *province* SE Gabon
Haut-Ogooué, Le *see* Haut-Ogooué
Haut-Ogooué, Province du *see* Haut-Ogooué
165 K4 **Haut-Rhin** ◈ *department* NE France
131 H2 **Hauts Plateaux** *plateau* Algeria/Morocco
Haut-Zaïre *see* Haut-Congo
82 C2 **Hau′ula** *var.* Hauula. O′ahu, Hawai′i, USA 21°36′N 157°54′W
Hauula *see* Hau′ula
179 I12 **Hauzenberg** Bayern, SE Germany 48°39′N 13°37′E
73 B10 **Havana** Illinois, N USA 40°18′N 90°03′W
Havana *see* La Habana
161 J8 **Havant** S England, UK 50°51′N 00°59′W
81 J12 **Havasu, Lake** ⊠ Arizona/California, W USA
155 E12 **Havdrup** Roskilde, E Denmark 55°33′N 12°08′E
178 H5 **Havel** ≈ NE Germany
163 F11 **Havelange** Namur, SE Belgium 50°23′N 05°14′E

◆ Country
● Country Capital
◇ Dependent Territory
○ Dependent Territory Capital
◈ Administrative Regions
✈ International Airport
▲ Mountain
▲▲ Mountain Range
Volcano
≈ River
◎ Lake
⊠ Reservoir

INDEX

◆ Country
● Country Capital
◇ Dependent Territory
○ Dependent Territory Capital
◇ Administrative Regions
✕ International Airport
▲ Mountain
▲ Mountain Range
♦ Volcano
↔ River
◎ Lake
▨ Reservoir

◆ Country   ◇ Dependent Territory   ✕ Administrative Regions   ▲ Mountain   ⊚ Volcano   ⊚ Lake
● Country Capital ○ Dependent Territory Capital ✈ International Airport   ▲ Mountain Range ▲▼ River   ⊡ Reservoir

◆ Country   ◇ Dependent Territory   ◈ Administrative Regions   ▲ Mountain   ◆ Volcano   ◎ Lake
● Country Capital   ○ Dependent Territory Capital × International Airport   ▲ Mountain Range   ◇ River   ◎ Reservoir

King Christian IX Land - Kohāt
INDEX
360

King Christian IX Land *see* Kong Christian IX Land
King Christian X Land *see* Kong Christian X Land
80 B5 **King City** California, W USA 36°12′N 121°09′W
75 G8 **King City** Missouri, C USA 40°03′N 94°31′W
82 G9 **King Cove** Alaska, USA 55°03′N 162°19′W
75 D12 **Kingfisher** Oklahoma, C USA 35°53′N 97°56′W
King Frederik VI Coast *see* Kong Frederik VI Kyst
King Frederik VIII Land *see* Kong Frederik VIII Land
117 H11 **King George Bay** *bay* West Falkland, Falkland Islands
292 D2 **King George Island** *var.* King George Land. *island* South Shetland Islands, Antarctica
58 F3 **King George Islands** *island group* Northwest Territories, C Canada
King George Land *see* King George Island
159 I3 **Kinghorn** UK 56°04′N 3°10′W
194 C8 **Kingisepp** Leningradskaya Oblast', NW Russian Federation 59°23′N 28°37′E
277 I8 **King Island** *island* Tasmania, SE Australia
56 B5 **King Island** *island* British Columbia, SW Canada
King Island *see* Kadan Kyun
Kingissepp *see* Kuressaare
220 G4 **King Khalid** ✈ (Ar Riyāḍ) Ar Riyāḍ, C Saudi Arabia 25°00′N 46°40′E
78 D2 **King Lear Peak** ▲ Nevada, W USA 41°13′N 118°30′W
293 L5 **King Leopold and Queen Astrid Land** *physical region* Antarctica
274 F3 **King Leopold Ranges** ▲▲ Western Australia
81 J11 **Kingman** Arizona, SW USA 35°12′N 114°02′W
75 D10 **Kingman** Kansas, C USA 37°39′N 98°07′W
286 G5 **Kingman Reef** ◇ *US territory* C Pacific Ocean
53 M8 **Kingnait Fiord** *coastal sea feature* Nunavut, NE Canada
64 F7 **King of Prussia** Pennsylvania, USA 40°05′N 75°24′W
135 H8 **Kingombe** Maniema, E Dem. Rep. Congo 02°37′S 26°39′E
276 F3 **Kingoonya** South Australia 30°56′S 135°20′E
292 F6 **King Peninsula** *peninsula* Antarctica
83 H7 **King Salmon** Alaska, USA 58°41′N 156°39′W
78 C3 **Kings Beach** California, W USA 39°13′N 120°02′W
160 F9 **Kingsbridge** UK 50°17′N 3°46′W
80 D6 **Kingsburg** California, W USA 36°30′N 119°33′W
80 F6 **Kings Canyon** *valley* California, USA
81 D9 **Kings Canyon** *valley* California, USA
161 I7 **Kingsclere** UK 51°19′N 1°15′W
161 J3 **Kings Cliffe** UK 52°34′N 0°30′W
276 G6 **Kingscote** South Australia 35°41′S 137°36′E
141 J7 **Kingscote** KwaZulu-Natal, South Africa 30°01′S 29°22′E
King's County *see* Offaly
158 D8 **Kingscourt** Cavan, Ireland 53°54′N 6°48′W
292 D2 **King Sejong** *South Korean research station* Antarctica
277 L5 **Kingsford Smith** ✈ (Sydney) New South Wales, SE Australia 33°58′S 151°09′E
57 H9 **Kingsgate** British Columbia, SW Canada 48°58′N 116°09′W
160 G4 **Kingsland** UK 52°15′N 2°48′W
69 L3 **Kingsland** Georgia, SE USA 30°48′N 81°41′W
161 H2 **Kingsley** UK 53°01′N 1°59′W
74 F6 **Kingsley** Iowa, C USA 42°35′N 95°58′W
161 L3 **King's Lynn** *var.* Bishop's Lynn, Kings Lynn, Lynn, Lynn Regis. E England, UK 52°45′N 00°24′E
Kings Lynn *see* King's Lynn
67 I7 **Kings Mountain** North Carolina, SE USA 35°15′N 81°20′W
274 E3 **King Sound** *sound* Western Australia
79 I2 **Kings Peak** ▲ Utah, W USA 40°43′N 110°27′W
67 H5 **Kingsport** Tennessee, S USA 36°32′N 82°33′W
80 D6 **Kings River** ≈ California, W USA
277 J10 **Kingston** Tasmania, SE Australia 42°57′S 147°18′E
62 F4 **Kingston** Ontario, SE Canada 44°14′N 76°30′W
90 F8 **Kingston** ● (Jamaica) E Jamaica 17°58′N 76°48′W
278 C11 **Kingston** Otago, South Island, New Zealand 45°20′S 168°45′E
65 M3 **Kingston** Massachusetts, NE USA 41°59′N 70°43′W
75 G9 **Kingston** Missouri, C USA 39°36′N 94°02′W
80 I3 **Kingston** Nevada, USA 39°13′N 117°04′W
65 H3 **Kingston** New York, NE USA 41°55′N 74°00′W
73 H11 **Kingston** Ohio, N USA 39°28′N 82°54′W
65 L4 **Kingston** Rhode Island, NE USA 41°28′N 71°31′W
66 F6 **Kingston** Tennessee, S USA 35°52′N 84°30′W
81 H9 **Kingston Peak** ▲ California, W USA 35°43′N 115°54′W
160 G6 **Kingston Seymour** UK 51°24′N 2°52′W
277 H6 **Kingston Southeast** South Australia 36°51′S 139°53′E
159 M9 **Kingston upon Hull** *var.* Hull. E England, UK 53°45′N 00°20′W
161 K6 **Kingston upon Thames** SE England, UK 51°26′N 00°18′W
91 M3 **Kingstown** ● (Saint Vincent and the Grenadines) Saint Vincent, Saint Vincent and the Grenadines 13°09′N 61°14′W
Kingstown *see* Dún Laoghaire
67 J8 **Kingstree** South Carolina, SE USA 33°40′N 79°50′W
290 G4 **Kings Trough** *undersea feature* E Atlantic Ocean
62 A6 **Kingsville** Ontario, S Canada 42°03′N 82°43′W
70 G9 **Kingsville** Texas, SW USA 27°32′N 97°53′W
160 F9 **Kingswear** UK 50°21′N 3°34′W
161 H6 **Kingswood** UK 51°27′N 2°31′W
160 G4 **Kington** UK 52°12′N 3°01′W
67 L4 **King William** Virginia, NE USA 37°42′N 77°03′W
52 G8 **King William Island** *island* Nunavut, N Canada Arctic Ocean
138 G9 **King William's Town** *var.* King, Kingwilliamstown. Eastern Cape, S South Africa 32°53′S 27°24′E
Kingwilliamstown *see* King William's Town
67 J2 **Kingwood** West Virginia, NE USA 39°27′N 79°43′W
214 B6 **Kınık** İzmir, W Turkey 39°05′N 27°25′E
158 B10 **Kinitty** Offaly, Ireland 53°06′N 7°43′W
135 C9 **Kinkala** Le Pool, S Congo 04°18′S 14°49′E
253 E10 **Kinka-san** *headland* Honshū, C Japan 38°17′N 141°34′E
279 H5 **Kinleith** Waikato, North Island, New Zealand 38°16′S 175°53′E
158 F1 **Kinlocheil** UK 56°51′N 5°20′W
158 G1 **Kinloch Rannoch** UK 56°42′N 4°11′W
155 F10 **Kinna** Älvsborg, S Sweden 57°32′N 12°42′E
156 F3 **Kinnaird Head** *var.* Kinnairds Head. *headland* NE Scotland, UK 58°39′N 03°22′W
Kinnairds Head *see* Kinnaird Head
155 F11 **Kinnared** Halland, S Sweden 57°01′N 13°04′E
158 C9 **Kinnegad** Westmeath, Ireland 53°27′N 7°06′W
Kinneret, Yam *see* Tiberias, Lake
235 G10 **Kinniyai** Eastern Province, NE Sri Lanka 08°30′N 81°11′E
153 H8 **Kinnula** Länsi-Soumi, C Finland 63°24′N 25°E
251 H5 **Kino-kawa** ≈ Honshū, SW Japan
55 H6 **Kinoosao** Saskatchewan, C Canada 57°06′N 101°02′W
163 G9 **Kinrooi** Limburg, NE Belgium 51°09′N 05°48′E
159 H2 **Kinross** C Scotland, UK 56°14′N 03°27′W
156 F6 **Kinross** *cultural region* C Scotland, UK
157 B11 **Kinsale** *Ir.* Cionn tSáile. Cork, SW Ireland 51°42′N 08°32′W
154 B7 **Kinsarvik** Hordaland, S Norway 60°22′N 06°43′E
135 D9 **Kinshasa** *prev.* Léopoldville. ● Kinshasa, W Dem. Rep. Congo 04°21′S 15°16′E
135 D9 **Kinshasa** *off.* Ville de Kinshasa, *var.* Kinshasa City. ◐ *region* (Dem. Rep. Congo) SW Dem. Rep. Congo
135 D9 **Kinshasa** ✈ Kinshasa, SW Dem. Rep. Congo 04°23′S 15°30′E
Kinshasa City *see* Kinshasa
189 K6 **Kins'ka** ≈ SE Ukraine
75 C10 **Kinsley** Kansas, C USA 37°55′N 99°26′W
67 L6 **Kinston** North Carolina, SE USA 35°16′N 77°35′W
132 G7 **Kintampo** W Ghana 08°06′N 01°40′W
161 I6 **Kintbury** UK 51°23′N 1°26′W
276 C1 **Kintore, Mount** ▲ South Australia 26°30′S 130°24′E
158 E4 **Kintour** UK 55°41′N 6°03′W
156 E7 **Kintyre** *peninsula* W Scotland, UK
156 E7 **Kintyre, Mull of** *headland* W Scotland, UK 55°16′N 05°46′W
256 C4 **Kin-u** Sagaing, C Myanmar (Burma) 22°47′N 95°36′E
58 E4 **Kinushseo** ≈ Ontario, C Canada
57 H3 **Kinuso** Alberta, W Canada 55°19′N 115°23′W
158 A10 **Kinvarra** Galway, Ireland 53°08′N 8°56′W
234 F4 **Kinwat** Mahārāshtra, C India 19°37′N 78°12′E
136 B6 **Kinyeti** ▲ S Sudan 03°56′N 32°52′E
179 C12 **Kinzig** ≈ SW Germany
280 F8 **Kioa** *island* N Fiji
Kioga, Lake *see* Kyoga, Lake
75 D11 **Kiowa** Kansas, C USA 37°01′N 98°29′W
75 F13 **Kiowa** Oklahoma, C USA 34°43′N 95°54′W
Kiparissía *see* Kyparissía
62 D1 **Kipawa, Lac** ◎ Québec, SE Canada
190 H3 **Kipen'** Leningradskaya Oblast', Russian Federation
137 C11 **Kipengere Range** ▲▲ SW Tanzania
137 A11 **Kipili** Rukwa, W Tanzania 07°30′S 30°39′E
137 F9 **Kipini** Coast, SE Kenya 02°30′S 40°30′E
55 H10 **Kipling** Saskatchewan, S Canada 50°04′N 102°45′W
82 G7 **Kipnuk** Alaska, USA 59°56′N 164°02′W
159 K9 **Kippax** UK 53°46′N 1°22′W
158 G3 **Kippen** UK 56°07′N 4°10′W
157 D9 **Kippure** *Ir.* Cipiúr. ▲ E Ireland 53°10′N 06°22′W
160 B2 **Kippure** ▲ Ireland 53°11′N 6°20′W
135 I12 **Kipushi** Katanga, SE Dem. Rep. Congo 11°45′S 27°20′E
281 K3 **Kirakira** *var.* Kaokaona. San Cristobal, SE Solomon Islands 10°28′S 161°54′E
234 G5 **Kirandul** *var.* Bailādila. Chhattīsgarh, C India 18°46′N 81°18′E
235 F8 **Kīranūr** Tamil Nādu, SE India 11°37′N 79°10′E
191 H12 **Kiraw** *Rus.* Kirovo. Homyel'skaya Voblasts', SE Belarus 51°30′N 29°25′E
191 H10 **Kirawsk** *Rus.* Kirovsk; *prev.* Startsy. Mahilyowskaya Voblasts', E Belarus 53°16′N 29°29′E
187 L6 **Kiraz** İzmir, Turkey 38°14′N 28°12′E
181 E11 **Kirberg** Hessen, Germany 8°10′N 50°19′E
190 D4 **Kirbla** Läänemaa, W Estonia 58°45′N 23°57′E
71 J6 **Kirbyville** Texas, SW USA 30°39′N 93°53′W
187 K2 **Kircasalih** Edirne, Turkey 41°24′N 26°48′E
177 L4 **Kirchbach** *var.* Kirchbach in Steiermark. Steiermark, SE Austria 46°55′N 15°40′E
Kirchbach in Steiermark *see* Kirchbach
177 J3 **Kirchdorf an der Krems** Oberösterreich, N Austria 47°55′N 14°08′E
181 E12 **Kircheimbolanden** Rheinland-Pfalz, Germany 8°01′N 49°40′E
181 I9 **Kirchheilingen** Thüringen, Germany 10°42′N 51°11′E
181 G14 **Kirchheim** Baden-Württemberg, Germany 9°09′N 49°03′E
181 H13 **Kirchheim** Bayern, Germany 9°52′N 49°39′E
181 G10 **Kirchheim** Hessen, Germany 9°34′N 50°50′E
Kirchheim *see* Kirchheim unter Teck
179 D12 **Kirchheim unter Teck** *var.* Kirchheim. Baden-Württemberg, SW Germany 48°39′N 09°28′E
181 E9 **Kirchhundem** Nordrhein-Westfalen, Germany 8°06′N 51°06′E
180 G4 **Kirchlinteln** Niedersachsen, Germany 9°19′N 52°57′E
180 H3 **Kirchwerder** Hamburg, Germany 10°12′N 53°25′E
Kirdzhali *see* Kŭrdzhali
193 I7 **Kirenga** ≈ S Russian Federation
193 I7 **Kirensk** Irkutskaya Oblast', C Russian Federation 57°37′N 107°54′E
Kirghizia *see* Kyrgyzstan
229 L4 **Kirghiz Range** *Rus.* Kirgizskiy Khrebet; *prev.* Alexander Range. ▲▲ Kazakhstan/Kyrgyzstan
Kirghiz SSR *see* Kyrgyzstan
Kirghiz Steppe *see* Kazakhskiy Melkosopochnik
Kirgizskaya SSR *see* Kyrgyzstan
Kirgizskiy Khrebet *see* Kirghiz Range
135 E8 **Kiri** Bandundu, W Dem. Rep. Congo 01°29′S 19°00′E
Kiriath-Arba *see* Hebron
284 G4 **Kiribati** *off.* Republic of Kiribati. ◆ *republic* C Pacific Ocean
Kiribati, Republic of *see* Kiribati
214 G8 **Kırıkhan** Hatay, S Turkey 36°30′N 36°20′E
214 E5 **Kırıkkale** Kırıkkale, C Turkey 39°50′N 33°31′E
214 E5 **Kırıkkale** ◐ *province* C Turkey
194 F8 **Kirillov** Vologodskaya Oblast', NW Russian Federation 59°52′N 38°24′E
Kirin *see* Jilin
137 D8 **Kirinyaga** *prev.* Mount Kenya. ⋀ C Kenya 0°02′S 37°19′E
194 D8 **Kirishi** *var.* Kirisi. Leningradskaya Oblast', NW Russian Federation 59°28′N 32°02′E
250 D8 **Kirishima-yama** ▲ Kyūshū, SW Japan 31°58′N 130°51′E
Kirisi *see* Kirishi
285 N1 **Kiritimati** ✈ Kiritimati, E Kiribati 02°00′N 157°30′W
285 N1 **Kiritimati** *prev.* Christmas Island. *atoll* Line Islands, E Kiribati
280 D4 **Kiriwina Island** *Eng.* Trobriand Island. *island* SE Papua New Guinea
280 D4 **Kiriwina Islands** *var.* Trobriand Islands. *island group* S Papua New Guinea
187 L5 **Kırkağaç** Manisa, Turkey 39°06′N 27°40′E
159 H6 **Kirkbean** UK 54°55′N 3°37′W
159 I9 **Kirkby** UK 53°29′N 2°54′W
159 L10 **Kirkby in Ashfield** UK 53°05′N 1°16′W
159 K8 **Kirkby Malzeard** UK 54°10′N 1°39′W
159 L7 **Kirkby Moorside** UK 54°16′N 0°56′W
159 J7 **Kirkby Stephen** UK 54°28′N 2°21′W
159 I3 **Kirkcaldy** E Scotland, UK 56°07′N 03°10′W
159 I5 **Kirkcambeck** UK 55°00′N 2°44′W
158 F6 **Kirkcolm** UK 54°58′N 5°05′W
159 H4 **Kirkconnel** UK 55°23′N 4°00′W
158 G6 **Kirkcowan** UK 54°54′N 4°36′W
159 H6 **Kirkcudbright** S Scotland, U 54°50′N 04°03′W
156 E7 **Kirkcudbright** *cultural region* S Scotland, UK
Kirkee *see* Khadki
154 E7 **Kirkenær** Hedmark, S Norway 60°27′N 12°04′E
152 I3 **Kirkenes** *Fin.* Kirkkoniemi. Finnmark, N Norway 69°43′N 30°02′E
158 G6 **Kirkinner** UK 54°49′N 4°27′W
158 G3 **Kirkintilloch** UK 55°55′N 4°10′W
152 C3 **Kirkjubæjarklaustur** Sudhurland, S Iceland 63°46′N 18°03′W
Kirk-Kilissa *see* Kırklareli
Kirkkoniemi *see* Kirkenes
153 H10 **Kirkkonummi** *Swe.* Kyrkslätt. Uusimaa, S Finland 60°06′N 24°20′E
58 F7 **Kirkland Lake** Ontario, S Canada 48°10′N 80°02′W
214 B4 **Kırklareli** *prev.* Kirk-Kilissa. Kırklareli, NW Turkey 41°45′N 27°12′E
214 B4 **Kırklareli** ◐ *province* NW Turkey
159 H3 **Kirkliston** UK 55°57′N 3°24′W
278 D10 **Kirkliston Range** ▲▲ South Island, New Zealand
158 F6 **Kirkmaiden** UK 54°41′N 4°55′W
159 I6 **Kirkoswald** UK 54°46′N 2°42′W
159 H5 **Kirkpatrick Durham** UK 55°01′N 3°54′W
62 A1 **Kirkpatrick Lake** ◎ Ontario, S Canada
293 I6 **Kirkpatrick, Mount** ▲ Antarctica 84°37′S 164°36′E
75 H8 **Kirksville** Missouri, C USA 40°12′N 92°35′W
159 I1 **Kirkton of Glenisla** UK 56°44′N 3°17′W
159 I1 **Kirkton of Kingoldrum** UK 56°40′N 3°05′W
217 J3 **Kirkūk** *var.* Karkūk, Kerkuk. N Iraq 35°28′N 44°26′E
217 K5 **Kir Kush** E Iraq 33°42′N 45°15′E
80 C1 **Kirkville** California, USA 38°55′N 121°48′W
156 G3 **Kirkwall** NE Scotland, UK 58°59′N 02°58′W
138 F10 **Kirkwood** Eastern Cape, S South Africa 33°23′S 25°19′E
80 E3 **Kirkwood** California, USA 38°42′N 120°04′W
75 J10 **Kirkwood** Missouri, C USA 38°35′N 90°24′W
Kirman *see* Kermān
Kir Moab *see* Al Karak
Kir of Moab *see* Al Karak
196 E3 **Kirov** Kaluzhskaya Oblast', W Russian Federation 54°02′N 34°17′E
195 I9 **Kirov** *prev.* Vyatka. Kirovskaya Oblast', NW Russian Federation 58°35′N 49°39′E
Kīrov *see* Balpyk Bi
Kirovabad *see* Gäncä
Kirovabad *see* Panj
Kirovakan *see* Vanadzor
195 L9 **Kirovgrad** Sverdlovskaya oblasť, Russian federation
Kīrov/Kirova *see* Kopbirlik
Kirovo *see* Kiraw
Kirovo *see* Beshariq
195 I9 **Kirovo-Chepetsk** Kirovskaya Oblast', NW Russian Federation 58°33′N 50°06′E
189 I5 **Kirovohrad** *Rus.* Kirovograd; *prev.* Kirovo, Yelizavetgrad, Zinov'yevsk. Kirovohrads'ka Oblast', C Ukraine 48°30′N 31°17′E
Kirovohrad *see* Kirovohrads'ka Oblast'
189 I5 **Kirovohrads'ka Oblast'** *var.* Kirovohrad, *Rus.* Kirovogradskaya Oblast'. ◐ *province* C Ukraine
Kirovo/Kirovograd *see* Kirovohrad
190 I3 **Kirovsk** Leningradskaya Oblast', Russian Federation
194 E3 **Kirovsk** Murmanskaya Oblast', NW Russian Federation 67°37′N 33°38′E
189 M5 **Kirovs'k** Luhans'ka Oblast', E Ukraine 48°40′N 38°39′E
Kirovsk *see* Kirawsk, Belarus
Kirovsk *see* Babadaýhan, Turkmenistan
195 I9 **Kirovskaya Oblast'** ◐ *province* NW Russian Federation
189 M5 **Kirov'ske** Donets'ka Oblast', E Ukraine 48°12′N 38°20′E
189 K9 **Kirovs'ke** *Rus.* Kirovskoye. Respublika Krym, S Ukraine 45°13′N 35°12′E
Kirovskiy *see* Balpyk Bi
Kirovskiy *see* Ust'yevoye
Kirovskoye *see* Kyzyl-Adyr
Kirovskoye *see* Kirovs'ke
218 D1 **Kırpaşa** *Gk.* Karpasía, *var.* Karpas Peninsula. *peninsula* NE Cyprus
228 C6 **Kirpili** Ahal Welaýaty, C Turkmenistan 39°31′N 57°13′E
159 I1 **Kirriemuir** E Scotland, UK 56°38′N 03°01′W
195 J8 **Kirs** Kirovskaya Oblast', NW Russian Federation 59°22′N 52°20′E
197 H4 **Kirsanov** Tambovskaya Oblast', W Russian Federation 52°40′N 42°48′E
214 E6 **Kirşehir** *anc.* Justinianopolis. Kirşehir, C Turkey 39°09′N 34°08′E
214 E6 **Kirşehir** ◐ *province* C Turkey
230 F8 **Kīrthar Range** ▲▲ S Pakistan
79 K6 **Kirtland** New Mexico, SW USA 36°43′N 108°21′W
161 K2 **Kirton** UK 52°55′N 0°03′W
181 G10 **Kirtorf** Hessen, Germany 9°07′N 50°46′E
152 F5 **Kiruna** *Lapp.* Giron. Norrbotten, N Sweden 67°50′N 20°16′E
135 H8 **Kirundu** Orientale, NE Dem. Rep. Congo 0°45′S 25°28′E
Kirun/Kirun' *see* Chilung
75 D9 **Kirwin Reservoir** ⊠ Kansas, C USA
197 I2 **Kirya** Chavash Respubliki, W Russian Federation 55°04′N 46°50′E
253 B12 **Kiryū** Gunma, Honshū, S Japan 36°26′N 139°18′E
155 H9 **Kisa** Östergötland, S Sweden 58°N 15°39′E
253 C9 **Kisakata** Akita, Honshū, C Japan 39°12′N 139°55′E
Kisalföld *see* Little Alföld
134 H7 **Kisangani** *prev.* Stanleyville. Orientale, NE Dem. Rep. Congo 0°30′N 25°14′E
253 C14 **Kisarazu** Chiba, Honshū, S Japan 35°23′N 139°57′E
183 E11 **Kisbér** Komárom-Esztergom, NW Hungary 47°30′N 18°00′E
55 H10 **Kisbey** Saskatchewan, S Canada 49°41′N 102°39′W
192 F8 **Kiselevsk** Kemerovskaya Oblast', S Russian Federation 54°00′N 86°38′E
233 J6 **Kishanganj** Bihār, NE India 26°06′N 87°57′E
232 D6 **Kishangarh** Rājasthān, N India 26°33′N 74°52′E
Kishegyes *see* Mali Iđoš
133 I7 **Kishi** Oyo, W Nigeria 09°01′N 03°53′E
Kishinev *see* Chişinău
Kishiözen *see* Malyy Uzen'
251 H5 **Kishiwada** *var.* Kisiwada. Ōsaka, Honshū, SW Japan 34°28′N 135°22′E
222 G9 **Kīsh, Jazīreh-ye** *island* S Iran
227 I2 **Kishkenekol'** *prev.* Kzyltu, *Kaz.* Qyzyltū. Kokshetau, N Kazakhstan 53°39′N 72°22′E
232 E3 **Kishtwār** Jammu and Kashmir, NW India 33°20′N 75°49′E
137 C8 **Kisii** Nyanza, SW Kenya 0°40′S 34°47′E
137 E11 **Kisiju** Pwani, E Tanzania 07°25′S 39°20′E
Kisiwada *see* Kishiwada
Kisjenő *see* Chişineu-Criş
82 B9 **Kiska Island** *island* Aleutian Islands, Alaska, USA
Kiskapus *see* Copşa Mică
183 H11 **Kiskörei-víztároló** ⊠ E Hungary
Kis-Küküllo *see* Târnava Mică
183 G12 **Kiskunfélegyháza** *var.* Félegyháza. Bács-Kiskun, C Hungary 46°42′N 19°52′E
183 G12 **Kiskunhalas** *var.* Halas. Bács-Kiskun, S Hungary 46°26′N 19°29′E
183 G12 **Kiskunmajsa** Bács-Kiskun, S Hungary 46°30′N 19°46′E
197 H9 **Kislovodsk** Stavropol'skiy Kray, SW Russian Federation 43°55′N 42°45′E
137 G8 **Kismaayo** *var.* Chisimayu, Kismayu, *It.* Chisimaio. Jubbada Hoose, S Somalia 0°05′S 42°35′E
Kismayu *see* Kismaayo
251 K3 **Kiso-sanmyaku** ▲▲ Honshū, S Japan
187 H9 **Kíssamos** *prev* Kastélli. Kríti, Greece, E Mediterranean Sea 35°30′N 23°39′E
Kisseraing *see* Kanmaw Kyun
132 D6 **Kissidougou** Guinée-Forestière, S Guinea 09°15′N 10°08′W
69 M6 **Kissimmee** Florida, SE USA 28°17′N 81°24′W
69 M7 **Kissimmee, Lake** ◎ Florida, SE USA
69 M7 **Kissimmee River** ≈ Florida, SE USA
55 I7 **Kississing Lake** ◎ Manitoba, C Canada
183 G12 **Kistelek** Csongrád, SE Hungary 46°27′N 19°58′E
Kistna *see* Krishna
183 H12 **Kisújszállás** Jász-Nagykun-Szolnok, E Hungary 47°14′N 20°45′E
250 F4 **Kisuki** Shimane, Honshū, SW Japan 35°25′N 133°15′E
137 C8 **Kisumu** *prev.* Port Florence. Nyanza, W Kenya 0°02′N 34°42′E
Kisutzaneustadtl *see* Kysucké Nové Mesto
183 I10 **Kisvárda** *Ger.* Kleinwardein. Szabolcs-Szatmár-Bereg, E Hungary 48°13′N 22°03′E
137 E11 **Kiswere** Lindi, SE Tanzania 09°24′S 39°37′E
Kiszucaújhely *see* Kysucké Nové Mesto
132 D5 **Kita** Kayes, W Mali 13°00′N 09°28′W
295 L7 **Kitaa** ◐ *province* W Greenland
Kitab *see* Kitob
252 C5 **Kitahiyama** Hokkaidō, NE Japan 42°25′N 139°55′E
253 D12 **Kita-Ibaraki** Ibaraki, Honshū, S Japan 36°46′N 140°45′E
251 M10 **Kita-Iō-jima** *island* SE Japan
253 D9 **Kitakami** Iwate, Honshū, C Japan 39°18′N 141°05′E
253 D10 **Kitakami-gawa** ≈ Honshū, C Japan
253 E8 **Kitakami-sanchi** ▲▲ Honshū, C Japan
253 C11 **Kitakata** Fukushima, Honshū, C Japan 37°38′N 139°52′E
250 D5 **Kitakyūshū** *var.* Kitakyûsyû. Fukuoka, Kyūshū, SW Japan 33°51′N 130°49′E
Kitakyûsyû *see* Kitakyūshū
136 C7 **Kitale** Rift Valley, W Kenya 01°01′N 35°01′E
252 G3 **Kitami** Hokkaidō, NE Japan 43°52′N 143°51′E
252 F3 **Kitami-sanchi** ▲▲ Hokkaidō, NE Japan
253 D13 **Kita-ura** ◎ Honshū, S Japan
80 E3 **Kit Carson** California, USA 38°40′N 120°07′W
79 N3 **Kit Carson** Colorado, C USA 38°45′N 102°47′W
276 A4 **Kitchener** Western Australia 31°03′S 124°00′E
62 C5 **Kitchener** Ontario, S Canada 43°28′N 80°27′W
153 J8 **Kitee** Itä-Suomi, SE Finland 62°06′N 30°09′E
136 B6 **Kitgum** N Uganda 03°17′N 32°54′E
Kithareng *see* Kanmaw Kyun
Kíthira *see* Kýthira
Kíthnos *see* Kýthnos
54 G2 **Kitikmeot** ◐ *district* Northwest Territories, N Canada
56 B4 **Kitimat** British Columbia, SW Canada 54°05′N 128°38′W
152 H5 **Kitinen** ≈ N Finland
229 H7 **Kitob** *Rus.* Kitab. Qashqadaryo Viloyati, S Uzbekistan 39°06′N 66°47′E
188 E5 **Kitsman'** *Ger.* Kotzman, *Rom.* Cozmeni, *Rus.* Kitsman. Chernivets'ka Oblast', W Ukraine 48°30′N 25°50′E
250 D6 **Kitsuki** *var.* Kituki. Ōita, Kyūshū, SW Japan 33°24′N 131°36′E
62 D8 **Kittanning** Pennsylvania, NE USA 40°48′N 79°28′W
65 M1 **Kittery** Maine, NE USA 43°05′N 70°44′W
152 H5 **Kittilä** Lappi, N Finland 67°39′N 24°53′E
177 M2 **Kittsee** Burgenland, E Austria 48°06′N 17°03′E
137 E8 **Kitui** Eastern, S Kenya 01°25′S 38°00′E
Kituki *see* Kitsuki
137 C10 **Kitunda** Tabora, C Tanzania 06°47′S 33°13′E
56 B3 **Kitwanga** British Columbia, SW Canada 55°07′N 128°03′W
138 G1 **Kitwe** *var.* Kitwe-Nkana. Copperbelt, C Zambia 12°48′S 28°13′E
Kitwe-Nkana *see* Kitwe
177 H3 **Kitzbühel** Tirol, W Austria 47°27′N 12°23′E
177 H4 **Kitzbüheler Alpen** ▲▲ W Austria
181 I12 **Kitzingen** Bayern, SE Germany 49°45′N 10°11′E
233 I7 **Kiul** Bihār, NE India 25°10′N 86°06′E
280 A3 **Kiunga** Western, SW Papua New Guinea 06°10′S 141°15′E
152 H7 **Kiuruvesi** Kuopio, C Finland 63°38′N 26°40′E
82 G3 **Kivalina** Alaska, USA 67°44′N 164°32′W
152 H6 **Kivalo** *ridge* C Finland
188 E2 **Kivertsi** *Pol.* Kiwerce, *Rus.* Kivertsy. Volyns'ka Oblast', NW Ukraine 50°50′N 25°31′E
Kivertsy *see* Kivertsi
153 H8 **Kivijärvi** Länsi-Soumi, C Finland 63°09′N 25°04′E
155 G12 **Kivik** Skåne, S Sweden 55°40′N 14°15′E
190 F3 **Kiviõli** Ida-Virumaa, NE Estonia 59°20′N 27°00′E
Kivu, Lac *see* Kivu, Lake
121 L6 **Kivu, Lake** *Fr.* Lac Kivu. ◎ Rwanda/Dem. Rep. Congo
280 B4 **Kiwai Island** *island* SW Papua New Guinea
82 G4 **Kiwalik** Alaska, USA 66°01′N 161°50′W
Kiwerce *see* Kivertsi
Kiyev *see* Kyyiv
227 I4 **Kiyevka** Karaganda, C Kazakhstan 50°15′N 71°33′E
Kiyevskaya Oblast' *see* Kyyivs'ka Oblast'
Kiyevskoye Vodokhranilishche *see* Kyyivs'ke Vodoskhovyshche
214 B4 **Kīyīköy** Kırklareli, NW Turkey 41°37′N 28°07′E
227 H3 **Kiyma** Akmola, C Kazakhstan 51°37′N 67°31′E
114 G9 **Kiyú** Uruguay 34°39′S 56°45′W
195 L8 **Kizel** Permskaya Oblast', NW Russian Federation 58°59′N 57°37′E
195 H7 **Kizema** *var.* Kizëma. Arkhangel'skaya Oblast', NW Russian Federation 61°06′N 44°51′E
Kizëma *see* Kizema
Kizilagach *see* Elkhovo
214 E5 **Kızılcahamam** Ankara, N Turkey 40°28′N 32°37′E
214 E6 **Kızıl Irmak** ≈ C Turkey
Kızılkoca *see* Şefaatli
Kizil Kum *see* Kyzyl Kum
215 I7 **Kızıltepe** Mardin, SE Turkey 37°12′N 40°36′E
Ki Zil Uzen *see* Qezel Owzan, Rūd-e
197 I9 **Kizilyurt** Respublika Dagestan, SW Russian Federation 43°13′N 46°54′E
197 I9 **Kizlyar** Respublika Dagestan, SW Russian Federation 43°51′N 46°39′E
195 J10 **Kizner** Udmurtskaya Respublika, NW Russian Federation 56°19′N 51°37′E
Kizyl-Arvat *see* Serdar
Kizyl-Atrek *see* Etrek
Kizyl-Kaya *see* Gyzylgaýa
Kizyl-Su *see* Gyzylsuw
53 H7 **Cape Kjer** *headland* Nunavut, NE Canada
155 E8 **Kjerkøy** *island* S Norway
152 H3 **Kjøllefjord** Finnmark, N Norway 70°55′N 27°19′E
152 E5 **Kjøpsvik** Nordland, C Norway 68°06′N 16°21′E
258 F5 **Klabat, Teluk** *bay* Pulau Bangka, W Indonesia
184 E4 **Kladanj** ◐ Fedederacija Bosna I Hercegovina, E Bosnia and Herzegovina
261 K8 **Kladar** Papua, E Indonesia 08°14′S 137°46′E
183 B8 **Kladno** Střední Čechy, NW Czech Republic 50°10′N 14°05′E
185 H4 **Kladovo** Serbia, E Serbia 44°37′N 22°36′E
256 F8 **Klaeng** Rayong, S Thailand 12°48′N 101°41′E
177 J5 **Klagenfurt** *Slvn.* Celovec. Kärnten, S Austria 46°38′N 14°20′E
190 B7 **Klaipėda** *Ger.* Memel. Klaipeda, NW Lithuania 55°42′N 21°09′E
259 J9 **Klakah** Jawa, C Indonesia 07°55′S 113°12′E
Klaksvig *see* Klaksvík
154 B1 **Klaksvík** *Dan.* Klaksvig. Bordhoy, N Faeroe Islands 62°13′N 06°34′W
78 A1 **Klamath** California, W USA 41°31′N 124°02′W
76 C8 **Klamath Falls** Oregon, NW USA 42°14′N 121°47′W
78 B1 **Klamath Mountains** ▲▲ California/Oregon, W USA
76 B8 **Klamath River** ≈ California/Oregon, W USA
258 D3 **Klang** *var.* Kelang; *prev.* Port Swettenham. Selangor, Peninsular Malaysia 03°02′N 101°27′E
154 F6 **Klarälven** ≈ Norway/Sweden
183 B8 **Klášterec nad Ohří** *Ger.* Klösterle an der Eger. Ústecky Kraj, NW Czech Republic 50°24′N 13°10′E
259 I9 **Klaten** Jawa, C Indonesia 07°40′S 110°32′E
183 B9 **Klatovy** *Ger.* Klattau. Plzeňský Kraj, W Czech Republic 49°24′N 13°16′E
Klattau *see* Klatovy
Klausenburg *see* Cluj-Napoca
140 D8 **Klawer** Western Cape, South Africa 31°47′S 18°37′E
83 M8 **Klawock** Prince of Wales Island, Alaska, USA 55°33′N 133°06′W
162 J5 **Klazienaveen** Drenthe, NE Netherlands 52°43′N 07°E
Kleck *see* Klyetsk
182 E5 **Kłecko** Weilkopolskie, C Poland 52°37′N 17°27′E
182 F6 **Kleczew** Wielkopolskie, C Poland 52°22′N 18°12′E
56 C6 **Kleena Kleene** British Columbia, SW Canada 51°55′N 124°54′W
140 B2 **Klein Aub** Hardap, C Namibia 23°48′S 16°39′E
181 C14 **Kleinblittersdorf** Saarland, Germany 7°02′N 49°09′E
Kleine Donau *see* Mosoni-Duna
179 H8 **Kleine Elster** ≈ E Germany
Kleine Kokel *see* Târnava Mică
181 F8 **Kleinenberg** Nordrhein-Westfalen, Germany 8°59′N 51°35′E
163 F9 **Kleine Nete** ≈ N Belgium
181 G9 **Kleinenglis** Hessen, Germany 9°15′N 51°04′E
Kleines Ungarisches Tiefland *see* Little Alföld
140 C5 **Klein Karas** Karas, S Namibia 27°36′S 18°05′E
Kleinkopisch *see* Copşa Mică
141 L2 **Klein-Letaba** ≈ Limpopo, South Africa
Klein-Marien *see* Väike-Maarja
140 D10 **Kleinmond** Western Cape, South Africa 34°21′S 19°02′E
181 H12 **Kleinrinderfeld** Bayern, Germany 9°51′N 49°42′E
Kleinschlatten *see* Zlatna
138 C8 **Kleinsee** Northern Cape, W South Africa 29°43′S 17°03′E
140 G4 **Klein-Tswaing** North-West, South Africa 26°53′S 24°11′E
Kleinwardein *see* Kisvárda
186 F4 **Kleisoúra** Ípeiros, W Greece 39°21′N 20°52′E
155 A8 **Klepp** Rogaland, S Norway 58°46′N 05°39′E
138 G7 **Klerksdorp** North-West, N South Africa 26°52′S 26°39′E
141 I4 **Klerksdorp** North-West, South Africa 26°52′S 26°40′E
196 E3 **Kletnya** Bryanskaya Oblast', W Russian Federation 53°25′N 32°58′E
Kletsk *see* Klyetsk
180 B7 **Kleve** *Eng.* Cleves, *Fr.* Clèves; *prev.* Cleve. Nordrhein-Westfalen, W Germany 51°47′N 06°11′E
184 E6 **Kličevo** C Montenegro 42°45′N 18°58′E
191 H10 **Klichaw** *Rus.* Klichev. Mahilyowskaya Voblasts', E Belarus 53°29′N 29°21′E
Klichev *see* Klichaw
191 J10 **Klimavichy** *Rus.* Klimovichi. Mahilyowskaya Voblasts', E Belarus 53°37′N 31°58′E
185 L5 **Kliment** Shumen, NE Bulgaria 43°37′N 27°00′E
Klimovichi *see* Klimavichy
191 J11 **Klimovo** Bryanskaya Oblast', Russian Federation
154 G1 **Klimpfjäll** Västerbotten, N Sweden 65°05′N 14°50′E
196 F1 **Klin** Moskovskaya Oblast', W Russian Federation 56°19′N 36°45′E
184 G6 **Klina** Kosovo, S Serbia 42°38′N 20°35′E
183 A8 **Klínovec** *Ger.* Keilberg. ▲ NW Czech Republic 50°23′N 12°57′E
155 J10 **Klintehamn** Gotland, SE Sweden 57°22′N 18°15′E
197 J4 **Klintsovka** Saratovskaya Oblast', W Russian Federation 51°42′N 49°17′E
196 E3 **Klintsy** Bryanskaya Oblast', W Russian Federation 52°46′N 32°21′E
141 J5 **Klip** ≈ South Africa
155 F12 **Klippan** Skåne, S Sweden 56°08′N 13°10′E
152 E6 **Klippen** Västerbotten, N Sweden 65°50′N 15°07′E
140 G9 **Klipplaat** Eastern Cape, South Africa 33°01′S 24°20′E
140 D7 **Kliprand** Western Cape, South Africa 30°36′S 18°42′E
218 B2 **Klírou** W Cyprus 35°01′N 33°11′E
185 J6 **Klisura** Plovdiv, C Bulgaria 42°40′N 24°28′E
155 C11 **Klitmøller** Viborg, NW Denmark 57°01′N 08°29′E
184 C4 **Ključ** ◐ Federacija Bosna I Hercegovina, NW Bosnia and Herzegovina
182 F7 **Kłobuck** Śląskie, S Poland 50°56′N 18°55′E
182 F6 **Kłodawa** Wielkopolskie, C Poland 52°14′N 18°55′E
183 D8 **Kłodzko** *Ger.* Glatz. Dolnośląskie, SW Poland 50°27′N 16°37′E
154 E7 **Kløfta** Akershus, S Norway 60°04′N 11°06′E
185 H4 **Klokočevac** Serbia, E Serbia 44°19′N 22°11′E
190 D3 **Klooga** *Ger.* Lodensee. Harjumaa, NW Estonia 59°18′N 24°10′E
163 D9 **Kloosterzande** Zeeland, SW Netherlands 51°22′N 04°01′E
184 F8 **Klos** *var.* Klosi. Dibër, C Albania 41°30′N 20°07′E
Klosi *see* Klos
Klösterle an der Eger *see* Klášterec nad Ohří
177 L2 **Klosterneuburg** Niederösterreich, NE Austria 48°19′N 16°20′E
176 F4 **Klosters** Graubünden, SE Switzerland 46°54′N 09°52′E
174 C2 **Kloten** Zürich, N Switzerland 47°27′N 08°35′E
174 C2 **Kloten** ✈ (Zürich) Zürich, N Switzerland 47°25′N 08°36′E
181 C11 **Klotten** Rheinland-Pfalz, Germany 7°12′N 50°10′E
180 J5 **Klötze** Sachsen-Anhalt, C Germany 52°37′N 11°09′E
58 G2 **Klotz, Lac** ◎ Québec, NE Canada
179 I8 **Klotzsche** ✈ (Dresden) Sachsen, E Germany 51°06′N 13°44′E
54 A3 **Kluane Lake** ◎ Yukon Territory, W Canada
Kluang *see* Keluang
182 F7 **Kluczbork** *Ger.* Kreuzburg, Kreuzburg in Oberschlesien. Opolskie, S Poland 50°59′N 18°13′E
83 L6 **Klukwan** Alaska, USA 59°24′N 135°49′W
181 C12 **Klüsserath** Rheinland-Pfalz, Germany 6°51′N 49°50′E
180 J2 **Klütz** Mecklenburg-Vorpommern, Germany 11°10′N 53°58′E
Klyastitsy *see* Klyastsitsy
190 G7 **Klyastsitsy** *Rus.* Klyastitsy. Vitsyebskaya Voblasts', N Belarus 55°53′N 28°36′E
197 K2 **Klyavlino** Samarskaya Oblast', W Russian Federation 54°21′N 52°12′E
144 F6 **Klyaz'in** ≈ W Russian Federation
197 H1 **Klyaz'ma** ≈ W Russian Federation
191 F10 **Klyetsk** *Pol.* Kleck, *Rus.* Kletsk. Minskaya Voblasts', SW Belarus 53°04′N 26°38′E
229 J4 **Klyuchevka** Talasskaya Oblast', NW Kyrgyzstan 42°34′N 71°45′E
193 M6 **Klyuchevskaya Sopka, Vulkan** ⋀ E Russian Federation 56°03′N 160°38′E
193 M5 **Klyuchi** Kamchatskaya Oblast', E Russian Federation 56°18′N 160°44′E
155 B9 **Knaben** Vest-Agder, S Norway 58°46′N 07°04′E
155 F11 **Knäred** Halland, S Sweden 56°30′N 13°21′E
159 K8 **Knaresborough** N England, UK 54°01′N 01°35′W
159 J6 **Knarsdale** UK 54°52′N 2°30′W
180 I5 **Knesebeck** Niedersachsen, Germany 10°42′N 52°41′E
185 J5 **Knezha** Vratsa, NW Bulgaria 43°29′N 24°04′E
70 E5 **Knickerbocker** Texas, SW USA 31°18′N 100°35′W
74 B3 **Knife River** ≈ North Dakota, N USA
56 C7 **Knight Inlet** *inlet* British Columbia, W Canada
83 J6 **Knight Island** *island* Alaska, USA
160 G4 **Knighton** E Wales, UK 52°20′N 03°01′W
80 D3 **Knights Ferry** California, USA 37°49′N 120°40′W
78 B4 **Knights Landing** California, W USA 38°47′N 121°43′W
184 C4 **Knin** Šibenik-Knin, S Croatia 44°03′N 16°12′E
70 F7 **Knippal** Texas, SW USA
177 K4 **Knittelfeld** Steiermark, C Austria 47°14′N 14°50′E
161 I2 **Kniveton** UK 53°02′N 1°42′W
154 I7 **Knivsta** Uppsala, C Sweden 59°43′N 17°49′E
185 H5 **Knjaževac** Serbia, E Serbia 43°34′N 22°16′E
75 G9 **Knob Noster** Missouri, C USA 38°47′N 93°33′W
158 B9 **Knockcroghery** Roscommon, Ireland 53°34′N 8°06′W
160 A4 **Knocktopher** Kilkenny, Ireland 52°29′N 7°13′W
163 B9 **Knokke-Heist** West-Vlaanderen, NW Belgium 51°21′N 03°19′E
155 D10 **Knøsen** *hill* N Denmark
Knosós *see* Knossos
187 J10 **Knossos** *Gk.* Knosós. *prehistoric site* Kríti, Greece, E Mediterranean Sea
70 E5 **Knott** Texas, SW USA 32°21′N 101°35′W
159 K9 **Knottingley** UK 53°42′N 1°14′W
161 I4 **Knowle** UK 52°23′N 1°44′W
292 F3 **Knowles, Cape** *headland* Antarctica 71°45′S 60°20′W
73 E9 **Knox** Indiana, N USA 41°17′N 86°37′W
74 D2 **Knox** North Dakota, N USA 48°19′N 99°43′W
62 D7 **Knox** Pennsylvania, NE USA 41°13′N 79°33′W
283 M6 **Knox Atoll** *var.* Ņadikdik, Narikrik. *atoll* Ratak Chain, SE Marshall Islands
54 A6 **Knox, Cape** *headland* Graham Island, British Columbia, SW Canada 54°05′N 133°02′W
70 F4 **Knox City** Texas, SW USA 33°25′N 99°49′W
293 M6 **Knox Coast** *physical region* Antarctica
73 I10 **Knox Lake** ⊠ Ohio, N USA
69 J1 **Knoxville** Georgia, SE USA 32°44′N 83°58′W
73 B9 **Knoxville** Illinois, N USA 40°54′N 90°16′W
66 G6 **Knoxville** Tennessee, S USA 35°58′N 83°55′W
295 J7 **Knud Rasmussen Land** *physical region* N Greenland
Knüll *see* Knüllgebirge
181 G9 **Knüllgebirge** *var.* Knüll. ▲▲ C Germany
159 J10 **Knutsford** UK 53°18′N 2°22′W
190 G7 **Knyazevo** Pskovskaya Oblast', Russian Federation
Knyazhevo *see* Sredishte
Knyazhitsy *see* Knyazhytsy
191 H9 **Knyazhytsy** *Rus.* Knyazhitsy. Mahilyowskaya Voblasts', E Belarus 54°10′N 30°28′E
138 E10 **Knysna** Western Cape, SW South Africa 34°03′S 23°03′E
261 I5 **Koagas** Papua, E Indonesia 02°40′S 132°16′E
Koartac *see* Quaqtaq
258 G6 **Koba** Pulau Bangka, W Indonesia 02°30′S 106°26′E
250 D8 **Kobayashi** *var.* Kobayasi. Miyazaki, Kyūshū, SW Japan 32°00′N 130°58′E
Kobayasi *see* Kobayashi
Kobdo *see* Hovd
251 H5 **Kōbe** Hyōgo, Honshū, SW Japan 34°40′N 135°10′E
Kobelyaki *see* Kobelyaky
189 J4 **Kobelyaky** *Rus.* Kobelyaki. Poltavs'ka Oblast', NE Ukraine 49°10′N 34°13′E
155 F12 **København** *Eng.* Copenhagen; *anc.* Hafnia. ● (Denmark) Sjælland, København, E Denmark 55°43′N 12°34′E
155 F12 **København** *off.* Københavns Amt. ◐ *county* E Denmark
Københavns Amt *see* København
132 D3 **Kobenni** Hodh el Gharbi, S Mauritania 15°58′N 09°24′W
261 H5 **Kobi** Pulau Seram, E Indonesia 02°56′S 129°53′E
181 D11 **Koblenz** *prev.* Coblenz, *Fr.* Coblence; *anc.* Confluentes. Rheinland-Pfalz, W Germany 50°21′N 07°36′E
176 D3 **Koblenz** Aargau, N Switzerland 47°34′N 08°16′E
261 J6 **Kobowre, Pegunungan** ▲▲ Papua, E Indonesia
194 E9 **Kabozha** Novgorodskaya Oblast', W Russian Federation 58°48′N 35°00′E
Kobrin *see* Kobryn
261 J7 **Kobroor, Pulau** *island* Kepulauan Aru, E Indonesia
191 D11 **Kobryn** *Pol.* Kobryn, *Rus.* Kobrin. Brestskaya Voblasts', SW Belarus 52°13′N 24°21′E
83 H4 **Kobuk** Alaska, USA 66°54′N 156°52′W
83 H4 **Kobuk River** ≈ Alaska, USA
215 I4 **K'obulet'i** W Georgia 41°47′N 41°47′E
193 J6 **Kobyay** Respublika Sakha (Yakutiya), NE Russian Federation 63°36′N 126°33′E
187 K3 **Kocacesme** Çanakkale, Turkey 40°40′N 26°48′E
214 C4 **Kocaeli** ◐ *province* NW Turkey
185 H7 **Kočani** NE FYR Macedonia 41°55′N 22°25′E
187 L6 **Koçarlı** Aydın, Turkey 37°46′N 27°42′E
184 F4 **Koceljevo** Serbia, W Serbia 44°28′N 19°49′E
177 K6 **Kočevje** *Ger.* Gottschee. S Slovenia 45°41′N 14°48′E
233 K6 **Koch Bihār** West Bengal, NE India 26°19′N 89°26′E
193 H5 **Kochechum** ≈ N Russian Federation
181 G13 **Kocher** ≈ SW Germany
195 K8 **Kochevo** Komi-Permyatskiy Avtonomnyy Okrug, NW Russian Federation 59°37′N 54°16′E
250 F6 **Kōchi** *var.* Kôti. Kōchi, Shikoku, SW Japan 33°31′N 133°30′E
250 F6 **Kōchi** *off.* Kōchi-ken, *var.* Kôti. ◐ *prefecture* Shikoku, SW Japan
Kochi *see* Cochin
Kōchi-ken *see* Kōchi
53 J7 **Koch Island** *island* Nunavut, NE Canada
Kochiu *see* Gejiu
Kochkor *see* Kochkorka
229 L4 **Kochkorka** *Kir.* Kochkor. Narynskaya Oblast', C Kyrgyzstan 42°09′N 75°42′E
195 L4 **Kochmes** Respublika Komi, NW Russian Federation 66°10′N 60°46′E
197 I8 **Kochubey** Respublika Dagestan, SW Russian Federation 44°25′N 46°33′E
187 I5 **Kochýlas** ▲ Skýros, Vóreioi Sporádes, Greece, Aegean Sea 38°50′N 24°35′E
182 I6 **Kock** Lubelskie, E Poland 51°39′N 22°26′E
137 E8 **Kodacho** *spring/well* S Kenya 01°52′S 39°22′E
235 G10 **Koddiyar Bay** *bay* NE Sri Lanka
83 I8 **Kodiak** Kodiak Island, Alaska, USA 57°47′N 152°24′W
83 I8 **Kodiak Island** *island* Alaska, USA
232 B9 **Kodīnār** Gujarāt, W India 20°44′N 70°46′E
194 G6 **Kodino** Arkhangel'skaya Oblast', NW Russian Federation 63°36′N 39°54′E
193 H7 **Kodinsk** Krasnoyarskiy Kray, C Russian Federation 58°37′N 99°18′E
136 B4 **Kodok** Upper Nile, SE Sudan 09°51′N 32°07′E
188 G6 **Kodyma** Odes'ka Oblast', SW Ukraine 48°05′N 29°09′E
Koedoes *see* Kudus
140 F6 **Koegasbrug** Northern Cape, South Africa 29°18′S 22°21′E
163 B9 **Koekelare** West-Vlaanderen, W Belgium 51°07′N 02°58′E
Koeln *see* Köln
Koepang *see* Kupang
Ko-erh-mu *see* Golmud
163 F9 **Koersel** Limburg, NE Belgium 51°04′N 05°17′E
140 D4 **Koës** Karas, SE Namibia 25°59′S 19°08′E
250 A1 **Koesan** Ch'ungch'ŏng-bukto, South Korea 36°49′N 127°48′E
Koetai *see* Mahakam, Sungai
Koetaradja *see* Bandaaceh
81 I13 **Kofa Mountains** ▲▲ Arizona, SW USA
261 M7 **Kofarau** Papua, E Indonesia 07°29′S 140°28′E
229 I7 **Kofarnihon** *Rus.* Kofarnikhon; *prev.* Ordzhonikidzeabad, *Taj* Orjonikidzeobod, Yangi-Bazar. W Tajikistan 38°32′N 68°56′E
229 I8 **Kofarnihon** *Rus.* Kafirnigan. ≈ SW Tajikistan
Kofarnikhon *see* Kofarnihon
141 H6 **Koffiefontein** Free State, South Africa 29°24′S 25°01′E
261 H4 **Kofiau, Pulau** *var* Kafiau. *island* Kepulauan Raja Ampat, E Indonesia
187 I10 **Kófinas** ▲ Kríti, Greece, E Mediterranean Sea 34°58′N 25°03′E
218 C2 **Kofínou** *var.* Kophinou. S Cyprus 34°49′N 33°24′E
177 K4 **Köflach** Steiermark, SE Austria 47°04′N 15°04′E
133 H8 **Koforidua** SE Ghana 06°01′N 00°12′W
250 F4 **Kōfu** Tottori, Honshū, SW Japan 35°16′N 133°31′E
253 B13 **Kōfu** *var.* Kôhu. Yamanashi, Honshū, S Japan 35°41′N 138°33′E
253 C13 **Koga** Ibaraki, Honshū, S Japan 36°12′N 139°42′E
137 B10 **Koga** Tabora, C Tanzania 06°08′S 32°20′E
Kogălniceanu *see* Mihail Kogălniceanu
59 J3 **Kogaluk** ≈ Newfoundland and Labrador, E Canada
58 G2 **Kogaluk** ≈ Québec, NE Canada
192 F6 **Kogalym** Khanty-Mansiyskiy Avtonomnyy Okrug, C Russian Federation 62°13′N 74°34′E
155 F12 **Køge** Roskilde, E Denmark 55°28′N 12°12′E
178 G2 **Køge Bugt** *bay* E Denmark
133 J7 **Kogi** ◐ *state* C Nigeria
228 G6 **Kogon** *Rus.* Kagan. Buxoro Viloyati, C Uzbekistan 39°47′N 64°29′E
248 B7 **Kŏgŭm-do** *island* S South Korea
Kőhalom *see* Rupea
250 B1 **Kohan** Kangwŏn-do, South Korea 37°12′N 128°51′E
231 I4 **Kohāt** North-West Frontier Province, NW Pakistan 33°37′N 71°30′E

◆ Country
● Country Capital
◇ Dependent Territory
○ Dependent Territory Capital
◐ Administrative Regions
✈ International Airport
▲ Mountain
▲▲ Mountain Range
⋀ Volcano
≈ River
◎ Lake
⊠ Reservoir

◆ Country   ◇ Dependent Territory   ◆ Administrative Regions   ▲ Mountain   ▲ Volcano   ☺ Lake
● Country Capital   ○ Dependent Territory Capital   ✕ International Airport   ▲ Mountain Range   ✍ River   ☺ Reservoir

Kuliga - Labrit
INDEX
363

195 K9 **Kuliga** Udmurtskaya Respublika, NW Russian Federation 58°14′N 53°49′E
190 D4 **Kullamaa** Läänemaa, W Estonia 58°52′N 24°05′E
295 J7 **Kullorsuaq** var. Kuvdlorssuak. ◈ Kitaa, C Greenland
181 I8 **Küllstedt** Thüringen, Germany 10°17′N 51°17′E
74 D3 **Kulm** North Dakota, N USA 46°18′N 98°57′W
Kulm see Chełmno
228 C6 **Kul'mach** prev. Turkm. Isgender. Balkan Welaýaty, W Turkmenistan 39°04′N 55°49′E
179 F10 **Kulmbach** Bayern, SE Germany 50°07′N 11°27′E
Kulmsee see Chełmża
229 J7 **Kŭlob** Rus. Kulyab. SW Tajikistan 37°55′N 68°46′E
152 I6 **Kuloharju** Lappi, N Finland 65°51′N 28°10′E
190 J3 **Kulotino** Novgorodskaya Oblast', Russian Federation
195 H5 **Kuloy** Arkhangel'skaya Oblast', NW Russian Federation 64°55′N 43°35′E
192 D4 **Kuloy** ≈ NW Russian Federation
215 I6 **Kulp** Dıyarbakır, SE Turkey 38°32′N 41°01′E
Kulpa see Kolpa
132 G6 **Kulpawn** ≈ N Ghana
64 F7 **Kulpsville** Pennsylvania, USA 40°15′N 75°20′W
223 H8 **Kūl, Rūd-e** var. Kūl. ≈ S Iran
226 C5 **Kul'sary** Kaz. Qulsary. Atyrau, W Kazakhstan 46°59′N 54°02′E
233 J8 **Kulti** West Bengal, NE India 23°45′N 86°50′E
154 G1 **Kultsjön** ◎ N Sweden
214 E6 **Kulu** Konya, W Turkey 39°06′N 33°02′E
193 L5 **Kulu** ≈ E Russian Federation
192 F8 **Kulunda** Altayskiy Kray, S Russian Federation 52°33′N 79°04′E
227 J2 **Kulunda Steppe** Kaz. Qulyndy Zhazyghy, Rus. Kulundinskaya Ravnina. grassland Kazakhstan/Russian Federation
Kulundinskaya Ravnina see Kulunda Steppe
277 I6 **Kulwin** Victoria, SE Australia 35°04′S 142°37′E
Kulyab see Kŭlob
189 I2 **Kulykivka** Chernihivs'ka Oblast', N Ukraine 51°23′N 31°39′E
Kum see Qom
250 F6 **Kuma** Ehime, Shikoku, SW Japan 33°36′N 132°53′E
197 I8 **Kuma** ≈ SW Russian Federation
Kumafa see Kumawa, Pegunungan
253 B13 **Kumagaya** Saitama, Honshū, S Japan 36°09′N 139°22′E
252 C5 **Kumaishi** Hokkaidō, NE Japan 42°08′N 139°57′E
258 I6 **Kumai, Teluk** bay Borneo, C Indonesia
197 N4 **Kumak** Orenburgskaya Oblast', W Russian Federation 51°16′N 60°06′E
261 L4 **Kumamba, Kepulauan** island group E Indonesia
250 C7 **Kumamoto** Kumamoto, Kyūshū, SW Japan 32°49′N 130°41′E
250 D7 **Kumamoto** off. Kumamoto-ken. ◈ prefecture Kyūshū, SW Japan
Kumamoto-ken see Kumamoto
251 I6 **Kumano** Mie, Honshū, SW Japan 33°54′N 136°08′E
Kumanova see Kumanovo
185 H7 **Kumanovo** Turk. Kumanova. N Macedonia 42°08′N 21°43′E
278 D9 **Kumara** West Coast, South Island, New Zealand 42°39′S 171°12′E
274 D5 **Kumarina Roadhouse** Western Australia 24°46′S 119°39′E
233 K8 **Kumarkhali** Khulna, W Bangladesh 23°54′N 89°16′E
132 G8 **Kumasi** prev. Coomassie. C Ghana 06°41′N 01°40′W
261 I6 **Kumawa, Pegunungan** var. Kumafa. ▲▲ Papua, E Indonesia
Kumayri see Gyumri
134 A5 **Kumba** Sud-Ouest, W Cameroon 04°39′N 09°26′E
235 F9 **Kumbakonam** Tamil Nādu, SE India 10°59′N 79°24′E
261 M8 **Kumbe, Sungai** ≈ Papua, E Indonesia
Kum-Dag see Gumdag
251 H9 **Kume-jima** island Nansei-shotō, SW Japan
197 L3 **Kumertau** Respublika Bashkortostan, W Russian Federation 52°48′N 55°48′E
Kumillā see Comilla
195 N8 **Kuminskiy** Khanty-Mansiyskiy Avtonomnyy Okrug, C Russian Federation 58°42′N 65°56′E
80 H1 **Kumiva Peak** ▲ Nevada, W USA 40°24′N 119°16′W
239 H5 **Kumkuduk** Xinjiang Uygur Zizhiqu, W China 40°15′N 91°55′E
Kumkurgan see Qumqo'rg'on
155 G8 **Kumla** Örebro, C Sweden 59°08′N 15°09′E
214 C8 **Kumluca** Antalya, SW Turkey 36°23′N 30°17′E
178 H4 **Kummerower See** ◎ NE Germany
133 L6 **Kumo** Gombi, E Nigeria 10°03′N 11°14′E
226 G5 **Kumola** ≈ C Kazakhstan
256 D2 **Kumon Range** ▲▲ N Myanmar (Burma)
140 D5 **Kums** Karas, SE Namibia 28°07′S 19°40′E
234 D7 **Kumta** Karnātaka, W India 14°25′N 74°24′E
238 G4 **Kümük** Xinjiang Uygur Zizhiqu, W China
82 E3 **Kumukahi, Cape** headland Hawai'i, USA, C Pacific Ocean 19°31′N 154°48′W
197 J10 **Kumukh** Respublika Dagestan, SW Russian Federation 42°10′N 47°07′E
Kumul see Hami
250 A1 **Kŭmwang** Ch'ungch'ŏng-bukto, South Korea 37°00′N 127°36′E
197 H5 **Kumylzhenskaya** Volgogradskaya Oblast', SW Russian Federation 49°54′N 42°35′E
221 K3 **Kumzār** N Oman 26°19′N 56°26′E
Kunar see Konar
Kunashiri see Kunashir, Ostrov
252 I3 **Kunashir, Ostrov** var. Kunashiri. island Kuril'skiye Ostrova, SE Russian Federation
190 F3 **Kunda** Lääne-Virumaa, NE Estonia 59°31′N 26°33′E
232 G7 **Kunda** Uttar Pradesh, N India 25°43′N 81°31′E
234 D7 **Kundāpura** var. Coondapoor. Karnātaka, W India 13°39′N 74°41′E
135 I11 **Kundelungu, Monts** ▲▲ S Dem. Rep. Congo
Kundert see Hernád
280 B3 **Kundiawa** Chimbu, W Papua New Guinea 06°00′S 144°57′E
Kundla see Sāvarkundla
258 E4 **Kundur, Pulau** island W Indonesia
Kunduz see Kondoz
Kunduz/Kundūz see Kondoz
Kuneitra see Al Qunayṭirah
138 B4 **Kunene** ◈ district NE Namibia
138 A3 **Kunene** var. Cunene. ≈ Angola/Namibia see also Cunene
Kunene see Cunene
Künes see Xinyuan
238 E3 **Künes He** ≈ NW China
190 J2 **Kunevichi** Leningradskaya Oblast', Russian Federation
155 E10 **Kungälv** Västra Götaland, S Sweden 57°54′N 12°00′E
229 M4 **Kungei Ala-Tau** Rus. Khrebet Kyungëy Ala-Too, Kir. Küngöy Ala-Too. ▲▲ Kazakhstan/Kyrgyzstan
Küngöy Ala-Too see Kungei Ala-Tau
155 E10 **Kungsbacka** Halland, S Sweden 57°30′N 12°05′E
155 E9 **Kungshamn** Västra Götaland, S Sweden 58°21′N 11°15′E
155 H8 **Kungsör** Västmanland, C Sweden 59°25′N 16°05′E
134 E6 **Kungu** Equateur, NW Dem. Rep. Congo 02°47′N 19°12′E
195 K9 **Kungur** Permskaya Oblast', NW Russian Federation 57°24′N 56°56′E
256 C7 **Kungyangon** Yangon, SW Myanmar (Burma) 16°27′N 96°00′E
183 H11 **Kunhegyes** Jász-Nagykun-Szolnok, E Hungary 47°22′N 20°36′E
256 D4 **Kunhing** Shan State, E Myanmar (Burma) 21°17′N 98°26′E
250 D7 **Kunimi-dake** ▲ Kyūshū, SW Japan 32°31′N 131°01′E
231 J2 **Kunjirap Daban** var. Khūnjerāb Pass. pass China/Pakistan
Kunjirap Daban Khunjerāb Pass
Kunlun Mountains see Kunlun Shan
238 E6 **Kunlun Shan** Eng. Kunlun Mountains. ▲▲ NW China
239 H7 **Kunlun Shankou** pass C China
240 C7 **Kunming** var. K'un-ming; prev. Yunnan. province capital Yunnan, SW China 25°04′N 102°41′E
K'un-ming see Kunming
252 D5 **Kunnui** Hokkaidō, NE Japan 42°26′N 140°18′E
Kunø see Kunoy
195 M4 **Kunovat** ≈ Yamalo-Nenetskiy Avtonomyy Okrug, Russian federation
154 B1 **Kunoy** Dan. Kunø. island N Faeroe Islands
250 B4 **Kŭnp'o** South Korea 34°43′N 128°35′E
180 J5 **Kunrau** Sachsen-Anhalt, Germany 11°02′N 52°34′E
248 B6 **Kunsan** var. Gunsan, Jap. Gunzan. W South Korea 35°58′N 126°42′E
243 M1 **Kunshan** Jiangsu, China 31°14′N 120°34′E
183 G12 **Kunszentmárton** Jász-Nagykun-Szolnok, E Hungary 46°50′N 20°19′E
183 F12 **Kunszentmiklós** Bács-Kiskun, C Hungary 47°00′N 19°07′E
274 F3 **Kununurra** Western Australia 15°50′S 128°44′E
250 B2 **Kunwi** Kyŏngsang-bukto, South Korea 36°14′N 128°34′E
190 I7 **Kunya** Pskovskaya Oblast', Russian Federation
Kunyang see Pingyang
Kunya-Urgench see Këneurgench
Kunyé see Pins, Île des
258 J5 **Kunyi** Borneo, C Indonesia 03°23′S 119°20′E
181 H10 **Künzell** Hessen, Germany 9°43′N 50°33′E
181 H13 **Künzelsau** Baden-Württemberg, S Germany 49°22′N 09°43′E
243 M4 **Kuocang Shan** ▲▲ SE China
194 D3 **Kuoloyarvi** var. Luolajarvi. Murmanskaya Oblast', NW Russian Federation 66°58′N 29°13′E
153 I8 **Kuopio** Kuopio, C Finland 62°54′N 27°41′E
153 I8 **Kuopio** ◈ province C Finland
153 H8 **Kuortane** Länsi-Soumi, W Finland 62°48′N 23°30′E
153 I9 **Kuortti** Isäsuomi, E Finland 61°25′N 26°25′E
Kupa see Kolpa
260 E9 **Kupang** prev. Koepang. Timor, C Indonesia 10°13′S 123°38′E
83 I2 **Kuparuk River** ≈ Alaska, USA
Kupchino see Cupcina
181 H14 **Kupferzell** Baden-Württemberg, Germany 9°41′N 49°14′E
280 C4 **Kupiano** Central, S Papua New Guinea 10°06′S 148°12′E
274 F3 **Kupingarri** Western Australia 16°46′S 125°57′E
192 F7 **Kupino** Novosibirskaya Oblast', C Russian Federation 54°22′N 77°09′E
190 E7 **Kupiškis** Panevėžys, NE Lithuania 55°51′N 24°58′E
83 I8 **Kupreanof Island** island Alexander Archipelago, Alaska, USA
83 H9 **Kupreanof Point** headland Alaska, USA 55°34′N 159°36′W
184 D4 **Kupres** ◈ Federacija Bosna I Hercegovina, SW Bosnia and Herzegovina
189 L4 **Kup"yans'k** Rus. Kupyansk. Kharkivs'ka Oblast', E Ukraine 49°42′N 37°36′E
Kupyansk see Kup"yans'k
189 M4 **Kup"yans'k-Vuzlovyy** Kharkivs'ka Oblast', E Ukraine 49°40′N 37°41′E
238 E4 **Kuqa** Xinjiang Uygur Zizhiqu, NW China 41°43′N 82°58′E
Kür see Kura
215 L4 **Kura** Az. Kür, Geor. Mtkvari, Turk. Kura Nehri. ≈ SW Asia
103 J4 **Kuracki** NW Guyana 06°52′N 60°13′W
250 E5 **Kurahashi-jima** island SW Japan
Kura Kurk see Irbe Strait
229 I5 **Kurama Range** Rus. Kuraminskiy Khrebet. ▲▲ Tajikistan/Uzbekistan
Kuraminskiy Khrebet see Kurama Range
Kura Nehri see Kura
261 J5 **Kuran, Kepulauan** island group E Indonesia
191 F9 **Kuranyets** Rus. Kurenets. Minskaya Voblasts', C Belarus 54°33′N 26°57′E
250 G5 **Kurashiki** var. Kurasiki. Okayama, Honshū, SW Japan 34°35′N 133°44′E
234 H3 **Kurasia** Chhattīsgarh, C India 23°11′N 82°16′E
Kurasiki see Kurashiki
250 G4 **Kurayoshi** var. Kurayosi. Tottori, Honshū, SW Japan 35°27′N 133°52′E
Kurayosi see Kurayoshi
227 M4 **Kurchum** Kaz. Kürshim. Vostochnyy Kazakhstan, E Kazakhstan 48°35′N 83°37′E
227 M4 **Kurchum** ≈ E Kazakhstan
215 M5 **Kürdämir** Rus. Kyurdamir. C Azerbaijan 40°21′N 48°08′E
Kurdestan see Kordestān
217 I1 **Kurdistan** cultural region SW Asia
Kurd Kui see Kord Kūy
234 D5 **Kurduvādi** Mahārāshtra, W India 18°06′N 75°31′E
185 K7 **Kŭrdzhali** var. Kirdzhali, Kărdžali. Kŭrdzhali, S Bulgaria 41°39′N 25°23′E
185 K7 **Kŭrdzhali, Yazovir** ⊠ S Bulgaria
250 E5 **Kure** Hiroshima, Honshū, SW Japan 34°15′N 132°33′E
286 F3 **Kure Atoll** var. Ocean Island. atoll Hawaiian Islands, Hawaii, USA
214 E4 **Küre Dağları** ▲▲ N Turkey
228 B6 **Kurendag** rus Gora Kyuren. ▲ W Turkmenistan 39°05′N 55°09′E
Kurenets see Kuranyets
190 C5 **Kuressaare** Ger. Arensburg; prev. Kingissepp. Saaremaa, W Estonia 58°17′N 22°29′E
192 G5 **Kureyka** Krasnoyarskiy Kray, N Russian Federation 66°22′N 87°21′E
193 H5 **Kureyka** ≈ N Russian Federation
Kurgal'dzhino/Kurgal'dzhinsky see Korgalzhyn
195 N10 **Kurgan** Kurganskaya Oblast', C Russian Federation 55°30′N 65°20′E
196 G8 **Kurganinsk** Krasnodarskiy Kray, SW Russian Federation 44°55′N 40°45′E
195 N10 **Kurganskaya Oblast'** ◈ province C Russian Federation
Kurgan-Tyube see Qŭrghonteppa
190 G3 **Kurgolovo** Leningradskaya Oblast', Russian Federation
284 B3 **Kuria** prev. Woodle Island. island Tungaru, W Kiribati
Kuria Muria Bay see Ḥalānīyāt, Khalīj al
Kuria Muria Islands see Ḥalānīyāt, Juzur al
233 K7 **Kurigram** Rajshahi, N Bangladesh 25°49′N 89°39′E
261 L8 **Kurik** Papua, E Indonesia 08°12′S 140°15′E
153 G8 **Kurikka** Länsi-Soumi, W Finland 62°36′N 22°25′E
253 D9 **Kurikoma-yama** ▲ Honshū, C Japan 38°57′N 140°44′E
286 D2 **Kurile Basin** undersea feature NW Pacific Ocean
Kurile Islands see Kuril'skiye Ostrova
Kurile-Kamchatka Depression see Kurile Trench
286 D2 **Kurile Trench** var. Kurile-Kamchatka Depression. undersea feature NW Pacific Ocean
197 J5 **Kurilovka** Saratovskaya Oblast', W Russian Federation 50°39′N 48°02′E
193 M8 **Kuril'sk** Kuril'skiye Ostrova, Sakhalinskaya Oblats', SE Russian Federation 45°10′N 147°51′E
193 N8 **Kuril'skiye Ostrova** Eng. Kurile Islands. island group SE Russian Federation
89 H5 **Kurinwas, Río** ≈ E Nicaragua
Kurisches Haff see Courland Lagoon
Kurkund see Kilingi-Nõmme
196 G2 **Kurlovskiy** Vladimirskaya Oblast', W Russian Federation 55°25′N 40°39′E
136 C3 **Kurmuk** Blue Nile, SE Sudan 10°36′N 34°16′E
Kurna see Al Qurnah
181 H12 **Kürnach** Bayern, Germany 10°02′N 49°51′E
234 E6 **Kurnool** var. Karnul. Andhra Pradesh, S India 15°51′N 78°01′E
251 J2 **Kurobe** Toyama, Honshū, SW Japan 36°55′N 137°24′E
250 C6 **Kurogi** Fukuoka, Kyūshū, SW Japan 33°09′N 130°45′E
252 D7 **Kuroishi** var. Kuroisi. Aomori, Honshū, C Japan 40°37′N 140°34′E
Kuroisi see Kuroishi
253 C12 **Kuroiso** Tochigi, Honshū, S Japan 36°58′N 140°02′E
252 D5 **Kuromatsunai** Hokkaidō, NE Japan 42°40′N 140°18′E
250 F10 **Kuro-shima** island SW Japan
251 I5 **Kuroso-yama** ▲ Honshū, SW Japan 34°31′N 136°10′E
278 D11 **Kurow** Canterbury, South Island, New Zealand 44°44′S 170°29′E
261 I6 **Kur, Pulau** island E Indonesia
197 H8 **Kursavka** Stavropol'skiy Kray, SW Russian Federation 44°28′N 42°31′E
190 C7 **Kuršėnai** Šiauliai, N Lithuania 56°00′N 22°56′E
Kürshim see Kurchum
Kurshskaya Kosa/Kuršių Nerija see Courland Spit
196 F4 **Kursk** Kurskaya Oblast', W Russian Federation 51°44′N 36°47′E
196 F4 **Kurskaya Oblast'** ◈ province W Russian Federation
Kurskiy Zaliv see Courland Lagoon
184 G6 **Kuršumlija** Serbia, S Serbia 43°09′N 21°16′E
187 L3 **Kurşunlu** Bursa, Turkey 40°24′N 28°17′E
215 J7 **Kurtalan** Siirt, SE Turkey 37°58′N 41°36′E
195 N10 **Kurtamysh** Kurganskaya Oblast', C Russian Federation 54°51′N 64°46′E
Kurtbunar see Tervel
Kurt-Dere see Vŭlchidol
Kurtitsch/Kürtös see Curtici
Kurtty see Kurtty
227 K7 **Kurtty** var. Kurtty. ≈ SE Kazakhstan
153 H9 **Kuru** Länsi-Suomi, W Finland 61°51′N 23°46′E
134 H4 **Kuru** ≈ W Sudan
238 F4 **Kuruktag** ▲▲ NW China
140 G5 **Kuruman** Northern Cape, South Africa 27°27′S 23°26′E
138 E7 **Kuruman** Northern Cape, N South Africa 27°28′S 23°27′E
121 K9 **Kuruman** ≈ W South Africa
140 E4 **Kuruman** ≈ Northern Cape, South Africa
140 G5 **Kuruman Hills** ▲▲ Northern Cape, South Africa
250 C6 **Kurume** Fukuoka, Kyūshū, SW Japan 33°15′N 130°27′E
193 I8 **Kurumkan** Respublika Buryatiya, S Russian Federation 54°13′N 110°21′E
235 G10 **Kurunegala** North Western Province, C Sri Lanka 07°28′N 80°23′E
103 K6 **Kurupukari** C Guyana 04°39′N 58°39′W
195 K7 **Kur"ya** Respublika Komi, NW Russian Federation 61°38′N 57°12′E
226 B7 **Kuryk** var. Yeraliyev. Mangistau, SW Kazakhstan 43°12′N 51°43′E
250 C3 **Kuryongp'o** Kyŏngsang-bukto, South Korea 35°59′N 129°33′E
214 B7 **Kuşadası** Aydın, SW Turkey 37°50′N 27°16′E
214 A6 **Kuşadası Körfezi** gulf SW Turkey
250 B9 **Kusagaki-guntō** island SW Japan
Kusaie see Kosrae
227 J5 **Kusak** ≈ C Kazakhstan
Kusary see Qusar
256 E6 **Ku Sathan, Doi** ▲ NW Thailand 18°22′N 100°31′E
251 I4 **Kusatsu** var. Kusatu. Shiga, Honshū, SW Japan 35°02′N 136°00′E
Kusatu see Kusatsu
219 E10 **Kuseifa** Israel
216 B7 **Kuseifa** Southern, C Israel 31°15′N 35°01′E
180 J5 **Kusey** Sachsen-Anhalt, Germany 11°05′N 52°34′E
214 B5 **Kuş Gölü** ◎ NW Turkey
196 G7 **Kushchevskaya** Krasnodarskiy Kray, SW Russian Federation 46°35′N 39°40′E
251 I5 **Kushida-gawa** ≈ Honshū, SW Japan
250 C8 **Kushikino** var. Kusikino. Kagoshima, Kyūshū, SW Japan 31°45′N 130°16′E
250 D9 **Kushima** var. Kusima. Miyazaki, Kyūshū, SW Japan 31°28′N 131°14′E
251 I6 **Kushimoto** Wakayama, Honshū, SW Japan 33°28′N 135°45′E
252 H4 **Kushiro** var. Kusiro. Hokkaidō, NE Japan 42°58′N 144°24′E
230 D3 **Kūshk** Herāt, W Afghanistan 34°55′N 62°20′E
Kushka see Gushgy
Kushka see Serhetabat
226 G3 **Kushmurun** Kaz. Qusmuryn. Kostanay, N Kazakhstan 52°27′N 64°31′E
226 G2 **Kushmurun, Ozero** Kaz. Qusmuryn. ◎ N Kazakhstan
197 L2 **Kushnarenkovo** Respublika Bashkortostan, W Russian Federation 55°07′N 55°24′E
233 K8 **Kushtia** var. Kustia. Khulna, W Bangladesh 23°54′N 89°07′E
195 L9 **Kushva** Sverdlovskaya Oblast', C Russian Federation 58°14′N 59°36′E
Kusikino see Kushikino
Kusima see Kushima
Kusiro see Kushiro
82 F7 **Kuskokwim Bay** bay Alaska, USA
83 H5 **Kuskokwim Mountains** ▲▲ Alaska, USA
252 G4 **Kussharo-ko** var. Kussyaro. ◎ Hokkaidō, NE Japan
Küssnacht see Küssnacht am Rigi
176 D4 **Küssnacht am Rigi** var. Küssnacht. Schwyz, C Switzerland 47°03′N 08°25′E
Kussyaro see Kussharo-ko
Kustanay see Kostanay
Küstence/Küstendje see Constanţa
180 E4 **Küstenkanal** var. Ems-Hunte Canal. canal NW Germany
Kustia see Kushtia
Küstrin see Kostrzyn
260 G3 **Kusu** Pulau Halmahera, E Indonesia 0°51′N 127°41′E
260 B8 **Kuta** Pulau Lombok, S Indonesia 08°53′S 116°15′E
217 J3 **Kutabān** N Iraq 35°21′N 44°45′E
214 C6 **Kütahya** prev. Kutaia. Kütahya, W Turkey 39°25′N 29°56′E
214 C6 **Kütahya** var. Kutaia. ◈ province W Turkey
Kutai see Mahakam, Sungai
Kutaia see Kütahya
215 J4 **K'ut'aisi** W Georgia 42°16′N 42°42′E
Kūt al 'Amārah see Al Kūt
Kut al Hai/Kūt al Ḥayy see Al Ḥayy
Kut al Imara see Al Kūt
193 K6 **Kutana** Respublika Sakha (Yakutiya), NE Russian Federation 59°05′N 131°43′E
Kutaradja/Kutaraja see Bandaaceh
252 D5 **Kutchan** Hokkaidō, NE Japan 42°54′N 140°46′E
Kutch, Gulf of see Kachchh, Gulf of
Kutch, Rann of see Kachchh, Rann of
180 G3 **Kutenholz** Niedersachsen, Germany 9°20′N 53°29′E
184 C2 **Kutina** Sisak-Moslavina, NE Croatia 45°29′N 16°45′E
184 D2 **Kutjevo** Po»zega-Slavonija, NE Croatia 45°26′N 17°54′E
183 C8 **Kutná Hora** Ger. Kuttenberg. Střední Čechy, C Czech Republic 49°58′N 15°18′E
182 F6 **Kutno** Łódzkie, C Poland 52°14′N 19°23′E
195 N3 **Kutop'yugan** Yamalo-Nenetskiy Avtonomyy Okrug, Russian federation
Kuttenberg see Kutná Hora
135 E8 **Kutu** Bandundu, W Dem. Rep. Congo 02°42′S 18°10′E
233 L9 **Kutubdia Island** island SE Bangladesh
134 H2 **Kutum** Northern Darfur, W Sudan 14°10′N 24°40′E
229 M4 **Kuturgu** Issyk-Kul'skaya Oblast', E Kyrgyzstan 42°45′N 78°04′E
181 J9 **Kutzleben** Thüringen, Germany 10°45′N 51°12′E
64 E6 **Kutztown** Pennsylvania, USA 40°31′N 75°47′W
59 I3 **Kuujjuaq** prev. Fort-Chimo. Québec, E Canada 58°10′N 68°15′W
58 F4 **Kuujjuarapik** Québec, C Canada 55°07′N 78°09′W
Kuuli-Mayak see Guwlumaýak
190 E5 **Kuulse magi** ▲ S Estonia
152 I6 **Kuusamo** Oulu, E Finland 65°57′N 29°15′E
153 I9 **Kuusankoski** Kymi, S Finland 60°51′N 26°40′E
197 M4 **Kuvandyk** Orenburgskaya Oblast', W Russian Federation 51°27′N 57°18′E
Kuvango see Cubango
Kuvasay see Quvasoy
Kuvdlorssuak see Kullorsuaq
194 E10 **Kuvshinovo** Tverskaya Oblast', W Russian Federation 57°03′N 34°09′E
217 M9 **Kuwait** off. State of Kuwait, var. Dawlat al Kuwait, Koweit, Kuweit. ◆ monarchy SW Asia
Kuwait see Al Kuwayt
Kuwait Bay see Kuwayt, Jūn al
Kuwait City see Al Kuwayt
Kuwait, Dawlat al see Kuwait
Kuwait, State of see Kuwait
Kuwajleen see Kwajalein Atoll
251 J4 **Kuwana** Mie, Honshū, SW Japan 35°04′N 136°40′E
261 I4 **Kuwawin** Papua, E Indonesia 01°10′S 132°40′E
217 L6 **Kuwayt** E Iraq 32°26′N 47°12′E
217 N9 **Kuwayt, Jūn al** var. Kuwait Bay. bay E Kuwait
Kuweit see Kuwait
189 H7 **Kuyal'nyts'kyy Lyman** ◎ SW Ukraine
192 F7 **Kuybyshev** Novosibirskaya Oblast', C Russian Federation 55°28′N 77°55′E
Kuybyshev see Bolgar, Respublika Tatarstan, Russian Federation
Kuybyshev see Samara
189 L6 **Kuybysheve** Rus. Kuybyshevo. Zaporiz'ka Oblast', SE Ukraine 47°20′N 36°41′E
Kuybyshevo see Kuybysheve
Kuybyshev Reservoir see Kuybyshevskoye Vodokhranilishche
Kuybyshevskaya Oblast' see Samarskaya Oblast'
197 J2 **Kuybyshevskoye Vodokhranilishche** var. Kuibyshev, Eng. Kuybyshev Reservoir. ⊠ W Russian Federation
193 K5 **Kuydusun** Respublika Sakha (Yakutiya), NE Russian Federation 63°15′N 143°10′E
195 K10 **Kuyeda** Permskaya Oblast', NW Russian Federation 56°23′N 55°19′E
244 F4 **Kuye He** ≈ Shaanxi, China
Kūysanjaq see Koi Sanjaq
194 E5 **Kuyto, Ozero** var. Ozero Kujto. ◎ NW Russian Federation
238 F3 **Kuytun** Xinjiang Uygur Zizhiqu, NW China 44°25′N 84°55′E
193 H8 **Kuytun** Irkutskaya Oblast', S Russian Federation 54°18′N 101°28′E
193 H6 **Kuyumba** Evenkiyskiy Avtonomyy Okrug, C Russian Federation 61°00′N 97°07′E
103 J7 **Kuyuwini Landing** S Guyana 02°06′N 59°14′W
190 H2 **Kuyvozi** Leningradskaya Oblast', Russian Federation
Kuzi see Kuji
82 G4 **Kuzitrin River** ≈ Alaska, USA
190 H2 **Kuz'molovskiy** Leningradskaya Oblast', Russian Federation
197 I3 **Kuznetsk** Penzenskaya Oblast', W Russian Federation 53°06′N 46°27′E
188 E2 **Kuznetsovs'k** Rivnens'ka Oblast', NW Ukraine 51°21′N 25°51′E
194 F4 **Kuzomen'** Murmanskaya Oblast', NW Russian Federation 66°16′N 36°47′E
253 E8 **Kuzumaki** Iwate, Honshū, C Japan 40°04′N 141°26′E
155 D13 **Kværndrup** Fyn, C Denmark 55°10′N 10°31′E
152 F4 **Kvaløya** island N Norway
152 G3 **Kvalsund** Finnmark, N Norway 70°30′N 23°56′E
154 D5 **Kvam** Oppland, S Norway 61°42′N 09°43′E
197 M3 **Kvarkeno** Orenburgskaya Oblast', W Russian Federation 52°09′N 59°44′E
154 G2 **Kvarnbergsvattnet** var. Frostviken. ◎ N Sweden
184 A3 **Kvarner** var. Carnaro, It. Quarnero. gulf W Croatia
184 A3 **Kvarnerić** channel W Croatia
83 H8 **Kvichak Bay** bay Alaska, USA
152 F5 **Kvikkjokk** Lapp. Huhttán. Norrbotten, N Sweden 66°58′N 17°45′E
155 C8 **Kvitseid** Telemark, S Norway 59°23′N 08°31′E
152 C4 **Kvitøya** island NE Svalbard
135 D8 **Kwa** ≈ W Dem. Rep. Congo
133 H7 **Kwadwokurom** C Ghana 07°49′N 00°15′W
281 J2 **Kwailibesi** Malaita, N Solomon Islands 08°25′S 160°48′E
283 L5 **Kwajalein Atoll** var. Kuwajleen. atoll Ralik Chain, C Marshall Islands
103 L5 **Kwakoegron** Brokopondo, N Suriname 05°14′N 55°20′W
137 E9 **Kwale** Coast, S Kenya 04°10′S 39°27′E
133 J8 **Kwale** Delta, S Nigeria 05°51′N 06°29′E
141 L6 **KwaMbonambi** KwaZulu-Natal, South Africa 28°36′S 32°05′E
135 D8 **Kwamouth** Bandundu, W Dem. Rep. Congo 03°11′S 16°16′E
Kwando see Cuando
Kwangchow see Guangzhou
Kwangchu see Kwangju
248 B7 **Kwangju** off. Kwangju-gwangyŏksi, var. Guangju, Kwangchu, Jap. Kōshū. SW South Korea 35°09′N 126°53′E
250 A1 **Kwangju** Kyŏnggi-do, South Korea 37°25′N 127°16′E
Kwangju-gwangyŏksi see Kwangju
135 D10 **Kwango** Port. Cuango. ≈ Angola/Dem. Rep. Congo see also Cuango
Kwango see Cuango
Kwangsi/Kwangsi Chuang Autonomous Region see Guangxi Zhuangzu Zizhiqu
Kwangtung see Guangdong
Kwangyuan see Guangyuan
136 B7 **Kwania, Lake** ◎ C Uganda
Kwanza see Cuanza
133 I6 **Kwara** ◈ state SW Nigeria
261 J5 **Kwatisore** Papua, E Indonesia 03°14′S 134°57′E
139 I8 **KwaZulu/Natal** off. KwaZulu/Natal Province; prev. Natal. ◈ province E South Africa
KwaZulu/Natal Province see KwaZulu/Natal
Kweichow see Guizhou
Kweichu see Guiyang
Kweilin see Guilin
Kweisui see Hohhot
Kweiyang see Guiyang
139 H3 **Kwekwe** prev. Que Que. Midlands, C Zimbabwe 18°56′S 29°49′E
138 F5 **Kweneng** ◈ district S Botswana
Kwesui see Hohhot
82 G6 **Kwethluk** Alaska, USA 60°48′N 161°26′W
82 G7 **Kwethluk River** ≈ Alaska, USA
182 F4 **Kwidzyń** Ger. Marienwerder. Pomorskie, N Poland 53°44′N 18°55′E
82 G7 **Kwigillingok** Alaska, USA 59°52′N 163°08′W
280 C4 **Kwikila** Central, S Papua New Guinea 09°51′S 147°43′E
135 E9 **Kwilu** ≈ W Dem. Rep. Congo
Kwito see Cuito
261 I4 **Kwoka, Gunung** ▲ Papua, E Indonesia 0°34′S 132°25′E
134 E4 **Kyabé** Moyen-Chari, S Chad 09°28′N 18°54′E
277 J6 **Kyabram** Victoria, SE Australia 36°21′S 145°05′E
256 D7 **Kyaikkami** prev. Amherst. Mon State, S Myanmar (Burma) 16°03′N 97°36′E
256 C7 **Kyaiklat** Irrawaddy, SW Myanmar (Burma) 16°25′N 95°42′E
256 D6 **Kyaikto** Mon State, S Myanmar (Burma) 17°16′N 97°01′E
193 I8 **Kyakhta** Respublika Buryatiya, S Russian Federation 50°25′N 106°13′E
276 F5 **Kyancutta** South Australia 33°10′S 135°33′E
256 C6 **Kyangin** Irrawaddy, SW Myanmar (Burma) 18°20′N 95°15′E
257 H6 **Ky Anh** Ha Tinh, N Vietnam 18°05′N 106°16′E
256 C5 **Kyaukpadaung** Mandalay, C Myanmar (Burma) 20°50′N 95°08′E
256 B5 **Kyaukpyu** Arakan State, W Myanmar (Burma) 19°27′N 93°33′E
256 C4 **Kyaukse** Mandalay, C Myanmar (Burma) 21°33′N 96°06′E
256 C6 **Kyaunggon** Irrawaddy, SW Myanmar (Burma) 17°04′N 95°12′E
191 C9 **Kybartai** Pol. Kibarty. Marijampolė, S Lithuania 54°37′N 22°44′E
80 E2 **Kyburz** California, USA 38°46′N 120°18′W
232 E3 **Kyelang** Himāchal Pradesh, NW India 32°33′N 77°03′E
183 E9 **Kyjov** Ger. Gaya. Jihomoravský Kraj, SE Czech Republic 49°00′N 17°07′E
187 I7 **Kykládes** var. Kikládhes, Eng. Cyclades. island group SE Greece
70 G7 **Kyle** Texas, SW USA 29°59′N 97°52′W
156 E5 **Kyle of Lochalsh** N Scotland, UK 57°18′N 05°39′W
181 B11 **Kyll** ≈ W Germany
181 B11 **Kyllburg** Rheinland-Pfalz, Germany 6°35′N 50°02′E
186 G6 **Kyllíni** var. Killini. ▲▲ S Greece
187 I5 **Kými** Évvoia, C Greece 38°38′N 24°06′E
153 H9 **Kymi** ◈ province SE Finland
187 I5 **Kýmis, Ákrotírio** cape Évvoia, C Greece
153 I9 **Kymijoki** ≈ S Finland
195 L9 **Kyn** Permskaya Oblast', NW Russian Federation 57°48′N 58°38′E
277 I7 **Kyneton** Victoria, SE Australia 37°14′S 144°28′E
136 C7 **Kyoga, Lake** var. Lake Kioga. ◎ C Uganda
251 H3 **Kyōga-misaki** headland Honshū, SW Japan 35°46′N 135°13′E
277 M2 **Kyogle** New South Wales, SE Australia 28°37′S 153°00′E
248 C6 **Kyŏngju** Jap. Keishū. SE South Korea 35°49′N 129°09′E
Kyŏngsŏng see Sŏul
Kyōsai-tō see Kŏje-do
137 B8 **Kyotera** S Uganda 0°38′S 31°34′E
251 I4 **Kyōto** Kyōto, Honshū, SW Japan 35°01′N 135°46′E
251 H4 **Kyōto** off. Kyōto-fu, var. Kyōto Hu. ◈ urban prefecture Honshū, SW Japan
Kyōto-fu/Kyōto Hu see Kyōto
186 F7 **Kyparissía** var. Kiparissía. Pelopónnisos, S Greece 37°15′N 21°40′E
186 F7 **Kyparissiakós Kólpos** gulf S Greece
Kyperounda see Kyperoúnta
218 B2 **Kyperoúnta** var. Kyperounda. C Cyprus 34°57′N 33°02′E
Kypros see Cyprus
187 I4 **Kyrá Panagía** island Vóreies Sporádes, Greece, Aegean Sea
Kyrenia see Girne
Kyrenia Mountains see Beşparmak Dağları
Kyrgyz Republic see Kyrgyzstan
229 L5 **Kyrgyzstan** off. Kyrgyz Republic, var. Kirghizia; prev. Kirgizskaya SSR, Kirghiz SSR, Republic of Kyrgyzstan. ◆ republic C Asia
Kyrgyzstan, Republic of see Kyrgyzstan
Kyriat Gat see Qiryat Gat
178 G6 **Kyritz** Brandenburg, NE Germany 52°56′N 12°24′E
154 D3 **Kyrksæterøra** Sør-Trøndelag, S Norway 63°17′N 09°06′E
Kyrkslätt see Kirkkonummi
195 K5 **Kyrta** Respublika Komi, NW Russian Federation 64°03′N 57°41′E
197 M1 **Kyshtym** Chelyabinskaya Oblast', S Russian Federation 55°39′N 60°31′E
183 F9 **Kysucké Nové Mesto** prev. Horné Nové Mesto, Ger. Kisutzaneustadtl, Oberneustadtl, Hung. Kiszucaújhely. Žilinský Kraj, N Slovakia 49°18′N 18°48′E
188 G8 **Kytay, Ozero** ◎ SW Ukraine
186 G9 **Kýthira** var. Kíthira, It. Cerigo, Lat. Cythera. Kńythira, S Greece 41°39′N 26°30′E
187 H8 **Kýthira** var. Kíthira, It. Cerigo, Lat. Cythera. island S Greece
187 I7 **Kýthnos** Kńythnos, Kykládes, Greece, Aegean Sea 37°24′N 24°28′E
187 I7 **Kýthnos** var. Kíthnos, Thermiá, It. Termia; anc. Cythnos. island Kykládes, Greece, Aegean Sea
187 I7 **Kýthnou, Stenó** strait Kykládes, Greece, Aegean Sea
Kythréa see Değirmenlik
Kyungëy Ala-Too, Khrebet see Kungei Ala-Tau
Kyurdamir see Kürdämir
250 D7 **Kyūshū** var. Kyûsyû. island SW Japan
286 C4 **Kyushu-Palau Ridge** var. Kyusyu-Palau Ridge. undersea feature W Pacific Ocean
250 D7 **Kyūshū-sanchi** ▲▲ Kyūshū, SW Japan
185 H7 **Kyustendil** anc. Pautalia. Kyustendil, W Bulgaria 42°17′N 22°42′E
185 I7 **Kyustendil** ◈ province W Bulgaria
Kyûsyû see Kyūshū
Kyusyu-Palau Ridge see Kyushu-Palau Ridge
193 J4 **Kyusyur** Respublika Sakha (Yakutiya), NE Russian Federation 70°36′N 127°19′E
277 J6 **Kywong** New South Wales, SE Australia 34°59′S 146°42′E
189 H3 **Kyyiv** Eng. Kiev, Rus. Kiyev. ● (Ukraine) Kyyivs'ka Oblast', N Ukraine 50°26′N 30°32′E
Kyyiv see Kyyivs'ka Oblast'
189 H3 **Kyyivs'ka Oblast'** var. Kyyiv, Rus. Kiyevskaya Oblast'. ◈ province N Ukraine
189 H3 **Kyyivs'ke Vodoskhovyshche** Eng. Kiev Reservoir, Rus. Kiyevskoye Vodokhranilishche. ⊠ N Ukraine
153 H8 **Kyyjärvi** Länsi-Soumi, C Finland 63°02′N 24°34′E
192 G8 **Kyzyl** Respublika Tyva, C Russian Federation 51°45′N 94°28′E
229 J4 **Kyzyl-Adyr** var. Kirovskoye. Talasskaya Oblast', NW Kyrgyzstan 42°37′N 71°34′E
227 K6 **Kyzylagash** Almaty, SE Kazakhstan 45°20′N 78°45′E
228 C7 **Kyzylbair** Balkan Welaýaty, W Turkmenistan 38°13′N 55°38′E
Kyzyl-Dzhiik, Pereval see Uzbel Shankou
227 J2 **Kyzylkak, Ozero** ◎ NE Kazakhstan
227 L5 **Kyzylkesek** Vostochnyy Kazakhstan, E Kazakhstan 47°56′N 82°02′E
229 K6 **Kyzyl-Kiya** Kir. Kyzyl-Kyya. Batkenskaya Oblast', SW Kyrgyzstan 40°15′N 72°07′E
226 F4 **Kyzylkol', Ozero** ◎ C Kazakhstan
208 D3 **Kyzyl Kum** var. Kizil Kum, Qizil Qum, Uzb. Qizilqum. desert Kazakhstan/Uzbekistan
Kyzyl-Kyya see Kyzyl-Kiya
Kyzylrabat see Qizilravot
Kyzylrabot see Qizilrabot
Kyzylsu see Kyzyl-Suu
229 M4 **Kyzyl-Suu** prev. Pokrovka. Issyk-Kul'skaya Oblast', NE Kyrgyzstan 42°20′N 77°55′E
229 J6 **Kyzyl-Suu** var. Kyzylsu. ≈ Kyrgyzstan/Tajikistan
229 M4 **Kyzyl-Tuu** Issyk-Kul'skaya Oblast', E Kyrgyzstan 42°06′N 76°54′E
227 H5 **Kyzylzhar** Kaz. Qyzylzhar. Karaganda, C Kazakhstan 48°22′N 70°00′E
226 G7 **Kzyl-Orda** Kzyl-Orda, S Kazakhstan 44°54′N 65°31′E
226 F6 **Kzyl-Orda** ◈ province S Kazakhstan
Kzyltu see Kishkenekol'

L

116 E6 **La Adela** La Pampa, Argentina 39°06′S 64°06′E
116 F3 **La Carlota** Cordoba, Argentina 33°30′S 63°18′E
116 J4 **La Coronilla** Rocha, Uruguay 33°54′S 53°36′E
114 E3 **La Criolla** Entre Rios, Argentina 31°18′S 58°06′E
116 I4 **La Cruz** Florida, Uruguay 33°54′S 56°18′E
116 G1 **La Gallareta** Santa Fe, Argentina 29°36′S 60°30′E
116 B2 **La Higuera** Coquimbo, Chile 29°36′S 71°12′E
116 B3 **La Ligua** Valparaíso, Chile 32°30′S 71°18′E
116 E1 **La Madrid** Tucuman, Argentina 27°42′S 65°24′E
116 I3 **La Paloma** Durazno, Uruguay 32°54′S 55°36′E
116 J4 **La Paloma** Rocha, Uruguay 34°42′S 54°12′E
116 D3 **La Paz** Mendoza, Argentina 33°30′S 67°30′E
116 E1 **La Posta** Catamarca, Argentina 28°00′S 65°36′E
114 B8 **La Trinidad** Buenos Aires, Argentina 34°12′S 61°12′E
114 B7 **La Vanguardia** Santa Fe, Argentina 33°18′S 60°36′E
177 L1 **Laa an der Thaya** Niederösterreich, NE Austria 48°44′N 16°23′E
177 J2 **Laakirchen** Oberösterreich, N Austria 47°59′N 13°49′E
Laaland see Lolland
170 D6 **La Albuera** Extremadura, W Spain 38°43′N 06°49′W
171 H4 **La Alcarria** physical region C Spain
170 E8 **La Algaba** Andalucía, S Spain 37°27′N 06°01′W
171 H5 **La Almarcha** Castilla-La Mancha, C Spain 39°41′N 02°23′W
171 I4 **La Almunia de Doña Godina** Aragón, NE Spain 41°28′N 01°23′W
173 M1 **La Ametlla de Mar** Cataluña, Spain 40°54′N 0°48′E
85 K3 **Presa La Amistad** Mexico 29°26′N 101°04′W
85 K3 **La Amistad, Presa** ⊠ NW Mexico
190 D4 **Läänemaa** var. Lääne Maakond. ◈ province NW Estonia
Lääne Maakond see Läänemaa
190 F3 **Lääne-Virumaa** off Lääne-Viru Maakond. ◈ province NE Estonia
Lääne-Viru Maakond see Lääne-Virumaa
114 B9 **La Angelita** Buenos Aires, Argentina 34°16′S 60°59′W
84 F3 **Presa de La Angostura** Veracruz-Llave, Mexico 30°30′N 109°22′W
87 H6 **La Antigua** Veracruz-Llave, Mexico 19°20′N 96°18′W
85 N10 **La Antigua** Veracruz-Llave, Mexico
116 D2 **La Antigua, Salina** salt lake W Argentina
163 D9 **Laarne** Oost-Vlaanderen, NW Belgium 51°03′N 03°50′E
136 I4 **Laas Caanood** Sool, N Somalia 08°33′N 47°44′E
85 L7 **La Ascensión** Nuevo León, NE Mexico 24°15′N 99°53′W
136 H4 **Laas Dhaareed** Sanaag, N Somalia 10°12′N 46°09′E
103 H2 **La Asunción** Nueva Esparta, NE Venezuela 11°06′N 63°53′W
Laatokka see Ladozhskoye, Ozero
180 H6 **Laatzen** Niedersachsen, NW Germany 52°19′N 09°46′E
88 C4 **La Aurora** ✈ (Ciudad de Guatemala) Guatemala, C Guatemala 14°33′N 90°30′W
171 K10 **Laayoune** Algeria
130 C5 **Laâyoune** var. Aaiún. ● (Western Sahara) NW Western Sahara 27°10′N 13°11′W
215 I2 **Laba** ≈ SW Russian Federation
85 K4 **La Babia** Coahuila de Zaragoza, NE Mexico 28°39′N 102°00′W
59 H7 **La Baie** Québec, SE Canada 48°20′N 70°54′W
172 G2 **Labajos** Castilla y León, Spain 40°51′N 4°31′W
260 E8 **Labala** Pulau Lomblen, S Indonesia 08°30′S 123°27′E
112 D6 **La Banda** Santiago del Estero, N Argentina 27°44′S 64°14′W
La Banda Oriental see Uruguay
170 E3 **La Bañeza** Castilla-León, N Spain 42°18′N 05°54′W
86 C5 **La Barca** Jalisco, SW Mexico 20°20′N 102°33′W
115 K9 **La Barra** Rocha, Uruguay 34°22′S 53°46′W
86 B6 **La Barra de Navidad** Jalisco, C Mexico 19°12′N 104°38′W
168 E6 **La Barthe-de-Neste** Midi-Pyrénées, France 43°05′N 0°22′E
280 F8 **Labasa** prev. Lambasa. Vanua Levu, N Fiji 16°25′S 179°24′E
263 L8 **Labason** Mindanao, S Philippines 08°03′N 122°31′E
167 H2 **La Bassée** Nord-Pas-de-Calais, France 50°32′N 2°48′E
168 C6 **Labastide-Clairence** Aquitaine, France 43°26′N 1°15′W
168 F3 **Labastide-Murat** Midi-Pyrénées, France 44°39′N 1°34′E
169 L3 **La Bâtie-Neuve** Provence-Alpes-Côte d'Azur, France 44°34′N 6°12′E
164 E4 **la Baule-Escoublac** Loire-Atlantique, NW France 47°17′N 02°24′W
132 C5 **Labé** NW Guinea 11°19′N 12°17′W
Labe see Elbe
114 B9 **La Beba** Buenos Aires, Argentina 34°09′S 61°01′W
169 K4 **La Bégude-de-Mazenc** Rhône-Alpes, France 44°32′N 4°56′E
62 G2 **Labelle** Québec, SE Canada 46°15′N 74°43′W
69 M8 **La Belle** Florida, SE USA 26°45′N 81°26′W
54 B3 **Laberge, Lake** ◎ Yukon Territory, W Canada
Labes see Łobez
Labiau see Polessk
184 A3 **Labin** It. Albona. Istra, NW Croatia 45°05′N 14°10′E
196 G8 **Labinsk** Krasnodarskiy Kray, SW Russian Federation 44°39′N 40°43′E
168 E10 **La Bisbal de Falset** Cataluña, Spain 41°16′N 0°43′E
171 L3 **La Bisbal d'Empordà** Cataluña, NE Spain 41°58′N 03°02′E
191 I9 **Labkovichy** Rus. Lobkovichi. Mahilyowskaya Voblasts', E Belarus 53°50′N 31°45′E
263 L5 **Labo** Luzon, N Philippines 14°10′N 122°47′E
Laboehanbadjo see Labuhanbajo
85 I5 **La Boquilla del Conchos** Chihuahua, Mexico 27°33′N 105°24′W
Laborca see Laborec
114 A8 **Labordeboy** Santa Fe, Argentina 33°43′S 61°20′W
183 I9 **Laborec** Hung. Laborca. ≈ E Slovakia
176 C5 **La Borgne** ≈ S Switzerland
91 J6 **Laborie** SW Saint Lucia 13°45′N 61°00′W
135 C9 **La Bouenza** ◈ province S Congo
114 F2 **Labougle** Corrientes, Argentina 30°19′S 57°43′W
164 F8 **Labouheyre** Landes, SW France 44°12′N 00°55′W
116 F4 **Laboulaye** Córdoba, C Argentina 34°05′S 63°20′W
169 H2 **La Bourboule** Auvergne, France 45°35′N 2°45′E
59 K4 **Labrador** cultural region Newfoundland and Labrador, SW Canada
290 E2 **Labrador Basin** var. Labrador Sea Basin. undersea feature Labrador Sea
59 I5 **Labrador City** Newfoundland and Labrador, E Canada 52°56′N 66°52′W
59 K2 **Labrador Sea** sea NW Atlantic Ocean
Labrador Sea Basin see Labrador Basin
Labrang see Xiahe
102 D5 **Labranzagrande** Boyacá, C Colombia 05°34′N 72°34′W
114 C2 **La Brava** Santa Fe, Argentina 30°28′S 60°10′W
106 E5 **Lábrea** Amazonas, N Brazil 07°20′S 64°46′W
91 K8 **La Brea** Trinidad, Trinidad and Tobago 10°14′N 61°37′W
84 G7 **La Brecha** Sinaloa, Mexico 25°23′N 108°26′W
168 D3 **Labréde** Aquitaine, France 44°41′N 0°32′W
169 L5 **La Brillanne** Provence-Alpes-Côte d'Azur, France 43°55′N 5°53′E
164 F8 **Labrit** Landes, SW France 44°03′N 00°29′W

◆ Country
● Country Capital
◇ Dependent Territory
○ Dependent Territory Capital
◈ Administrative Regions
✈ International Airport
▲ Mountain
▲▲ Mountain Range
♨ Volcano
≈ River
◎ Lake
⊠ Reservoir

◆ Country	◇ Dependent Territory	◆ Administrative Regions	▲ Mountain	◉ Volcano	⊗ Lake
● Country Capital	○ Dependent Territory Capital	✈ International Airport	▲ Mountain Range	≈ River	⊠ Reservoir

◆ Country   ◇ Dependent Territory   ◈ Administrative Regions   ▲ Mountain   ◉ Lake
● Country Capital   ○ Dependent Territory Capital   ✈ International Airport   ▲ Mountain Range   ☒ Reservoir
   ✈ River

◆ Country ◇ Dependent Territory ✈ Administrative Regions ▲ Mountain ◬ Volcano ○ Lake
● Country Capital ◯ Dependent Territory Capital ✈ International Airport ▲ Mountain Range ≈ River ⊠ Reservoir

◆ Country
● Country Capital
◇ Dependent Territory
○ Dependent Territory Capital
◇ Administrative Regions
✕ International Airport
▲ Mountain
▲ Mountain Range
≈ Volcano
≈ River
☒ Lake
☒ Reservoir

◆ Country
● Country Capital
◇ Dependent Territory
○ Dependent Territory Capital
◆ Administrative Regions
✕ International Airport
▲ Mountain
▲ Mountain Range
◆ Volcano
⋙ River
⊚ Lake
⊡ Reservoir

◆ Country ◇ Dependent Territory ◈ Administrative Regions ▲ Mountain ◉ Volcano ◎ Lake
● Country Capital ○ Dependent Territory Capital ✕ International Airport ▲ Mountain Range ⟶ River ▣ Reservoir

◆ Country
● Country Capital
◇ Dependent Territory
◆ Dependent Territory Capital
◆ Administrative Regions
✈ International Airport
▲ Mountain
▲ Mountain Range
🌋 Volcano
↔ River
⊘ Lake
⊠ Reservoir

◆ Country	◇ Dependent Territory	◆ Administrative Regions	▲ Mountain	▲ Volcano	⊚ Lake
● Country Capital	◎ Dependent Territory Capital	✕ International Airport	▲ Mountain Range	⊲ River	⊟ Reservoir

Symbol	Meaning	Symbol	Meaning	Symbol	Meaning	Symbol	Meaning
◆	Country	◇	Dependent Territory	◈	Administrative Regions	▲	Mountain	★	Volcano	◻	Lake
●	Country Capital	○	Dependent Territory Capital	✈	International Airport	▲	Mountain Range	♣	River	◻	Reservoir

◆ Country
● Country Capital
◇ Dependent Territory
○ Dependent Territory Capital
▲ Administrative Regions
✈ International Airport
▲ Mountain
▲ Mountain Range
▲ Volcano
◀ River
◉ Lake
◉ Reservoir

◆ Country ● Country Capital ◇ Dependent Territory ○ Dependent Territory Capital ◆ Administrative Regions ✈ International Airport ▲ Mountain ▲ Mountain Range ▲ Volcano ✍ River ⊘ Lake ▣ Reservoir

◆ Country
◆ Country Capital
◇ Dependent Territory
○ Dependent Territory Capital
◆ Administrative Regions
✕ International Airport
▲ Mountain
▲ Mountain Range
▲ Volcano
✍ River
◎ Lake
▢ Reservoir

◆ Country	◇ Dependent Territory	✕ Administrative Regions	▲ Mountain	▲ Volcano	© Lake
● Country Capital	○ Dependent Territory Capital	✕ International Airport	▲ Mountain Range	♣ River	☒ Reservoir

◆ Country   ◇ Dependent Territory   ✕ Administrative Regions   ▲ Mountain   ⛰ Volcano   ☉ Lake
● Country Capital   ○ Dependent Territory Capital   ✈ International Airport   ▲ Mountain Range   ◆ River   ☒ Reservoir

◆ Country   ◇ Dependent Territory   ✕ Administrative Regions   ▲ Mountain   ⊙ Volcano   ◎ Lake
◆ Country Capital   ○ Dependent Territory Capital   ✕ International Airport   ▲ Mountain Range   ☐ River   ☐ Reservoir

◆ Country   ◇ Dependent Territory   ✕ Administrative Regions   ▲ Mountain   ✦ Volcano   ◎ Lake
● Country Capital ○ Dependent Territory Capital   ✈ International Airport   ▲ Mountain Range   ✍ River   ▭ Reservoir

Paranaíta - Pembina
INDEX
389

107 I6 **Paranaíta** Mato Grosso, W Brazil 09°35′S 57°01′W
113 J3 **Paranapanema, Rio** ≈ S Brazil
110 B10 **Paranapiacaba, Serra do** ▲▲ S Brazil
113 I3 **Paranavaí** Paraná, S Brazil 23°02′S 52°36′W
222 F4 **Parandak** Markazī, W Iran 35°19′N 50°40′E
187 I2 **Paranésti** var Paranestio. Anatolikí Makedonía kai Thráki, NE Greece 41°16′N 24°31′E
Paranestio see Paranésti
285 K7 **Paraoa** atoll Îles Tuamotu, C French Polynesia
110 G2 **Paraopeba** Minas Gerais, Brazil 19°18′S 44°25′W
278 G7 **Paraparaumu** Wellington, North Island, New Zealand 40°55′S 175°01′E
112 E2 **Parapeti, Río** ≈ SE Bolivia
104 I4 **Paraque, Cerro** ▲ W Venezuela 06°00′S 67°00′W
232 F9 **Parāsiya** Madhya Pradesh, C India 22°11′N 78°50′E
187 L9 **Paraspóri, Ákrotírio** cape Kárpathos, SE Greece
110 G8 **Parati** Rio de Janeiro, SE Brazil 23°15′S 44°42′W
107 L4 **Parauapebas** Pará, N Brazil 06°03′S 49°48′W
165 I5 **Paray-le-Monial** Saône-et-Loire, C France 46°27′N 04°07′E
Parbatsar see Parvatsar
234 E4 **Parbhani** Mahārāshtra, C India 19°16′N 76°51′E
178 G5 **Parchim** Mecklenburg-Vorpommern, N Germany 53°26′N 11°51′E
Parchwitz see Prochowice
182 I6 **Parczew** Lubelskie, E Poland 51°40′N 23°E
110 C5 **Pardo, Rio** ≈ S Brazil
183 D8 **Pardubice** Ger. Pardubitz. Pardubický Kraj, C Czech Republic 50°01′N 15°47′E
183 D8 **Pardubický Kraj** ⬖ region N Czech Republic
Pardubitz see Pardubice
191 D10 **Parechcha** Pol. Porzecze, Rus. Porech'ye. Hrodzyenskaya Voblasts', W Belarus 53°53′N 24°08′E
106 G8 **Parecis, Chapada dos** var. Serra dos Parecis. ▲▲ W Brazil
Parecis, Serra dos see Parecis, Chapada dos
172 C1 **Paredes** Porto, Portugal 41°12′N 8°20′W
170 F3 **Paredes de Nava** Castilla-León, N Spain 42°09′N 04°42′W
118 F4 **Pareditas** Mendoza, Argentina 33°56′S 69°04′W
87 J9 **Paredón** Chiapas, Mexico 16°02′N 93°52′W
282 F9 **Parem** island Chuuk, C Micronesia
283 J1 **Parem Island** island E Micronesia
278 F1 **Parengarenga Harbour** inlet North Island, New Zealand
164 F8 **Parentis-en-Born** Landes, SW France 44°22′N 01°04′W
Parenzo see Poreč
278 D11 **Pareora** Canterbury, South Island, New Zealand 44°28′S 171°12′E
260 C6 **Parepare** Sulawesi, C Indonesia 04°S 119°40′E
114 D6 **Parera** Entre Ríos, Argentina 32°48′S 58°53′W
186 E4 **Párga** Ípeiros, W Greece 39°18′N 20°19′E
153 G10 **Pargas** Swe. Parainen. Länsi-Soumi, SW Finland 60°18′N 22°20′E
170 A8 **Pargo, Ponta do** headland Madeira, Portugal, NE Atlantic Ocean 32°48′N 17°17′W
103 H3 **Pariaguán** Anzoátegui, NE Venezuela 08°51′N 64°43′W
104 H7 **Pariamanu, Río** ≈ E Peru
79 H5 **Paria River** ≈ Utah, W USA
Parichi see Parychy
86 C6 **Paricutín, Volcán** ⛰ C Mexico 19°25′N 102°20′W
89 I10 **Parida, Isla** island SW Panama
103 K4 **Parika** NE Guyana 06°51′N 58°25′W
153 J9 **Parikkala** Etelä-Suomi, SE Finland 61°33′N 29°34′E
103 H6 **Parima, Serra** var. Sierra Parima. ▲ Brazil/Venezuela 02°30′N 64°00′W see also Parima, Sierra
103 H6 **Parima, Sierra** var. Serra Parima. ▲ Brazil/Venezuela see also Parima, Serra
105 F9 **Parinacochas, Laguna** ◎ SW Peru
104 A4 **Pariñas, Punta** headland NW Peru 04°45′S 81°22′W
107 I3 **Parintins** Amazonas, N Brazil 02°38′S 56°45′W
167 H5 **Paris** anc. Lutetia, Lutetia Parisiorum, Parisii. ● (France) Paris, N France 48°52′N 02°19′E
285 M1 **Paris** Kiritimati, E Kiribati 01°55′N 157°30′W
75 G12 **Paris** Arkansas, C USA 35°17′N 93°46′W
77 I8 **Paris** Idaho, NW USA 42°14′N 111°24′W
73 D11 **Paris** Illinois, N USA 39°36′N 87°42′W
66 F3 **Paris** Kentucky, S USA 38°13′N 84°15′W
75 I9 **Paris** Missouri, C USA 39°28′N 92°00′W
66 C5 **Paris** Tennessee, S USA 36°19′N 88°20′W
71 I3 **Paris** Texas, SW USA 33°41′N 95°33′W
Parisii see Paris
89 K10 **Parita** Herrera, S Panama 08°01′N 80°30′W
89 K9 **Parita, Bahía de** bay S Panama
153 G9 **Parkano** Länsi-Suomi, W Finland 62°03′N 23°E
Parkan/Párkány see Štúrovo
75 E10 **Park City** Kansas, C USA 37°48′N 97°19′W
79 I2 **Park City** Utah, W USA 40°39′N 111°30′W
81 I12 **Parker** Arizona, SW USA 34°07′N 114°16′W
69 I4 **Parker** Florida, SE USA 30°07′N 85°36′W
74 E6 **Parker** South Dakota, N USA 43°24′N 97°08′W
53 I5 **Parker, Cape** headland Nunavut, NE Canada
81 J12 **Parker Dam** California, W USA 34°17′N 114°08′W
74 H6 **Parkersburg** Iowa, C USA 42°34′N 92°47′W
67 I2 **Parkersburg** West Virginia, NE USA 39°17′N 81°33′W
74 F4 **Parkers Prairie** Minnesota, N USA 46°09′N 95°19′W
263 M9 **Parker Volcano** ⛰ Mindanao, S Philippines 06°09′N 124°52′E
277 K5 **Parkes** New South Wales, SE Australia 33°10′S 148°10′E
161 M5 **Parkeston** UK 51°56′N 1°15′E
72 C4 **Park Falls** Wisconsin, N USA 45°57′N 90°25′W
80 C6 **Parkfield** California, USA 35°54′N 120°26′W
Parkhar see Farkhor
62 B5 **Parkhill** Ontario, S Canada 43°11′N 81°39′W
74 F3 **Park Rapids** Minnesota, N USA 46°55′N 95°03′W
74 E2 **Park River** North Dakota, N USA 48°24′N 97°44′W
74 E6 **Parkston** South Dakota, N USA 43°24′N 97°58′W
56 C8 **Parksville** Vancouver Island, British Columbia, SW Canada 49°13′N 124°13′W
79 L2 **Parkview Mountain** ▲ Colorado, C USA 40°19′N 106°08′W
64 D9 **Parkville** Maryland, USA 39°23′N 76°32′W
170 G5 **Parla** Madrid, C Spain 40°13′N 03°48′W
74 F4 **Parle, Lac qui** ⊠ Minnesota, N USA
186 G7 **Parlía Tyroú** Pelopónnisos, S Greece 37°17′N 22°50′E
80 D6 **Parlier** California, USA 36°37′N 119°32′W
234 E5 **Parli Vaijnāth** Mahārāshtra, C India 18°53′N 76°36′E
176 F8 **Parma** Emilia-Romagna, N Italy 44°50′N 10°20′E
73 I9 **Parma** Ohio, N USA 41°24′N 81°43′W
Parnahyba see Parnaíba
108 F3 **Parnaíba** var. Parnahyba. Piauí, E Brazil 02°58′S 41°46′W
291 F8 **Parnaíba Ridge** undersea feature C Atlantic Ocean
108 F4 **Parnaíba, Rio** ≈ NE Brazil
186 G5 **Parnassós** ▲▲ C Greece
278 F9 **Parnassus** Canterbury, South Island, New Zealand 42°41′S 173°18′E
276 F6 **Parndana** South Australia 35°48′S 137°13′E
187 H6 **Párnitha** ▲▲ C Greece
Parnon see Párnonas
186 G7 **Párnonas** var. Parnon. ▲▲ S Greece
190 D4 **Pärnu** Ger. Pernau, Latv. Pērnava; prev. Rus. Pernov. Pärnumaa, SW Estonia 58°24′N 24°32′E
190 E4 **Pärnu** var. Parnu Jõgi, Ger. Pernau. ≈ SW Estonia
190 D4 **Pärnu-Jaagupi** Ger. Sankt-Jakobi. Pärnumaa, SW Estonia 58°36′N 24°30′E
Parnu Jõgi see Pärnu
190 D5 **Pärnu Laht** Ger. Pernauer Bucht. bay SW Estonia
190 D4 **Pärnumaa** var. Pärnu Maakond. ⬖ province SW Estonia
Pärnu Maakond see Pärnumaa
233 K6 **Paro** W Bhutan 27°23′N 89°31′E
233 K6 **Paro** ✕ (Thimphu) W Bhutan 27°23′N 89°31′E
278 D9 **Paroa** West Coast, South Island, New Zealand 42°31′S 171°10′E
248 C5 **P'aro-ho** var. Hwach'ŏn-chŏsuji. ⊠ N South Korea
187 J7 **Pároikiá** prev. Páros. Páros, Kykládes, Greece, Aegean Sea 37°04′N 25°06′E
277 I3 **Paroo River** seasonal river New South Wales/Queensland, SE Australia
187 I7 **Páros** island Kykládes, Greece, Aegean Sea
Páros see Pároikiá
140 D10 **Parow** Western Cape, South Africa 33°54′S 18°36′E
79 H5 **Parowan** Utah, W USA 37°50′N 112°49′W
165 K7 **Parpaillon** ▲▲ SE France
176 F4 **Parpan** Graubünden, S Switzerland 46°46′N 09°32′E
116 B5 **Parral** Maule, C Chile 36°08′S 71°52′W
Parral see Hidalgo del Parral
277 L5 **Parramatta** New South Wales, SE Australia 33°49′S 150°59′E
67 M4 **Parramore Island** island Virginia, NE USA
85 K7 **Parras** var. Parras de la Fuente. Coahuila de Zaragoza, NE Mexico 25°26′N 102°07′W
Parras de la Fuente see Parras
172 B4 **Parreira** Santarém, Portugal 39°13′N 8°24′W
89 H8 **Parrita** Puntarenas, S Costa Rica 09°30′N 84°20′W
85 K3 **Parrita** Chihuahua, Mexico
53 J8 **Parry Bay** coastal sea feature Nunavut, NE Canada
53 H5 **Parry Channel** sea waterway Northwest Territories/Nunavut, N Canada
Parry group see Mukojima-rettō
62 C3 **Parry Island** island Ontario, S Canada
52 G5 **Parry Islands** Island group
295 I8 **Parry Islands** island group Nunavut, NW Canada
52 C6 **Parry Peninsula** Peninsula Northwest Territories, NW Canada
62 C3 **Parry Sound** Ontario, S Canada 45°21′N 80°03′W
180 J5 **Parsau** Niedersachsen, Germany 10°52′N 52°32′E
182 D4 **Parsęta** Ger. Persante. ≈ NW Poland
74 B2 **Parshall** North Dakota, N USA 47°57′N 102°07′W
75 F11 **Parsons** Kansas, C USA 37°20′N 95°15′W
66 C6 **Parsons** Tennessee, S USA 35°39′N 88°07′W
67 J2 **Parsons** West Virginia, NE USA 39°06′N 79°43′W
Parsonstown see Birr
178 I6 **Parsteiner See** ◎ NE Germany
175 E12 **Partanna** Sicilia, Italy, C Mediterranean Sea 37°43′N 12°54′E
176 F4 **Partenen** Graubünden, E Switzerland 46°58′N 10°01′E
181 G12 **Partenstein** Bayern, Germany 9°31′N 50°03′E
164 G5 **Parthenay** Deux-Sèvres, W France 46°39′N 00°13′W
155 F10 **Partille** Västra Götaland, S Sweden 57°43′N 12°12′E
175 E12 **Partinico** Sicilia, Italy, C Mediterranean Sea 38°03′N 13°07′E
183 F10 **Partizánske** prev. Šimonovany, Hung. Simony. Trenčiansky Kraj, W Slovakia 48°35′N 18°23′E
159 M10 **Partney** UK 53°11′N 0°07′E
159 H7 **Parton** UK 54°34′N 3°35′W
107 I1 **Paru de Oeste, Rio** ≈ N Brazil
277 H5 **Paruna** South Australia 34°45′S 140°43′E
103 M8 **Paru, Rio** ≈ N Brazil
230 G3 **Parvān** Pash. Parwān. ⬖ province E Afghanistan
234 H5 **Pārvatipuram** Andhra Pradesh, E India 17°01′N 81°47′E
232 D6 **Parvatsar** prev. Parbatsar. Rājasthān, N India 26°52′N 74°49′E
Parwān see Parvān
159 K10 **Parwich** UK 53°05′N 1°43′W
238 E9 **Paryang** Xizang Zizhiqu, W China 30°04′N 83°28′E
191 H11 **Parychy** Rus. Parichi. Homyel'skaya Voblasts', SE Belarus 52°48′N 29°25′E
138 G7 **Parys** Free State, C South Africa 26°55′S 27°28′E
81 D10 **Pasadena** California, W USA 34°09′N 118°09′W
71 I7 **Pasadena** Texas, SW USA 29°41′N 95°13′W
104 B3 **Pasaje** El Oro, SW Ecuador 03°23′S 79°50′W
215 K3 **P'asanauri** N Georgia 42°21′N 44°40′E
258 D6 **Pasapuat** Pulau Pagai Utara, W Indonesia 02°36′S 99°58′E
256 D5 **Pasawng** Kayah State, C Myanmar (Burma) 18°50′N 97°16′E
68 F4 **Pascagoula** Mississippi, S USA 30°21′N 88°32′W
68 F4 **Pascagoula River** ≈ Mississippi, S USA
188 E6 **Paşcani** Hung. Páskán. Iaşi, NE Romania 47°14′N 26°46′E
177 J2 **Pasching** Oberösterreich, N Austria 48°16′N 14°10′E
76 E5 **Pasco** Washington, NW USA 46°13′N 119°06′W
104 E6 **Pasco** off. Departamento de Pasco. ⬖ department C Peru
65 L3 **Pascoag** Rhode Island, USA 41°57′N 71°42′W
Pasco, Departamento de see Pasco
117 B11 **Pascua, Río** ≈ S Chile
165 H1 **Pas-de-Calais** ⬖ department N France
178 I5 **Pasewalk** Mecklenburg-Vorpommern, NE Germany 53°31′N 13°59′E
55 H6 **Pasfield Lake** ◎ Saskatchewan, C Canada
190 J2 **Pasha** Leningradskaya Oblast', Russian Federation
Pa-shih Hai-hsia see Bashi Channel
Pashkeni see Bolyarovo
Pashmakli see Smolyan
263 K5 **Pasig** Luzon, N Philippines 14°34′N 121°04′E
233 M5 **Pāsighāt** Arunāchel Pradesh, NE India 28°08′N 95°13′E
215 I5 **Pasinler** Erzurum, NE Turkey 39°59′N 41°41′E
Pasi Oloy, Qatorkŭhi see Zaalayskiy Khrebet
88 C2 **Pasión, Río de la** ≈ N Guatemala
258 D6 **Pasirganting** Sumatera, W Indonesia 02°04′S 100°51′E
Pasirpangarayan see Bagansiapiapi
258 E2 **Pasir Puteh** var. Pasir Putih. Kelantan, Peninsular Malaysia 05°50′N 102°24′E
Pasir Putih see Pasir Puteh
258 I4 **Pasir, Tanjung** cape East Malaysia
155 H10 **Påskallavik** Kalmar, S Sweden 57°10′N 16°25′E
Páskán see Paşcani
Paskevicha, Zaliv see Tushybas, Zaliv
182 G4 **Pasłęk** Ger. Preußisch Holland. Warmińsko-Mazurskie, NE Poland 54°03′N 19°40′E
182 G3 **Pasłęka** Ger. Passarge. ≈ N Poland
230 E9 **Pasni** Baluchistān, SW Pakistan 25°13′N 63°30′E
117 C9 **Paso de Indios** Chubut, Argentina 43°48′S 69°06′E
114 F9 **Paso Antolín** Colonia, Uruguay 34°12′S 57°47′W
114 F9 **Paso de la Horqueta** Colonia, Uruguay 34°12′S 57°52′W
114 D4 **Paso de la Laguna** Entre Ríos, Argentina 31°48′S 59°10′W
115 H4 **Paso de las Carretas** Uruguay 31°30′S 56°02′W
102 F4 **Paso del Caballo** Guárico, N Venezuela 08°19′N 67°08′W
115 K5 **Paso del Centurión** Cerro Largo, Uruguay 32°10′S 53°45′W
115 I4 **Paso del Cerro** Uruguay 31°31′S 55°46′W
114 G1 **Paso del León** Artigas, Uruguay 30°10′S 57°06′W
114 F5 **Paso de los Carros** Paysandú, Uruguay 31°59′S 57°25′W
118 E10 **Paso de los Indios** Neuquén, Argentina 38°32′S 69°25′W
114 G1 **Paso de los Libres** Corrientes, NE Argentina 29°43′S 57°09′W
115 H6 **Paso de los Toros** Tacuarembó, C Uruguay 32°45′S 56°30′W
Pasoeroean see Pasuruan
118 B8 **Paso Hondo** Bío-Bío, Chile 36°55′S 72°32′W
115 I5 **Paso Pereira** Cerro Largo, Uruguay 32°28′S 55°14′W
85 J8 **Paso Real** Oaxaca, Mexico
80 B7 **Paso Robles** California, W USA 35°37′N 120°42′W
55 H8 **Pasquia Hills** ▲▲ Saskatchewan, S Canada
231 J5 **Pasrūr** Punjab, E Pakistan 32°12′N 74°42′E
111 I2 **Passabém** Minas Gerais, Brazil 19°17′S 43°13′W
72 D2 **Passage Island** island Michigan, N USA
117 H11 **Passage Islands** island group W Falkland Islands
52 E5 **Passage Point** headland Banks Island, Northwest Territories, NW Canada 73°31′N 115°12′W
65 H6 **Passaic** New Jersey, USA 40°51′N 74°08′W
Passarge see Pasłęka
186 E4 **Passarón** ancient monument Ípeiros, W Greece
Passarowitz see Požarevac
110 G4 **Passa Tempo** Minas Gerais, Brazil 20°40′S 44°30′W
179 I12 **Passau** Bayern, SE Germany 48°34′N 13°28′E
110 G7 **Passa Vinte** Minas Gerais, Brazil 22°13′S 44°15′W
68 F4 **Pass Christian** Mississippi, S USA 30°19′N 89°15′W
175 G13 **Passero, Capo** headland Sicilia, Italy, C Mediterranean Sea 36°40′N 15°09′E
263 L7 **Passi** Panay Island, C Philippines 11°05′N 122°37′E
115 M1 **Passo do Sobrado** Rio Grande do Sul, Brazil 29°45′S 52°17′W
113 I6 **Passo Fundo** Rio Grande do Sul, S Brazil 28°16′S 52°20′W
113 I6 **Passo Fundo, Barragem de** ⊠ S Brazil
115 I1 **Passo Novo** Rio Grande do Sul, Brazil 29°41′S 55°32′W
110 F7 **Passo Quatro** Minas Gerais, Brazil 22°23′S 44°58′W
113 I6 **Passo Real, Barragem de** ⊠ S Brazil
110 D4 **Passos** Minas Gerais, NE Brazil 20°45′S 46°38′W
262 G5 **Passu Keah** island S Paracel Islands
169 M1 **Passy** Rhône-Alpes, France 45°55′N 6°41′E
191 F8 **Pastavy** Pol. Postawy, Rus. Postavy. Vitsyebskaya Voblasts', NW Belarus 55°07′N 26°50′E
104 D2 **Pastaza** ⬖ province E Ecuador
104 D3 **Pastaza, Río** ≈ Ecuador/Peru
112 E10 **Pasteur** Buenos Aires, E Argentina 35°10′S 62°14′W
229 I6 **Pastigav** Rus. Pastigov. W Tajikistan 39°27′N 69°16′E
Pastigov see Pastigav
102 A7 **Pasto** Nariño, SW Colombia 01°12′N 77°17′W
79 J6 **Pastora Peak** ▲ Arizona, SW USA 36°48′N 109°10′W
114 D6 **Pastor Britos** Entre Ríos, Argentina 32°46′S 58°53′W
170 G5 **Pastrana** Castilla-La Mancha, C Spain 40°24′N 02°55′W
259 J9 **Pasuruan** prev. Pasoeroean. Jawa, C Indonesia 07°38′S 112°44′E
190 D7 **Pasvalys** Panevėžys, N Lithuania 56°03′N 24°24′E
183 G11 **Pásztó** Nógrád, N Hungary 47°57′N 19°41′E
282 E9 **Pata** var. Patta. atoll Chuuk Islands, C Micronesia
79 I10 **Patagonia** Arizona, SW USA 31°32′N 110°45′W
117 C10 **Patagonia** semi arid region Argentina/Chile
Patalung see Phatthalung
232 C7 **Pātan** Gujarāt, W India 23°51′N 72°11′E
232 F8 **Pātan** Madhya Pradesh, C India 23°19′N 79°41′E
260 G4 **Patani** Pulau Halmahera, E Indonesia 0°19′N 128°46′E
Patani see Pattani
188 E9 **Pătâriagele** prev. Pătîriagele. Buzău, SE Romania 45°19′N 26°21′E
Patavium see Padova
276 G3 **Patawarta Hill** ▲ South Australia 30°57′S 138°42′E
166 G7 **Patay** Centre, France 48°03′N 1°42′E
55 M7 **Patchepawapoka River** ≈ Ontario, C Canada
277 H6 **Patchewollock** Victoria, SE Australia 35°24′S 142°11′E
65 J6 **Patchogue** New York, USA 40°46′N 73°01′W
160 G6 **Patchway** UK 51°32′N 2°34′W
278 G6 **Patea** Taranaki, North Island, New Zealand 39°48′S 174°35′E
278 G6 **Patea** ≈ North Island, New Zealand
133 J7 **Pategi** Kwara, C Nigeria 08°39′N 05°46′E
137 F9 **Pate Island** var. Patta Island. island SE Kenya
171 I6 **Paterna** País Valenciano, E Spain 39°30′N 00°24′W
172 E9 **Paterna de Rivera** Andalucía, Spain 36°31′N 5°52′W
177 J4 **Paternion** Slvn. Špatrjan. Kärnten, S Austria 46°40′N 13°43′E
175 G12 **Paternò** anc. Hybla, Hybla Major. Sicilia, Italy, C Mediterranean Sea 37°34′N 14°55′E
140 D9 **Paternoster** Western Cape, South Africa 32°49′S 17°53′E
76 D3 **Pateros** Washington, NW USA 48°01′N 119°55′W
65 H5 **Paterson** New Jersey, NE USA 40°55′N 74°12′W
76 D5 **Paterson** Washington, NW USA 45°56′N 119°37′W
278 B13 **Paterson Inlet** inlet Stewart Island, New Zealand
162 I4 **Paterswolde** Drenthe, NE Netherlands 53°07′N 06°32′E
232 E3 **Pathānkot** Himāchal Pradesh, N India 32°16′N 75°43′E
Pathein see Bassein
77 K8 **Pathfinder Reservoir** ⊠ Wyoming, C USA
256 E8 **Pathum Thani** var. Patumdhani, Prathum Thani. Pathum Thani, C Thailand 14°03′N 100°29′E
259 I8 **Pati** Jawa, C Indonesia 06°45′S 111°00′E
102 B7 **Patía** var. El Bordo. Cauca, SW Colombia 02°07′N 76°57′W
232 E4 **Patiāla** var. Puttiala. Punjab, NW India 30°21′N 76°27′E
102 A7 **Patía, Río** ≈ SW Colombia
260 G4 **Patinti, Selat** strait Maluku, E Indonesia
282 B1 **Pati Point** headland NE Guam 13°36′N 144°39′E
Pătîriagele see Pătâriagele
104 C7 **Pativilca** Lima, W Peru 10°44′S 77°45′W
256 C2 **Pātkai Bum** var. Patkai Range. ▲▲ Myanmar (Burma)/India
Patkai Range see Pātkai Bum
187 K7 **Pátmos** Pátmos, Dodekánisa, Greece, Aegean Sea 37°18′N 26°32′E
187 K7 **Pátmos** island Dodekánisa, Greece, Aegean Sea
233 I7 **Patna** var. Azimabad. state capital Bihār, N India 25°36′N 85°11′E
158 G5 **Patna** UK 55°21′N 4°30′W
234 H4 **Patnāgarh** Orissa, E India 20°42′N 83°12′E
263 L7 **Patnongon** Panay Island, C Philippines 10°56′N 122°03′E
215 J6 **Patnos** Ağrı, E Turkey 39°14′N 42°52′E
113 I5 **Pato Branco** Paraná, S Brazil 26°20′S 52°40′W
73 E12 **Patoka Lake** ◎ Indiana, N USA
152 H3 **Patoniva** Lapp. Buoddobohki. Lappi, N Finland 69°44′N 27°01′E
184 F9 **Patos** var. Patosi. Fier, SW Albania 40°40′N 19°37′E
Patos see Patos de Minas
109 D11 **Patos de Minas** var. Patos. Minas Gerais, NE Brazil 18°35′S 46°32′W
118 D6 **Patos de San Pedro, Río** ≈ Maule, Chile
Patosi see Patos
115 N4 **Patos, Lagoa dos** lagoon S Brazil
116 D2 **Patquía** La Rioja, C Argentina 30°02′S 66°54′W
186 F6 **Pátra** Eng. Patras; prev. Pátrai. Dytikí Ellás, S Greece 38°14′N 21°45′E
186 F6 **Patraïkós Kólpos** gulf S Greece
Pátrai/Patras see Pátra
152 A2 **Patreksfjördhur** Vestfirdhir, W Iceland 65°33′N 23°54′W
70 D4 **Patricia** Texas, SW USA 32°34′N 102°00′W
117 A11 **Patricio Lynch, Isla** island S Chile
110 A2 **Patrimônio** Minas Gerais, Brazil 19°24′S 48°36′E
110 C1 **Patrocínio** Minas Gerais, Brazil 18°57′S 46°59′W
Patta see Pata
Patta Island see Pate Island
256 F11 **Pattani** var. Patani. Pattani, SW Thailand 06°50′N 101°20′E
256 F8 **Pattaya** Chon Buri, S Thailand 12°57′N 100°53′E
63 K2 **Patten** Maine, NE USA 45°58′N 68°27′W
180 H3 **Pattensen** Niedersachsen, Germany 10°08′N 53°19′E
180 H6 **Pattensen** Niedersachsen, Germany 9°46′N 52°16′E
80 C4 **Patterson** California, W USA 37°27′N 121°07′W
68 D5 **Patterson** Louisiana, S USA 29°41′N 91°18′W
80 F3 **Patterson, Mount** ▲ California, W USA 38°27′N 119°16′W
72 F5 **Patterson, Point** headland Michigan, N USA 45°58′N 85°39′W
175 G12 **Patti** Sicilia, Italy, C Mediterranean Sea 38°08′N 14°58′E
175 G12 **Patti, Golfo di** gulf Sicilia, Italy
152 H7 **Pattijoki** Oulu, W Finland 64°41′N 24°40′E
287 I3 **Patton Escarpment** undersea feature E Pacific Ocean
75 G8 **Pattonsburg** Missouri, C USA 40°03′N 94°08′W
42 B4 **Patton Seamount** undersea feature NE Pacific Ocean
56 B1 **Pattullo, Mount** ▲ British Columbia, W Canada 56°18′N 129°43′W
87 H3 **Patuca, Río** ≈ E Honduras
233 K8 **Patuakhali** var. Patukhali. Barisal, S Bangladesh 22°20′N 90°20′E
Patukhali see Patuakhali
Patumdhani see Pathum Thani
86 D6 **Pátzcuaro** Michoacán de Ocampo, SW Mexico 19°30′N 101°38′W
88 C4 **Patzicía** Chimaltenango, S Guatemala 14°38′N 90°52′W
164 F9 **Pau** Pyrénées-Atlantiques, SW France 43°18′N 00°22′W
164 F7 **Pauillac** Gironde, SW France 45°12′N 00°44′W
256 C4 **Pauk** Magwe, W Myanmar (Burma) 21°25′N 94°30′E
111 I4 **Paula Cândido** Minas Gerais, Brazil 20°53′S 42°58′W
52 D7 **Paulatuk** Northwest Territories, NW Canada 69°23′N 124°W
88 G3 **Paulayá, Río** ≈ NE Honduras
68 F2 **Paulding** Mississippi, S USA 32°01′N 89°01′W
73 G9 **Paulding** Ohio, N USA 41°08′N 84°34′W
169 I2 **Paulhac** Auvergne, France 45°18′N 3°21′E
169 I6 **Paulhan** Languedoc-Roussillon, France 43°32′N 3°27′E
110 C8 **Paulínia** São Paulo, Brazil 22°45′S 47°10′W
74 F6 **Paullina** Iowa, C USA 42°58′N 95°41′W
108 H6 **Paulo Afonso** Bahia, E Brazil 09°21′S 38°14′W
82 G9 **Pauloff Harbor** var. Pavlor Harbour. Sanak Island, Alaska, USA 54°26′N 162°43′W
141 I5 **Paul Roux** Free State, South Africa 28°18′S 27°57′E
64 F8 **Paulsboro** New Jersey, USA 39°50′N 75°14′W
75 E13 **Pauls Valley** Oklahoma, C USA 34°46′N 97°14′W
81 E12 **Pauma Valley** California, USA 33°18′N 116°59′W
256 C6 **Paungde** Pegu, C Myanmar (Burma) 18°30′N 95°30′E
Pauni see Paoni
232 F4 **Pauri** Uttaranchal, N India 30°08′N 78°48′E
Pautalia see Kyustendil
261 M5 **Pauwasi** ≈ Papua, E Indonesia
195 L8 **Pavda** Sverdlovskaya oblast', Russian federation
222 D4 **Pāveh** Kermānshāhān, NW Iran 35°02′N 46°15′E
196 G3 **Pavelets** Ryazanskaya Oblast', W Russian Federation 53°47′N 39°22′E
176 E7 **Pavia** anc. Ticinum. Lombardia, N Italy 45°10′N 09°10′E
172 C5 **Pavia** Évora, Portugal 38°54′N 8°01′W
166 F4 **Pavilly** Haute-Normandie, France 49°34′N 0°58′E
190 B6 **Pāvilosta** Liepāja, W Latvia 56°52′N 21°12′E
195 H9 **Pavino** Kostromskaya Oblast', NW Russian Federation 59°10′N 46°09′E
185 K5 **Pavlikeni** Veliko Tŭrnovo, N Bulgaria 43°14′N 25°20′E
227 J2 **Pavlodar** Pavlodar, NE Kazakhstan 52°21′N 76°59′E
227 J2 **Pavlodar** off. Pavlodarskaya Oblast', Kaz. Pavlodar Oblysy. ⬖ province NE Kazakhstan
Pavlodar Oblysy/Pavlodarskaya Oblast' see Pavlodar
Pavlograd see Pavlohrad
189 K5 **Pavlohrad** Rus. Pavlograd. Dnipropetrovs'ka Oblast', E Ukraine 48°32′N 35°50′E
Pavlor Harbour see Pauloff Harbor
227 I3 **Pavlovka** Akmola, C Kazakhstan 51°22′N 72°35′E
197 L2 **Pavlovka** Respublika Bashkortostan, W Russian Federation 55°28′N 56°36′E
197 I4 **Pavlovka** Ul'yanovskaya Oblast', W Russian Federation 52°40′N 47°08′E
197 H2 **Pavlovo** Nizhegorodskaya Oblast', W Russian Federation 55°59′N 43°03′E
196 G5 **Pavlovsk** Voronezhskaya Oblast', W Russian Federation 50°26′N 40°08′E
196 G7 **Pavlovskaya** Krasnodarskiy Kray, SW Russian Federation 46°06′N 39°52′E
189 J5 **Pavlysh** Kirovohrads'ka Oblast', C Ukraine 48°54′N 33°20′E
114 B7 **Pavón** Santa Fe, Argentina 33°15′S 60°24′W
114 G9 **Pavón** Uruguay 34°17′S 56°55′W
114 B7 **Pavón Arriba** Santa Fe, Argentina 33°19′S 60°50′W
176 G8 **Pavullo nel Frignano** Emilia-Romagna, C Italy 44°19′N 10°52′E
190 H5 **Pavy** Pskovskaya Oblast', Russian Federation
75 F11 **Pawhuska** Oklahoma, C USA 36°42′N 96°21′W
160 G7 **Pawlett** UK 51°11′N 3°0′W
67 K9 **Pawleys Island** South Carolina, SE USA 33°27′N 79°07′W
65 I4 **Pawling** New York, USA 41°34′N 73°36′W
256 D5 **Pawn** ≈ C Myanmar (Burma)
73 C11 **Pawnee** Illinois, N USA 39°35′N 89°34′W
75 E11 **Pawnee** Oklahoma, C USA 36°21′N 96°50′W
79 M2 **Pawnee Buttes** ▲ Colorado, C USA 40°49′N 103°58′W
75 F8 **Pawnee City** Nebraska, C USA 40°06′N 96°09′W
75 C10 **Pawnee River** ≈ Kansas, C USA
73 F8 **Paw Paw** Michigan, N USA 42°12′N 86°09′W
73 F8 **Paw Paw Lake** Michigan, N USA 42°12′N 86°16′W
65 L3 **Pawtucket** Rhode Island, NE USA 41°52′N 71°22′W
Pax Augusta see Badajoz
187 I10 **Paximádia** island SE Greece
Pax Julia see Beja
186 E5 **Paxoí** island Iónia Nisiá, Greece, C Mediterranean Sea
83 J5 **Paxson** Alaska, USA 62°58′N 145°27′W
229 I6 **Paxtakor** Jizzax Viloyati, C Uzbekistan 40°21′N 67°54′E
159 J3 **Paxton** UK 55°46′N 2°06′W
73 D10 **Paxton** Illinois, N USA 40°27′N 88°06′W
194 E7 **Pay** Respublika Kareliya, NW Russian Federation 61°10′N 34°24′E
256 C6 **Payagyi** Pegu, SW Myanmar (Burma) 17°28′N 96°32′E
176 C4 **Payerne** Ger. Peterlingen. Vaud, W Switzerland 46°49′N 06°57′E
76 F7 **Payette** Idaho, NW USA 44°04′N 116°55′W
76 F7 **Payette River** ≈ Idaho, NW USA
195 L2 **Pay-Khoy, Khrebet** ▲▲ NW Russian Federation
172 D7 **Paymogo** Andalucía, Spain 37°45′N 7°20′W
Payne see Kangirsuk
58 G2 **Payne, Lac** ◎ Québec, NE Canada
74 G4 **Paynesville** Minnesota, N USA 45°22′N 94°42′W
258 J3 **Payong, Tanjung** cape East Malaysia
Payo Obispo see Chetumal
168 F3 **Payrac** Midi-Pyrénées, France 44°48′N 1°28′E
114 E5 **Paysandú** Paysandú, W Uruguay 32°21′S 58°05′W
114 G5 **Paysandú** ⬖ department W Uruguay
164 F4 **Pays de la Loire** ⬖ region NW France
79 I8 **Payson** Arizona, SW USA 34°13′N 111°19′W
79 H3 **Payson** Utah, W USA 40°02′N 111°43′W
195 L3 **Payyer, Gora** ▲ NW Russian Federation 66°49′N 64°33′E
Payzawat see Jiashi
215 I4 **Pazar** Rize, NE Turkey 41°10′N 40°53′E
214 D4 **Pazarbaşı Burnu** headland NW Turkey 41°12′N 30°18′E
214 G7 **Pazarcık** Kahramanmaraş, S Turkey 37°31′N 37°19′E
185 J7 **Pazardzhik** prev. Tatar Pazardzhik. Pazardzhik, SW Bulgaria 42°11′N 24°21′E
102 D5 **Paz de Ariporo** Casanare, E Colombia 05°54′N 71°52′W
184 A3 **Pazin** Ger. Mitterburg, It. Pisino. Istra, NW Croatia 45°14′N 13°56′E
185 H7 **Pčinja** ≈ N Macedonia
284 D9 **Pea** Tongatapu, S Tonga 21°10′S 175°14′W
75 E10 **Peabody** Kansas, C USA 38°10′N 97°06′W
65 M2 **Peabody** Massachusetts, USA 42°32′N 70°56′W
56 F2 **Peace** ≈ Alberta/British Columbia, W Canada
Peace Garden State see North Dakota
54 F5 **Peace Point** Alberta, C Canada 59°11′N 112°12′W
57 H2 **Peace River** Alberta, W Canada 56°15′N 117°18′W
69 L7 **Peace River** ≈ Florida, SE USA
56 F8 **Peachland** British Columbia, SW Canada 49°49′N 119°48′W
78 G7 **Peach Springs** Arizona, SW USA 35°33′N 113°27′W
Peach State see Georgia
66 F9 **Peachtree City** Georgia, SE USA 33°24′N 84°36′W
283 N2 **Peacock Point** point SE Wake Island
157 H9 **Peak District** physical region C England, UK
277 K4 **Peak Hill** New South Wales, SE Australia 32°39′S 148°12′E
161 K3 **Peakirk** UK 52°38′N 0°16′W
132 C10 **Peak, The** ▲ C Ascension Island
170 G7 **Peal de Becerro** Andalucía, S Spain 37°55′N 03°08′W
283 M1 **Peale Island** island N Wake Island
79 J4 **Peale, Mount** ▲ Utah, W USA 38°26′N 109°13′W
81 E10 **Pearblossom** California, USA 34°30′N 117°55′W
83 H2 **Peard Bay** bay Alaska, USA
69 I3 **Pea River** ≈ Alabama/Florida, S USA
71 I7 **Pearland** Texas, SW USA 29°33′N 95°17′W
82 C2 **Pearl City** O'ahu, Hawai'i, USA 21°24′N 157°58′W
82 B2 **Pearl Harbor** inlet O'ahu, Hawai'i, USA, C Pacific Ocean
Pearl Islands see Perlas, Archipiélago de las
Pearl Lagoon see Perlas, Laguna de
68 E4 **Pearl River** ≈ Louisiana/Mississippi, S USA
70 F8 **Pearsall** Texas, SW USA 28°54′N 99°07′W
69 K3 **Pearson** Georgia, SE USA 31°18′N 82°51′W
81 F8 **Pearsonville** California, USA 35°49′N 117°52′W
141 H9 **Pearston** Eastern Cape, South Africa 32°35′S 25°08′E
52 G3 **Peary Channel** sea waterway Nunavut, N Canada
161 M4 **Peasenhall** UK 52°16′N 1°27′E
70 F3 **Pease River** ≈ Texas, SW USA
161 L7 **Peasmarsh** UK 50°58′N 0°40′E
58 E4 **Peawanuk** Ontario, C Canada 54°55′N 85°31′W
139 K3 **Pebane** Zambézia, NE Mozambique 17°14′S 38°10′E
80 A4 **Pebble Beach** California, USA 36°34′N 121°57′W
117 H10 **Pebble Island** island N Falkland Islands
117 I10 **Pebble Island Settlement** Pebble Island, N Falkland Islands 51°20′S 59°40′W
184 F6 **Peć** Alb. Pejë, Turk. Ipek. Kosovo, S Serbia 42°40′N 20°19′E
70 G5 **Pecan Bayou** ≈ Texas, SW USA
68 C5 **Pecan Island** Louisiana, S USA 29°39′N 92°26′W
113 K5 **Peças, Ilha das** island S Brazil
73 C8 **Pecatonica River** ≈ Illinois/Wisconsin, N USA
176 E5 **Peccia** Ticino, S Switzerland 46°24′N 08°39′E
172 C8 **Pechão** Faro, Portugal 37°03′N 7°52′W
Pechenegi see Pechenihy
Pechenezhskoye Vodokhranilishche see Pecheniz'ke Vodoskhovyshche
194 E2 **Pechenga** Fin. Petsamo. Murmanskaya Oblast', NW Russian Federation 69°34′N 31°14′E
189 L3 **Pechenihy** Rus. Pechenegi. Kharkivs'ka Oblast', E Ukraine 49°49′N 36°57′E
189 L3 **Pecheniz'ke Vodoskhovyshche** Rus. Pechenezhskoye Vodokhranilishche. ⊠ E Ukraine
195 K5 **Pechora** Respublika Komi, NW Russian Federation 65°09′N 57°09′E
195 K7 **Pechora** ≈ NW Russian Federation
Pechora Bay see Pechorskaya Guba
Pechora Sea see Pechorskoye More
195 J3 **Pechorskaya Guba** Eng. Pechora Bay. bay NW Russian Federation
195 I2 **Pechorskoye More** Eng. Pechora Sea. sea NW Russian Federation
188 A7 **Pecica** Ger. Petschka, Hung. Ópécska. Arad, W Romania 46°09′N 21°06′E
70 C5 **Pecos** Texas, SW USA 31°25′N 103°30′W
60 E7 **Pecos River** ≈ New Mexico/Texas, SW USA
183 F13 **Pécs** Ger. Fünfkirchen, Lat. Sopianae. Baranya, SW Hungary 46°05′N 18°11′E
89 K10 **Pedasí** Los Santos, S Panama 07°36′N 80°04′W
Pedde see Pedja
277 J10 **Pedder, Lake** ◎ Tasmania, SE Australia
118 D2 **Pedegua** Valparaíso, Chile 32°23′S 71°06′W
91 H6 **Pedernales** SW Dominican Republic 18°02′N 71°41′W
86 D6 **Pedernales** Michoacán de Ocampo, Mexico 19°08′N 101°28′W
103 I3 **Pedernales** Delta Amacuro, NE Venezuela 09°58′N 62°15′W
70 G6 **Pedernales River** ≈ Texas, SW USA
112 B5 **Pedernales, Salar de** salt lake N Chile
110 A7 **Pederneiras** São Paulo, Brazil 22°23′S 48°46′W
Pedhoulas see Pedoulás
103 M6 **Pédima** var. Malavate. SW French Guiana 03°15′N 54°08′W
276 E1 **Pedirka** South Australia 26°41′S 135°11′E
260 G3 **Pediwang** Pulau Halmahera, E Indonesia 01°29′N 127°57′E
190 F4 **Pedja** var. Pedja Jõgi, Ger. Pedde. ≈ E Estonia
Pedja Jõgi see Pedja
218 B2 **Pedoulás** var. Pedhoulas. W Cyprus 34°58′N 32°51′E
111 J4 **Pedra Bonita** Minas Gerais, Brazil 20°30′S 42°24′E
109 F9 **Pedra Azul** Minas Gerais, NE Brazil 16°02′S 41°17′W
111 J4 **Pedra do Anta** Minas Gerais, Brazil 20°36′S 42°43′W
110 F3 **Pedra do Indaià** Minas Gerais, Brazil 20°15′S 45°13′W
111 J4 **Pedra Dourada** Minas Gerais, Brazil 20°49′S 42°10′W
170 D2 **Pedrafita, Porto de** var. Puerto de Piedrafita. pass NW Spain
132 B9 **Pedra Lume** Sal, NE Cape Verde 16°47′N 22°54′W
110 E7 **Pedralva** Minas Gerais, Brazil 22°14′S 45°28′W
115 L4 **Pedras Altas** Rio Grande do Sul, Brazil 31°44′S 53°35′W
89 I9 **Pedregal** Chiriquí, W Panama 09°04′N 79°25′W
102 E2 **Pedregal** Falcón, N Venezuela 11°04′N 70°08′W
110 B3 **Pedregulho** São Paulo, Brazil 20°16′S 47°29′W
115 L5 **Pedreiras** Rio Grande do Sul, Brazil 32°02′S 53°03′W
110 C8 **Pedreiras** São Paulo, Brazil 22°43′S 46°55′W
85 J7 **Pedriceña** Durango, C Mexico 25°08′N 103°46′W
110 B2 **Pedrinópolis** Minas Gerais, Brazil 19°13′S 47°28′W
116 F6 **Pedro Luro** Buenos Aires, Argentina 39°36′S 63°00′E
172 G7 **Pedro Abad** Andalucía, Spain 37°58′N 4°27′W
110 C10 **Pedro Barros** São Paulo, Brazil 24°15′S 47°22′W
113 L4 **Pedro Barros** São Paulo, S Brazil 24°12′S 47°22′W
83 I7 **Pedro Bay** Alaska, USA 59°47′N 154°06′W
112 B3 **Pedro de Valdivia** var. Oficina Pedro de Valdivia. Antofagasta, N Chile 22°33′S 69°38′W
111 I7 **Pedro do Rio** Rio de Janeiro, Brazil 22°20′S 43°08′W
172 C6 **Pedrógão** Beja, Portugal 38°07′N 7°39′W
172 D3 **Pedrógão** Castelo Branco, Portugal 40°05′N 7°14′W
114 B1 **Pedro Gómez Cello** Santa Fe, Argentina 30°02′S 60°18′W
113 H3 **Pedro Juan Caballero** Amambay, E Paraguay 22°34′S 55°41′W
111 H2 **Pedro Leopoldo** Minas Gerais, Brazil 19°38′S 44°03′W
170 G6 **Pedro Muñoz** Castilla-La Mancha, C Spain 39°25′N 02°56′W
235 G9 **Pedro, Point** headland NW Sri Lanka 09°54′N 80°08′E
111 H6 **Pedro Teixeira** Minas Gerais, Brazil 21°43′S 43°44′W
118 F5 **Pedro Vargas** Mendoza, Argentina 34°37′S 68°28′W
277 H5 **Peebinga** South Australia 34°56′S 140°56′E
159 I4 **Peebles** SE Scotland, UK 55°40′N 03°15′W
73 H12 **Peebles** Ohio, N USA 38°57′N 83°23′W
156 F7 **Peebles** cultural region SE Scotland, UK
65 H5 **Peekskill** New York, NE USA 41°17′N 73°54′W
158 G8 **Peel** W Isle of Man 54°13′N 04°04′W
52 A7 **Peel** ≈ Northwest Territories/Yukon Territory, NW Canada
52 E5 **Peel Point** headland Victoria Island, Northwest Territories, NW Canada 73°22′N 114°33′W
53 H6 **Peel Sound** passage Nunavut, N Canada
178 H4 **Peene** ≈ NE Germany
163 G9 **Peer** Limburg, NE Belgium 51°08′N 05°29′E
62 D4 **Pefferlaw** Ontario, S Canada 44°18′N 79°11′W
172 D2 **Pega** Guarda, Portugal 40°26′N 7°09′W
278 F9 **Pegasus Bay** bay South Island, New Zealand
218 A2 **Pégeia** var. Peyia. SW Cyprus 34°52′N 32°24′E
177 K4 **Peggau** Steiermark, SE Austria 47°10′N 15°20′E
179 G10 **Pegnitz** Bayern, SE Germany 49°45′N 11°33′E
179 G11 **Pegnitz** ≈ SE Germany
171 J6 **Pego** País Valenciano, E Spain 38°51′N 00°08′W
172 B5 **Pegões Velhos** Setúbal, Portugal 38°41′N 8°40′W
256 C6 **Pegu** var. Bago. Pegu, SW Myanmar (Burma) 17°18′N 96°31′E
256 C6 **Pegu** ⬖ division S Myanmar (Burma)
261 J3 **Pegun, Pulau** island Kepulauan Mapia, E Indonesia
161 N7 **Pegwell Bay** bay UK
283 J2 **Pehleng** Pohnpei, E Micronesia
133 I6 **Péhonko** C Benin 10°14′N 01°57′E
116 F5 **Pehuajó** Buenos Aires, E Argentina 35°48′S 61°53′W
116 F5 **Pehuajó** Buenos Aires, Argentina 35°54′S 61°42′E
245 K7 **Peicheng** China 34°28′N 117°58′E
Pei-ching see Beijing/Beijing Shi
180 I6 **Peine** Niedersachsen, C Germany 52°19′N 10°14′E
Pei-p'ing see Beijing/Beijing Shi
Peipsi Järv/Peipus-See see Peipus, Lake
190 F4 **Peipus, Lake** Est. Peipsi Järv, Ger. Peipus-See, Rus. Chudskoye Ozero. ◎ Estonia/Russian Federation
169 N5 **Peéra-Cava** Provence-Alpes-Côte d'Azur, France 43°56′N 7°22′E
187 H6 **Peiraías** prev. Piraiévs, Eng. Piraeus. Attikí, C Greece 37°57′N 23°42′E
113 J3 **Peixe, Rio do** ≈ S Brazil
245 J7 **Peixian** Jiangsu, China 34°26′N 116°34′E
107 J7 **Peixoto de Azevedo** Mato Grosso, W Brazil 10°18′S 55°03′W
258 G5 **Pejantan, Pulau** island W Indonesia
Pejë see Peć
256 G5 **Pèk** var. Xieng Khouang; prev. Xiangkhoang. Xiangkhoang, N Laos 19°19′N 103°23′E
185 H4 **Pek** ≈ E Serbia
259 H8 **Pekalongan** Jawa, C Indonesia 06°54′S 109°37′E
258 D4 **Pekanbaru** var. Pakanbaru. Sumatera, W Indonesia 0°31′N 101°27′E
73 C10 **Pekin** Illinois, N USA 40°34′N 89°38′W
Peking see Beijing/Beijing Shi
Pelabohan Kelang/Pelabuhan Kelang see Pelabuhan Klang
258 D3 **Pelabuhan Klang** var. Kuala Pelabohan Kelang, Pelabohan Kelang, Pelabuhan Kelang, Port Klang, Port Swettenham. Selangor, Peninsular Malaysia 02°57′N 101°24′E
259 F8 **Pelabuhan Ratu, Teluk** bay Jawa, SW Indonesia
175 E14 **Pelagie, Isole** island group SW Italy
Pelagosa see Palagruža
68 E2 **Pelahatchie** Mississippi, S USA 32°19′N 89°48′W
258 J7 **Pelaihari** var. Pleihari. Borneo, C Indonesia 03°48′S 114°45′E
169 M4 **Pelat, Mont** ▲ SE France 44°16′N 06°46′E
188 B8 **Peleaga, Vârful** prev. Vîrful Peleaga. ▲ W Romania 45°23′N 22°52′E
Peleaga, Vîrful see Peleaga, Vârful
193 I7 **Peleduy** Respublika Sakha (Yakutiya), NE Russian Federation 59°39′N 112°36′E
62 A7 **Pelee Island** island Ontario, S Canada
91 M1 **Pelée, Montagne** ▲ N Martinique 14°47′N 61°10′W
62 B7 **Pelee, Point** headland Ontario, S Canada 41°56′N 82°30′W
260 E4 **Pelei** Pulau Peleng, N Indonesia 01°26′S 123°27′E
Peleliu see Beliliou
260 E4 **Peleng, Pulau** island Kepulauan Banggai, N Indonesia
260 E4 **Peleng, Selat** strait Sulawesi, C Indonesia
69 J3 **Pelham** Georgia, SE USA 31°07′N 84°09′W
183 C9 **Pelhřimov** Ger. Pilgram. Vysočina, C Czech Republic 49°26′N 15°14′E
83 L7 **Pelican** Chichagof Island, Alaska, USA 57°52′N 136°05′W
285 N2 **Pelican Lagoon** ◎ Kiritimati, E Kiribati
74 H2 **Pelican Lake** ◎ Minnesota, N USA
74 G3 **Pelican Lake** ◎ Minnesota, N USA
72 C5 **Pelican Lake** ◎ Wisconsin, N USA
54 F7 **Pelican Mountains** ▲▲ Alberta, W Canada
90 E1 **Pelican Point** Grand Bahama Island, N Bahamas 26°39′N 78°09′W
140 A2 **Pelican Point** headland W Namibia 22°55′S 14°25′E
74 F3 **Pelican Rapids** Minnesota, N USA 46°34′N 96°04′W
Pelican State see Louisiana
57 N3 **Pelikan Narrows** Saskatchewan, C Canada 55°11′N 102°51′W
187 J5 **Pelinaío** ▲ Chíos, E Greece 38°31′N 26°01′E
Pelinnaeum see Pelinnaío
186 F4 **Pelinnaío** anc. Pelinnaeum. ruins Thessalía, C Greece
184 G8 **Pelister** ▲ SW FYR Macedonia 41°00′N 21°12′E
184 D6 **Pelješac** peninsula S Croatia
152 H5 **Pelkosenniemi** Lappi, NE Finland 67°06′N 27°30′E
180 D7 **Pelkum** Nordrhein-Westfalen, Germany 7°44′N 51°38′E
140 D6 **Pella** Northern Cape, South Africa 29°02′S 19°09′E
74 H7 **Pella** Iowa, C USA 41°24′N 92°55′W
186 G3 **Pélla** site of ancient city Kentrikí Makedonía, N Greece
66 E8 **Pell City** Alabama, S USA 33°35′N 86°17′W
116 F5 **Pellegrini** Buenos Aires, Argentina 36°24′S 61°06′E
118 G10 **Pellegrini, Lago** ◎ Río Negro, Argentina
152 G5 **Pello** Lappi, NW Finland 66°47′N 24°E
178 D3 **Pellworm** island N Germany
54 B2 **Pelly** ≈ Yukon Territory, NW Canada
53 I8 **Pelly Bay** Nunavut, N Canada 68°38′N 89°45′W
54 B2 **Pelly Crossing** Yukon Territory, NW Canada
54 B3 **Pelly Mountains** ▲▲ Yukon Territory, W Canada
52 G7 **Pelly Point** headland Nunavut, NW Canada
Pélmonostor see Beli Manastir
79 K8 **Pelona Mountain** ▲ New Mexico, SW USA 33°40′N 108°06′W
Peloponnese/Peloponnesus see Pelopónnisos
186 G7 **Pelopónnisos** Eng. Peloponnese. ⬖ region S Greece
186 G7 **Pelopónnisos** var. Morea, Eng. Peloponnese; anc. Peloponnesus. peninsula S Greece
175 G12 **Peloritani, Monti** anc. Pelorus and Neptunius. ▲▲ Sicilia, Italy, C Mediterranean Sea
175 G12 **Peloro, Capo** var. Punta del Faro. headland S Italy 38°15′N 15°39′E
Pelorus and Neptunius see Peloritani, Monti
115 M4 **Pelotas** Rio Grande do Sul, S Brazil 31°45′S 52°20′W
113 J6 **Pelotas, Rio** ≈ S Brazil
152 G4 **Peltovuoma** Lapp. Bealdovuopmi. Lappi, N Finland 68°23′N 24°12′E
169 J2 **Pélussin** Rhône-Alpes, France 45°25′N 4°41′E
196 M7 **Pelym** Sverdlovskaya oblast', Russian federation
196 M8 **Pelym** Sverdlovskaya oblast', Russian federation
195 M7 **Pelym** ≈ C Russian Federation
63 K3 **Pemadumcook Lake** ◎ Maine, NE USA
259 H8 **Pemalang** Jawa, C Indonesia 06°53′S 109°07′E
258 H4 **Pemangkat** var. Pamangkat. Borneo, C Indonesia 01°11′N 109°00′E
Pemar see Paimio
258 C3 **Pematangsiantar** Sumatera, W Indonesia 02°59′N 99°01′E
137 F13 **Pemba** prev. Port Amelia, Porto Amélia. Cabo Delgado, NE Mozambique 13°S 40°35′E
137 F10 **Pemba** ⬖ region E Tanzania
137 F10 **Pemba** island E Tanzania
137 F13 **Pemba, Baia de** inlet NE Mozambique
137 E10 **Pemba Channel** channel E Tanzania
274 D8 **Pemberton** Western Australia 34°27′S 116°09′E
56 D8 **Pemberton** British Columbia, SW Canada 50°19′N 122°49′W
74 E1 **Pembina** North Dakota, N USA 48°58′N 97°14′W
74 E1 **Pembina** ≈ Canada/USA

◆ Country
● Country Capital
◇ Dependent Territory
○ Dependent Territory Capital
⬖ Administrative Regions
✕ International Airport
▲ Mountain
▲▲ Mountain Range
⛰ Volcano
≈ River
◎ Lake
⊠ Reservoir

◆ Country ● Country Capital ◇ Dependent Territory ○ Dependent Territory Capital ◆ Administrative Regions ✕ International Airport ▲ Mountain ▲ Mountain Range ▲ Volcano ♆ River ◎ Lake ⊡ Reservoir

◆ Country   ● Country Capital   ◇ Dependent Territory   ○ Dependent Territory Capital   ✕ Administrative Regions   ✕ International Airport   ▲ Mountain   ▲ Mountain Range   ▲ Volcano   ☒ River   ☒ Lake   ☒ Reservoir

INDEX
393

Qaraoy - Raijua, Selat
INDEX
395

Qaraoy *see* Karaoy
Qaraqoyyn *see* Karakoyyn, Ozero
Qara Qum *see* Garagum
Qarasū *see* Karasu
Qaratal *see* Karatal
Qarataū *see* Karatau, Khrebet, Kazakhstan
Qarataū *see* Karatau, Zhambyl, Kazakhstan
Qaraton *see* Karaton
136 *J4* **Qardho** *var.* Kardh, *It.* Gardo. Bari, N Somalia *09°34′N 49°30′E*
222 *D1* **Qareh Chāy** N Iran
222 *E1* **Qareh Sū** NW Iran
Qariateïne *see* Al Qaryatayn
Qarkilik *see* Ruoqiang
229 *H7* **Qarluq** *Rus.* Karluk. Surkhondaryo Viloyati, S Uzbekistan *38°17′N 67°39′E*
229 *K7* **Qarokŭl** *Rus.* Karakul'. E Tajikistan *39°07′N 73°33′E*
229 *K7* **Qarokŭl** *Rus.* Ozero Karakul'. ◎ E Tajikistan
Qarqan *see* Qiemo
238 *F5* **Qarqan He** NW China
Qarqannah, Juzur *see* Kerkenah, Îles de
Qarqaraly *see* Karkaralinsk
230 *F2* **Qarqīn** Jowzjān, N Afghanistan *37°25′N 66°03′E*
Qars *see* Kars
Qarsaqbay *see* Karsakpay
229 *H7* **Qarshi** *Rus.* Karshi; *prev.* Bek-Budi. Qashqadaryo Viloyati, S Uzbekistan *38°54′N 65°48′E*
228 *G7* **Qarshi Cho'li** *Rus.* Karshinskaya Step. *grassland* S Uzbekistan
228 *G7* **Qarshi Kanali** *Rus.* Karshinskiy Kanal. *canal* Turkmenistan/Uzbekistan
218 *F2* **Qartaba** Lebanon
Qaryatayn *see* Al Qaryatayn
Qāsh, Nahr al *see* Gash
229 *H7* **Qashqadaryo Viloyati** *Rus.* Kashkadar'inskaya Oblast'. ◐ *province* S Uzbekistan
Qasigianguit *see* Qasigiannguit
295 *K8* **Qasigiannguit** *var.* Qasigianguit, *Dan.* Christianshåb. ◐ Kitaa, C Greenland
Qaşīm, Minţaqat *see* Al Qaşīm
244 *F2* **Qasq** Inner Mongolia, China *40°26′N 111°04′E*
Qasr al Hir Ash Sharqī *see* Ḩayr ash Sharqī, Qaşr al
217 *H5* **Qaşr 'Amīj** C Iraq *33°30′N 41°52′E*
217 *I6* **Qaşr Darwīshāh** C Iraq *32°36′N 43°27′E*
222 *C4* **Qaşr-e Shīrīn** Kermānshāhān, W Iran *34°32′N 45°36′E*
129 *H4* **Qasr Farâfra** W Egypt *27°00′N 27°59′E*
Qassim *see* Al Qaşīm
220 *F9* **Qa'ţabah** SW Yemen *13°51′N 44°42′E*
216 *C5* **Qaţanā** *var.* Katana. Dimashq, S Syria *33°27′N 36°04′E*
221 *H4* **Qatar** *off.* State of Qatar, *Ar.* Dawlat Qaţar. ◆ *monarchy* SW Asia
Qatar, State of *see* Qatar
Qatrana *see* Al Qaţrānah
222 *G7* **Qaţrūyeh** Fārs, S Iran *29°08′N 54°42′W*
Qattara Depression/Qaţţārah, Munkhafaḑ al *see* Qaţţâra, Monkhafad el
129 *H3* **Qaţţâra, Monkhafad el** *var.* Munkhafaḑ al Qaţţārah, *Eng.* Qattara Depression. *desert* NW Egypt
Qattinah, Buhayrat *see* Ḩimş, Buḩayrat
Qaydār *see* Qeydār
Qāyen *see* Qā'en
229 *I6* **Qayroqqum** *Rus.* Kayrakkum. NW Tajikistan *40°16′N 69°46′E*
229 *I6* **Qayroqqum, Obanbori** *Rus.* Kayrakkumskoye Vodokhranilishche. ⊠ NW Tajikistan
215 *L6* **Qazangödağ** *Rus.* Gora Kapydzhik, *Turk.* Qapiciğ Dağı. ▲ SW Azerbaijan *39°18′N 46°00′E*
217 *K5* **Qazānīyah** *var.* Dhū Shaykh. E Iraq *33°39′N 45°33′E*
Qazaqstan/Qazaqstan Respublikasy *see* Kazakhstan
215 *K3* **Qazbegi** *Rus.* Kazbegi. NE Georgia *42°39′N 44°36′E*
230 *G9* **Qāzi Ahmad** *var.* Kazi Ahmad. Sind, SE Pakistan *26°19′N 68°08′E*
215 *M5* **Qazimämmäd** *Rus.* Kazi Magomed. SE Azerbaijan *40°03′N 48°56′E*
Qazris *see* Cáceres
222 *E3* **Qazvīn** *var.* Kazvin. Qazvīn, N Iran *36°16′N 50°E*
280 *F7* **Qelelevu Lagoon** *lagoon* NE Fiji
129 *J5* **Qena** *var.* Qinā; *anc.* Caene, Caenepolis. E Egypt *26°12′N 32°49′E*
184 *F10* **Qeparo** Vlorë, S Albania *40°04′N 19°49′E*
Qeqertarssuaq *see* Qeqertarsuaq
295 *K8* **Qeqertarsuaq** *var.* Qeqertarssuaq, *Dan.* Godhavn. ◐ Kitaa, S Greenland
295 *K8* **Qeqertarsuaq** *island* W Greenland
295 *K8* **Qeqertarsuup Tunua** *Dan.* Disko Bugt. *inlet* W Greenland
Qerveh *see* Qorveh
223 *H9* **Qeshm** Hormozgān, S Iran *26°58′N 56°17′E*
223 *H9* **Qeshm** *var.* Jazīreh-ye Qeshm, Qeshm Island. *island* S Iran
Qeshm Island/Qeshm, Jazīreh-ye *see* Qeshm
222 *E3* **Qeydār** *var.* Qaydār. Zanjān, NW Iran *36°50′N 47°40′E*
222 *E3* **Qezel Owzan, Rūd-e** *var.* Ki Zil Uzen, Qi Zil Uzun. NW Iran
222 *D3* **Qezel Owzan, Rūd-e** NW Iran
Qian *see* Guizhou
245 *K3* **Qianan** China *39°50′N 117°41′E*
243 *M5* **Qiancang** China *27°35′N 120°31′E*
242 *E5* **Qiancheng** China *27°12′N 109°49′E*
Qiandaohu *see* Chun'an
Qiandao Hu *see* Xin'anjiang Shuiku
243 *J7* **Qianjia** China *25°12′N 116°09′E*
242 *G3* **Qianjiang** Hubei, C China *30°23′N 112°58′E*
242 *E3* **Qianjiang** Sichuan, C China *29°30′N 108°45′E*
242 *E9* **Qian Jiang** S China
243 *L3* **Qianli Gang** ▲▲ Zhejiang, China
240 *C4* **Qianning** *var.* Gartar. Sichuan, C China *30°27′N 101°24′E*
243 *M3* **Qianqing** China *30°08′N 120°24′E*
243 *J2* **Qianshan** Anhui, China *30°22′N 116°20′E*
245 *N2* **Qian Shan** ▲▲ NE China
243 *N4* **Qiansuo** China *28°42′N 121°27′E*
242 *A3* **Qianwei** *var.* Yujin. Sichuan, C China *29°15′N 103°52′E*
242 *B5* **Qianxi** Guizhou, S China *27°00′N 106°01′E*
244 *E7* **Qianxian** Shaanxi, China *34°19′N 108°08′E*
242 *E5* **Qianyang** China *27°19′N 110°06′E*
Qiaotou *see* Datong
Qiaowa *see* Muli
239 *I4* **Qiaowan** Gansu, N China *40°37′N 96°40′E*
243 *M4* **Qiaoxiajie** China *28°10′N 120°33′E*
Qibilī *see* Kebili
242 *G6* **Qidong** China *26°47′N 112°07′E*
243 *M1* **Qidong** Jiangsu, China *31°29′N 121°23′E*
238 *F6* **Qiemo** *var.* Qarqan. Xinjiang Uygur Zizhiqu, NW China *38°09′N 85°30′E*
245 *J5* **Qihe** Shandong, China *36°28′N 116°28′E*
242 *C4* **Qijiang** *var.* Gunan. Chongqing Shi, C China *29°01′N 106°40′E*
238 *G3* **Qijiaojing** Xinjiang Uygur Zizhiqu, NW China *43°29′N 91°35′E*
245 *K1* **Qilaotu Shan** ▲▲ Hebei, China
230 *G6* **Qila Saifullāh** Baluchistān, SW Pakistan *30°45′N 68°08′E*
239 *J5* **Qilian** *var.* Babao. Qinghai, C China *38°09′N 100°08′E*
208 *C4* **Qilian Shan** *var.* Kilien Mountains. ▲▲ N China
243 *H6* **Qiling** China *26°18′N 114°07′E*
243 *I8* **Qiling** China *24°05′N 115°27′E*
295 *J7* **Qimusseriarsuaq** *Dan.* Melville Bugt, *Eng.* Melville Bay. *bay* NW Greenland
Qinā *see* Qena
244 *C7* **Qin'an** Gansu, C China *34°49′N 105°50′E*
Qincheng *see* Nanfeng
Qing *see* Qinghai
243 *H9* **Qingcheng** China *23°42′N 113°02′E*
244 *D6* **Qingcheng** Gansu, China *36°01′N 107°32′E*
245 *L6* **Qingdao** *var.* Ching-Tao, Ch'ing-tao, Tsingtao, Tsintao, *Ger.* Tsingtau. Shandong, E China *36°31′N 120°55′E*
242 *A4* **Qingfu** China *28°27′N 104°33′E*
Qinggil *see* Qinghe
245 *J3* **Qingguang** China *39°12′N 117°02′E*
239 *I6* **Qinghai** *var.* Chinghai, Koko Nor, Qing, Qinghai Sheng, Tsinghai. ◐ *province* C China
239 *J6* **Qinghai Hu** *var.* Ch'ing Hai, Tsing Hai, *Mong.* Koko Nor. ◎ C China
Qinghai Sheng *see* Qinghai
238 *G2* **Qinghe** *var.* Qinggil. Xinjiang Uygur Zizhiqu, NW China *46°42′N 90°19′E*
244 *F5* **Qingjian** *var* Kuanzhou, *prev* Xiuyan. Shaanxi, C China *37°10′N 110°09′E*
245 *L8* **Qingjiang** China *33°35′N 119°01′E*
243 *M4* **Qingjiang** China *28°17′N 121°06′E*
242 *E3* **Qing Jiang** C China
Qingkou *see* Ganyu
242 *B6* **Qinglong** *var.* Liancheng. Guizhou, S China *25°49′N 105°10′E*
245 *K2* **Qinglong** Hebei, E China *40°24′N 118°57′E*
243 *M2* **Qingpu** China *31°05′N 121°00′E*
243 *H4* **Qingshanshi** China *28°28′N 113°10′E*
242 *A3* **Qingshen** China *29°48′N 103°49′E*
244 *C7* **Qingshui** Gansu, China *34°27′N 106°04′E*
244 *G3* **Qingshuihe** Inner Mongolia, China *39°34′N 111°23′E*
239 *I7* **Qingshuihe** Qinghai, C China *33°47′N 97°10′E*
244 *C5* **Qingshui He** Ningxia, China
242 *E6* **Qingshui Jiang** Guizhou, China
242 *C5* **Qingshui Jiang** Guizhou, China
243 *H8* **Qingtang** China *24°12′N 113°55′E*
243 *M4* **Qingtian** Zhejiang, China *28°05′N 120°11′E*
244 *C4* **Qingtongxia** Ningxia, China *37°31′N 106°00′E*
244 *C4* **Qingtonxia Shuiku** ⊠ Ningxia, China
245 *J4* **Qingxian** Hebei, China *38°20′N 116°29′E*
244 *G5* **Qingxu** Shanxi, China *37°22′N 112°13′E*
244 *D6* **Qingyang** *var.* Xifeng. Gansu, C China *35°46′N 107°35′E*
Qingyang *see* Jinjiang
243 *L5* **Qingyuan** China *27°37′N 119°04′E*
248 *B2* **Qingyuan** *var.* Qingyuan Manzu Zizhixian. Liaoning, NE China *42°08′N 124°55′E*
Qingyuan Manzu Zizhixian *see* Qingyuan
245 *J5* **Qingyun** China *37°47′N 117°23′E*
243 *H8* **Qingyun Shan** ▲▲ Guangdong, China
238 *G7* **Qingzang Gaoyuan** *var.* Xizang Gaoyuan, *Eng.* Plateau of Tibet. *plateau* W China
242 *C6* **Qingzhen** Guizhou, China *26°20′N 106°16′E*
245 *K5* **Qingzhou** *prev.* Yidu. Shandong, E China *36°41′N 118°29′E*
244 *G6* **Qin He** C China
245 *L3* **Qinhuangdao** Hebei, E China *39°57′N 119°31′E*
242 *D10* **Qin Jiang** ▲▲ Guangxi, China
244 *E8* **Qin Ling** ▲▲ C China
244 *G6* **Qinxian** *var.* Qin Xian. Shanxi, C China *36°46′N 112°42′E*
Qin Xian *see* Qinxian
245 *H7* **Qinyang** Henan, C China *35°05′N 112°56′E*
242 *D10* **Qinzhou** Guangxi Zhuangzu Zizhiqu, S China *22°09′N 108°36′E*
242 *D10* **Qinzhou Wan** *bay* Guangxi, China
245 *K3* **Qinzhuang** China *39°35′N 119°05′E*
Qiong *see* Hainan
240 *F10* **Qionghai** *prev.* Jiaji. Hainan, S China *19°12′N 110°26′E*
242 *A2* **Qionglai** Sichuan, C China *30°24′N 103°28′E*
240 *C4* **Qionglai Shan** ▲▲ C China
Qiongxi *see* Hongyuan
240 *F9* **Qiongzhou Haixia** *var.* Hainan Strait. *strait* S China
237 *J3* **Qiqihar** *var.* Ch'i-ch'i-ha-erh, Tsitsihar; *prev.* Lungkiang. Heilongjiang, NE China *47°23′N 124°E*
Qir *see* Qīr-va-Kārzīn
238 *D6* **Qira** Xinjiang Uygur Zizhiqu, NW China *37°05′N 80°45′E*
Qir'awn, Buḩayrat al *see* Qaraoun, Lac de
222 *G8* **Qīr-va-Kārzīn** *var* Qir. Fārs, S Iran *28°27′N 53°04′E*
216 *B7* **Qiryat Gat** *var.* Kyriat Gat. Southern, C Israel *31°37′N 34°47′E*
216 *C5* **Qiryat Shemona** Northern, N Israel *33°13′N 35°35′E*
244 *D7* **Qishan** Shaanxi, China *34°16′N 107°23′E*
Qishlaq *see* Garmsār
221 *I8* **Qishn** SE Yemen *15°29′N 51°44′E*
216 *B6* **Qishon, Naḩal** N Israel
Qita Ghazzah *see* Gaza Strip
238 *G3* **Qitai** Xinjiang Uygur Zizhiqu, NW China *44°N 89°34′E*
242 *A8* **Qiubei** Yunnan, China *24°01′N 104°07′E*
245 *M5* **Qixia** Shandong, China *37°10′N 120°30′E*
245 *H7* **Qixian** *var.* Qi Xian, Zhaoge. Henan, C China *35°35′N 114°10′E*
245 *I7* **Qixian** Henan, China *34°19′N 114°28′E*
244 *G5* **Qixian** Shanxi, China *37°13′N 112°11′E*
Qi Xian *see* Qixian
242 *G6* **Qiyang** China *26°35′N 111°52′E*
Qizān *see* Jīzān
243 *I3* **Qizhou** China *30°04′N 115°20′E*
Qizil Qum/Qizilqum *see* Kyzyl Kum
229 *L8* **Qizilrabot** *Rus.* Kyzylrabot. SE Tajikistan *37°29′N 74°44′E*
228 *F6* **Qizilravot** *Rus.* Kyzylrabat. Buxoro Viloyati, C Uzbekistan *40°35′N 62°09′E*
Qi Zil Uzun *see* Qezel Owzan, Rūd-e
217 *J3* **Qizil Yār** N Iraq *35°26′N 44°12′E*
Qoghaly *see* Kugaly
Qogir Feng *see* K2
222 *F4* **Qom** *var.* Kum, Qum. Qom, N Iran *34°43′N 50°54′E*
Qomisheh *see* Shahreẕā
Qomolangma Feng *see* Everest, Mount
222 *F5* **Qom, Rūd-e** C Iran
Qomsheh *see* Shahreẕā
Qomul *see* Hami
Qondūz *see* Kondoz
Qongyrat *see* Konyrat
Qoqek *see* Tacheng
Qorabowur Kirlari *see* Karabaur', Uval
Qoradaryo *see* Karadar'ya
228 *D3* **Qorajar** *Rus.* Karadzhar. Qoraqalpoghiston Respublikasi, NW Uzbekistan *43°34′N 58°35′E*
228 *G6* **Qorako'l** *Rus.* Karakul'. Buxoro Viloyati, C Uzbekistan *39°27′N 63°45′E*
141 *J8* **Qora Mouth** Eastern Cape, South Africa *32°27′S 28°41′E*
228 *E4* **Qorao'zak** *Rus.* Karauzyak. Qoraqalpoghiston Respublikasi, NW Uzbekistan *43°07′N 60°03′E*
228 *C3* **Qoraqalpog'iston** *Rus.* Karakalpakya. Qoraqalpog'iston Respublikasi, NW Uzbekistan *44°45′N 56°06′E*
228 *D4* **Qoraqalpog'iston Respublikasi** *Rus.* Respublika Karakalpakstan. ◐ *autonomous republic* NW Uzbekistan
Qorgazhyn *see* Korgalzhyn
216 *B2* **Qornet es Saouda** ▲ NE Lebanon *36°06′N 34°06′E*
228 *G6* **Qorowulbozor** *Rus.* Karaulbazar. Buxoro Viloyati, C Uzbekistan *39°28′N 64°49′E*
222 *D4* **Qorveh** *var.* Qerveh, Qurveh. Kordestān, W Iran *35°09′N 47°48′E*
Qosshaghyl *see* Koschagyl
Qostanay/Qostanay Oblysy *see* Kostanay
222 *G8* **Qoţbābād** Fārs, S Iran *28°52′N 53°40′E*
223 *H8* **Qoţbābād** Hormozgān, S Iran *27°49′N 56°00′E*
218 *G1* **Qoubaïyât** Lebanon
216 *C4* **Qoubaïyât** *var.* Al Qubayyāt. N Lebanon *37°00′N 34°30′E*
Qoussantina *see* Constantine
Qowowuyag *see* Cho Oyu
228 *E4* **Qozonketkan** *Rus.* Kazanketken. Qoraqalpogh'iston Respublikasi, W Uzbekistan *42°59′N 59°21′E*
228 *E4* **Qozoqdaryo** *Rus.* Kazakdar'ya. Qoraqalpoghiston Respublikasi, NW Uzbekistan *43°26′N 59°47′E*
65 *K2* **Quabbin Reservoir** ⊠ Massachusetts, NE USA
180 *E5* **Quakenbrück** Niedersachsen, NW Germany *52°41′N 07°57′E*
64 *F6* **Quakertown** Pennsylvania, NE USA *40°26′N 75°17′W*
277 *I6* **Quambatook** Victoria, SE Australia *35°52′S 143°28′E*
70 *F3* **Quanah** Texas, SW USA *34°17′N 99°46′W*
257 *I7* **Quang Ngai** *var.* Quangngai, Quang Nghia. Quang Ngai, C Vietnam *15°09′N 108°50′E*
Quangngai *see* Quang Ngai
Quang Nghia *see* Quang Ngai
257 *I6* **Quang Tri** *var.* Triêu Hai. Quang Tri, C Vietnam *16°46′N 107°11′E*
Quanjiang *see* Suichuan
243 *K1* **Quanjiao** China *32°06′N 118°15′E*
Quan Long *see* Ca Mau
238 *D6* **Quanshuigou** China/India *35°40′N 79°28′E*
160 *G7* **Quantock Hills** ▲▲ UK
243 *L7* **Quanzhou** *var.* Ch'uan-chou, Tsinkiang; *prev.* Chin-chiang. Fujian, SE China *24°56′N 118°31′E*
242 *F7* **Quanzhou** Guangxi Zhuangzu Zizhiqu, S China *25°59′N 111°02′E*
243 *L8* **Quanzhou Gang** *harbor* Fujan, China
55 *I9* **Qu'Appelle** Saskatchewan, S Canada
59 *H1* **Quaqtaq** *prev.* Koartac. Québec, NE Canada *60°50′N 69°30′W*
115 *H2* **Quaraí** Rio Grande do Sul, S Brazil *30°38′S 56°25′W*
114 *G1* **Quaraí, Rio** *Sp.* Río Cuareim. Brazil/Uruguay *see also* Cuareim, Río
Quaraí, Rio *see* Cuareim, Río
260 *C5* **Quarles, Pegunungan** ▲▲ Sulawesi, C Indonesia
Quarnero *see* Kvarner
167 *J8* **Quarré-les-Tombes** Bourgogne, France *47°22′N 3°59′E*
175 *B10* **Quartu Sant' Elena** Sardegna, Italy, C Mediterranean Sea *39°15′N 09°12′E*
81 *E9* **Quartz Hill** California, USA *34°39′N 118°13′W*
80 *I6* **Quartzite Mountain** ▲ Nevada, USA *37°31′N 116°19′W*
81 *I13* **Quartzsite** Nevada, USA *33°40′N 114°14′W*
74 *I7* **Quasqueton** Iowa, C USA *42°23′N 91°45′W*
110 *G7* **Quatis** Rio de Janeiro, Brazil *22°25′S 44°16′W*
137 *G10* **Quatre Bornes** W Mauritius *20°15′S 57°28′E*
137 *I9* **Quatre Bornes** Mahé, NE Seychelles
161 *H4* **Quatt** UK *52°29′N 2°21′W*
215 *M4* **Quba** *Rus.* Kuba. N Azerbaijan *41°22′N 48°30′E*
Qubba *see* Ba'qūbah
223 *I3* **Qūchān** *var.* Kuchan. Khorāsān-Razavī, NE Iran *37°12′N 58°28′E*
141 *K6* **Qudeni** KwaZulu-Natal, South Africa *28°36′S 30°52′E*
277 *K6* **Queanbeyan** New South Wales, SE Australia *35°24′S 149°17′E*
63 *J1* **Québec** *var.* Quebec. *province capital* Québec, SE Canada *46°50′N 71°15′W*
62 *G1* **Québec** *var.* Quebec. ◐ *province* SE Canada
114 *F5* **Quebracho** Paysandú, W Uruguay *31°58′S 57°53′W*
118 *D3* **Quebrada de Alvarado** Valparaíso, Chile *33°03′S 71°07′W*
180 *J7* **Quedlinburg** Sachsen-Anhalt, C Germany *51°48′N 11°09′E*
216 *C7* **Queen Alia** ✈ ('Ammān) 'Ammān, C Jordan
56 *D7* **Queen Bess, Mount** ▲ British Columbia, SW Canada *51°15′N 124°29′W*
54 *A7* **Queen Charlotte** British Columbia, SW Canada *53°18′N 132°04′W*
117 *H11* **Queen Charlotte Bay** *bay* West Falkland, W Falkland Islands
54 *A7* **Queen Charlotte Islands** *Fr.* Îles de la Reine-Charlotte. *island group* British Columbia, SW Canada
56 *A6* **Queen Charlotte Sound** *sea area* British Columbia, W Canada
56 *B7* **Queen Charlotte Strait** *strait* British Columbia, W Canada
75 *H8* **Queen City** Missouri, C USA *40°24′N 92°34′W*
71 *J4* **Queen City** Texas, SW USA *33°09′N 94°09′W*
295 *I8* **Queen Elizabeth Islands** *Fr.* Îles de la Reine-Élisabeth. *island group* Nunavut, N Canada
293 *L6* **Queen Mary Coast** *physical region* Antarctica
132 *E10* **Queen Mary's Peak** ▲ C Tristan da Cunha
52 *G8* **Queen Maud Gulf** *gulf* Arctic Ocean
293 *H6* **Queen Maud Mountains** ▲▲ Antarctica
159 *H5* **Queensberry** ▲ UK *55°16′N 3°37′W*
52 *G4* **Queens Channel** *sea waterway* Nunavut, N Canada
275 *J5* **Queensland** ◐ *state* N Australia
286 *D7* **Queensland Plateau** *undersea feature* N Coral Sea
277 *J9* **Queenstown** Tasmania, SE Australia *42°06′S 145°33′E*
278 *B11* **Queenstown** Otago, South Island, New Zealand *45°01′S 168°44′E*
141 *I8* **Queenstown** Eastern Cape, South Africa *31°54′S 26°53′E*
138 *G9* **Queenstown** Eastern Cape, S South Africa *31°52′S 26°50′E*
64 *D10* **Queenstown** Maryland, USA *38°57′N 76°58′W*
Queenstown *see* Cobh
76 *B3* **Queets** Washington, NW USA *47°31′N 124°19′W*
114 *F5* **Queguay** Paysandú, Uruguay *32°05′S 57°55′W*
114 *F5* **Queguay Grande, Río** W Uruguay
108 *G7* **Queimadas** Bahia, E Brazil *10°59′S 39°38′W*
111 *H8* **Queimados** Rio de Janeiro, Brazil *22°43′S 43°34′W*
172 *D2* **Queiriz** Guarda, Portugal *40°44′N 7°27′W*
135 *D11* **Quela** Malanje, NW Angola *09°18′S 17°07′E*
118 *C1* **Quelen, Punta** *point* Coquimbo, Chile
172 *C8* **Quelfes** Faro, Portugal *37°03′N 7°49′W*
139 *J3* **Quelimane** *var.* Kilimane, Kilmain, Quilimane. Zambézia, NE Mozambique *17°53′S 36°51′E*
118 *C7* **Quella** Maule, Chile *36°04′S 72°05′W*
117 *B8* **Quellón** Isla de Chiloé, Chile *43°12′S 73°48′E*
Quelpart *see* Cheju-do
110 *G7* **Queluz** São Paulo, Brazil *22°32′S 44°46′W*
79 *K8* **Quemado** New Mexico, SW USA *34°18′N 108°29′W*
70 *E8* **Quemado** Texas, SW USA *28°58′N 100°36′W*
90 *G5* **Quemado, Punta de** *headland* E Cuba *20°13′N 74°07′W*
Quemoy *see* Chinmen Tao
116 *F5* **Quemú Quemú** La Pampa, Argentina *36°06′S 63°42′E*
112 *E10* **Quemú Quemú** La Pampa, E Argentina *36°03′S 63°36′W*
118 *B10* **Quepe** Araucanía, Chile *38°51′S 72°37′W*
118 *B10* **Quepe, Río** Araucanía, Chile
234 *C6* **Quepem** Goa, W India *15°13′N 74°03′E*
89 *H8* **Quepos** Puntarenas, S Costa Rica *09°28′N 84°10′W*
Que Que *see* Kwekwe
116 *H6* **Quequén** Buenos Aires, E Argentina *38°30′S 58°44′W*
116 *G6* **Quequén Grande, Río** E Argentina
116 *G6* **Quequén Salado, Río** E Argentina
Quera *see* Chur
86 *E5* **Querétaro** Querétaro de Arteaga, C Mexico *20°36′N 100°24′W*
168 *G7* **Quérigut** Midi-Pyrénées, France *42°42′N 2°06′E*
84 *E3* **Querobabi** Sonora, NW Mexico *30°02′N 111°02′W*
89 *H8* **Quesada** *var.* Ciudad Quesada, San Carlos. Alajuela, N Costa Rica *10°19′N 84°26′W*
170 *G7* **Quesada** Andalucía, S Spain *37°52′N 03°05′W*
241 *H3* **Queshan** Henan, C China *32°48′N 114°03′E*
56 *E5* **Quesnel** British Columbia, SW Canada *52°59′N 122°30′W*
54 *D8* **Quesnel Lake** ◎ British Columbia, SW Canada
79 *L5* **Questa** New Mexico, SW USA *36°41′N 105°37′W*
164 *E4* **Questembert** Morbihan, NW France *47°39′N 02°24′W*
112 *C3* **Quetena, Río** SW Bolivia
230 *F6* **Quetta** Baluchistān, SW Pakistan *30°15′N 67°E*
Quetzalcoalco *see* Coatzacoalcos
Quetzaltenango *see* Quezaltenango
104 *B2* **Quevedo** Los Ríos, C Ecuador *01°02′S 79°27′W*
84 *G8* **Península de Quevedo** *peninsula* Sinaloa, Mexico
88 *B4* **Quezaltenango** *var.* Quetzaltenango. Quezaltenango, W Guatemala *14°50′N 91°30′W*
87 *K10* **Quezaltenango** *off.* Departamento de Quezaltenango, *var.* Quetzaltenango. ◐ *department* SW Guatemala
Quezaltenango, Departamento de *see* Quezaltenango
88 *D4* **Quezaltepeque** Chiquimula, SE Guatemala *14°38′N 89°25′W*
263 *J8* **Quezon** Palawan, W Philippines *09°13′N 118°01′E*
263 *K5* **Quezon City** Luzon, N Philippines *14°39′N 121°02′E*
245 *J7* **Qufu** Shandong, E China *35°37′N 117°05′E*
172 *B2* **Quiaios** Coimbra, Portugal *40°13′N 8°51′W*
135 *C11* **Quibala** Cuanza Sul, NW Angola *10°44′S 14°58′E*
135 *C11* **Quibaxe** *var.* Quibaxi. Cuanza Norte, NW Angola *08°30′S 14°36′E*
Quibaxi *see* Quibaxe
102 *B5* **Quibdó** Chocó, W Colombia *05°40′N 76°38′W*
164 *E4* **Quiberon** Morbihan, NW France *47°30′N 03°07′W*
164 *E4* **Quiberon, Baie de** *bay* NW France
102 *E3* **Quíbor** Lara, N Venezuela *09°55′N 69°35′W*
88 *C3* **Quiché** *off.* Departamento del Quiché. ◐ *department* W Guatemala
Quiché, Departamento del *see* Quiché
180 *H2* **Quickborn** Schleswig-Holstein, Germany *9°54′N 53°44′E*
118 *A10* **Quidico** Bío-Bío, Chile *38°15′S 73°30′W*
115 *H4* **Quiebra Yugos** Uruguay *31°40′S 56°10′W*
87 *H9* **Quiechapa** Oaxaca, Mexico *16°26′N 96°15′W*
181 *C13* **Quierschied** Saarland, Germany *7°03′N 49°19′E*
163 *D11* **Quiévrain** Hainaut, S Belgium *50°25′N 03°41′E*
84 *G7* **Quila** Sinaloa, C Mexico *24°24′N 107°11′W*
135 *C13* **Quilengues** Huíla, SW Angola *14°09′S 14°04′E*
Quilimane *see* Quelimane
118 *C1* **Quilimarí** Coquimbo, Chile *32°07′S 71°30′W*
105 *F8* **Quillabamba** Cusco, C Peru *12°49′S 72°41′W*
106 *D10* **Quillacollo** Cochabamba, C Bolivia *17°26′S 66°16′W*
112 *B3* **Quillagua** Antofagasta, N Chile *21°33′S 69°32′W*
165 *H9* **Quillan** Aude, S France *42°52′N 02°11′E*
118 *B10* **Quillen** Araucanía, Chile *38°28′S 72°24′W*
57 *N6* **Quill Lakes** ◎ Saskatchewan, S Canada
116 *B3* **Quillota** Valparaíso, C Chile *32°54′S 71°16′W*
114 *E9* **Quilmes** Buenos Aires, Argentina *34°43′S 58°16′W*
115 *M4* **Quilombo** Rio Grande do Sul, Brazil *31°32′S 52°28′W*
115 *L5* **Quilombo** Rio Grande do Sul, Brazil *32°17′S 53°25′W*
235 *E10* **Quilon** *var.* Kolam, Kollam. Kerala, SW India *08°57′N 76°37′E*
277 *I1* **Quilpie** Queensland, C Australia *26°39′S 144°15′E*
230 *G3* **Quil-Qala** Bāmīān, N Afghanistan *35°13′N 67°02′E*
118 *B9* **Quilquen** Araucanía, Chile *38°06′S 72°43′W*
243 *K3* **Quimen** China *29°47′N 117°33′E*
112 *E6* **Quimilí** Santiago del Estero, C Argentina *27°35′S 62°25′W*
116 *F1* **Quimilí** Santiago del Estero, Argentina *27°48′S 62°24′E*
106 *G10* **Quimome** Santa Cruz, E Bolivia *17°45′S 61°15′W*
164 *D4* **Quimper** *anc.* Quimper Corentin. Finistère, NW France *48°00′N 04°05′W*
Quimper Corentin *see* Quimper
164 *E4* **Quimperlé** Finistère, NW France *47°52′N 03°33′W*
76 *B3* **Quinault** Washington, NW USA *47°27′N 123°53′W*
76 *B3* **Quinault River** Washington, NW USA
118 *C7* **Quinchamávida** Maule, Chile *36°07′S 72°03′W*
78 *C3* **Quincy** California, W USA *39°56′N 120°56′W*
69 *J4* **Quincy** Florida, SE USA *30°35′N 84°34′W*
73 *A10* **Quincy** Illinois, N USA *39°56′N 91°24′W*
65 *L2* **Quincy** Massachusetts, NE USA *42°15′N 71°00′W*
76 *D4* **Quincy** Washington, NW USA *47°13′N 119°51′W*
102 *B6* **Quindío** *off.* Departamento del Quindío. ◐ *province* C Colombia
102 *B6* **Quindío, Nevado del** ▲ C Colombia *04°42′N 75°25′W*
112 *D8* **Quines** San Luis, C Argentina *32°15′S 65°46′W*
167 *L8* **Quingey** Franche-Comté, France *47°06′N 5°53′E*
82 *G7* **Quinhagak** Alaska, USA *59°45′N 161°55′W*
132 *B5* **Quinhámel** W Guinea-Bissau *11°52′N 15°52′W*
Qui Nhon/Quinhon *see* Quy Nhơn
Quinindé *see* Rosa Zárate
71 *H4* **Quinlan** Texas, SW USA *32°54′N 96°08′W*
118 *C2* **Quinquimo** Valparaíso, Chile *32°27′S 71°19′W*
115 *M5* **Quinta** Rio Grande do Sul, S Brazil *32°05′S 52°18′W*
172 *C3* **Quintã** Castelo Branco, Portugal *39°47′N 8°12′W*
115 *H4* **Quintana** Salto, Uruguay *31°24′S 56°22′W*
170 *G6* **Quintanar de la Orden** Castilla-La Mancha, C Spain *39°36′N 03°03′W*
87 *M6* **Quintana Roo** ◐ *state* SE Mexico
118 *C3* **Quintay** Valparaíso, Chile *33°13′S 71°40′W*
118 *C2* **Bahia Quintero** *bay* Valparaíso, Chile
171 *I4* **Quinto** Aragón, NE Spain *41°25′N 00°31′W*
176 *E5* **Quinto** Ticino, S Switzerland *46°32′N 08°44′E*
75 *F12* **Quinton** Oklahoma, C USA *35°07′N 95°22′W*
116 *E4* **Quinto, Río** C Argentina
135 *B10* **Quinzau** Dem. Rep. Congo, NW Angola *06°50′S 12°48′E*
62 *D1* **Quinze, Lac des** ◎ Québec, SE Canada
87 *H8* **Quiotepec** Oaxaca, Mexico *17°38′N 96°37′W*
173 *K6* **Quipar** Murcia, Spain
135 *C13* **Quipungo** Huíla, C Angola *14°49′S 14°29′E*
116 *B5* **Quirihue** Bío Bío, C Chile *36°15′S 72°35′W*
110 *E8* **Quirim** São Paulo, Brazil *23°02′S 45°38′W*
135 *E12* **Quirima** Malanje, NW Angola *10°51′S 18°06′E*
277 *L4* **Quirindi** New South Wales, SE Australia *31°29′S 150°40′E*
103 *H3* **Quiriquire** Monagas, NE Venezuela *09°59′N 63°14′W*
62 *B2* **Quirke Lake** ◎ Ontario, S Canada
112 *F10* **Quiroga** Buenos Aires, E Argentina *35°18′S 61°22′W*
86 *D6* **Quiroga** Michoacán de Ocampo, Mexico *19°40′N 101°32′W*
170 *D2* **Quiroga** Galicia, NW Spain *42°28′N 07°15′W*
Quiróm, Salar *see* Pocitos, Salar
104 *B4* **Quiroz, Río** NW Peru
137 *F13* **Quissanga** Cabo Delgado, NE Mozambique *12°24′S 40°33′E*
139 *I6* **Quissico** Inhambane, S Mozambique *24°42′S 34°44′E*
70 *E3* **Quitaque** Texas, SW USA *34°22′N 101°03′W*
137 *F12* **Quiterajo** Cabo Delgado, NE Mozambique *11°37′S 40°22′E*
115 *N2* **Quitéria** Rio Grande do Sul, Brazil *30°26′S 52°04′W*
69 *K3* **Quitman** Georgia, SE USA *30°46′N 83°33′W*
68 *F2* **Quitman** Mississippi, S USA *32°02′N 88°43′W*
71 *I4* **Quitman** Texas, SW USA *32°37′N 95°26′W*
104 *C1* **Quito** ● (Ecuador) Pichincha, N Ecuador *0°14′S 78°30′W*
Quito *see* Mariscal Sucre
84 *D2* **Quitovac** Sonora, Mexico *31°31′N 112°45′W*
86 *C6* **Quitupan** Jalisco, Mexico *19°55′N 102°52′W*
108 *H4* **Quixadá** Ceará, E Brazil *04°57′S 39°04′W*
139 *L2* **Quixaxe** Nampula, NE Mozambique *15°15′S 40°07′E*
243 *H8* **Qujiang** *var.* Maba. Guangdong, S China *24°47′N 113°34′E*
242 *C3* **Qu Jiang** C China
243 *L4* **Qu Jiang** SE China
242 *A7* **Qujing** Yunnan, SW China *25°39′N 103°52′E*
141 *I9* **Quko** Eastern Cape, South Africa *32°41′S 28°10′E*
Qulan *see* Kulan
228 *G5* **QuljuqtovTog'lari** *Rus.* Gory Kul'dzhuktau. ▲▲ C Uzbekistan
Qulsary *see* Kul'sary
Qulyndy Zhazyghy *see* Kulunda Steppe
Qum *see* Qom
Qumälisch *see* Lubartów
239 *H7* **Qumar He** C China
239 *I7* **Qumarlêb** *var.* Yuegaitan. Qinghai, C China *34°06′N 95°54′E*
Qumisheh *see* Shahreẕā
229 *H8* **Qumqo'rg'on** *Rus.* Kumkurgan. Surkhondaryo Viloyati, S Uzbekistan *37°54′N 67°31′E*
Qunaytirah/Qunayţirah, Muḩāfaẓat al *see* Al Qunayţirah
228 *D4* **Qŭnghirot** Qoraqalpoghiston Respublikasi, NW Uzbekistan *43°01′N 58°49′E*
282 *F9* **Quoi** *island* Chuuk, C Micronesia
53 *H8* **Quoich** Nunavut, NE Canada
138 *D10* **Quoin Point** *headland* SW South Africa *34°48′S 19°39′E*
140 *E10* **Quoin Point** *point* Western Cape, South Africa
276 *G4* **Quorn** South Australia *32°22′S 138°03′E*
229 *J6* **Qŭqon** Farghona Viloyati, E Uzbekistan *40°34′N 70°55′E*
Qurein *see* Al Kuwayt
229 *I8* **Qŭrghonteppa** *Rus.* Kurgan-Tyube. SW Tajikistan *37°51′N 68°42′E*
Qurlurtuuq *see* Kugluktuk
Qurveh *see* Qorveh
Qusair *see* Quseir
215 *M4* **Qusar** *Rus.* Kusary. NE Azerbaijan *41°26′N 48°27′E*
Quşayr *see* Al Quşayr
129 *J5* **Quseir** *var.* Al Quşayr, Qusair. E Egypt *26°05′N 34°16′E*
222 *C2* **Qūshchī** Āžarbāyjān-e Gharbi, N Iran *37°59′N 45°05′E*
229 *H6* **Qŭshrabot** Samarqand Viloyati, C Uzbekistan *40°15′N 66°40′E*
242 *E6* **Qu Shui** Hunan, China
Qusmuryn *see* Kushmurun, Kostanay, Kazakhstan
Qusmuryn *see* Kushmurun, Ozero
Quţayfah/Qutayfe/Quteife *see* Al Quţayfah
Quthing *see* Moyeni
52 *E7* **Quunnguq Lake** ◎ Northwest Territories, NW Canada
229 *J6* **Quvasoy** *Rus.* Kuvasay. Farg'ona Viloyati, E Uzbekistan *40°17′N 71°53′E*
Quwair *see* Guwēr
244 *G6* **Quwo** China *35°38′N 111°28′E*
Quxar *see* Lhazê
Quxar *see* Lhazê
Qu Xian *see* Quzhou
238 *G9* **Qūxü** *var.* Xoi. Xizang Zizhiqu, W China *29°25′N 90°48′E*
245 *I4* **Quyang** Hebei, China *38°22′N 114°25′E*
Quyang *see* Jingzhou
257 *J9* **Quy Chanh** Ninh Thuân, S Vietnam *11°28′N 108°53′E*
257 *J8* **Quy Nhơn** *var.* Quinhon, Qui Nhon. Binh Đinh, C Vietnam *13°47′N 109°11′E*
229 *H6* **Qŭytosh** Jizzakh Viloyati, C Uzbekistan *40°13′N 67°19′E*
243 *L4* **Quzhou** *var.* Qu Xian. Zhejiang, SE China *28°55′N 118°54′E*
Qyteti Stalin *see* Kuçovë
Qyzyltū *see* Kishkenekol'
Qyzylzhar *see* Kyzylzhar

R

Raa Atoll *see* North Maalhosmadulu Atoll
177 *J2* **Raab** Oberösterreich, N Austria *48°19′N 13°40′E*
177 *K4* **Raab** Austria/Hungary
Raab *see* Rába
Raab *see* Győr
177 *K1* **Raabs an der Thaya** Niederösterreich, E Austria *48°51′N 15°28′E*
152 *H7* **Raahe** *Swe.* Brahestad. Oulu, W Finland *64°42′N 24°31′E*
162 *H6* **Raalte** Overijssel, E Netherlands *52°23′N 06°16′E*
163 *F8* **Raamsdonksveer** Noord-Brabant, S Netherlands *51°42′N 04°54′E*
53 *H3* **Raanes Peninsula** *Peninsula* Nunavut, N Canada
152 *H6* **Raanujärvi** Lappi, NW Finland *66°39′N 24°40′E*
156 *D5* **Raasay** *island* NW Scotland, UK
136 *J3* **Raas Caseyr** *headland* NE Somalia *11°51′N 51°16′E*
190 *E3* **Raasiku** *Ger.* Rasik. Harjumaa, NW Estonia *59°22′N 25°11′E*
184 *B3* **Rab** *It.* Arbe. Primorje-Gorski Kotar, NW Croatia *44°46′N 14°46′E*
184 *B3* **Rab** *It.* Arbe. *island* NW Croatia
260 *C8* **Raba** Sumbawa, S Indonesia *08°27′S 118°45′E*
183 *E11* **Rába** *Ger.* Raab. Austria/Hungary *see also* Raab
184 *A3* **Rabac** Istra, NW Croatia *45°03′N 14°09′E*
170 *D2* **Rábade** Galicia, NW Spain *43°07′N 07°37′W*
136 *B2* **Rabak** White Nile, C Sudan *13°12′N 32°44′E*
280 *D4* **Rabaraba** Milne Bay, SE Papua New Guinea *10°00′S 149°50′E*
168 *G5* **Rabastens** Midi-Pyrénées, France *43°50′N 1°45′E*
164 *G8* **Rabastens-de-Bigorre** Hautes-Pyrénées, S France *43°23′N 00°10′E*
175 *I14* **Rabat** W Malta *35°51′N 14°25′E*
130 *F2* **Rabat** *var.* al Dar al Baida. ● (Morocco) NW Morocco *34°02′N 06°51′W*
Rabat *see* Victoria
280 *D2* **Rabaul** New Britain, E Papua New Guinea *04°13′S 152°11′E*
Rabbah Ammon/Rabbath Ammon *see* 'Ammān
74 *B4* **Rabbit Creek** South Dakota, N USA
62 *D1* **Rabbit Lake** ◎ Ontario, S Canada
280 *F8* **Rabi** *prev.* Rambi. *island* N Fiji
220 *D5* **Rābigh** Makkah, W Saudi Arabia *22°51′N 39°E*
88 *C3* **Rabinal** Baja Verapaz, C Guatemala *15°05′N 90°26′W*
258 *B4* **Rabi, Pulau** *island* NW Indonesia, East Indies
183 *G9* **Rabka** Małopolskie, S Poland *49°38′N 20°E*
234 *D6* **Rabkavi** Karnātaka, W India *16°40′N 75°03′E*
Râbniţa *see* Rîbniţa
177 *L3* **Rabnitz** E Austria
194 *E5* **Rabocheostrovsk** Respublika Kareliya, NW Russian Federation *64°58′N 34°46′E*
66 *G7* **Rabun Bald** ▲ Georgia, SE USA *34°58′N 83°18′W*
128 *F6* **Rabyānah** SE Libya *24°07′N 21°58′E*
128 *E5* **Rabyānah, Ramlat** *var.* Rebiana Sand Sea, Şaḩrā' Rabyānah. *desert* SE Libya
Rabyānah, Şaḩrā' *see* Rabyānah, Ramlat
188 *E7* **Răcăciuni** Bacău, E Romania *46°20′N 27°00′E*
Racaka *see* Riwoqê
175 *F13* **Racalmuto** Sicilia, Italy, C Mediterranean Sea *37°25′N 13°44′E*
188 *D9* **Răcari** Dâmboviţa, SE Romania *44°37′N 25°43′E*
Răcari *see* Durankulak
188 *B9* **Răcăşdia** *Hung.* Rakasd. Caraş-Severin, SW Romania *44°58′N 21°36′E*
176 *D8* **Racconigi** Piemonte, NE Italy *44°45′N 07°41′E*
73 *I12* **Raccoon Creek** Ohio, N USA
51 *N7* **Race, Cape** *cape* Newfoundland, Newfoundland and Labrador, E Canada
68 *D5* **Raceland** Louisiana, S USA *29°43′N 90°36′W*
65 *N3* **Race Point** *headland* Massachusetts, NE USA *42°03′N 70°14′W*
218 *G2* **Rachaaïne** Lebanon
80 *J6* **Rachel** Nevada, USA *37°39′N 115°45′W*
257 *H10* **Rach Gia** Kiên Giang, S Vietnam *10°01′N 105°05′E*
256 *G10* **Rach Gia, Vinh** *bay* S Vietnam
132 *D2* **Rachid** Tagant, C Mauritania *18°48′N 11°41′W*
182 *G5* **Raciąż** Mazowieckie, C Poland *52°46′N 20°04′E*
183 *F8* **Racibórz** *Ger.* Ratibor. Śląskie, S Poland *50°05′N 18°10′E*
73 *D8* **Racine** Wisconsin, N USA *42°42′N 87°50′W*
72 *H2* **Racine Lake** ◎ Ontario, S Canada
160 *F8* **Rackenford** UK *50°57′N 3°38′W*
80 *D1* **Rackerby** California, USA *39°26′N 121°20′W*
183 *F12* **Ráckeve** Pest, C Hungary *47°10′N 18°58′E*
Rácz-Becse *see* Bečej
220 *F9* **Radā'** *var.* Ridā'. W Yemen *14°24′N 44°49′E*
117 *D10* **Rada Tilly** Chubut, Argentina *45°54′S 67°30′E*
184 *G6* **Radan** ▲ SE Serbia *42°59′N 21°31′E*
188 *E6* **Rădăuţi** *Ger.* Radautz, *Hung.* Rádóc. Suceava, N Romania *47°49′N 25°58′E*
188 *E5* **Rădăuţi-Prut** Botoşani, NE Romania *48°14′N 26°47′E*
Radautz *see* Rădăuţi
Radbusa *see* Radbuza
183 *A9* **Radbuza** *Ger.* Radbusa. SE Czech Republic
66 *E4* **Radcliff** Kentucky, S USA *37°50′N 85°57′W*
216 *G2* **Radd, Wādī ar** *dry watercourse* N Syria
155 *E8* **Råde** Østfold, S Norway *59°21′N 10°53′E*
177 *K5* **Radeče** *Ger.* Ratschach. C Slovenia *46°01′N 15°10′E*
Radein *see* Radenci
188 *D3* **Radekhiv** *Pol.* Radziechów, *Rus.* Radekhov. L'vivs'ka Oblast', W Ukraine *50°17′N 24°39′E*
Radekhov *see* Radekhiv
177 *L4* **Radenci** *Ger.* Radein; *prev.* Radinci. NE Slovenia *46°36′N 16°02′E*
177 *J4* **Radenthein** Kärnten, S Austria *46°48′N 13°42′E*
181 *D9* **Radevormwald** Nordrhein-Westfalen, Germany *7°21′N 51°12′E*
67 *I5* **Radford** Virginia, NE USA *37°07′N 80°34′W*
232 *C7* **Rādhanpur** Gujarāt, W India *23°52′N 71°49′E*
114 *F8* **Radial Conchillas** Colonia, Uruguay *34°06′S 58°00′W*
Radinci *see* Radenci
197 *J3* **Radishchevo** Ul'yanovskaya Oblast', W Russian Federation *52°49′N 47°54′E*
58 *F5* **Radisson** Québec, E Canada *53°47′N 77°35′W*
141 *J3* **Radium** Limpopo, South Africa *25°05′S 28°19′E*
57 *H8* **Radium Hot Springs** British Columbia, SW Canada *50°39′N 116°09′W*
188 *B7* **Radna** *Hung.* Máriaradna. Arad, W Romania *46°05′N 21°41′E*
185 *K6* **Radnevo** Stara Zagora, C Bulgaria *42°17′N 25°58′E*
157 *F10* **Radnor** *cultural region* E Wales, UK
Radnót *see* Iernut
Rádóc *see* Rădăuţi
179 *D13* **Radolfzell am Bodensee** Baden-Württemberg, S Germany *47°43′N 08°58′E*
182 *H7* **Radom** Mazowieckie, C Poland *51°23′N 21°08′E*
191 *B12* **Radom** ◐ *province* C Poland
188 *D10* **Radomireşti** Olt, S Romania *44°06′N 25°00′E*
182 *G7* **Radomsko** *Rus.* Novoradomsk. Łódzkie, C Poland *51°04′N 19°25′E*
188 *G3* **Radomyshl'** Zhytomyrs'ka Oblast', N Ukraine *50°30′N 29°16′E*
185 *H7* **Radoviš** *prev.* Radovište. E Macedonia *41°39′N 22°26′E*
Radovište *see* Radoviš
154 *A6* **Radøy** *island* S Norway
177 *I3* **Radstadt** Salzburg, NW Austria *47°24′N 13°31′E*
276 *E5* **Radstock, Cape** *headland* South Australia *33°11′S 134°18′E*
174 *G4* **Raduha** ▲ N Slovenia *46°24′N 14°46′E*
191 *E9* **Radun'** *Rus.* Radun'. Hrodzyenskaya Voblasts', W Belarus *54°03′N 25°00′E*
192 *F6* **Raduzhnyy** Khanty-Mansiyskiy Avtonomnyy Okrug, C Russian Federation *62°03′N 77°28′E*
190 *D7* **Radviliškis** Šiaulai, N Lithuania *55°48′N 23°32′E*
55 *H10* **Radville** Saskatchewan, S Canada *49°28′N 104°19′W*
220 *D4* **Radwá, Jabal** ▲ W Saudi Arabia *24°31′N 38°21′E*
183 *I8* **Radymno** Podkarpackie, SE Poland *49°57′N 22°49′E*
188 *D3* **Radyvyliv** Rivnens'ka Oblast', NW Ukraine *50°07′N 25°12′E*
Radziechów *see* Radekhiv
182 *F5* **Radziejów** Kujawsko-pomorskie, C Poland *52°36′N 18°33′E*
182 *I6* **Radzyń Podlaski** Lubelskie, E Poland *51°48′N 22°37′E*
54 *F4* **Rae** Northwest Territories, NW Canada
52 *D8* **Rae** Nunavut, NW Canada
232 *G6* **Rāe Bareli** Uttar Pradesh, N India *26°14′N 81°14′E*
Rae-Edzo *see* Edzo
67 *K7* **Raeford** North Carolina, SE USA *34°59′N 79°15′W*
53 *I9* **Rae Isthmus** *headland* Nunavut, NE Canada
54 *E3* **Rae Lake** ◎ Northwest Territories, NW Canada
163 *H10* **Raeren** Liège, E Belgium *50°42′N 06°06′E*
53 *H8* **Rae Strait** *strait* Nunavut, N Canada
278 *G6* **Raetihi** Manawatu-Wanganui, North Island, New Zealand *39°29′S 175°16′E*
285 *J8* **Raevavae** *var* Raivavae. *island* Îles Australes, SW French Polynesia
Rafa *see* Rafah
114 *G9* **Rafael Pevazza** San Jose, Uruguay *34°30′S 56°48′E*
114 *A4* **Rafaela** Santa Fe, E Argentina *31°16′S 61°25′W*
216 *A7* **Rafah** *var.* Rafa, Rafaḩ, *Heb.* Rafiaḩ, *var.* Raphiah. SW Gaza Strip *31°18′N 34°15′E*
134 *G5* **Rafaï** Mbomou, SE Central African Republic *05°01′N 23°51′E*
110 *B8* **Rafard** São Paulo, Brazil *23°01′S 47°32′W*
220 *F2* **Rafḩah** Al Ḩudūd ash Shamālīyah, N Saudi Arabia *29°41′N 43°29′E*
Rafiaḩ *see* Rafah
223 *H7* **Rafsanjān** Kermān, C Iran *30°25′N 56°E*
134 *H4* **Raga** Western Bahr el Ghazal, SW Sudan *08°28′N 25°41′E*
63 *K5* **Ragged Island** *island* Maine, NE USA
61 *M10* **Ragged Island Range** *island group* S Bahamas
278 *G4* **Raglan** Waikato, North Island, New Zealand *37°48′S 174°54′E*
160 *G5* **Raglan** UK *51°46′N 2°53′W*
68 *B4* **Ragley** Louisiana, S USA *30°31′N 93°13′W*
190 *H3* **Raglicy** Novgorodskaya Oblast', Russian Federation
Ragnit *see* Neman
175 *G13* **Ragusa** Sicilia, Italy, C Mediterranean Sea *36°56′N 14°42′E*
Ragusa *see* Dubrovnik
Ragusavecchia *see* Cavtat
260 *E6* **Raha** Pulau Muna, C Indonesia *04°50′S 122°43′E*
191 *H10* **Rahachow** *Rus.* Rogachëv. Homyel'skaya Voblasts', SE Belarus *53°03′N 30°03′E*
121 *L4* **Rahad** *var.* Nahr ar Rahad. W Sudan
Rahad, Nahr ar *see* Rahad
Rahaeng *see* Tak
158 *C9* **Raharney** Westmeath, Ireland *53°31′N 7°06′W*
219 *D9* **Rahat** Israel
216 *B7* **Rahat** Southern, C Israel *31°20′N 34°43′E*
129 *L6* **Rahaţ, Ḩarrat** *lava flow* W Saudi Arabia
180 *F5* **Rahden** Nordrhein-Westfalen, Germany *8°37′N 52°26′E*
231 *H7* **Rahīmyār Khān** Punjab, SE Pakistan *28°27′N 70°21′E*
154 *E7* **Råholt** Akershus, S Norway *60°16′N 11°10′E*
171 *K10* **Rahouia** Algeria
Rahovec *see* Orahovac
65 *H6* **Rahway** New Jersey, USA *40°36′N 74°17′W*
285 *I6* **Raiatea** *island* Îles Sous le Vent, W French Polynesia
114 *D5* **Raíces** Entre Ríos, Argentina *31°54′S 59°16′W*
234 *E6* **Rāichūr** Karnātaka, C India *16°15′N 77°20′E*
Raidestos *see* Tekirdağ
233 *J7* **Rāiganj** West Bengal, NE India *25°38′N 88°11′E*
234 *H3* **Raigarh** Chhattīsgarh, C India *21°53′N 83°28′E*
114 *G9* **Raigón** Uruguay *34°21′S 56°39′W*
260 *D9* **Raijua, Selat** *strait* Nusa Tenggara, S Indonesia

◆ Country
● Country Capital
◇ Dependent Territory
○ Dependent Territory Capital
◐ Administrative Regions
✈ International Airport
▲ Mountain
▲▲ Mountain Range
Volcano
River
◎ Lake
⊠ Reservoir

◆ Country
● Country Capital
◇ Dependent Territory
○ Dependent Territory Capital
✦ Administrative Regions
✈ International Airport
▲ Mountain
▲ Mountain Range
☒ Volcano
♒ River
○ Lake
☒ Reservoir

◆ Country
● Country Capital
◇ Dependent Territory
○ Dependent Territory Capital
◆ Administrative Regions
✕ International Airport
▲ Mountain
▲ Mountain Range
▨ Volcano
✦ River
○ Lake
☒ Reservoir

◆ Country ◇ Dependent Territory ◆ Administrative Regions ▲ Mountain ◢ Volcano ◎ Lake
● Country Capital ○ Dependent Territory Capital ✕ International Airport ▲▲ Mountain Range ≈ River ⊟ Reservoir

◆ Country
● Country Capital
◇ Dependent Territory
○ Dependent Territory Capital
◈ Administrative Regions
✕ International Airport
▲ Mountain
▲▲ Mountain Range
▲ Volcano
≈ River
○ Lake
□ Reservoir

◆ Country ◇ Dependent Territory ◈ Administrative Regions ▲ Mountain ▲ Volcano ◎ Lake
● Country Capital ○ Dependent Territory Capital ✈ International Airport ▲ Mountain Range ↗ River ◉ Reservoir

Stampalia - Suárez
INDEX
411

Stampalia see Astypálaia
75 H14 Stamps Arkansas, C USA 33°22′N 93°30′W
152 E5 Stamsund Nordland, C Norway 68°07′N 13°50′E
75 G8 Stanberry Missouri, C USA 40°12′N 94°33′W
293 H3 Stancomb-Wills Glacier glacier Antarctica
141 J4 Standerton Mpumalanga, E South Africa 26°57′S 29°14′E
159 I9 Standish UK 53°35′N 2°40′W
72 G7 Standish Michigan, N USA 43°59′N 83°58′W
161 H2 Standon UK 52°55′N 2°17′W
66 F4 Stanford Kentucky, S USA 37°30′N 84°40′W
77 J4 Stanford Montana, NW USA 47°08′N 110°15′W
161 L6 Stanford le Hope UK 51°30′N 0°25′E
155 J10 Stånga Gotland, SE Sweden 57°16′N 18°30′E
154 E6 Stange Hedmark, S Norway 60°40′N 11°05′E
139 H8 Stanger KwaZulu/Natal, E South Africa 29°20′S 31°18′E
159 J6 Stanhope UK 54°45′N 2°01′W
Stanimaka see Asenovgrad
Stanislau see Ivano-Frankivs'k
80 D3 Stanislaus River ≈ California, W USA
Stanislav see Ivano-Frankivs'k
Stanislavskaya Oblast' see Ivano-Frankivs'ka Oblast'
Stanisławów see Ivano-Frankivs'k
Stanke Dimitrov see Dupnitsa
277 J9 Stanley Tasmania, SE Australia 40°48′S 145°18′E
117 J11 Stanley var. Port Stanley, Puerto Argentino. ○ (Falkland Islands) East Falkland, Falkland Islands 51°45′S 57°56′W
159 H2 Stanley UK 56°28′N 3°27′W
76 G7 Stanley Idaho, NW USA 44°12′N 114°58′W
74 B2 Stanley North Dakota, N USA 48°19′N 102°23′W
64 A10 Stanley Virginia, NE USA 38°34′N 78°30′W
72 B5 Stanley Wisconsin, N USA 44°58′N 90°54′W
135 D9 Stanley Pool var. Pool Malebo. lake section of river Congo/Dem. Rep. Congo
235 E8 Stanley Reservoir ⊠ S India
Stanleyville see Kisangani
88 E2 Stann Creek ◐ district SE Belize
Stann Creek see Dangriga
159 K5 Stannington UK 55°06′N 1°40′W
193 J7 Stanovoy Khrebet ⛰ SE Russian Federation
176 D4 Stans Unterwalden, C Switzerland 46°57′N 08°23′E
161 K5 Stansted ✈ (London) Essex, E England, UK 51°53′N 00°16′E
277 M2 Stanthorpe Queensland, E Australia 28°35′S 151°52′E
161 L4 Stanton UK 52°19′N 0°54′E
66 G4 Stanton Kentucky, S USA 37°51′N 83°51′W
72 G7 Stanton Michigan, N USA 43°19′N 85°04′W
74 E7 Stanton Nebraska, C USA 41°57′N 97°13′W
74 C3 Stanton North Dakota, N USA 47°19′N 101°22′W
70 D5 Stanton Texas, SW USA 32°07′N 101°47′W
161 H5 Stanway UK 51°59′N 1°55′W
76 C3 Stanwood Washington, NW USA 48°14′N 122°22′W
189 N5 Stanychno-Luhans'ke Luhans'ka Oblast', E Ukraine 48°39′N 39°30′E
162 H5 Staphorst Overijssel, E Netherlands 52°38′N 06°12′E
161 I2 Stapleford UK 52°55′N 1°16′W
161 L7 Staplehurst UK 51°09′N 0°33′E
62 A6 Staples Ontario, S Canada 42°09′N 82°34′W
74 G3 Staples Minnesota, N USA 46°21′N 94°47′W
74 C7 Stapleton Nebraska, C USA 41°29′N 100°40′W
70 G5 Star Texas, SW USA 31°27′N 98°16′W
182 H7 Starachowice Świętokrzyskie, C Poland 51°04′N 21°02′E
Stara Kanjiža see Kanjiža
183 H9 Stará L'ubovňa Ger. Altlublau, Hung. Ólubló. Prešovský Kraj, E Slovakia 49°19′N 20°40′E
184 F3 Stara Pazova Ger. Altpasua, Hung. Ópazova. Vojvodina, N Serbia 44°59′N 20°10′E
Stara Planina see Balkan Mountains
185 K6 Stara Reka ≈ C Bulgaria
188 F4 Stara Synyava Khmel'nyts'ka Oblast', W Ukraine 49°39′N 27°39′E
188 D2 Stara Vyzhivka Volyns'ka Oblast', NW Ukraine 51°27′N 24°25′E
Staraya Belitsa see Staraya Byelitsa
191 H9 Staraya Byelitsa Rus. Staraya Belitsa. Vitsyebskaya Voblasts', NE Belarus 54°42′N 29°38′E
197 J2 Staraya Mayna Ul'yanovskaya Oblast', W Russian Federation 54°36′N 48°57′E
191 H11 Staraya Rudnya Rus. Staraya Rudnya. Homyel'skaya Voblasts', SE Belarus 52°50′N 30°17′E
194 D9 Staraya Russa Novgorodskaya Oblast', W Russian Federation 57°59′N 31°18′E
185 K6 Stara Zagora Lat. Augusta Trajana. Stara Zagora, C Bulgaria 42°26′N 25°39′E
74 F4 Starbuck Minnesota, N USA 45°36′N 95°31′W
285 H4 Starbuck Island prev. Volunteer Island. island E Kiribati
75 I13 Star City Arkansas, C USA 33°56′N 91°52′W
160 F8 Starcross UK 50°37′N 3°27′W
184 C4 Staretina ⛰ W Bosnia and Herzegovina
Stargard in Pommern see Stargard Szczeciński
182 C4 Stargard Szczeciński Ger. Stargard in Pommern. Zachodnio-pomorskie, NW Poland 53°20′N 15°02′E
281 K4 Star Harbour harbor San Cristobal, SE Solomon Islands
Stari Bečej see Bečej
184 C5 Stari Grad It. Cittavecchia. Split-Dalmacija, S Croatia 43°11′N 16°36′E
260 E6 Staring, Teluk var. Teluk Wawosungu. bay Sulawesi, C Indonesia
194 E10 Staritsa Tverskaya Oblast', W Russian Federation 56°28′N 34°51′E
69 L4 Starke Florida, SE USA 29°56′N 82°07′W
66 C8 Starkville Mississippi, S USA 33°27′N 88°49′W
179 F13 Starnberg Bayern, SE Germany 48°00′N 11°19′E
179 F13 Starnberger See ◎ SE Germany
Starobel'sk see Starobil's'k
189 M6 Starobesheve Donets'ka Oblast', E Ukraine 47°45′N 38°01′E
189 M4 Starobil's'k Rus. Starobel'sk. Luhans'ka Oblast', E Ukraine 49°16′N 38°56′E
191 F11 Starobin var. Starobyn. Minskaya Voblasts', S Belarus 52°44′N 27°28′E
Starobyn see Starobin
196 E3 Starodub Bryanskaya Oblast', W Russian Federation 52°30′N 32°56′E
182 F4 Starogard Gdański Ger. Preussisch-Stargard. Pomorskie, N Poland 53°57′N 18°29′E
227 H7 Staroikan Yuzhnyy Kazakhstan, S Kazakhstan 43°09′N 68°34′E
Starokonstantinov see Starokostyantyniv
188 F4 Starokostyantyniv Rus. Starokonstantinov. Khmel'nyts'ka Oblast', NW Ukraine 49°43′N 27°13′E
196 G7 Starominskaya Krasnodarskiy Kray, SW Russian Federation 46°31′N 39°03′E
190 G3 Staropolye Leningradskaya Oblast', Russian Federation
185 L4 Staro Selo Rom. Satul-Vechi; prev. Star-Smil. Silistra, NE Bulgaria 43°58′N 26°32′E
196 F7 Staroshcherbinovskaya Krasnodarskiy Kray, SW Russian Federation 46°36′N 38°42′E
197 M3 Starosubkhangulovo Respublika Bashkortostan, W Russian Federation 53°05′N 57°22′E
80 I1 Star Peak ▲ Nevada, W USA 40°31′N 118°09′W
Star-Smil see Staro Selo
160 F9 Start Point headland SW England, UK 50°13′N 03°38′W
Startsy see Kirawsk
Starum see Stavoren
195 N3 Staryy Nadym Yamalo-Nenetskiy Avtonomyy Okrug, Russian federation
191 G10 Staryya Darohi Rus. Staryye Dorogi. Minskaya Voblasts', S Belarus 53°02′N 28°16′E
Staryye Dorogi see Staryya Darohi
191 J11 Staryye Yurkovichi Bryanskaya Oblast', Russian Federation
195 J10 Staryye Zyatsy Udmurtskaya Respublika, NW Russian Federation 57°22′N 52°42′E
189 K9 Staryy Krym Respublika Krym, S Ukraine 45°03′N 35°06′E
196 F4 Staryy Oskol Belgorodskaya Oblast', W Russian Federation 51°21′N 37°52′E
188 C4 Staryy Sambir L'vivs'ka Oblast', W Ukraine 49°27′N 23°00′E
178 G7 Stassfurt var. Staßfurt. Sachsen-Anhalt, C Germany 51°51′N 11°35′E
Staßfurt see Stassfurt
183 H8 Staszów Świętokrzyskie, C Poland 50°33′N 21°07′E
74 H7 State Center Iowa, C USA 42°01′N 93°09′W
64 B6 State College Pennsylvania, NE USA 40°48′N 77°52′W
80 F2 Stateline California, USA 38°58′N 119°57′W
65 H6 Staten Island island New York, NE USA
Staten Island see Estados, Isla de los
69 K4 Statenville Georgia, SE USA 30°42′N 83°00′W
69 L2 Statesboro Georgia, SE USA 32°28′N 81°47′W
States, The see United States of America
67 I6 Statesville North Carolina, SE USA 35°46′N 80°54′W
155 D8 Stathelle Telemark, S Norway 59°01′N 09°40′E
160 G5 Staunton UK 51°49′N 2°39′W
73 C11 Staunton Illinois, N USA 39°00′N 89°47′W
67 K3 Staunton Virginia, NE USA 38°10′N 79°05′W
160 G5 Staunton on Wye UK 52°06′N 2°55′W
155 A8 Stavanger Rogaland, S Norway 58°58′N 05°43′E
159 K10 Staveley UK 53°16′N 1°21′W
163 H11 Stavelot Dut. Stablo. Liège, E Belgium 50°24′N 05°56′E
155 D8 Stavern Vestfold, S Norway 58°58′N 10°01′E
Stavers Island see Vostok Island
161 H5 Staverton UK 51°55′N 2°10′W
162 F4 Stavoren Fris. Starum. Friesland, N Netherlands 52°52′N 05°22′E
197 H8 Stavropol' prev. Voroshilovsk. Stavropol'skiy Kray, SW Russian Federation 45°02′N 41°58′E
Stavropol' see Tol'yatti
197 H8 Stavropol'skaya Vozvyshennost' ⛰ SW Russian Federation
197 H8 Stavropol'skiy Kray ◐ territory SW Russian Federation
187 H3 Stavrós Kentrikí Makedonía, N Greece 40°39′N 23°43′E
187 I9 Stavrós, Akrotírio cape Kríti, Greece, E Mediterranean Sea
187 J7 Stavrós, Akrotírio headland Náxos, Kykládes, Greece, Aegean Sea 37°12′N 25°32′E
187 I2 Stavroúpoli prev. Stavroúpolis. Anatolikí Makedonía kai Thráki, NE Greece 41°12′N 24°45′E
Stavroúpolis see Stavroúpoli
189 H4 Stavyshche Kyyivs'ka Oblast', N Ukraine 49°23′N 30°10′E
277 I7 Stawell Victoria, SE Australia 37°06′S 142°52′E
182 I4 Stawiski Podlaskie, NE Poland 53°22′N 22°08′E
62 C4 Stayner Ontario, S Canada 44°25′N 80°05′W
80 F2 Steamboat Nevada, USA 39°23′N 119°45′W
79 K2 Steamboat Springs Colorado, C USA 40°28′N 106°51′W
66 F5 Stearns Kentucky, S USA 36°39′N 84°27′W
82 G5 Stebbins Alaska, USA 63°30′N 162°15′W
181 B10 Steckenborn Nordrhein-Westfalen, Germany 6°21′N 50°38′E
180 I6 Stederdorf Niedersachsen, Germany 10°15′N 52°21′E
176 F4 Steeg Tirol, W Austria 47°15′N 10°18′E
75 J11 Steele Missouri, C USA 36°04′N 89°49′W
74 C3 Steele North Dakota, N USA 46°51′N 99°55′W
292 F3 Steele Island island Antarctica
73 C12 Steeleville Illinois, N USA 38°00′N 89°39′W
141 K3 Steelpoort Mpumalanga, South Africa 24°43′S 30°12′E
141 K3 Steelpoort ≈ Limpopo, South Africa
64 D7 Steelton Pennsylvania, USA 40°14′N 76°50′W
75 I10 Steelville Missouri, C USA 37°57′N 91°21′W
163 D8 Steenbergen Noord-Brabant, S Netherlands 51°35′N 04°19′E
Steenkool see Bintuni
54 E5 Steen River Alberta, W Canada 59°37′N 117°17′W
162 H5 Steenwijk Overijssel, N Netherlands 52°47′N 06°07′E
160 F7 Steep Holm island UK
117 G10 Steeple Jason island Jason Islands, NW Falkland Islands
266 E6 Steep Point headland Western Australia 26°09′S 113°11′E
188 F6 Ştefăneşti Botoşani, NE Romania 47°44′N 27°15′E
Stefanie, Lake see Ch'ew Bahir
52 F6 Stefansson Island island Nunavut, N Canada
188 G7 Ştefan Vodă Rus. Suvorovo. SE Moldova 46°33′N 29°39′E
117 C9 Steffen, Cerro ▲ S Chile 44°27′S 71°42′W
176 D4 Steffisburg Bern, C Switzerland 46°47′N 07°38′E
181 J12 Stegaurach Bayern, Germany 10°50′N 49°52′E
155 F13 Stege Storstrøm, SE Denmark 54°59′N 12°18′E
191 I9 Stegrimovo Smolenskaya Oblast', Russian Federation
188 B7 Ştei Hung. Vaskohsziklás. Bihor, W Romania 46°34′N 22°28′E
Steier see Steyr
Steierdorf/Steierdorf-Anina see Anina
179 J14 Steiermark off. Land Steiermark, Eng. Styria. ◐ state C Austria
Steiermark, Land see Steiermark
181 I12 Steigerwald hill range C Germany
180 G5 Steimbke Niedersachsen, Germany 9°23′N 52°39′E
163 G10 Stein Limburg, SE Netherlands 50°58′N 05°45′E
Stein see Stein an der Donau
Stein see Kamnik, Slovenia
176 G4 Steinach Tirol, W Austria 47°07′N 11°30′E
Steinamanger see Szombathely
177 K2 Stein an der Donau var. Stein. Niederösterreich, NE Austria 48°25′N 15°35′E
181 G11 Steinau Hessen, Germany 9°28′N 50°19′E
180 F2 Steinau Niedersachsen, Germany 8°53′N 53°41′E
Steinau an der Elbe see Ścinawa
55 J10 Steinbach Manitoba, S Canada 49°32′N 96°40′W
163 H13 Steinfort Luxembourg, W Luxembourg 49°39′N 05°55′E
180 D6 Steinfurt Nordrhein-Westfalen, Germany 7°21′N 52°09′E
181 F8 Steinhausen Nordrhein-Westfalen, Germany 8°32′N 51°35′E
181 J10 Steinheid Thüringen, Germany 11°05′N 50°28′E
181 F11 Steinheim Hessen, Germany 8°55′N 50°27′E
180 I5 Steinhorst Niedersachsen, Germany 10°24′N 52°41′E
180 G5 Steinhude Niedersachsen, Germany 9°21′N 52°27′E
178 D6 Steinhuder Meer ◎ NW Germany
154 E2 Steinkjer Nord-Trøndelag, C Norway 64°01′N 11°29′E
140 C6 Steinkopf Northern Cape, South Africa 29°16′S 17°44′E
Stejarul see Karapelit
163 D9 Stekene Oost-Vlaanderen, NW Belgium 51°13′N 04°04′E
141 H4 Stella North-West, South Africa 26°33′S 24°52′E
180 H3 Stelle Niedersachsen, Germany 10°07′N 53°23′E
138 D10 Stellenbosch Western Cape, SW South Africa 33°56′S 18°51′E
162 D7 Stellendam Zuid-Holland, SW Netherlands 51°48′N 04°01′E
83 K6 Steller, Mount ▲ Alaska, USA 60°36′N 142°49′W
174 C7 Stello, Monte ▲ Corse, France, C Mediterranean Sea 42°49′N 09°24′E
174 D3 Stelvio, Passo dello pass Italy/Switzerland
165 J2 Stenay Meuse, NE France 49°29′N 05°12′E
178 G6 Stendal Sachsen-Anhalt, C Germany 52°36′N 11°52′E
190 C6 Stende Talsi, NW Latvia 57°09′N 22°33′E
276 F6 Stenhouse Bay South Australia 35°15′S 136°58′E
178 G2 Stenløse Frederiksborg, E Denmark 55°47′N 12°13′E
155 G10 Stensjön Jönköping, S Sweden 57°36′N 14°42′E
155 G9 Stenstorp Västra Götaland, S Sweden 58°15′N 13°45′E
159 I3 Stenton UK 55°57′N 2°36′W
155 E9 Stenungsund Västra Götaland, S Sweden 58°05′N 11°49′E
Stepanakert see Xankändi
215 K4 Step'anavan N Armenia 41°00′N 44°27′E
180 J2 Stepenitz ≈ N Germany
74 D5 Stephan South Dakota, N USA 44°12′N 99°25′W
74 E2 Stephen Minnesota, N USA 48°27′N 96°54′W
75 H14 Stephens Arkansas, C USA 33°25′N 93°04′W
278 F7 Stephens, Cape headland D'Urville Island, Marlborough, SW New Zealand 40°42′S 173°56′E
64 B9 Stephens City Virginia, NE USA 39°03′N 78°10′W
277 H4 Stephens Creek New South Wales, SE Australia 31°51′S 141°30′E
278 G7 Stephens Island island C New Zealand
114 B7 Stephenson Santa Fe, Argentina 33°24′S 60°33′W
72 E5 Stephenson Michigan, N USA 45°27′N 87°36′W
59 L7 Stephenville Newfoundland, Newfoundland and Labrador, SE Canada 48°33′N 58°34′W
70 G5 Stephenville Texas, SW USA 32°12′N 98°13′W
227 H8 Step' Nardara Kaz. Shardara Dalasy; prev. Shaidara. grassland S Kazakhstan
197 I8 Stepnoye Stavropol'skiy Kray, SW Russian Federation 44°18′N 44°34′E
227 I2 Stepnyak Akmola, N Kazakhstan 52°52′N 70°49′E
285 K2 Steps Point headland Tutuila, W American Samoa 14°23′S 170°46′W
181 H11 Sterbfritz Hessen, Germany 9°37′N 50°19′E
186 G5 Stereá Ellás Eng. Greece Central. ◐ region C Greece
141 J6 Sterkfonteindam ⊠ Free State, South Africa
141 J2 Sterkrivier ≈ Limpopo, South Africa
141 I7 Sterkspruit Eastern Cape, South Africa 30°32′S 27°22′E
138 G8 Sterkspruit Eastern Cape, SE South Africa 30°31′S 27°22′E
197 L3 Sterlibashevo Respublika Bashkortostan, W Russian Federation 53°19′N 55°12′E
83 I6 Sterling Alaska, USA 60°32′N 150°51′W
79 N2 Sterling Colorado, C USA 40°37′N 103°12′W
73 C9 Sterling Illinois, N USA 41°47′N 89°42′W
75 D10 Sterling Kansas, C USA 38°12′N 98°12′W
70 E5 Sterling City Texas, SW USA 31°50′N 101°00′W
73 H8 Sterling Heights Michigan, N USA 42°34′N 83°01′W
64 C10 Sterling Park Virginia, NE USA 39°00′N 77°24′W
79 N2 Sterling Reservoir ⊠ Colorado, C USA
68 C1 Sterlington Louisiana, S USA 32°42′N 92°05′W
197 L3 Sterlitamak Respublika Bashkortostan, W Russian Federation 53°39′N 56°00′E
Sternberg see Šternberk
183 E9 Šternberk Ger. Sternberg. Olomoucký Kraj, E Czech Republic 49°45′N 17°20′E
181 F14 Sternenfels Baden-Württemberg, Germany 8°51′N 49°03′E
221 J9 Stēroh Suquṭrā, S Yemen 12°21′N 53°50′E
182 D6 Stęszew Wielkopolskie, C Poland 52°16′N 16°41′E
Stettin see Szczecin
Stettiner Haff see Szczeciński, Zalew
57 J6 Stettler Alberta, SW Canada 52°21′N 112°40′W
73 J10 Steubenville Ohio, N USA 40°21′N 80°37′W
161 K5 Stevenage E England, UK 51°55′N 00°14′W
66 E7 Stevenson Alabama, S USA 34°52′N 85°50′W
76 C5 Stevenson Washington, NW USA 45°43′N 121°54′W
83 I7 Stevenson Entrance strait Alaska, USA
72 C6 Stevens Point Wisconsin, N USA 44°32′N 89°33′W
158 G4 Stevenston UK 55°38′N 4°46′W
83 I4 Stevens Village Alaska, USA 66°01′N 149°02′W
76 G5 Stevensville Montana, NW USA 46°30′N 114°05′W
155 F13 Stevns Klint headland E Denmark 55°15′N 12°25′E
56 B2 Stewart British Columbia, W Canada 55°58′N 129°52′W
54 B2 Stewart ≈ Yukon Territory, NW Canada
54 B2 Stewart Crossing Yukon Territory, NW Canada 63°22′N 136°37′W
117 C14 Stewart, Isla island S Chile
278 B13 Stewart Island island S New Zealand
275 J4 Stewart, Mount ▲ Queensland, E Australia 20°11′S 145°29′E
158 G4 Stewarton UK 55°40′N 4°30′W
54 A2 Stewart River Yukon Territory, NW Canada 63°17′N 139°24′W
80 A1 Stewarts Point California, USA 38°39′N 123°24′W
75 G9 Stewartsville Missouri, C USA 39°45′N 94°30′W
57 M7 Stewart Valley Saskatchewan, S Canada 50°34′N 107°47′W
74 H5 Stewartville Minnesota, N USA 43°51′N 92°29′W
180 F5 Steyerberg Niedersachsen, Germany 9°02′N 52°34′E
Steyerlak-Anina see Anina
161 K8 Steyning UK 50°53′N 0°20′W
141 I5 Steynsrus Free State, South Africa 27°57′S 27°34′E
177 J2 Steyr var. Steier. Oberösterreich, N Austria 48°02′N 14°26′E
177 J2 Steyr ≈ NW Austria
159 J4 Stichill UK 55°38′N 2°27′W
159 M10 Stickford UK 53°07′N 0°01′E
74 D6 Stickney South Dakota, N USA 43°24′N 98°23′W
180 J7 Stiege Sachsen-Anhalt, Germany 10°53′N 51°40′E
162 G3 Stiens Friesland, N Netherlands 53°15′N 05°45′E
Stif see Sétif
75 F12 Stigler Oklahoma, C USA 35°16′N 95°08′W
175 H10 Stigliano Basilicata, S Italy 40°24′N 16°13′E
155 I8 Stigtomta Södermanland, C Sweden 58°48′N 16°47′E
56 A1 Stikine ≈ British Columbia, W Canada
Stilida/Stilís see Stylída
155 D12 Stilling Århus, C Denmark 56°04′N 10°00′E
74 H4 Stillwater Minnesota, N USA 45°03′N 92°48′W
80 H2 Stillwater Nevada, USA 39°31′N 118°33′W
75 E12 Stillwater Oklahoma, C USA 36°07′N 97°03′W
80 H2 Stillwater Range ⛰ Nevada, W USA
62 G5 Stillwater Reservoir ⊠ New York, NE USA
175 I12 Stilo, Punta headland S Italy 38°27′N 16°36′E
161 K3 Stilton UK 52°29′N 0°17′W
75 G12 Stilwell Oklahoma, C USA 35°48′N 94°37′W
184 G6 Štimlje Kosovo, S Serbia 42°27′N 21°03′E
70 E1 Stinnett Texas, SW USA 35°49′N 101°27′W
185 H7 Štip E FYR Macedonia 41°45′N 22°10′E
Stira see Stýra
159 H3 Stirling C Scotland, UK 56°07′N 03°57′W
274 D8 Stirling Range ⛰ Western Australia
158 G2 Stirlingshire cultural region C Scotland, UK
154 E3 Stjørdalshalsen Nord-Trøndelag, C Norway 63°27′N 10°57′E
Stochód see Stokhid
179 D13 Stockach Baden-Württemberg, S Germany 47°51′N 09°01′E
161 I7 Stockbridge UK 51°06′N 1°29′W
70 G7 Stockdale Texas, SW USA 29°14′N 97°57′W
180 I2 Stockelsdorf Schleswig-Holstein, Germany 10°39′N 53°54′E
177 L2 Stockerau Niederösterreich, NE Austria 48°24′N 16°13′E
155 I8 Stockholm ● (Sweden) Stockholm, C Sweden 59°17′N 18°03′E
155 J8 Stockholm ◐ county C Sweden
160 G8 Stockland UK 50°50′N 3°04′W
Stockmannshof see Pļaviņas
159 J10 Stockport NW England, UK 53°25′N 02°10′W
159 K9 Stocksbridge UK 53°29′N 1°36′W
291 F9 Stocks Seamount undersea feature C Atlantic Ocean
80 C3 Stockton California, W USA 37°56′N 121°19′W
75 D9 Stockton Kansas, C USA 39°27′N 99°17′W
75 G10 Stockton Missouri, C USA 37°43′N 93°49′W
72 C3 Stockton Island island Apostle Islands, Wisconsin, N USA
75 G10 Stockton Lake ⊠ Missouri, C USA
80 C3 Stockton Metropolitan ✈ California, USA 37°54′N 121°14′W
159 K7 Stockton-on-Tees var. Stockton on Tees. N England, UK 54°34′N 01°19′W
Stockton on Tees see Stockton-on-Tees
70 D6 Stockton Plateau plain Texas, SW USA
75 C8 Stockville Nebraska, C USA 40°33′N 100°20′W
154 H4 Stöde Västernorrland, C Sweden 62°27′N 16°34′E
Stodolichi see Stadolichy
191 J9 Stodolishche Smolenskaya Oblast', Russian Federation
257 H8 Stœng Trĕng prev. Stung Treng. Stœng Trêng, NE Cambodia 13°31′N 105°58′E
184 G8 Stogovo Karaorman ⛰ W FYR Macedonia
161 L6 Stoke UK 51°26′N 0°37′E
Stoke see Stoke-on-Trent
160 F9 Stoke Fleming UK 50°19′N 3°36′W
161 I3 Stoke Golding UK 52°34′N 1°24′W
161 H2 Stoke-on-Trent var. Stoke. C England, UK 53°N 02°10′W
159 K7 Stokesley UK 54°28′N 1°12′W
277 I8 Stokes Point headland Tasmania, SE Australia 40°09′S 143°55′E
161 H2 Stoke-upon-Trent UK 53°00′N 2°11′W
188 D2 Stokhid Pol. Stochód, Rus. Stokhod. ≈ NW Ukraine
Stokhod see Stokhid
152 B3 Stokkseyri Sudhurland, SW Iceland 63°49′N 21°00′W
152 E4 Stokmarknes Nordland, C Norway 68°34′N 14°55′E
Stol see Veliki Krš
184 D6 Stolac ◐ Federacija Bosna I Hercegovina, S Bosnia and Herzegovina
Stolbce see Stowbtsy
181 B10 Stolberg var. Stolberg im Rheinland. Nordrhein-Westfalen, W Germany 50°45′N 06°15′E
181 J8 Stolberg Sachsen-Anhalt, Germany 10°57′N 51°34′E
Stolberg im Rheinland see Stolberg
193 J3 Stolbovoy, Ostrov island NE Russian Federation
Stolbtsy see Stowbtsy
191 F12 Stolin Rus. Stolin. Brestskaya Voblasts', SW Belarus 51°53′N 26°51′E
154 F7 Stöllet var. Norra Ny. Värmland, C Sweden 60°24′N 13°15′E
180 E3 Stollhamm Niedersachsen, Germany 8°22′N 53°31′E
Stolp see Słupsk
Stolpe see Słupia
Stolpmünde see Ustka
180 G5 Stolzenau Niedersachsen, Germany 9°04′N 52°31′E
186 G4 Stómio Thessalía, C Greece 39°51′N 22°45′E
161 H2 Stone UK 52°54′N 2°08′W
62 E2 Stonecliffe Ontario, SE Canada 46°12′N 77°58′W
156 G5 Stonehaven NE Scotland, UK 56°59′N 02°14′W
157 H12 Stonehenge ancient monument Wiltshire, S England, UK
159 H4 Stonehouse UK 55°40′N 3°59′W
66 F8 Stone Mountain ▲ Georgia, SE USA 33°48′N 84°10′W
55 J9 Stonewall Manitoba, S Canada 50°08′N 97°20′W
80 H6 Stonewall Flat salt lake Nevada, USA
67 J2 Stonewood West Virginia, NE USA 39°15′N 80°18′W
158 F6 Stoneykirk UK 54°49′N 4°59′W
62 A6 Stoney Point Ontario, S Canada 42°18′N 82°32′W
152 E4 Stonglandseidet Troms, N Norway 69°03′N 17°06′E
132 E10 Stonybeach Bay bay Tristan da Cunha, SE Atlantic Ocean
78 B3 Stony Creek ≈ California, W USA
132 E10 Stonyhill Point headland S Tristan da Cunha
62 E4 Stony Lake ◎ Ontario, SE Canada
57 I5 Stony Plain Alberta, SW Canada 53°31′N 114°04′W
65 H2 Stony Point New York, USA 42°33′N 73°45′W
67 I6 Stony Point North Carolina, SE USA 35°51′N 81°04′W
62 F5 Stony Point headland New York, NE USA 43°50′N 76°18′W
55 H5 Stony Rapids Saskatchewan, C Canada 59°14′N 105°48′W
83 H6 Stony River Alaska, USA 61°48′N 156°37′W
161 J5 Stony Stratford UK 52°03′N 0°51′W
Stony Tunguska see Podkamennaya Tunguska
58 E6 Stooping ≈ Ontario, C Canada
180 G2 Stör ≈ N Germany
154 G7 Storå Örebro, S Sweden 59°44′N 15°10′E
155 F8 Stora Gla ◎ C Sweden
155 E8 Stora Le Nor. Store Le. ◎ Norway/Sweden
152 F5 Stora Lulevatten ◎ N Sweden
152 F6 Storavan ◎ N Sweden
194 A4 Storavan lakes Norrbotten, Sweden
154 J7 Storby Åland, SW Finland 60°12′N 19°33′E
154 B4 Stordalen Møre og Romsdal, S Norway 62°22′N 07°00′E
155 E13 Storebælt var. Store Bælt, Eng. Great Belt, Storebelt. channel Baltic Sea/Kattegat
Store Bælt see Storebælt
Storebelt see Storebælt
155 H10 Storebro Kalmar, S Sweden 57°36′N 15°30′E
155 F13 Store Heddinge Storstrøm, SE Denmark 55°19′N 12°24′E
Store Le see Stora Le
154 D4 Støren Sør-Trøndelag, S Norway 63°02′N 10°16′E
152 A3 Storfjorden fjord S Norway
155 G8 Storfors Värmland, C Sweden 59°33′N 14°16′E
152 E6 Storforshei Nordland, C Norway 66°25′N 14°25′E
Storhammer see Hamar
178 G5 Störkanal canal N Germany
154 F3 Storlien Jämtland, C Sweden 63°18′N 12°10′E
53 I4 Cape Storm headland Nunavut, N Canada
277 J10 Storm Bay inlet Tasmania, SE Australia
141 H8 Stormberg Eastern Cape, South Africa 31°17′S 26°17′E
141 I7 Stormberg ≈ Eastern Cape, South Africa
74 F6 Storm Lake Iowa, C USA 42°38′N 95°12′W
74 F6 Storm Lake ◎ Iowa, C USA
156 D4 Stornoway NW Scotland, UK 58°13′N 06°23′W
Storojineţ see Storozhynets'
152 C4 Storøya island NE Svalbard
195 J7 Storozhevsk Respublika Komi, NW Russian Federation 61°56′N 52°18′E
Storozhinets see Storozhynets'
188 E5 Storozhynets' Ger. Storozynetz, Rom. Storojineţ, Rus. Storozhinets. Chernivets'ka Oblast', W Ukraine 48°11′N 25°42′E
Storozynetz see Storozhynets'
161 K7 Storrington UK 50°54′N 0°27′W
152 E5 Storriten ▲ C Norway 68°09′N 17°12′E
65 K3 Storrs Connecticut, NE USA 41°48′N 72°15′W
154 E5 Storsjøen ◎ S Norway
154 I6 Storsjön ◎ C Sweden
154 G3 Storsjön ◎ C Sweden
152 F3 Storslett Troms, N Norway 69°45′N 21°03′E
154 E5 Storsølnkletten ▲ S Norway 61°52′N 11°32′E
152 F4 Storsteinnes Troms, N Norway 69°13′N 19°14′E
155 E13 Storstrøm var. Storstrøms Amt. ◐ county SE Denmark
Storstrøms Amt see Storstrøm
152 G6 Storsund Norrbotten, N Sweden 65°36′N 20°40′E
153 D8 Storsylen ▲ S Norway 63°07′N 12°10′E
154 F4 Storsylen Swe. Sylarna. ▲ Norway/Sweden 63°00′N 12°14′E
152 F5 Stortoppen ▲ N Sweden 67°33′N 17°27′E
154 H1 Storuman Västerbotten, N Sweden 65°05′N 17°10′E
154 H1 Storuman ◎ N Sweden
154 H6 Storvik Gävleborg, C Sweden 60°37′N 16°30′E
154 I7 Storvreta Uppsala, C Sweden 59°58′N 17°42′E
180 F3 Stotel Niedersachsen, Germany 8°36′N 53°27′E
161 K5 Stotfold UK 52°00′N 0°13′W
181 J9 Stotternheim Thüringen, Germany 11°03′N 51°04′E
55 H10 Stoughton Saskatchewan, S Canada 49°40′N 103°01′W
65 L3 Stoughton Massachusetts, NE USA 42°07′N 71°06′W
73 C8 Stoughton Wisconsin, N USA 42°56′N 89°12′W
157 G12 Stour ≈ E England, UK
157 I11 Stour ≈ S England, UK
161 H4 Stourbridge UK 52°28′N 2°08′W
161 M6 Stour ≈ UK
75 H10 Stover Missouri, C USA 38°26′N 92°59′W
155 D11 Støvring Nordjylland, N Denmark 56°53′N 09°52′E
159 I4 Stow UK 55°42′N 2°51′W
191 F10 Stowbtsy Pol. Stolbce, Rus. Stolbtsy. Minskaya Voblasts', C Belarus 53°29′N 26°44′E
71 J7 Stowell Texas, SW USA 29°47′N 94°22′W
161 M4 Stowmarket E England, UK 52°05′N 00°54′E
185 M5 Stozher Dobrich, NE Bulgaria 43°27′N 27°49′E
158 C6 Strabane Ir. An Srath Bán. W Northern Ireland, UK 54°49′N 07°27′W
158 F2 Strachur UK 56°10′N 5°04′W
180 D3 Strackholt Niedersachsen, Germany 7°38′N 53°22′E
160 A2 Stradbally Laois, Ireland 53°01′N 7°09′W
161 M4 Stradbroke UK 52°19′N 1°16′E
158 C8 Stradone Cavan, Ireland 53°59′N 7°14′W
181 B8 Straelen Nordrhein-Westfalen, Germany 6°16′N 51°27′E
75 H11 Strafford Missouri, C USA 37°16′N 93°07′W
277 J9 Strahan Tasmania, SE Australia 42°10′S 145°18′E
183 B9 Strakonice Ger. Strakonitz. Jihočeský Kraj, S Czech Republic 49°14′N 13°55′E
Strakonitz see Strakonice
178 H4 Stralsund Mecklenburg-Vorpommern, NE Germany 54°18′N 13°06′E
163 G9 Stramproy Limburg, SE Netherlands 51°12′N 05°43′E
138 D10 Strand Western Cape, SW South Africa 34°06′S 18°50′E
154 B4 Stranda Møre og Romsdal, S Norway 62°18′N 06°56′E
140 C7 Strandfonteinpunt point Northern Cape, South Africa
158 A7 Strandhill Sligo, Ireland 54°16′N 8°36′W
158 F7 Strangford UK 54°22′N 5°30′W
158 E7 Strangford Lough Ir. Loch Cuan. inlet E Northern Ireland, UK
155 I8 Strängnäs Södermanland, C Sweden 59°22′N 17°02′E
158 B6 Stranorlar Ir. Srath an Urláir. Donegal, NW Ireland 54°48′N 07°46′W
158 F6 Stranraer S Scotland, UK 54°54′N 05°02′W
57 N7 Strasbourg Saskatchewan, S Canada 51°05′N 104°58′W
165 L3 Strasbourg Ger. Strassburg; anc. Argentoratum. Bas-Rhin, NE France 48°35′N 07°45′E
79 M3 Strasburg Colorado, C USA 39°42′N 104°13′W
74 C4 Strasburg North Dakota, N USA 46°07′N 100°10′W
73 I10 Strasburg Ohio, N USA 40°35′N 81°31′W
64 A10 Strasburg Virginia, NE USA 38°59′N 78°21′W
188 G7 Străşeni var. Strasheny. C Moldova 47°07′N 28°37′E
Strasheny see Străşeni
177 J4 Strassburg Kärnten, S Austria 46°54′N 14°21′E
Strassburg see Strasbourg, France
Strassburg see Aiud, Romania
163 H13 Strassen Luxembourg, S Luxembourg 49°37′N 06°05′E
177 I3 Strasswalchen Salzburg, C Austria 47°59′N 13°19′E
62 C5 Stratford Ontario, S Canada 43°22′N 81°00′W
278 G6 Stratford Taranaki, North Island, New Zealand 39°20′S 174°16′E
80 D6 Stratford California, W USA 36°10′N 119°47′W
65 I5 Stratford Connecticut, USA 41°11′N 73°08′W
74 G7 Stratford Iowa, C USA 42°16′N 93°55′W
75 E13 Stratford Oklahoma, C USA 34°48′N 96°57′W
70 D1 Stratford Texas, SW USA 36°21′N 102°05′W
72 C6 Stratford Wisconsin, N USA 44°53′N 90°13′W
Stratford see Stratford-upon-Avon
161 I4 Stratford-upon-Avon var. Stratford. C England, UK 52°12′N 01°41′W
158 G3 Strathblane UK 55°58′N 4°18′W
277 J10 Strathgordon Tasmania, SE Australia 42°49′S 146°04′E
57 J7 Strathmore Alberta, SW Canada 51°05′N 113°20′W
80 E7 Strathmore California, W USA 36°07′N 119°04′W
62 B5 Strathroy Ontario, S Canada 42°57′N 81°40′W
156 F3 Strathy Point headland N Scotland, UK 58°36′N 04°04′W
158 G2 Strathyre UK 56°19′N 4°19′W
160 E8 Stratton UK 50°50′N 4°31′W
79 N3 Stratton Colorado, C USA 39°16′N 102°34′W
63 J3 Stratton Maine, NE USA 45°08′N 70°25′W
161 J5 Stratton Audley UK 51°55′N 1°07′W
53 I5 Stratton Inlet coastal sea feature Nunavut, NE Canada
65 J1 Stratton Mountain ▲ Vermont, NE USA 43°05′N 72°55′W
179 H12 Straubing Bayern, SE Germany 48°53′N 12°35′E
178 I6 Strausberg Brandenburg, E Germany 52°34′N 13°52′E
80 E2 Strawberry California, USA 38°48′N 120°09′W
80 E3 Strawberry California, USA 38°12′N 120°01′W
76 E6 Strawberry Mountain ▲ Oregon, NW USA 44°18′N 118°43′W
74 I6 Strawberry Point Iowa, C USA 42°40′N 91°31′W
79 I3 Strawberry Reservoir ⊠ Utah, W USA
79 I3 Strawberry River ≈ Utah, W USA
80 E1 Strawberry Valley California, USA 39°34′N 121°06′W
70 G4 Strawn Texas, SW USA 32°33′N 98°30′W
185 H7 Straža ▲ Bulgaria/FYR Macedonia 42°16′N 22°13′E
183 F10 Strážov Hung. Sztrazsó. ▲ NW Slovakia 48°59′N 18°29′E
276 E4 Streaky Bay South Australia 32°49′S 134°13′E
276 E4 Streaky Bay bay South Australia
161 K6 Streatham UK 51°25′N 0°08′W
73 C9 Streator Illinois, N USA 41°07′N 88°50′W
Streckenbach see Świdnik
183 F9 Stredné Slovensko ◐ region C Slovakia
Strednogorie see Pirdop
183 C9 Středočeský Kraj ◐ region C Czech Republic
160 G7 Street UK 51°07′N 2°44′W
74 D3 Streeter North Dakota, N USA 46°37′N 99°23′W
71 H5 Streetman Texas, SW USA 31°52′N 96°19′W
188 C9 Strehaia Mehedinţi, SW Romania 44°37′N 23°10′E
Strehlen see Strzelin
185 J6 Strelcha Pazardzhik, C Bulgaria 42°28′N 24°21′E
192 G7 Strelka Krasnoyarskiy Kray, C Russian Federation 58°05′N 92°54′E
194 F4 Strel'na ≈ NW Russian Federation
190 E5 Strenči Ger. Stackeln. Valka, N Latvia 57°38′N 25°42′E
179 E14 Strengen Tirol, W Austria 47°07′N 10°25′E
176 E6 Stresa Piemonte, NE Italy 45°52′N 08°32′E
Streshin see Streshyn
191 H11 Streshyn Rus. Streshin. Homyel'skaya Voblasts', SE Belarus 52°43′N 30°07′E
159 J9 Stretford UK 53°27′N 2°19′W
181 I11 Streufdorf Thüringen, Germany 10°41′N 50°21′E
154 A1 Streymoy Dan. Strømø. island N Faeroe Islands
192 F6 Strezhevoy Tomskaya Oblast', C Russian Federation 60°39′N 77°37′E
155 D12 Strib Fyn, C Denmark 55°33′N 09°47′E
183 A9 Stříbro Ger. Mies. Plzeňský Kraj, W Czech Republic 49°44′N 12°55′E
280 A3 Strickland ≈ SW Papua New Guinea
Striegau see Strzegom
Strigonium see Esztergom
162 E7 Strijen Zuid-Holland, SW Netherlands 51°45′N 04°34′E
114 B5 Strobel Entre Ríos, Argentina 32°03′S 60°37′W
117 C11 Strobel, Lago ◎ S Argentina
116 F7 Stroeder Buenos Aires, Argentina 40°18′S 62°48′E
186 E7 Strofádes island Iónioi Nísoi, Greece, C Mediterranean Sea
Strofilia see Strofyliá
187 H5 Strofyliá var. Strofilia. Évvoia, C Greece 38°49′N 23°25′E
180 F5 Ströhen Niedersachsen, Germany 8°42′N 52°32′E
158 B9 Strokestown Roscommon, Ireland 53°47′N 8°06′W
178 H5 Strom ≈ NE Germany
180 E7 Stromberg Nordrhein-Westfalen, Germany 8°12′N 51°48′E
175 G11 Stromboli ⊼ Isola Stromboli, SW Italy 38°48′N 15°13′E
175 G11 Stromboli, Isola island Isole Eolie, S Italy
156 E5 Stromeferry N Scotland, UK 57°20′N 05°35′W
156 F3 Stromness N Scotland, UK 58°57′N 03°18′W
Strømø see Streymoy
154 I5 Strömsbruk Gävleborg, C Sweden 61°52′N 17°19′E
75 E8 Stromsburg Nebraska, C USA 41°06′N 97°36′W
155 G11 Strömsnäsbruk Kronoberg, S Sweden 56°35′N 13°45′E
155 E8 Strömstad Västra Götaland, S Sweden 58°56′N 11°11′E
154 G3 Strömsund Jämtland, C Sweden 63°51′N 15°35′E
154 G2 Ströms Vattudal valley N Sweden
158 F3 Strone UK 55°59′N 4°54′W
75 I14 Strong Arkansas, C USA 33°06′N 92°19′W
Strongilí see Strongylí
175 I11 Strongoli Calabria, SW Italy 39°17′N 17°03′E
73 I9 Strongsville Ohio, N USA 41°18′N 81°50′W
187 N8 Strongylí var. Strongilí. island SE Greece
156 G3 Stronsay island NE Scotland, UK
158 F1 Strontian UK 56°41′N 5°34′W
161 H5 Stroud C England, UK 51°46′N 02°15′W
75 E12 Stroud Oklahoma, C USA 35°45′N 96°39′W
64 F5 Stroudsburg Pennsylvania, NE USA 40°59′N 75°12′W
64 F5 Stroudsburg Pennsylvania, USA 40°59′N 75°12′W
155 C11 Struer Ringkøbing, W Denmark 56°29′N 08°37′E
184 G8 Struga SW FYR Macedonia 41°11′N 20°40′E
Strugi-Kranyse see Strugi-Krasnyye
194 C9 Strugi-Krasnyye var. Strugi-Kranyse. Pskovskaya Oblast', W Russian Federation 58°19′N 29°09′E
140 E10 Struisbaai bay Western Cape, South Africa
185 I7 Struma Gk. Strymónas. ≈ Bulgaria/Greece see also Strymónas
Struma see Strymónas
160 D5 Strumble Head headland SW Wales, UK 52°01′N 05°05′W
185 H8 Strumeshnitsa Mac. Strumica. ≈ Bulgaria/FYR Macedonia
185 H8 Strumica E FYR Macedonia 41°27′N 22°39′E
Strumica see Strumeshnitsa
185 I7 Strumyani Blagoevgrad, SW Bulgaria 41°41′N 23°13′E
181 I9 Struth Thüringen, Germany 10°18′N 51°13′E
73 J9 Struthers Ohio, N USA 41°03′N 80°36′W
185 J6 Stryama ≈ C Bulgaria
141 J2 Strydpoort Mountains ⛰ Limpopo, South Africa
187 H2 Strymónas Bul. Struma. ≈ Bulgaria/Greece see also Struma
Strymónas see Struma
187 H3 Strymonikós Kólpos gulf N Greece
188 C4 Stryy L'vivs'ka Oblast', NW Ukraine 49°16′N 23°51′E
188 C4 Stryy ≈ W Ukraine
182 D7 Strzegom Ger. Striegau. Wałbrzych, SW Poland 50°59′N 16°20′E
182 D5 Strzelce Krajeńskie Ger. Friedeberg Neumark. Lubuskie, W Poland 52°52′N 15°30′E
183 F8 Strzelce Opolskie Ger. Gross Strehlitz. Opolskie, SW Poland 50°31′N 18°19′E
277 H2 Strzelecki Creek seasonal river South Australia
276 G2 Strzelecki Desert desert South Australia
182 E7 Strzelin Ger. Strehlen. Dolnośląskie, SW Poland 50°48′N 17°03′E
182 F5 Strzelno Kujawsko-pomorski, C Poland 52°38′N 18°11′E
183 H8 Strzyżów Podkarpackie, SE Poland 49°52′N 21°46′E
Stua Laighean see Leinster, Mount
69 N7 Stuart Florida, SE USA 27°12′N 80°15′W
74 G7 Stuart Iowa, C USA 41°30′N 94°19′W
74 D6 Stuart Nebraska, C USA 42°36′N 99°08′W
67 J5 Stuart Virginia, NE USA 36°38′N 80°19′W
56 D4 Stuart ≈ British Columbia, SW Canada
82 G5 Stuart Island island Alaska, USA
56 D4 Stuart Lake ◎ British Columbia, SW Canada
278 B11 Stuart Mountains ⛰ South Island, New Zealand
276 E2 Stuart Range hill range South Australia
Stubaital see Neustift im Stubaital
155 E13 Stubbekøbing Storstrøm, SE Denmark 54°53′N 12°04′E
91 M3 Stubbs Saint Vincent, Saint Vincent and the Grenadines 13°08′N 61°09′W
177 K3 Stübming ≈ E Austria
185 K7 Studen Kladenets, Yazovir ⊠ S Bulgaria
278 D11 Studholme Canterbury, South Island, New Zealand 44°44′S 171°08′E
161 H8 Studland UK 50°38′N 1°56′W
161 H4 Studley UK 52°16′N 1°53′W
Stuhlweissenberg see Székesfehérvár
Stuhm see Sztum
55 K7 Stull Lake ◎ Ontario, C Canada
Stung Treng see Stœng Trĕng
196 G2 Stupino Moskovskaya Oblast', W Russian Federation 54°54′N 38°06′E
75 H9 Sturgeon Missouri, C USA 39°13′N 92°16′W
62 C2 Sturgeon ≈ Ontario, S Canada
72 E6 Sturgeon Bay Wisconsin, N USA 44°51′N 87°21′W
62 C2 Sturgeon Falls Ontario, S Canada 46°22′N 79°57′W
58 C6 Sturgeon Lake ◎ Ontario, S Canada
72 D4 Sturgeon River ≈ Michigan, N USA
66 C4 Sturgis Kentucky, S USA 37°33′N 87°58′W
73 F9 Sturgis Michigan, N USA 41°48′N 85°25′W
74 A5 Sturgis South Dakota, N USA 44°24′N 103°30′W
184 C3 Šturlić ◐ Federacija Bosna I Hercegovina, NW Bosnia and Herzegovina
161 H8 Sturminster Newton UK 50°55′N 2°17′W
183 F11 Štúrovo Hung. Párkány; prev. Parkan. Nitriansky Kraj, SW Slovakia 47°49′N 18°40′E
161 M6 Sturry UK 51°17′N 1°07′E
277 H3 Sturt, Mount hill New South Wales, SE Australia
274 G3 Sturt Plain plain Northern Territory, N Australia
276 G1 Sturt Stony Desert desert South Australia
141 I9 Stutterheim Eastern Cape, South Africa 32°34′S 27°25′E
138 G9 Stutterheim Eastern Cape, S South Africa 32°35′S 27°26′E
179 D12 Stuttgart Baden-Württemberg, SW Germany 48°47′N 09°12′E
75 I13 Stuttgart Arkansas, C USA 34°30′N 91°32′W
152 B2 Stykkishólmur Vesturland, W Iceland 65°04′N 22°43′W
186 G5 Stylída var. Stilida, Stilís. Stereá Ellás, C Greece 38°55′N 22°37′E
188 E2 Styr Rus. Styr'. ≈ Belarus/Ukraine
187 I6 Stýra var. Stira. Évvoia, C Greece 38°10′N 24°13′E
Styria see Steiermark
Su see Jiangsu
Sua see Sowa
260 F8 Suai W EastTimor 09°19′S 125°16′E
102 C5 Suaita Santander, C Colombia 06°07′N 73°30′W
129 K8 Suakin var. Sawakin. Red Sea, NE Sudan 19°06′N 37°17′E
243 N7 Suao Jap. Suō. N Taiwan 24°33′N 121°48′E
Suao see Suau
138 F4 Sua Pan var. Sowa Pan. salt lake NE Botswana
84 F4 Suaqui Grande Sonora, NW Mexico 28°22′N 109°52′W
112 E7 Suardi Santa Fe, C Argentina 30°32′S 61°58′W
102 B6 Suárez Cauca, SW Colombia 02°55′N 76°41′W

◆ Country
● Country Capital
◇ Dependent Territory
○ Dependent Territory Capital
◐ Administrative Regions
✈ International Airport
▲ Mountain
⛰ Mountain Range
⊼ Volcano
≈ River
◎ Lake
⊠ Reservoir

◆ Country
● Country Capital
◇ Dependent Territory
○ Dependent Territory Capital
■ Administrative Regions
✈ International Airport
▲ Mountain
▲ Mountain Range
🌋 Volcano
♒ River
◉ Lake
▨ Reservoir

◆ Country
● Country Capital
◇ Dependent Territory
○ Dependent Territory Capital
◆ Administrative Regions
✕ International Airport
▲ Mountain
▲ Mountain Range
◈ Volcano
♣ River
⊠ Lake
⊟ Reservoir

◆ Country
● Country Capital
◇ Dependent Territory
○ Dependent Territory Capital
⊕ Administrative Regions
✕ International Airport
▲ Mountain
▲ Mountain Range
⊠ Volcano
♒ River
⊚ Lake
⊞ Reservoir

◆ Country
● Country Capital
◇ Dependent Territory
○ Dependent Territory Capital
◈ Administrative Regions
✕ International Airport
▲ Mountain
▲ Mountain Range
◭ Volcano
♒ River
◎ Lake
□ Reservoir

◆ Country	◇ Dependent Territory	✕ Administrative Regions	▲ Mountain	◓ Volcano	◒ Lake
● Country Capital	○ Dependent Territory Capital	✈ International Airport	▲ Mountain Range	✍ River	☒ Reservoir

◆ Country
○ Country Capital
◇ Dependent Territory
○ Dependent Territory Capital
▲ Administrative Regions
✕ International Airport
▲ Mountain
▲ Mountain Range
⛰ Volcano
♠ River
○ Lake
⬚ Reservoir

Üroteppa - Varallo
INDEX
421

229 I6 **Üroteppa** Rus. Ura-Tyube. NW Tajikistan 39°55´N 68°57´E
172 D4 **Urra** Portalegre, Portugal 39°14´N 7°24´W
102 B5 **Urrao** Antioquia, W Colombia 06°16´N 76°10´W
172 E1 **Urrós** Bragança, Portugal 41°21´N 6°28´W
Ursat'yevskaya see Xovos
181 H12 **Urspringen** Bayern, Germany 9°40´N 49°54´E
Urt see Gurvantes
197 M3 **Urtazym** Orenburgskaya Oblast', W Russian Federation 52°12´N 58°48´E
84 G5 **Uruàchic** Chihuahua, Mexico 27°52´N 108°14´W
109 B9 **Uruaçu** Goiás, C Brazil 14°38´S 49°06´W
86 D6 **Uruapan** var. Uruapan del Progreso. Michoacán de Ocampo, SW Mexico 19°26´N 102°04´W
Uruapan del Progreso see Uruapan
104 F7 **Urubamba, Cordillera** ▲▲ C Peru
104 F7 **Urubamba, Río** ≈ C Peru
111 I3 **Urucânia** Minas Gerais, Brazil 20°22´S 42°45´W
107 H2 **Urucará** Amazonas, N Brazil 02°30´S 57°45´W
114 G1 **Uruguaiana** Rio Grande do Sul, S Brazil 29°45´S 57°05´W
Uruguai, Rio see Uruguay
115 L5 **Uruguay** Cerro Largo, Uruguay 32°29´S 53°31´W
115 H6 **Uruguay** off. Oriental Republic of Uruguay; prev. La Banda Oriental. ◆ republic E South America
114 E8 **Uruguay** var. Rio Uruguai, Río Uruguay. ≈ E South America
Uruguay, Oriental Republic of see Uruguay
Uruguay, Río see Uruguay
Urumchi see Ürümqi
Urumi Yeh see Orūmīyeh, Daryācheh-ye
238 F3 **Ürümqi** var. Tihwa, Urumchi, Urumqi, Urumtsi, Wu-lu-k'o-mu-shi, Wu-lu-mu-ch'i; prev. Ti-hua. Xinjiang Uygur Zizhiqu, NW China 43°52´N 87°31´E
Urumtsi see Ürümqi
Urundi see Burundi
282 B1 **Uruno Point** headland NW Guam 13°37´N 144°50´E
193 M8 **Urup, Ostrov** island Kuril'skiye Ostrova, SE Russian Federation
Urusan see Ulsan
197 K2 **Urussu** Respublika Tatarstan, W Russian Federation 54°34´N 53°23´E
278 G5 **Uruti** Taranaki, North Island, New Zealand 38°57´S 174°32´E
112 C1 **Uru Uru, Lago** ◎ W Bolivia
103 I5 **Uruyén** Bolívar, SE Venezuela 05°40´N 62°26´W
Ūrūzgān see Orūzgān
167 H6 **Ury** Île-de-France, France 48°20´N 2°36´E
252 E3 **Uryū-gawa** ≈ Hokkaidō, NE Japan
252 E3 **Uryū-ko** ◎ Hokkaidō, NE Japan
197 H5 **Uryupinsk** Volgogradskaya Oblast', SW Russian Federation 50°51´N 41°59´E
Ürzhar see Urdzhar
195 I10 **Urzhum** Kirovskaya Oblast', NW Russian Federation 57°09´N 49°56´E
188 E9 **Urziceni** Ialomiţa, SE Romania 44°43´N 26°39´E
250 D6 **Usa** Ōita, Kyūshū, SW Japan 33°31´N 131°22´E
191 G9 **Usa** Rus. Usa. ≈ C Belarus
195 K4 **Usa** ≈ NW Russian Federation
172 E6 **Usagre** Extremadura, Spain 38°21´N 6°10´W
214 C6 **Uşak** prev. Ushak. Uşak, W Turkey 38°42´N 29°25´E
214 C6 **Uşak** var. Ushak. ◐ province W Turkey
140 B1 **Usakos** Erongo, W Namibia 22°01´S 15°32´E
137 E9 **Usambara Mountains** ▲▲ NE Tanzania
137 C11 **Usangu Flats** wetland SW Tanzania
117 I11 **Usborne, Mount** ▲ East Falkland, Falkland Islands 51°35´S 58°57´W
178 I4 **Usedom** island NE Germany
181 A12 **Useldange** Diekirch, C Luxembourg 49°47´N 05°59´E
Ushachi see Ushachy
191 G8 **Ushachy** Rus. Ushachi. Vitsyebskaya Voblasts', N Belarus 55°11´N 28°37´E
Ushak see Uşak
192 G2 **Ushakova, Ostrov** island Severnaya Zemlya, N Russian Federation
Ushant see Ouessant, Île d'
Üsharal see Ucharal
191 J11 **Ushcherp'ye** Bryanskaya Oblast', Russian Federation
250 C8 **Ushibuka** var. Usibuka. Kumamoto, Shimo-jima, SW Japan 32°12´N 130°00´E
Ushi Point see Sabaneta, Puntan
227 K6 **Ushtobe** Kaz. Üshtöbe. Almaty, SE Kazakhstan 45°15´N 77°59´E
Üshtöbe see Ushtobe
117 D14 **Ushuaia** Tierra del Fuego, S Argentina 54°48´S 68°19´W
83 I5 **Usibelli** Alaska, USA 63°54´N 148°41´W
Usibuka see Ushibuka
181 F11 **Usingen** Hessen, Germany 8°32´N 50°20´E
280 B3 **Usino** Madang, N Papua New Guinea 05°40´S 145°31´E
195 K4 **Usinsk** Respublika Komi, NW Russian Federation 66°01´N 57°37´E
160 G6 **Usk** UK 51°42´N 2°54´W
Uskočke Planine/Uskokengebirge see Gorjanci
Uskoplje see Gornji Vakuf
160 G6 **Usk** ≈ UK
Üsküb/Üsküp see Skopje
196 G4 **Usman'** Lipetskaya Oblast', W Russian Federation 52°04´N 39°41´E
190 B6 **Usmas Ezers** ◎ NW Latvia
190 I7 **Usmyn'** Pskovskaya Oblast', Russian Federation
195 K8 **Usol'ye** Permskaya Oblast', NW Russian Federation 59°27´N 56°33´E
193 H8 **Usol'ye-Sibirskoye** Irkutskaya Oblast', C Russian Federation 52°48´N 103°40´E
118 F2 **Uspallata** Mendoza, Argentina 32°35´S 69°20´W
118 F2 **Uspallata, Sierra de** ▲▲ Mendoza, Argentina
87 I8 **Uspanapa, Río** ≈ SE Mexico
227 I4 **Uspenskiy** Karaganda, C Kazakhstan 48°45´N 72°46´E
86 C6 **Uspero** Michoacán de Ocampo, Mexico
165 H6 **Ussel** Corrèze, C France 45°33´N 02°18´E
193 L9 **Ussuriysk** prev. Nikol'sk, Nikol'sk-Ussuriyskiy, Voroshilov. Primorskiy Kray, SE Russian Federation 43°48´N 131°59´E
195 M4 **Ust' -Voykar** Yamalo-Nenetskiy Avtonomyy Okrug, Russian federation
196 M10 **Ust'-Bagaryak** Chelyabinskaya oblasť, Russian federation
214 F4 **Usta Burnu** headland N Turkey 41°58´N 34°30´E
230 G7 **Usta Muhammad** Baluchistān, SW Pakistan 28°07´N 68°00´E
168 C6 **Ustaritz** Aquitaine, France 43°24´N 1°27´W
193 I8 **Ust'-Barguzin** Respublika Buryatiya, S Russian Federation 53°28´N 109°00´E
193 M6 **Ust'-Bol'sheretsk** Kamchatskaya Oblast', E Russian Federation 52°48´N 156°12´E
197 H5 **Ust'-Buzulukskaya** Volgogradskaya Oblast', SW Russian Federation 50°12´N 42°06´E
190 H7 **Ust'-Dolyssy** Pskovskaya Oblast', Russian Federation
183 B8 **Ustecký Kraj** ◐ region NW Czech Republic
175 F11 **Ustica, Isola d'** island S Italy
193 H7 **Ust'-Ilimsk** Irkutskaya Oblast', C Russian Federation 57°57´N 102°30´E
183 B8 **Ústí nad Labem** Ger. Aussig. Ústecký Kraj, NW Czech Republic 50°41´N 14°04´E
183 D8 **Ústí nad Orlicí** Ger. Wildenschwert. Pardubický Kraj, C Czech Republic 49°58´N 16°24´E
Ustinov see Izhevsk
184 E5 **Ustiprača** ◐ Republika Srpska, SE Bosnia and Herzegovina
192 E6 **Ust'-Ishim** Omskaya Oblast', C Russian Federation 57°42´N 70°58´E
182 E3 **Ustka** Ger. Stolpmünde. Pomorskie, N Poland 54°35´N 16°50´E
193 N5 **Ust'-Kamchatsk** Kamchatskaya Oblast', E Russian Federation 56°14´N 162°28´E
227 L3 **Ust'-Kamenogorsk** Kaz. Öskemen. Vostochnyy Kazakhstan, E Kazakhstan 49°58´N 82°36´E
193 M6 **Ust'-Khayryuzovo** Koryakskiy Avtonomnyy Okrug, E Russian Federation 57°07´N 156°37´E
227 M3 **Ust'-Koksa** Respublika Altay, S Russian Federation 50°15´N 85°45´E
195 J7 **Ust'-Kulom** Respublika Komi, NW Russian Federation 61°42´N 53°42´E
193 H7 **Ust'-Kut** Irkutskaya Oblast', C Russian Federation 56°49´N 105°32´E
193 J4 **Ust'-Kuyga** Respublika Sakha (Yakutiya), NE Russian Federation 69°59´N 135°27´E
196 G8 **Ust'-Labinsk** Krasnodarskiy Kray, SW Russian Federation 44°40´N 40°46´E
193 K6 **Ust'-Maya** Respublika Sakha (Yakutiya), NE Russian Federation 60°27´N 134°28´E
193 K5 **Ust'-Nera** Respublika Sakha (Yakutiya), NE Russian Federation 64°28´N 143°01´E
193 J7 **Ust'-Nyukzha** Amurskaya Oblast', S Russian Federation 56°30´N 121°32´E
193 I4 **Ust'-Olenëk** Respublika Sakha (Yakutiya), NE Russian Federation 73°03´N 119°34´E
193 L5 **Ust'-Omchug** Magadanskaya Oblast', E Russian Federation 61°07´N 149°17´E
193 H8 **Ust'-Ordynskiy** Ust'-Ordynskiy Buryatskiy Avtonomnyy Okrug, S Russian Federation 52°50´N 104°42´E
196 H8 **Ust'-Ordynskiy Buryatskiy Avtonomnyy Okrug** ◐ autonomous district S Russian Federation
194 G6 **Ust'-Pinega** Arkhangel'skaya Oblast', NW Russian Federation 64°09´N 41°55´E
192 G4 **Ust'-Port** Taymyrskiy (Dolgano-Nenetskiy) Avtonomnyy Okrug, N Russian Federation 69°42´N 84°25´E
185 L7 **Ustrem** prev. Vakav. Yambol, E Bulgaria 42°01´N 26°28´E
183 I9 **Ustrzyki Dolne** Podkarpackie, SE Poland 49°26´N 22°36´E
Ust'-Sysol'sk see Syktyvkar
195 J5 **Ust'-Tsil'ma** Respublika Komi, NW Russian Federation 65°25´N 52°09´E
Ust Urt see Ustyurt Plateau
195 H7 **Ust'ya** ≈ NW Russian Federation
193 M6 **Ust'yevoye** prev. Kirovskiy. Kamchatskaya Oblast', E Russian Federation 54°06´N 155°48´E
189 I6 **Ustynivka** Kirovohrads'ka Oblast', C Ukraine 47°58´N 32°32´E
226 D7 **Ustyurt Plateau** var. Ust Urt, Uzb. Ustyurt Platosi. plateau Kazakhstan/Uzbekistan
Ustyurt Platosi see Ustyurt Plateau
194 F9 **Ustyuzhna** Vologodskaya Oblast', NW Russian Federation 58°50´N 36°25´E
238 F3 **Usu** Xinjiang Uygur Zizhiqu, NW China 44°27´N 84°37´E
260 D5 **Usu** Sulawesi, C Indonesia 02°34´S 120°58´E
250 E7 **Usuki** Ōita, Kyūshū, SW Japan 33°07´N 131°48´E
88 E5 **Usulután** Usulután, SE El Salvador 13°20´N 88°26´W
88 D5 **Usulután** ◐ department SE El Salvador
87 J7 **Usumacinta, Río** ≈ Guatemala/Mexico
Usumbura see Bujumbura
U.S./USA see United States of America
141 J1 **Usutu** Limpopo, South Africa 22°34´S 28°35´E
190 I7 **Usvyaty** Pskovskaya Oblast', Russian Federation
261 K6 **Uta** Papua, E Indonesia 04°28´S 136°03´E
79 I4 **Utah** off. State of Utah, also known as Beehive State, Mormon State. ◐ state W USA
79 H3 **Utah Lake** ◎ Utah, W USA
Utaidhani see Uthai Thani
152 H7 **Utajärvi** Oulu, C Finland 64°45´N 26°25´E
Utamboni see Mitemele, Río
Utaradit see Uttaradit
258 D2 **Utara, Selat** strait Peninsular Malaysia
252 E4 **Utashinai** var. Utasinai. Hokkaidō, NE Japan 43°32´N 142°03´E
Utasinai see Utashinai
261 K6 **Uta, Sungai** ≈ Papua, E Indonesia
284 D7 **'Uta Vava'u** island Vava'u Group, N Tonga
79 N6 **Ute Creek** ≈ New Mexico, SW USA
191 E8 **Utena** Utena, E Lithuania 55°30´N 25°34´E
79 N6 **Ute Reservoir** ⊠ New Mexico, SW USA
256 E7 **Uthai Thani** var. Muang Uthai Thani, Udayadhani, Utaidhani. Uthai Thani, W Thailand 15°22´N 100°03´E
230 F9 **Uthal** Baluchistān, SW Pakistan 25°53´N 66°37´E
64 F1 **Utica** New York, NE USA 43°06´N 75°15´W
171 I6 **Utiel** País Valenciano, E Spain 39°33´N 01°13´W
57 H3 **Utikuma Lake** ◎ Alberta, W Canada
88 G3 **Utila, Isla de** island Islas de la Bahía, N Honduras
Utina see Udine
109 F8 **Utinga** Bahia, E Brazil 12°05´S 41°07´W
Utirik see Utrik Atoll
189 K7 **Utlyuts'kyy Lyman** bay S Ukraine
250 C7 **Uto** Kumamoto, Kyūshū, SW Japan 32°42´N 130°40´E
155 I8 **Utö** Stockholm, C Sweden 58°55´N 18°19´E
70 F7 **Utopia** Texas, SW USA 29°30´N 99°31´W
190 H3 **Utorgosh** Novgorodskaya Oblast', Russian Federation
162 F7 **Utrecht** Lat. Trajectum ad Rhenum. Utrecht, C Netherlands 52°06´N 05°07´E
139 H7 **Utrecht** KwaZulu/Natal, E South Africa 27°40´S 30°20´E
162 F6 **Utrecht** ◐ province C Netherlands
170 E8 **Utrera** Andalucía, S Spain 37°10´N 05°47´W
283 L5 **Utrik Atoll** var. Utirik, Utrōk, Utrōnk. atoll Ratak Chain, N Marshall Islands
173 K2 **Utrillas** Aragón, Spain 40°49´N 0°51´W
Utrōk/Utrōnk see Utrik Atoll
155 A8 **Utsira** island SW Norway
152 H3 **Utsjoki** var. Ohcejohka. Lappi, N Finland 69°54´N 27°01´E
253 C12 **Utsunomiya** var. Utunomiya. Tochigi, Honshū, S Japan 36°36´N 139°53´E
197 I7 **Utta** Respublika Kalmykiya, SW Russian Federation 46°22´N 46°03´E
256 E6 **Uttaradit** var. Utaradit. Uttaradit, N Thailand 17°38´N 100°05´E
232 F4 **Uttarkāshi** Uttaranchal, N India 30°45´N 78°19´E
232 F5 **Uttar Pradesh** prev. United Provinces, United Provinces of Agra and Oudh. ◐ state N India
161 H2 **Uttoxeter** UK 52°54´N 1°51´W
91 I8 **Utuado** C Puerto Rico 18°17´N 66°41´W
238 F2 **Utubulak** Xinjiang Uygur Zizhiqu, W China 46°50´N 86°15´E
82 G2 **Utukok River** ≈ Alaska, USA
Utunomiya see Utsunomiya
281 I5 **Utupua** island Santa Cruz Islands, E Soloman Islands
226 C3 **Utva** ≈ NW Kazakhstan
283 H10 **Utwe Harbor** harbor Kosrae, E Micronesia
Uubulan see Hayrhan
239 M1 **Uulbayan** var. Dzüünbulag. Sühbaatar, E Mongolia 46°30´N 112°22´E
194 B9 **Uulu** Estonia
190 D5 **Uulu** Pärnumaa, SW Estonia 58°15´N 24°32´E
295 K8 **Uummannaq** var. Umanak, Umanaq. ◐ Kitaa, C Greenland
Uummannarsuaq see Nunap Isua
Uusikaarlepyy see Nykarleby
153 G10 **Uusikaupunki** Swe. Nystad. Länsi-Soumi, SW Finland 60°48´N 21°25´E
195 J10 **Uva** Udmurtskaya Respublika, NW Russian Federation 56°41´N 52°15´E
184 F5 **Uvac** ≈ W Serbia
70 F7 **Uvalde** Texas, SW USA 29°14´N 99°49´W
235 G11 **Uva Province** ◐ province SE Sri Lanka
191 I11 **Uvaravichy** Rus. Uvarovichi. Homyel'skaya Voblasts', SE Belarus 52°36´N 30°44´E
102 E6 **Uvá, Río** ≈ E Colombia
Uvarovichi see Uvaravichy
197 H4 **Uvarovo** Tambovskaya Oblast', W Russian Federation 51°58´N 42°13´E
192 E6 **Uvat** Tyumenskaya Oblast', C Russian Federation 59°11´N 68°37´E
284 C10 **Uvea, Île** island N Wallis and Futuna
137 A10 **Uvinza** Kigoma, W Tanzania 05°08´S 30°23´E
135 I9 **Uvira** Sud Kivu, E Dem. Rep. Congo 03°24´S 29°05´E
141 K7 **Uvongo** KwaZulu-Natal, South Africa 30°50´S 30°24´E
239 H1 **Uvs** ◐ province NW Mongolia
192 G8 **Uvs Nuur** var. Ozero Ubsu-Nur. ◎ Mongolia/Russian Federation
250 E6 **Uwa** Ehime, Shikoku, SW Japan 33°22´N 132°29´E
250 E6 **Uwajima** var. Uwazima. Ehime, Shikoku, SW Japan 33°13´N 132°32´E
128 G7 **'Uwaynāt, Jabal al** var. Jebel Uweinat. ▲ Libya/Sudan 21°51´N 25°01´E
Uwazima see Uwajima
Uweinat, Jebel see 'Uwaynāt, Jabal al
261 M7 **Uwimmerah, Sungai** ≈ Papua, E Indonesia
62 D4 **Uxbridge** Ontario, S Canada 44°07´N 79°07´W
161 J6 **Uxbridge** UK 51°33´N 0°29´W
Uxellodunum see Issoudun
Uxin Qi see Dabqig
87 L5 **Uxmal, Ruinas** ruins Yucatán, SE Mexico
205 J3 **Uy** ≈ Kazakhstan/Russian Federation
226 F7 **Uyaly** Kzylorda, S Kazakhstan 44°22´N 61°16´E
193 K4 **Uyandina** ≈ NE Russian Federation
239 J2 **Uyanga** var. Ongi. Övörhangay, C Mongolia 46°30´N 102°18´E
Üydzen see Manlay
Uyeda see Ueda
192 G2 **Uyedineniya, Ostrov** island N Russian Federation
133 K8 **Uyo** Akwa Ibom, S Nigeria 05°00´N 07°57´E
239 H2 **Üyönch** Hovd, W Mongolia 46°04´N 92°05´E
227 I7 **Uyuk** Zhambyl, S Kazakhstan 43°46´N 70°55´E
221 J7 **'Uyūn** SW Oman 17°19´N 53°50´E
112 C2 **Uyuni** Potosí, W Bolivia 20°27´S 66°48´W
112 C2 **Uyuni, Salar de** wetland SW Bolivia
228 F5 **Uzbekistan** off. Republic of Uzbekistan. ◆ republic C Asia
Uzbekistan, Republic of see Uzbekistan
229 K7 **Uzbel Shankou** Rus. Pereval Kyzyl-Dzhiik. pass China/Tajikistan
228 B6 **Uzboý** prev. Rus Imeni 26 Bakinskikh Komissarov, Turkm. 26 Baku Komissarlary Adyndaky. Balkan Welaýaty, W Turkmenistan 39°24´N 54°04´E
191 F10 **Uzda** Rus. Uzda. Minskaya Voblasts', C Belarus 53°29´N 27°10´E
168 F2 **Uzerche** Limousin, France 45°25´N 1°34´E
165 J8 **Uzès** Gard, S France 44°00´N 04°25´E
229 K5 **Uzgen** Kir. Özgön. Oshskaya Oblast', SW Kyrgyzstan 40°42´N 73°17´E
188 G2 **Uzh** ≈ N Ukraine
Uzhgorod see Uzhhorod
188 B5 **Uzhhorod** Rus. Uzhgorod; prev. Ungvár. Zakarpats'ka Oblast', W Ukraine 48°36´N 22°19´E
192 G7 **Uzhur** Krasnoyarskiy Kray, S Russian Federation 55°18´N 89°36´E
Uzi see Uji
184 F5 **Užice** prev. Titovo Užice. Serbia, W Serbia 43°52´N 19°51´E
Uzin see Uzyn
196 G3 **Uzlovaya** Tul'skaya Oblast', W Russian Federation 54°01´N 38°15´E
179 D14 **Uznach** Sankt Gallen, NE Switzerland 47°12´N 09°00´E
227 K7 **Uzunagach** Almaty, SE Kazakhstan 43°08´N 76°20´E
214 B4 **Uzunköprü** Edirne, NW Turkey 41°18´N 26°40´E
190 C7 **Užventis** Šiaulai, C Lithuania 55°49´N 22°38´E
189 H4 **Uzyn** Rus. Uzin. Kyyivs'ka Oblast', N Ukraine 49°52´N 30°27´E
226 G2 **Uzynkol'** prev. Lenin, Leninskoye. Kustanay, N Kazakhstan 54°05´N 65°23´E

V

Vääksy see Asikkala
138 F8 **Vaal** ≈ C South Africa
152 H7 **Vaala** Oulu, C Finland 64°34´N 26°49´E
141 I4 **Vaal Dam** ⊠ South Africa
141 H5 **Vaalhartsdam** ◎ Northern Cape, South Africa
153 I9 **Vaalimaa** Etelä-Suomi, SE Finland 60°34´N 27°49´E
163 H10 **Vaals** Limburg, SE Netherlands 50°46´N 06°01´E
141 J2 **Vaalwater** Limpopo, South Africa 24°10´S 28°06´E
153 G8 **Vaasa** Swe. Vasa; prev. Nikolainkaupunki. Länsi-Soumi, W Finland 63°07´N 21°39´E
162 H6 **Vaassen** Gelderland, E Netherlands 52°18´N 05°59´E
190 D7 **Vabalninkas** Panevėžys, NE Lithuania 55°59´N 24°45´E
168 G5 **Vabre** Midi-Pyrénées, France 43°41´N 2°26´E
183 F11 **Vác** Ger. Waitzen. Pest, N Hungary 47°46´N 19°08´E
113 J6 **Vacaria** Rio Grande do Sul, S Brazil 28°31´S 50°52´W
80 C2 **Vacaville** California, W USA 38°21´N 121°59´W
115 K2 **Vaccacahy** Rio Grande do Sul, Brazil 30°26´S 54°22´W
165 J8 **Vaccarès, Étang de** ◎ SE France
90 G6 **Vache, Île à** island SW Haiti
137 G11 **Vacoas** W Mauritius 20°18´S 57°29´E
76 C4 **Vader** Washington, NW USA 46°23´N 122°58´W
154 B6 **Vadheim** Sogn Og Fjordane, S Norway 61°12´N 05°48´E
218 C2 **Vadili** Gk. Vatilí. C Cyprus 35°09´N 33°39´E
232 C8 **Vadodara** prev. Baroda. Gujarāt, W India 22°19´N 73°14´E
152 I3 **Vadsø** Fin. Vesisaari. Finnmark, N Norway 70°07´N 29°47´E
155 G9 **Vadstena** Östergötland, S Sweden 58°26´N 14°55´E
176 F4 **Vaduz** ● (Liechtenstein) W Liechtenstein 47°08´N 09°32´E
Vág see Váh
194 G7 **Vaga** ≈ NW Russian Federation
154 D5 **Vågåmo** Oppland, S Norway 61°52´N 09°06´E
184 B4 **Vaganski Vrh** ▲ W Croatia 44°24´N 15°32´E
154 A1 **Vágar** Dan. Vågø. island W Faeroe Islands
Vágbeszterce see Považská Bystrica
155 G10 **Vaggeryd** Jönköping, S Sweden 57°30´N 14°10´E
155 I8 **Vagnhärad** Södermanland, C Sweden 58°57´N 17°32´E
Vågø see Vágar
170 C4 **Vagos** Aveiro, N Portugal 40°33´N 08°42´W
172 B2 **Vagos** Aveiro, Portugal 40°33´N 8°41´W
Vágsellye see Sal'a
152 E4 **Vågsfjorden** fjord N Norway
154 A5 **Vågsøy** island S Norway
Vágújhely see Nové Mesto nad Váhom
183 E11 **Váh** Ger. Waag, Hung. Vág. ≈ W Slovakia
153 G8 **Vähäkyrö** Länsi-Suomi, W Finland 63°04´N 22°05´E
285 K7 **Vahitahi** atoll Îles Tuamotu, E French Polynesia
Váhtjer see Gällivare
172 C4 **Vaiamonte** Portalegre, Portugal 39°06´N 7°31´W
Vaidei see Vulcan
66 B9 **Vaiden** Mississippi, S USA 33°19´N 89°42´W
235 F9 **Vaigai** ≈ SE India
166 D7 **Vaiges** Pays de la Loire, France 48°03´N 0°28´W
181 F14 **Vaihingen** Baden-Württemberg, Germany 8°58´N 48°56´E
118 A2 **Vaihu** Easter Island, Chile, E Pacific Ocean 27°10´S 109°22´W
190 E5 **Väike Emajõgi** ≈ S Estonia
190 E4 **Väike-Maarja** Ger. Klein-Marien. Lääne-Virumaa, NE Estonia 59°07´N 26°16´E
Väike-Salatsi see Mazsalaca
79 L3 **Vail** Colorado, C USA 39°36´N 106°20´W
167 H9 **Vailly** Centre, France 46°52´N 2°44´E
167 I4 **Vailly-sur-Aisne** Picardie, France 49°25´N 3°31´E
284 D9 **Vaina** Tongatapu, S Tonga 21°12´S 175°10´W
190 C4 **Väinameri** prev. Muhu Väin, Ger. Moon-Sund. sea E Baltic Sea
153 I9 **Vainikkala** Etelä-Suomi, SE Finland 60°54´N 28°18´E
190 B7 **Vaiņode** Liepāja, SW Latvia 56°25´N 21°52´E
235 E9 **Vaippār** ≈ SE India
285 N4 **Vairao** Tahiti, W French Polynesia 17°48´S 149°17´W
165 J8 **Vaison-la-Romaine** Vaucluse, SE France 44°15´N 05°04´E
284 C9 **Vaitupu** Île Uvea, E Wallis and Futuna 13°14´S 176°09´W
284 C4 **Vaitupu** atoll C Tuvalu
Vajdahunyad see Hunedoara
Vajdej see Vulcan
134 G3 **Vakaga** ◐ prefecture NE Central African Republic
185 I6 **Vakarel** Sofiya, W Bulgaria 42°35´N 23°40´E
Vakav see Ustrem
196 G10 **Vakfıkebir** Trabzon, NE Turkey 41°03´N 39°19´E
192 F6 **Vakh** ≈ C Russian Federation
Vakhon, Qatorkŭhi see Nicholas Range
229 I8 **Vakhsh** SW Tajikistan 37°46´N 68°48´E
229 I8 **Vakhsh** ≈ SW Tajikistan
195 H9 **Vakhtan** Nizhegorodskaya Oblast', W Russian Federation 58°00´N 46°43´E
154 B6 **Vaksdal** Hordaland, S Norway 60°29´N 05°45´E
195 H5 **Vaksha** ≈ NW Russian Federation
Valachia see Wallachia
172 B4 **Valada** Santarém, Portugal 39°05´N 8°46´W
172 B1 **Valadares** Porto, Portugal 41°06´N 8°38´W
174 B3 **Valais** Ger. Wallis. ◐ canton SW Switzerland
184 G9 **Valamarës, Mali i** ▲ SE Albania 40°48´N 20°31´E
195 J9 **Valamaz** Udmurtskaya Respublika, NW Russian Federation 57°36´N 52°07´E
185 H8 **Valandovo** SE FYR Macedonia 41°20´N 22°33´E
183 E9 **Valašské Meziříčí** Ger. Wallachisch-Meseritsch, Pol. Wałeckie Międzyrzecze. Zlínský Kraj, E Czech Republic 49°29´N 17°57´E
187 I5 **Valáxa** island Vóreies Sporádes, Greece, Aegean Sea
169 M4 **Valberg** Provence-Alpes-Côte d'Azur, France 44°06´N 6°56´E
155 F8 **Vålberg** Värmland, C Sweden 59°24´N 13°12´E
172 C3 **Valbom** Castelo Branco, Portugal 39°58´N 7°40´W
172 D2 **Valbom** Guarda, Portugal 40°47´N 7°08´W
169 L3 **Valbonnais** Rhône-Alpes, France 44°54´N 5°54´E
168 C6 **Valcarlos** Navarra, Spain 43°06´N 1°18´W
188 C8 **Vâlcea** prev. Vîlcea. ◐ county SW Romania
116 E7 **Valcheta** Río Negro, Argentina 40°48´S 66°12´E
63 I3 **Valcourt** Québec, SE Canada 45°28´N 72°18´W
Valdai Hills see Valdayskaya Vozvyshennost'
170 F2 **Valdavia** ≈ N Spain
194 E9 **Valday** Novgorodskaya Oblast', W Russian Federation 57°57´N 33°20´E
194 D9 **Valdayskaya Vozvyshennost'** var. Valdai Hills. hill range W Russian Federation
170 E5 **Valdecañas, Embalse de** ⊠ W Spain
172 E4 **Valdefuentes** Extremadura, Spain 39°16´N 6°07´W
190 C6 **Valdemārpils** Ger. Sassmacken. Talsi, NW Latvia 57°23´N 22°36´E
155 H9 **Valdemarsvik** Östergötland, S Sweden 58°13´N 16°35´E
170 G5 **Valdemoro** Madrid, C Spain 40°12´N 03°40´W
170 G6 **Valdepeñas** Castilla-La Mancha, C Spain 38°46´N 03°24´W
173 H7 **Valdepeñas de Jaén** Andalucía, Spain 37°35´N 3°49´W
170 E3 **Valderaduey** ≈ NE Spain
170 F3 **Valderas** Castilla-León, N Spain 42°05´N 05°27´W
168 G5 **Valderiés** Midi-Pyrénées, France 44°01´N 2°14´E
171 J4 **Valderrobres** var. Vall-de-roures. Aragón, NE Spain 40°53´N 00°08´E
117 F8 **Valdés, Península** peninsula SE Argentina
104 C1 **Valdéz** var. Limones. Esmeraldas, NW Ecuador 01°13´N 79°00´W
83 J6 **Valdez** Alaska, USA 61°08´N 146°21´W
Valdia see Weldiya
169 M2 **Val d'Isère** Savoie, E France 45°23´N 07°03´E
116 B7 **Valdivia** Los Lagos, C Chile 39°50´S 73°13´W
118 D4 **Valdivia de Paine** Región Metropolitana, Chile 33°49´S 70°52´W
165 H3 **Val-d'Oise** ◐ department N France
58 F7 **Val-d'Or** Québec, SE Canada 48°06´N 77°42´W
69 K3 **Valdosta** Georgia, SE USA 30°49´N 83°16´W
154 D6 **Valdres** physical region S Norway
76 F7 **Vale** Oregon, NW USA 43°59´N 117°15´W
188 B6 **Valea lui Mihai** Hung. Érmihályfalva. Bihor, NW Romania 47°31´N 22°08´E
172 C4 **Vale de Açor** Portalegre, Portugal 39°15´N 7°55´W
172 B6 **Vale de Água** Setúbal, Portugal 37°54´N 8°35´W
172 B1 **Vale de Cambra** Aveiro, Portugal 40°51´N 8°24´W
172 B3 **Vale de Paredes** Leiria, Portugal 39°42´N 9°03´W
172 B7 **Vale de Santiago** Beja, Portugal 37°45´N 8°25´W
172 C6 **Vale de Vargo** Beja, Portugal 37°59´N 7°25´W
172 C4 **Vale do Peso** Portalegre, Portugal 39°21´N 7°39´W
172 D3 **Vale Feitoso** Castelo Branco, Portugal 40°04´N 6°59´W
56 F6 **Valemount** British Columbia, SW Canada 52°46´N 119°17´W
109 H8 **Valença** Bahia, E Brazil 13°22´S 39°06´W
170 C3 **Valença do Minho** Viana do Castelo, N Portugal 42°02´N 08°38´W
108 F5 **Valença do Piauí** Piauí, E Brazil 06°26´S 41°46´W
165 H5 **Valençay** Indre, C France 47°10´N 01°31´E
165 J7 **Valence** anc. Valentia, Valentia Julia, Ventia. Drôme, E France 44°56´N 04°54´E
171 I6 **Valencia** País Valenciano, E Spain 39°29´N 00°24´W
81 D9 **Valencia** California, USA 34°27´N 118°37´W
102 F3 **Valencia** Carabobo, N Venezuela 10°12´N 68°02´W
171 I6 **Valencia** Cat. València. ◐ province País Valenciano, E Spain
171 I6 **Valencia** ✈ Valencia, E Spain
170 D6 **Valencia de Alcántara** Extremadura, W Spain 39°25´N 07°14´W
170 F3 **Valencia de Don Juan** Castilla-León, N Spain 42°17´N 05°31´W
171 J6 **Valencia, Golfo de** var. Gulf of Valencia. gulf E Spain
Valencia, Gulf of see Valencia, Golfo de
157 A11 **Valencia Island** Ir. Dairbhre. island SW Ireland
Valencia/València see País Valenciano
165 I1 **Valenciennes** Nord, N France 50°21´N 03°32´E
188 E9 **Vălenii de Munte** Prahova, SE Romania 45°11´N 26°02´E
169 L5 **Valensole** Provence-Alpes-Côte d'Azur, France 43°50´N 5°59´E
Valentia see Valence, France
Valentia see País Valenciano
Valentia Julia see Valence
165 K4 **Valentigney** Doubs, E France 47°27´N 06°49´E
74 C6 **Valentine** Nebraska, C USA 42°53´N 100°31´W
70 B6 **Valentine** Texas, SW USA 30°35´N 104°30´W
115 I7 **Valentines** Uruguay 33°16´S 55°07´W
Valentine State see Oregon
176 E7 **Valenza** Piemonte, NW Italy 45°01´N 08°37´E
154 E6 **Våler** Hedmark, S Norway 60°39´N 11°52´E
102 E3 **Valera** Trujillo, NW Venezuela 09°21´N 70°38´W
286 G8 **Valerie Guyot** Undersea Feature S Pacific Ocean
172 C7 **Vales Mortos** Beja, Portugal 37°48´N 7°30´W
Valetta see Valletta
190 E5 **Valga** Ger. Walk, Latv. Valka. Valgamaa, S Estonia 57°48´N 26°04´E
190 E5 **Valgamaa** var. Valga Maakond. ◐ province S Estonia
Valga Maakond see Valgamaa
169 J4 **Valgorge** Rhône-Alpes, France 44°35´N 4°07´E
172 D2 **Valhelhas** Guarda, Portugal 40°24´N 7°24´W
89 J9 **Valiente, Península** peninsula NW Panama
175 B8 **Valinco, Golfe de** gulf Corse, France, C Mediterranean Sea
184 F4 **Valjevo** Serbia, W Serbia 44°17´N 19°54´E
Valjok see Válljohka
173 M1 **Valjunquera** Aragón, Spain 40°57´N 0°01´E
190 E5 **Valka** Ger. Walk. Valka, N Latvia 57°48´N 26°01´E
Valka see Valga
153 H9 **Valkeakoski** Länsi-Suomi, W Finland 61°17´N 24°05´E
153 I9 **Valkeala** Etelä-Suomi, S Finland 60°55´N 26°49´E
163 G10 **Valkenburg** Limburg, SE Netherlands 50°52´N 05°50´E
163 G9 **Valkenswaard** Noord-Brabant, S Netherlands 51°21´N 05°29´E
191 D9 **Valkininkai** Alytus, S Lithuania 54°22´N 24°51´E
189 K4 **Valky** Kharkivs'ka Oblast', E Ukraine 49°51´N 35°40´E
87 M5 **Valladolid** Yucatán, SE Mexico 20°39´N 88°13´W
170 F3 **Valladolid** Castilla-León, NW Spain 41°39´N 04°45´W
170 F3 **Valladolid** ◐ province Castilla-León, N Spain
165 K8 **Vallauris** Alpes-Maritimes, SE France 43°34´N 07°03´E
Vall-de-roures see Valderrobres
171 I5 **Vall D'Uxó** País Valenciano, E Spain 39°49´N 00°15´W
155 C8 **Valle** Aust-Agder, S Norway 59°13´N 07°33´E
170 F2 **Valle** Cantabria, N Spain 43°14´N 04°16´W
88 E5 **Valle** ◐ department S Honduras
170 G5 **Vallecas** Madrid, C Spain 40°23´N 03°37´W
85 L5 **Vallecillo** Nuevo León, Mexico 26°40´N 100°00´W
79 K5 **Vallecito Reservoir** ⊠ Colorado, C USA
174 B4 **Valle d'Aosta** ◐ region NW Italy
172 G8 **Valle de Abdalagís** Andalucía, Spain 36°56´N 4°41´W
86 E6 **Valle de Bravo** México, S Mexico 19°19´N 100°08´W
84 B1 **Valle de Guadalupe** Jalisco, W Mexico North America
102 G3 **Valle de Guanape** Anzoátegui, N Venezuela 09°54´N 65°41´W
86 C6 **Valle de Juàrez** Jalisco, Mexico 19°56´N 102°56´W
102 G3 **Valle de La Pascua** Guárico, N Venezuela 09°15´N 66°00´W
102 B6 **Valle del Cauca** off. Departamento del Valle del Cauca. ◐ province W Colombia
Valle del Cauca, Departamento del see Valle del Cauca
85 H5 **Valle de Olivos** Chihuahua, Mexico 27°12´N 106°17´W
86 D5 **Valle de Santiago** Guanajuato, C Mexico 20°25´N 101°15´W
85 H5 **Valle de Zaragoza** Chihuahua, N Mexico 27°25´N 105°50´W
102 C2 **Valledupar** Cesar, N Colombia 10°31´N 73°16´W
132 B3 **Vallée de Ferlo** ≈ NW Senegal
112 D1 **Vallegrande** Santa Cruz, C Bolivia 18°30´S 64°06´W
118 C2 **Valle Hermoso** Valparaíso, Chile 32°26´S 71°14´W
85 N6 **Valle Hermoso** Quintana Roo, Mexico
87 M6 **Valle Hermoso** Quintana Roo, Mexico 19°11´N 88°31´W
86 G1 **Valle Hermoso** Tamaulipas, C Mexico 25°39´N 97°49´W
80 B2 **Vallejo** California, W USA 38°08´N 122°16´W
114 B5 **Valle María** Entre Ríos, Argentina 31°59´S 60°35´W
87 H8 **Valle Nacional** Oaxaca, Mexico 17°47´N 96°19´W
116 B1 **Vallenar** Atacama, N Chile 28°35´S 70°44´W
155 I8 **Vallentuna** Stockholm, C Sweden 59°32´N 18°05´E
169 I4 **Valleraugue** Languedoc-Roussillon, France 44°05´N 3°38´E
166 C8 **Vallet** Pays de la Loire, France 47°10´N 1°16´W
175 J13 **Valletta** prev. Valetta. ● (Malta) E Malta 35°54´N 14°31´E
81 F11 **Valle Vista** California, USA 33°45´N 116°54´W
129 I5 **Valley of the Kings** headland Egypt
81 C8 **Valley Acres** California, USA 35°12´N 119°24´W
81 E12 **Valley Center** California, USA 33°13´N 117°02´W
75 E10 **Valley Center** Kansas, C USA 37°49´N 97°22´W
74 E3 **Valley City** North Dakota, N USA 46°57´N 97°58´W
76 D8 **Valley Falls** Oregon, NW USA 42°28´N 120°16´W
Valleyfield see Salaberry-de-Valleyfield
67 J3 **Valley Head** West Virginia, NE USA 38°33´N 80°01´W
80 D3 **Valley Home** California, USA 37°50´N 120°55´W
70 G5 **Valley Mills** Texas, SW USA 31°36´N 97°27´W
129 I5 **Valley of the Kings** ancient monument E Egypt
74 F6 **Valley Springs** South Dakota, N USA 43°34´N 96°28´W
66 E3 **Valley Station** Kentucky, S USA 38°06´N 85°52´W
65 I6 **Valley Stream** New York, USA 40°40´N 73°43´W
57 H3 **Valleyview** Alberta, W Canada 55°02´N 117°17´W
71 H4 **Valley View** Texas, SW USA 33°27´N 97°08´W
116 G5 **Vallimanca, Arroyo** ≈ E Argentina
152 H4 **Válljohka** var. Valjok. Finnmark, N Norway 69°40´N 25°52´E
175 G10 **Vallo della Lucania** Campania, S Italy 40°13´N 15°15´E
169 L2 **Valloire** Rhône-Alpes, France 45°10´N 6°26´E
169 J4 **Vallon-Pont-d'Arc** Rhône-Alpes, France 44°24´N 4°24´E
176 B4 **Vallorbe** Vaud, W Switzerland 46°43´N 06°21´E
169 L3 **Vallouise** Provence-Alpes-Côte d'Azur, France 44°51´N 6°29´E
171 K4 **Valls** Cataluña, NE Spain 41°18´N 01°15´E
154 H5 **Vallsta** Gävleborg, C Sweden 61°30´N 16°25´E
154 I6 **Vallvik** Gävleborg, C Sweden 61°10´N 17°15´E
57 M9 **Val Marie** Saskatchewan, S Canada 49°15´N 107°44´W
190 E5 **Valmiera** Est. Volmari, Ger. Wolmar. Valmiera, N Latvia 57°34´N 25°26´E
80 J1 **Valmy** Nevada, USA 40°48´N 117°08´W
170 G2 **Valnera** ▲ N Spain 43°08´N 03°39´W
164 F2 **Valognes** Manche, N France 49°31´N 01°28´W
Valona see Vlorë
Valona Bay see Vlorës, Gjiri i
170 C4 **Valongo** var. Valongo de Gaia. Porto, N Portugal 41°11´N 08°30´W
Valongo de Gaia see Valongo
170 F3 **Valoria la Buena** Castilla-León, N Spain 41°48´N 04°33´W
191 F9 **Valozhyn** Pol. Wołożyn, Rus. Volozhin. Minskaya Voblasts', C Belarus 54°05´N 26°32´E
170 D3 **Valpaços** Vila Real, N Portugal 41°36´N 07°17´W
116 B3 **Valparaíso** Valparaíso, C Chile 33°05´S 71°18´W
85 J9 **Valparaíso** Zacatecas, C Mexico 22°49´N 103°28´W
86 C3 **Valparaíso** Zacatecas, Mexico 22°46´N 103°34´W
69 H4 **Valparaiso** Florida, SE USA 30°30´N 86°28´W
73 E9 **Valparaiso** Indiana, N USA 41°28´N 87°04´W
116 B3 **Valparaíso** off. Región de Valparaíso. ◐ region C Chile
Valparaíso, Región de see Valparaíso
Valpo see Valpovo
184 E2 **Valpovo** Hung. Valpo. Osijek-Baranja, E Croatia 45°40´N 18°25´E
169 I6 **Valras-Plage** Languedoc-Roussillon, France 43°15´N 3°17´E
165 J7 **Valréas** Vaucluse, SE France 44°22´N 05°00´E
141 I5 **Vals** ≈ Free State, South Africa
Vals see Vals-Platz
232 C9 **Valsād** prev. Bulsar. Gujarāt, W India 20°40´N 72°55´E
Valsbaai see False Bay
261 H5 **Valse Pisang, Kepulauan** island group E Indonesia
176 E5 **Vals-Platz** var. Vals. Graubünden, S Switzerland 46°39´N 09°09´E
261 K8 **Vals, Tanjung** headland Papua, SE Indonesia 08°26´S 137°35´E
152 I7 **Valtimo** Itä-Suomi, E Finland 63°39´N 28°49´E
186 F5 **Váltou** ▲▲ C Greece
197 H7 **Valuyevka** Rostovskaya Oblast', SW Russian Federation 46°48´N 43°49´E
196 F5 **Valuyki** Belgorodskaya Oblast', W Russian Federation 50°11´N 38°07´E
79 H2 **Val Verda** Utah, W USA 40°51´N 111°53´W
170 A10 **Valverde** Hierro, Islas Canarias, Spain, NE Atlantic Ocean 27°48´N 17°55´W
81 E11 **Val Verde** California, USA 33°51´N 117°15´W
170 D8 **Valverde del Camino** Andalucía, S Spain 37°35´N 06°45´W
172 D3 **Valverde del Fresno** Extremadura, Spain 40°13´N 6°52´W
81 E10 **Valyermo** California, USA 34°27´N 117°51´W
155 D12 **Vamdrup** Vejle, C Denmark 55°26´N 09°18´E
154 G6 **Våmhus** Dalarna, C Sweden 61°07´N 14°30´E
153 G9 **Vammala** Länsi-Soumi, SW Finland 61°20´N 22°55´E
Vámosudvarhely see Odorheiu Secuiesc
215 J6 **Van** Van, E Turkey 38°30´N 43°23´E
71 I4 **Van** Texas, SW USA 32°31´N 95°38´W
215 K6 **Van** ◐ province E Turkey
215 K5 **Vanadzor** prev. Kirovakan. N Armenia 40°49´N 44°29´E
71 H4 **Van Alstyne** Texas, SW USA 33°25´N 96°34´W
77 K5 **Vananda** Montana, NW USA 46°22´N 106°58´W
185 J1 **Vânători** Hung. Héjjasfalva; prev. Vînători. Mureş, C Romania 46°14´N 24°56´E
285 K7 **Vanavana** atoll Îles Tuamotu, SE French Polynesia
Vana-Vändra see Vändra
193 H6 **Vanavara** Evenkiyskiy Avtonomnyy Okrug, C Russian Federation 60°19´N 102°19´E
75 G12 **Van Buren** Arkansas, C USA 35°28´N 94°25´W
63 L1 **Van Buren** Maine, NE USA 47°07´N 67°57´W
75 I11 **Van Buren** Missouri, C USA 37°00´N 91°00´W
63 L3 **Vanceboro** Maine, NE USA 45°31´N 67°25´W
67 L6 **Vanceboro** North Carolina, SE USA 35°16´N 77°06´W
66 G3 **Vanceburg** Kentucky, S USA 38°36´N 84°40´W
Vanch see Vanj
56 D8 **Vancouver** British Columbia, SW Canada 49°13´N 123°06´W
76 C5 **Vancouver** Washington, NW USA 45°38´N 122°39´W
56 D9 **Vancouver** ✈ British Columbia, SW Canada 49°03´N 123°00´W
54 B9 **Vancouver Island** island British Columbia, SW Canada
Vanda see Vantaa
261 K5 **Van Daalen** ≈ Papua, E Indonesia
73 C11 **Vandalia** Illinois, N USA 38°57´N 89°05´W
75 I9 **Vandalia** Missouri, C USA 39°18´N 91°29´W
73 G11 **Vandalia** Ohio, N USA 39°53´N 84°12´W
141 I4 **Vanderbijlpark** Gauteng, South Africa 26°42´S 27°49´E
71 H8 **Vanderbilt** Texas, SW USA 28°45´N 96°37´W
73 G8 **Vandercook Lake** Michigan, N USA 42°11´N 84°23´W
56 D4 **Vanderhoof** British Columbia, SW Canada 53°54´N 124°00´W
63 H5 **Vanderwhacker Mountain** ▲ New York, NE USA 43°54´N 74°06´W
274 G2 **Van Diemen Gulf** gulf Northern Territory, N Australia
Van Diemen's Land see Tasmania
190 E4 **Vändra** Ger. Fennern; prev. Vana-Vändra. Pärnumaa, SW Estonia 58°39´N 25°00´E
Vandsburg see Więcbork
76 B10 **Van Duzen River** ≈ California, W USA
141 J4 **Vandyksdrif** Mpumalanga, South Africa 26°05´S 29°19´E
191 D8 **Vandžiogala** Kaunas, C Lithuania 55°07´N 23°55´E
85 L8 **Vanegas** San Luis Potosí, C Mexico 23°53´N 100°55´W
Vaner, Lake see Vänern
155 F8 **Vänern** Eng. Lake Vaner; prev. Lake Vener. ◎ S Sweden
155 F9 **Vänersborg** Västra Götaland, S Sweden 58°16´N 12°22´E
154 C6 **Vang** Oppland, S Norway 61°07´N 08°34´E
139 M9 **Vangaindrano** Fianarantsoa, SE Madagascar 23°21´S 47°35´E
215 J6 **Van Gölü** Eng. Lake Van; anc. Thospitis. salt lake E Turkey
281 I2 **Vangunu** island New Georgia Islands, NW Solomon Islands
70 B5 **Van Horn** Texas, SW USA 31°03´N 104°51´W
281 I5 **Vanikolo** var. Vanikoro. island Santa Cruz Islands, E Solomon Islands
Vanikoro see Vanikolo
280 A2 **Vanimo** Sandaun, NW Papua New Guinea 02°40´S 141°17´E
193 L8 **Vanino** Khabarovskiy Kray, SE Russian Federation 49°10´N 140°18´E
234 D7 **Vānīvilāsa Sāgara** ◎ SW India
229 J7 **Vanj** Rus. Vanch. S Tajikistan 38°22´N 71°27´E
188 B9 **Vânju Mare** prev. Vînju Mare. Mehedinţi, SW Romania 44°25´N 22°52´E
62 G3 **Vankleek Hill** Ontario, SE Canada 45°32´N 74°39´W
Van, Lake see Van Gölü
154 J2 **Vännäs** Västerbotten, N Sweden 63°54´N 19°43´E
154 J2 **Vännäsby** Västerbotten, N Sweden 63°55´N 19°53´E
164 E4 **Vannes** anc. Dariorigum. Morbihan, NW France 47°40´N 02°45´W
152 F3 **Vanna** island N Norway
165 K6 **Vanoise, Massif de la** ▲▲ E France
141 J5 **Van Reenen** Free State, South Africa 28°22´S 29°23´E
141 J6 **Van Reenens Pass** pass South Africa
261 K5 **Van Rees, Pegunungan** ▲▲ Papua, E Indonesia
140 D8 **Vanrhynsdorp** Western Cape, South Africa 31°37´S 18°44´E
138 D9 **Vanrhynsdorp** Western Cape, SW South Africa 31°36´S 18°45´E
140 D8 **Vanrhynspas** pass Northern Cape, South Africa
67 H4 **Vansant** Virginia, NE USA 37°13´N 82°03´W
154 G7 **Vansbro** Dalarna, C Sweden 60°32´N 14°15´E
155 B9 **Vanse** Vest-Agder, S Norway 58°04´N 06°40´E
53 J9 **Vansittart Island** island Nunavut, NE Canada
141 I7 **Van Stadensrus** Free State, South Africa 29°59´S 27°01´E
153 H10 **Vantaa** Swe. Vanda. Etelä-Suomi, S Finland 60°18´N 25°01´E
153 H10 **Vantaa** ✈ (Helsinki) Etelä-Suomi, S Finland 60°18´N 25°01´E
76 D4 **Vantage** Washington, NW USA 46°55´N 119°55´W
280 G8 **Vanua Balavu** prev. Vanua Mbalavu. island Lau Group, E Fiji
281 M1 **Vanua Lava** island Banks Islands, N Vanuatu
280 F8 **Vanua Levu** island N Fiji
280 E8 **Vanua Levu Barrier Reef** reef C Fiji
Vanua Mbalavu see Vanua Balavu
281 J6 **Vanuatu** off. Republic of Vanuatu; prev. New Hebrides. ◆ republic SW Pacific Ocean
267 I5 **Vanuatu** island group SW Pacific Ocean
Vanuatu, Republic of see Vanuatu
280 G9 **Vanua Vatu** island Lau Group, E Fiji
73 G10 **Van Wert** Ohio, N USA 40°52´N 84°34´W
140 F7 **Van Wyksvlei** Northern Cape, South Africa 30°21´S 21°49´E
140 F7 **Vanwyksvleidam** ⊠ Northern Cape, South Africa
140 F4 **Van Zylsrust** Northern Cape, South Africa 26°52´S 22°03´E
280 C10 **Vao** Province Sud, S New Caledonia 22°40´S 167°29´E
168 G5 **Vaour** Midi-Pyrénées, France 44°04´N 1°48´E
Vapincum see Gap
188 G5 **Vapnyarka** Vinnyts'ka Oblast', C Ukraine 48°31´S 28°44´E
172 C7 **Vaqueiros** Faro, Portugal 37°23´N 7°44´W
85 M9 **Vaqueras** San Luis Potosí, Mexico 21°42´N 99°45´W
165 K8 **Var** ◐ department SE France
165 K8 **Var** ≈ SE France
155 F9 **Vara** Västra Götaland, S Sweden 58°16´N 12°57´E
Varadinska Županija see Varaždin
190 F6 **Varakļani** Madona, C Latvia 56°36´N 26°40´E
176 D6 **Varallo** Piemonte, NE Italy 45°51´N 08°16´E

◆ Country
● Country Capital
◇ Dependent Territory
○ Dependent Territory Capital
◐ Administrative Regions
✈ International Airport
▲ Mountain
▲▲ Mountain Range
⛰ Volcano
≈ River
◎ Lake
⊠ Reservoir

W

◆ Country ● Country Capital ◇ Dependent Territory ○ Dependent Territory Capital ◈ Administrative Regions ✕ International Airport ▲ Mountain ▲ Mountain Range ▲ Volcano ~ River ○ Lake ○ Reservoir

◆ Country	◇ Dependent Territory	◆ Administrative Regions	▲ Mountain	▼ Volcano	◎ Lake
● Country Capital	○ Dependent Territory Capital	✕ International Airport	▲ Mountain Range	← River	■ Reservoir

Picture credits

◆ Country	◇ Dependent Territory	⟡ Administrative Regions	▲ Mountain	⛰ Volcano	⊙ Lake
● Country Capital	○ Dependent Territory Capital	✕ International Airport	▲ Mountain Range	⤳ River	▨ Reservoir

NORTH AMERICA

 CANADA

 UNITED STATES OF AMERICA

 MEXICO

 BELIZE

 COSTA RICA

El Salvador

 GUATEMALA

HONDURAS

 GRENADA

 HAITI

 JAMAICA

 ST KITTS & NEVIS

 ST LUCIA

 ST VINCENT & THE GRENADINES

 TRINIDAD & TOBAGO

 COLOMBIA

AFRICA

 URUGUAY

 CHILE

 PARAGUAY

 ALGERIA

 EGYPT

 LIBYA

 MOROCCO

 TUNISIA

 LIBERIA

 MALI

 MAURITANIA

 NIGER

 NIGERIA

 SENEGAL

 SIERRA LEONE

 TOGO

 BURUNDI

 DJIBOUTI

 ERITREA

 ETHIOPIA

 KENYA

 RWANDA

 SOMALIA

 SUDAN

EUROPE

 SOUTH AFRICA

 SWAZILAND

 ZAMBIA

 ZIMBABWE

 DENMARK

 FINLAND

 ICELAND

 NORWAY

 MONACO

 ANDORRA

 PORTUGAL

 SPAIN

 ITALY

 SAN MARINO

 VATICAN CITY

 AUSTRIA

 BOSNIA & HERZEGOVINA

 CROATIA

 MACEDONIA

 MONTENEGRO

 SERBIA

 BULGARIA

 GREECE

 MOLDOVA

ASIA

 ARMENIA

 AZERBAIJAN

 GEORGIA

 TURKEY

 IRAQ

 ISRAEL

 JORDAN

 LEBANON

 IRAN

 KAZAKHSTAN

 KYRGYZSTAN

 TAJIKISTAN

 TURKMENISTAN

 UZBEKISTAN

 AFGHANISTAN

 PAKISTAN

 TAIWAN

 JAPAN

 MYANMAR (BURMA)

 CAMBODIA

 LAOS

 PHILIPPINES

 THAILAND

 VIETNAM

AUSTRALASIA & OCEANIA

 MAURITIUS

 SEYCHELLES

 AUSTRALIA

 NEW ZEALAND

 PAPUA NEW GUINEA

 FIJI

 SOLOMON ISLANDS

 VANUATU